HER MEMORIES OF THIS HOUSE WERE AS POIGNANT AS HIS OWN.

"Lally, I have a question for you, and I want you to think carefully before you answer."

"Ask me your question, Nathan."

"Would you want to return to England?"

Her answer came immediately. "To do that, after all we have endured in New Orleans, would be a betrayal. Of ourselves and of those dear to us. Even with the heartbreak, what we have here is more important and more satisfying than anything we had in England. Why do you think I would even consider such an idea?"

"I have watched you search the past to find comfort."

"Lighting Sabbath candles? Attending a Sabbath service? Do you call that searching the past? No, Nathan. That is accepting my heritage."

Nathan clasped his cousin's hands. "Lally, do you still believe that what we lost could be some sort of punishment?"

"No, Nathan, I do not. But never again will I ignore what I am. Never again will I pretend to be something I'm not."

LEWIS ORDE

DREAMS of GOLD

ZEBRA BOOKS
KENSINGTON PUBLISHING CORP.

For Kay,
whose eyes are
sharper than mine.
I hope!

Prologue

By nine-fifty, the Atlanta air felt like an oven's breath. Yesterday, beneath a merciless late-August sun, the temperature had soared to ninety degrees. Only a fool would bet against it eclipsing that mark today. The two thousand men surrounding the City Hall building were too excited to heed such discomfort. Standing shoulder to shoulder in the street, or squatting on the low roofs of nearby storage buildings, they struggled to catch a glimpse of events taking place in the first-floor courtroom. They were witnesses to history, seeing through the windows hell beckon with a sulphurous finger to the corrupt and evil murderer of a pure young girl.

Bells rang to clear the way for a streetcar. The mob parted just enough to allow passage. Instead of showing impatience, the conductor waved at the men closest to his vehicle. The murder trial had taken twenty-one days so far, and the Georgia Electric Company had long ago given up hope of maintaining a schedule for streetcars that passed the building. Nor did passengers display annoyance at delays. Like everyone else in Atlanta, they understood the magnitude of this trial. All agreed that justice was far more important than punctuality.

"Be a verdict today!" a dungaree-clad man yelled triumphantly at the conductor.

"Case hasn't gone to the jury yet."

"Will today, and they won't waste no time either. Twelve

good Christian men are going to send that godless pervert straight to the bottomless pit! You mark my words!"

"Tomorrow," another man yelled, "you'll be able to get your streetcar through here like grease through a goose!"

The conductor laughed out loud. "Company will sure be glad to hear that."

Behind the streetcar rolled a black Pierce Arrow that had made the journey from the suburb of Inman Park. A bearded, white-haired man occupied the passenger seat. His gaze swept across the same crowd he had seen every day of the trial. They reminded him of spectators at a fight. Silence fell over the crowd. Every eye followed the black Pierce Arrow. When it stopped, the driver got out and ran around to open the passenger door. The white-haired man stood up slowly, taking time to adjust the jacket of his light gray suit. His face, like his body, was thin. Deep lines furrowed his brow and crept out from his dark brown eyes. He stared again at the crowd, marveling at the hatred that continued to exist in this city. Four years had passed since the bloody race riots of 1906 had splashed Atlanta's name across the world's newspapers. That had not been enough. These people still needed someone to hate. The white-haired man understood why. In the past decade, thousands of tenant farmers had been forced off their land to find unfamiliar, unsatisfying work at factories and mills. Angry and frustrated, and with a fervor whipped up by skillful propaganda, they had sought a scapegoat for all their troubles, a sacrificial offering to which they could attach their own sins and sufferings.

Well, they'd found one now, that was for sure.

Two men barred the way into the City Hall building. One carried a notebook, the other a camera. "The case should go to the jury today," said the reporter from the Atlanta *Constitution*. "You still think they'll return an innocent verdict?"

"I have the utmost faith in the American judicial system."

"Did you read the leader in this week's edition of *Awaken*, demanding a boycott of any store owned by a non-Georgian?"

Fire glowed in the brown eyes. The speech became clipped.

The words flowed quicker, each cut off in the rush to reach the next. An accent grew more noticeable, an inflection that had its roots a long way from the Blue Ridge Mountains. "The publisher of that scurrilous newspaper has made such shameful demands many times before. I suppose I should congratulate him for elevating hatemongering to an art in his search for political success, but I would remind him that even *Awaken*'s most loyal readers must be long bored with tales of babies buried in convent grounds, Negroes practicing cannibalism when the moon is full, and temples used for satanism. Now if you will excuse me. . . ."

Back straight, dignity evident in every step, he walked past the two men into the building. There, the scene was equally chaotic. Policemen and reporters filled the corridors. Inside the courtroom, every square inch of spectator space was taken. Duplicates of the men who filled the street sat squashed together on the benches. More fight lovers, the white-haired man thought, but these were the lucky ones with ringside seats. Some waved newspapers in front of sweaty faces. Others sought a cooling breeze from slowly moving fans. Every window was wide open. Groups of men stood by each one, talking with the crowd outside.

Five chairs were positioned at the defense counsel table. Four were occupied. Three of the men sitting there were lawyers. The fourth was the defendant. The white-haired man touched the defendant's shoulder as he slipped into the chair beside him.

"Did you sleep well?"

"As well as possible after nearly three months in a cell."

"Tonight you'll sleep better, when this nonsense is finally done with and you're back home again."

"I hope."

"You will." The white-haired man gazed across the courtroom to the jury box, where the panel was being seated for the day. They looked a far better class than the ruffians who filled the street outside and clogged the spectator benches. The jury included bank tellers and salesmen, shipping clerks and cashiers, intelligent men who could think and analyze, separate truth from the lies and innuendoes that had saturated the testimony set before them. Men who could tell fact from fiction. He reined in his enthusiasm before it ran away. In his search for hope, was he placing too much emphasis on appearance? Did a better education and a more sophisticated background really enable these jurors to see realities which the mob, blinded by bigotry, could never recognize? Or were they victims of the same fears and prejudices that controlled their less polished cousins?

"All rise!"

The bailiff called the court to order. The judge sat down, and the case entered its twenty-second day with the continuation of closing arguments. The spectators joined in. Each point made by the defense counsel was booed; each prosecution point met with a lusty cheer. Twice the judge stopped proceedings and threatened to have the courtroom cleared.

At three-fifteen, the jury began deliberations. Ninety minutes later, they returned a unanimous verdict: Guilty of murder. Applause erupted. At every open window, men leaned out to shout "Guilty!" The roar from the crowd outside eclipsed all else. The judge glared at the wall of faces staring in and ordered the bailiff to close the windows. The noise dulled to a low rumble. Inside the courtroom, the temperature jumped.

From the defense table, the white-haired man watched the prosecutor approach the jury box and poll each juror with the words: "Is this your verdict?" Each time a juror answered, "It is," the white-haired man flinched.

The chief defense counsel leaned across and whispered, "We'll start work immediately for a new trial. This mockery of justice will never be allowed to stand."

His words seemed to bring some comfort to the defendant, who nodded in acknowledgment, but the white-haired man found little solace in such a prospect. Only by calling on reserves of inner strength had he endured the lengthy trial, but now his resolve was gone. In total shock, he could think of nothing but the blackness that gaped before him. The jurors, educated men though they might be, were too scared to return anything but a guilty verdict. The judge, too intimidated to do otherwise, would surely proscribe death by hanging. A wild and angry mob had dictated the outcome of this trial from start to finish, coercing both jury and judge. That same rage—fueled by fear and prejudice, hate and frustration, ignorance and stupidity—would sweep everything before it like a mighty tidal wave. Sweep aside appeals. Sweep aside petitions for a retrial. Sweep the defendant right onto the scaffold.

Waves of pain beat down on the white-haired man. For one insane moment, he found himself envying the rednecks who filled the benches and the street outside. Those people were lucky. They understood from an early age the futility of life, whereas it had taken him seventy-eight years to come to terms with it.

How smart he'd always thought he was, believing he alone grasped the real meaning—the true purpose—of tragedy. Grief was merely a part of life's greater plan. Strong men like himself did not wilt from grief. They grew more vital by overcoming it, as he had always done.

Being orphaned at an early age. He had overcome that.

Losing a young, beloved wife. He had endured that.

Having everything ripped away from him in a cruel, calamitous conflict that had torn a nation apart. He had even survived that. And he had risen again, stronger than ever, to succeed in a new city.

Only now did he realize that those afflictions had been insignificant. It had taken this trial to make him fully comprehend the meaning of tragedy.

In a shameful travesty of justice, his son had been convicted of a horrifying murder. And the city he had helped rebuild from ashes was going to hang his innocent son because it was too frightened to do anything else!

Part One

1851–1853

Chapter One

Dense fog enveloped London, a gray, viscous blanket woven from the smoke of a million household fires and the sooty steam of a thousand trains. The steady beat of horses' hooves on roads of granite block was swallowed by the darkness, and the keenest eye could see little farther than ten yards.

Along Fleet Street, an omnibus rolled slowly eastward. The driver, perched high at the front of the vehicle, peered left and right, constantly alert for danger, while from a small footboard by the door the conductor bellowed destinations into the gloom in the hope of attracting passengers. Without warning, a hansom cab darted from the shadows. At the last instant, just as collision appeared inevitable, the omnibus driver pulled his two-horse team to the left. The cab rumbled past with less than a foot to spare before evaporating once more into the eddying murk.

Sitting at the back of the crowded omnibus, Nathan Solomon braced himself against the abrupt maneuver. The journey had been like this all the way from Bloomsbury, a perilous game of blindman's buff with all manner of horse-drawn vehicles materializing and vanishing in the wink of an eye like monsters in a nightmare.

Next to Nathan, his cousin Leonora gripped his arm for support. "Has this fog made us very late?" she asked.

Settling back, Nathan checked his pocket watch. "It is only ten minutes past six, Lally. We still have plenty of time."

"Thank God it is March and not November."

Nathan nodded understandingly. The fog would disperse soon, once the early-spring sun went to work on it. In the grim days of November, it covered the city all day long.

Once more, as it crossed Farringdon Street, the omnibus veered sharply. Nathan's high hat fell from his head to roll on the grimy floor. Leonora picked it up and returned it to her cousin. Nathan brushed dirt from the dark blue silk that matched his frock coat and checkered trousers. Around him, other men wore the somber tones that were gaining favor in mid-Victorian Britain, but Nathan refused to dress so conservatively. Just nineteen—New Year's Day was also his birthday—he felt too young to clothe himself in the austerity of middle age.

The omnibus stopped. "Ludgate Hill!" the conductor shouted. "This is Ludgate Hill!"

Nathan and Leonora alighted and walked back down the hill toward the intersection with Farringdon Street. Passing the same police officer they saw every weekday morning at this time, Nathan offered a cordial "Good morning, Constable!" The man responded by touching a white-gloved hand to the brim of his hat. The cousins always welcomed the constable's presence. Despite the illusion of affluence created by the shops lining Ludgate Hill, and the grandeur of St. Paul's Cathedral which overshadowed the entire area, they could never forget that some of London's most deplorable and dangerous slums lay only a short walk away.

They stopped halfway down the hill, outside a shop that occupied double premises. High plate-glass windows displayed clothing in various stages of manufacture surrounded by bolts of fine English wool and Irish poplin, boots, hats, shirts, hose, gloves, and riding gear. Written in gilt letters above the windows were the words: S. SOLOMON AND SONS, TAILORS, DRAPERS, HOSIERS, HATTERS, BOOT AND SHOE MAKERS.

Nathan unlocked the door. He lit the gas lamps that provided the shop and the tailoring workroom behind it with a yellow, smoky light then turned his attention to the huge stove at the rear of the premises. After removing the previous day's ashes, he laid the foundation for a new fire. Once the kindling was ablaze, he added coal. As a cozy warmth spread through the shop, Nathan and Leonora removed their hats and coats and began preparing S. Solomon and Sons for another business day.

They finished their chores shortly after seven o'clock. From beneath a counter Nathan took the latest edition of Charles Dickens's magazine, *Household Words*. Nathan bought everything published by Dickens, whether it was an installment of a new book or the miscellany of poetry, fiction, and essays contained in his journals, and he eagerly awaited this time each morning, the precious minutes between the completion of his tasks and the opening of the shop, when he could read a few pages. Sitting by the stove, he opened the magazine.

"Please read to me, Nathan," Leonora said.

"A young lady should be able to read for herself, Lally." Nathan's nickname for his cousin was a throwback to her birth. He had been two and a half then, and despite his earnest attempts to pronounce her name it had emerged from his mouth as Lally. Later, when pronunciation improved, he retained the use of Lally, preferring it to his cousin's full name. So did Leonora.

"The stories always sound better when my handsome older cousin reads them for me," Leonora answered with an impish smile.

Nathan's stomach tightened. He could see his father in Leonora's smile. Nathan had inherited Jacob Solomon's tall and rangy build, but his features were those of his mother, a long and narrow face, eager brown eyes, and straight, light brown hair. Somehow his father's looks had skipped sideways, settling not in the son but in the niece. Leonora had Jacob Solomon's round, open face, his thick mop of curling black hair, and his eyes. Whenever laughter filled Leonora's soulful brown eyes with light, Nathan could see his father best.

"Do come on, Nathan," Leonora said impatiently. "Please read to me before the others get here."

Nathan read for ten minutes, until, one by one, the staff of S. Solomon and Sons arrived. Tailors disappeared into the workroom. Sales clerks took up their positions. The postman delivered a handful of letters which Nathan carried up a short flight of stairs to the office, setting them on a desk that overlooked the trading area.

Just before seven-thirty, Nathan and Leonora stood by the front door. Exactly on the half hour, it opened again. Three men entered. One was in his early fifties, a short, portly man whose red face was framed by thick gray hair and frizzy whiskers. The remaining two were in their twenties.

"Good morning, Uncle Samuel. Good morning, cousin David, cousin Alfred."

Samuel Solomon gave his niece and nephew a curt nod before continuing into the shop where he watched with satisfaction the frenzied activity caused by his arrival. He clapped his hands. The sales clerks formed a straight line. Samuel inspected them, scrutinizing everything from the neatness of their clothing to the cleanliness of their fingernails. More than once Nathan had seen his uncle send an employee home because he judged the man's appearance to be unsatisfactory, and then deduct wages for the time he was absent. Samuel Solomon ran his shop like a field marshal commanding an army, and his employees were as afraid for their jobs as any soldier ever feared military discipline.

Today, Samuel was satisfied by what he saw. He clapped his hands once more, and the clerks scurried back to their positions. Followed by David, Alfred, Nathan, and Leonora, he climbed the stairs to the office where he sat at the desk and opened that morning's mail. Separating correspondence from bills, he began to read. Slowly his face turned a deep shade of scarlet.

"Do you know what these are?" He brandished two sheets of heavy paper covered with copperplate script. "Complaints! Complaints from customers whose clothes were not ready when promised! Let me remind you of something—the trading house of S. Solomon and Sons was not built on a foundation of broken pledges, and I will not see its reputation deteriorate because of such poor business practices. David, tell those laggards in the workroom that if they fail to complete their tasks more quickly, we will not hesitate to advertise for tailors who do."

David's chest swelled. "I will attend to it immediately."

Watching David hurry down the stairs on his mission of reprimand, Nathan was struck by the strong resemblance between Samuel Solomon and his older son. Like Samuel, David combined a lack of height with plumpness. His brown hair was yet to go gray, but his face was just as inflamed as his father's, his blue eyes equally sharp. Nor did the likeness stop at the purely physical. Both men offset bodily shortcomings with an abundance of arrogance and intimidation. Samuel's instructions would be carried out with interest, for David let pass no opportunity to flaunt authority over those subordinate to him.

"Alfred, you and Nathan inspect the shipment of cloth that was delivered last night. I am sick and tired of the mills foisting their rubbish on to us." Samuel never gave his younger son the tasks he assigned to David. Alfred was too easygoing to crack the whip over employees, too much of a hedonist to accept major responsibility. While David, at twenty-six, was soon to marry the daughter of a wealthy spice merchant, Alfred, two years his junior, showed no signs of settling down. He passed his time at dance rooms, racetracks, and prize fights, caring little for the business that afforded him such indulgences. He worked, Samuel had once decided, as if he were doing his father a favor. Samuel was thankful that his two sons had arrived in such an order. David had inherited his father's values. The shop would be in good hands when Samuel could no longer control it.

"Leonora, help in the workroom today. We do not want any more orders being late."

"Yes, Uncle Samuel."

Finally, Samuel turned to Nathan. "When you've finished inspecting the cloth, go to Mary McBride. She was to have six shirts ready by today. Here is what we owe her."

Nathan counted the money his uncle gave him. As always, was astounded. "One shilling and sixpence, Uncle Samuel? Eighteen pennies for making up half a dozen shirts?"

Samuel glared across the desk at his nephew. "Your task is to collect those shirts from Mary McBride. Please be so kind as to leave the matter of payment to my discretion."

Nathan could not drop the subject so easily. "How is the poor woman expected to exist on threepence a shirt? Especially when she has to buy her own needles and thread."

"Nathan, whenever I listen to you, I hear your father speak." Samuel shook his head in despair. "My brother Jacob, may he rest in peace, also had a head so full of ideals that no room remained for common sense. God only knows what would have happened had I not been able to employ him. He would have had to support himself as an old-clothes man in Petticoat Lane, or by working for a slop seller in Poplar or Blackwall. And as for you—you would have been out in the street, peddling cakes or fruit. Maybe the experience would have done you good."

Nathan gritted his teeth. Whenever Samuel encountered a disagreeable trait in his nephew, he invariably produced a comparison between Nathan and Jacob Solomon. He treated Leonora the same, likening a failing in the girl with a shortcoming in her mother Rachel, Samuel's sister. Nathan and Leonora had to accept Samuel's word, for their own memories were brief. Both sets of parents had died together eleven years earlier, in 1840, victims of one of the many accidents that plagued the early days of rail travel. Samuel and his wife, Harriet, had taken in the orphaned cousins, raising them, to outside appearances, as their own; Leonora's surname had even been changed to Solomon. But all too often they were reminded of their real station. While David and Alfred completed educations at private schools, Nathan and Leonora were put to work at the shop on Ludgate Hill. Every odd job fell to them. No matter how foul the weather, they opened the shop before six-thirty each morning. They swept, cleaned, and polished; they delivered and collected. And when Samuel ran out of work for his niece and nephew, he sent them out to drive a small, hat-shaped carriage that had the company's name emblazoned across every square inch of space. Samuel adored such eye-catching publicity. Advertisements for the shop decorated buildings and the walls of railway stations. He also considered himself a poet, and rarely a week passed without a magazine or newspaper carrying one of his carefully crafted rhymes extolling the praises of S. Solomon and Sons.

"Help Alfred with inspecting that cloth, Nathan, then collect those shirts. And hurry up about it. We do not have all day."

Nathan followed his cousin into the storeroom. They set a bolt of cloth on the cutting table and started to unroll it, seeking imperfections in the fabric. "You should know better than to discuss money with my father," Alfred said. "What are you trying to do to him, bring on a heart seizure?"

"It seems neither fair nor honorable to pay the woman only threepence a shirt."

"Since when does fairness or honor apply to business? If the trade establishes threepence as the accepted price, we would be foolish and irresponsible to pay a farthing more." Alfred notched a length of string through the fabric selvage to mark a flaw. "You should care only about what my father pays you."

Nathan looked across the cutting table at his cousin. Unlike David, Alfred bore no resemblance at all to his father. Samuel's younger son was tall and slim. His blue eyes sparkled, and his full mouth smiled easily. He was a young man who enjoyed life immensely, and he treated only his own gratification seriously. "Why do I even need money, Alfred? I live in your home and I eat with your family. Your father's money is surplus to my needs. Mary McBride has to feed three children on threepence a shirt. She certainly cannot rely on her good-for-nothing husband."

"Nathan, grow up! Do you think God created class distinction by accident? Do you believe that chance decrees one family should be illiterate peasants while in another family's veins flows aristocratic blood? Or that one family should be poor workers employed by another family—a wealthy merchant family?"

"We should still help those less fortunate than ourselves."

Alfred laughed. "We do. We pay them threepence a shirt."

Nathan felt his temper rise. He failed to understand how anyone could be as callous as Alfred, making jokes about the pain he saw around him. "I mean *really* help."

"The downtrodden are intended to be downtrodden. To help them be anything else would upset the natural order of things. Sometimes, Nathan, I believe you must be a Chartist." Alfred pointed across the table. "You missed a flaw there. Keep your mind on your work and we will all be better off."

They finished checking the cloth just after nine. Nathan donned his hat and coat and left the shop. The fog had lifted. The March sun shone through weakly. Despite the warmth of the coat, he shivered. In many ways, the fog had been a blessing, a disguise behind which London hid its ugliness, its manure-filled streets and dirty buildings. The grimy red brick and granite depressed him. Even the city's wealthy areas, where residents brightened the exterior of their homes with stucco, failed to escape the cycle of smoke and soot and fog. Nathan had lived his entire life in London. He knew nothing else, yet he also knew that somewhere there had to be something better.

He rode an omnibus to Saffron Hill, where he entered a maze of narrow courts and alleys. The breeze carried the stench of Fleet Ditch. Nathan held a scented handkerchief to his face, but even lavender failed to disguise the foulness of the broad, open sewer that carried waste to the Thames. He recalled the cholera epidemic that had raged two years before. In London alone, three thousand people had died during the summer of 1849. Saffron Hill would be a fertile breeding ground for another such outbreak. So would the Devil's Acre in Westminster, the rookeries of St. Giles, Jacob's Island in Bermondsey, or any one of London's countless slums where sanitation was virtually unknown.

Mary McBride dwelled with her husband and three children in one room on the ground floor of a crumbling house. Her husband worked as a long-song seller, hawking his yards of topical lyrics on London's streets. He squandered his meager earnings in the closest gin palace and came home drunk and reeking only to sleep. Mary's nimble fingers provided the family's sole means of support. As well as sewing for S. Solomon and Sons, she took in work from other shops.

Nathan rapped on the door of the rented room. "Mary McBride, I am here for S. Solomon and Sons' shirts."

The door swung back. Mary McBride was in her twenties, but the stoop of her thin body, the lines in her face, and the twisted hands with which she held the shirts made her appear twice that. Three small children, unwashed and wearing little more than rags, clung to her soiled skirt. Inside the room, bedding was strewn across the floor. Nathan felt a surge of pity for this woman, and when he handed her the one shilling and sixpence his uncle had given him, he did something he had never done before: he added a shilling of his own money.

"Thank you, sir." Mary accompanied the words with a tiny curtsy. "You're very kind, sir. Thank you."

Nathan left the building as quickly as he could. He hoped she used the money to buy food before her husband took it for drink, and then he felt angry that S. Solomon and Sons should contribute to such pitiful living conditions by paying only three-pence a shirt. Of course, his uncle would never see it that way. Nor would David, or Alfred. They would claim that without the threepence a shirt, Mary McBride and her brood would starve to death. And they would believe every word of it!

And without Samuel Solomon's beneficence, would Nathan and Leonora, the orphaned cousins, have starved? As Nathan pondered the question, a work of Charles Dickens came to mind, the story of another orphan named Oliver Twist. Neither

Nathan nor Leonora were hungry or abused, but they could find other similarities between their own situation and that of Dickens's ragged street urchin. When Nathan had read the book to Leonora, they had taken Oliver's phrase—"Please, sir, I want some more"—for their own, repeating it to each other as though it were some magic password. For a while, they had even referred to their uncle as Mr. Bumble, because they recognized many of the fat-witted, bumptious beadle's characteristics in Samuel Solomon.

Little wonder, Nathan mused, that he felt such empathy for Mary McBride. They both lived on crumbs that dropped from the same rich man's table.

Samuel Solomon lived on the northwest corner of Russell Square, in a stuccoed house built at the beginning of the century. Terra-cotta ornaments brightened up the exterior, but the inside of the house remained dim. The small windows, mementos of the structure's Georgian heritage, restricted sunlight. Even during the day, artificial illumination was necessary.

The gaslight, installed only the previous year, cast its yellow glow over the dining room, lending a soft luster to oak paneling and heavy mahogany furniture. Samuel occupied the top of the long dining table. At the other end sat Harriet Solomon. Alfred faced Nathan and Leonora across the middle. David was absent, dining at the home of his fiancée, Charlotte Sonnenfeld, in nearby Bedford Square.

As a maid cleared away the last of the dishes, Alfred pushed back his chair and stood. "Where are you going?" Samuel asked.

"Dancing." Alfred walked to the ornate marble fireplace and stood rubbing his hands in the warmth of the flames.

"Alfred, it would benefit you to view life in the same responsible manner as your brother David. In Charlotte, he has found a young lady from a fine family of whom your mother and I approve. While you waste your time with such shallow and insignificant pleasures as dancing, David enhances his prospects at the home of his future father-in-law."

"Perhaps I will be fortunate enough to find such a suitable young lady at Kate Hamilton's or the Argyll Rooms. Who is to know"—Alfred smiled at his father—"I might even find her waiting for me one evening this summer at Cremorne Gardens."

Samuel found no amusement in his son's mocking humor. "Rest assured, Alfred, any woman you find in such low places will not be welcome in this house."

"In that case, I will try to remember not to bring her home. Good night, Father. Mother." He stooped to kiss Harriet on the cheek, then fixed his gaze on Nathan. "Would you care to join me tonight? At nineteen, you should be learning the social grace of dancing. How will you ever sweep a beautiful woman off her feet without knowing how to dance the polka or quadrille?"

It was the first time Alfred had ever made such an offer. Nathan's interest flared. Often, he lay in bed listening for the sound of a cab stopping outside the house, the closing of the door, and Alfred's footsteps on the stairs; weary footsteps, it seemed, as if he had exhausted himself in his pursuit of enjoyment. Sometimes, when working together in the shop, Alfred described his outings, and Nathan listened spellbound to tales of dance floors filled with bewitching women, fiery horses flying around a track, fortunes won or lost on the turn of a card or the roll of a wheel, and bruising battles between combatants in a prize fight. Alfred's escapades aroused jealousy. Nathan could not wait to be old enough, and independent enough, to sample the pleasures that his cousin took for granted.

Before Nathan could respond, Samuel answered firmly on his behalf. "Never mind the polka and quadrille. Nathan has to open the shop in the morning. He retires early. You would do well to follow his example."

"I will bear it in mind," Alfred said as he left the room.

Letting out his breath in a long sigh, Samuel looked down the length of the table to his wife. "Do you hear how your son scorns me? A million young men in London would sell their souls to the devil for the opportunity of belonging to a family like this, and Alfred makes fun of it all."

Harriet sought to change the subject. Twenty-eight years of marriage had taught her that Samuel hated nothing more than having his dignity teased. He was a man who set vast importance on respectability. His position in life—encompassing his roles as family head, owner of a thriving business, and dignitary of the Maiden Lane Synagogue in Covent Garden—was his most prized possession. David had inherited his father's sense of propriety, but Alfred had not. The younger son delighted in poking fun at both his father and brother, enjoying it all the more when he could see how much it vexed them.

"I had a cab take me to Hyde Park this afternoon to see the Crystal Palace," Harriet told Samuel. "It really is the most exquisite and daring piece of architecture I have ever seen, tiers and tiers of slender columns and arches, and all that glass sparkling so brightly in the sunlight. It fills one's heart with pride to know that England can produce such an edifice."

Samuel's irritation at his younger son abated as he listened to his wife praise the enormous iron-and-glass structure that would house the Great Exhibition of the Works of Industry of All Nations. The Crystal Palace had captured public imagination like nothing before it. Crowds had filled Hyde Park to watch massive columns and girders hoisted into the air, four hundred tons of glass panes fitted into place. Forty countries were sending more than fifteen-thousand exhibitors, and for five months London would be the industrial and scientific showcase of the world.

"May we go on May Day to the exhibition opening, Samuel? Queen Victoria will perform the opening ceremony."

Leonora added her voice. "May we, Uncle Samuel? May we?"

Samuel made a show of pondering the request. He chewed his lower lip and stared into space for several seconds before giving his answer. "I think we would be wise to wait until the exhibition has been open for a while. Let us allow the annoying little problems of birth to be resolved before we visit."

"I will take you on opening day, Lally," Nathan promised.

Samuel turned a cold stare on his nephew. "Nathan, your cousin's name is Leonora. I am certain she would appreciate being called that."

Leonora shook her head. "I like Nathan to call me Lally. He has always called me that, even before we came to live here. It is his secret name for me."

"In that case, *I* would appreciate Nathan using your proper name. Only common people delight in nicknames, Leonora. Young ladies do not. Or do you secretly wish to be common?"

Face flushed with embarrassment, Leonora excused herself and left the room. Samuel continued talking as if nothing had happened. "Common people will be all you'll see on opening day. It will be a madhouse, hundreds of thousands pouring into Hyde Park just to glimpse the royal procession. I suppose the problem with London becoming the scientific and industrial center of the world"—his face broke into a smile as he saw a way to tease his nephew—"is that any member of the hoi polloi with a shilling in his pocket will be able to visit the exhibition."

Already angry at his uncle's treatment of Leonora, Nathan could not resist the bait. "Do you really believe that working people have no curiosity? Do you believe that they have no interest in expanding their worlds? Or do you just believe that they should not be allowed to do so?"

"Do you see how Nathan jumps to defend workers, Harriet? He is their champion. If it were up to him, S. Solomon and Sons would be a charitable institution that paid shirtmakers a guinea a shirt and tailors a shilling for every stitch they put in a pair of trousers. We would not be able to sell a coat for less than a hundred guineas, and who in their right mind, I ask you, would pay that?" Samuel folded his linen napkin and stood up. "I will be in my study, composing a patriotic advertisement to coincide with the opening of the exhibition. Please see to it that I am not disturbed."

As the door closed, Harriet touched her nephew's hand. "Do not take your uncle's words too much to heart, Nathan. Despite his brusqueness, you are his brother's son, and Leonora is his sister's daughter. He cares for you both deeply."

Although unable to fully accept his aunt's assurance, Nathan found comfort in her gentle touch. Outside of Leonora, Harriet Solomon was the only member of the household he truly liked. She had none of Samuel's or David's stuffy pride. Nor did she share Alfred's biting humor. Harriet Solomon was a kind-hearted woman who had made Nathan's eleven-year stay with the family tolerable.

Following the deaths of their parents, Nathan, at eight, and Leonora at six, had been plunged into an unfamiliar environment. While their own parents had lived modestly, their adopted family enjoyed wealth, and they exchanged their roles as only children in small homes for anonymity in a large house where they were never certain of their welcome. A sense of impersonality pervaded Russell Square. The vastness of the house intimidated them. Servants performed work their mothers had done. Most importantly of all, parental love was replaced by an uncle's neglect and the relentless teasing of their cousins.

Harriet, alone, had shown tenderness. At first, she eased their loss by weaving magical tales of their parents being in a place where no pain or sadness existed. She intervened on their behalf during squabbles with her own sons. Only with her husband could she not intercede. When Samuel decided that his nephew should leave school to work in the shop, Harriet argued that he should be given the same educational opportunities as David and Alfred. That battle she could not win. Samuel was adamant. He would never allow Nathan to occupy a position equal to his own sons. Samuel's brother, Jacob, had been a lowly sales clerk. In turn, his son, although brought up in Samuel's household, would follow in his father's footsteps.

"I do believe that Uncle Samuel cares for us." The lie came easily. Nathan did not wish to distress his aunt by disagreeing with her. "I just never cease to be astonished by the blindness of people to the misery of those less fortunate than themselves."

"You have your father's values, Nathan. He also wept for the hungry and the lame." Harriet's brown eyes clouded as some past moment came to mind. "I was nineteen when I was introduced to your uncle. He was five years older than me and seemed so wise, so confident. His father was a cloth merchant, but even at twenty-four Samuel was scheming to go far beyond that. Soon after we were married, he started a modest establishment in the Minories. He worked sixteen hours a day in it, learning from everything he did. And in eighteen thirty-six, with money he had saved and borrowed, he opened the big shop on Ludgate Hill. Your uncle is a very ambitious and clever man, and sometimes it was difficult to realize that he and your father were brothers."

When Nathan regarded his aunt quizzically, she shook her head. "Do not mistake my meaning, Nathan. Your father was as intelligent as his brother, but they were different men. Where Samuel was impatient, your father waited. Samuel browbeat while Jacob persuaded. And where Samuel ignored the beggar, your father dipped into his pocket. We moved here two years after Samuel opened the shop on Ludgate Hill. I would be a liar if I said I would happily exchange this beautiful house for something smaller and less elegant, but often during my marriage I have wished that Samuel were a little less successful, a little less money-conscious, and a little more like his brother had been."

Harriet walked from the dining table to the fireplace. Each of the two pillars supporting the mantelpiece was topped by a lion's head. She turned the nose of the right-hand head. A deep, long drawer slid out from the base of the pillar. Nathan stared; he had never suspected the existence of such a hiding place. "It is here Uncle Samuel keeps the money he hides from the tax collector," Harriet said. "Come, see for yourself."

Joining his aunt, Nathan looked down into the drawer. Gold coins gleamed dully in the gaslight. "There must be a hundred sovereigns there," he whispered.

"More than two hundred," Harriet answered. "Your uncle had this fireplace created when we first moved to Russell Square."

"Why does he keep this money here?"

"To look at it. These coins feed his vanity. Earnings on which he has not paid taxes proves that he has outwitted the income tax inspector, and mastering that official gives your uncle the same satisfaction as getting the best of any deal."

Lifting a handful of coins, Nathan let them filter through his fingers. He had never seen so much money in his entire life. "What does Uncle Samuel do with this?"

"Occasionally he uses a portion to buy something for personal enjoyment, but mostly he allows it to sit here and accumulate."

"Why did you show me this, Aunt Harriet?"

"To demonstrate the difference between your father and your uncle. Your father would have used this gold to help others. He would have considered it sinful to let money remain here while a short distance away people starved. And that is why I sometimes wish your Uncle Samuel was more like your father." Hearing footsteps, Harriet closed the drawer. The lion's nose tripped back into the upright position. By the time Samuel entered the room, Nathan and his aunt were once more sitting at the table.

"Please listen to this verse," Samuel said. "I have entitled it 'A letter to Britannia.' It is to be included in the *Times* on the day the Great Exhibition opens. Tell me whether or not you feel it strikes the proper patriotic note." He cleared his throat and began to read from the sheet of paper he held:

> "Britannia, again, the sun shines on thee,
> From city to city, from sea to sea.
> Men flock from afar to drink their fill

Of your scientific discoveries and industrial skill.
Britannia, we salute you, you are truly blessed,
With the greatness and vision for which others quest.
May God keep smiling on all Britons,
                    Yours sincerely, S. Solomon and Sons."

Face alive with a beaming smile of pleasure, Samuel awaited the opinions of his audience. Harriet clapped her hands lightly. Nathan seemed thoughtful for a few seconds, then said, "Uncle Samuel, you have fully captured the patriotism engendered by the exhibition, but would not the last two lines sound less forced and artificial if they read like this:

"May God bless you and keep you safe from all ill.
Sincerely, S. Solomon and Sons of Ludgate Hill."

Samuel repeated the fresh lines, nodding in approval. "A fine suggestion, Nathan. Perhaps all that time you spend reading does have some advantages." He left the room to return to his study and revise the advertisement.

In bed that night, Nathan pondered Harriet's words. Jacob Solomon would have used the gold to help the poor, just as Nathan, his son, had tried to help Mary McBride. Knowing that he so closely resembled his father filled Nathan with pleasure.

And then, just before falling asleep, Nathan puzzled over the incongruities presented by his uncle. How could a man who so brazenly exposed his patriotism across the pages of newspapers take such delight in cheating his country out of a measly seven percent income tax?

Chapter Two

March yielded to April. The days lengthened. The sun provided warmth as well as light. In parks and gardens, flowers and trees in vivid bloom added a blaze of color. Leaf by leaf and bud by bud, London shrugged off the drabness of its winter coat and assumed the brilliant mantle of spring.

Nathan welcomed the change of season. Dawn's light, rather than cold, fog-shrouded darkness, made the early-morning journey with Leonora from Bloomsbury to Ludgate Hill less depressing. Even the red-brick buildings, so dreary in winter's frigid gloom, seemed brighter and more attractive when warmed by the sun.

The greatest difference, however, was in the people. Wherever Nathan turned, he saw foreigners. The city overflowed with them, all drawn by the imminent opening of the Great Exhibition of the Works of Industry of All Nations. Men and women in unfamiliar clothes appeared in increasing numbers, gazing at monuments and buildings while discussing them in guttural Dutch and German or the musical swiftness of one of the Romance languages. Often, Nathan found himself stopped on the street by people asking in various accents for directions to some notable site. London, the very symbol of English history and culture, had been transformed into the crossroads of the world.

Samuel Solomon was quick to capitalize on the influx of

foreigners. Four days before the exhibition opened, he held a meeting in the shop. "This week, London becomes the center of the universe, and it will remain so for the five months the exhibition lasts. Hundreds of thousands will flock here not only to visit the exhibition but to see for themselves what makes the British masters of the world."

Leonora volunteered information she had read in that morning's newspaper. "A special train-and-boat service is bringing visitors here from Paris. Imagine that, eleven hours of continuous travel is all it takes to go from Paris to London."

David laughed scornfully. "Nelson must be turning in his grave at the thought of the French reaching England so easily. And then being welcomed with open arms once they get here!"

"Never mind Nelson," Alfred said. "Pity the poor old Duke of Wellington. As the ranger of Hyde Park he will see it overrun by the very people he made his reputation fighting. Maybe he'll poke a battery of cannon from the windows of Apsley House and blow the damned Frenchies right back across the Channel."

Samuel clapped his hands. "You need to concern yourselves with one thing only. At S. Solomon and Sons, a Frenchman's coins will buy just as much as the gold and silver of an Englishman. The same applies to any foreign visitor. We are traders, nothing else. So kindly leave your boorish jokes for comics at Evans's or the Garrick's Head Tavern."

Following his penchant for publicity, Samuel created signs in different languages to welcome visitors to London and invite them to shop at S. Solomon and Sons. Some signs he placed in the shop's enormous windows. He hired sandwich men to display other placards within a one-mile radius of the shop. The three largest billboards of all—in German, Dutch, and French—he reserved for the hat-shaped carriage. From dawn to dusk, Nathan drove the mobile advertisement around London's busiest streets.

The promotion worked. Tourists filled the shop, buying hats and gloves and scarves and canes from an overworked staff.

From his office above the selling floor, Samuel observed it all, watching and listening for any comment or action that could be construed as a slur against the overseas visitors responsible for the dramatic surge in business. Money was to be made from this exhibition, and he would not allow a single penny to slip away.

But in the privacy of Russell Square, where words could not jeopardize a sale, Samuel's tolerance underwent a transformation. Each night, he regaled Harriet with scornful descriptions of that day's foreign customers, and when he paused for breath his sons rushed in to fill the void. Very soon, the family's mockery found a point of focus. While all visitors from abroad provided amusing anecdotes for the dinner table, one group stood out from the rest. Visiting London in greater numbers than ever before were Americans. Their clothes and talk made them noticeable. So did their actions. Boasting loudly of earth-shaking products, American exhibitors had ordered extensive space at the Crystal Palace. Adjectives such as *greatest, finest, largest,* and *fastest* accompanied every deed. To the British, secure in an extensive history, the Americans with their youthful brashness and perpetual clamor were heaven-sent objects of ridicule.

"A very peculiar couple from New York visited the shop this afternoon," David related over dinner as the exhibition ended its first week. His words were meant for both his mother and his fiancée, Charlotte Sonnenfeld, who was dining with the family. "The man seemed normal. Indeed, until he opened his mouth, he might have been mistaken for an Englishman. But the woman wore the most bizarre clothes I have ever seen. A wide straw hat, a short velvet coat buttoned tightly around the waist, a frilled skirt that barely reached her knees—"

"Her legs were bare?" Charlotte's brown eyes widened. Disbelief covered her round face.

"Would that her legs had only been bare!" David cried. "Believe me when I tell you they looked far worse! Below the skirt they were concealed by the most hideous garment ever designed—trousers that blossomed full at the knee and then tapered down to skin-tight dimensions at the ankle."

"She called them bloomers," Alfred explained, "and claimed that they were becoming the epitome of fashion in New York."

"Bloomers?" Harriet experimented with the word, saying it three times as though repetition would make it more palatable. "What kind of name for a garment is a bloomer?"

"It sounds like something you would see at a flower show," Leonora quipped. She glanced at Nathan as if seeking approval. He chuckled.

David dismissed his cousin's joke with a sharp glance. "The garment is named after its creator, a Mrs. Bloomer. And this American woman resplendent in her bloomers had the gall to state that any English lady who cares about her appearance will soon be demanding identical garments."

Charlotte sniffed. "Mark my words, I care very deeply about my appearance but you will never see me wearing such things."

"I am grateful to hear that." David smiled at Charlotte and felt his skin tingle when she smiled back. He and Charlotte had met through the machinations of their fathers, who saw in such a union the merger of two affluent families, but even had they not been introduced, David was certain they would have found each other. There was so much he and Charlotte shared. Fate would have drawn them together had their fathers not done so.

Short with a leaning to plumpness, Charlotte did not possess a beauty to drive men wild. She was not a young woman, David knew, who would turn his brother Alfred's head. That did not concern him. At twenty-six, he appreciated the existence of more important qualities than physical attractiveness. The wealth he and Charlotte would inherit from their respective families, and the power they would create with that wealth, would more than compensate for any slights inflicted by a fickle nature.

Yes, he and Charlotte would be very happy. So would their children. After all, given a choice, what kind of parents would a child prefer? David's eyes rested on his brother. Handsome and profligate parents, like Alfred and any woman he chose for his wife? Or—his gaze moved on to Nathan—parents who were compassionate to the point of folly?

David had no doubt that he was destined to lead the next generation of the Solomon family. If his birthright had not already placed him in that position, his intelligence, ambition, and sense of values would have done.

The entire family, with the exception of Nathan who remained busy driving the hat-shaped carriage, and Leonora who sewed in the workroom, visited the exhibition during its second week. They spent the day there, and when they returned home they were fully loaded with fresh ammunition.

"What arrogant folk those Americans are," Samuel declared. "To reserve so much space and talk with such braggadocio about the products they will show, and when all is said and done they have nothing to show at all! Some carriages and rocking chairs! Model ships! And a representation of that floating church for seamen. *Punch* was right when it said the United States needed only a few square feet of exhibition space. Just place the Colt revolvers over the soap, and pile the Cincinnati pickles on top of the Virginia honey, and every treasure of American art and manufacture can be displayed in a very compact area."

"Those carriages have none of the elegance of an English chaise," Alfred observed. "They look as though they should be pulled not by horses but by oxen. And all that flour and copper ore . . . ! Why would anyone want to look at that?"

David offered a faint apology for American shortcomings, an excuse that in itself contained an insult. "I suppose we should take into account that the Americans are still a relatively primitive people. For God's sake, they have been looking after their own affairs for only seventy-five years. When they have a history as long and as noble as our own, perhaps their exhibits will rival those of Britain."

The exhibition was six weeks old before Samuel allowed his niece and nephew a day off to visit the Crystal Palace. With their uncle's words—"remember, I expect you to work extra hard in the future to compensate for this day of idleness"—echoing in their ears, Nathan and Leonora traveled to Hyde Park.

Enchantment began the instant they entered the main building and gazed up at leafy elms that soared majestically toward the curving canopy of glass. Pushed and buffeted by the crowd, they strolled along the vast central avenue, admiring ornate crystal fountains and groups of statuary, all brilliantly lit by the June sun. They explored galleries of art and machinery, furnishings and jewelry that had come all this way from countries as diverse as Russia and Australia, India and Bohemia. They marveled at a printing press that produced ten thousand copies hourly of the *Illustrated London News*. They viewed with fascination a steam hammer that could be calibrated to smash a gigantic boulder or lightly crack an egg. They enjoyed music made by a grand organ of forty-five hundred pipes, and they laughed delightedly as a silent-alarum bedstead dumped its occupant into a bath of cold water. And for fully two minutes, eyes fixed wide in awe, they stared at the Koh-i-noor diamond sitting regally inside its gilded iron cage.

It was the American section of the exhibition, though, which they visited after lunching at one of the Schweppes refreshment rooms, that intrigued them the most. Having heard the caustic reports of their uncle and cousins, they expected to find little, but the month that had passed since the family's visit had given the Americans time to fill their stands. Nathan's eyes flew from heavy machinery to carriages, weapons, furniture. Leonora gazed at delicate jewelry and art. Neither knew where to look first.

As they stopped to admire a group of unpretentious but exquisitely formed ornaments, a hand dropped onto Nathan's shoulder. Turning, he looked into the face of a tall, burly man.

"You're feasting your eyes on gold there, lad. Glorious California gold."

Nathan trembled with excitement. Two years before, he had avidly read newspaper reports about the California Gold Rush. Hundreds of Englishmen had sailed for America, fleeing cholera at home for gold fever in California. Now he could see for himself what the fuss had been about. "Is it true that all a man has to do is dip his hands in any stream to collect this gold?"

Humor mixed with mischief in the American's blue eyes. "Why would a man get his hands wet for a scattering of dust when with a shovel he can dig up two pounds of the stuff before breakfast each morning?" He took a simple bracelet from the display and set it gently in Leonora's hands. "Tell me that's not the most gorgeous thing you've ever seen or touched."

Leonora nodded. Such simplicity contained a world of beauty. The knowledge that the gold in this ornament had come all the way from California made her heart beat quicker. She passed the bracelet to Nathan. He caressed it lovingly. This was how gold should be used, to bring joy to the eye and the soul. Not to be hidden away in darkness like Uncle Samuel's hoard of sovereigns.

Similar cordiality awaited the cousins at all the American displays. When they stared curiously at a farm machine, a man with a Viking's flaxen hair said, "That's the McCormick reaper, capable of harvesting an acre of grain in an hour. When enough McCormick reapers are in farmers' hands, you'll see hunger become a footnote for the history books."

An older man showed photographs and daguerreotypes of such clarity that Leonora felt she was looking through a window at a real scene, while a straight-backed man in a blue-and-gold uniform explained to a large crowd the operating mechanism of Samuel Colt's revolver. Nathan and Leonora took in every action, every word. The Americans were not a bit like the absurd caricatures their uncle and cousins had painted. They were an open, friendly people, justifiably proud of the products they had brought from across the Atlantic and almost childishly eager to show them. They warmed to each American they met, and before leaving the exhibition that evening they took personal pleasure in watching a locksmith from Boston pick a supposedly unpickable English lock and collect a two hundred-pound reward for doing so.

Over dinner, Harriet asked her niece and nephew how they had enjoyed their visit. Leonora's reply was enthusiastic. "You should all go again. The American exhibit is finished now, and it is nothing like Uncle Samuel described it. Why, they have a machine, the McCormick reaper, that will revolutionize farming."

Samuel smiled at Leonora's intensity. "The Great Exhibition must be greater than any of us realized," he said, looking around the table to see who would share his joke. "In just a few hours, it has turned a girl from the city into an agricultural expert."

Leonora fell silent. Nathan, stung by Samuel's mockery, jumped to his cousin's defense. "If you could understand the benefits of this new machine, you would praise, not scorn. This reaper can harvest more than an acre of grain in a single hour." Words leaped from his mouth in a parody of the flaxen-haired American. "Farming will become much more productive, and hunger will be a thing of the past, a footnote in history books—"

"As long as the farmers who use this machine have an unlimited supply of slave labor to do their work." Samuel regarded his nephew indulgently. "Nathan, how can you find anything to admire in a country where slavery is an honored institution? Why, even your Mister Dickens had little good to say about the Americans when he visited the country eight years ago. What were his comments . . . ?"

David quickly supplied the answer for his father. "Pigs roamed the streets. Ribald slander was the stock in trade of a licentious press. The men hawked and spat everywhere and, worst of all, they were dull."

"Thank you, David. If you respect dull fellows so, Nathan, you must be a dullard yourself."

"It seems to me, Uncle Samuel," Nathan retorted, "that there is scant difference between American slavery and the niggardly wages paid by English shopkeepers! Perhaps American slaves are even less exploited than British workers. After all, slaves represent an investment for their owners, and as such are provided with food in their stomachs and a roof over their heads. Workers in this country all too often do not earn enough to furnish themselves with such basic living necessities because their employers feel that they can always hire someone else."

Samuel exploded. "In all my life, I have never witnessed such rudeness and ingratitude! Go to your room, sir! I will not be insulted so in my own home!"

Nathan stood up, kissed his aunt and Leonora good night, bowed stiffly to his uncle, and left the dining room.

He sat in his room for an hour, staring through the window at Russell Square. He was familiar with Charles Dickens's criticism of the United States in *American Notes,* and his attacks on the country as a nation of swindlers in the novel, *Martin Chuzzlewit.* Nathan had always accepted Dickens's words as fact, because he had no reason to believe otherwise. Until today, when he had met, for the first time, a group of Americans. They were not dull. Nor were they uncouth. And Dickens's prose, no matter how much enjoyment it had brought in the past, was nothing more than one man's opinion. What Nathan had witnessed today with his own eyes eclipsed any story Dickens could ever write.

The Crystal Palace was more than home to the greatest show in history. More than the blending of a million square feet of glass with iron columns, girders, sash bars, and an architect's imagination. For Nathan, the Crystal Palace had assumed a meaning far removed from science and industry and commerce. It signified a crux in his life, the crossroads between what he had always craved and what he now knew he could attain.

The Crystal Palace had opened his eyes to the wonders of the world and had shown him that there was indeed something better.

Chapter Three

David Solomon married Charlotte Sonnenfeld on the last Sunday of June, beneath the traditional marriage canopy of the Maiden Lane Synagogue in Covent Garden. The ceremony was followed by dinner at the Sonnenfeld home in Bedford Square. Sixty guests—family members, friends, and business associates—lavished presents upon the newlyweds. The bride's parents gave five hundred pounds. Samuel, not to be outdone, contributed an identical sum.

Nathan could never remember seeing his uncle in such an expansive mood. Samuel told everyone that he could not have invested five hundred pounds in a better cause than the future of his son and daughter-in-law. Furthermore, he would be delighted to give a similar amount when his younger son married. He would even, Nathan was amazed to hear, endow his nephew and niece with respectable wedding gifts should they decide at some future date to take a wife or husband. Not five hundred pounds, of course, but something befitting the only son of his dearly loved late brother, Jacob, and the only daughter of his late sister, Rachel.

By Monday morning, the wedding splendor was no more than a memory. Reality was the rumbling omnibus ride to Ludgate Hill and the preparation of S. Solomon and Sons for another business day. Samuel entered the shop promptly at seven-thirty. His face showed none of the previous day's joy and excitement. He was as stern a taskmaster as ever, reproving one sales clerk for scuffed shoes, and another for a tiny stain on his waistcoat. Worse was to come when he reached his office. On reading in that morning's mail a letter of complaint from a naval captain whose uniforms were made by S. Solomon and Sons, Samuel trembled with rage.

"David, look in the records to see which scoundrel made this customer's coat and send him packing!"

"David is not here, Father," Alfred responded.

Samuel lifted his face from the letter to glare at his son for contradicting him. Then he remembered. David and Charlotte were traveling by train later that morning to Brighton, on the Sussex coast. A pity. He would sorely miss his older son for the week he and his new bride would be away.

"Would you like me to attend to the matter?" Alfred asked.

Samuel shook his head. Alfred did not possess the firmness to handle staff discipline. "Never mind, I will do it myself. I have plenty of other work to keep you occupied."

Nathan left the shop at nine o'clock to make deliveries and collections. He was glad to get out. His uncle's mood was as acerbic today as it had been buoyant only yesterday. It was if he had suddenly realized that he was five hundred pounds poorer, and would be even more so should his younger son, nephew, and niece decide to marry. Nathan wondered what figure befitted the only son of Samuel's dearly loved late brother. He would be astonished if his uncle gave as much as ten pounds for his nephew's wedding. But then he had been dumbfounded to hear Samuel even mention the prospect of such a gift.

Among the errands for that day was the collection of six completed shirts from Mary McBride and the delivery of enough blue calico to make six more. Walking through Saffron Hill, Nathan blotted out the squalor by estimating how many shirts at threepence each Mary would have to make to earn ten pounds. Eight hundred. An astounding figure, until he calculated how many shirts she needed to make to earn the five hundred pounds Samuel had given to David and Charlotte. No person lived long enough to produce that many shirts.

A group of boys and girls, all dirty and dressed in ragged clothing, cavorted in front of the rundown house where the seamstress lived. As Nathan approached, they clustered around him, hands outstretched. Resolutely, he pushed his way through and entered the house to knock loudly on the ground-floor door.

"Mary McBride! I am here for S. Solomon and Sons!"

The door slammed back against the wall. Nathan found himself facing a tall, heavy, red-haired man. John McBride, for once, was home. "What do you want?"

Nathan angled his face away. McBride's breath, fanned by gin and bad teeth, was fearsome. "I would like to see Mary McBride."

"You would, would you? And would you be one of her—"

"John . . . !" Mary pushed her thin body between the two men. "This is the young gentleman who brings me work! Will you leave him alone for God's sake!" She turned to Nathan. "I am truly sorry, sir. He came home not long ago and was trying to sleep. He is not well, you know."

Nathan looked past Mary to John McBride. Alcohol flushed his pockmarked face. Anger filled his bloodshot eyes. His body swayed like a poplar in the wind. Nathan translated "not well" to mean completely drunk. How was it possible, so soon after yesterday's grandeur, to be standing in a place like this? "You have some shirts ready for me, Mrs. McBride?"

"Yes, sir. And do you have more work for me?"

Nathan handed over the blue calico. While McBride glared, Mary took the fabric into the room and returned with the finished shirts. Nathan handed over the one shilling and six-pence his uncle had given to him. After a moment's considera-tion, he added a shilling of his own money.

"God bless you, sir," Mary whispered.

McBride jumped forward, shoving his wife out of the way to

get at Nathan. "I saw that! Money you gave her, money above what she earned for making your shirts."

Nathan retreated, shirts raised like a shield. McBride knocked them aside. As Mary screamed, a fist crashed into Nathan's face, just below his right eye. He staggered back into the wall. Large red hands reached out. Fingers closed around his throat. The pockmarked face drew close to his own, and McBride's breath swept over him like a breeze from Fleet Ditch.

"You think your money can get you anything you want, do you? I know what kind of blackguard you are, sneaking in when honest men are working. I'll teach you a lesson you'll never forget!"

McBride's fingers became steel bands, squeezing ever tighter. Nathan's eyes bulged. His ears popped. Panic guided him where experience could not. His right knee flew into McBride's groin. The grip around his neck fell away. McBride's groan became a scream as Nathan's head flashed forward to butt him in the face. Blood pouring from a shattered nose, McBride fell to his knees. As Nathan stared at the writhing figure, shocked by the violence he had wrought and simultaneously elated, Mary pushed him toward the door.

"He is a very jealous man. I beg you not to be here when he recovers."

"What about you?"

"I've cleaned my man after many a fight. By the time you come for your shirts next week, he would have been in two more fights and he will not even remember who he fought. Now go."

Nathan ran from the house. Outside, the same children still played. When they stretched out grimy hands again, he scattered half a dozen pennies among them and made his escape while they fought in the dirt for the coins. By the time he reached Ludgate Hill, he could barely see with his right eye. He pushed open the shop door. Alfred, engaged in showing a customer a gold-topped walking stick, saw him first.

"What in heaven's name happened to you?"

Before he could reply, Nathan saw his reflection in a mirror. A purple bruise obscured his right eye. Blood spattered the front of his coat.

Samuel's voice echoed across the trading floor. "Come up here!" Nathan ran up the stairs to his uncle's office. Every eye in the shop followed; every ear strained to listen. "How dare you enter this establishment in such a disgusting state? Have you no regard for our patrons' sensibilities?"

"I was attacked."

Samuel snatched away the shirts and inspected them carefully. "I suppose I should be grateful that you had the common sense not to bleed on these."

"This blood is not mine. It is that of Mary McBride's husband. He was drunk and assaulted me. I defended myself."

"Clean yourself up, then take the carriage out. I do not want you in this shop looking like a common street brawler."

Nathan returned downstairs and entered the workroom. While Leonora tried to wash the bloodstains from his clothing, Alfred pestered him for details of the incident. Holding a cold, wet cloth to his eye, Nathan related exactly what had happened.

"Do you always give this woman extra money?"

"Sometimes. She cannot possibly feed herself and her children on what she earns."

"Do you give all our workers gratuities?"

"No. Only Mary McBride. She is far worse off than all the others. Besides, I cannot afford to be so philanthropic as to help everyone."

Alfred stroked his chin thoughtfully. "Perhaps you should let this be a valuable lesson on life to you, cousin. Study it and learn from it. Giving the woman the required one shilling and sixpence would not have infuriated McBride. It was the extra shilling that precipitated his rage. He saw something in that generosity. He thought you were paying for his wife's favors—"

"No man would pay for Mary McBride's favors."

"Take advice from someone better versed in worldly ways. Leave the status quo as it is. When you try to help people by giving them ideas above their stations, this is what happens." Alfred took Nathan's face in his hands. "That is an eye to be proud of. You could claim you fought fifty rounds with Bendigo of Nottingham, and no one would dare disbelieve you."

Chuckling, Alfred walked away. Leonora continued scrubbing the bloodstains. "Status quo," she scoffed. "Alfred does not know what he is talking about. You should help people less fortunate than yourself. He is wrong and you are right."

Nathan managed an awkward smile. "Thank you, but being right does not make my eye hurt any less."

Nathan returned to Saffron Hill the next Monday. The swelling around his eye had diminished but his face still bore the mark of John McBride's fist. As he knocked on the door, he prayed that the Irishman was not at home.

Mary McBride opened the door. On seeing Nathan she burst into an incoherent apology. "I'm sorry, sir, so sorry. But my children, they had to eat."

"What are you talking about?"

"Your calico shirts. My John, he came to last week, sir, after you'd left. He took the money you gave me. Took everything he could find and he left me, sir. Left me and the children without a penny, and we haven't seen him since. We didn't have a thing to eat, sir. Not a thing."

Mary's rapid shift of focus left Nathan confused. He grasped for the one familiar subject. "What about the calico shirts?"

"That's what I'm telling you, sir. We had no money to buy food with. So I made up the shirts and sold them. I'm sorry, sir. I'll pay you back, but we had to eat, didn't we?"

"Of course you had to eat." Nathan cursed himself for his thoughtless actions. He should have given Mary no money at all in sight of her drunken husband. "Do not worry. I will bring you more calico, and you will make the shirts again."

"I'll pay you back, sir. I promise you I'll pay you back."

"I know you will." He handed Mary the money his uncle had given to him for the finished shirts. "Take that. But if your husband comes back, do not let him see it."

He left with Mary's promises of repayment following him. He was certain she meant every word, and he was just as certain that she would never be able to keep such a pledge. The poor woman was trapped between conscience and a poverty that mocked it.

Samuel Solomon was not as understanding as his nephew. When Nathan recounted what had happened, his uncle regarded him with amazement. "You promised the woman that you would give her more calico? More of *my* calico?"

"How else will she be able to make the shirts?"

"The shirts are no longer important, Nathan. We will give the work to another seamstress and inform the customer that completion of his order will be a week late. Our concern now is the course we follow regarding Mary McBride." Nathan stared blankly, and Samuel added, "She stole from us. She purloined property belonging to S. Solomon and Sons."

"For mercy's sake, she was starving. Her husband had run off with every penny she owned. She had children to feed."

David, who had returned to the shop that morning after his week with Charlotte in Brighton, added his opinion. "Two wrongs never make a right, Nathan. Because she was the victim of a robbery does not give her the right to steal from us."

Nathan looked from father to son. "Have neither of you any compassion? Mary did not steal. She borrowed, and she means to pay us back. She had to sell something to have money for food, and the shirts were all she had." Nathan's eyes gleamed as he recognized a reason his uncle and cousin would understand. "What use to S. Solomon and Sons is a seamstress who starves to death?"

David rejected the argument with blunt logic. "Seamstresses are like pennies—a shilling buys you a dozen."

"I will consider what is to be done," Samuel told his nephew. "Now go about your business."

Samuel's decision was given that night. When the dinner dishes were cleared, he stood with his back to the fireplace, surveying his wife, his sons and daughter-in-law, his niece and nephew. "Tomorrow morning before I go to the shop, I will visit the police and have Mary McBride arrested as a thief."

"What?" Nathan cried. He scanned the table for a face that showed the horror he felt. David and Charlotte wore expressions of smug righteousness. Alfred's face bore the trace of a smile as if he found the episode a huge joke, another amusing chapter in his libertine way of life. Leonora appeared frightened. Only in his aunt's eyes did Nathan detect pity. Harriet had never known hunger, but she, like her nephew, could empathize with those who endured it every day.

"Aunt Harriet, please tell Uncle Samuel he must not act in such a harsh manner."

Harriet said nothing. Samuel, smiling in satisfaction, tucked his thumbs into the waistband of his trousers. "Nathan, your aunt and I are fortunate in that we recognize and understand our responsibilities. I would no sooner tell your aunt how to manage this household than she would tell me how to manage my business. There is much you do not grasp about the operation of a business, and I have no doubt that there is much you never will grasp. But let me assure you that I have not taken the step of prosecuting Mary McBride lightly. Nor have I taken it on my own. I have conferred with other shop owners. We all face similar problems, and if one of us is seen to give in to a worker taking liberties like this, all our livelihoods will be in danger."

Samuel filed a complaint at the police station. Mary McBride was arrested and charged. When the case came before the magistrate, Nathan was called to testify. Entering the witness box, he looked at Mary. Ice ran down his back. Where were her children? Who was caring for them? Were they even being looked after? In that moment, as he gazed at the pitiful woman in the dock, Nathan hated his uncle more than any person in the world.

The prosecutor guided him through the events leading to the sale of the six shirts. Nathan tried to slant his testimony in Mary's favor. He volunteered details of helping the seamstress with money of his own, hoping that he could paint a sympathetic picture of a woman in desperate need.

The prosecutor seized on the information. "You were in the habit of adding your own money to that paid by your uncle?"

"I was."

"So, even your munificence added to your uncle's fair payment for work received was not enough for this woman. She had to steal the shirts as well, and sell them as her own."

Nathan looked past the prosecutor to where his uncle sat. Instead of father and son, Samuel and David could be twins with their plump, pink faces wreathed in complacent smiles at the sight of a British court grinding inexorably toward its inevitable conclusion. "She sold the shirts only because her husband had stolen everything she owned."

"That is what she told you, and that is what you believed."

When Nathan left the witness box, he avoided looking at Mary. He had not helped her at all. He had painted shades of gray only to learn the court was interested in nothing but black and white. Mary McBride had stolen goods; therefore, she must go to prison.

The magistrate asked Mary whether she had anything to say on her own behalf. Her statement was brief. "I know I did wrong by selling those shirts, sir, but I had children to feed, didn't I? And how was I supposed to feed them with no money to buy food? That's all I have to say."

The magistrate cleared his throat. "The evidence presented in this case leaves me to draw but one inescapable conclusion. And that is that you, sir"—he pointed at Samuel—"are the one who should be in the dock. It is you who should be accused of a crime, not the wretched woman you have caused to come before me."

"Me?" Color deserted Samuel's face.

"Yes, sir! You! Theft entails intent to deprive a man permanently of his rightful possessions. I am quite satisfied that Mrs. McBride had no such intent. Your own nephew has testified how she promised to repay you. More than anything in the world she wanted to compensate you for what you had lost."

Samuel jumped to his feet. "That is a very easy claim to make when you are on trial for your liberty!"

"Be silent, sir! And sit down!"

Samuel, shocked at the cold ferocity of the magistrate's voice, dropped back onto the seat.

"This woman has three children. Because her worthless husband absconded with every penny she owned, she was forced to resort to unorthodox methods to feed those children. Still, I am certain in my own mind that she never meant to deprive you of your property permanently." The magistrate's gray eyes skewered Samuel. "I am in no position to comment on the often despicable treatment by shopkeepers of their sweated labor— that does not fall within the jurisdiction of this court—but what I would like to know, sir, is whether you have within your body a single shred of human kindness, a single ounce of decency?"

Nathan hid a smile behind a raised hand.

"I think not," the magistrate continued, when Samuel failed to answer. "That lack of pity can be the only reason you brought this outrageous charge. I find the defendant not guilty."

Samuel viewed Mary's acquittal as a personal humiliation. The moment he returned to the shop, he called David and Nathan to his office. "David, make certain that Mary McBride receives no more work. Contact every shopkeeper we know and brand her as a thief and troublemaker. If she wants work to feed her grubby urchins, she will have to find it in another town."

After David left, Samuel turned to Nathan. "Today was the most embarrassing day of my life. I hold you accountable."

"I fail to understand, Uncle Samuel, how I can be blamed for what the magistrate described as your lack of pity."

"You deliberately misled the magistrate with your evidence. You made the McBride woman look like a saint, while you did your damnedest to paint me as an ogre."

"I told the truth."

"The truth? You helped a thief go free while you smeared the reputation of an honest, upright man. Understand this, Nathan. Only the memory of my brother Jacob prevents me from turning you out into the street and letting you fend for yourself. Good God, if he only knew how you had stabbed me in the back today. . . ."

"My father would have done exactly as I did."

Samuel laughed scornfully. "Your father would have put family loyalty—allegiance to me, his brother, his own flesh and blood—above all else. Do not deceive yourself for a moment into thinking he would have done otherwise."

Nathan stood his ground. "Uncle Samuel, you use my father's memory like a tool. When you wish to belittle me, you compare what you consider a fault of mine to a fault my father allegedly had. You bring up his name only to hurt me. Well, sir, I do not believe a single word you say about my father. He was nothing like you at all. He would never have supported your exploitation of working people. He would have placed honesty and fairness above family loyalty. Believe me, Uncle, it is your actions, not mine, that would make him turn in his grave."

"Get out of my sight! Begone, before I forget that you are my brother's son."

Nathan did not eat with the family that night. Instead, he went up to his room where he filled a leather case with clothing. Then he sat by the window, waiting. Shortly before nine o'-clock, he saw Alfred leave the house. Minutes later, there was a knock on the bedroom door. Nathan opened it. In the hallway stood Leonora. She held a tray covered by a linen napkin.

"What do you want, Lally?"

Uninvited, she stepped into the bedroom and set the tray on a table. Her dark brown eyes took in the leather case in the center of the bed but she made no reference to it. "I brought you a sandwich and a cup of chocolate."

"Thank you."

"Is there anything else you need?" Again, her eyes flicked to the leather case.

"No, thank you. I will eat the sandwich and then go to bed." He gave his cousin a wan, forced smile. "You should go to bed as well. We must rest in order to open the shop for our loving uncle tomorrow morning."

He kissed Leonora on the cheek and closed the door. As her footsteps receded along the hall, Nathan felt tears burn his eyes. Leonora did not deserve to be deceived in this manner. Resuming his position at the window, he swore he would find a way to make it up to her.

Thirty minutes later, Nathan heard his aunt retire for the night. His uncle followed an hour later. Nathan remained at the window for two more hours. At twenty minutes before one, a hansom cab brought Alfred home. Nathan followed his cousin's footsteps up the stairs and along the corridor. He waited another fifty minutes, until one-thirty, when the house was absolutely silent. Clutching the leather case, he tiptoed downstairs, crossed the hall to the dining room and quietly closed the door.

Holding a lighted candle, he approached the marble fireplace. The right-hand lion's nose turned easily. The drawer slid out. Nathan scooped up gold sovereigns, counting as he poured them into his case. One hundred and twenty-nine. Less than the amount he had first seen, but more than enough for his needs. The drawer slid closed, and the lion's nose clicked back into place. For an instant total silence cloaked the dining room, then Nathan heard an echo. Another click, the opening of the door leading to the hall.

The candle flickered as Nathan spun around. Leonora, fully

dressed, stood in the doorway. "What are you doing here, Lally?"

"I want to go with you."

Nathan stood perfectly still, uncertain what to do. Moments into the greatest adventure of his life, indecision plagued him.

"I knew you were leaving when I saw the case on your bed. Take me with you," Leonora said more insistently.

"How can I take you when I do not know where I am going?"

"Of course you know. You are going to America."

Nathan blinked. He had not given any thought about where he would go. He just wanted to leave his uncle's home. Now, hearing Leonora mention America, it suddenly seemed so clear and obvious. "When I am settled in America I will get word to you."

"When you are settled, you will forget all about me."

The accusation pained Nathan. Leonora was the closest person in the world to him. "You know I would never do that. I care too much about you."

"If you really care, you will not leave me here alone."

"It will be too hard for you. You are a girl. I promise——" He broke off, heart pounding as another figure appeared behind Leonora. Harriet's white nightgown swept the floor. A frilly nightcap covered her hair. She was dressed for sleep, but there was nothing tired about her demeanor. In the candlelight that danced across her face, her eyes shone with excitement. It was the excitement, Nathan feared, that came with catching a thief.

"You are both fortunate that your uncle sleeps so heavily and your cousin Alfred is too exhausted by his pleasures to be disturbed by the noise you make." Harriet stepped into the room and closed the door. "Nathan, I knew you would finally leave this house tonight."

"You knew?" was all he could say.

A faint smile appeared. "Did you never guess my real reason for revealing that secret drawer?"

"What secret drawer?" Leonora asked.

Nathan ignored her. "To show me the difference between my father and my uncle?"

"I wanted you to know where money was. I did not want you fleeing with no means of support." Harriet looked inside the drawer and closed it again, checking the alignment of the lion's nose. "When I first showed you the money, I believed you would take it and leave within a week. When you did not, I wondered if I had misjudged you. Perhaps you were not as unhappy in this house as you seemed to be. But after today's incident, I knew you could not possibly remain here one more day."

Nathan swallowed hard. Never had his aunt's true motive occurred to him. "I will repay the money, I promise you that."

Harriet seemed not to hear. "Where will you go, Nathan?"

Leonora answered. "America. We have wanted to see America ever since we visited the Crystal Palace."

Nathan glared at his cousin in exasperation "I have already said that I will get word to you when I am settled. The journey to America is too dangerous for a girl of sixteen—"

"Seventeen! I became seventeen a few days after David's wedding. I am only thirty months younger than you, Nathan."

"Take Leonora with you," Harriet urged. "Like flowers, you will both blossom better out of the shade of this house."

When Nathan continued to vacillate, Leonora walked to the door. "Very well, I will see if Uncle Samuel agrees that you should take me with you."

Nathan was on her in a flash, dragging her back into the center of the room. "All right, you may come with me." Barely were the words out of his mouth than Leonora stood on tiptoe to kiss him on the cheek.

Harriet pushed her niece and nephew to the front door. She hugged each one farewell, understanding how apprehensive they must feel. No matter how miserable the house in Russell Square had been, its familiarity brought comfort. Facing them now was the unknown. "Go," she whispered. "Be brave and take the first step quickly. The second and third steps will be easier."

They walked down to the street. When they looked back, the door was closed. Nathan breathed in the clear night air. Squaring his shoulders and gripping the gold-laden case tightly, he began to walk with long, fast strides. His legs felt strong, his mind alert. Nineteen years old, and for the first time in his life he was in complete charge of his own destiny.

"I cannot keep up with you," Leonora complained. "My legs are shorter than yours, and this skirt was not made for hiking."

"That was why I wanted to send word later. You will hamper me, Lally, then neither of us will escape." Nonetheless, he slowed his pace.

After half a mile, they reached a cab stand. Nathan gave instructions to the driver, who stared at them with astonishment. "What would a young gentleman and lady such as yourselves want with Saffron Hill?"

Nathan's voice turned sharp. "Never mind what I would want with Saffron Hill, just take me there."

"Yes, sir!"

The cab pulled away from the stand and headed toward Saffron Hill. Following Nathan's directions, the driver navigated narrow alleys that barely allowed his vehicle passage. Outside Mary McBride's home, the cab stopped. Nathan got down and entered the decaying house. The seamstress answered his summons, too tired to show surprise at the unexpected, late-night visit. Nathan followed her into the single room. The three children, huddled together on a tattered straw mattress, slept peacefully.

Nathan spilled sovereigns on to the floor and began counting. "Use this money to make a new life for yourself." He reached forty-three, one third of the total taken from his uncle's treasure trove, and returned the remainder to the case. "Far away from where anyone will ever find you, especially your husband and my uncle."

"God bless you, sir," Mary whispered.

"I hope He does." Without another word, Nathan left the house and rejoined Leonora in the waiting cab. "Now take us to Euston Station."

Just after three o'clock, the cab deposited the young couple at the London terminus for the North Western Railway. Nathan led the way into the building. A timetable indicated that a train leaving at six o'clock would stop at Birmingham, Crewe, and Newton, where a connection could be made to the Liverpool and Manchester line. Nathan bought tickets to the port city of Liverpool, then he and Leonora sat down to wait.

"Our absence will be discovered in two hours," Leonora whispered, although they were almost alone in the vast station building. "The maid will knock on our doors as she always does. When she receives no reply, she will call Uncle Samuel. Do you think he will suspect Aunt Harriet of helping us?"

Nathan shook his head. "His vanity will never allow him to believe that a member of his own household would oppose him."

The number of people in the station increased. Every footstep snatched at Nathan's and Leonora's attention. Each new approach made them expect to see a policeman bearing down. Nathan wished he had a book to occupy his mind. He walked around, seeking discarded reading material. A rolled-up copy of the previous Sunday's *News of the World* was all he could find. By the time he and Leonora boarded the train at five-fifty, they had both read every single word of the newspaper's eight pages.

The train left Euston precisely at six, as London shrugged off the night. Sitting by the window, Nathan watched buildings glide past and smelled smoke from the engine. "Uncle Samuel will certainly know about our disappearance now," he told Leonora.

Leonora pictured events at Russell Square. A shiver ran down her back as she envisaged her uncle glaring at the empty drawer. "Do you think he will summon the police?"

"Of course he will. If he unleashes the full majesty of the law on some pitiable wretch for stealing a shilling's worth of calico, he will not hesitate to do the same to a scoundrel of a nephew who has made off with more than one hundred pounds."

"Two scoundrels. A nephew *and* a niece."

"Two scoundrels." he said and squeezed his cousin's hand. Wearily, he closed his eyes. From memories of childhood, he summoned the image of his father's face. His favorite image, that of his father laughing; the same image he saw whenever Leonora smiled or laughed. Jacob Solomon had laughed often, a happy man who could find more contentment in a single slice of bread than his brother Samuel would ever discover in an entire bakery.

Bathed by the memory of his father's laughter, Nathan's fears began to fade. Samuel Solomon was wrong. His brother Jacob was not turning in his grave over his son's actions. He approved of them, and he was laughing at the justice of it all.

The journey took eight hours. Worry returned the instant Nathan and Leonora stepped from the train at Liverpool's Lime Street Station. Were the police awaiting their arrival? Had their aunt inadvertently betrayed them? Or had their uncle, recalling Nathan's infatuation with the American exhibits at the Crystal Palace, concluded that his nephew and niece would flee to a port from where ships sailed to the United States?

Exuding a confidence he did not feel, Nathan strode along the platform. Leonora held onto his arm, desperately trying to keep up. In the forecourt of the busy station, they came under the scrutiny of two men dressed in black. As the men approached, Nathan's pulse jumped. He searched for an avenue of escape.

"Emigrating, are you, sir?" asked the taller of the two. Before Nathan could reply, the man removed the leather case from his hand. "Don't you worry about a thing, sir, we'll take you and your young lady to a fine lodging house that'll look after all your needs until you sail."

"Return that case at once!" Nathan reached for the case,

only to be blocked by the second man, a short, stocky individual who exhibited a disarming affability.

"Never turn down the offer of a friend, sir. Liverpool's an awful city, where emigrants like yourselves are taken advantage of by unscrupulous runners and dishonest lodging house keepers. We'll make sure you're comfortable until your ship sails."

"We do not have passage on a ship yet."

"You don't? Well, it's lucky you found us. We'll take care of that for you as well. Where is it you're going, New York?"

Nathan's head reeled. He was a stranger here. The wide streets and classically styled granite buildings were unlike anything he had ever seen. These men spoke an English he barely understood. He and Leonora had boarded a train for Liverpool, but instead of being English in England's second city, they might just as well be strangers marooned in some faraway foreign land. Only one thing remained clear. Without that case and the money it contained, they would be penniless. He lunged again for the case, this time determined to brook no hindrance. His shoulder sent the smaller man spinning away, and his fingers closed around the arm holding the case.

"Release that case at once, or it will be the worse for you!"

The case dropped to the ground. As Nathan stooped to retrieve it, he heard Leonora's shout of warning. The second man leaped on his back. Nathan bent sharply at the waist, sending his attacker flying over his head. As he straightened up, two strong hands locked his arms behind his back. A deep voice laden with authority said, "What's going on here?"

Nathan relaxed. The hold slackened. He turned around to face a police constable. "I was trying to get my case from these rogues."

The taller man pushed himself between Nathan and the constable. "He asked us to carry his case here, to the station. And when we got here, he refused to pay us."

"That is a lie!" Leonora protested. "My cousin and I have just arrived in Liverpool from London."

The constable turned to Leonora. He looked at her dress and

coat, rumpled from the lengthy train journey, and he knew who told the truth. "What are you doing in Liverpool?"

"Sailing to America. These scoundrels snatched our case, then promised to take us to a fine lodging house where we could stay until we sailed. When we told them that we had not booked passage on any ship, they offered to do that for us as well."

"I'm sure they did. You would have paid twice the normal fare, and you would have been booked on a ship that sails in a month or more, so you would have been forced to stay for weeks in a rat-infested hellhole whose owner pays them a commission." He glowered at the two men. "Get away, you vermin. Ply your swindling trade out of my sight."

Watching the two men walk away, Nathan remembered their warning. "Are they unscrupulous runners?"

"They are indeed. Gangs such as them wait to pounce like packs of wolves at Lime Street Station, or at the docks where ships bring America-bound men and women from Ireland. Pretending to help, they snatch away luggage and carry it to some lodging house where they have an arrangement with the owner. The poor emigrants cannot get their luggage back without payment of an exorbitant porter's fee, then the lodging house owner robs them even further. The only difference between pirates and runners is that pirates, if they're caught, face a date with the hangman."

Nathan rethought his own opinion of himself. Leaving the house in Russell Square that morning, he had felt like a fully grown man, capable of molding his own destiny. In London, surrounded by all that was familiar, he might have been. In the strange environs of Liverpool he was a lamb among lions. How would he cope in America? Unless he quickly shed his coat of wool and sprouted teeth and claws, he would be devoured.

"Would you be good enough to suggest where we could stay?"

The constable gave directions to the Wayfarer's, a hostel close to Prince's Dock. "It's owned by James Mulcahy, an honest man. In Liverpool these days, when there's so much money to be made from robbing emigrants, an honest man is all too rare."

Nathan and Leonora found the Wayfarer's to be a converted warehouse capable of accommodating six hundred emigrants waiting to sail. One shilling a day purchased a bed and three meals. The beds were clean, fifty to a large dormitory. Twelve such dormitories, separated by gender, plus a kitchen and dining area, comprised the hostel. They paid a week's money in advance.

James Mulcahy, the hostel owner, advised them on the supplies they would need for the lengthy voyage. "Food is included in your passage money, but half the time it's not to your taste. Take your own." He also told them what would not be needed. "Merchants will try to sell you everything from telescopes so you can see land before anyone else does to clubs, guns, and knives in case you're attacked by pirates. You don't need any of that. And don't let anyone tell you that your English gold's no good in America. If you change it here you'll be swindled."

That night, Nathan watched the men with whom he shared the dormitory secure their valuables, the life savings they were taking to America. Some slipped bags of money under pillows, others tied it to their bodies. Before going to sleep, Nathan folded his sovereigns into a scarf which he wrapped tightly around his waist.

Next morning, he and Leonora visited an emigration broker. Inside the office, a dozen men studied a notice tacked to the wall. The two runaways joined them. The notice was a sailing schedule of the shipping lines represented by the broker. Most ships went to New York. A few listed Baltimore as a destination, while one sailed to Quebec. Nathan's eyes took in a scattering of other North American ports, and he shook his head in wonder.

"So many ships, Lally. One sails every day. Are that many people leaving Britain?"

"Do you not remember that story in the newspaper you found at Euston? About eighteen fifty-one being the busiest year ever for emigration to America? What is to keep people here? Poverty? Disease? You and I have led sheltered lives, Nathan. Barring Uncle Samuel's workers, we have mixed only with people on the Solomon family's level. They are the exception. The Mary McBrides are the rule."

Nathan listened to the conversations around him. Everyone, it seemed, was sailing to New York. He knew nothing about it. Nor did he know about other American cities. He knew only of California, where a man could find two pounds of gold before breakfast each morning. The memory of his conversation with the American exhibitor made him smile. The man had exaggerated, of course, but even hyperbole had appeal.

"Look!" Leonora's finger pointed at the list. "There! Right at the bottom!"

Nathan's eyes slid down the shipping list. Suddenly they stopped. Sailing in four days for the city of New Orleans was an American packet named *The Wandering Jew*. He smiled. The smile became a chuckle, then a loud, body-shaking laugh. Heads turned from the shipping schedule to the young man who considered its contents so amusing.

"What is it you find so funny, boy?" a black-haired man asked in a lilting, musical voice.

Nathan's eyes remained fixed on the name of the ship sailing to New Orleans. *The Wandering Jew*. "My cousin and I have just discovered our true identities." Leaving the puzzled Welshman to ponder that answer, he approached a clerk's window.

"New Orleans, please. What is it like?"

"A beautiful city with a moderate climate."

"Can a man find work there?"

"All the work he can manage. It's a major port."

Nathan nodded. Somehow, he had known it would be like that. "I wish to book two passages on *The Wandering Jew*."

"What class?"

Nathan considered the question. With more than eighty sovereigns, they could afford the best, but who knew when they would come into more money? "The cheapest."

Five minutes later, Nathan left the office with two steerage tickets in his hand. "Four days," he told Leonora as they walked toward the Wayfarer's. "Just four days and we will be gone."

The four days passed in a flurry of activity. Nathan bought provisions, while Leonora purchased practical clothing for the voyage. They underwent a mandatory medical examination that comprised nothing more than a doctor peering into their mouths and eyes, and ascertaining that each had two arms and legs. Almost before they realized it, they were eating their last breakfast at the Wayfarer's. *The Wandering Jew* would sail on that evening's tide. In an hour, they had to leave the hostel and board the New Orleans-bound packet.

Nathan asked James Mulcahy for paper. He wrote to his uncle in London. After begging Samuel's pardon for any distress his and Leonora's sudden flight had caused, he apologized for the removal of the one hundred and twenty-nine gold sovereigns. "I do not use the word *theft*," he wrote, "because I have no intention of depriving you permanently of your money." Reading the sentence through, he chuckled. Perhaps his uncle would be able to appreciate the irony of it.

He finished the letter by promising to repay every penny. He did not mention giving some of the money to Mary McBride, nor did he indicate his destination. If Samuel chose to visit Liverpool and search through the passenger list of every ship, he might learn of his niece's and nephew's whereabouts. Nathan doubted that his uncle would bother with such a monumental task. Samuel would just wash his hands of them both, say "Good riddance to bad rubbish," and comfort himself by pointing out some shared shortcoming between Nathan and Leonora and their parents.

After signing the letter, he wrote Samuel's name and address on the envelope and handed it to Mulcahy. "I ask a favor of you. Wait a week and then post this."

"I'll gladly do that for you." Mulcahy shook Nathan's hand and wished him luck.

Carrying his leather case and balancing on his shoulder a

large wooden chest containing provisions for the voyage, Nathan left the hostel and walked toward Prince's Dock and *The Wandering Jew*'s berth. Leonora, using both hands to carry a case full of her own clothing, kept pace with him. Within two hundred yards of starting the journey, two men wrestled the chest and case away from Nathan. A third took Leonora's case.

"Which ship are you sailing on, sir? We'll see you get there all right."

"None of your damned business which ship we're sailing on! Now put our belongings down, or it will be the worse for you."

Ignoring the threat, the three runners walked off with the baggage. Quite calmly, Nathan withdrew from his coat pocket a small, elaborately designed pistol. Pointing the short-barreled weapon at the head of the closest runner, he commanded in a loud, firm voice, "Stop or I shoot."

The three men stopped. Mouths agape in shock and fear, they turned around. "Right, sir. We'll put your stuff down, sir."

Nathan watched them place the baggage carefully on the ground. "Now be off with you."

"Yes, sir." One of the men touched his cap respectfully, then they all turned and ran. Nathan waited until they were out of sight before replacing the pistol in his pocket. Lifting their baggage once more, he and Leonora continued their journey.

Four o'clock that afternoon found them leaning against the bulwark of *The Wandering Jew* as a steam tug towed the stubby, square-rigged ship from the walled enclosure of Prince's Dock. Their baggage was stowed in the cramped steerage quarters between decks. The gold coins Nathan carried on his person.

In the middle of the River Mersey, the ship dropped anchor. "Roll call!" sailors shouted. "All emigrants assemble for roll call! When you hear your name, show your ticket!"

Four-hundred men, women, and children crowded into the ship's waist. Names were chanted in a rhyming sequence by the second mate, a brawny red-haired man in a tight blue coat. As the first emigrants stepped forward to show their tickets, sailors armed with long, pointed poles went below. By the time roll call reached names starting with the letter M, they had returned. With them were half a dozen stowaways whose hiding places had been no defense against the sharpened poles. The stowaways were thrown into a rowing boat for the journey back to shore.

"Nathan Solomon, come on, come on!"

Nathan and Leonora stepped forward, tickets held out for inspection. The second mate glanced at them before moving on. They returned to the crowd. Nathan shifted his attention aft, to the quarterdeck. Protected by rope barriers from the emigrants, a dozen cabin passengers watched roll call. Nathan had seen some of them embark, their baggage carried by porters, their arrival greeted by the captain himself. In contrast, steerage passengers had been herded on board like cattle. Nathan would wager every one of his gold sovereigns that the cabin passengers would not be sleeping on the rough wooden bunks that were the lot of the emigrants. For a moment he regretted not paying the extra money for a cabin. He could have afforded to do so. He and Leonora could have traveled in comfort like the pampered men and women who now stood on the quarterdeck. Then he remembered his logic for traveling cheaply. Who knew when he would earn money again?

His eyes fixed on a plump, bearded man who stared intently at the chaotic scene in the ship's waist. What thoughts crossed that man's mind as he watched the emigrants? Was he mocking them or was he pitying them? What work did he do that allowed him to sail in the comfort of a cabin? His gray coat and trousers and his round-brimmed black hat gave him the air of a merchant. Had he come by his money as a shopkeeper, like Samuel Solomon? Or, like Nathan, had he come by it through theft?

"Look up there, Nathan!"

He heard Leonora's excited voice and felt her hand tugging his sleeve. High above the deck, red-shirted sailors danced nimbly through the rigging. Topsails snapped open and filled with wind. To cheers from the passengers, *The Wandering Jew* began its journey down the Mersey toward the Irish Sea.

Nathan resumed his position at the bulwark. Other emigrants surrounded him. Some sang. Some cried. And some just stood silently as the umbilical cord connecting them with home was severed. Nathan concentrated on a moment from the immediate past, recalling with satisfaction the expression of terror on the faces of the three runners as they stared down the barrel of his pistol. How many emigrants reacted in such a forthright manner to the runners' villainy?

He had followed most of James Mulcahy's advice. He had refused to change English gold in Liverpool. He had bought food but had not weighed himself and Leonora down with articles that would prove useless. Only in one area had he rejected the hostel owner's counsel—the purchase of a weapon. Nathan had seen the pistol in a gunsmith's window. Inquiring about it, he learned that the pistol had been made in Philadelphia by a man named Deringer. It had come to Liverpool in the possession of a sailor aboard an American ship. Nathan deemed it fitting that he should return the weapon to its homeland.

The memory of the runners' faces prompted a tight smile. Slipping his hand into his pocket, Nathan fondled the pistol's walnut stock and silver mounting. He was learning. He was losing his wool coat and growing teeth and claws.

Chapter Four

Life aboard *The Wandering Jew* settled quickly into a routine. Each dawn, a sailor lit the large stove of the emigrants' galley, above the main hatches. Each evening, a bucket of salt water doused the fire. All day long, scores of pots and pans simmered on the stove as emigrants cooked meals, either from ship's rations or from provisions they had brought aboard. Nathan and Leonora ate the ship's oatmeal, potatoes, and sea biscuits, while refusing the heavily salted pork. Thanks to John Mulcahy, they had their own supply of preserved meats, sausages, and cheeses.

Outside of cooking and eating, there was little to do. Most of the steerage passengers kept busy with their families, and those sailing alone regarded Nathan and Leonora suspiciously when they tried to start a conversation. Nathan fared no better with the sailors who worked in the ship's waist where the emigrants gathered. They struck him as brutal men who constantly harangued each other with oaths and violent threats. Luckily, the weather was fair and the two cousins spent much of each day sunning themselves in a longboat while Nathan read aloud from the magazines and books he had bought for the voyage.

On the third day out, the cry of "Land ho!" echoed across the ship. People crowded the starboard side. Far away, a shadowy peak rose hazily from the sea. Next to Leonora and Nathan, a young woman lifted up a small girl. "Look, darling, there lies America. We're almost there."

From behind came the laughter of *The Wandering Jew*'s second mate. "America's still as far away as the moon. What you're seeing is Cape Clear, Ireland. Don't you peasants even recognize your own country?" Grinning broadly at the disappointment he had created, the red-haired officer swaggered toward the quarterdeck, unhooking the rope barrier to gain access.

Leonora burned with anger. The second mate was well suited to supervising *The Wandering Jew*'s fierce crew. His threats and oaths were louder and fouler than those of anyone else, and more than once Leonora had seen him swing a rope's end at a seaman. Nor was his abuse reserved for sailors. Among his duties was overseeing the allocation of rations to the steerage passengers, a task he performed with ill humor, saving the choicest food for those who made a show of acknowledging his authority.

"Do not let that man's malice upset you," she told the woman. "To reach America, we first have to pass Ireland."

The woman regarded Leonora with eyes of deepest blue. "Would you be an expert on sailing around the world then?"

"No. But I did study geography."

"Geography? What is geography?"

"Geography teaches about the world's countries and peoples. I learned geography at school."

"Ah, school." The woman's grave expression disappeared. The blue eyes reflected enlightenment and hope. "I never had any school, but my little girl will. In America, my Frances will go to school and grow up to be as clever as her mother is ignorant."

Leonora recalled other times she had seen the woman, between decks or cooking at the emigrants' stove. Always, she had been accompanied only by the little girl, never by a man. "Is your husband not sailing with you?"

"No. My Michael went to America in eighteen forty-eight.

Three months ago, he sent money for me to join him." She glanced down at the girl, black-haired like herself, who stood serenely on the gently rolling deck. "Won't Michael be surprised when he sees Frances? She wasn't even born when he left home."

Leonora marveled at the young Irishwoman. Her own and Nathan's courage in crossing the ocean paled beside this woman's pluck. Leonora asked her name.

"Rose Meagher. From Tipperary. And who would you be?"

"I am Leonora Solomon. And this is my cousin, Nathan."

"Solomon? You're not Irish."

"We come from London."

The women's cordiality vanished in a flash. "London, is it? What are you doing here with the likes of us?" Her shrill voice attracted a dozen people, women dressed like herself in shawls and long skirts, and men whose garments spoke of farm work. "With your fine clothes and your fine speech and your knowledge of *geography,* you should be there"—she gestured toward the quarterdeck—"with the other *gentlefolk.*"

Leonora stepped back, confused by the venom that suddenly colored the woman's voice, and scared by the crowd it had drawn. Nathan understood perfectly. He and Leonora had no business between decks with the mostly Irish emigrants; they should be with the other Englishmen. The woman's husband, Michael Meagher, had gone to America in 1848, right after Ireland had been devastated by the potato famine. Meagher's wife, finally on the way to joining him in exile, viewed every Englishman as a foe. So, apparently, did almost every steerage passenger.

One strapping individual with a wide, rosy face and bright blue eyes pushed his way to the front of the crowd. A battered black hat covered a tangle of curly brown hair. Knee breeches ended above bulging bare calves. Ignoring Leonora, he speared Nathan's chest with a stubby finger. "Is it not enough that you have driven us from our homes and our country? Now you spy on our flight as well!"

Nathan had seen him often since leaving Liverpool, a bear of a man whose forceful personality overwhelmed those around him. He ruled the emigrants' kitchen, claiming one corner of the stove for himself and throwing aside the pans of anyone who dared contest him. At night, between decks, he played a fiddle, alternating melancholy airs that brought tears to the eyes with lively jigs that lent energy to the oldest legs.

"My cousin and I sail to America for the same reason you do. To find a better life." As Nathan spoke, he reached into his coat pocket to caress the pistol's walnut stock. He hesitated to use the weapon except as a last resort, but by God he would use it to protect Leonora and himself. "Besides, what makes you think you're worth spying on, you loud country oaf!"

The big man shook his head, unable to decide whether he was being reasoned with or insulted. He scrutinized Nathan's blue checkered trousers and silk waistcoat. "Why would a man dressed as finely as yourself be needing a better life?"

Before Nathan could think of an answer, Leonora's voice rang out. "You make a mistake to judge a man by what he wears. For all we know, you could be lord of some manor, a wealthy landowner too frugal to spend money on stockings. Your clothes mean nothing, and neither do my cousin's."

"A wealthy lord . . . !" The big man swung around to the other men and women. "Did you hear? William Patrick Flaherty, born and raised in a mud hut in Tullamore, could be a wealthy lord!"

A man next to Flaherty tugged his forelock and bowed deeply. A woman in a shabby black dress curtsied. Flaherty's laughter rolled across the deck. Nathan removed his hand from his pocket. He glanced at Leonora whose quickness of thought had saved the day. Her face was flushed with excitement; her small jaw jutted out with an aggressive confidence.

Leonora's poise was contagious. Nathan was ready when Flaherty turned around again. "In London I worked for a tailor. On leaving his employment, I helped myself to a complete wardrobe to compensate for years of abuse and niggardly wages."

"A tailor, eh?"

"Indeed. And among this tailor's customers was the Earl of Clarendon. It was the earl's clothes to which I helped myself."

Flaherty's eyes blazed at the name of Ireland's oppressor. "Whatever you stole, it was not enough!" He strode away, shaking with laughter.

The crowd dispersed, leaving Nathan and Leonora alone at the bulwark. "Thank you, Lally. Your quick wits saved us."

"Seeing your hand in your pocket quickened my wit. You should have bought new clothes for yourself as well as for me. What you wear, even if it is the proceeds of larceny, belongs not between decks but with pampered cabin passengers."

Nathan had to agree. Lying in the longboat, he sometimes amused himself by watching the cabin passengers. Four women, carrying parasols to protect them from the sun, paraded up and down the quarterdeck as if enjoying a summer stroll in Hyde Park. Three young men played cards constantly, breaking only to give an order for drinks to the steward. And the portly, bearded man in gray was always there. He spent most of his time on deck reading from newspapers he kept below in his cabin. Occasionally, he watched the activities of the emigrants, as if studying them.

He was watching now, Nathan noticed. Had he seen the earlier confrontation? If so, how had that fitted in to his studies?

That evening, Nathan became a celebrity. William Patrick Flaherty paraded him between decks, saying "I want you to meet the lad who stole the Earl of Clarendon's clothes." One man protested that he had seen the Earl of Clarendon with his own eyes, and he was a fat dwarf whose clothes would never fit a tall, slim young man like Nathan. Flaherty laughed off the objection. "My young friend is a tailor with a tailor's skills and cunning. Do you think he would not know how to alter the earl's clothes to fit his own shape?'' The man made no more complaints. Flaherty's word was law.

Before he fell asleep that night, Nathan turned to Leonora who occupied the next bunk. "For the first time since leaving Liverpool," he told her, "I feel that we belong on this ship."

He awoke just before dawn, holding on to the edge of the bunk to avoid being thrown from it. The cries and groans of tortured bodies came from all around, and with his first conscious breath he drew in the sour smell of sickness. He looked at Leonora. She lay curled up, one hand clutching her stomach, the other pressed to her mouth. When he touched her shoulder, she moaned and gestured for him to leave her alone. Holding a hand to his mouth, he pushed his way past listless bodies and climbed the stairs toward the hatch.

Cold spray slashed his face as he stuck his head outside. Gaining the deck, he held on to a mast for support. Whitecaps spat spray at banks of clouds scudding low across the sky. The ship pitched and tossed like a cork in the blustery wind. No women carried parasols on the quarterdeck today; no men played cards. Nathan made his way cautiously to the huge stove above the main hatches. It was cold. Using a piece of tarred canvas, he struggled for five minutes to start the fire. As he debated going back between decks for his own breakfast, another figure emerged. It was Flaherty, carrying his coffeepot.

"You and me are the only ones with stomach enough for this weather," the Irishman shouted above the wind. Filling his pot from the freshwater cask, he set it on the corner of the stove where the fire glowed brightest. "Did you not bring your own coffeepot with you? Never mind, there's enough in mine for two. You won't want to be going between decks again for a while, not with that stink of hell down there."

No sooner were the words out of his mouth than the ship dipped into a deep trough. A huge wave crashed over the bow. Water cascaded across the deck to soak both men through to the skin. The coffeepot flew off the stove, spilling its contents on the deck. With a hiss of protest, Nathan's fire died.

The wind carried a peal of mean, familiar laughter. The second mate stood five yards away. His red hair was plastered to his head. His blue coat clung wetly to his body. A broad grin covered his face. "Welcome to the Western Ocean, my lads. After a week of this, those of you who haven't been washed overboard will be wishing you'd stayed at home with your pigs."

"We need a fire for cooking!" Nathan yelled.

The second mate pointed to the sodden stove. "Not in this weather. You'll have to make do with eating food that doesn't need cooking. Those of you who feel like eating, that is."

"What about the ship's captain?" Flaherty demanded, reaching out to grab something solid as the packet dropped into another trough. "What about the cabin passengers? Are you telling us that they'll have to eat cold food?"

"Don't fret yourselves about Captain Franklin and the others. The ship's cook will do for them. His kitchen's sheltered."

"Then he can cook for us as well!"

"Really?" The second mate was in his element. The violent pitching of the ship gave him a distinct advantage over landsmen. While they clutched for support, he enjoyed every roll and lurch. "If you paid twenty pounds for the voyage and ate in the dining room like gentlemen, he might. But the cook hasn't set sail yet who'll use his fire for steerage scum."

"We'll see," Nathan said. "We'll see what he's got to say about it after we've spoken with the captain."

"That'll surely make the cook shake with terror."

"And we'll tell him about you," Flaherty shouted. "Make no mistake about that."

"You do that. Do it right now. And when you report me to Captain Franklin, be sure to get my name right. It's Johnson, Jack Johnson. Second mate of *The Wandering Jew!*"

"Did you hear that?" Flaherty asked Nathan. "It's Jack Johnson you've got to tell the captain about."

"Me?"

"Who else? To be captain of a ship like this, a man must be

a gentleman. You dress and talk like one. He'll listen to you more readily than he'll listen to a farm boy like me."

Johnson interrupted their discussion. "Well, do you want to see the captain or not? I'll be happy to show you the way."

Nathan and Flaherty approached the quarterdeck. The ship's first mate had the helm. He challenged them the moment they unhooked the rope barrier. "Steerage passengers aren't allowed past that rope! Get back where you belong!"

"Let them pass," Johnson called out. "Two emigrants to speak to Captain Franklin! I'll take them through." He accompanied the words with a broad wink. The first mate laughed, but the joke was lost on Nathan and Flaherty.

Johnson knocked on the door of the captain's cabin. When a voice commanded "Come in," the second mate opened the door and pushed both men through. "Two emigrants to air grievances, sir!"

Captain John Franklin had company, the bearded man Nathan had seen reading newspapers on the quarterdeck. They sat together in the mahogany-paneled salon that adjoined the captain's sleeping quarters while the steward served breakfast. Steam rose from coffee. The enticing smell of freshly cooked sausages taunted Nathan's and Flaherty's own hunger.

"What do you men want?" Franklin demanded.

Flaherty nudged Nathan to speak. "Captain, scores of men, women, and children are sick. They need a doctor and medicine."

Franklin savored the aroma of his coffee before sipping it. "We do not carry a doctor on this voyage. As for medicine, Mister Johnson will supply you with whatever he thinks you need." Nathan glanced at the second mate. A less likely physician he could not imagine. "Is there something else?" Franklin asked.

"Yes, Captain. The weather is too stormy for us to light the emigrants' stove. We need a fire for hot food, and with your permission, Captain, we would like to use the cook's fire."

"You can't light the emigrants' stove and you'd like permission to use the galley, would you?" A sharp nasal twang distorted Captain Franklin's speech. His eyes sparkled as if he, too, shared Jack Johnson's esoteric joke.

"Yes, Captain. The passengers would surely appreciate it."

"Passengers!" Franklin slammed a fist on the table. Color flooded his face. "Passengers occupy cabins. Between decks is cargo. Eastward-bound, my cargo is cotton and sugar as supplied by merchants like Mister Lowensohn here." He inclined his head to the bearded man. "Westward-bound, emigrants comprise my cargo."

"Cargo?" Nathan asked in disbelief. "Sir, *The Wandering Jew* carries people between her decks, not cargo."

"She carries emigrants!" Franklin fired back. "Men who are failures in their own land fleeing to another country where, undoubtedly, they will repeat their inadequacies. Emigrants are the bane of a shipping man's life! They bring in no money while expecting everything to be done for them."

"Then why do you carry them?"

"Ballast. I carry emigrants to provide ballast, otherwise my ship would ride badly. And ballast requires neither use of the cook's stove nor any other special treatment."

Nathan's anger rose. Abuse from the second mate was one thing; he had to be coarser and tougher than the sailors in order to control them. It was another matter to suffer such rudeness from the ship's captain, a gentleman. "Sir, whatever you consider emigrants to be, I would remind you that they are still free people. If you mistreat them, I will make certain that the proper authorities hear of it the instant we reach New Orleans!"

Flaherty, who had so far taken no part in the dispute, chose that moment to add his own, less refined opinion. "There's four hundred of us between decks, Captain. Your crew numbers about forty. We can take over this ship any time we feel like it."

The bearded man whom Nathan now knew as Lowensohn flinched at the prospect. Franklin was not so easily swayed. The nasal tone took on a quiet note of menace. "The sea laws that govern crews apply also to passengers. I've had mutinous emigrants tied in the rigging and flogged before now, and I've battened the hatches leading to the steerage and let troublesome emigrants suffocate in their own filth. I will not imperil my ship for ballast. Mister Johnson, escort these emigrants back to where they belong."

Grabbing Nathan and Flaherty by the collars, Jack Johnson marched them out of the cabin to the rope barrier. "Don't come the wrong side of this rope again," he warned, "or you'll be sorry you ever set sail."

Nathan shook himself free. His blood chilled at a terrifying prospect. Supposing his uncle and Charles Dickens were right? What if the American exhibitors he had met at the Crystal Palace were the exception, and these unfair, violent men the rule?

The storm lasted another three days. Nathan and Flaherty assumed control of steerage. Jack Johnson supplied them with two jugs of strong-smelling amber liquid which he claimed was a remedy for seasickness. Flaherty sampled the medicine and pronounced it to be rum-based. He shared the jugs between the worst sufferers. A dozen people declared they felt better; another thirty were demonstrably worse.

A cleaning brigade was organized from those men fit enough to work. They mopped between decks and carried the slops topside to be cast overboard. To those who resisted such sanitary measures, Nathan explained that he had witnessed the effects of cholera. In the cramped steerage quarters, the faintest hint of disease would be catastrophic. Sometimes, Nathan's reasoning failed to sway men who regarded filth and open sewers as a fact of life. Against such obstinacy, Flaherty's strength, and his willingness to use it, succeeded.

While the men cleaned, healthy women prepared food for those who could eat. Rose Meagher took charge of that and soon found herself in conflict with Jack Johnson. She brought her complaints to Nathan and Flaherty. "The second mate knows we cannot use the stove in this rough weather, so he takes a wicked pleasure in giving out food which needs cooking before it can be eaten. The devil take him."

Nathan gazed longingly at the galley where the ship's cook prepared hot food for the cabin passengers and crew. They ate fresh meat, cut from livestock slaughtered at sea. They enjoyed eggs collected each morning from the ship's chicken pens.

"And when I ask him what use food is when there's no fire," Rose continued, "he says that with his help anyone with money can get a meal properly cooked in the galley."

Flaherty quashed that idea immediately. "If we had money, we would not be traveling like convicts, would we? Besides, why should we pay again for what we have paid already?"

"That swine had the nerve to tell me that I could have all the hot food I want for myself and my Frances if . . ." Rose Meagher's voice failed her for a second. "If I was nice to him."

Flaherty bristled. Such an insult to Rose represented an insult to all of Ireland. "Is there nothing in the ship's rations that does not need a fire?" Nathan asked.

"Biscuits. For the poor folk who could afford to bring no food of their own, biscuits are all they have to eat."

Leonora, freshly recovering from seasickness, touched her cousin's arm. "I would be happy to share our food with others."

Nathan nodded. "All those with private stores will share their food. Leonora and I will start with our supplies."

Flaherty forgot about Johnson. He clapped Nathan on the shoulder. "Good lad! Despite your English talk and your fancy clothes, you've got honest blood in you!"

On the fourth morning, the wind dropped. The sea fell. At noon, the sun broke through. By midafternoon, Nathan found it difficult to believe that there had ever been a storm. Only blue sky could be seen. The wind, while enough to fill the ship's square sails, caused nothing more than a gentle swell. Sailors shone brass and holystoned the decks. Fire glowed once more in the emigrants' stove. Gaunt figures emerged from between decks. Hollow eyes stared out from wan, haggard faces as seasickness victims caught their first breath of fresh air in days.

The cabin passengers also reappeared. The four women with their parasols paraded along the quarterdeck again. The three men resumed their card game. And Mr. Lowensohn, whose goods were carried by *The Wandering Jew* on its eastbound crossing, returned with his newspapers. He had lost no weight during the storm, Nathan noticed. He had continued to eat well, enjoying cooked food with the captain and other cabin passengers. Lowensohn looked positively stout, just like a merchant should look.

As Nathan stared, Lowensohn glanced up from his newspaper. For a second, his pale blue eyes locked with those of the younger man. The distance was too far for Nathan to be certain, but he swore he could see the trace of a smile on Lowensohn's round face. The proud, self-righteous smile that colored a merchant's face when his carriage drove past the hovel of a working man.

Nathan decided there and then that he despised all merchants. From his uncle, who exploited his own family, to this man Lowensohn who had remained plump and well fed while only yards away hundreds of his fellow human beings had gone hungry for want of a cooking fire.

Whatever he eventually did with his life, Nathan decided, he would never become a merchant!

Following the storm, *The Wandering Jew* encountered a long stretch of favorable weather. Monotony again became the principal enemy. Nathan, having read the magazines and newspapers he had bought in Liverpool, tried to exchange them without success. Many of the emigrants could not read, and those who could had not brought reading material.

"Why not trade your magazines and newspapers there?" Leonora suggested, pointing to the quarterdeck.

"I would rather be bored senseless, Lally, than be forced to transact any business with those people."

Fortunately for Nathan, his alliance with Flaherty occupied much of his time. They assigned cleaning tasks, settled fights, and created diversions to relieve the tedium. Entertainment became a priority. Flaherty sought out anyone with a musical instrument, a voice, or the ability to dance. All were pressed into a nightly show that began once the evening meal finished. Performers were rated by the loudness of the applause, with the winner receiving the contents of a hat that was passed around the audience. One night Leonora, with a quavering voice, raced through "Greensleeves" in a desperate attempt to keep up with Flaherty's increasingly fast fiddle accompaniment. Another night, Nathan chanted a morbid ballad called "Sam Hall," which he had learned from his cousin Alfred, who had heard it sung at London drinking clubs earlier that year.

The most popular turn was a young Italian couple. The wife sang Neapolitan songs in a lilting contralto while the husband accompanied her on an accordion. After they had been judged winners for the third time, the captain's steward made the journey from the quarterdeck to the ship's waist to request that the Italians play and sing for the cabin passengers. They were gone for an hour. When they returned, Flaherty greeted them.

"How much did they give you?"

The man opened his hand. Inside were a half-dozen pennies. Flaherty snatched them away and held them out for Nathan to see. He turned to the quarterdeck. "You mean and miserable devils! You'll not be getting anyone from here to entertain you again!"

The incident with the Italian couple did nothing to lessen Nathan's dislike of the cabin passengers. Nor did his opinion of the ship's officers improve with the weather. Jack Johnson remained the bane of the ship's waist. While supervising the daily distribution of rations, he ridiculed the lame and sick, humiliated men by making them beg for food, and shamed women who sailed alone by loudly offering them extra if they behaved nicely to him. Nathan did his best to ignore the second mate, but the ploy was doomed to failure. Because of the depletion of their personal provisions during the storm, he and Leonora were forced to rely more on the ship's rations. Johnson, understanding that their earlier charity now forced them to come to him for food, reveled in their predicament. Each time Nathan lined up, the mate exhibited an overdone politeness that reeked of insolence. "Captain Franklin sends his compliments and says to be sure and inform him if anything displeases you, sir. You do know the way to his cabin, don't you?"

"I know the way," Nathan replied. "And you can be damned sure that I'll be paying the captain another visit if necessary."

"And you can be just as damned sure I'll be there to see it!"

Four weeks out of Liverpool, another storm overtook *The Wandering Jew*. This time, the emigrants in steerage fared much better. Most had found their sea legs. Those who had not were looked after by the healthy. The sleeping quarters were cleaned out twice a day, in the morning and in the evening, and there was little of the stink of sickness that had accompanied the first storm. Even cooking could be performed after Flaherty found two carpenters, traveling with their tools, to erect a shelter that shielded the emigrants' fire from all but the fiercest weather.

When, after four days, the skies cleared, the emigrants flooded back on deck. The nightly entertainment started once again. Loud applause greeted every act, no matter how mundane, as the audience made up for lost nights. Rose Meagher approached Nathan and Leonora and pointed to the quarterdeck. In the past, cabin passengers had always turned out in strength to watch the shows. Tonight, only two of the card players were visible. "Once I envied those people," Rose said. "No more. They may have wealth and comfort, but they lack our spirit. They had no one to help them through the storm as we did."

As Rose walked away, Leonora whispered to Nathan, "Who could have dreamed, two months ago, that one day I would feel so close to a peasant's wife from Tipperary?"

"Life has many twists and turns. Some good, some bad. Who is to know in which direction our next turn will take us?"

"We have both been through the bad turns, Nathan. From now on, every turn life takes will be in a good direction." Leonora touched her heart. "I can feel it here."

Nathan squeezed her hand. "I hope so, Lally. I hope so."

Next morning, life took a savagely bitter turn. As women worked around the emigrants' stove, a high-pitched shriek split the air. A second of pure silence followed, then Rose Meagher's voice soared octaves above the ensuing turmoil.

"Frances! Frances! Holy Mother of God . . . Frances!"

Nathan, who was sipping coffee, dropped his cup onto the deck and shoved his way through the mob milling around the stove. In the center, Rose, still screaming her daughter's name, cradled the little girl's head in her arms. The child's normally pale face was deathly white. Her breathing came in ragged gasps. Steam rose from her sodden clothing. On the deck beside her rolled a large black pot. Next to the pot lay a dozen potatoes.

As Nathan knelt beside Rose, a hand clawed his shoulder. He looked up into a young woman's terrified face. "I couldn't help it, sir. The little girl, she was running between our legs—"

Flaherty appeared at the woman's side and wrapped a calming arm around her. "No one's blaming you, Kathryn."

Nathan returned his attention to Frances. Rose cried softly as she hugged her daughter to her bosom. The child's breathing weakened. Nathan knew little about medicine, but he understood that the child's clothes had to be removed to ascertain the extent of the scalding. He looked up at the ring of faces surrounding the scene. All he saw were moving lips and moving hands as women prayed and crossed themselves.

"Lally!" he shouted. "Help Rose to undress Frances." He climbed to his feet, pushed through the crowd and ran toward the quarterdeck. The second mate met him at the rope barrier. "Mister Johnson, we have a child severely scalded! We need medicine!"

"Wait there." Johnson disappeared into the galley, emerging a minute later with a glass jar that contained turquoise-colored paste. "Put this on the child's burns. It's all we have."

As he glanced at the second mate's florid face, Nathan swore he saw concern. Could he be wrong about the man, he wondered as he ran back with the salve. Beneath Jack Johnson's cruel and coarse exterior, did there beat a heart?

The crowd parted for Nathan. Rose and Leonora had stripped the sodden clothes from the girl. Although Nathan tried to avert his eyes from the naked body, he could not help seeing the blazing area of cooked flesh that stretched from the front of her tiny thighs across her abdomen and up to her neck. By some miracle, her face had escaped the torrent of scalding water. In repose, chalk-white skin framed by ringlets of black hair, it was the face of an angel.

Rose rubbed the salve gently onto the burned skin. As she worked, her lips kept time, reciting novenas in a soft monotone. "Bring blankets from below," Leonora whispered to Nathan. Once the salve was applied, Leonora helped Rose carry the naked child to the shelter of the bulwark, out of the way of the sailors who worked in the ship's waist. When Nathan returned with blankets, Rose set the child on them.

"Go away, all of you," Rose urged, as if seeing the onlookers for the first time. "There's nothing for you here."

Some women returned to their pots and pans. Others drifted back to where they could watch from a distance. Two women stood by the rope barrier, passing information to cabin passengers. Nathan found himself standing next to Flaherty.

"What happened?" Nathan asked.

"The woman Kathryn had just lifted a pot full of cooked potatoes from the stove when little Frances ran between her legs. Kathryn lost her balance. A terrible, terrible thing."

Leonora left Rose to join her cousin. The shine had deserted her dark eyes. Her face looked worn, her shoulders drooped. "Rose will nurse the child up here. I will stay with her."

"How is she?" Nathan asked.

"Her breathing has become more regular, but she remains unconscious. Who knows what pain she is being spared? And what pain she will have to endure once the shock wears off?"

If the shock wears off, Nathan mused, but he was loath to voice such pessimism.

"How is the little girl?"

Leonora turned around to find the second mate standing behind her. "Has the salve helped?" Johnson asked.

"Yes, thank you," Leonora answered, struggling to conquer her surprise. Like Nathan minutes earlier, she believed she saw beneath Jack Johnson's coarse exterior the husk of a decent man.

"You tell that woman that if the child's pain becomes too great, I have a bottle of laudanum."

"Thank you. I will."

All day long and into the evening, Frances remained comatose. At ten that night, consciousness returned. She began whimpering. The whimper changed to a cry and then a scream as her senses registered the full extent of her injuries. The screaming diminished only when her tortured body no longer had the strength to sustain it. Rose rubbed in more of the turquoise salve and rocked her daughter back and forth. When her tired arms could no longer comfort the child, Leonora took over.

Long after midnight, when the ship was silent, Leonora opened the hatch and descended the steps. Feeling her way carefully in the dark, she approached Nathan's bunk and gently touched his shoulder. When he continued to sleep, she shook him harder.

"Nathan, come upstairs quickly. Rose has disappeared."

"Disappeared?" His startled question roused others from their sleep. They raised themselves to listen.

"Frances began crying again. Rose put on more and more salve until the poor child was covered with it. Nothing helped. Remembering what Mister Johnson said about laudanum, I offered to get some. Instead, Rose carried Frances in her arms toward the quarterdeck to search for him. That must have been fifteen minutes ago, and I have not seen her since."

Nathan put on his coat. Carrying a lantern, he marched toward the steps leading up to the deck. Behind came Leonora, Flaherty, and a dozen other men and women who had been awakened. "Search everywhere," he hissed. "And pray she has not jumped overboard and taken the child with her!"

The search party spread out across the deck, checking inside storage bins, behind coils of rope, in any area large enough to conceal a body. Nathan and Flaherty approached the quarterdeck. "We search for the woman whose child was scalded this morning," Nathan called out to the officer on watch. "She went to seek laudanum from Mister Johnson."

"I gave her permission to pass." Seeing Flaherty unhook the rope barrier, he demanded, "What do you think you're doing? You emigrants cannot come up here!"

"Try to stop us," Flaherty retorted.

The ship's officer grabbed a wooden club as if to defend the sanctity of the quarterdeck. Flaherty knocked aside the club and grasped the man's coat lapels, drawing him up on tiptoe. "Show us the way to Johnson's cabin and be bloody quick about it."

The man needed no further urging. A quivering finger and a quaking voice gave Flaherty the information he wanted. Moments later, Flaherty's fist pounded the door of Jack Johnson's cabin. When no answer came, the Irishman's shoulder slammed into the door. It withstood two assaults. On Flaherty's third charge, the lock gave. The door flew open. Flaherty stumbled into the small cabin. Behind came Nathan, eyes registering the scene illuminated by his flickering lantern. On the floor, lying like some long-forgotten parcel, was the shawl-wrapped figure of Frances Meagher. Johnson, half sitting, half lying on his bunk, was forcing himself into his trousers. Behind him, pressed between his body and the cabin wall, Rose Meagher lay completely naked. Dried tears streaked her cheeks. Her eyes were screwed closed as if blotting out everything around her.

The second mate's face reflected a mixture of disbelief and fury. "What the hell do you mean by breaking in like this?"

"What do *we* mean?" Flaherty was virtually speechless. His mouth opened and closed as if he were gasping for breath. At last he managed: "What do *you* mean by having Rose Meagher here?"

Johnson's face changed. The anger vanished. A smirk appeared, a slow, sly smile that hinted at secrets between men. "Have you never had a woman want you?" Johnson asked.

Rose's eyes shot wide open. "He made me—"

Johnson laughed harshly. "What are you going to believe? A man's truth or the lies of a trollop who was begging for it!"

"He's lying!" Rose screamed. "For laudanum he made me—"

The back of Johnson's hand silenced her. Before the sound of the slap faded, Nathan's hand dipped into the pocket of his coat to reappear holding the pistol he had bought in Liverpool.

"Stand up."

The sight of the weapon froze Johnson. He sat on the edge of the bunk, one hand gripping the top of his trousers. "You don't have the damned nerve."

"Stand up!"

This time Nathan roared. Specks of flint dotted his brown eyes. Johnson stood, pulling his trousers all the way up. Rose Meagher came to life. Wrapping a blanket around herself, she leaped from the bed and lifted the body of her scalded daughter. For ten seconds, she crooned to the child and rocked her gently in her arms. Suddenly, the expression on her face changed from love to horror. She shrieked, a strange guttural sound that started deep within her throat and finished bouncing around the confines of the cabin.

"Frances! My Frances is dead!"

Nathan's mind went blank with outrage. Flaherty snatched the gun from his grasp, raised it to eye level and squeezed the trigger. In the millisecond it took for the hammer to drop, Johnson flung himself to the side. The ball missed his head by inches and smashed into the cabin wall. As the echo of the shot died away, a new voice intruded.

"Stand very still. I know how to deal with troublemakers on my ship!"

Flaherty swung around to face the new threat. Captain John Franklin stood in the doorway. Next to him was the watch officer. Behind them, half a dozen cabin passengers, headed by the merchant Lowensohn, filled the companionway. Each of Captain Franklin's hands held a pistol. As Flaherty's empty weapon came to bear, the index finger of Franklin's right hand twitched. Thunder filled the cabin once again. Flaherty bellowed in pain and fell back onto Johnson's bunk, left hand clutching his right arm. Franklin spared him no more than a fleeting glance before spearing Nathan with hard brown eyes.

"Do you also wish to taste a one-ounce ball? Or do you have more sense than your reckless friend?"

"He was unarmed!" Nathan protested. "His weapon was empty."

"Only because he had done his damnedest to kill my second mate with it. Are you all right, Mister Johnson?"

"Yes, sir." Bare chested, and still holding up his trousers, Johnson walked past Nathan to stand beside his captain.

"What happened here?"

"That woman came to me for laudanum, sir. Her child had been burned this morning. While I was getting the laudanum, these two smashed the door in and tried to kill me."

"That is an outright lie!" Nathan stated.

"Be quiet! I would believe a thousand second mates before I accepted a single word from a mutinous emigrant."

Nathan refused to be browbeaten into silence. His future depended on what happened in the next few minutes. If the ship's captain chose to believe the lies of Jack Johnson, then Nathan's great adventure could end up in some stinking jail. Or worse. And what would happen to Leonora, who had begged and connived her way into being taken along? If he went to jail, she would be left alone and helpless in a foreign, hostile land.

"The one truthful statement in Johnson's pack of lies is that Rose Meagher came for laudanum," Nathan said. "She was gone for so long we became anxious. When Mister Flaherty and myself entered this cabin, we found your second mate taking advantage of Rose Meagher, while her child lay dying on the floor."

Jack Johnson laughed. "This emigrant spends all his time reading, Captain. You can see for yourself what kind of an imagination it has given him."

"I do not believe for an instant such a scurrilous accusation against one of my officers," Franklin said. He turned to the watch officer. "Confine these men. I'll decide what is to be done with them in the morning. A rigorous lesson in marine law might dissuade other emigrants from similar foolish action."

Nathan gazed beseechingly at Rose Meagher, willing her to break out of her grief and shock long enough to support his story. Instead, it was the merchant Lowensohn who spoke.

"Lower your weapon, Captain Franklin. Unlike you, I believe everything this young man has to say, just as I disbelieve every word uttered by your scoundrel of a second mate."

Franklin turned in disbelief. "You would do well to remain within your area of expertise, Mister Lowensohn."

"As long as *The Wandering Jew* carries my goods, it remains within my area of expertise." Lowensohn delivered the clipped, angry words in a harsh accent. "I am ashamed for saying nothing earlier about the appalling manner in which emigrants are treated on this ship. Now, I can keep silent no longer. If you take any action against these men other than to redress their justifiable grievances, you will never carry another bale of cotton for the factoring firm of Gershon Lowensohn."

Still Franklin made no move to comply. The undischarged pistol remained trained on Nathan.

"Did you hear me, Captain? I do not make an idle threat. I make a solemn promise."

Franklin turned the pistol aside and lowered the hammer. He

motioned for the watch officer to assist Flaherty. Nathan rushed to help Rose.

"She's dead," Rose murmured. "My precious little girl is dead. What will I tell my Michael now?"

"Her husband," Nathan whispered to Lowensohn, who had followed him to Rose's side. "He went to America three years ago. He had never seen the child."

Lowensohn fixed Rose with a solemn stare. "You will tell him that you are both young enough to have other children. Many other children. And they will be American children, born not in a country of bitter poverty but in a land of plenty."

Rose looked up from Frances's still body. Her eyes passed over the round, bearded face of Gershon Lowensohn but she saw nothing. The shock that protected her from the full agony of losing her child shut out everything around her.

Rose Meagher's shock lasted through the following evening, when the emigrants congregated to witness the little girl's burial. Supported by Leonora, Rose stared dully at two sailors who stood by the bulwark. Between them, on a plank, rested the tiny body of her daughter. An American flag with its thirty-one stars shielded the body from view.

"Do you know the captain asked me what flag I preferred?" Rose asked Leonora. "Did he expect me to say I wanted a Union Jack to cover my dear Frances? Stupid man."

Leonora patted the bereaved mother's arm. Rose might believe she was whispering but her voice was shrill enough to cut across Captain Franklin's recital of the Twenty-third Psalm.

"Where is that swine Jack Johnson?" Rose demanded.

"In chains," Leonora answered softly. "He'll get his just deserts for what he did."

"It should be him beneath that flag, not my little daughter." She looked at the captain as he intoned the psalm's final two lines. "I wish we had a priest here. God won't listen to a ship's captain like He'll listen to a priest."

"God listens to everyone."

"He pays more attention to what a priest says."

Leonora said no more. It was best to agree with everything Rose said, then she would not interrupt the service and it would be over that much quicker. Looking away from Franklin and the two sailors with their flag-shrouded charge, she caught Nathan's eye. She had never seen him so somber. His hands were clasped in front of his stomach, his eyes downcast. Beside him stood William Patrick Flaherty, his right arm supported by a sling. Flaherty had been lucky. The ball from Captain Franklin's pistol had passed through the fleshy part of his upper right arm without damaging bone or nerve. Laudanum dulled the pain.

From Flaherty, Leonora's eyes moved to Gershon Lowensohn, who stood three feet to Franklin's right. Lowensohn was the only cabin passenger to come down into the ship's waist to attend the funeral. The others watched from the quarterdeck. Nathan had related in detail Lowensohn's ultimatum to the ship's captain, describing his own amazement at learning there existed merchants who differed vastly from the stereotype he had formed on the basis of Samuel Solomon.

Captain Franklin finished the Twenty-third Psalm. After a five-second pause during which the only sound was the creaking of the ship, Gershon Lowensohn began reciting familiar words.

> "I will lift up mine eyes unto the hills
> from whence cometh my help . . ."

Leonora knew the hymn in both English and Hebrew. The Hundred and twenty-first Psalm had always been her favorite, sung often when she had gone with her uncle's family to the synagogue in Maiden Lane. Unlike her, Nathan had never enjoyed those visits. He maintained that they had no business accepting the existence of a warm and loving God—how could they believe after their parents had been taken from them? When she replied that she found comfort in being part of a group of people who held that something mightier than themselves existed, Nathan laughed. "Do not let Uncle Samuel hear you say that," he warned. "He will never agree to the existence of something greater than himself."

Hearing the particular psalm now, with its memory of a rare warm moment in her uncle's home, soothed Leonora. Silently, she accompanied Lowensohn through to the final lines:

> "The Lord shall guide thy going out and thy coming in,
> from this time forth and for ever more."

Captain Franklin gave a barely imperceptible nod. The two sailors lifted the end of the plank. The tiny body slipped out from beneath the Stars and Stripes and plummeted thirty feet to the water below.

"Frances!" Rose Meagher screamed. Before Leonora could react, the bereaved mother dashed toward the side of the ship. The two sailors tried to stop her. She fought her way past them and heaved herself up onto the bulwark. For an instant she rocked back and forth. Once more she screamed her daughter's name, then she dove into the sea. The sailors peered over the side. They could see no sign of either Rose or her daughter. The Atlantic had taken them both.

The two deaths cast a pall over the ship. Three other emigrants had died since leaving Liverpool, but their passing had affected only their immediate families. Rose Meagher's grief-stricken plunge touched the heart of everyone. Nathan and Leonora spent hours sitting silently in the longboat, as if debating the wisdom of starting this adventure. Flaherty's boisterousness deserted him. Even Captain Franklin appeared to mellow. He was seen between decks, talking to steerage passengers, and when a short but violent squall rocked *The Wandering Jew,* he ordered the ship's cook to make his stove available.

A week after Rose's death, Gershon Lowensohn visited the ship's waist. Carrying beneath one arm a pile of newspapers, he stopped by the longboat where Nathan sat with Leonora.

"Young man, I seem to have exhausted my supply of reading matter. Would you be willing to exchange some of your own newspapers and magazines with me?"

"I would be happy to do so, Mister Lowensohn. Please give me a few minutes to fetch them." Nathan went below and collected from his trunk every newspaper and magazine he had purchased in Liverpool. Hurrying back on deck, he found Lowensohn describing New Orleans to Leonora. Nathan listened intently. Hearing the merchant speak at length left a jarring note. When Lowensohn paused, Nathan commented on it.

"Forgive me for being so personal, but last week, in the second mate's cabin, I could have sworn you spoke with the accent of a German. At Frances Meagher's funeral as well. Now you sound as American as Captain Franklin."

"I have lived in the United States for more than twenty years, therefore I try to speak like an American. I lived in Jamaica for two years before that, and there my ambition was to speak like you, like an Englishman. But when my emotions rise, I speak English with my native accent, that of a Bavarian. Young man, I congratulate you on your talent for placing accents."

"Thank you." The merchant did not have such a plump face after all, Nathan decided. Pugnacious was a better word, a square, solid face that had filled with the years but which still bore the distinct character of a fighter. "These past months in London gave me many opportunities to sharpen that talent."

"Yes, the Great Exhibition. I consider myself fortunate to have been in England on business at such a time. I spent two days at the exhibition before boarding this ship for the voyage home. A fascinating experience. A wonderful city, London. Why did you young people leave?"

"We are orphans, sir," Leonora replied calmly. "Our parents died in a railway accident. Our uncle did his duty by bringing us up, but he accepted the charge with bad grace. We decided it was time to leave him."

"I see. Tell me, with all the ships that leave Liverpool for so many other ports, why would you select New Orleans?"

Nathan answered. "It was my cousin's choice, sir. She thought, and I agreed wholeheartedly with her, that the name of this ship described us perfectly."

"In that case, we have much in common. Read those newspapers well and you will have a reasonable idea of what you can expect in your new home." He turned and walked away.

Nathan sorted through the newspapers. "Listen to these quaint names, Lally. The New Orleans *Daily Delta,* the *Daily Crescent,* the *Bee,* and"—he choked with laughter—"the *Daily Picayune.* What on earth is a Picayune?"

She snatched a copy of the bilingual *Bee* from his grasp, her dark eyes gleaming with excitement as she read from the English section. "They have an opera, Nathan. They have theater. They even have gaslighting. . . ."

"What did you expect? A primitive village? They have other things as well, though," he added, holding open a page of the *Picayune.* "Listen, two men died in a fight in a tavern on Gallatin Street, wherever that is."

"We will not be going there," Leonora said primly.

"And Jacques Fontaine killed Alain Prossant in a duel."

"A duel? Surely dueling is illegal—"

"In England, but not in New Orleans. That was just one of six duels to happen on the same day. The others, it says here, were declared finished after the drawing of first blood."

Leonora paled. "Perhaps it is only men of French descent who duel," she said hopefully.

Gershon Lowensohn visited the ship's waist again the next day. Nathan and Leonora peppered him with questions. Yes, dueling was common, not just among Creoles but among men of every background. One avoided it by neither offering offense nor being quick to take it. And no decent person ever went anywhere near Gallatin Street.

"What about this?" Leonora asked, indicating a report in the *Daily Crescent* about the possibility of a slave uprising.

Lowensohn shrugged. "Editors need to find ways to sell their newspapers."

"Do you have slaves?" Nathan asked.

"A number of Negroes work for me."

The simple admission came as a shock. After Lowensohn's intervention with Captain Franklin, they had regarded the merchant as a merciful man. "How can you own another human being?" asked Leonora.

A trace of harshness colored Lowensohn's speech. "Do not speak so distastefully of what you do not fully understand."

"I understand enough to know that slavery is wrong. It was wrong when the children of Israel were enslaved by the Egyptians, and it is just as wrong now."

The anger disappeared as Lowensohn asked "How old are you?"

Leonora stuck her chin out. "Seventeen."

"You have very powerful opinions for one so young. The Negroes in my employ are treated better than many white workers. They have been with me for ten years, and each is like family."

"In England, we heard tales of abuse," Nathan began.

"Regrettably, abuse does occur, but the slave owner who practices it is cutting off his own nose to spite his face. After all, does it make sense for a man to invest thousands of dollars in workers and then mistreat that investment?"

Lowensohn's question recalled for Nathan his own argument with Samuel Solomon. Had he not used similar rationalization when claiming that American slaves were probably better off than free British workers? Nonetheless, it made the concept of slavery no easier to accept.

When Lowensohn returned the following day to ask what else they had learned from the Louisiana papers, Leonora drew him again on the topic of slavery. Lowensohn's voice contained more than a trace of a German accent when he answered.

"Your tone brims with self-righteousness, young lady, as if you somehow think the country of your birth is better because it does not have slavery. Which country do you think initiated the slave trade? Were you blind to the iron rings set into the Liverpool piers where slaves were held before being transported to the Colonies? The British have no right to feel superior to Americans for any reason, not when Baron Lionel Rothschild, after twice being elected to Parliament, is still unable to take his seat because he wishes to be sworn in on the Old Testament, and not on the true faith of a Christian. You will not find such prejudice in New Orleans. Our people are accepted by both Creole and Yankee society, and you should be thankful for it."

Leaving Nathan and Leonora to ponder that, Lowensohn returned to the quarterdeck.

Eight weeks to the day after leaving Liverpool, *The Wandering Jew* docked at New Orleans. Nathan stood with Leonora at the bulwark, admiring the wide sweep of the Mississippi as it curved north to Jefferson Parish and south to St. Bernard. Directly opposite, across the shining water, lay the settlement of Algiers. They had never seen so many boats. Oceangoing sailing ships and screw-powered vessels fought with river sternwheelers and sidewheelers for berthing space. Oar-propelled rafts and small arks darted between their larger cousins. Liverpool, with its concrete piers and docks and sense of order, was the epitome of harmony compared with the turmoil represented by New Orleans. Most striking was the profusion of dark faces. Negroes loaded and unloaded cargo, carried merchandise to warehouses, drove wagons, and engaged in a dozen other occupations. While they toiled, they communicated with each other in a patois neither Leonora nor Nathan could understand. If it were not for a huge sign with the city's name on it, they could have been forgiven for believing Captain Franklin had erred in his navigation and brought *The Wandering Jew* not to New Orleans but to Africa.

While steerage passengers waited for immigration officers to board, the cabin passengers disembarked. Gershon Lowensohn was among the first down the gangplank. Nathan and Leonora watched the merchant stumble momentarily as his feet touched firm ground for the first time in eight weeks. Recovering quickly, he looked up, acknowledging the cousins with a wave of the hand before following the Negro porter carrying his baggage to the point where people waited for arriving passengers.

A lump formed in Leonora's throat as she watched Lowensohn throw his arms around a stout woman before kissing and hugging a teenaged boy and three girls. Lowensohn was arriving home to people he loved, while she and Nathan were stepping into the unknown. They may have made friends on the ship, but such friendships were doomed to end when the voyage ended. Lowensohn was a prime example of that. During the latter part of the voyage, he had visited them daily, speaking freely of his youth in Bavaria, his two years in Jamaica, and his twenty years in the United States, beginning in New York before peddling in the South and finally settling in New Orleans. Both Leonora and Nathan noticed that he never invited them to his cabin and they understood why. A cabin passenger's ticket gave him leave to visit steerage passengers, but not the other way around.

Two hours passed before the steerage passengers were allowed to leave the boat. William Patrick Flaherty, right arm still in a sling, sought out Nathan and Leonora. "America's a very big country. In all likelihood we'll never see each other again." He held out his left hand. "Good luck to you both."

"Good luck to you as well."

As Flaherty held Nathan's hand, he winked. "I've also seen the Earl of Clarendon. No tailor in the world could have altered his clothes to fit yourself."

"Why did you accept my story?"

"Because you told it well, that's why. You brought a smile to my face, which is a rare thing for an Englishman to do for an

Irishman. And as it turned out, you weren't such a terrible fellow after all." With a cheerful wave, he strode toward the gangplank, eager to start his new life.

The two cousins were among the last to disembark. Twilight was falling as they carried their belongings down the gangplank, but the dock remained as busy as ever. Their legs wobbled when they exchanged the roll of water for the firmness of ground. Their lungs felt heavy. Only now did they realize how stifling the air was. Aboard the ship, a breeze had always been present. On land, the air hung like a suffocating blanket. The simple exertion of descending the gangplank made them both perspire.

Nathan swatted at an insect that brushed against his cheek. "We had better find a place to stay quickly, before these things eat us alive."

"As long as it is not on Gallatin Street." Leonora looked around for someone to give directions. She saw only Negroes, and she did not feel comfortable asking one of them. At last she spotted a tall, dark-haired man who stood gazing at *The Wandering Jew*. Followed by Nathan, she approached the man. Before she could seek directions, the man asked a question of his own.

"Were you passengers on that ship?" His Irish accent was soft, as though blunted by time in America.

"We were," Leonora answered.

"My name is Michael Meagher. My wife Rose was to have sailed on that ship, with our daughter Frances. Did you notice them during the voyage? Do you know if they are still on board?"

Leonora's heart throbbed. Unable to speak, she looked to her cousin for help. "I fear I have distressing news for you, sir."

Meagher listened wordlessly. "I thank you for all you did on behalf of my wife and daughter," he said when Nathan finished. "Does the man responsible remain on board?"

"The second mate, Jack Johnson? Yes, he is held in chains by order of Captain Franklin."

"Thank you." Meagher approached the ship and ran up the gangplank. Leonora took two steps, as though to follow him.

"Watch out!" Nathan pulled her back as a black carriage drawn by two horses came dangerously close.

The carriage stopped. The Negro coachman jumped down. He bore no resemblance to the sweaty, ill-clothed laborers who thronged the dock. A well-brushed broadcloth suit covered a starched shirt. A new beaver hat topped his neatly cut gray hair. Gleaming boots protected his feet. Nor did the coachman's speech resemble the laborers' unintelligible slang. "Do I have the honor of addressing Master Nathan Solomon?"

Too stunned to do anything else, Nathan nodded.

White teeth gleamed in the coachman's black face. "Allow me to introduce myself. I am Moses and I have come to lead you and Mistress Leonora from this desert to the promised land."

"What?" Nathan murmured.

"Compliments of Master Gershon and Mistress Anna Lowensohn, sir. They would be honored to have you both as house guests."

Chapter Five

Driven briskly by Moses, the carriage transported Nathan and Leonora to the Garden District, a section of New Orleans built on layers of fertile alluvial silt washed up by Mississippi floods. Enough daylight remained for them to see large, newly built houses. Magnolias, live oaks, and sycamore trees surrounded the houses, and the air was redolent with the scent of unfamiliar flowers. Reaching Prytania Street, the carriage rolled through a gate in an ornate cast-iron fence and entered a garden ablaze with crepe myrtles and rose bushes before halting in front of a white two-story house. The house was built four feet above ground level and was reached by steps leading up to a high covered porch supported by circular columns. The porch continued around both sides of the house, as did the balcony on the upper floor. As Nathan descended onto a marble carriage block, he decided that this was how temples in ancient Greece must have looked.

Gershon Lowensohn appeared on the porch, accompanied by the woman who had met him at the wharf. Arm in arm, they walked down the steps. "Welcome to Waverley," Gershon said.

Nathan needed only a moment to understand why the name sounded so familiar. "Despite our many conversations on board ship, sir, you never mentioned that you were an admirer of Sir Walter Scott."

Gershon's dour face softened. "Every English-speaking Orleanian is an admirer of Scott. Especially my wife, Anna. Anna, these are the English cousins I told you about, who no longer cared to be in their wicked uncle's charge."

"Welcome to our home," Anna Lowensohn said. "We worried that Moses would be unable to find you when he returned to the wharf."

"No matter how much I would like to claim such thoughtfulness was mine," Gershon said, "you are here at the insistence of my wife. When I described how you stood up to the ship's captain and that rascal of a second mate, Anna berated me for not thinking to invite you myself. But you have to understand that my mind was on other matters, such as seeing my family for the first time in many months."

Leonora curtsied slightly to the woman, as if meeting royalty. Nathan offered his hand. Anna gripped it with a dry firmness that came as no surprise. Like her husband, Anna exuded a manner that deterred flippancy and foolishness. Given to stoutness, her gray hair was pulled back from a round, red face to form a tidy bun. Keen brown eyes scrutinized whatever came before them. "My cousin and I thank you for your kindness," Nathan told her. "I doubt if you will ever understand just how grateful we were to hear Moses identify himself and his mission."

The brown eyes lost their sharpness. The round face broke into a smile so warm that Nathan was sure she understood exactly. "My husband and I have four children. If, for some terrible reason, they were forced to undertake a hazardous journey similar to the one you and your cousin have just completed, we would hope that someone would be kind enough to care for them."

"Besides," added Gershon to Nathan, "on board that ship, you proved that you were an exceptional young man, both capable and compassionate. I can always find room in my business for such sterling qualities."

Anna clapped her hands. "You must both be starving. Dinner is waiting, and so are our children, who are most eager to meet you." She ushered them up the steps to the porch, while Gershon instructed Moses to bring in the luggage. They entered the house through a wide hall from which a sweeping stairway curved up to the second floor. Anna led the way into a long, oblong drawing room divided by an arch into double parlors. The ceilings were far higher than any Nathan had seen before. He guessed them to be eighteen feet, which made the elegant mahogany and rosewood Louis XVI tables, chairs, and couches look like furniture from a doll's house. On smooth plaster walls, long mirrors rested in gilded mounts. The pine floor, like that in the hallway, gleamed with a high luster and was as black as coal.

Waiting in the far parlor were the children Nathan and Leonora had seen at the wharf. The three girls shared a sofa, sitting primly with their hands folded in their laps. The boy, older and more sure of himself, stood by the fireplace, studying a marble-and-bronze clock set inside an arched case. He turned away from the clock as the guests entered the room.

"Welcome to Waverley. I am Henry, my father's only son—"

Gershon Lowensohn's dry laugh interrupted Henry. "Next he will tell you that he is our only child to have finished school."

"I am." Henry squared his shoulders and stood as straight as he could. At fifteen, he was already an inch taller than his father, possessing a slender, willowy build that would fill out as adolescence passed. His eyes were blue, and his face, beneath a wild mop of dark curly hair, was almost triangular in shape, lending him a permanently inquisitive appearance. "Not only have I finished school, but I work with my father. I am, if I say so myself, absolutely indispensable to him."

Anna Lowensohn chuckled. "Without Henry, the business would surely fall apart."

"Henry works to get an understanding for commerce," Gershon explained. "In a year or two, he will attend university."

"And when he finishes there, he will surely tell you everything you are doing wrong," Leonora joked, feeling that she liked Henry already.

"He tells me that already, without the aid of a university education," Gershon said. He indicated the three girls sitting on the sofa. "Those beautiful young ladies are our daughters. Miriam"—the oldest girl stood up and curtsied—"is fourteen years old today."

"Congratulations," Nathan said and the fourteen-year-old's face turned red beneath her wavy, shoulder-length golden hair.

"That is Sarah, who is twelve, and Martha who is nine."

Sarah and Martha also curtsied, but when Sarah sat down again, Martha remained standing. "I am named after the wife of our country's first president. What do you think of that?"

Before Nathan or Leonora could reply, Henry offered his opinion. "Our English guests think that when you grow up, you will probably marry a man with wooden teeth!"

Martha swung toward her tormentor, but Anna was quicker. Stepping in front of Martha, she said, "You young ladies were allowed to stay up late tonight as a special treat because your father was coming home, and because we had guests. Now it is time for you to go to bed."

The two younger girls curtsied once more and left the room. Anna looked at her oldest daughter. "Surely I do not have to leave?" Miriam protested. "Today is my birthday. I am only a year younger than Henry, and I am thoroughly grown up—"

"But I work, while you still attend school," Henry reminded his sister.

"You make it sound as if you have worked for many years when it is, in fact, only a few months."

Anna interceded to break up another brewing battle. "You may stay up until we have finished eating," she told Miriam.

"Eat slowly," Miriam whispered to Nathan. Henry overheard the whisper and winked mischievously. "Eat quickly," he urged the two cousins, "and I will see you never want for anything."

Leonora's gaze locked with Nathan's. The constant bickering

among the three sisters and their older brother bore the hallmark of a close and loving family, something neither Leonora nor Nathan had ever known.

Despite Henry's entreaty, they ate slowly. For the first time in the nine weeks they were sitting at a proper dining table, and they basked in the attention paid to them by two Negro maids named Naomi and Bathsheba. The food, bearing the hint of unfamiliar, piquant spices, was unlike anything they had eaten in England. When Leonora remarked upon the tastiness of the meal, Anna explained that the family was fortunate to have a cook named Delilah, who prepared the finest food in all of New Orleans. Anna called Delilah from the kitchen. A huge woman with skin of velvet ebony entered the dining room. Like the maids, she covered her head with a red *tignon*.

"It seems quite coincidental," Leonora observed after Delilah returned to the kitchen, "that all of your servants have biblical names."

"There is no coincidence at all," Gershon answered. "There is also Rebecca our housekeeper, and Samson, a giant of a man who tends to the gardens. Anna and I gave our Negroes biblical names when we bought them ten years ago. We bought them"—he smiled at Leonora's expression of distaste that people could be traded like commodities—"to give them their liberty, and they have worked for us ever since as free men and women of color."

Leonora's sour expression changed to embarrassment as she recalled her confrontation with Gershon on board *The Wandering Jew*. She had never guessed that the Negroes who worked for him were free.

"Slavery is illegal in England, is it not?" Henry asked.

"England has a different form of slavery," Nathan answered. "That of merchants enslaving their workers."

Hardly was the reply out of Nathan's mouth before Henry was ready with a question about Queen Victoria. And when that was answered, he had another, about the British parliamentary system. Between answering, Nathan barely had time to eat. He could see that Miriam also had questions, but she was no match for her brother's tenacity. Nathan felt sorry for her. From his pocket, he pulled out one of the gold sovereigns he had taken from Samuel Solomon's treasure trove and passed it to the girl.

"Happy fourteenth birthday."

Miriam accepted the coin with a squeal of delight. When she showed it to her father, he gave Nathan a quizzical glance. "That is a considerable sum of money."

Nathan shrugged. "A young lady is only fourteen once."

"May I have Moses drive our guests around New Orleans tomorrow?" Henry asked.

"I thought you were indispensable to your father's business," Anna reminded her son.

Gershon pretended to consider the request. "I think I will be able to manage without Henry for one day, Anna."

"May I go as well?" Miriam asked. The question was intended for Gershon, but Miriam's green eyes were fixed on Nathan.

Anna started to say that Miriam had to attend school the following day, but Gershon waved aside her objection. "Did you not hear what Nathan just said, Anna? A young lady is only fourteen once. Missing one day's instruction in art and music will not irreparably ruin her education."

After dinner, Anna showed Leonora and Nathan to rooms on the upper floor of the house. Their bags had been unpacked, the clean clothes hung away, the dirty clothes removed for washing. Tired, but unwilling yet to sleep on the tall-post curly maple beds that beckoned so invitingly, they sat in Leonora's room and tried to come to terms with their good fortune.

"Did I not tell you on board the ship," Leonora said, "that every turn our lives took would be a good one?"

"You did indeed, Lally. But who"—Nathan spread his hands out wide—"could have foreseen this? The odd thing is, I despised Gershon Lowensohn when I first saw him. He struck me as being every despicable thing a merchant could be. And now look at him! And look at us!"

"That was thoughtful of you to give Miriam a gold sovereign for her birthday. How many do we have left?"

"Enough. Besides, I do not think we have to worry about money. I will be working soon. Remember, our benefactor can always use a young man with my qualities."

Leonora's voice took on a bantering note. "Perhaps he sees you as a suitor for Miriam."

"Do you really think so?"

"Of course not. I was only teasing. But I do believe Miriam might be thinking in those terms. She is fourteen, you know, and thoroughly grown up."

"How many times did she remind us of the fact?"

"Perhaps that is the reason she insisted so on accompanying us tomorrow. She has her father twisted around her little finger, and now that she is fourteen and thoroughly grown up, she wants you around her little finger as well." Leonora stopped talking as she saw the life leave Nathan's face. His mouth dropped and his eyes dulled. She asked what was wrong.

"I just had a vision of Michael Meagher. While we laugh over our good fortune, that poor devil is grieving for his wife and the child he never saw."

Leonora stroked her cousin's hand, feeling a tremendous sympathy for him. Nathan cared for everyone who came into his life. It was a trait Leonora loved. "I think we should both get some sleep. We have a busy day tomorrow."

"Good night, Lally." Nathan kissed his cousin on the cheek and went to his own room. Despite his tiredness, half an hour passed before he fell asleep beneath the *mosquitaire* that protected him from insects. And when he did, he dreamed a curious, incoherent fantasy in which the wealthy Lowensohns of New Orleans became intertwined with the ill-fated Meagher family. At the very end of the illusion, a woman ran toward him, arms outstretched. Brilliant sunshine flooded her face and he could see Miriam. Every feature was perfectly clear, curling golden hair, glowing green eyes flecked with amber, fair skin, and high cheekbones that would allow her to age gracefully. But when she passed beneath a tree, dark shadows distorted her features. The golden hair became black, the green eyes turned flat blue. And then Nathan saw Rose Meagher in that moment of grief and madness before plunging to her death.

After breakfast the next morning, Moses brought the carriage around to the front of the house. Unhesitatingly, Miriam sat herself down next to Nathan, leaving Henry to sit beside Leonora.

"How was your first night of sleep on American soil?" Miriam asked as the carriage rolled onto Prytania Street.

"Rather warm," Leonora answered.

"Summer and early autumn can try the patience, but you will soon grow accustomed to it," Henry assured her.

"The warmth of New Orleans is far better than the terrible weather in the North," Miriam said. "Do you know that in New York snow begins falling in October and does not stop until the following May? It is so cold that even the harbor freezes over, and no ships can go in or out."

"Who told you that?" Nathan wanted to know.

"Our father. He and mother lived in New York many years ago. They met there."

"Believe only half of everything Miriam says," Henry advised. "Like all girls, she has a tendency to exaggerate."

Miriam glared angrily at her brother. "I do not! And even if I did, it would not detract from the fact that New Orleans is still a far more pleasant town than New York."

"For once my sister is right," Henry said. "In fact, I will go so far as to say that any southern town is finer than any northern town. Southern people are more honest, southern weather is more amenable, and southern ground is more appreciative of a planter's effort. How much sugar and cotton is grown up north?"

Following Henry's instructions, Moses drove to the old quarter of the city. Alighting from the carriage, they stood with their backs to the Mississippi. Henry pointed to an immense bronze statue of a solidier astride a rearing horse. "I think you may know of that man. Andrew Jackson, our seventh president. Before being elected president, he gained a certain fame for leading the American army that routed the British in the Battle of New Orleans thirty-six years ago."

Miriam saw an opportunity to score against her brother. "Henry, stop boring our guests with the tales of gore you find so fascinating. Nathan and Leonora want to see the sights that make New Orleans so remarkable. They are not interested in who spilled blood."

"Very well. You be the guide."

"Certainly. And I will be a better one than you." Miriam motioned across the square to a large, stucco-covered building with a high central tower and belfries at each end. "That is the St. Louis Cathedral. Next to it"—she pointed to a structure of cement-covered brick, built in Hispano-Moorish style—"is the Cabildo, the seat of government. Inside the Cabildo occurred the transfer of the Louisiana Territory from France to the United States. And those"—she indicated long, four-story, red-brick buildings on either side of the square—"are the newly constructed Pontalba buildings, where many people can live quite privately within the same walls." Smiling impishly, she turned back to Henry. "Well? Am I a good guide?"

"You left out one item of major importance."

"I did?"

"You neglected to mention that in the Cabildo is the bronze death mask of Napoleon Buonaparte, cast from a mold taken of his head shortly after his death."

Miriam shook her head and spoke to Nathan. "Sometimes, I wonder how Martha, Sarah, and I could possibly have such a repulsive brother. I have asked our mother frequently, but she fails to understand as well."

"In turn," Henry responded as he returned to the carriage,

"I am always puzzled over how I could have three such thoroughly boring and unimaginative sisters."

As Moses continued the tour of New Orleans, brother and sister took turns at being guide. Miriam pointed out elegant public buildings, hotels, and the Théâtre d'Orléans, while Henry reserved his comments for more common places of entertainment. He seemed to know the location of every dance hall, gambling club, and drinking den in the city, and when they stopped for coffee at a stall in the French Market, Nathan questioned Henry on his knowledge.

Henry's answer was simple. "A young man in New Orleans is expected to know these things. How will he ever find enjoyment otherwise?"

"You, a fifteen-year-old boy, visit such places?" Leonora asked in disbelief.

Miriam laughed mockingly. "Of course he does not. Our parents would never allow him to do so. He has learned about them from men he meets while working in our father's business, and he makes believe that he, too, goes there."

Henry grimaced at his sister but he made no attempt to contradict her.

When they resumed the tour, Henry instructed Moses to drive to a cemetery. Nathan and Leonora stared in morbid curiosity at the multitude of vaults and monuments. "The dead have to be interred above ground," Henry explained, "because in New Orleans a grave digger would find water soon after he stuck his spade into the earth. It is bad enough that a man has to die, surely he should not be expected to swim his way to heaven as well."

As the carriage rolled along Esplanade Avenue, the northern boundary of the French Quarter, Henry called for Moses to stop. A dozen Negro men and women stood on the *banquette*. The women wore brightly colored calico dresses and dazzling silk bandannas; the men were outfitted in suits with vests and ties, white shirts, and well-shined shoes.

"That is a slave depot," Henry explained. "A slave dealer's

office. When slaves are not at an auction, they stand outside the depot in their best clothes so that they may be inspected." Leonora's face whitened. Nathan stared dispassionately, his mind on the sharp rebuke Gershon Lowensohn had given aboard *The Wandering Jew*. What right, indeed, did the English have to criticize anyone else?

Henry stuck his head through the carriage window. "Moses, what do you think of those specimens?"

From above came words that shocked the two English cousins. "A more scruffy bunch of niggers I have never seen, Master Henry. I wouldn't give you a dollar for the best of them."

Laughing, Henry ducked his head back inside the carriage. Seeing the expressions on his guests' faces, he felt he had to explain. "Moses is a free man of color who can read and write. He considers himself far above the bondsmen you see there."

"Is he as free as you or me?" Leonora asked tightly.

"He is still bound by certain legal restrictions, otherwise he may do as he pleases."

"Many free men of color, wealthy enough to do as they see fit, are slave owners themselves," Miriam offered.

Leonora sucked in her breath at that information. "Where do slaves come from to be auctioned?" Nathan asked. "I understood that their importation was now illegal."

"It is," Henry replied, "but some are still brought in by smugglers who feel the risk of apprehension is worth the reward. Others are sent down from states farther north for sale here. New Orleans is the largest slave-trading center in the country."

"Slavery is a fact of life," Miriam said. "Although the Lowensohn family does not own slaves, we do not criticize those who do. After all, our livelihood comes from planters whose own prosperity rests on the backs of bondsmen."

Henry thrust his head through the window once more. "Moses, before we return home, take us to The Oaks!"

The carriage rolled forward a few yards before Miriam shouted at Moses to halt. She glared at her brother. "I have tolerated you showing Nathan and Leonora every place of sin in New Orleans, but our father will be furious if you take them to The Oaks!"

Henry laughed at his sister's protest. "It is one o'clock in the afternoon, Miriam. Nothing will be happening beneath The Oaks at this time. Our fair city's blood lust is either settled in the evening, when offense is given, or first thing in the morning when both parties have had a good night's sleep."

"Do you refer to dueling?" Nathan asked. Henry nodded. "Have you ever seen one?"

"No. My father, as Miriam would be very quick to point out, forbids me to do so. But one day, when I am old enough to do as I wish . . ." In the confines of the carriage he flourished an imaginary sword.

Miriam sat stiffly, arms folded across her chest. Nathan, in the next seat, could feel her tension, and knew that Henry had overstepped the mark in the teasing of his sister. Despite the tormenting that went on between them, Miriam was clearly frightened by the prospect of her brother being involved in a duel. "I think, Henry, that it might be best if we returned to your father's home without visiting this place."

"I promise that you will see nothing. All I want is for you to experience the sensation of this place."

"It is a place of death," Miriam argued.

"Duels are rarely fought to the death, Miriam," Henry said with the exaggerated patience one uses in speaking to a child who is slow to understand. "The drawing of first blood usually ends the duel, and then both contestants, honor satisfied, become the best of friends again."

"What do you think, Lally? Should we humor Henry by viewing this meeting place for men who have been insulted, or should we cater to Miriam's obvious distaste for . . ." He turned to Henry once more. "What do you call this place?"

"The Oaks. The Dueling Oaks."

"I do not care whether you go or not!" Miriam burst out. "Do whatever you wish!"

Instantly, Henry hammered with his fist on the outside of the carriage. Moses cracked the whip and the journey continued.

Henry was mistaken. When the coach neared the towering line of live oaks beneath which the majority of New Orleans's matters of honor were settled, Moses pulled back sharply on the reins. "Master Henry! I see a crowd gathered beneath The Oaks. Maybe twenty or thirty men."

Excitement illuminated Henry's face. He swung back the door and jumped out. "Come on, Nathan! Now is your opportunity to witness some exceptional swordplay!"

Nathan hesitated momentarily, torn between his own curiosity and Miriam's distress. "Go," Leonora told him. "Miriam and I will remain here."

Needing no second urging, Nathan strode after Henry. "What kind of swords are used?"

"Sometimes a broadsword, a weapon to cut and slash. But usually the *colichemarde,* a light and slender sword. In the hands of an expert, it becomes lightning."

They reached the crowd and eased their way through. Two men in trousers and open-necked shirts faced each other across a distance of twenty yards. One was tall and slim, a strikingly handsome man with pale skin and jet black, wavy hair; the other was shorter, stocky, with tousled red hair and a heavy, brutal face. Seconds attended both men. Oblivious to the chatter of spectators offering and accepting bets in English and French on the duel's outcome, Nathan stared at the scene unfolding before him. He did not have to wonder what insult, what grudge, or what offense had caused this meeting. He knew.

Henry's voice was hushed with awe as he said, "They are not using the *colichemarde.* They are using pistols."

Nathan watched seconds press cocked pistols into both hands of their champions. A man acting as referee issued instructions in a firm voice. "I will count from one to five. You may begin firing at the count of one, and you will cease firing at five, to reload if necessary. If either of you opens fire before the count of one or continues to fire after the count of five, he will be deemed to have violated the *Code Duello* and he will be shot down for the poltroon that he is."

The referee retreated ten paces. The two duelists stood with pistols at their sides.

"One!"

Nathan jumped in surprise as the red-haired man threw up his right hand and fired. Splinters flew from the oak tree ten yards behind his adversary.

"Two!"

The pale-skinned man brought up the pistol in his right hand just as the red-haired man raised his left. The two weapons discharged simultaneously, filling the air with a crashing report that slammed like thunder into Nathan's eardrums. The red-haired man remained upright, a grim smile of triumph etched upon his coarse face as he saw his foe stagger back. Blood stained the right sleeve of the pale man's shirt. The discharged pistol dropped from nerveless fingers.

"Three!"

Face contorted with pain, the wounded man breathed deeply and struggled to regain his balance. With excruciating slowness, his uninjured left hand began to rise, the pistol in it traversing the ground, the legs of the red-haired man, his groin, his stomach, his chest, and finally his face.

"Turn sideways!" shouted the red-haired man's second. "Turn sideways and present a smaller target!"

"Four!"

The hammer fell. A final roaring explosion bounced back off the line of oaks. The red-haired man flung his hands up to his face as if to ward off the ball. He was too late. Blood gushed from between his fingers. Bone and brain sprayed out in a fine mist from his shattered forehead, and his body was picked up by an unseen hand and flung back five yards.

Nathan's stomach rolled. Clasping a hand to his mouth, he pushed his way through the excited, applauding crowd. Followed by Henry, he ran toward the carriage a hundred yards away. Moses saw him coming and clambered down to help. Leonora and Miriam also jumped down.

Leonora held out her hands to stop Nathan's mad rush. His face was ghostly white. She touched his sweat-covered brow. It was cold, deathly cold. "What happened?"

Nathan, eyes wild, shook his head. "Get us out of here!" he shouted at Moses. "Take us away from this place of madness."

The coachman helped Nathan into the carriage. The two girls followed him. Henry brought up the rear, his excitement dulled by the blood he had seen shed and his concern for Nathan.

All through the journey back to Prytania Street, Leonora tried to elicit information from her cousin. He said nothing. He just stared at her, every so often shaking his head as if unable to fully believe what his eyes had witnessed. Miriam pressed her brother for information. In a whisper, he told her what he and Nathan had seen.

Miriam turned pale. "I hope you are satisfied now, Henry Lowensohn. Just look what your stupidity has done for Nathan."

Henry lapsed into silence.

Back at Waverley, Leonora assuaged Anna Lowensohn's concern by saying that Nathan had fallen victim to the heat. "I am quite certain he will be all right in a few hours, thank you."

Leonora helped Nathan up to his room. She removed his boots and made him comfortable on the bed. Then she sat by him, holding his hands and massaging them gently. "I know what you saw," she said softly. "Henry told us during the ride home. Now you will have to do your best to forget about it."

Nathan closed his eyes and licked his lips. "Henry knows what he thinks I saw. He has no idea what I really saw."

"Nathan, I do not understand you. You are making no sense."

"Do you remember last night, Lally? Rose Meagher's husband? Michael Meagher?"

"Yes, of course I remember the poor man. What about him?"

Nathan swallowed hard, picturing once more the bloody scene beneath The Oaks. "Michael Meagher has his satisfaction now."

Leonora gasped loudly. "That duel—it was between him and Jack Johnson?"

"The very same. So help me God, as much as I despised the man, I can take no pleasure in his death."

"Neither can I." Leonora saw that a trace of color had returned to her cousin's face; the sweating had diminished. Sharing the terrible secret had lessened his own horror. "Nathan, please make me a promise. Swear to me that you will never participate in one of those stupid, terrible duels."

"I promise, Lally. I promise that I will be slow to give offense and even slower to take it."

Leonora recognized the sincerity in Nathan's warm brown eyes and kissed him gently on the cheek.

Helped by the friendship and generosity of the Lowensohn family, Nathan and Leonora soon felt at home. Only one aspect of New Orleans bothered them. That was the weather, an uncomfortable mix of heat and humidity that frequently robbed the body of energy and the mind of thought. Drenching downpours that regularly turned streets into raging torrents brought only temporary relief. The instant the rain stopped the temperature climbed, and the air hung like a damp, clammy curtain.

Two weeks after the cousins' arrival, a tremendous storm battered the city for two days. Flood waters inundated low-lying areas. Ferocious gusts of wind tore up trees and damaged buildings. When the storm passed and residents began the task of cleaning up, Nathan had a question for Leonora.

"Do you remember what that clerk at the emigration broker's office in Liverpool told us, Lally?"

"That New Orleans was a beautiful city with a moderate

climate? Well"—she started to laugh—"give him credit for being half right."

Nathan began working for Gershon Lowensohn, whose countinghouse was located at the bottom of Canal Street, the wide thoroughfare separating the old Creole quarter of New Orleans from the newer American section. Gershon worked closely with several planters. Among his functions as a cotton factor was buying whatever supplies the planters needed and arranging their shipment to the respective plantations; when necessary, he even arranged for the purchase and shipment of slaves. Sometimes, he acted as banker, lending money to his planters to tide them over the hard times that came with the production of an annual crop. Most important, though, he acted as an intermediary between plantation owners and the business world. In New Orleans he received cotton from the planters and sold it for the best possible price. In return, he charged the planters a commission of two and a half percent.

Although the first bales of the annual cotton crop reached New Orleans in mid-August, it was not until late September, coinciding with Nathan joining Gershon, that the season began in earnest. Each edition of the city's business newspaper, the *Price–Current*, carried details of shipments scheduled to arrive on board river steamers. Cotton receipts increased steadily, and by December the river was thick with steamboats waiting to unload their white cargo.

"The busy period lasts until March," Gershon told Nathan, "when it slows to a trickle that finally ceases in May. From late spring through the end of summer, the cotton trade takes a well-deserved rest."

Nathan watched river steamers line up to unload their cargo of cotton onto the wharf. There, a clerk labeled the bales with the marks of both planter and factor. From the wharf, the bales were transported to one of the twenty cotton presses operating in New Orleans where a steam press reduced them in size ready for final shipping to clients in New York and Europe.

With Henry Lowensohn, Nathan learned to grade the raw

cotton into classifications ranging from inferior to fine. "If you err," Gershon said as he handed each young man a six-ounce sample of cotton, "always be sure to err on the side of the man whose interests you represent."

Nathan tore the sample apart and rubbed it between his fingers. "Good fair."

Henry performed the same ritual. "Low middling."

Gershon raised his eyebrows. "Those two verdicts leave much in between. Henry, I hope you represent the buyer. And Nathan, you had better be the planter's man. I rate this sample as nothing better, and nothing worse, than middling fair."

Gershon also took the two young men on his visits to the planters. Sometimes they rode in a carriage. To the more distant plantations, they traveled by steamer. Nathan, by far preferring this employment to the menial labor he had performed for his uncle in London, learned quickly. Gershon congratulated him frequently on his astuteness. "Within a few years you will be able to leave me and go into business on your own account."

"I would be happy to remain with you. I have never known a finer employer." He knew how fortunate he was to have been befriended by Gershon. He and Leonora lived comfortably in the Garden District, while less fortunate steerage passengers who arrived in New Orleans, like those fleeing Ireland, finished up in the run-down shanties and cramped tenements of the Irish Channel, between Camp Street and the river.

Gershon smiled at the compliment and the pledge of loyalty it contained. "Do not forget Henry. Now, he treats working for me as a novelty, but once he attends university he will begin anticipating the day he succeeds me. The two of you have become good friends, and the best way for you to remain such is for you to work in separate places. Besides, I think you would provide stimulating competition for Henry."

While Nathan learned from Gershon Lowensohn, Leonora was taken under the wing of Anna Lowensohn. In New Orleans, Leonora was not expected to perform the mindless tasks she had done in London for her Uncle Samuel. Instead, she kept herself busy by helping Anna manage Waverley. Most specifically, she acted as governess for the three girls. She assisted with their schoolwork, shared with them her skill at sewing and embroidery, and kept them entertained for hours on end with stories about England and the voyage across the Atlantic. Sarah and Martha, especially, liked listening to Leonora's stories. They pressed her for more and more, and Leonora had to invent tales to satisfy the appetites of the two younger girls. She understood their craving for such accounts of distant places. The farthest they had traveled from New Orleans was to the resorts on Lake Pontchartrain, where wealthy Orleanians escaped the oppressive city summer. They envied Miriam, who, as a special birthday treat the previous year, had accompanied their father on a steamboat to Natchez. And all three girls were intensely jealous of Henry, who had been as far as Charleston and Savannah.

The position of governess became much more than a simple task. Leonora grew close to the girls, finding in each distinctly separate qualities. Miriam was by far the prettiest and the most vain. She spent hours on end in front of a mirror while she tried on different clothes and arranged her golden hair in a variety of styles. With each change, she wanted to hear Leonora's opinion.

"Leonora, do you think my hair looks best in curls or drawn back in a classical Grecian look?

"Leonora, which color dress becomes my complexion most? A royal blue or a dark green?

"Leonora, which locket is most complimentary to my neck, the silver or the gold . . . ?"

The oldest girl's narcissim never failed to amuse Leonora. "It does not matter which coiffure, which color dress, or which locket you choose, Miriam. You will break young men's hearts no matter what."

"Have you broken many?"

Leonora shook her head. "Not one."

Miriam appeared saddened by the news. "That is a shame. Has your own been broken?"

Leonora answered with an enigmatic smile.

Neither of the other girls shared Miriam's conceit. Nor did they possesses her stunning looks. Sarah was by far the most solemn of the three sisters. She took her schoolwork seriously, and any advice she sought from Leonora concerned academic subjects rather than fashion. Frequently, Leonora could see a young Anna in the middle girl—short and somewhat stocky with straight dark brown hair and a plump, round face.

There was nothing solemn about Martha. The nine-year-old girl with unruly brown hair and perpetually sparkling blue eyes was almost boyish in her actions. If there was any mischief to be found, Martha would discover it. In Leonora's first days at Waverley, she had to coax the girl down from the upper branches of an oak tree which she had climbed to inspect a bird's nest, and she had to mend a dress Martha ripped while sliding down the invitingly shiny mahogany balustrade leading from Waverley's upper floor to the entrance hall. But it was Martha, mimicking Miriam's infatuation with her own reflection, who opened Leonora's eyes to what she had failed to see for herself.

"Leonora . . ." Standing in front of a mirror in the drawing room, the youngest girl ran a hand through her hair and gave a remarkably accurate impersonation of her oldest sister's slow, soft speech. "Does this coiffure suit me best? Or do you think I should wear it"—busy fingers ripped through the hair, turning it into wild bush that sprouted in a hundred different directions—"like this?"

Holding in her laughter, Leonora studied the effect. "I suppose it all depends on whom you are trying to impress."

"Why, your cousin Nathan, of course."

"Why would you want to impress Nathan?"

Martha's impersonation became so sharp that Leonora could swear she was hearing Miriam. "Because he's so handsome. I just adore him. And if he doesn't feel the same about me, I'll die. I swear it, I'll just die."

Leonora knew that no nine-year-old girl, no matter how strong an imagination she possessed, could invent those words and sentiments. She had heard the lines said by someone else. When Nathan returned from work that evening, Leonora shared her knowledge with him. "You have an admirer."

"Miriam?"

Leonora felt disappointed that he knew. "Who told you?"

"Do you think I am blind, Lally? Miriam finds excuses to visit the countinghouse when I am working there. She tries to monopolize me when I am here. It seems that I cannot move a step without falling over her. And if that were not enough, when I walk in the garden, Martha dances along behind me singing that Miriam loves Nathan."

"Perhaps it is I who am blind. How do you feel about it?"

"Flattered, and just a little wishful that Miriam was four or five years older. When she is nineteen, she will be a very beautiful young woman. But then she will have a hundred young men chasing after her and she will forget all about me."

"If I were Miriam I would never forget about you."

"You are very precious, Lally. No man could wish for a more loyal, more wonderful cousin."

Before Nathan could notice the single tear that blossomed in the corner of her right eye, Leonora turned away. Nathan would never see her as anything more than a cousin, not when he could afford to be so cavalier about Miriam's affections. He would never admit it, not even to himself, but Leonora swore that some of his cousin Alfred's rakish characteristics were beginning to surface in Nathan. After working from dawn to dusk in London, and having no time for his own leisure, he was acting like a man released from prison. The diversions of New Orleans beckoned to him, and he was sampling them eagerly.

Leonora was jealous. She, too, had worked from dawn to dusk for Samuel Solomon, but she felt just as confined in New Orleans as she had in London. As a girl, she could not go out alone, as Nathan did. Nor was she taken by Gershon Lowensohn to such prestigious institutions as the Boston Club, where business deals were made; as a member, he had taken both Henry and Nathan there. When Leonora went out, it was as part of the Lowensohn family. For dinner, to a play, occasionally to a dance organized by one of the associations Gershon supported. The young men to whom she was introduced at those dances held little attraction for her. Sons of Gershon's friends or business associates, they all seemed quite dull. Especially so when compared with Nathan.

Yes, Leonora could easily understand what Miriam found so attractive in Nathan. She had felt the same way for many years.

With the approach of Christmas, Waverley began to echo with the sound of festivity. Guests visited the big house. Gifts were exchanged. Anna Lowensohn spent time discussing special menus with Delilah. The feeling of the season even wound its way into Leonora's relationship with the three girls. When they spoke of the gifts they hoped to receive, Leonora felt puzzled. Observing Christmas was alien to her. In London she had seen the season celebrated all around her but she had never felt part of it. Her uncle's family respected the holiday and gave their servants time off, but they never commemorated it themselves. She took her questions to Gershon Lowensohn.

"On the ship, at the service for little Frances Meagher, you recited the One hundred and twenty-first Psalm. You admit to being a Jew, yet in my three months in this house I have never known anyone here to attend a synagogue. Now I am even further confused to find that you celebrate Christmas."

"I know many psalms and prayers by heart. Their essence is quite beautiful and I find their words uplifting, but they do not make me want to immerse myself in the superstitious beliefs of my ancestors. I left all that behind when I left Germany."

"You make it sound as if Judaism—or any religion, for that

matter—is tantamount to paganism. In London, I attended the synagogue regularly, and I never felt like a pagan."

"That was England, where Jews still do not feel fully accepted. In Germany and other European countries, where such acceptance is even less forthcoming, religion remains important as a defensive bond against outside negative influences. Here, in New Orleans, no such negative influences exist. No groups pressure us. We are accepted in every level of society, and we have been allowed to prosper. Therefore, some of us have felt safe in finally shedding the trappings of fear and superstition that kept us locked within ghetto walls for so many centuries."

"But there are synagogues in New Orleans."

"A German one, a Sephardic one. If you wish to attend, please do not allow my sentiments to stop you. Tell Nathan the same. If he wishes to attend, he is more than free to do so."

Leonora contemplated the dilemma. Despite the mention of Nathan, she realized that Gershon's words affected only her. Nathan cared little for any religious heritage. Only she did. Or so she thought, because the more she considered Gershon's reasoning, the more sense she found in it. Finally, she said, "Your family has made us most welcome, and we wish to do only as you do."

Gershon smiled as if he had just been paid the greatest of compliments. "Thank you. I hope neither of you regrets it."

Chapter Six

When Nathan turned twenty on New Year's Day, 1852, he viewed the occasion not so much as a celebration of being a year older but as an opportunity to review the previous year's accomplishments. His outstanding achievement of 1851 was gaining his independence. In one decisive moment, he had cast off the shackles. Cast them off from Leonora, too, although he remembered with no little shame and embarrassment the moment he had tried to dissuade her from joining him in his flight. Leaving her alone in their uncle's home would have condemned her to a life of misery, for which he would never have forgiven himself. Here, helping Anna Lowensohn manage Waverley and befriending the three Lowensohn girls, Leonora was as happy as he had ever known her.

Nathan felt pleased at the way he had adapted to New Orleans. The food, whether cooked by Delilah or eaten at one of the city's excellent restaurants, no longer seemed strange; indeed, he often wondered how he could have endured English cuisine which, in retrospect, seemed bland to the point of boredom. He had picked up enough French to make himself understood when he ventured into the *Vieux Carré*, the old, original section of the city. Even the weather was bearable, now that winter had arrived. It was a winter unlike any he had known. One day, warmth and brilliant sunshine fooled a man into thinking spring had dawned; the next day, a damp, bone-chilling wind drove people into shelter.

Such cold was not so different to his memories of London, but there all similarity ended. Instead of being a drab, smog-laden stretch of misery, winter in New Orleans represented the height of the commercial and social seasons. With the first frost, and the simultaneous disappearance of the mosquitoes, the city had burst into life. More river steamers than ever lined up at the levee to disgorge their cargoes. Merchants returned from New York with the latest lines. Businessmen traveled down from northern cities to conduct deals. Pleasure-seeking Orleanians filled the opera house and theaters, attended balls, and chanced their luck at the tables of the city's opulent gambling clubs.

Gambling intrigued Nathan. It was a curiosity aroused initially by the stories of his cousin Alfred, told during slack times at S. Solomon and Sons. When Henry Lowensohn, during that first day's tour of New Orleans, had taken such pains to identify the locations of gambling houses, Nathan had silently vowed to visit them. He needed to find out for himself whether Alfred's thrilling account of gambling was fact or wishful fiction.

The first establishments he tried, soon after beginning work for Gershon Lowensohn, were the popular keno parlors, where numbered balls were pulled from a globe and players covered the corresponding numbers on cards. Nathan found no excitement in the parlors with their dirty tables and stink of tobacco or beer. Success at keno stemmed from sheer luck. He wanted something more challenging. From keno parlors, he progressed to clubs where any number of games of chance were played. First he watched and then he tried his own luck at games as diverse as *vingt-et-un* and roulette, *écarté*, poker, and brag. He grew to prefer poker, finding in it just the right combination of luck and skill. He gained far more satisfaction in the winning of a hand through his own ability than in the actual gain of money. Always he made certain to remember the exact sequence of cards so that he could thrill Henry the following morning.

Henry was as avid a listener to Nathan's tales as Nathan, himself, had been to those of Alfred.

In the new year, as he turned twenty, Nathan discovered Mercier's, a club occupying the second floor of a building on Chartres near the intersection with Conti. Owned by a plump, middle-aged Parisian named Georges Mercier, the club was as elegant as the keno parlors had been vulgar. Brocade drapes cloaked the windows. Elaborate chandeliers furnished light. Ornate flower arrangements added life and color. The men who played at Mercier's embodied a cross-section of New Orleans. At the roulette wheel, stoic Yankee businessmen bet against flamboyant Creoles whose families had lived through French and Spanish jurisdictions before Louisiana's sale to the United States. Sunburned sugar and cotton planters played poker against pallid, somberly clad merchants from St. Louis and Cincinnati.

Nathan became a regular at Mercier's. He concentrated on the poker games. At first, he merely watched, gauging the expertise of the players. After two weeks of watching, on a blustery late January night, he sat in on his first game. His three opponents were an elderly Creole lawyer with shoulder-length white hair and a long, sad face, a cotton planter, and a Whig politician. Early in the game, Nathan raised while holding nothing. The bet was called, his bluff exposed. An hour later, after raising heavily again, he was trapped in another bluff. The lawyer, the planter, and the politician exchanged knowing glances. This young newcomer was easy to figure out; now they could take him. A dozen hands later, Nathan made one more large raise. Another bluff. Or so his opponents thought. When they raised in turn, he raised right back. He left the table soon after, pockets bulging with other people's money.

"They were like three wolves scenting a helpless prey," he told Henry the following morning as they watched bales of cotton coming off the ships. "Twice they had caught me bluffing, and they were certain they had caught me again."

"They did not catch you bluffing," Henry pointed out. "You allowed them to catch you."

Nathan laughed. "They did not know that."

Gershon walked past at that moment and asked to share the joke. Henry blurted out that Nathan had won three hundred dollars the previous night. Gershon rocked back and forth as he digested that piece of news. His voice took on a guttural edge. "If providence continues to smile so brightly upon you, you may soon no longer need to work in the cotton trade."

"I cannot see myself being so lucky again," Nathan said, trying to recover the situation. "It was a stroke of luck. Normally I win or lose a few dollars, nothing more."

Gershon nodded and gave Nathan a slight smile. "Good. I am uncertain whether I would like my son and my daughters to be exposed to a man who makes a habit of gambling quite so rashly."

The warning etched itself in Nathan's memory. Never before had the merchant commented on how he used his free time. He entered and left Waverley as he chose, reporting to no one. Now Gershon had made known his displeasure, and only a fool would ignore it. Nathan damned the arrogance that had made him recount his exploits to Henry. He would not be so indiscreet again. Setting the example for Henry that Alfred had once set for him risked Gershon's friendship, a rapport Nathan valued highly. The Lowensohns had treated him and Leonora like their own flesh and blood, opening their home and their hearts to them. Although Nathan knew he would have no trouble earning enough money to rent a comfortable home for himself and Leonora, he did not want to leave Waverley. The Lowensohn home with all the love and kindness it contained was a foundation for the good life he hoped to build for himself and Leonora, and he would be a fool to reject it for the flash of adoration in a boy's eyes.

There and then he decided that he would no longer tease Henry's imagination. When the boy was old enough to do as he pleased, that would be another matter. Nor, he resolved, almost as an afterthought, would he even gamble for a while. No matter how much he knew he would miss the newfound excitement! Such a concession was a small sacrifice to retain Gershon's goodwill.

Nathan chose an opportune time to indulge Gershon Lowensohn's dislike for gambling. The New Orleans social season provided a profusion of other diversions. With the Lowensohns, Nathan and Leonora saw *Richard III* and *Hamlet* on successive nights at the St. Charles theater, with Junius Booth playing both title roles. The following week, they attended a production of Rossini's *William Tell* at the Théâtre d'Orléans with the family.

"Do you and Leonora find it disconcerting," Gershon Lowensohn asked during the first intermission of *William Tell*, "to hear this opera sung in French and not Italian?"

"Not at all," Nathan answered, "because we have never heard it sung in Italian."

Gershon appeared mystified. "But Italian is the original language . . ."

"This is our first opera," Leonora said, "and we are enjoying it immensely, no matter what language is being used."

Nathan was enjoying not only the opera but the people in the audience. At the St. Charles theater, the audience had been drawn mostly from the American section of the city. At the Théâtre d'Orléans, Creoles comprised the majority. They were very different to the people above Canal Street. The men, stylish in full dress coats and white kid gloves, affected an elegance the Americans lacked, while the women, clothed in latest Parisian fashions, seemed to Nathan the most beautiful he had ever seen. Certainly they were far more attractive than their American counterparts who, for the most part, appeared dowdy and anemic by comparison. Creole women presented striking pictures with glowing skin, sparkling eyes, and jet-black lustrous hair elaborately arranged with colored ribbons, ornamental pins, or a solitary flower whose charm paled beside that of its wearer.

During the next two weeks, Nathan had the opportunity to admire many more Creole women when he and Leonora watched productions of Verdi's *Nabucco* and Meyerbeer's *Les Huguenots* at the Théâtre d'Orléans. When Swedish nightingale Jenny Lind arrived in the city toward the end of February, they saw her, too. New Orleans was offering them the opportunity to compensate for all the culture and entertainment they had been denied while living with their uncle, and they were determined to take advantage of every offering. And when they tired of music and drama, the city's hectic rush toward Mardi Gras provided other forms of fun. It seemed that there was always some kind of a parade passing through the streets. One morning, the city's firemen marched proudly along Canal Street, showing off their uniforms and sparkling equipment. In the afternoon, masked men and women filled the streets of the *Vieux Carré,* inviting everyone they saw to join their procession. In London, Nathan and Leonora had never seen such gaiety. While enjoyable it was still foreign to them and needed explanation.

Gershon provided it. "Carnival is the one time of the year that New Orleans goes mad. When Lent begins on Ash Wednesday, sobriety descends upon the city. Until then, the carnival reigns supreme, reaching its climax on Mardi Gras. Sadly, the past few years have tarnished the carnival's charm. Where women once leaned from balconies to throw roses or bonbons to marchers, now bags of flour are thrown. Some rascals even throw lime and mud. I fear that unless some responsible organization takes charge soon, the tradition will cease, and the city will be the poorer for it. I urge you to see it while you still can."

On the afternoon of Mardi Gras, Moses drove Nathan, Leonora, Henry, and Miriam to the *Vieux Carré.* Along Royal Street passed hundreds of masked marchers in every kind of costume. Harlequins paraded with mythical beasts, Indians walked side by side with Spanish noblemen from the time of Cortez. On the *banquette,* praline sellers, flower vendors, and purveyors of rice cakes offered their wares to the crowd of onlookers among whom every shade of skin was evident. Negroes with the darkest of complexions, lighter-skinned mulattoes, and quadroons with fairer coloring yet, stood shoulder to shoulder with planters and slave dealers. From the balconies of houses flew bags of flour to burst on the heads and shoulders of marchers. Loud cheers greeted each strike. Sometimes the aim from the balconies contained more enthusiasm than accuracy, and a bag of flour would burst on the shoulders of a spectator. Then it would be the turn of marchers to make good-natured fun of the unfortunate victim.

"I agree with your father," Nathan yelled above the commotion to Miriam and Henry, "that it would be a terrible shame for this excitement and happiness to die away. England has hundreds of years of history and pageantry, but I swear it has nothing to equal this!"

Miriam, who had placed herself between Nathan and Leonora, pressed against him. "Look over there!" She pointed to a man resplendent in a devil's costume. Red silk cloaked his body, red horns protruded from his head, and a long red tail poked out from beneath his shimmering red cape. "Do you believe the devil exists, Nathan?"

"Not in that form."

"What form do you think he takes?" she asked, drawing closer.

Nathan's shirt collar tightened uncomfortably around his neck. His cheeks burned and his heart pounded at the sudden closeness of this audacious fourteen-year-old girl. Henry and Leonora, standing at the other side of her, had no idea what was taking place. They were too interested in the procession to care what happened elsewhere. "I am certain that the devil does not have horns and a tail, for one thing."

"What does the devil have?"

"Ringlets of beautiful golden hair"—he turned to look into

her face—"and green eyes filled with mischief and temptation."

Miriam blushed. "I think you are very rude."

"And you are very precocious." For the first time, a sharp edge affected Nathan's voice.

Miriam recoiled, as if from a bee. In the five months Nathan had lived at Waverley, he had never talked to her in this manner. He had always found the time to answer her questions, to help with schoolwork should she need it. Now he spoke sharply. "I thought you were my friend," she replied.

"I am. But even friendships must be occasionally scrutinized and adjusted if necessary." Just then, Henry and Leonora hooted with laughter as a bag of flour burst like a bomb on the devil's red silk headpiece. Nathan smiled. "That is the devil's reward for his mischief and temptation. Do you wish for flour, or worse, to defile your beautiful golden hair?"

Before Miriam could answer, another bag was launched from a second-floor balcony. This time the thrower's aim was poor. Instead of arcing through the air to land among the marchers, the bag of flour fell toward the *banquette*. Leonora screamed in shock as white powder covered her head and shoulders. Nathan looked up. Two-dozen people filled the balcony from where the missile had been launched. One young man leaned over.

"Excusez-moi!"

Nathan glared at the young man. His words were remorseful, but there was nothing repentant about the smile that lit his handsome face. "Do you see the anguish your foolishness has caused this young lady?" he demanded in English, neither knowing nor caring whether the young man understood.

The young man shrugged his shoulders expressively. His dark brown eyes gleamed with excitement. "Sir, if you would—"

Nathan did not hear the remainder of the young man's speech. He was too concerned with Leonora, who had begun to cry. Tears streaked the mask of white that covered her face. Holding her tightly, he guided her through the crowd to where

Moses waited with the carriage. He had forgotten all about Miriam, who followed with Henry. As the carriage began to move, Nathan tenderly wiped the flour from his cousin's face.

"If you could only see yourself, Lally. You look like one of the clowns in the procession."

Leonora sniffed back tears. "I do not feel so funny."

"That's better. It is only flour, after all," he said, remembering Gershon's comments about young rascals throwing lime or mud at the marchers. "A bath will make you as good as new. But next time we will make sure to ascertain the accuracy of those who stand on balconies above us."

"Did you understand the Creole's offer?" Henry asked.

"I was not listening. Was it important?"

"He said that if you wanted satisfaction for any distress he had caused your ladyfriend, he was at your disposal."

Nathan shuddered. He still remembered every moment of the meeting beneath The Oaks between Jack Johnson and Michael Meagher. To have challenged the Creole to a duel would have solved nothing. It would have merely compounded the young man's stupidity by making Nathan an accessory to it.

A tight smile broke through Leonora's streaky white mask. "If I were your lady friend instead of your cousin, would you have sought satisfaction?"

"Of course he would not," Miriam responded, flashing an impish smile at Nathan. "Your cousin does not know the meaning of romance."

"Perhaps that is because he has not yet found anyone worth being romantic over," Leonora said sweetly. Miriam bit her lip and did not say another word for the remainder of the journey to the Garden District.

When told about the incident, Gershon and Anna Lowensohn expressed gratitude that nothing worse had happened; the wild abandon of Mardi Gras too often led to bloodshed and heartbreak. A bath removed the flour from Leonora's hair and skin, and when she sat down to dinner she looked none the worse for wear. She was even able to joke about the experience, saying, "If people think my clothes are Mardi Gras costumes fit only to pelt with flour, perhaps it is time I spoke sternly to the dressmaker!"

Nathan noticed that Miriam remained unusually quiet during the meal. The moment it was finished, she excused herself and went to her room. Nathan suspected that she felt scorned, both by his own reaction to her closeness and Leonora's cutting remark. Although he regretted any damage to Miriam's feelings, he believed it was for the best. Her infatuation, unless checked as it had been today, would only grow and be that much harder to deal with. He and Leonora had been cruel to be kind.

After dinner, when Gershon began a chess game with his son, and Anna and Leonora busied themselves with embroidery, Nathan decided to return on his own to the *Vieux Carré*. Tonight, the carnival ended and he wished to witness the final festivities.

The final moments were more than Nathan bargained for. A jostling mass of humanity filled every street of the French Quarter. Music blared from every direction. Masked and costumed figures pushed him from the *banquette* into the road and then back again. He could not even find refuge in restaurants, where every seat and table was filled. He stood in a coffee house on Conti for fifteen minutes, sipping a glass of cognac, until the din drove him out. Forcing his way through the undiminished throng, he walked along Conti toward the river, before turning left onto Chartres. A familiar door offered sanctuary from the crowd. Nathan stepped inside and walked up a flight of stairs. Reaching the top, he relished the peace that suddenly surrounded him. Heavy brocade curtains eliminated the outside noise while elaborate chandeliers illuminated a scene that was as tranquil as the street was chaotic.

Although more than a month had passed since Nathan's last visit to Mercier's, he did not take the nearest empty chair and begin to play immediately. He behaved as he had done before, drifting from table to table to watch different games, assessing the skill of potential adversaries. Half an hour passed before he decided which game he wished to join once an empty chair presented itself. At a table far removed from the windows overlooking Chartres, five men played poker. Three wore the somber clothes of men from above Canal Street; in front of each was an ample supply of money. In front of the fourth man, the same white-haired Creole lawyer who had lost to Nathan a month earlier, remained only a handful of dollars, while the fifth player, a tall silkily handsome man with a flamboyant vest and a narrow black bow tie, possessed a pile of money that depicted him as the evening's clear winner. Nathan positioned himself behind the man in the colorful vest, eager to see how he played. The man turned around and asked Nathan if he would be kind enough to stand elsewhere. He was superstitious, he explained, and considered it bad luck to have anyone standing behind him.

Nathan moved immediately. All professional gamblers were superstitious, and he had no doubt that the man who asked him to move was a professional. The boats that plied the Mississippi from New Orleans to St. Louis were full of such men. This one had left the river to seek easy pickings in the gambling houses of a city caught up in carnival. Looking forward to pitting his skill against such a player, Nathan took up a position behind the Creole lawyer, reasoning that he would be the first to fold.

The lawyer lasted two more hands. He won the first when his aggressive opening bet caused everyone to fold. The small triumph lent wings to his courage. He wagered everything when he drew a third king to complement the two he had been given. The gambler, on his own deal, then drew a third ace to match the pair he had already. Showing the winning hand, he pulled in the pot, sorting coins into different denominations and stacking them neatly in front of him. Wordlessly, the lawyer stood, bowed formally to his adversaries, and left the table.

The gambler's eyes, pale gray and calculating, switched to Nathan. He motioned toward the vacant chair, indicating that it was Nathan's if he wanted it. Before Nathan could accept, a figure brushed past him and dropped into the empty seat. A face wreathed in a familiar carefree smile turned to look up at him. A voice brimming with an equally familiar repentant tone repeated the apology Nathan had heard earlier that day on Royal Street.

"Excusez-moi."

Nathan bit back the protest that formed on his lips. The young man had been only too willing to seek a duel over the badly aimed bag of flour that had hit Leonora. An objection now about his rude behavior would prompt another such challenge, perhaps more forceful this time. In his enthusiasm, the young Creole did not even recognize Nathan as the man to whom he had made the earlier offer. He probably made such offers of satisfaction a dozen times a day. Nathan accepted the apology with a nonchalant *"Ne riens, monsieur."*

The young Creole played cards as rashly as he seemed to do everything else. After casually spilling money onto the table, he bet with a wild abandon that had little to do with the hands he held. One by one, the three Americans dropped out. With each passing, the man in the flashy vest looked to Nathan, standing diagonally behind the young Creole. Each time, Nathan rejected the invitation to sit in. He had no wish to be caught between a shrewd professional gambler and an outright fool intent on throwing his money away.

The youth's money continued to diminish as he persisted in betting wildly. He did not seem to mind at all. He sat slouched in the chair, right hand holding the cards away from his chest, not caring who could see. Every few seconds, he ran the slim fingers of his left hand through thick and curly black hair, as if impatient with the pace of the game. Or nervous. Nathan wondered if he had been drinking. His face was flushed, and his dark brown eyes shone with a disturbing recklessness.

There was nothing reckless about his opponent's gray eyes. They studied every card, every movement of money into the center of the table, and every nervous motion of the Creole youth. When the gambler sensed that his opponent was ready to commit his remaining money in one do-or-die attempt, those gray eyes narrowed to slits of total concentration.

Nathan edged closer as the Creole picked up the five cards dealt to him by the gambler. Two red queens showed. Pushing all his money into the center of the table, he demanded three more cards. He drew another queen and—Nathan held back a gasp; the young man's luck had changed at last!—a pair of sixes. Nathan's gaze moved across the table, then back to the young Creole as he noticed the abrupt transformation taking place. The slouch had gone. So had the wildness in the eyes, the nervous brushing of the hair.

Unbidden, the Creole set down his hand to expose the full house. Jumping to his feet, he reached across the table like a striking snake to snatch the deck from the gambler's grasp. "With what wonderful cards from the bottom of the deck," he asked in lightly accented English, "were you preparing to reward yourself this time?" He turned the deck upside down. The bottom two cards were fours. "Would you care to bet against my belief that the other two fours are in your hand, my dishonest friend?"

"Do you call me a cheat, sir?"

"No. I call you a thief. A scoundrel only cheats when he plays a game for nothing. When he plays for money, he steals."

Outrage colored the gambler's face. His voice rose. Other games stopped as players swung around to look. "How dare you slander me so, sir? I'll make you retract that statement if it's the last thing I do!" The final words were accompanied by a stinging slap across the young Creole's face.

The Creole snapped to attention and gave the gambler a stiff and formal bow. "I am at your service, sir." Turning to Nathan, whose seat at the table he had usurped, he spoke in French. *"Monsieur, je vous prie d'être mon temoin."*

Nathan's face went blank. *"Monsieur, je ne comprends pas—"*

"Excuse me, sir, for assuming you understood French. My name is Antoine Vanson, and I ask that, as you bore witness to this thief's wickedness, you honor me by acting as my second."

Nathan swallowed hard. He knew that if he refused Antoine Vanson's request, the next challenge might be flung at him.

Before he could decide, the gambler demanded to know Antoine Vanson's choice of weapons. "The *colichemarde,*" the Creole answered immediately. "With its point I will brand you as a thief and a liar."

Relief flooded over Nathan. It would not be a fight with pistols, a duel to the death as that between Jack Johnson and Michael Meagher. In that relief, he could even recognize the justice and ethics of Antoine Vanson's promise to brand the villainous gambler with a mark of Cain. "Where and when will this meeting take place?" he asked, already planning to arrange an absence from Gershon Lowensohn's countinghouse.

"Here and now."

"What about The Oaks? What about daylight?"

"Why travel to The Oaks when there is a perfectly adequate courtyard downstairs? And why wait for daylight when gaslight and torches will suffice?"

Antoine led the way down to a large courtyard that lay behind the building. Nathan followed. Behind came the gambler and one of the club's waiters who had offered to second him. Bringing up the rear were a dozen of the club's members, eager to witness the duel. In the courtyard, Antoine shrugged himself out of his coat and handed it to Nathan. The gambler stripped down to his gaudy vest. Georges Mercier, the club owner, brought out two swords.

"Select one for me," Antoine instructed Nathan.

"I know nothing about them."

Antoine smiled at his second's reluctance. "They are identical. I have settled matters of honor here before."

Nathan studied the swords. They were thirty inches long, with triangular-sectioned blades tapering to a point. He chose one and offered it, handle first, to Antoine who took it in his right hand. The narrow silver blade whistled as the young Creole slashed first one way and then the other. He looked across the intervening space to the gambler who tested his own sword with his left hand. Light shone down from windows facing the courtyard. Each of the dozen spectators held a glowing lantern.

"What other function do I have as your second?"

"To ensure that my body, if I lose, is returned to my family." Antoine roared with laughter as Nathan's face paled. "Have you no sense of humor, my friend?"

"Only when something strikes me as humorous."

Georges Mercier brought the duelists together. They crossed swords, the young Creole in black trousers and brilliant white shirt facing the older gambler whose silk vest emitted a myriad of shimmering colors in the moving light.

"En garde!"

The ring of steel filled the courtyard as the gambler jumped onto the attack, slashing at Antoine's head, then thrusting for his body. Each cut and riposte was met by Antoine's sword, so perfectly positioned that for a moment Nathan believed the Creole to be telepathic, to know the target of the gambler's sword even before the man himself had decided. Antoine continued to allow the gambler to carry the duel, parrying every stroke with an easy expertise that grew more pronounced with each passing second. Two minutes passed in this manner, until Antoine decided it was time to end the contest. After parrying a thrust at his chest, he suddenly went onto the attack, using a withering combination of strokes to force his opponent into a corner of the courtyard.

"Sir . . ." The lightly accented voice was as teasing as the point of his *colichemarde*. "I have given you every chance to carry the fight to me. Now I will carry it to you." Antoine's sword glimmered again, darting toward his opponent's right shoulder. As the gambler parried, Antoine's sword changed direction, curving in one sudden scintillating flash of lightning around and under and through the other man's defense. Steel tinkled on stone as the gambler dropped his weapon and clutched at his face. Blood poured from his left ear where Antoine's sword had struck the lobe.

"Voila!" Tossing his weapon to Nathan, Antoine acknowledged the applause of the onlookers with a slight bow.

Georges Mercier approached the beaten duelist. *"Monsieur,* when you feel comfortable enough to move, I would appreciate you leaving these premises and never returning. Mercier's has no room for men of your low character."

Antoine led the way back up to the club. Champagne corks popped. Antoine proposed the toast with as much flourish as he wielded the *colichemarde.* "To the thrill of the duel!"

Georges Mercier responded with a salute of his own. "And to the sword of Antoine Vanson. May it always remain as sharp as his eyes! For the life of me, I did not see that rogue cheat."

"You knew before you sat down?" Nathan asked.

Antoine smiled. "I trust you can now excuse my rudeness. The white-haired gentleman whose place I took is my father. I saw that man rob my father, and what kind of son stands idly by while his father is so badly treated?"

Nathan remembered the Creole lawyer's final hand. He had been dealt three kings while his opponent had helped himself to three aces. Unknown to Nathan, Antoine must have watched the entire episode, seething with anger and yearning for revenge. "Where is your father now?" Nathan asked, looking around but failing to spot the white-haired man.

"The *Code Duello* forbids a blood relative being in close proximity to an affair of honor. It is quite strict about that. Besides, my father knew I would emerge successful."

"I won a considerable sum of money from your father on my last visit here, a few weeks ago."

"I am sure you won it honestly." Antoine's smile broadened. "You seconded me admirably, yet I do not even know your name."

"Nathan. Nathan Solomon."

Holding the champagne in his left hand, Antoine extended his right. "Nathan Solomon, I am honored to make your acquaintance."

"You made my acquaintance earlier today."

"I did?" Puzzlement replaced the smile.

"You even offered me satisfaction."

Antoine's confusion increased. "I am sorry, but I do not—"

"On Royal, where your poorly aimed missile covered my cousin Leonora with flour."

"Mon Dieu! A thousand apologies. But in truth"—quite unexpectedly he began to laugh—"my aim was not that poor. I was trying to attract that young lady's attention. I intended to land the bag of flour at her feet, but I was jostled as I threw." He walked away from Nathan to return a few seconds later with half a dozen long-stemmed roses in full bloom which he had taken from a silver vase on one of the tables. "Give these to your cousin Leonora, with all my regrets, and with the hope that one day she will graciously allow me the opportunity to personally make amends for my boorish behavior of this afternoon."

Nathan took the roses back to Waverley, placing them in a vase with a card bearing Leonora's name. He went to bed smiling. Leonora had found an admirer, and he had found a friend.

By morning, the red roses had wilted. Nonetheless, Leonora was delighted with them and eager to know the name of her admirer. Laughing at her curiosity—and at the anticipation of her shock and surprise when she eventually learned that her admirer was the same Creole who had doused her so liberally with flour—Nathan refused to provide the information she requested.

"You will have to be patient, Lally," he said as he prepared to leave Waverley for the countinghouse on Canal Street. "Perhaps this evening, over dinner, I will divulge his identity."

"Patient . . . ! When an unknown admirer sends flowers, patience flees before them!" Exasperated, she brandished the roses in Nathan's face like a weapon.

"Be careful with his flowers or I will tell him of the cavalier manner in which you treated them."

"And I will tell him how you teased me. If he is the gallant man I hope he is," she cried, suddenly imbued with the spirit and tradition of her adopted city, "he will challenge you to a duel."

Nathan continued laughing. "Of that I have little doubt."

It was the longest day Leonora had known. No man had sent her flowers before and she doubted that she had the endurance to wait until dinner to learn who he was. The suspense would turn her into a nervous wreck! She mentioned the roses to Anna, who smiled indulgently as if recalling some romantic moment from her youth. She shared her secret with the three girls and received three different reactions. Martha danced through the house, singing that Leonora had a beau, while Sarah accepted the news quite dispassionately. Miriam reacted with wishful envy.

"I long for the day a handsome admirer sends me roses."

"How do you know my admirer is handsome?"

"Of course he is. An admirer who is chivalrous enough to send roses must be handsome."

Leonora speculated that even now the girl pictured Nathan bringing her flowers. "When you are a little older, Miriam, handsome men will stand in line to send you roses."

"Do you really think so?" Hope brightened her emerald eyes.

Leonora nodded. There was no question about it. Miriam already possessed much of the beauty of the woman she would soon become. Tall and slender, she moved with the grace of a gazelle, her shoulder-length golden hair flowing as she walked like wheat in the wind. One day, the tiny flecks of amber that punctuated the green of her eyes would attract men like a magnet drew metal. And Leonora was certain that when the day came, Nathan would be in the very vanguard of Miriam's admirers. He would fight his way to the head of the line, asking with each step how he could have ever failed to notice her.

That was always the trouble, Leonora mused. People never seemed to notice what was right beneath their noses.

Despite Leonora's fears that having to wait the entire day would drive her mad, dinner found her sane, and just as impatient. "You promised . . . !" she reminded Nathan the instant they sat down. The vase with the red roses graced the table in front of her.

"I did indeed. But I thought by now you would have guessed the gentleman's identity. You do know him, after all."

"I do?" Leonora appeared puzzled.

"He is the Creole who turned your hair white."

"What?" Puzzlement gave way to indignity. "You accepted roses from a such a villain?"

"The roses were an apology. He was trying to attract your attention by bursting the bag at your feet, but someone jarred his arm as he threw."

Leonora's outrage gave way to a sunburst of a smile. "What is his name, Nathan? And is he as handsome as I hope he is?"

"Vanson. Antoine Vanson. And he is very handsome."

Gershon Lowensohn paid attention. "Vanson? Does his father practice law on Chartres?"

"The father is a lawyer. Do you know him?"

"If it is the man I am thinking of, he has a reputation as an intense gambler. Not always a very successful one. How did you meet him?"

"At Mercier's. Both the father and the son."

"I see," Gershon said disapprovingly. "In the son's case, it seems that the apple has not fallen far from the tree."

Nathan felt glad at having omitted the details of his role as Antoine's second. Gershon would have become even frostier had he known about the duel. Gershon's reservations, however, had no effect on Leonora. "Would you offer Antoine Vanson my gratitude and tell him that I forgive him for his atrocious aim?"

Nathan carried the message when he returned to Mercier's the next night. Antoine was there, eager to hear how his peace offering had been received. When he learned that Leonora forgave him, he beamed with joy. "Can you understand, Nathan Solomon, how ironic it would be to bear a beautiful woman's anger, when the cause of that anger was intended as a compliment?"

"Your sense of the romantic is too strong for me to fully comprehend."

"That is because your Yankee background prohibits you from understanding."

"I come from London."

Antoine made a dismissive gesture with his hand. "English, Yankee . . . there is little difference. In New Orleans, Creole men alone can fully comprehend the poignant pain of romance. In the matter of women, outside the *Vieux Carré* exist only cold fish."

Nathan was amused by his new friend's grandiloquence. While the impassioned statements that sprang from his lips seemed perfectly acceptable, similar pronouncements from a Yankee would have been nothing short of bombastic. Suddenly he burst out laughing. When Antoine asked the reason for such mirth, he answered, "I am laughing because I cannot believe that I am actually agreeing with you!"

Antoine stared, still unable to discern what was so funny. Nathan threw his own words at him. "Have you no sense of humor, my friend?"

At last, a smile touched the Creole's face. *"Touché"*

Instead of playing cards, they spent the evening talking, cementing their burgeoning friendship by learning more about each other. Nathan quickly discovered that their ages were almost identical—Antoine had been born just three months before him. Hearing Nathan describe his and Leonora's flight from England and the tyranny of their uncle, Antoine nodded approvingly as though such dramatic actions were in keeping with the Creole manner. In turn, Antoine spoke about himself. When he mentioned studying the Napoleonic Code at his father's law practice on Chartres, Nathan knew that Gershon Lowensohn had been correct.

"My father is a very lonely and unhappy man," Antoine explained. "He married late, when he was thirty-five, and he loved my mother deeply. When she died six years ago, after twenty-seven years of blissfully happy marriage, my father's world disintegrated. The only interest he has outside his law practice is establishments like this. He finds an excitement in gambling that removes him temporarily from the sadness in which he lives. That is why I, as the only person who can protect him, will tolerate no man taking advantage of him as that riverboat gambler tried to do. I only scarred that cur, but if necessary I would have killed him."

The simple statement was chillingly believable, and Nathan wondered if Antoine had already killed to defend his father from such predators. Such a responsibility struck Nathan as both awe-inspiring and appalling. "Have you no brothers or sisters to help you?"

"Many, but not here. My oldest brother, Alphonse—he is twelve years older than me—lives in Paris. He left New Orleans seven years ago, when he married. Another brother, Marcel, eight years my senior, is married to the daughter of Étienne St. Croix, a wealthy sugar planter, and now lives on the plantation which he expects one day to inherit. They have one child, my brother Marcel and his miserable wife Micaela, a daughter two years old who my father dearly loves but rarely sees."

"Why does your father not travel there to see them?"

"He would not go without an invitation, and only in the autumn is such an invitation forthcoming. That is when Marcel holds the annual party to which he invites all his friends and tells them to invite their friends. Then my father rushes there because it is his only opportunity to see his granddaughter."

"Do they never come to New Orleans?"

"Marcel does, to visit his mistress." He smiled at the shock on Nathan's face. "If you were married to Micaela St. Croix, you would also have a mistress. But obviously he does not bring the child with him on such journeys. In fact, I doubt if Marcel even cares whether or not my father ever sees his granddaughter. And then, of course, there is my sister, Marie-Louise."

"Yes?" Nathan prompted when Antoine's voice faded, and his eyes took on a wistful expression.

"My mother's death broke my father's heart the first time. I fear that Marie-Louise will break it for him a second and irreparable time."

"What has she done?"

"Marie-Louise is my father's favorite child. She is his only daughter. Because she bears a startling resemblance to our mother, she could always do whatever she wished with my father. This has been especially true since our mother's death. A year ago, when she turned eighteen, she expressed a desire to visit Europe. The Grand Tour. What could my father do but accede, although it was obvious that the possibility of her remaining there tore the poor man apart?"

"She has not come back?"

"She stays with my brother Alphonse and his family. Every so often a ship from Europe brings news of the wonderful time she is having. She is feted at the homes of barons and counts. She flies around a dance floor in the arms of handsome hussars and cavalry officers. Dashing young men ply her with gifts from Cartier's. Why would she exchange all that for the boring company of an old and unhappy man?"

"Because she is his daughter," Nathan said immediately. "And because he gave her everything long before these Parisian Lotharios turned her head with baubles."

Antoine rested his hand on Nathan's arm. "You possess great understanding. More than that, you have a passionate heart, and I always believed that to be solely a Creole trait." A sparkle suddenly shone in his eyes, driving out the somberness. "But enough about my family's unhappiness. Tell me more about your charming cousin Leonora. Has she truly forgiven me for dousing her with flour? And when will you allow me to meet her?"

"Allow you?"

"Certainly. You are her protector."

At first, Antoine's words amused Nathan. He could just picture Leonora when he told her that it was up to him whom she did or did not meet. Her face would blaze with outrage and she would throw at his head the first thing that came to hand. But as Nathan journeyed home from the *Vieux Carré* to the Garden District, he began to think differently. Antoine was perfectly correct. Nathan was Leonora's only family—relatives in England meant nothing now—and as such he was accountable for her welfare. What happened to Leonora would be a reflection upon him. As gallant and likable as Antoine Vanson was, did Nathan really want his seventeen-year-old cousin associating with him? Gershon Lowensohn's caveat against the Vanson family carried far more significance for Leonora than it did for Nathan.

At twenty, Nathan knew he could take care of himself when it came to choosing friends. He was not so certain that the same applied to his younger cousin.

Nathan found his dilemma eased by the pressure of work. With spring approaching, the armada of ships bringing cotton to the wharf rushed toward a seasonal climax. Nathan's days grew increasingly longer and more hectic as he oversaw the thousand details between unloading raw cotton and sending it on the way to eventual customers. He started work before dawn each day and continued until dark. After dinner, he wanted only to rest. The serenity of a chess game at Waverley seemed suddenly more appealing than the excitement of gambling. More importantly, it provided him with an excuse not to face another request from Antoine Vanson for an introduction to Leonora. He was not afraid for himself; it was on Leonora's behalf that he showed cowardice.

Leonora said no more about Antoine, although Nathan noticed that she carefully pressed each of the red roses into a book.

Many years from now, she would have those dried flowers to look at. They would help her remember her first Mardi Gras when an errant bag of flour had burst upon her head, and she would recall what little she had seen and heard of her first admirer.

Gershon Lowensohn noticed the change in Nathan's habits and felt pleased. A month after Mardi Gras, as they sat down to play chess in the rear parlor, he asked, "Is it really fatigue that keeps you from going out each night, or have you finally learned that I was correct in saying our city's gambling houses are not fit places for a young man of character?"

Nathan opened the game by moving his king's pawn forward two squares. "I met a man of exemplary character at such a club—"

"Young Vanson?" Gershon advanced his own king's pawn.

"Yes, Antoine. I know I would enjoy him as my friend, but he wished to meet Leonora formally. That is why I stay home, to avoid having to make the introduction."

"You are wise. A cultural gulf exists between Americans and Catholic Creoles. Some have crossed it, such as Louisiana's principal candidates for the United States Senate, John Slidell, a New York-born Episcopalian, and Judah Benjamin, a Charleston Jew. Both have Creole wives, although Benjamin's wife now lives in Paris with their child and he sees them only once a year." He broke off, head cocked at the sound of a bell. "John Slidell and Judah Benjamin are exceptions to the rule, Nathan, a rule proclaiming that Creoles and Americans do not mix. Creoles will never cease to believe that we envy Creole society and its alleged Franco/Spanish aristocratic blood, while above Canal Street we will never stop thinking that Creoles envy American business acumen, ingenuity, and good common sense."

Nathan advanced his queen's knight to threaten the black pawn. "But I would still like to share Antoine's friendship. In the few hours I spent with him, I found him to be fascinating. I feel there is much I could learn from him."

"You have to make the decision, Nathan. You could be his friend and choose to ignore his overtures toward Leonora—"

He broke off as footsteps sounded on the black pine floor. Anna Lowensohn entered the rear parlor. "Nathan, a young gentleman wishes to speak with you—"

Before she could complete the introduction, Antoine Vanson walked past her into the room. "Forgive this intrusion, but I had not seen you for almost a month. I worried that you had fallen sick."

Nathan rose, the game forgotten. "Thank you for your consideration. I am well, as you can see. My absence from Mercier's has been occasioned not by illness but by work." His eyes moved from Antoine's face to the enormous bouquet of red roses he carried, and he said the first thing that came into his mind. "Are they for me, in case I was sick?"

Antoine's laugh rippled across the room. "I would bring you something more meaningful, like a bottle of good Madeira to help you over your malady. No, these are for your cousin Leonora. It seemed a waste of effort to come all the way here from the *Vieux Carré* and not make a point of seeing her."

From the corner of his eye, Nathan saw Gershon watching how he would cope with the situation. "Leonora may have already retired, Antoine. I am certain that if you give them to Mrs. Lowensohn, she will make sure Leonora receives them first thing in the morning."

"That will not be necessary, cousin. I will be more than happy to take them myself."

Nathan, the Lowensohns, and Antoine turned toward the doorway. Leonora stood there, hands held together in front of her long black skirt. Her dark, curly hair rested on her shoulders, contrasting strongly with the bright white of the blouse she wore. A turquoise-laced shawl covered her shoulders.

Antoine stepped forward, the roses held out. "I thought you were beautiful that day I tried to catch your attention with the bag of flour, but now I see that my first impression merely cheated me. You are more than beautiful. You are exquisitely divine. Please accept these flowers as a token of my adoration."

Face flushed with pleasure and excitement, Leonora stretched out trembling hands for the flowers. She lifted them to her nose and breathed in deeply. Their sweetness overpowered her, just as Antoine Vanson threatened to do. His handsome looks, the devilish sparkle in his eyes, his elegance of dress and manner were everything she had ever dreamed of in a beau.

Antoine turned to Nathan. "I will be attending a ball this Saturday at the Armory Hall, and I would be honored if you would allow me to ask your charming cousin to accompany me."

Nathan's reservations dissolved in the face of Antoine's eloquently phrased question. "Certainly. I can think of no gentleman better suited to be the escort of my beloved cousin."

Some of Leonora's infatuation disappeared. "Do you intend to ask me as well?" she wanted to know. "Perhaps I do not want to go with you to the Armory Hall, no matter how fit an escort my beloved cousin considers you to be."

Antoine's dark brown eyes narrowed in momentary surprise. "Forgive me, but to have asked you without first obtaining your cousin's permission would have been a breach of courtesy."

"I understand," Leonora said, not certain that she did.

"Will you accompany me to the ball?"

"Thank you. I would love to accompany you."

Nathan watched Antoine raise Leonora's free hand to his lips. It seemed inconceivable that this sophisticated young man was the same sword-wielding terror who had marked the professional gambler. He turned to look at Gershon, who had remained sitting by the freshly started chess game as if expecting Nathan to return at any moment. A mixture of emotions played across the cotton factor's face. A slight smile curled his lips, but his blue eyes remained wary. He had spelled out a warning to Nathan, and had then watched Nathan disregard it completely. Nathan and Leonora were intent on crossing the gulf between the two cultures. He hoped they succeeded without too much pain.

Chapter Seven

After being taken to the ball, Leonora talked of nothing else. She repeated every compliment Antoine had given her as they rode by cabriolet from Waverley to the Armory Hall. She recounted the welcome she'd received from Antoine's friends, who told her how lucky she was to have been asked by him to a ball; he had never looked at any girl but a Creole before. She described Antoine as a divine dancer, so perfect at the waltz, quadrille, polka, and lancier that her own mistakes went unnoticed. She related the entire menu of the midnight meal that renewed the dancers' strength, and with a catch in her voice she spoke of the return ride to Waverley. "Antoine is a perfect gentleman. He helped me down and walked me to the door, and before he left he gave me this." Proudly, she flaunted the single pearl that hung from a gold chain around her slender throat.

Nathan knew about the evening's final moments before Leonora made them public. He had waited in the front parlor until three in the morning when the cabriolet carrying Antoine and Leonora stopped by the marble carriage block. He had watched Antoine present her with the necklace and had seen the embrace and brushing kiss that followed. Remaining in the parlor, he had listened to the rustle of Leonora's skirt as she ascended the curving staircase to the upper floor, and had wondered how she would react if she knew he had seen. She would accuse him of spying and meddling in her affairs, and she would hate him for it. But spying and meddling were his duties. As her older cousin, as her only relative for all practical purposes, he had an obligation to ensure no harm befell her. Leonora might not understand, but Antoine would. After all, had he not charged Nathan with such responsibility in the first place?

Antoine became a regular visitor to Waverley, arriving once a week in the cabriolet to escort Leonora to a ball, the theater, or dinner. The grace and gallantry with which he charmed Leonora worked equally well on the rest of the household. He soon broke through Gershon Lowensohn's wall of reserve. After only a couple of visits the two were talking with the ease of long-standing friends. Even Miriam forgot momentarily her infatuation with Nathan, finding a completely different attraction in Antoine Vanson's Gallic allure. Instead of asking Leonora about her cousin, she began to pester her about Antoine.

Nathan, too, fell under the young Creole's spell, but for vastly disparate reasons. He saw Antoine more often than did Leonora and the Lowensohns, and in surroundings very different to Waverley. At Mercier's, when old Jean-Pierre Vanson gambled, Nathan saw Antoine watch hawklike for any man who dared take advantage of his father. When he found such men, he never hesitated to challenge them. Twice in the following month, Nathan seconded his friend in Mercier's courtyard. A cut on the arm ended one duel; a pierced shoulder halted the other.

"Have you ever fought a duel to the death?" Nathan asked after the second encounter.

"Just once," Antoine replied casually.

"You killed a man who cheated at cards?"

"My God, no! A card cheat's punishment is a wound to the hand with which he deals or a scar on his face to mark him as a dishonest rogue. The scoundrel I ran through had grievously offended the young lady I was escorting to a ball."

"How did he offend her?"

"I overheard him remark to his companions that my escort danced with all the grace of a cart horse."

"Was your escort upset that you challenged him?"

"Upset?" Antoine regarded Nathan as though he were mad. "She would have had it no other way. Had I failed to challenge him, I would have lost all credibility in her eyes."

"How old were you then?"

"It was a year ago. I was nineteen."

"A year ago, I was in London, where I had no idea that young men of my age settled differences with such finality."

Antoine smiled at the irony presented to him. "You tease me with a bewildering dilemma, Nathan. You second me willingly, yet I sense that you do so with total disapproval."

Nathan no longer knew whether he disapproved or not. Viewed through the perspective of his English background, dueling was abhorrent, the result of a communications breakdown between otherwise sane men. Yet in the light of New Orleans tradition, it became understandable. Even acceptable. He found a sense of justice in the idea of a cheat's hand, the tool of his trade, being injured, or a scar left across his face to warn other potential victims. "My wise namesake, King Solomon, would have approved of such justice, Antoine. And against all tenets of good common sense, there is something oddly romantic about the notion of a man risking his life to protect a woman's honor."

Antoine found the admission worthy of applause. He clapped his hands together half a dozen times, then rested them on Nathan's shoulders. "Does it not make your heart rest easily to know that your delightful cousin is in the care of such a man?"

"It does." But even as he spoke Nathan questioned how wise he had been to allow the relationship between Leonora and this gracious but dangerous man to progress so far. Surely he could have found a way to hinder their meetings. Yet if Leonora's safety worried him, how much more secure could she be than in the company of a man such as Antoine? A brave young man who would challenge anyone foolish enough to offend her? Furthermore, what right did he have to keep his cousin from a man whose company he found increasingly exciting? Being with Antoine was like a drug, heady and invigorating when administered, but leaving a hollow, aching emptiness when it was withdrawn. Those evenings when Nathan stayed at home, he found himself wondering what was occurring at Mercier's. More importantly, what was Antoine doing?

Antoine allowed his hands to remain on Nathan's shoulders. "If you have already started to accept such a basic Creole tradition as chivalry, perhaps it is time to continue your education and transform you into a proper gentleman."

"I already am a gentleman."

"Mon ami, heaven forbid that my words offend your ears, but what passes for a gentleman in London does not necessarily pass here. Oh, it is easy enough to fool the Yankees above Canal Street, but to be regarded as a gentleman in the *Vieux Carré* one must possess style, elegance, and panache."

Notwithstanding Antoine's reputation as a duelist, Nathan would never have found offense in the remark. Not when it was accompanied by the bright twinkle that added devilment to the Creole's dark brown eyes. Antoine seemed to find a vast degree of fun in everything he did. He possessed a joy of life that Nathan envied, deriving the maximum pleasure from every opportunity. On the dance floor, he expended more energy than anyone else; in a restaurant, he found immense satisfaction in even the simplest dish. Nathan wondered if he would have enjoyed a similar lust for life had his own youth been less unhappy? If his parents had not died so young? If he had not been brought up by an uncle to whom the duty was so obviously an onerous charge? And if he had not been born in London, but here, in New Orleans, where fun and enjoyment seemed so much more an accepted part of life?

No point would be served by daydreaming. He was in New Orleans now, being offered the chance to make up for much of the pleasure he had missed. Only a fool or a curmudgeon would reject it. "Your words would never offend me, Antoine. I would be eternally grateful if you would show me how to be accepted as a gentleman in the *Vieux Carré* as well as above Canal Street."

Six months earlier, when Nathan and Leonora had arrived in New Orleans, Gershon Lowensohn had taken them under his wing and helped them gain a foothold in their new country. Now Antoine Vanson appointed himself as Nathan's mentor. He claimed his task was to make Nathan recognizable as a gentleman in the French Quarter, and he took it seriously. His first act in that role was to forbid Nathan from ever again speaking English once he crossed below Canal Street.

"You have a basic understanding of French. Now see how quickly you will become fluent when you realize that you can no longer fall back onto English to make yourself understood."

Initially, Nathan struggled. He composed his thoughts in English, then hesitated while he translated those thoughts into the language in which he would express them. In restaurants, Antoine goaded him with: "The food will grow cold and the wine will turn sour while you dither." At dance halls, Antoine teased him by saying, "These beautiful girls will be old women by the time you ask them onto the floor." And at Metairie racetrack, Antoine murmured caustically, "The race will be over before you share with us the secret of which horse you wish to bet on." But as hard as Nathan tried, he still shaped thoughts in English.

The transformation came after a month, at Mercier's. Sitting in a game of draw poker, Nathan was dealt three aces. He bet heavily. Two players fell, leaving only one man facing him. The man's name was Raymonde Perrault, and he had been introduced to Nathan by Antoine only that evening. In his thirties, with olive skin and coal-black eyes set in a lean face, Perrault was dressed so fastidiously that Nathan felt slovenly by comparison. He wore a suit of green broadcloth, a bright white shirt, and a black cravat around his throat. The edge of a lace handkerchief showed from one sleeve. Rings adorned the slender, artistic fingers of both hands. Very slowly, those beringed fingers counted out enough money to equal Nathan's bet. A second passed, then they pushed out another equal amount to raise.

Nathan glanced at his cards again. Three aces filled him with confidence. After matching the raise, he translated his English thoughts into halting French. *"Monsieur,* I think you are trying to steal this hand. I would be a fool to let you do so."

A humorless smile passed across the man's face. "I never steal a hand, *monsieur.* I always win within the rules."

Nathan felt Antoine's fingers press on his shoulder, as if in warning. He asked for two cards, a queen and a five; no help at all. Across the table, Perrault indicated that he would play the five cards he had been dealt.

"Your bet, *monsieur,"* Perrault said.

Nathan stared hard at Perrault. The smile had gone, leaving his face devoid of expression. The eyes resembled chips of granite. "I still think you are trying to steal this hand," Nathan said. He counted out twenty dollars, half of that which remained in front of him.

"I would be grateful if you would cease using that word." Perrault raised another twenty dollars. "I never steal."

Again, Nathan felt the pressure of Antoine's hand. He paid no heed. His mind was absorbed with the game. He wished he had more money, so he could raise again and teach this cold-faced dandy a lesson he would never forget. Claiming he did not steal! Of course he stole! He was trying to do so now, trying to win this game with a gigantic bluff. Refusing to take any cards, raising each bet and hoping Nathan's spine would fold. Not with three aces it would not! Nathan pushed out his last twenty dollars.

"I call."

Perrault set down his cards. Nathan, with a beaming smile exposed his three aces and reached for the pot. Perrault's hand stopped him. Despite their slimness, the bejeweled fingers had surprising strength. Their grip on Nathan's hand was like a vise. "Perhaps you would do well to look at my cards, *monsieur.*"

Nathan looked. The smile fell from his face. His jaw dropped. Perrault's five hearts mocked him. He had not been bluffing after all.

Nathan laughed bitterly and looked up at Antoine. "And all the time I thought he was trying to steal the hand . . . !"

Perrault stood. Two steps took him around the table to confront Nathan. "If words alone do not make my feelings clear, *monsieur,* then my sword possesses a most eloquent tongue."

Antoine stepped forward quickly, putting himself between the suddenly threatening figure of the dandified Raymonde Perrault and the still-seated Nathan. *"Monsieur* Perrault, my friend is not totally familiar with our language. . . ." He swung around to Nathan and broke his own rule by hissing in English. "Apologize to him at once! Tell him you meant nothing by your comment."

Recognizing the urgency in Antoine's voice, Nathan reacted instantly. A torrent of French poured from his lips. *"Monsieur,* forgive me if I have offended you. That was never my intention."

The dark eyes remained like stone. "When a man tells you once he does not like to be accused of stealing . . ."

"It was an expression, an unfortunate one I now realize. I should have said that I thought you were trying to win the game through bluff. I apologize for any distress I have caused you."

"I accept your apology, *monsieur.* I also accept your money." Perrault bowed formally and left the table. As he walked toward the door leading down to Chartres, he exchanged greetings with half a dozen men who had witnessed the brief confrontation.

"Do you know what you just did?" Antoine asked.

"Yes. . . ." Nathan gave a puzzled smile. "For the first time, I thought in French. When I apologized to him, when I asked him to pardon me, my thoughts were in French."

Antoine regarded Nathan as though he had taken leave of his senses. Then he began to laugh. "You just insulted not once but three times the finest swordsman in New Orleans, and all you can say is that you thought in French?"

A cold wave swept over Nathan. "What would have happened if I had not thought in French? If I had hesitated while trying to form my apology first in English?"

"I would have now been preparing to second you, and wondering how to relay news of your death to your charming cousin Leonora. Raymonde Perrault is a *maître d'armes*, my impetuous friend. A master of arms, greater possibly than *Pépé Lulla* and Bastile Croquère. My own skill stems from his expertise as a tutor. He is rumored to be responsible for thirty of the souls who repose in Saint Louis Cemetery."

"Why did you not warn me?"

"Did you not feel my fingers caress your shoulder?"

"I thought you were advising caution in my betting."

Antoine stared into his friend's eyes. "Tell me, are you thinking now in French, or have you reverted to English?"

"French," Nathan answered instantly. "Being accepted as a gentleman while in the *Vieux Carré* is nowhere near as important as being safe. Safety here depends on quickness of mind——"

"And only by thinking in French can a man be assured of that quickness. You learned a valuable lesson tonight, my friend."

"Two valuable lessons. I also learned that it is wise to listen to a *maître d'armes* when he suggests that you stop accusing him of theft."

Antoine burst out laughing. "And do not forget the night's third lesson, that of believing a man is bluffing when he is most assuredly not."

Throughout the spring of 1852, the friendship between the two young men blossomed. Nathan became a part of Antoine's life, accompanying him to dances and racetracks, restaurants, and gambling houses. Antoine introduced Nathan to his social circle as the Englishman he was transforming into a Creole. As Antoine's friend, Nathan was accepted everywhere. It soon became obvious that the Vanson name carried influence within the Creole community. One day, Antoine reeled off the list of family accomplishments. A hundred and twenty-seven years earlier, two Vanson brothers had been among the original French settlers. One had died defending *Nouvelle Orleans* from an Indian attack, while the other had become wealthy as an indigo planter. Antoine's great-grandfather had witnessed the ceremony ceding Louisiana to the United States. And Antoine's own father, Jean-Pierre Vanson, had fought under Andrew Jackson to repel the British in the Battle of New Orleans. "We may appear to live apart from the rest of the country, Nathan, but the Vansons—indeed, all Creoles—are an integral part of these United States."

As the weather turned warmer and the mosquitoes returned, they traveled along the Shell Road to the resorts on Lake Pontchartrain. Sometimes, Leonora accompanied them. They made a happy trio, walking arm in arm by the lakeshore with Leonora striding along confidently in the center, smiling first at one escort and then the other as if deciding which one she preferred. But when Antoine was not beside her, Leonora's attitude changed. The smile gave way to a frown, and confidence became uncertainty.

"Does he ever talk about me?" Leonora demanded of Nathan when they were alone at Waverley.

"He always talks of you. Whenever we meet, his first words concern your welfare."

"I don't mean that. I mean . . ." Leonora's voice died as she tried to decide what she really did mean. Finally she came out with, "I am jealous of you, Nathan. Jealous that Antoine believes your company is so obviously preferable to mine."

"That is absurd."

"Is it? Then why does he see so much more of you than me?"

"Because I represent a challenge to him. He has sworn to

transform me into a gentleman. That must surely be a difficult task, which is why he has to see me so often."

"While I despair, all you can do is joke."

"Forgive me, Lally. I do not mean to make light of your feelings." Nathan understood his cousin's concern. She had no idea where she stood with Antoine. He continued to see her once a week, and when he was with her, his behavior was as gracious as ever. He showered her with compliments and gifts, and made her feel like the only girl in his life. Yet Nathan knew Antoine also courted other young women. Had he not been introduced to some of them?

Nathan feared that Antoine found Leonora something of a novelty. Everything about her was different from other young women he saw. Nathan hoped that when the Creole grew tired of her, he would set her feet back on the ground with the utmost gentleness.

Toward the end of June, four months after their first meeting, Antoine invited Nathan to dinner at his father's home on Esplanade. Nathan was struck by the vast difference between Jean-Pierre Vanson's home and the classically styled Waverley, with its lush garden shielding the house from the street. Built when the Garden District was still the Livaudais family estate, and the grand Greek-revival houses now upon it no more than visions in the minds of ambitious clerks and shopkeepers, the Vanson home was three stories high and planned around a central courtyard. On opposite sides of the same rooms, French doors opened onto lacework balconies that offered views of busy Esplanade or the serenity of the courtyard. Depending on the mood, one could choose to be a part of a busy city or cut oneself off from it completely simply by crossing the room. The furnishings also differed. At Waverley, every ornament, every clock or bauble, looked as if it had been placed in its position only after careful consideration. In the Vanson home, knickknacks filled almost every spare inch of space. Tiny silver eggcups with attached spoons covered one table; on another table danced a dozen small glass figurines.

Jean-Pierre led the way through to the rear gallery that overlooked the courtyard and invited his son and guest to sit down at a cherry drop-leaf table. Nathan thought the old man appeared far more comfortable in the relaxed surroundings of his home than he did in the intense atmosphere of a gambling club. Perhaps it was the light that spilled into the courtyard, but his hair seemed whiter and thicker, his brown eyes sharper.

As they sat at a table, an elderly Negro woman, hair covered by the ever-present *tignon*, set down a tray carrying three grenadine-filled glasses, a bowl of lemons, a lemon press, and a pitcher. After making pink lemonade, she offered the first glass to Vanson. He tasted it, smiled at the elderly woman and said, "Thank you, Rosa."

The woman made a second glass for Antoine, then a third for Nathan. As he accepted it, he became sharply aware of the single outstanding difference between Waverley and this house. It was not the design, nor was it the ambience. At Waverley, the Negroes who waited on the Lowensohn family were free men and women who could take their labor wherever they chose. Here, the woman in the *tignon* who made pink lemonade was a slave, a bond servant who had been purchased like any piece of livestock.

That single difference grew more evident over dinner. The Vanson home was full of Negro servants to cater to the needs of Jean-Pierre and his two guests. A butler in a tailcoat poured wine. Maids served the food. A young boy worked the cypress *punkah,* the shoofly fan that swung above the dinner table to cool the air and discourage flies from pestering the diners.

After dinner, the three men retired to a parlor overlooking the courtyard. The room was dominated by a large painting of a gray-haired woman. On the opposite wall hung a smaller portrait of the same woman, but painted many years before, when her hair was still dark. As the butler finished pouring

Madeira, Nathan asked Antoine's father how many slaves he owned.

"Eight," Jean-Pierre answered. "That many are necessary to run a house this size."

"How long have they worked for you?"

"Some have been a part of this family for more than thirty years. Rosa, who served us with refreshing pink lemonade when you arrived, came to us when I married my dear wife." His eyes flicked to the large painting, and all at once Nathan saw the sadness that Antoine had described at their first meeting. Since Nathan's arrival at the house, Jean-Pierre had been the gracious host, caring only for the welfare of his guest. It was clearly a role he had happily filled many times during his life. Now, mention of his wife had replaced pleasure with pain.

Antoine stepped in quickly, hoping to divert his father's attention from memories that would lead only to sadness. "The boy who operated the *punkah* is the son of a man and woman who have been with us for fifteen years. His father is a coachman and his mother works in the kitchen. They are all dedicated to my father and fear what will happen to them should he ever die."

Nathan recalled Gershon Lowensohn's words aboard *The Wandering Jew*, long before he revealed that his Negro servants were free men and women. He had claimed that each was like family. Now Antoine and his father were making the same claim. "How can a slave"—the question escaped from Nathan's mouth before he had a chance to consider its wisdom—"ever feel a part of the family which enslaves him?"

"Nathan, you come from a different country." Antoine's voice carried a note of admonition. "You do not yet fully understand our ways, just as some of those newcomers from above Canal Street do not fully understand. It is the black man's lot to be dominated by the white man. Even the Bible tells us so. The black race is incapable of looking after itself. They are our childlike inferiors. Slavery is merely the way for us to shoulder our responsibilities toward them."

Another comment surfaced in Nathan's memory, one made by Miriam Lowensohn during that first day's tour of New Orleans. Slavery was a fact of life in the city. Although the Lowensohns did not own slaves, they did not criticize those who did; their livelihood, after all, came from planters whose own prosperity rested on the backs of bondsmen. The same now applied to Nathan. Antoine Vanson was his friend. In a true friend, you accepted the bad points as well as the good.

Jean-Pierre continued to stare at the large painting, mesmerized by the memories it contained. "Your mother, Antoine, always stressed that the happiness of slaves was a reflection on the family that owned them. She was a very wise woman."

Antoine fidgeted in his seat, as if uncomfortable at his father's rambling. Nathan stood up and positioned himself in front of the painting. Despite the fact that Antoine's mother had been in her fifties when the portrait was painted, it was obvious that she had been a very beautiful woman. Graying hair, parted at the center, was pulled back from an oval face. Full lips curved up in a soft smile. Above a straight nose, dark brown eyes shone down to bathe Nathan with a warmth that made him feel cheated at being denied the opportunity to meet the subject of the painting.

"Madame Mathilde Vanson, my wife, sat for that seven years ago," Jean-Pierre explained, "just a year before the Almighty in his wisdom took her from us. What times we had when she was with us. This house rang with music, and laughter was heard in every room. Each night, I ask God to let me live long enough to hear those sounds again, when Marie-Louise returns." He saw Nathan peering at the name of the artist. "It was painted by Jacques Amans, a Belgian portraitist who keeps a studio in New Orleans."

Nathan studied the canvas for another minute before crossing the room to the smaller painting. It took his breath away. If he had thought Madame Mathilde Vanson beautiful as a woman in her fifties, as a girl of no more than eighteen she was striking. Lustrous jet black hair fell softly from a center parting before being drawn back into a bun. The face was that of a Renaissance madonna, with gently curving lips and dark smiling eyes. The overall picture was one of serenity, but as Nathan stared, he fancied he saw something else in those eyes. A smoldering fire that threatened at any moment to burst into flame and consume the canvas on which it depended for life.

Nathan dropped his eyes to a corner of the portrait and found the name of Jacques Amans again. It took him a moment to register the incongruity. He stepped back and swung around to face Antoine and his father. "How can Jacques Amans have been responsible for this painting? The portrait of Madame Vanson as a young lady must have been painted thirty-five years ago . . . ?"

Jean-Pierre gave a dry laugh. "That painting was done little more than a year ago."

"How can that be? Madame Vanson has been—"

"That painting is not of my mother," Antoine said. "It is of my sister, Marie-Louise. She sat for it shortly before sailing for Europe."

Nathan turned to look again at the portrait. The face seemed even more enticing, the smile more alluring, the smoldering fire in the eyes even closer to bursting into vivid flame. It was no wonder that Marie-Louise could do as she wished with her father. No wonder she was feted at the homes of barons and counts. No wonder handsome hussars and cavalry officers stood in line to dance with her. If Jacques Amans's skill as a portrait painter had captured even a trace of Marie-Louise Vanson's loveliness, then she was the most radiantly beautiful creature Nathan had ever seen.

At evening's end, Antoine saw Nathan to the *banquette*. "You speak like a Creole, you dress with Creole style," Antoine told his friend. "Only one thing now stands between Nathan Solomon of London and full acceptance as a gentleman in the *Vieux Carré*."

"I thought the invitation to your father's home signified that acceptance."

"It was the prelude to acceptance. Full acceptance requires you to be a skillful swordsman, capable of defending his own honor or the honor of a lady."

Nathan started to laugh. "Antoine, you know me better than that. I would never challenge any man—"

"If your reputation becomes that flawless, no man will ever challenge you. Besides, every Creole gentleman takes lessons from one of the *maître d'armes*. Fencing is a skill, as much a social grace as the ability to dance. The best swordsmen always make the best dancers."

Nathan found himself helpless against such persuasion. "Lead on, Antoine. Introduce me to your *maître d'armes*."

"I think an introduction will be unnecessary. You have made his acquaintance once already."

Raymonde Perrault taught fencing in Exchange Alley, the short thoroughfare running from Canal to Conti. He was one of many instructors who maintained rooms there, and as Nathan walked for the first time along the flagstoned alley the noise coming from open windows was nerve-racking. Cries of *"En garde!"* and shouts of triumph punctuated the whistling of small-swords and the ringing echo of broadswords as hundreds of dueling-conscious Orleanians honed their skills.

Perrault remembered Nathan from their meeting at Mercier's. "Do you come to learn swordsmanship because you have offended other men by accusing them of stealing from you at cards?"

"No, *monsieur*. To avoid ever repeating that particular mistake, I have worked assiduously to improve my knowledge of French. I seek your skill because my good friend Antoine Vanson swears that you are the best teacher in all New Orleans."

Perrault inclined his narrow head in recognition of the tribute. "Let us learn if the pupil is worthy of the teacher."

The first lesson covered the fundamentals of edged-weapon defense. Standing in a line with three other novices and holding a wooden stick shaped like a broadsword, Nathan repeatedly executed the four basic guard positions, the parries against a cutting attack. By the end of the lesson, his right arm was ready to drop from its socket. In the next lesson, he learned guard positions five through eight, the false-edge parries made against the thrust. Perrault confronted each novice in turn. Almost at will, he thrust a rod through their guard positions, jabbing the point painfully into their rib cages. Each time he shouted, "If that had been a real weapon, you would not be bruised. You would be dead! Practice those parries until even I cannot penetrate them, because the time is not far off when they might save your life!"

From broadswords, tuition moved to the *colichemarde,* the smallsword with the triangular blade hollowed out on all three sides for lightness and speed. In Perrault's hand, the *colichemarde* had a life of its own, flashing sideways to parry, darting forward in a lunge or riposte, and crashing down like a bolt of lightning in the culmination of a *balestra.*

"When you leave here," Perrault yelled after Nathan failed to parry a lunge, "fall onto your knees before the Holy Virgin in Saint Louis Cathedral and offer up a prayer of gratitude to the men who designed the mask and padded jacket you wear today. A hundred years ago, before the mask and jacket, the punishment for such a basic mistake would have been instant death!"

Nathan took every opportunity to practice. Antoine provided good and willing competition. Watched by old Jean-Pierre Vanson, the two friends faced each other for an hour at a time in the courtyard of the home on Esplanade. Nathan found an increasing enjoyment in the sport, discovering skills he never dreamed he owned. Fencing exercised his mind as well as his body, and the sense of achievement from winning a point against the far more experienced Antoine equalled any exhilaration he had ever known. Afterward, exhausted and soaked in perspiration, they sat on the rear gallery, sipping cold pink lemonade and discussing the just-completed bout.

One summer Sunday, on the shore at Lake Pontchartrain, Nathan and Antoine terrified Leonora with a fencing display. A carefree summer outing changed abruptly with the start of an argument between the two friends over the merits of the Mississippi. When Antoine praised the river as the most magnificent stretch of water in the world, Nathan turned away as if to hide a laugh.

"My dear Antoine, you could lose the Mississippi in the River Thames that runs through London."

Antoine bristled. "How dare you insult the Mississippi so? Were you not such a good friend, I would not hesitate to run you through for such insolence."

To Leonora's horror, Nathan ignored the warning. "Antoine, you have sipped too much dirty water from that little stream you call a river. It has addled your brain."

Swords appeared, and before Leonora's terrified gaze the two friends began to thrust and parry. She had no idea that the whole scene had been prearranged just for her benefit, nor did she realize that the swords Antoine produced so readily from the open carriage which had brought them from New Orleans had small buttons affixed to their points.

"Do you take back your insult?" Antoine cried out as he began a *flèche*, a running attack that drove Nathan back.

"Never!" Nathan darted to one side, deflected the thrusting sword and launched his own attack. "The Mississippi is a stream of horses' piss!"

Leonora watched in horror, trying to scream but too paralyzed with fear to find her voice. After fifteen seconds, she managed to shriek, "Stop it! Stop it at once, I say!"

Both swords dropped immediately. The sweaty faces of the duelists turned to Leonora. "You behave like children to fight over something as ridiculous as a comparison between the Mississippi and the Thames. And you . . . !" She glared fiercely at Nathan. "How can you possibly defend the Thames when you know it is the repository for every piece of sewage in London?"

Laughing, Nathan proffered the sword to his cousin. "See the point, Lally? A button covers it. No one will be hurt with these swords. We do not duel. We practice. We indulge in the art of fencing. It is a skill all gentlemen should know."

"Such practicing is beyond my comprehension," Leonora said, "because when you rehearse killing, as you two constantly do, it is only a matter of time before you actually have to do it."

Antoine flexed the sword between his hands. "I fear you will never adapt as well as your cousin to our traditions, Leonora. A Creole lady thrills to the sight of gentlemen drawing swords, especially if they are fighting over her."

"In that case, I do not wish to adapt. Dueling is the height of stupidity." Tears brimming in her eyes, she turned on Nathan. Her voice rose as anger replaced anxiety. "Do you not remember our first day in this city, how sick you became after seeing Rose Meagher's husband kill that seaman? What did you promise that day—that you would be slow to give offense and even slower to take it?" Without waiting for an answer, she flounced away to the carriage and climbed in. Head turned away, she let the tears fall. She could find no art or skill in a fight—even a practice fight—between the two young men she loved.

Antoine gave Nathan a puzzled smile. Nathan shrugged his shoulders. What right had Leonora to bring up what happened a year ago? There was no comparison between the bloody battle with pistols fought by Michael Meagher and Jack Johnson and the elegant skill of fencing.

Perhaps Antoine was right, and Leonora would never adapt to Creole customs. Nathan thought that a pity, because he felt entirely at home with them.

At Waverley, Nathan turned from pupil to tutor, sharing with Henry Lowensohn the skill he had acquired. Each new move he learned from Raymonde Perrault and perfected against Antoine, he passed on to Henry, who was an avid learner. Leonora never watched the contests. Whenever the ring of steel echoed across the garden at Waverley, she sat up in her room, refusing to come down until the sparring had finished.

Other household members were not so vehemently opposed. Miriam watched at every opportunity, green eyes wide in adoration as Nathan turned defense into attack. Another regular viewer was Gershon Lowensohn. He saw nothing wrong in young men knowing how to defend themselves; he worried only when such skill was coupled with rashness. He did not consider Nathan rash. However, he was not so certain about Nathan's friend. During his years in New Orleans, Gershon had seen many men like Antoine, men who breathed the *Code Duello* with every mouthful of fresh air. They never failed to frighten him.

Chapter Eight

In mid-September, as New Orleans began to shake itself awake from its summer hiatus, Antoine invited the two cousins to his brother Marcel's annual party at the sugar plantation a dozen miles below the city.

Nathan and Leonora traveled by carriage with Antoine and his father. Jean-Pierre Vanson proved to be a talkative passenger. He pointed out homes along the way, adding little anecdotes about the owners. He commented on Leonora's clothing, saying that the pale blue of her full skirt and tight bodice made her dark hair and eyes even more stunning. In turn, Leonora complimented Jean-Pierre on his outfit, a loose-fitting frock coat worn over a bright yellow vest, a nankeen blouse and light gray trousers.

"You dress like a dandy, Monsieur Vanson. You will be the most elegant man at your son's party."

The old man beamed with pleasure. "If I were forty years younger," he told Leonora, "I would be your most ardent suitor."

Nathan understood why Jean-Pierre was in such high spirits. Today he would see his granddaughter. Marcel's two-year-old daughter, Josephine, was Jean-Pierre's only grandchild in the United States. In Paris, the oldest Vanson son, Alphonse, had already fathered three boys, but Jean-Pierre had yet to set eyes on any of them. He was too old to undertake the lengthy voyage to France, and neither Alphonse nor his wife showed any sign of wanting to sail in the other direction. Nathan felt a twinge of pity for the old man. One son gave him no opportunity to see his grandchildren, while the other offered invitations like a royal summons. Even Marie-Louise, the daughter on whom Jean-Pierre doted, had deserted him. Of four children, only Antoine demonstrated loyalty, and his devotion was so fierce that it almost compensated for the apathy of the other three.

The carriage reached Marcel Vanson's home just after midday. A long avenue led through fields high with sugar cane in which toiled dozens of Negroes. In the distance, almost on the banks of the Mississippi, rose the two chimneys of the plantation's sugar house, where cane juice was boiled down and granulated, ready to be shipped to New Orleans. Nathan looked out with interest. The sugar trade worked to a different timetable than the cotton industry. For almost sixty years—ever since a man named Étienne de Boré first succeeded in granulating Louisiana cane—the state's sugar growers had raced the calendar, ready to give the order to cut the instant they sensed the first frost. Only one miscalculation was needed, one unexpected cold snap, and then the stench of sour cane would cover the fields, heralding a sugar planter's failure.

At the end of the avenue stood a two-story brick mansion surrounded by gardens filled with colorful plants and flowers. Spanish moss draped the branches of majestic live oaks. In front of the high porch, carefully cultivated rose bushes filled the air with a heady fragrance. To one side stood the carriages of a dozen earlier arrivals.

A tall Negro in a scarlet coachman's uniform waited by the marble carriage block in front of the house. The instant the carriage stopped, he opened the door to help passengers alight. Marcel and Micaela Vanson came down from the porch to greet their guests. Eight years older than Antoine, Marcel bore little physical resemblance to his brother. Where Antoine was lithe and graceful, Marcel was squat and muscular. A thick black beard covered a red face in which the dominant feature was a fleshy hook of a nose. Above it, dark brown eyes glittered from the shelter of fierce, bushy brows. Micaela, by contrast, was thin and ashen-faced. Her brown hair was wispy, irritability colored her thin lips. Nathan recalled Antoine mentioning Marcel's visits to his mistress in New Orleans; a beautiful woman must make a welcome change to the pale harridan he had married. He wondered what could have initially attracted Marcel to Micaela until he remembered it was her father who owned the plantation. Wealth had a way of beautifying the plain.

Both Marcel and Micaela kissed Jean-Pierre on the cheek, but there was little affection in the greeting. When Marcel told his father he looked well, the old man simply nodded and asked where his granddaughter was.

"In the house. Micaela will show you."

"Thank you. I would like to see her." Following Micaela, Jean-Pierre climbed the porch stairs and entered the house.

Marcel shook his brother's hand. When introduced to Nathan and Leonora, he repeated their names, as if familiarizing himself with them. Then he turned away to greet more guests.

"You will have to forgive my brother," Antoine told Nathan and Leonora. "He was never known for delicacy of speech. But his hospitality . . . now that is something else. And that is what we came here to enjoy. The least we can do is eat and drink at his expense."

On the lawn behind the house, tables were covered with fine linen and silver cutlery. Half a dozen Negro women in red *tignons* scurried between the tables and the kitchen, carrying enormous dishes of food. Men in scarlet uniforms offered drinks from trays. In the middle of all this activity, Jean-Pierre Vanson appeared with his young granddaughter, an old man stooping to hold the hand of a child. A broad smile covered his lined face; life sparkled in his normally tired eyes. Antoine turned to Nathan and Leonora.

"If today's invitation were just for me, I would not bother to come. My brother's temper can be foul and his wife is a shrew.

But to see my father this happy, a journey of a thousand miles would not be onerous."

As more guests arrived, Nathan and Leonora drew closer together. Beside Antoine and his father, they knew no one. Only as the meal was about to be served did Nathan see the first familiar face, and then it was Leonora who brought it to his attention. "What a shame, Antoine's father won't be the most elegant man here after all," she told Nathan. "Look at that coxcomb talking to Marcel. He must have risen before dawn to dress so finely."

Nathan saw a familiar lean and swarthy face. "Make fun of that coxcomb only in your softest tones, Leonora. He is Raymonde Perrault, to whom Antoine and I go for fencing instruction."

As Leonora watched, Perrault clapped Marcel on the shoulder, and the two men began to laugh. "He must be a very popular man. Marcel has given him more time than he has given anyone else."

"All *maître d'armes* are popular. They attract admirers in the same way great actors and singers do."

Leonora continued to watch Perrault. He was never alone for a moment. When he ended the conversation with Marcel, another man waited for him. Before he finished talking to that man, two more men stood in line. All through the meal, people approached his table. When the meal ended, half a dozen, then a dozen, and finally fifty or more men began to chant Perrault's name.

Nathan leaned across Leonora to talk to Antoine. "Why do they call for him?"

"They want an exhibition of his skill. He gives one wherever he is invited. It is expected. Everyone who calls for him seeks the honor of being chosen as his partner."

Rings glinting in the sunlight, Perrault raised a hand in acknowledgment. A silence descended as the men waited to learn whom he would select. Perrault's gaze moved slowly across the guests until it reached the table where Nathan sat with Antoine, Leonora, and Jean-Pierre. Nathan's heart leaped as the black eyes met his own. No! Perrault would make him look a fool in front of all these people! The beringed hand seemed to point right at him. Heart racing, Nathan started to stand.

"Antoine," Perrault called. "A contest between you and me will provide fine entertainment for these good people."

Nathan sank back, relieved, as Antoine rose to his feet. The spectators formed a ring around the two opponents. Marcel Vanson produced a pair of masks and two *colichemardes* with buttoned points on which he smeared red fluid. The first man to score three touches would be the winner. While Perrault cut the air experimentally with the blade, Antoine approached Leonora. Pinned to one sleeve of her bodice was a bright yellow ribbon. "May I wear your colors, my lady?"

A burning tide swept through Leonora's body. As much as she loathed the idea of dueling, Antoine's offer to champion her momentarily replaced her fear with excitement. Without hesitation, she removed the yellow ribbon and handed it to him. He tied the ribbon around the hilt of his sword, kissed Leonora's hand, and stepped out to meet his challenger.

Excited shouts rang out as the exhibition began. Nathan kept one eye on the two figures inside the human ring; the other he reserved for the people standing next to him. Jean-Pierre observed the contest with the same interest he exhibited when Antoine and Nathan sparred in the courtyard of the house on Esplanade. Leonora was agitated. Her hands were clenched, her lips compressed. She watched as anxiously as if the two men were fighting not with impotent blades but with real swords.

A cry went up as Perrault evaded Antoine's guard and touched the point of his sword to the younger man's left arm. The red fluid on the button left a vivid smear on the white fabric of the blouse. First blood.

Another cry greeted Perrault's second touch. Bright red colored the right shoulder of Antoine's blouse. One more strike and the contest would be over. Nathan concentrated on the battle, willing Antoine on, shouting in exultation when his friend executed a *botte du paysan,* grasping the forte of the blade in his left hand and striking sharply at Perrault's sword before thrusting through the opening produced by the maneuver. A red smudge discolored Perrault's white blouse.

"Did you see that?" Jean-Pierre shouted in Nathan's ear. "The pupil has bested the master!"

Nathan nodded excitedly. One more touch and Antoine would even the score. Two more and he would win!

Perrault removed his mask for a moment to wipe his brow. He smiled, as if commending his opponent, but the expression contained all the warmth of a January blizzard. The two men assumed the guard position once more. Lightning flashed and the third and final red blossom appeared as if by magic on Antoine's blouse, right above the heart. Antoine stared down at the mark, stunned by the speed with which it had materialized.

A heavy hand descended on Nathan's shoulder. *"Monsieur,* I understand from my brother that you, too, are a proficient swordsman. I would deem it an honor to face you in a contest."

Nathan turned around. The first words Marcel Vanson had spoken to him all day constituted a challenge. "Pardon me if I refuse, but my stomach is still so full from your hospitality that I fear I would disappoint you."

"I cannot accept a refusal. My curiosity is aroused by my brother's tales of an Englishman who aspires to be a Creole. An English Hebrew, no less."

Nathan stiffened. For the first time in New Orleans, his background had been thrown into his face. And by the brother of his dearest friend.

Marcel's face twisted into a scowl. "Creole," he sneered and looked at his father. "Does this Hebrew not understand that no Creole flees from a challenge? Perhaps now you and my brother will see how you shame our name by befriending him."

Catching hold of Marcel's arm, Nathan said, "I accept your invitation, *monsieur.* My stomach is not so full after all. Your food, I must confess, was not good enough to fill it."

Antoine returned. He had removed the yellow ribbon from his sword. Unaware of the clash between his brother and Nathan, he held it out to Leonora. "I apologize for disgracing the colors you so graciously gave me."

She touched Antoine's stained shirt. "I thank God only that those are not real bloodstains."

Pushing his way through the spectators, Marcel clapped his hands for attention. "My brother Antoine is involved in an interesting experiment to transform Nathan Solomon, an English Hebrew, into a Creole gentleman." A burst of laughter greeted the announcement. Marcel smiled smugly, letting the laughter die away on its own accord before speaking again. "He has taught this Hebrew how to tell good wine from bad, but even a trained monkey is capable of doing that. I will now test the true success of this experiment by learning if this Hebrew can fight like a Creole gentleman. I will see whether *Monsieur* Solomon, a blood descendant of King Saul and King David, has inherited their legendary battle skills."

"I will stop this at once!" Antoine said. "I did not invite you to my brother's home to be insulted so!"

Nathan held Antoine back. "I can take care of myself."

Leonora had not understood all of Marcel's proclamation, but she had heard Nathan's name, and that frightened her. She demanded to know what was happening. In whispered English, Nathan informed her of Marcel's challenge, and squeezed her hand reassuringly. "He is all bluster. The smallsword expertise I learned from Raymonde Perrault will bring me swift victory."

Marcel Vanson had a surprise in store for Nathan. Instead of retaining the *colichemardes* from the previous contest, he brought forth a pair of wooden sticks shaped like broadswords, but much heavier and more unwieldy than those used by Nathan in his first visit to Raymonde Perrault's fencing academy. The bout began. The delicate skills Nathan had learned from Perrault afforded him little protection against Marcel's furious attack. Swinging the sword-shaped stick like a club, Marcel smashed aside Nathan's guard, overwhelming the attempted parries with brute force. Time and again the heavy stick cracked into Nathan's arms and ribs. Each time a bellowed taunt rang out. "That would have cost you an arm, King Solomon! Look out, there goes your hand! You have just been cut in two, my Hebrew prince!"

Even when Nathan did successfully parry and launch his own cutting attack, his blows caused Marcel no discomfort. With a smallsword, Nathan knew he could have held his own. But with wooden broadswords, Marcel's strength was the overwhelming factor. After two minutes, the sword was too heavy for Nathan to hold. Down his left side, bruised ribs ached sharply with each motion. Sensing the end of the bout, Marcel swung a huge two-handed cut toward Nathan's head. Desperately, Nathan raised his own weapon to parry. The sheer power of Marcel's blow ripped the sword from Nathan's grasp and smashed it to the ground. Marcel's stroke continued and Nathan felt his head explode as the wooden sword smashed into it. Leaning on his weapon, Marcel mocked the prostrate figure of his opponent.

"Where, I ask, is the wisdom of Solomon now?"

Leonora rushed to Nathan's side. Antoine was quicker. Bending over his fallen friend, he helped him to his feet, then turned to face his brother.

"Marcel, if you are that familiar with the Bible to talk so intimately of Saul, David, and Solomon, you will know there is no more dangerous a foe than a brother turned enemy. That is what you accomplished today by insulting my friends."

"Friends? A Vanson does not befriend these people! A Vanson does not wear the colors of a heathen woman when he fights another Creole! Who do you think you are, Antoine, some knight templar in *Ivanhoe* who has succumbed to the wiles of a Hebrew witch and fallen in love with her? If that is your predicament, remember this—while blood runs warm through my body, the Vanson name will not be humiliated by an alliance with a member of that cursed race."

"Your blood may run cold sooner than you think." Supporting Nathan, and followed by his father and Leonora, Antoine headed for the carriage. From behind came Marcel's taunting laughter.

The carriage ride back to New Orleans was a nightmare. To minimize movement, Nathan sat wedged between Antoine and the side of the carriage, but each bump sent a new spasm of pain piercing through his side and head. Antoine was profuse in his apologies and his vows of reprisal. "One day, I will finally forget that we come from the same mother and father, and I will teach him a long overdue lesson!" Suddenly he laughed. "You are lucky, my friend, because you only needed to tolerate him for a few hours. I have suffered his rudeness all my life."

Leonora turned sideways to look at Jean-Pierre and remembered the old man walking with his granddaughter. The day had a ray of sunshine after all. "Did you enjoy your grandchild's company?"

"Very much, but the visit was too short. I fear that she will forget me by the time we meet again." He gazed at Nathan. "I also apologize for Marcel. He sneers at the idea of you adapting to Creole culture when it is he and that skinny harridan of a wife who need lessons in gentility and breeding."

Despite his own discomfort, Nathan felt another moment of sympathy for Jean-Pierre. How hard was it for a man of his age to come to terms with the knowledge that three of his children cared so little for him? When he considered the way they treated him, what icy hand clawed at his heart?

On reaching the house on Esplanade, Jean-Pierre found a letter waiting. While Antoine, Nathan, and Leonora watched, he read it through. Slowly, he lifted his eyes to stare at his son.

"God has listened to my prayers, Antoine. Even as we speak, a ship carrying Marie-Louise approaches New York. In two weeks at the most, she will be here among us." Energy surged through the tired body. "We must make plans, Antoine. This house will ring again with music, and laughter will be heard in every room."

* * *

The fight with Marcel Vanson left Nathan sore. Bruises covered his arms and shoulders. His ribs ached whenever he breathed deeply or made a sudden movement. A vivid purple welt spread across the left side of his forehead, and he felt fortunate that his skull had not been cracked by Marcel's final, savage blow. When Anna and Gershon Lowensohn asked the cause of such injuries, Nathan said he had been thrown from a horse while visiting the home of Antoine's brother. Leonora supported the story. The Lowensohns, having no reason to believe otherwise, accepted it.

The duplicity did not succeed for long. Two days after the trip to the sugar plantation, Antoine visited the countinghouse on Canal Street. He found Nathan making entries in a ledger. Setting a bottle of cognac on the desk, Antoine said, "You look as if you would welcome an interruption."

"I would welcome relief from my aches and pains."

Antoine surveyed the discolored forehead. "You wear your bruises well, like badges of valor. How did Leonora take all this? Is she distressed? Is there anything I can do for her?"

"I am battered, and all you can do is ask about Leonora?"

"While I like and respect you as a friend, I am captivated by your cousin. I adore her. Did you not see the way I fought Raymonde Perrault? I scored a touch against him, which few men do, and the reason I fought so skillfully was because Leonora's ribbon flew from the handle of my sword."

Despite his soreness, Nathan chuckled. "You really believed you were fighting for Leonora?"

"Of course. Her love lent wings to my sword." He paused to greet Gershon Lowensohn who entered the room at that moment. "It was a pity that you had no such motivation in your battle with my blustering bully of a brother. Then he, not you, might be wearing these bruises."

Aware of Gershon standing within earshot, Nathan changed the subject. "Should I carry a message to Leonora for you?"

"Tell her everything I said. Everything, do you understand? I will return tomorrow to learn her answer."

As Antoine left, Gershon studied Nathan. "There was no horse? Or was your fall in addition to a fight?"

"There was no horse," Nathan answered quietly. "I fought with Antoine's brother."

"Over what?"

"It was supposed to be an amiable contest of skill. Instead, Marcel decided to make it a definitive lesson."

"That you do not belong among the Creoles?"

"Precisely."

"You, of course, will ignore the lesson."

Nathan nodded. "Marcel is a minority. Besides, he lives too far away to be a nuisance."

"I hope for your sake that you are right."

That evening, walking with Leonora in the garden, Nathan repeated Antoine's message. Her dark eyes widened; color flushed her cheeks. "He fought so well because my ribbon flew from his sword? My love lent wings to his sword? He adores me?"

"Those are his exact words."

Leonora sat on a bench and closed her eyes. "Oh, Nathan, I knew he felt that way, but I wanted to hear him say it."

"What do you want me to tell him?"

"That I adore him, too." She kissed Nathan on the cheek and danced away beneath the trees, arms wrapped around herself as if pretending she were in Antoine's embrace. Nathan watched for a few seconds, delighted for his cousin. He had worried that her interest in Antoine would lead to heartbreak. Now that he had been proved wrong he could not be more pleased.

When Antoine returned the next morning to the counting-house, his first words were to ask Nathan how he felt. "There, be satisfied that I have inquired after your welfare. Now please tell me how Leonora responded to my message."

"She danced away as if she were the belle of a thousand balls. In truth, Antoine, I have never seen my cousin so happy."

"Did she give any indication of her feelings for me?"

"She did." Nathan felt a little embarrassed at relaying Leonora's message. "She said she adores you, too."

Antoine accepted it in a very matter-of-fact manner. "Good. Then you will not be averse to my marrying her."

Nathan raised a hand. "Wait a moment. You do not ask that question of me. You ask it of Leonora."

"But you are the closest she has to a guardian—"

"It does not matter what I am. I cannot give you permission to marry her."

"Then may I have your permission to ask her?"

"Certainly, but . . ."

"What concerns you? Do you worry that I will be unable to care for Leonora? Perhaps we Vansons are not as wealthy as your adopted family, but we are certainly not paupers. Once I begin to practice law, my income will be more than adequate."

Nathan held out a hand. "It isn't that at all, Antoine."

"Then what is it?"

"I worry about your brother."

"Marcel?" Antoine laughed. "He is a surly, toothless dog, with a bark more fearful than his bite." He looked hard at Nathan. "Surely you do not fear him."

"Only a fool would ignore the threats he made. All I ask is that you wait awhile before you make plans to marry my cousin. Give Marcel's rage a chance to cool. After your sister returns to New Orleans might be a more propitious time."

Antoine considered the request for several seconds before agreeing. "Perhaps you are right. Everyone loves Marie-Louise. Everyone will be happy when she returns, even my surly dog of a brother. I will allow time for the excitement of Marie-Louise's return to abate before I ask for Leonora's hand, but mark my words, you will see that you have nothing to fear."

The soreness left Nathan's body slowly. Work at the wharf was arduous, and enjoyable pursuits such as dancing and riding were out of the question. Most of all, he missed his fencing lessons. When he felt well enough, Raymonde Perrault's fencing academy would be his first stop.

Two weeks passed before he set out for Exchange Alley. The bruise on his forehead had gone. His arms were strong enough once more to wield a sword. Antoine accompanied him to Perrault's rooms. When the two friends entered, Perrault broke off from instructing newcomers in the basic guard positions. *"Monsieur* Vanson, you are welcome here. Your companion is not."

Nathan bristled as though he had been slapped in the face. Antoine held out a hand to steady him. "Why not?"

"The lessons a man learns here are to help him acquit himself with honor, as you did when you competed against me at your brother's home. *Monsieur* Solomon, however, not only failed to acquit himself with honor in his contest, but he brought shame to me with a display that was little short of spineless. He fought with all the bravery and courage of a craven coward."

Nathan stepped forward, jaw clenched, discomfort forgotten in the face of this insult. Before he could issue any denial to the charges, Antoine grabbed his arm and pulled him back. "Are you a fool, Nathan? You saw what he did to me, and I am ten times the swordsman you will ever be. He would cut you to ribbons."

"I will not be called a coward."

"Let him call you whatever he wishes. Names cannot hurt like a sword does." Antoine hustled Nathan out of the building and into Exchange Alley. Through open windows came the clash of steel on steel and the accompanying cries of battle. To Nathan's ears, they sounded like a thousand jeers all aimed at him.

Chapter Nine

In early October, a week after Nathan's clash with Raymonde Perrault, the Vanson household was thrown into turmoil. The reason was the return from Paris of Marie-Louise. The ship bringing her from Europe had docked eight days earlier in New York. She had spent two days in New York before traveling on the newly completed railroad to St. Louis, from where she took the steamboat down the Mississippi.

After giving his daughter two days to recover from all the traveling, Jean-Pierre held a day-long open house. All of New Orleans was invited to stop by and welcome his daughter home. Nathan and Leonora arrived by open phaeton midway through the afternoon to find the house full. As they stepped inside, Nathan held his cousin back. "Listen," was all he said. Leonora listened. From all around, from every room in the house, it seemed, came laughter. Mingling with the laughter was music. Jean-Pierre's dream had been fulfilled.

Antoine pushed through the crowd. He kissed Leonora before grasping her and Nathan by the hands and pulling them deeper into the house. "I have told my sister all about my English friends. She is most eager to meet you."

The two cousins followed Antoine through the house and into the courtyard. The music grew louder. In one corner of the courtyard, a string quartet played unnoticed. All attention was focused on Jean-Pierre, a vital Jean-Pierre who smiled and laughed and talked animatedly with those around him, and the young woman who stood by his side.

"My sister, Marie-Louise," Antoine said proudly to Leonora.

"She is very lovely. Do you not think so, Nathan?"

Nathan barely heard his cousin's question. Every fiber of his attention was fixed on the young woman in the pale yellow, hooped taffeta skirt who stood next to Jean-Pierre. Never before had he beheld such beauty. Even the strikingly elegant women he had seen at the Théâtre d'Orléans faded beside Antoine's younger sister. Taller than Leonora, Marie-Louise possessed a deportment that added elegance to even the most modest movement. The simple turning of her head carried the poise of a dancer executing a faultless pirouette. Her face was the palest Nathan had ever seen. Set against the lustrous black hair that cascaded gently to her shoulders, her skin seemed almost translucent. Widely spaced dark brown eyes cast a liquid, luminous allure.

Seeing the newcomers, Jean-Pierre reached out to draw them close. "This, Marie-Louise, is Leonora, the English girl who has so bewitched your brother. And here is Nathan, her cousin, whom Antoine is trying his hardest to transform into a Creole."

Marie-Louise glanced at Leonora before dismissing her in favor of Nathan. There was more to interest her in the tall young man with the lean, earnest face. She smiled at him. "An Englishman into a Creole, eh? That sounds a tantalizing challenge, even for one as determined and chimerical as my brother. How well is Antoine succeeding in his task?"

The smile warmed Nathan's face. It was like stepping from a cool, dark room into the bright spring day. "Surely you see the results before you. If you met me on the *banquette*, would you not consider me a Creole before you considered me an Englishman?"

Angling her head, Marie-Louise touched a finger to her chin. "To look at you . . . ? Yes, perhaps you could pass for Creole.

To listen to you . . . ? Again, perhaps. But the real question is, do you have the necessary refinement?"

Nathan glanced around the courtyard. The musicians were playing a gentle, lilting melody. "We would be foolish to allow such lovely music to go to waste. Will you give me the honor of dancing with me?"

The smile broadened into a golden ray of sunshine. "I would be delighted to dance with you. You are as gallant as any Creole gentleman I have ever met."

Bowing in acknowledgment, Nathan held out a hand. Marie-Louise's touch was as delicious as her smile. His heart hammered in anticipation of holding this young woman in his arms, but before he could turn expectation into fact, he heard a familiar voice demanding loudly, *"Ou est ma soeur?* Where is my sister? I have ridden all the way from my plantation to see her!"

Jean-Pierre's guests parted as Marcel Vanson pushed his way through. He barely acknowledged his father before striding to where Marie-Louise stood with Nathan. Placing his hands on her shoulders, he kissed her on the cheek. "Welcome home, sister. You look well. Traveling must agree with you."

"Merci." Marie-Louise stepped back from the embrace, soft eyes flicking over Marcel's coarse, bearded face. "You also look well, brother. Growing sugar must agree with you."

"It is most unfortunate," said Nathan, whose mood of joyful anticipation had changed abruptly to surging anger, "that growing sugar has not sweetened your brother's disposition."

First Marcel scowled, then he laughed. "Well, well, look who is here. Is your presence another part of my young brother's experiment to turn a sow's ear into a silk purse? I thought I had cured him of that notion. I understand Raymonde Perrault does not care much for the idea either. After all"—he pivoted as he spoke, addressing everyone in the courtyard—"one cannot really blame a celebrated *maître d'armes* for having nothing to do with such a spineless coward as our Hebrew prince here."

Antoine pushed forward. "Did you put Perrault up to that?"

"I had no need to do so. He saw for himself what a poltroon

your friend is. Why you continue to soil our name by associating with him and his cousin is beyond my understanding." He turned back to Marie-Louise. "Sister, when you tire of this house, Micaela and I want you to visit us. We have many friends who have heard much about your beauty and your charm. Men from good Creole families are drawing lots to be the first to meet you. Please, do not shame the Vanson name as your brother tries to do." Marcel glared at his father. "You, too, shame our heritage by encouraging these friendships," he said before striding away.

"Give our regards to your mistress on the Ramparts!" Antoine yelled after his brother. "We all know she is the real reason for your visit to New Orleans!"

Marcel swung around. Venom blazed from his eyes. Nathan thought a fight would erupt there and then. For five seconds, the two brothers faced each other, then Marcel turned once more and pushed his way through the crowd.

Nathan looked down to find Marie-Louise's hand still clasped inside his own. The musicians continued playing the same slow melody. He drew Marie-Louise into the center of the courtyard and began to dance. "Your comment about sugar failing to sweeten my brother's disposition demonstrates that you have wit as well as gallantry," Marie-Louise said.

"Such qualities are easy to acquire in the presence of a lovely lady. Did I offend you by speaking of your brother so?"

"Not at all. My absence did not cause me to forget the kind of man Marcel is. Antoine told me what happened between the two of you. Like all bullies, Marcel enjoys hurting and humiliating people. He did it to you at his home, and he tried to do it again just now. But here, in my father's home, he failed."

Emboldened by the quick closeness he had formed with Marie-Louise, Nathan asked, "Will you journey to your brother's home to meet the men who have drawn lots for the privilege of being introduced to you?"

"Perhaps." Marie-Louise smiled coquettishly. "Would you draw lots for the privilege of meeting me?"

"Had I not been offered this opportunity, I would have done anything for such a privilege. Certainly so after seeing the portrait of you by Jacques Amans. When I looked upon that—"

"You thought the Blessed Virgin had sat for *Monsieur* Amans." Playfulness sparkled in Marie-Louise's dark brown eyes. Nathan saw in the flesh the same smoldering fire he had first seen in the Amans portrait. The Belgian artist had captured the young woman's inner soul on canvas.

"No, not the Blessed Virgin. The opposite. I saw a sprite, a scamp. I saw an ambush for any man unwary enough to gaze too closely into those bewitching eyes."

Amused by Nathan's description, Marie-Louise gave a deep, throaty chuckle. "Are you such an unwary man, my Hebrew prince?"

Nathan realized that Marie-Louise had used Marcel's name for him, but he felt neither anger nor humiliation. From Antoine's sister, such a title was honorable. "Perhaps."

"Gaze into my eyes."

Nathan did so and once again discerned the smoldering fire that Amans had captured so accurately. Marie-Louise asked what he saw. "Quicksand," he answered. "A trap from which a man would never escape, no matter how hard he struggled."

"How hard would you struggle?"

"Would you think the worse of me if I told you I would lay down my arms and surrender immediately?"

Marie-Louise gave that deep, sensual chuckle again. The sound sent shivers cascading down Nathan's spine. This young woman was eighteen, the same age as Leonora, yet centuries separated them.

The music stopped, and Nathan returned Marie-Louise to her father. Antoine and Leonora joined them. A servant offered wine. Marie-Louise raised a glass to her brother. "Antoine, you have succeeded in transforming your friend Nathan into as fine a gentleman as ever set foot in the *Vieux Carré*. But then I think that you must have had some promising raw material to work with."

"Your brother had very promising material," Jean-Pierre said. "Especially when it came to playing poker."

Remembering the first time he had played cards with Antoine's father, Nathan laughed. "That night I merely enjoyed the traditional good fortune of a beginner."

Jean-Pierre would have none of it. "Good players make their own good fortune, whether they are novices or veterans."

For the rest of the afternoon, Nathan was forced to share Marie-Louise with other guests. Friends pressed around to ask how she had enjoyed her years in Paris, and curious to know how the French capital compared with New Orleans. She chatted gaily, but often her gaze sought out Nathan. When their eyes met, he felt a current flow between them, and he hated those other people who believed they had the right to occupy Marie-Louise's time.

Nathan and Leonora left the Vanson home as twilight changed to night. Antoine saw them to their phaeton. When Nathan mentioned the change he had seen in Jean-Pierre, Antoine nodded. "I knew Marie-Louise would have such a positive effect on him, but she has also brought news that saddens him. In Paris, Alphonse's wife has just learned that she is expecting her fourth child, another grandchild who my father will never see."

When Leonora was settled inside the phaeton, Nathan drew his friend to one side. "Once I gave you permission to approach my cousin. Now I would like you to return the favor and give me permission to approach your sister."

"Approach her as often as you wish. I want you to consume every moment of her time."

"Why?"

"Do you think I want her being introduced to friends of my brother Marcel?"

Laughing, Nathan climbed into the phaeton. He flicked the reins and the two-horse team began the journey to the Garden District. Leonora sat quietly as they rolled through the streets of the *Vieux Carré*. Only as they crossed the wide expanse of

Canal Street did she find her voice. "Does your heart pound, Nathan? Is there a hollow feeling in your stomach?"

He turned to face at her. "What do you mean?"

"Do you feel as I do when I think of Antoine? When you think of Marie-Louise, does your head float two feet above your body?"

Smiling, Nathan returned his attention to the road. "No, not two feet, Lally. Ten feet is more like it!"

Nathan saw Marie-Louise again three days later, when Antoine invited him and Leonora for dinner. Throughout the meal, Nathan could do nothing but admire his friend's sister. He neglected the food set in front of him while he listened to every word she said. He spent long moments staring at her while pretending to be absorbed in something else. When she looked directly at him or spoke to him, he could barely control the hammering of his heart and the unnerving movement of his stomach. At the end of each course, an amused Jean-Pierre, observing the barely touched plate in front of Nathan, asked if he felt all right.

Two days after that, Nathan saw Marie-Louise yet again, when the Creole brother and sister and the two English cousins dined at Moreau's. Nathan spent the evening comparing Marie-Louise's charms with those of every other woman in the restaurant. Creole belles filled Moreau's, but none could hold a candle to Antoine's sister. Perhaps the year in Paris had given her added elegance, an extra veneer of refinement, taught her how to make the most of the beauty with which nature had blessed her. Nathan could not put his finger on it. He only knew that Antoine's sister was the fairest young lady he had ever set eyes on.

That night, after returning to Waverley, Nathan asked Leonora to walk with him in the garden. "I have seen Marie-Louise three times, Lally, and I know I am deeply in love with her. But I need the opportunity to tell her so. And I need to know if her passions have formed as quickly as mine have done."

Leonora smiled tenderly at her cousin. She was seeing a new side to him, a facet of his personality that had been born the moment he set eyes on Marie-Louise. "If you love her as you say you do, she will know. And if she loves you, she will find a way to tell you so."

Nathan stared glumly at the moonlit garden. An odd sensation possessed him, unlike anything he had ever known. He found its strangeness both elating and frightening. "Does she compare me with the dashing escorts she knew in Paris? If so, how do I fare? Am I as suave, as witty and charming? As graceful?"

"How can you doubt yourself so? I suspect there is not a man in all of France who could measure up to you."

"Most of all, Lally, I want to be alone with her." As Nathan expressed the wish, he wondered if it would ever come true. Antoine was always sure to be nearby. He took his responsibility as Marie-Louise's brother very seriously. The best Nathan could hope for was a few minutes alone with Marie-Louise on the dance floor, when the partner-switching intricacies of the quadrille were exchanged for the simpler, more private steps of the waltz, the new dance that was so rapidly gaining popularity.

No young lady could have wished for a more zealous guardian than Antoine. As fall progressed and New Orleans embarked upon its annual social season, Nathan continued to see Marie-Louise, but always as part of the familiar foursome. There were parties at the Vanson home. There were theater and opera outings, dinners, dances. Always, Antoine managed to keep control. Every moment that Nathan spent with Marie-Louise, he could feel his friend's eyes upon him.

Such a lack of privacy failed to dim Nathan's ardor. Each hour he spent in Marie-Louise's company pushed him deeper in love with her. Each minute away from her constituted an eternity. He moped around the Lowensohn house on Prytania Street and the countinghouse on Canal Street. Whenever Gershon or Anna asked what was wrong, he simply shrugged his shoulders and said he felt fine. Eventually, they asked Leonora. Her answer that Nathan had been hit by a bolt out of the blue named Marie-Louise Vanson fetched a mixed reaction. Anna was amused to see the normally assured young man in such a turmoil. Gershon, showing more practicality than his wife, foresaw problems. The next day in the countinghouse, he broached them to Nathan.

"Please do not misunderstand me. I am happy for you in your feelings for this young lady, but if Marcel Vanson beat you black and blue to dissuade you from associating with his family, what do you think he will do if he learns you are madly in love with his sister?"

"My love for Marie-Louise overwhelms any fear I may have of Marcel. Besides, he is a blowhard who will do nothing."

"You hope," Gershon said ominously.

Henry, who had overheard the brief conversation, sidled up to Nathan. "If it should come to a duel, may I have the honor of attending you as your second?"

For once, Nathan failed to be amused by the boy's banter. "There will be no duels," he answered curtly.

The news of Nathan's infatuation with Marie-Louise affected one other member of the family. Miriam's interest in Antoine had lasted only a few weeks before reverting to her first love, to Nathan. She found reasons to be where he was, to talk to him, to follow him into the garden whenever he sought a moment to himself, and she returned to pestering Leonora with questions about him. The instant Nathan's preoccupation with Marie-Louise became known, Miriam underwent a transformation. She ignored him whenever he spoke to her, and angled her head away when she passed him in the house. When Leonora brought her cousin the news that Miriam no longer mentioned his name, Nathan nodded.

"In gaining one love, Lally, I fear I have lost another."

"She will recover." As Leonora gave the guarantee, she recalled the day Nathan had brought home roses from Antoine.

Miriam, showing a wistful jealousy, had yearned for an admirer to send her such bouquets, and Leonora had promised that one day men would stand in line to do so. When that day came, she had believed Nathan would be in the vanguard of Miriam's admirers.

Well, she had been wrong. She had not taken into account that before Miriam grew old enough to attract Nathan, he would meet Marie-Louise.

Unlike the previous year, Leonora saw nothing unusual in the celebration of Christmas within the Lowensohn household. She understood now that the family treated it simply as a secular holiday, an occasion for exchanging gifts and good wishes. The same was not true of the Vanson home, where Leonora and Nathan were invited to spend Christmas day. There, old Jean-Pierre, Antoine, and Marie-Louise commemorated the advent of Christmas by attending midnight mass at St. Louis Cathedral.

Nathan and Leonora arrived at Esplanade just after midday, with gifts for the entire family. Jean-Pierre seemed surprised until he remembered that his young guests were not Creole. "For us, Christmas is a serious occasion," he explained. "It is not our tradition to exchange gifts until New Year's Day, sometimes not until Three Kings' Day." When he saw the disappointment on the faces of Leonora and Nathan, he softened his stance. "I think that we can bend tradition just this once, especially as I know that my children already have gifts for you."

For Jean-Pierre, Nathan and Leonora had a gold-topped ebony cane. To Antoine, Nathan gave a gold watch and chain, while Leonora presented him with an initialed ring. In turn Antoine gave Nathan a gold breast pin and Leonora a fan with a silver-and-pearl handle, and matching combs for her hair. Immediately, she sought a mirror to see how the combs looked.

Marie-Louise joined her, adjusting the combs in Leonora's dark, wavy hair until she was satisfied with their position.

When Marie-Louise returned from helping Leonora, Nathan handed her a long, slim box. Inside rested a wide bracelet that glowed with the deep green fire of emeralds. Marie-Louise gasped with pleasure and excitement. "Thank you. I have never seen anything so exquisite."

"Show Nathan what you have for him," Jean-Pierre prodded.

Doubt replaced Marie-Louise's exhilaration. "I am almost embarrassed to do so. My gift seems so mundane . . ."

Nathan spoke encouragingly. "Nothing associated with you could ever be mundane."

"Even your graciousness does not reassure me. But . . ." From a table Marie-Louise fetched a package the size of a book. "Once you expressed admiration for the original, so I took the liberty of having a copy made for you. Beside your gift, though, I fear this pales into insignificance."

After carefully removing the wrapping, Nathan gazed down at a copy of the Jacques Amans portrait of Marie-Louise that hung on the wall of the parlor overlooking the courtyard. The artist had done a faithful reproduction, right down to the fire lurking in the dark brown eyes. "You could have chosen nothing lovelier, nothing more fitting," he said softly, for in that instant he learned the answers to so many questions. Leonora had been right. If Marie-Louise felt strongly for him, she would find a way to let him know. By presenting him with such a gift, she had just done precisely that.

He looked from facsimile to actuality. The fire no longer smoldered in Marie-Louise's eyes. It had burst into vibrant flame. "Do you really mean that?" she asked.

"With all my heart."

The Christmas meal was the most memorable Nathan had ever eaten. The food was delicious—snapper in oyster sauce, truffled turkey, veal scalloped with mushrooms—but what made it really unforgettable for Nathan was finally knowing that Marie-Louise's feelings were as fervent as his own. Each time he lifted his eyes from his plate he found her looking at him as if she, too, understood. Once he caught Leonora's gaze. She gave him a muted smile, her own reminder that she had told him so.

Following the meal, Jean-Pierre announced that he wanted to try out his new gold-topped walking cane. "Which of you charming young ladies wishes to accompany an old man on a stroll?"

Both Marie-Louise and Leonora accepted. Nathan and Antoine moved from the dining room to the parlor, where they sat on the balcony overlooking Esplanade. Despite being Christmas, the temperature was comfortable. The *banquette* was full of men and women. Soon, Jean-Pierre came into view. He had Marie-Louise on one arm and Leonora on the other. Every few yards, as he passed someone he knew, he waved with the gold-topped cane and wished them a merry Christmas.

"My father is the happiest man in the world at this moment," Antoine said. "He is realizing the dream of every red-blooded Creole man, to have a beautiful woman on each arm. See how other men regard him. They know Marie-Louise, but they are uncertain about Leonora. They wonder whether Vanson the lawyer has taken a young wife."

Nathan's eyes followed the old man. He had a lively spring to his step as if the company of the two young women had caused years to fall away. "If I were you, Antoine, I would hurry."

"Eh?" Antoine leaned over the ironwork balcony for a better look. "What do you mean?"

"Marry Leonora quickly."

"What, before my father does decide to take her as his young wife?" Antoine's laughter stopped as suddenly as it had started. He stared oddly at his friend. "You are serious. Are you really scared by the preposterous notion that my father will decide to marry your cousin?"

"Of course I am not frightened by such a notion."

"Then why would you now rush me into marrying Leonora, when only a short time ago you were counseling patience because you feared Marcel's reaction and his rage?"

"Like Marcel, I concern myself with the tradition that is so strong within your family. But I worry for a different reason. You are older than Marie-Louise, so tradition would dictate that you must marry first. Once you are married, I will be able to marry Marie-Louise. With your father's permission, of course."

"You crafty devil! The moment my father returns with our brides-to-be, we will tell him. Provided"—Antoine slapped Nathan on the shoulder—"that he does not run off with mine!"

Jean-Pierre returned fifteen minutes later, declaring that his new gold-topped ebony walking cane functioned admirably. "Of course," he said, sitting on the balcony with his son and Nathan, while Marie-Louise and Leonora remained inside adjusting their hair, "it might have been performing not for me but for the two beautiful young ladies who graced my arms."

"It is about those two beautiful young ladies that Nathan and I wish to talk with you," Antoine told his father.

"Oh?" The old man's eyes twinkled with anticipation and pleasure. "You have plans for them?"

"I intend to marry Leonora—"

"And I would like permission to ask for Marie-Louise's hand."

Jean-Pierre clapped his hands and stood up. "Wonderful! Wonderful! I can think of no finer Christmas gift. I will send them out to you. In the meantime, I will be downstairs, seeking our best bottle of champagne."

He disappeared into the parlor. The two suitors exchanged glances. Nathan tried to give a confident smile, but the trembling in his stomach allowed only an expression of anxiety.

"Nathan, will we be brothers-in-law or cousins?"

"Is there a law that says we cannot be both?"

"Not to my knowledge."

Marie-Louise led Leonora out onto the balcony. "Papa said you wished to speak to us."

"My dear friend Nathan desires to marry you, sister. Having known him for almost a year, I can furnish him with the highest references."

"And I," Nathan said, turning to Leonora, "can furnish similarly impeccable references for Antoine."

The two young women glanced at each other as if seeking some explanation. "Will you marry Antoine?" Nathan asked his cousin.

Leonora looked first to her cousin, then to Antoine, as if unsure whom to answer. "I will," she said to each in turn.

"Marie-Louise, will you marry Nathan?"

No uncertainty affected Marie-Louise's answer. With dark eyes fixed firmly on Nathan, she said, "I will."

Returning to the balcony with a freshly opened bottle of champagne and five glasses, Jean-Pierre found both young couples embracing. Below, on the *banquette,* men and women interrupted their Christmas strolls to stare up at the happy scene, to smile, and then applaud.

"Am I to assume," he asked, "that I may now pour this?"

The two embraces broke apart. Jean-Pierre raised his own glass. "To my new son and my new daughter. Welcome to the Vanson family. I cannot wait to send out news. Even Alphonse will surely come from Paris for such a doubly joyous event."

Leonora broke the news to the Lowensohns the next afternoon. When the family relaxed in the rear parlor after lunch, she announced that she was betrothed to Antoine Vanson. Gershon and Henry looked up from the chessboard on which they played. Anna ceased her embroidery. Miriam set down her book, and Martha and Sarah forgot the puzzle they were jointly solving.

Anna was the first to react. She stood up, walked over to

Leonora and embraced her. "Congratulations. That is wonderful news. Antoine is a charming and sincere young man."

Gershon followed his wife's example. "We could derive no more pleasure from your news if you were related to our family by blood. Let us know whatever we can do to help."

Henry stepped forward to kiss Leonora on the cheek, then came Miriam, and finally the two younger girls. "Where will you live once you are married?" Anna asked.

"Antoine mentioned that he would continue to live in his father's home until he finishes his studies and can practice law on his own."

"Moving from the Garden District to the *Vieux Carré*, eh?" Gershon said. He felt glad that his fears had been groundless and that the transition had been made without pain.

"When will the marriage be?" Miriam asked. She pictured a splendid spring day, when warm Gulf breezes mixed with winter's final crispness. Already she wondered what she would wear. She would be nearing sixteen; the wedding would serve as her coming-out party. Maybe Nathan would tear his eyes away from his Creole paramour and finally notice her. Finally appreciate her.

"Next September or October, perhaps."

"Why so long a delay?" Anna asked.

"Antoine's oldest brother, Alphonse, lives in Paris. His wife is expecting their fourth child in the spring. *Monsieur* Vanson prays they will attend the wedding, and bring their children with them because he has never seen any of his French grandchildren. He wants to give them enough time for the child to be born and all necessary traveling arrangements to be made."

Gershon nodded understandingly. He smiled at Nathan. "I cannot imagine you having any trouble giving your cousin away. After all, she is marrying your dearest friend."

"As much as I would like to give Leonora away, I will have to forego the pleasure. I have more pressing business that day."

"What could be more pressing than your cousin's marriage?"

"Lally's marriage to Antoine will comprise just one half of a double wedding. Marie-Louise and I"—Nathan's face became wreathed in a smile—"will be standing right next to them."

Choking back sobs, Miriam ran from the room.

During the next two days, Leonora tried several times to talk to Miriam. Each time, Miriam turned her head away. Losing her patience at last, Leonora grabbed the golden-haired girl by the arm and swung her around.

"Please do not ignore me. I want to talk with you about the way you are behaving. I think I understand why you are upset."

"What do you care?"

"It is because I care that I dislike seeing you so troubled."

Miriam sniffed. "When you came to New Orleans, we gave you a home. We welcomed you with open arms into our family. You knew how I felt about Nathan, and despite this knowledge you did nothing to stop him falling in love with Antoine's sister. Don't say you care about me when you so obviously do not."

Stunned into silence, Leonora could do nothing but watch Miriam stalk away.

News of the double betrothal aroused strong reaction in one other quarter. Five days after Christmas, Jean-Pierre Vanson received a letter from his son, Marcel. After reading it, he showed it to Antoine. That evening, after making certain that Leonora and Marie-Louise were busy elsewhere, Antoine took Nathan into the parlor and told him of the letter's contents. "My brother gives us half of his approval. He writes that he does not care what I do. If I wish to disgrace our name, that is my concern. But he will never allow his only sister to marry a Hebrew. He will do everything in his power to make certain that such a match never takes place."

"What can he do?" Nathan asked.

"Absolutely nothing, because before he can get to you, he knows that he must come through me. And he would never attempt that." He filled two glasses with wine. "To us. To my brother's confusion. And to the New Year, which shall surely be our year. Yours and mine, and Leonora's and Marie-Louise's."

Nathan lifted his glass in response. As the New Year was celebrated, he would turn twenty-one. Midnight tomorrow would present a double cause for celebration. He forgot all about Marcel as a new thought spread warmth through his body. He, Antoine, Leonora, and Marie-Louise were celebrating the birth of 1853 at a New Year's ball in the St. Louis Hotel. As midnight struck, he and Marie-Louise would be in each other's arms. Nathan could think of no finer way to begin what would undoubtedly be the most memorable year of his life.

Chapter Ten

By New Year's Eve, the double engagement was common knowledge. At the St. Louis Hotel, Nathan, Marie-Louise, Antoine, and Leonora were the center of attention. As they entered the ballroom, men and women pressed forward to offer congratulations. On the dance floor, they were constantly interrupted by other dancers eager to wish them well. Even while sitting in a loge to refresh themselves with wine they failed to find privacy. People clustered around to learn more details of this unusual double match. A brother and sister from a respected Creole family marrying non-Creole cousins.

Not only non-Creole, but English.

Et non seulement les Anglais, mais encore les Juifs!

Nathan and Leonora lost track of the dozens of people to whom they were introduced. Even when they managed to remember some of the names, they had no hope of ever being able to match those names to faces. Questions flew at them in rapid succession. A young woman in a blue silk dress wanted to know whether both brides intended to order their wedding gowns from Paris or have them made in New Orleans. Her escort asked if the two couples would live in the old quarter or above Canal Street, where the administrative and commercial heart of New Orleans now lay.

"Will you be married in Saint Louis Cathedral?" asked a tall, thin man with a flourishing black mustache.

"Of course," Antoine answered breezily. "Where else does a Creole marry?"

"What about your children?" demanded the young woman who had inquired about wedding gowns. "Yours and Marie-Louise's? They will be raised as Catholics, will they not?" She switched her attention to Leonora. "Have you and your cousin started studying to convert to Catholicism?"

Leonora's eyes widened. Before she could speak, Antoine's fingers closed gently on her arm. "There is no immediate need for Leonora and Nathan to convert," he answered. "After all, Judah P. Benjamin did not convert when he married Natalie Saint Martin, and surely we can do no better than follow the example of such a prominent citizen of Louisiana."

Antoine's reply seemed to satisfy the young woman in the blue silk dress. The tone of questioning turned lighthearted. Would the children of these two unions consider English or French their first language? Would their allegiance be to the Union Jack or the Stars and Stripes? Nowhere did Nathan notice the faintest trace of hostility. Marcel Vanson was alone in his hatred, and being alone, he was powerless.

When dancing paused for food and refreshments to be served, Nathan took Leonora by the hand and left the ballroom. In less than an hour, 1852 would be over. The coming year would see him replaced as Leonora's guardian by Antoine. Before this year was out, he wanted to be alone with his cousin. Never mind the easy way Antoine had glossed over the possibility of conversion. Nathan had seen the shock that suddenly plagued Leonora. Before it was too late, he wanted to know exactly how she felt.

They walked to the hotel's rotunda. Beneath the huge dome built from thousands of hollow earthenware pots was a simple platform. Tonight, on New Year's Eve, the platform was empty. In a day or two, though, slaves would be auctioned from it, just as they would be sold from a similar platform in the St. Charles Hotel, and at a dozen other places in New Orleans. Nathan leaned against the edge of the platform and gazed at his cousin.

"The possibility of converting to Catholicism troubles you, does it not?"

Very slowly, Leonora nodded. "I understood all the time that Antoine was a Catholic, but it never entered my mind that people might expect me to adopt his religion."

"Does the religion of your birth really mean so much to you? You seem to have accepted the Lowensohn family's ambivalent attitude toward it, even to exchanging Christmas presents."

"Yes, I accepted it, but I was never able to completely cast aside my own heritage. Do you not care about relinquishing the religion into which you were born? Do you not feel that you are tearing out a piece of your soul?"

"If Marie-Louise asked me to change my faith, I would do so. And I would be as devout a Catholic as I was a Jew," Nathan said with a smile. "In other words, I would regard Catholicism as nothing more than a superstition conveniently adopted to please the woman I love." He looked closely at Leonora. "If Antoine were not so accommodating, would you still want to marry him?"

Leonora felt helpless. "I do not know. I have had no time to consider such a situation."

"You must think about it. Suppose that between now and the wedding, Antoine changes his mind. What if, in six or nine months, he no longer views Judah Benjamin as such a noble model?"

Panic welled up deep within Leonora, sweeping away all attempts at analysis. How could she answer such an important question when she could not even marshal her thoughts?

"Think, Lally. Make up your mind before it is too late."

Leonora looked at her hands and tried to decide what was more important—her love for Antoine or the memory of a faith she had all but forgotten. "Antoine," she whispered. "Antoine means more to me."

"Good," Nathan said and led her back to the ballroom.

Midnight came amid a clamor of revelry. Merrymakers filled the dance floor. Marie-Louise kissed Nathan twice, once to celebrate the New Year, the second time to commemorate his twenty-first birthday. Nathan held her close, unwilling to relinquish the embrace. The year of 1853 was only moments old and already he was wishing it away. Wishing his way past spring, past summer. He wanted it to be fall, when Alphonse Vanson would be here with his family, and he could make Marie-Louise his own.

Antoine and Leonora approached them. Leonora kissed her cousin on the cheek and wished him both a happy New Year and a happy birthday. "When we celebrate next year," Antoine said to Nathan, "we will be old married couples. Perhaps we should make the most of this one, eh?"

"I am quite looking forward to celebrating the next New Year as part of an old married couple."

"Had you made any other response, I would have considered it an unpardonable insult to my fair sister," Antoine responded. "Leonora finds it warm in here, so we are going outside to sample the air. Will you join us?"

"We will stay," Marie-Louise replied. "Nathan wants to enjoy every moment of his last New Year's ball before becoming part of an old married couple."

Hardly had Leonora and Antoine left when Nathan spotted a familiar figure. Raymonde Perrault slowly circled the ballroom, stopping at almost every group to offer seasonal greetings. He shook hands solemnly with men and formally kissed the hands of women. Watching him come nearer, Nathan prepared for the snub of being publicly ignored by the renowned fencing master. Had he known Perrault was at the ball, he would have heeded Antoine's suggestion to take the air. It was too late now to walk out. Perrault would see him do so and would know the reason why.

Perrault stopped at the couple standing next to Nathan and Marie-Louise. A few words were exchanged, a man's hand shaken, a woman's hand kissed, then he moved on.

"*Monsieur* Solomon, how pleasant to see you." Perrault extended a white-gloved hand through which showed the outlines of his many rings. "Please allow me to wish you and your charming lady a most happy New Year."

Nathan was shaken by the recognition. The last time the two men had met, Perrault had labeled him a spineless coward and had banished him from his fencing academy. Now, in a ballroom full of people, where such a snub would be magnified a thousandfold, the *maître d'armes* had acknowledged him. Nathan took Perrault's hand in his own. "Thank you. A happy New Year to you as well."

"I understand that you have become betrothed. Allow me to offer you my congratulations." The black and white of Perrault's evening dress made him appear even more sinister than Nathan remembered. His olive skin seemed darker, his black eyes more piercing. He turned to Marie-Louise and raised her hand gently to his lips. "I congratulate you as well, *mademoiselle.*"

"*Merci, monsieur.*"

"Perhaps I could be so bold as to kiss the bride in advance. After all"—Perrault's bleak smile sent shivers racing down Marie-Louise's back—"in my dangerous profession, who is to know whether I will still be alive to claim a kiss at your wedding?" Dropping Marie-Louise's hand, he clasped her face and kissed her full on the lips.

Marie-Louise jumped back, her shriek echoing around the suddenly silent ballroom. Nathan reacted instinctively. Grabbing Perrault with his left hand, he swung him around and punched him in the face with his right. The blow sent the smaller man sprawling onto the floor. He rose slowly, touching a finger to his face, below his left eye, where the mark of Nathan's fist bloomed quickly against the dark skin.

"A slap, *Monsieur* Solomon, is all a gentleman would have needed to convey a feeling of offense. A punch is the mark of a man beneath contempt. But you, as we all know, are no gentleman. Nonetheless, I will overlook this violation of the dueling code, just as I will overlook the fact that a man of your social standing is not worthy of my time and attention. You will hear from my second in the morning. Enjoy the dancing,"

Perrault said turning to leave, "for you may not be dancing with such grace and agility tomorrow night."

The crowd parted to let Perrault through. Those closest to Nathan retreated as though he were afflicted with the plague. The stupidity that made a man challenge a fencing master might be contagious. Marie-Louise clutched his arm and whispered in his ear, "You are very brave, *mon cher*. Very brave and very gallant to challenge a man who insults me so."

At that moment, Nathan considered himself neither brave nor gallant. He regarded himself as a fool.

Five minutes later, Antoine returned with Leonora. "Did you hear the news?" he blurted out excitedly. "Some imbecile here, with either too much wine in his stomach or an urgent desire in his heart to meet Saint Peter, just challenged Raymonde Perrault to a duel."

Smiling weakly, Nathan responded with the words Antoine had once spoken to him. *"Monsieur, je vous prie d'être mon témoin."*

Antoine's face blanched. *"You* challenged Perrault? Why?"

Nathan explained. Leonora trembled as she listened. Antoine blotted out the revelry around him and tried to understand why Perrault would have acted so disrespectfully to Marie-Louise. He could find no reason at all. Even drunk, Perrault would never have committed such an ungentlemanly deed. "Go home now and sleep, Nathan. You will need all your rest. I will come in the morning, to hear Perrault's second give details of the duel."

Nathan returned to Waverley with Leonora, leaving Antoine to take Marie-Louise home. Instead of going to bed, he sat in the front parlor. Leonora repeated Antoine's advice, but Nathan paid no heed. "My mind is too occupied to allow me to sleep."

"Why did you have to challenge him?"

"I will allow no man to treat Marie-Louise so shamefully. Besides, had I not challenged him"—remembering a conversation with Antoine, Nathan realized just how much he had adopted his friend's values—"I would have lost all credibility in her eyes."

"Do you remember a promise you made to me on our first full day in New Orleans?"

"That I would be slow to give offense and slower to take it? I remember, Lally. But that was before I met Marie-Louise."

At two-thirty, Gershon Lowensohn entered the front parlor. Awakened from his sleep by voices, he had come to investigate. He listened to Nathan's story, face growing more solemn with every detail. When Nathan finished, Gershon declared that a way out still existed. "Although I abhor the stupidity of dueling, I am familiar with the code by which duels are fought. In it there is a provision for an apology to be made."

Nathan shook his head. "I will defend Marie-Louise's honor. If I do not, I will be unworthy of her."

"And if by doing so you are killed, then what use will you be to her?"

"I will not be killed. The drawing of first blood will settle this affair."

"I hope you are right. In the meantime, I would suggest that you sleep. You need to be rested and alert to face such a skillful opponent as Raymonde Perrault."

Nathan went upstairs to bed. He fell asleep immediately but it was a slumber filled with dreams. The recurrent theme of each vision was blood, starting with a scratch on the chest of a man whose face he could not see. Then a cut from which dripped tiny red droplets. Then a deeper cut, followed by a savage gash from which blood pumped with arterial force. He sat up in bed. Sweat covered his body. A scream trembled on his lips which he barely managed to control. He rarely dreamed. What did this one mean? Lying back, he fell asleep again, this time an undisturbed rest from which he did not awaken until eight-thirty, when Rebecca, the Lowensohns' housekeeper, entered the room.

"Master Nathan, you have a gentleman caller."

"Who?"

"*Monsieur* Vanson. He waits for you in the front parlor."

"Thank you. Please tell him that I will be down directly." Nathan waited for Rebecca to leave before climbing out of bed. He dressed hurriedly. Antoine had agreed to be his second, and Nathan did not wish to make him cool his heels.

Five minutes after Rebecca's summons, Nathan descended the wide curving staircase. The familiar noises of the house came to him. From the kitchen came the voice of Delilah, the cook, chiding one of the maids for some infraction. Through the open windows, he heard Anna Lowensohn giving instructions to Samson, the gardener. As he crossed the hall to the double parlor, he forced what he hoped was an assured smile. No second should expect his champion to be anything but confident.

"Good morning, Antoine!" he cried out as he entered the front parlor. "Perrault's second has not yet appeared, so perhaps our master of arms has thought better of accepting my challenge."

"I would be most grateful, *Monsieur* Solomon, if you would not confuse me with my irresponsible younger brother."

The smile fell from Nathan's face. It was not Antoine Vanson who awaited him in the parlor. It was Marcel. "Do you second *Monsieur* Perrault?"

Marcel bowed. "I have the honor to do so. I assume from your greeting that my brother will second you. Most interesting, brothers seconding opponents in a duel. Perhaps even a first in the annals of New Orleans."

The chime of a bell echoed through the house. Nathan heard Rebecca cross the hall to open the door. Moments later, Antoine was shown into the front parlor. Like Nathan, he stopped in amazement when he recognized Marcel.

"You are Perrault's second?" Antoine demanded. Before his brother could answer, Antoine grabbed Nathan's arm. "Now do you understand the riddles? Why do you think Perrault banished you from his academy? And why do you think he treated Marie-Louise so disrespectfully last night? Because my brother, imposing on a friendship, asked him to do so! Marcel has exploited his association with Perrault to achieve his own objective of terminating your interest in Marie-Louise." He turned back to his brother. "I was wrong about you. I considered you no more fearsome than a surly, toothless dog. I should have taken into account your devious qualities."

Marcel's red face remained impassive. "I come in my capacity as Raymonde Perrault's second. As the challenged party, it is his privilege to choose weapons. He chooses, of course, his favorite weapon—the *colichemarde*."

"Time and place?" Antoine asked.

"Three this afternoon. Beneath The Oaks."

"Will the drawing of first blood suffice?"

Although Marcel directed his answer to Antoine, he looked at Nathan, giving the young Englishman a chilling smile that turned his heart to a block of solid ice. "Raymonde Perrault fights only to the death." Marcel bowed deeply and, without another word, left the house.

From the rear parlor, where they had listened to every word, emerged Gershon and Henry. Gershon's somber face was grimmer than ever, a counterpoint to the flush of excitement that colored his son's cheeks. "You are insane," Gershon said, "to proceed with this duel. I urge you to reconsider your refusal last night to take advantage of the provision allowing you to apologize. The drawing of first blood will not suffice today. This duel is to the death, and the odds surely favor your opponent. For God's sake, he taught you everything you know. How can you hope to defeat him?"

Within Nathan, rival forces struggled for supremacy. His English background agreed with Gershon. To settle an argument with a sword was insane! How could he hope to defeat the man who had taught him how to use that sword? If he had only that English upbringing to consider, he would apologize, no matter the cost in humiliation. But he had a Creole experience to take into account. Although far shorter than his English background, it was more recent, and therefore stronger; and because of Marie-Louise, it held his soul in an iron grip. "This is not a lesson where a teacher will humiliate his pupil. It is a duel of honor that will be won by the man with virtue on his side."

"And you believe you are that man," Gershon said.

"I do. That is why I will win."

Gershon's face became stern. "Leave here now, before your cousin awakes. It will be miserable enough for me to tell her how foolish pride cost you your life. At least, spare her the prelude to your folly."

Nathan shook hands with Gershon and Henry before following Antoine outside to where a carriage waited. As he climbed in, he heard Henry's voice calling his name. The youth ran down the steps and clutched the carriage door. "My father says I cannot watch you, Nathan, but I swear I will be there. Please . . ." Tears misted Henry's blue eyes. "Please win."

Nathan patted his hand. "Henry, I promise you I will win. The prize is too great for me to contemplate doing otherwise."

Antoine signaled to the driver and the carriage began to move. "What you do is right," Antoine said as they passed through the gate onto Prytania Street. "You are acting precisely the way I would act in a similar situation."

"Then why does your chin rest on your knees?"

"Because my heart, like that of *Monsieur* Lowensohn, is heavy at the prospect of seeing Leonora torn apart by the grief of losing you."

The Oaks held a macabre familiarity for Nathan. He had not visited the place since the day he had seen Michael Meagher kill Jack Johnson. That was fifteen months ago, yet every branch of every tree remained vivid in his memory.

Today, The Oaks played host to a festive crowd. When Nathan arrived with Antoine at twenty minutes before the appointed hour, some four-dozen men had already congregated. More continued to turn up by carriage or horseback until Nathan estimated their number to be at least a hundred. Raymonde Perrault had many friends and admirers, all of whom expected to witness a faultless display of swordsmanship culminating in a graceful kill.

"Gentlemen, regrettably I must spoil your enjoyment."

"What was that?" Antoine asked.

"Just thinking aloud." Nathan smiled as he finally spotted a familiar face. Henry worked his way through the crowd until he achieved a good position at the front. Aside from Antoine, the lad was the only supporter Nathan had. He would do his best not to disappoint him.

Perrault arrived with Marcel Vanson at five minutes before three. Approaching Nathan, he said, "You surprise me. From a coward such as yourself, I expected to receive an apology. Once on the field of honor, of course, it is too late to offer one."

"The only apology I shall make to you is for having skewered your heart on my sword."

Perrault's black eyes gleamed. *"Bon chance."*

The two combatants removed their coats. Nathan clenched his teeth against the damp cold that suddenly assailed him. Antoine whispered advice in Nathan's ear. "Keep taunting him like that. You may cause him to be careless."

An elderly man acting as referee stepped forward, holding two *colichemardes* by the blades. Nathan chose one. Taking the other, Perrault pranced around and slashed the air. With each whistling stroke, a burst of applause erupted from the onlookers.

"Bravo!" Nathan called out. "You are a magnificent dancer. Can you fight as well?"

A single peal of laughter greeted the question. Nathan looked gratefully at Henry, blessing him for showing such pluck. Perrault instantly ceased his display. A thundercloud crossed his swarthy face. "You will pay for such taunts, my friend. Your end will not be easy. I shall make of you an example that will send my admirers home happy."

Nathan gathered courage for one final barb. "Your admirers

will go home carrying you. They will strip those rings from your fingers and curse your memory when they learn that your jewels, like the pompous dandy who wore them, are worthless fakes!"

"Enough!" Perrault cried. "Let us begin!"

The referee brought the swords of the two men together. Stepping back, he dropped his arm. Almost immediately, Nathan felt a nest of hornets savage his left shoulder. He looked down, amazed to see blood staining his shirt. Simultaneously, he heard the onlookers applaud Perrault's first triumph.

Perrault stepped back to admire his artistry. "Before I am finished, I shall hear you beg for a final, merciful thrust."

Nathan swallowed hard, fighting down the panic and the fear that suddenly exploded within him. "Your last thought will be that you taught me too well." He raised his sword. The blades crossed again. Nathan began a *flèche*, a powerful running attack that drove Perrault before him. After three steps, he sensed a weakness and lunged for his opponent's chest. Perrault gracefully parried the stroke, turning Nathan's sword to one side, and answered with a swift riposte. Lightning struck the outside of Nathan's right bicep. His sword dropped as molten lead filled the muscles of his arm.

"Raise your weapon!" Perrault shouted. "Protect yourself! There is no glory in defeating an unworthy opponent!"

Nathan tightened his grip around the *colichemarde*'s hilt. The sword was no longer light and pliant. In his pain-racked hand, it was as heavy and cumbersome as a limb from one of the oaks that witnessed the contest. He brought up the sword once more. Laughing, Perrault brushed it aside. The point of his weapon sliced across Nathan's left cheek, leaving a shallow cut from which blood oozed. Another movement left a similar incision on Nathan's right cheek. Nathan's eyes darted from side to side as they tried to follow the streak of quicksilver in Perrault's hand. Analogies flashed through his mind. Perrault was a toreador with Nathan as his bull; his sword was a paintbrush in a master's hand and Nathan was his canvas. Each movement, each new daub of color on Nathan's skin or clothes, brought forth another shout of approval from the *maître*'s host of admirers.

Those shouts grew louder as Perrault pressed forward. Nathan fell away, frantically parrying every stroke. The ground rose behind him. His shoulders pressed against one of the massive oaks. Mouth widening in triumph, Perrault launched a *balestra*. Nathan's weak counter merely deflected the lunge. Instead of finding Nathan's heart, the point of Perrault's sword drove through the right side of his chest.

Blood filled Nathan's mouth. Each breath became a searing burst of flame. Perrault's face swam in and out of focus as he pulled the blade free. Leaning against the oak, Nathan awaited the *coup de grace*. He had no strength to parry again. Tears streaked his face as he wept over the anguish his death would cause. In a few moments, his life would be over, but others would be left to carry the burden of grief. Leonora, who would have no family at all. Marie-Louise, how long would she mourn before she found another man to marry? Antoine and Henry. They would leave this place together, to inform those Nathan loved of his passing.

Antoine . . . ! As Perrault drew back his arm for the final thrust, a vision flashed before Nathan. The exhibition at Marcel Vanson's sugar plantation! Antoine had scored against Perrault with a well-executed *botte du paysan*. Could Nathan duplicate that feat now?

Perrault's sword leaped forward. Gathering up the last of his strength, Nathan gripped the forte of his own *colichemarde* with his left hand and struck abruptly at Perrault's sword. As Perrault's blade whipped sideways, Nathan, performing the stroke impeccably, thrust through the gap the maneuver had created.

The shouting died. A heavy silence dropped like a blanket over The Oaks. The narrow-bladed sword fell from Raymonde Perrault's right hand. He collapsed onto his knees, left hand clawing futilely at the shining sliver of steel protruding from his chest. His eyes opened wide, and the expression he carried into eternity was one of total disbelief.

Nathan stared in fascination at the body of his former tutor. He was aware of the crowd, shocked into silence by the defeat of their hero, slowly dispersing. All except two. Antoine and Henry raced toward him. Nathan tried to raise his arms, tried to shout that his twenty-first birthday would not be his dying day after all, but the effort proved too much. Consciousness fled, and he slipped slowly to the ground.

Nathan was carried back to Waverley like a triumphant soldier. Gershon, torn between relief and disbelief at the outcome of the duel, summoned the family doctor, a white-haired pink-faced man named Edward Mathieson. The doctor examined Nathan and dressed his injuries, expressing concern for the chest wound. Nathan could breathe only with the greatest difficulty. Mathieson suspected that Perrault's sword had pierced the right lung. Recovery rested as much with the grace of God as it did with medical skill.

Within a day, Nathan's body burned with fever. He slipped in and out of consciousness. Anna Lowensohn, Leonora, and Marie-Louise, who stayed at the house, took turns sitting by the bed, waiting for a flash of semiwakefulness when they could get him to open his mouth and swallow a morsel of food or drink to sustain the strength required to fight the fever. Miriam offered to share the duty. Leonora, recalling the golden-haired girl's outburst on learning of Nathan's betrothal to Marie-Louise, demurred, saying three people were enough. Miriam insisted, and Leonora hesitatingly agreed. When Miriam first sat beside Nathan's bed, Leonora stayed with her. She saw nothing to cause her concern. Miriam was interested only in his recovery; her concern for his well-being had dissipated any animosity she might have held toward him. From then on, Miriam sat alone.

On the fifth day, Nathan opened his eyes. For the first time since the fever's onset he could recognize the person at the side of his bed. Golden hair came into focus. Green eyes smiled at him. His voice was nothing more than a croaking whisper that sent pain swirling through his chest. "Miriam? Is that you?"

"It is." She touched his forehead. The fire had died. She stood up and ran from the room, shouting at the top of her voice: "Come upstairs! Nathan recognized me! He spoke to me! His fever has gone! Come upstairs!"

Within a minute, excited people filled the room. Nathan could even see the black faces of household servants. Leonora bent over the bed to kiss his forehead. Marie-Louise's cool hands caressed his unshaven cheeks while she examined every feature of his face. Flesh had fallen from him. His gauntness spoke of suffering. Tears spilled from Marie-Louise's eyes. Her fragrance tantalized Nathan's senses. He grew uncomfortably aware of his own smell. Days of alternately sweating and shivering had left him with the sour, sweaty odor of a Girod Street tavern on a hot, wet August night. He clutched at the bedclothes, trying to draw them tighter around himself and cut off the smell lest those around him be offended.

Anna Lowensohn's face filled his vision. "Are you hungry?"

The question prompted rumblings deep within his stomach. "Hungry enough"—he persevered despite the chest pain that even the simple act of speaking brought—"to eat every piece of food Delilah can prepare."

"Good. First we will feed you, then we will have you bathed. Moses has already gone to bring Doctor Mathieson so we may have a professional opinion that you are truly recovering."

"How long—"

"Has passed since you proved yourself to be the finest swordsman in all of New Orleans? Six days."

The answer came from Nathan's right. He turned to see Antoine standing beside the bed. "You . . . brought me back here?"

"With Henry's assistance."

"Perrault's supporters . . . no trouble?"

"Only with one. On the morning after your victory, Marcel and I returned to The Oaks to settle our own long-standing feud."

Nathan switched to a whispered French. "What happened?"

Antoine bent low, his mouth close to Nathan's ear. "I defeated him, of course."

Nathan closed his eyes as a different kind of pain swept over him. "You . . . killed . . . your . . . own . . . brother?"

"No, I did not kill him. And for remaining alive, he has you and Leonora to thank."

"I do not understand."

"When a family member dies, Creole tradition requires a year of full mourning followed by a year of half mourning. Even the pleasure of running Marcel through—which I had ample opportunity to do—would have been poor consolation for delaying my marriage to Leonora and Marie-Louise's marriage to you. I left him with enough scars to ensure that he never bothers me again."

Nathan opened his eyes once more. "Or me."

"No one, my friend, will ever bother you again. The man who ended Raymonde Perrault's career is safe from any challenge."

Nathan's recovery was an arduous process. The minor injuries to his arms and shoulders, the nicks on his face, the dozen little cuts and puncture wounds that Perrault had intended as precursors to the killing thrust, healed swiftly, leaving nothing more than fine scars. The injury to the chest was more complicated. Two months after the duel, when the wound's entry point was nothing more noticeable than an uneven pink blemish, fatigue plagued him. While New Orleans celebrated Mardi Gras, he lay in bed, propped up against pillows, resting. When he walked around the room, or was helped downstairs to sit in the garden, his energy quickly evaporated. As hard as he breathed, his blood never seemed to find enough oxygen to supply energy to his muscles. Even thinking drained his strength. Dr. Mathieson explained that the fault lay with the injured lung. It was not yet functioning properly. Perhaps it never would. Nathan's mind filled with nightmarish visions of himself as half a man, unable to do so much as walk for five minutes before being forced to sit down and rest. He would be no prize for Marie-Louise. Beautiful and young, she would tire of him within a week of their marriage. Who could blame her? Nathan certainly could not. She deserved far better than being married to a cripple, even if his injury resulted from a duel fought to protect her honor. When she visited him every day, she was everything he could ever want: compassionate, caring, concerned for his recovery. But he wondered whether, deep down, she questioned the future.

Such feelings of inadequacy extended also to the Lowensohn family. Gershon Lowensohn's busiest time as a cotton factor was between late September and March. Nathan's injury had stopped him working for the second half of the season. Without such work, how could he ever pay back the Lowensohn family's kindness? When he discussed the subject one afternoon with Leonora, she accused him of being foolish.

"Do you think Gershon Lowensohn keeps a separate ledger in which he has one column for any kindness he has shown us, and another column for any work we have done in return for him and his family? And do you think that just because you are ill for a month or so, Marie-Louise will love you any less? She is confident that you will recover. The worst enemy you have is yourself. Do not let that adversary destroy the happiness you have worked so hard to find."

Leonora's reprimand stung. Nathan's mental attitude improved, but that was only half the battle. A rebuke could not repair physical damage. No matter how positive his thoughts, the damage to his right lung continued to heal at a snail's pace.

In late April, Jean-Pierre Vanson received a letter carried by Atlantic steamer from his son in Paris. Alphonse, his wife, and their four children, including the baby girl born the third week of March, would be delighted to attend Marie-Louise's wedding. They were booking passage on a steamer for the middle of September, and expected to arrive in New Orleans early in October.

That evening, accompanied by his son and daughter, Jean-Pierre carried the letter to the Lowensohn home. He told Nathan and Leonora that, with Alphonse's acceptance, firm arrangements could finally be made for the double wedding. A date was set, October the twenty-ninth, the final Saturday of the month. Then Jean-Pierre broached the one sensitive subject of the proposed wedding. "When you kneel in Saint Louis Cathedral, you should have knowledge of the faith in which you exchange your vows. I think it fitting that you take tuition in Catholicism."

Nathan received his future father-in-law's suggestion with a nod of the head. Accepting Catholicism mattered little to him. As he had told Leonora beneath the rotunda of the St. Louis Hotel, he simply regarded it as exchanging one superstition for another. He understood, however, that the proposal presented an entirely different problem for his cousin. As he looked at her, he hoped she remembered the vow she had made.

She did. "If Antoine wishes me to take such tuition," Leonora told Jean-Pierre, "I will do so."

The elderly Creole smiled. "Thank you, my child. Thank you as well, Nathan, for being so understanding."

The news from Paris and the setting of a date for the double wedding had the most beneficial effect of all on Nathan. Each day he felt physical improvement. His breath came easier. The pain in the right side of his chest decreased until it was little more than a tiny, almost unnoticeable twinge, and when he sucked air in deeply—experimentally at first and then with a growing confidence—he could swear he felt his right lung expand. Energy returned. He began taking walks to build up his stamina, each one longer than its predecessor. The weather accommodated him. The spring rains were late this year and he could walk the streets without having to wade through masses of sodden garbage washed up from overflowing gutters.

Twice a week, on Monday and Thursday, he and Leonora visited the Presbytere next to St. Louis Cathedral where *Abbé* Francois, a dry, old Creole priest, instructed them in the fundamentals of Catholicism. When they left the Presbytere after each lesson, Nathan asked Leonora how she felt. If the meetings with the priest upset her, he would speak to Jean-Pierre and find some way around this need to learn Catholicism. But Leonora always answered his concern by saying she felt fine. Eventually Nathan stopped asking. He was satisfied that Leonora's love for Antoine overcame her original reluctance to compromise the faith into which she had been born.

Chapter Eleven

At the end of May, the spring rains finally came, falling with a fury that made up for their lateness. For hours on end, water dropped from leaden skies. Garbage flowed across the *banquettes*. Bursts of scalding sunshine created a steamy mist. Before the ground could dry, more rain lashed the city. With nowhere to run, water collected in pools where it grew stagnant and acquired a green velvet scum. In this fetid Turkish bath, mosquitoes—the annual curse of New Orleans—flourished as never before.

Gershon Lowensohn declared that he had never known the mosquitoes to be so annoying. He complained about them at the office, where he worked beneath a net-covered frame, and at home where similar protection shrouded the beds. "Night is the time I look forward to the most," he said over dinner one evening toward the end of June, when Antoine and Marie-Louise were present. "It is paradise to lie within the security of a net and hear those irksome pests whining outside as they try to find a way in."

Anna made light of her husband's protests. "You claim that every year is the worst for mosquitoes. Your blood is too sweet. Mosquitoes smell it through your skin and cannot resist it."

"Is that the reason mosquitoes bite people? Because of the sweetness of their blood?" Leonora asked. She knew Gershon had a liking for sweet foods. Even as he groused about the mosquitoes he enjoyed a second helping of dessert, a heavy bread pudding with a rich brandy sauce. Leonora did not have such a sweet tooth, and the mosquitoes did not torment her as badly as they pestered Gershon. The same held true for Nathan.

"What else could it be?" Anna responded. "The sugar a man eats must affect the flavor of his blood, and it is blood these pests are after."

"They are even worse in the *Vieux Carré* than here," Antoine said. "You cannot open a window without having a swarm fly in. My father, too, must have sweet blood as he is continually being bitten by these pests."

"We should be grateful they do nothing worse than cause an itch," Nathan said. "Imagine our woe if they stung like bees."

"I pray that this current affliction ends soon," Marie-Louise said. "Otherwise, instead of blessing our marriage, my brother Alphonse will be cursing us all for causing him to come here."

"Perhaps mosquitoes are the reason he left New Orleans in the first place," Henry offered. "Do they have mosquitoes in Paris?"

"I do not remember them."

Antoine sighed. "Summer in New Orleans is a miserable time. The weather is abominable. Lethargy invades the body. Flies pester honest men, and food spoils so quickly that it causes illness. I read just last week of a dozen sailors and laborers dying from eating bad food. Newcomers are most affected by our wretched summer. Unaccustomed to the heat, and living in pitiable circumstances, they pass diseases to each other with the generosity of people exchanging Christmas gifts."

While Nathan and Leonora once again reflected on their good fortune at having avoided such awful living conditions, Gershon said, "It was not long ago that all New Orleans—not just the Irish Channel—was ravaged by disease. In eighteen thirty-seven, twin epidemics of cholera and yellow fever created havoc here."

Nathan remembered cholera ravaging London's slums. The

idea of it coupled with another disease was too horrifying to dwell on. "Could such pestilence happen again?"

"No. Conditions have improved too much for it to gain a foothold. Why, only this morning the *Crescent* declared that Bronze John—"

"Bronze John?" Leonora queried.

"Yellow fever turns a white man's skin yellow or bronzelike. As I was saying, only this morning the *Crescent* declared Bronze John to be an obsolete idea in New Orleans. Epidemics flourish only where people live like swine. They cannot thrive," Gershon said with a degree of smugness, "in a civilized city such as the New Orleans we live in today," He clapped his hands briskly. "Now, when we have two soon-to-be-married couples at our table, let us talk about something more pleasant than disease."

Miriam, taking the cue from her father, asked Leonora and Marie-Louise about the wedding dresses they were having made, and mosquitoes, food poisoning, and epidemics were quickly forgotten.

The summer storms continued. Daily downpours flooded streets. Arrows of lightning darted from glowering clouds. Drumrolls of thunder rocked the city. In impoverished areas like Lynch's Row in the Irish Channel, where entire families slept in a single room, and battalions of ill-paid clerks sought cheap lodging, the number of deaths rose. Newspapers attributed the fatalities to a variety of illnesses. Food poisoning continued to be a favorite cause. Inflammation of the lungs was also popular, as were enteritis and congestion of the brain. The city's overcrowded conditions, the newspapers agreed, were conducive to such sicknesses. Even when death crossed the border between poverty and wealth, the newspapers continued to blame easily acceptable causes. Never once did they hint at the possibility of an epidemic. To launch that kind of panic would serve only to upset the city's commercial development, and without the advertising and support from commerce, newspapers would soon stop publishing.

In the third week of July, as they prepared to travel from the Garden District to the countinghouse on Canal Street, Gershon and Nathan noticed that Moses looked unwell. Despite the heat, the Negro coachman shivered as he held open the carriage door. When Gershon asked if he felt all right, Moses replied, "A touch of the chill and a headache is all, Master Gershon. It has been with me two or three days and is coming to a head."

That evening, when he collected the two men, Moses still shivered. When Gershon suggested that he go to bed the instant they reached home, Moses gave a wide smile and said he intended to do just that. "Right after I've eaten supper, Master Gershon. Delilah's been cooking calves head with brain sauce, and that'll cure a sick man quicker than any doctor's medicine."

"I think we have no need to worry," Gershon told Nathan as Moses set the carriage in motion. "Any man with an appetite that strong cannot be sick."

Over dinner, Gershon joked with Delilah about the healing qualities of her cooking. "There's nothing wrong with Moses now," the cook answered. "He's in the kitchen stuffing himself with second helpings of everything. How he'll sleep with all that food lying inside of his belly is beyond me."

But as dinner finished, Rebecca, the housekeeper, rushed into the dining room with the news that Moses had collapsed. Gershon followed Rebecca to the servants' quarters. There he found Moses being helped to his feet by the gardener. "Put him to bed," Gershon told Samson. "I will summon Doctor Mathieson."

"No need, Master Gershon," Moses protested as he struggled to stand without help. "I'll be all right. Just a chill is all."

Gershon gave the coachman the benefit of the doubt and was pleased the following morning when Moses brought the carriage to the front of the house. The shivering had stopped. The headache had gone. His legs showed no sign of weakness.

The coachman's recovery lasted for two days. On the third morning, he failed to rise from his bed. When Rebecca took Gershon and Anna through to the servants' quarters, they found Moses convulsed in pain. His skin was on fire, his eyes bloodshot. He screamed for water, but when Rebecca brought it, he struck out at her as though she were the devil. This time, Gershon had no compunction about sending for Edward Mathieson.

The doctor dosed Moses with quinine and promised to return the following day. Mathieson's next visit found Moses in far worse condition. His veins were distended as though about to rupture. His lips, gums, and nose oozed blood. He retched black, bloodstained vomit.

Forty-eight pain-filled hours later, Moses died, one of four hundred and twenty-nine people exhibiting similar symptoms to expire that week. On the day of his death, the *Delta* defied the city's commercial powers by admitting that New Orleans was firmly in the grip of a yellow-fever epidemic.

Suddenly death was all around. Another seven hundred people perished in the last week of July, and the words "epidemic," "Yellow Fever," and "Bronze John" were on everyone's lips. Medical men and laymen argued about the cause. Some claimed it was effluvia from the ground which had been disturbed by the digging of canals around the city. Their answer was to burn barrels of tar and fire cannon from street corners to drive away the pestilential vapor. Others maintained the fever originated in rotting wood, while another school of thought blamed the epidemic on specks of matter that floated in the air, so minute they could not be seen. In the New Orleans of 1853, no one thought to blame the insignificant mosquito which continued to breed abundantly in perfect conditions provided by persistent heavy rains and inadequate drainage.

The wealthy tried to run from the accursed city, but few found shelter elsewhere. New Orleans was rife with plague, and armed men protected other communities from those pariahs they thought might carry the sickness. In the Vanson household, the first official word of the fever prompted Jean-Pierre to write to his son Alphonse, urging him not to sail with his family for New Orleans. The double wedding would be delayed, he wrote, until the epidemic was over. When death had finished this visit, the marriages of Antoine to Leonora and Marie-Louise to Nathan would be a symbol of the city's renewed life. As long as they all survived, he mused, but he did not include that thought in the letter. As he signed his name, Jean-Pierre realized that the letter would never reach his son in time. No ships were leaving New Orleans; the city was cut off from the world. He tore it up and prayed that Alphonse would read in Paris of the epidemic and have the good sense to delay his voyage.

At the beginning of August, when the week's fatalities fell just short of a thousand, Jean-Pierre felt the disease's first embrace. For two days he concealed the shiver, headache, and aching bones from his son and daughter. The spasm passed, and he congratulated himself on overcoming the disease. The improvement lasted one day. Rosa, the elderly slave who had been with the family since Jean-Pierre's marriage, found her master moaning and writhing on his bed. An unhealthy color tinged his skin; blood seeped from his gums. Rosa called Antoine and Marie-Louise. The doctor they summoned confirmed their worst fears. Bronze John had visited the house on Esplanade.

Alarmed by his father's sickness, Antoine sought help. Leaving Marie-Louise with the old man, he rode on horseback to the Garden District. The city had an ominous strangeness. The peddlers were gone, the shops closed. No vendors advertised their wares with lusty cries. Yet the waterlogged streets remained busy with doctors driving their cabs from patient to patient, and funeral processions following one after another. Smoke from burning tar barrels filled the air. The crash of cannon shook the eardrums. Above all rose the smell of death, the odor of rotting flesh and bursting corpses that flowed, it seemed, from every house Antoine passed. Finally, he understood the folly of the belief that only the unacclimated and the poor fell victim to New Orleans's regular visitations from the fever. In the summer of 1853, Bronze John respected no caste barriers. Creoles and Negroes, once regarded as immune from such native diseases, fell as quickly as any American businessman in the Garden District or newly arrived immigrant in the Irish Channel.

Nathan opened the door. Antoine had not seen Nathan or Leonora for two days—the plague had restrained even the most ardent relationships—and his English friend's appearance shocked him. Sweat covered his face, his shirt clung to his body like a damp rag. The instant Nathan recognized the visitor, the grimmest scenario sprang to mind. "Is it Marie-Louise?"

"No. She remains well. It is . . ." Antoine choked back tears, the first time Nathan had ever seen him show such emotion. "It is my father who is ill. The fever has struck him down."

Nathan invited Antoine inside and quickly closed the door. The air was stifling. Antoine could feel perspiration spring instantly from his pores. "You are not alone. The fever has struck this house a second time."

Like Nathan, Antoine feared the worst. "Leonora?"

"No. Henry. He has been ill for two days now. Doctor Mathieson has ordered us to close every window to keep out the effluvia he believes to be responsible for the disease. What is being done for your father?"

"Our doctor has treated him with quinine and has bled him with cruel cups, but nothing helps."

Nathan shuddered. A cruel cup was a device containing sharp blades that were pressed into the flesh. He was grateful that Dr. Mathieson did not subscribe to the dubious practice of bleeding a patient. "I shall call Leonora so you may see with your own eyes that she remains well." He led Antoine into the front parlor. The young Creole dropped into a wing chair and looked around. He had always found the Lowensohn home to be a happy, lively place, but that was only a memory now.

Today, he felt only grief and trepidation. His own home was the same. After his father died, and he had little doubt that Jean-Pierre would succumb, who would follow? Marie-Louise? Himself? Or would fate be doubly cruel by leaving him alone? As he sat in the wing chair, Antoine swore to kill himself if that occurred.

Hearing light footsteps cross the entrance hall, he stood up. Leonora entered the parlor and rushed into Antoine's open arms. Dampness spotted her yellow taffeta dress. Her face shone with perspiration, and her dark hair curled damply. "Nathan told me about your father. I am so sorry."

"Thank you. This house is not without tragedy either."

"In these grim days, is any house in New Orleans without tragedy?"

"How safe are you all to remain here where the fever has struck twice? You could have caught it from the coachman, and you may still catch it from Henry. Those of you who are not ill should think about fleeing New Orleans."

"Who would accept us? Other towns have placed an embargo on all people and goods from New Orleans. Besides, our doctor does not believe the fever can be passed from one person to another. He is among the school that believes the germ to be carried in the vapor that rises from the ground."

"Our doctor thinks differently. I sometimes wonder if any doctor really knows."

"You and Marie-Louise could leave. Surely your brother's plantation is a healthier spot than the city."

"I have heard that my brother has given guns to certain trusted slaves and ordered them to open fire on any boat that even comes close to his landing."

"But if he knew it was you—"

Antoine laughed. "Then he would give them cannon. No, *ma chère*, we are not running from this plague." A sudden vitality filled Antoine as he understood the reason he had journeyed from the *Vieux Carré* to the Garden District. He had come to draw strength from Leonora so that he could return it to her.

"We shall endure it as my family has endured other such pestilential visits before. With God's help, my father and Henry will recover, and we will still be married in ten more weeks."

Leonora held Antoine as tightly as she could and she prayed that he was right. She prayed to both the God she had known in the religion of her birth, and to the holy figures of the religion she was adopting to please this man she loved.

Leonora's prayers and Antoine's assurances were only partially effective. Henry Lowensohn showed signs of recovery. His temperature fell and the aches in his body diminished. Gershon and Anna praised Dr. Mathieson for ordering the windows closed to bar entry of the disease-carrying effluvia.

The drastic measures preferred by the Creole doctor attending the Vanson household met with less success. Despite the bleeding by cruel cups, Jean-Pierre died two days later, racked by blazing fever and crying out for Mathilde, the wife he had lost seven years before. The funeral service, conducted in the crashing din of a thunderstorm, was as brief as decently possible. The elderly lawyer who had lived with so much dignity was laid to rest with a bare minimum of it. But these were unusual times. Compared with most of the funerals taking place in New Orleans that summer, Jean-Pierre's hasty interment in an aboveground vault beside his beloved wife was a stately ceremony. Each week, hundreds of bodies were heaved into shallow common graves over which a scattering of earth was thrown. Within days, that earth had shifted, exposing bloated corpses to the jaws of flies which seemed to multiply by the minute.

The house on Esplanade, which, since Marie-Louise's return, had been a place of joy, assumed a funereal atmosphere. Gloom stood in every corner, heartbreak sat on every chair. Wearing black, Antoine and Marie-Louise shared a sofa, holding hands like two young children thrown into the terrifying world of orphans. Servants tiptoed around them, frightened of disturbing whatever memories they were exploring. In normal times, the death of a man like Jean-Pierre Vanson would have drawn hundreds of mourners. The house would have been filled with friends and business associates eager to pay respects to the family. But these were not normal times, and the only visitors Antoine and Marie-Louise had in the time following their father's death were Nathan and Leonora. Even Marcel did not come. The messenger Antoine sent to the sugar plantation returned with the message undelivered after two men fired warning shots at him.

On the day after the funeral, Antoine and Marie-Louise spoke for the first time of the double marriage planned for the end of October. Neither of the English cousins had broached the subject because they assumed that the ceremony would be postponed. The words they heard stunned them.

"Last night, after you left to return home, my sister and I talked about our future. Creole tradition requires a lengthy mourning period—"

"We Vansons are bound by such tradition," Marie-Louise broke in as her brother faltered. She knew Antoine was a young man of tremendous character, but these trying days tore the strength from even the most vital men. In such grief-laden situations, women were often stronger. "That tradition includes a certain amount of superstition. Our father is dead in the flesh, but his spirit, until it is finally called away, will remain in this house where he lived for so long."

"You believe in ghosts?" Leonora burst out.

"We believe in spirits. Both Antoine and I feel the spirit of our dear *père* around us in this house. We feel it, and we hear his words when he speaks. He has told us that he desires my marriage to you, Nathan, and Antoine's marriage to you, Leonora, to continue as planned. While he is here, he yearns to see us living in this house as two married couples, and he prays that he will not be called away before both Leonora and I are mothers to children who carry Vanson blood."

Nathan clasped Marie-Louise's hands. He remembered the train journey from London to Liverpool when he had pictured his father laughing at the justice of his son's treatment of Samuel Solomon. Now, holding the hands of the young woman he loved, he could feel the spirit of Jean-Pierre Vanson. He could see the lawyer's lined face that had shown happiness only when his daughter returned from Paris. Like Marie-Louise, he could hear the old man's voice saying it was his dearest wish for the two marriages to take place on the intended date. And when he looked at Leonora, and saw the serene expression on her face, he knew that the same vision was making itself known to her.

The two cousins returned to the Lowensohn home in a mood inappropriate to the grief around them. The epidemic was at its fiercest. Barely a house in New Orleans had been spared its scathing lash, yet they were both content. Momentarily, they felt aloof from the misery, as if the vision of Jean-Pierre protected them from the effects of the very disease that had ended his own life.

That protection endured until they stepped into the still, humid air of Waverley. From the upper floor of the house, a woman's shriek of grief cascaded down the curving staircase. Gershon, his face pale and somber, emerged from the front parlor and walked slowly toward Nathan and Leonora with the news that Henry had suffered a relapse. The fever had returned. With it had come a savage delirium that had transformed the boy into a screaming, violent fiend who lashed out at anyone who came near.

The convulsions had ended only thirty minutes earlier, when Henry had died.

Neither Nathan nor Leonora had ever known such grief. The heartache they had seen in the Vanson home was nothing like it. Even the memories of their own anguish thirteen years before over the deaths of their parents paled beside the suffering and torment they saw in the Lowensohn home. There was a special agony reserved for parents who outlived their children.

After Henry's burial, Gershon sat for hours at the table in the parlor where he had played chess with his son, stroking his beard meditatively. Once, Nathan saw the cotton factor setting up the game, then moving both black and white pieces. "This was an opening Henry favored," Gershon explained when he noticed Nathan watching. "He liked to bring his queen into the game immediately, hoping he could use its power to force me into making a mistake."

Nathan recalled the ploy from the times he had played Henry. "Premature queen play helps an opponent deploy his own men."

"Precisely, but you could not tell that to Henry. It was something he had to learn for himself. Eventually, he would have done so. Sit down, Nathan. See if you can do better."

Nathan took the seat opposite Gershon. If chess was to be the tool Gershon used to help himself over this tragedy, Nathan was more than willing to cooperate.

Anna Lowensohn also sought refuge in memories. She visited Henry's bedroom, where he had died. Sometimes Leonora followed her in. The older woman was always grateful for the company. She sat in a chair by the window overlooking the front garden and talked about Henry. She also spent time in the kitchen, helping Delilah to prepare Henry's favorite dishes, as though by eating them the family would be drawn a little closer to the boy. But the preparation of fine food, once so simple in a city that prided itself on mouth-watering cuisine, was no longer easy. The French Market—the morning haunt of cooks seeking fresh meat, live seafood, delicious fruits and vegetables—was now almost deserted, another victim of the epidemic. Those able to eat had to make do with whatever they could find.

Of the three girls, fourteen-year-old Sarah and eleven-year-old Martha, found support in each other's company. Sarah, under Leonora's tuition, had become a skillful embroideress; now she spent hours sharing her talent with her younger sister. Only Miriam appeared to have no escape from grief. She sat on the front porch, rocking back and forth, eyes half closed as she gazed wistfully over the garden. Leonora joined her, but the moment she sat down, she wondered how to start a conversation. A high-pitched whine close to her right ear provided the answer.

"Are you not bothered by these flies, Miriam?"

Miriam's golden hair shimmered as she shook her head. "I have sour blood."

"Sour blood?"

"Surely you have heard my mother's philosophy."

Remembering the dinner conversation when Marie-Louise and Antoine had been present, Leonora nodded. She and Nathan must have sour blood, too, as neither of them was overly pestered by the mosquitoes. "Why do you spend so much time out here?"

"I like to dream. When I hear the wheels of a carriage or the sound of a horse's hooves on Prytania Street, I pretend it is Henry returning. And I think of things to say to him."

"What kind of things?"

For an instant the pain left Miriam's face. The green eyes sharpened. Leonora swore she saw the trace of a smile. "Nasty things. Those same unkind words we always said to each other."

Leonora was shocked. "Why?"

Miriam turned to face Leonora. "I understand now that when Henry teased me, it was his way of showing he loved me. When I teased him, and when I shouted at him, it was the same. You do not have to tell someone you love them. There are other ways of showing it. Unfortunately"—the smile departed—"we do not always realize we love people until it is too late."

Leonora glanced down, amazed to find Miriam's hand inside her own. She did not remember taking it.

"I envy you because you have Antoine," Miriam said. "I envy Nathan, too. I envy everyone who loves and is loved, and I pray each night and each morning that nothing happens to destroy that love. Especially now."

Leonora said nothing, content just to sit in the chair and hold

Miriam's hand. During the past few months, the oldest girl had grown up, turned from a petulant child into a mature, understanding woman. Two events had caused the transformation. First the duel, when Nathan had hovered between life and death; then this tragedy, the loss of her only brother. Leonora hoped that no more adversity occurred to temper Miriam's character.

Six days after Henry's burial, further tragedy struck the Lowensohn household. In the week when yellow-fever fatalities first eclipsed one thousand, Sarah and Martha fell ill within twelve hours of each other. Dr. Mathieson, mystified how the fever could have penetrated the tightly closed doors and windows, treated the two girls with quinine. Their progress followed that of their brother. A period of recovery lifted hopes before a relapse dashed them. A week after contracting the disease, they died, again within twelve hours of each other.

Anna Lowensohn did not attend the double funeral. She remained in bed, heavily sedated, with Miriam and Leonora beside her. Nathan accompanied Gershon as he said farewell to his younger daughters. Henry's death had aged him ten years; the girls' deaths added another twenty. Gershon's once round face was haggard. His stocky frame had shrunk. Halfway through the short burial ceremony, Nathan reached out to support the older man as his body trembled and he threatened to fall. On the return trip from the busy cemetery, Gershon spoke only one sentence. In a voice choked with sadness, he asked, "How many of us, Nathan, will still be alive when this pestilence ends?"

Nathan made no reply. He had heard a similar sentiment just two days before, the last time he and Leonora had called at the Vanson home. Henry's death, coming so soon after their father's passing, had saddened the Vansons immensely. When Nathan and Leonora brought word that Martha and Sarah were stricken with the fever, Antoine's and Marie-Louise's determination faltered.

"There is scarcely a family in all of New Orleans unaffected by this plague," Marie-Louise had said. "Who is to know if any of us will be alive on the day we are to be married?"

Sitting rigidly in his chair, Nathan had concealed as best he could the shiver that speared his back. "We will be wed," he told Marie-Louise in a quiet but firm tone. "I swear we will be wed, even if we are all dying of this accursed fever."

Nathan recalled that vow now, as the carriage in which he and Gershon rode made its mournful way back from the cemetery. The idea of yellow fever denying him marriage to Marie-Louise seared his mind with terror. If he failed to marry the young woman he had traveled halfway across the world to find, his entire life would have been wasted!

Dinner was served at the customary time that evening. Anna, Gershon, Miriam, Leonora, and Nathan occupied their usual places. The seats once filled by Henry, Martha, and Sarah stood empty, reminders of what the family had lost. The food tasted of sawdust to Nathan. After one mouthful he set down his fork and pushed his plate away. Anna, still dazed by sedatives, stared at her plate while Miriam and Leonora sat quietly, their food untouched. Gershon, alone, ate properly, finishing each course as he did every night. A man of habit, he might, by following his daily customs, keep one hand on sanity while the world around him went mad. Even when the meal was over, Gershon did not neglect his custom of complimenting Delilah on her cooking.

After Delilah had left the dining room, Gershon turned to the other four people at the table. "I am weary. Burying three children in two weeks is excessively tiring. Please excuse me, but I think I shall retire." He stood up and walked from the room.

When Anna looked in on him half an hour later, he was asleep. Closing the bedroom door quietly, she went downstairs to the rear parlor and opened the wicker chest where Sarah had kept her embroidery. She found the last piece on which the girl had worked, a half-finished tablecloth decorated with colorful birds. Sighing at the memories contained in the illustrations of bluejays and cardinals, Anna pulled colored thread through a needle and started to sew. One by one, Miriam, Leonora, and Nathan came in to say good night. At midnight, Rebecca asked if she could do anything before she went to bed. Anna shook her head, content to sit in the candelabra's flickering light and finish her daughter's work.

She carried on with the embroidery until almost one o'clock. Then she carefully folded the tablecloth and replaced it in the wicker chest. She felt better. The embroidery had provided a medium through which she could contact her two dead daughters. With each stitch she had heard their voices. Martha had begged her not to be sad. And Sarah . . . Anna dabbed at her eyes as she climbed the stairs. Sarah had complained when she had used the wrong color thread, had told her that she'd intended using a vermillion there, not the soft red Anna had chosen. Anna would tell that story to Gershon in the morning. Perhaps she would even tell it to him now, if he were awake.

She opened the bedroom door and stepped inside. Candlelight spilled across the room, illuminating the protective *baire* that covered the bed. Through the netting, Anna saw the outline of Gershon's body. He had not moved since she looked in on him. Concerned, she moved closer, lifted the edge of the netting, and held the candle over his face. His eyes were fixed wide open, staring but unseeing. She touched his forehead. It was cold. Stifling a cry, she stepped back. Her husband had been dead all the time she had been embroidering, all the time she had been carrying on her conversation with Sarah and Martha. Dead, perhaps, even when she had looked in on him that first time.

Early next morning, Dr. Edward Mathieson diagnosed the cause of Gershon's death as heart seizure. Yellow fever had not claimed him as a victim; he had died of a broken heart. Nathan, alone, made the now familiar journey to the cemetery which had, with such ghastly swiftness, become home to so many of the Lowensohn family. As the coffin containing Gershon's body was placed inside the vault, tears scalded Nathan's cheeks. His anguish was as strong as that which he recalled feeling for his own parents. There seemed to be no end to this horrifying plague. Those the affliction did not smite directly, it struck down, like Gershon, through other means.

When Nathan returned from the cemetery, he was appalled to see Mathieson's cab in front of the Lowensohn home. Surely not another! Was no one to be left alive at this house? Wearily, he climbed the steps to the porch. How much more of this could a man take before going mad?

Leonora met him in the hall with the news that she had called Mathieson. "It is not the fever, Nathan. This time, the sickness is grief. Ever since you left for the cemetery, Miriam has lain in her room, screaming like an animal in pain, while her mother has thrown herself around like a madwoman, shrieking at God that he was punishing her when she had done nothing wrong. Rebecca and I had to restrain her before she harmed herself."

Mathieson came down to say he had given opium to Anna and her daughter. "I have also told the housekeeper to open all windows. Closing them does not seem to keep out the effluvia that carries this disease. If we are all doomed to die, we might as well suffer the least discomfort while doing so."

Nathan escorted the doctor to his cab and watched as he drove away to his next patient. He could not criticize the man's mordant attitude. Mathieson had studied so he could save lives. For the past few weeks he had done little but watch people die. Irony was his best defense. Hearing his name called, he turned around. Leonora came down from the porch to stand beside him. "Nathan, had it not been for the Lowensohn family's kindness, we might have been among the first victims of this epidemic—"

"I think, Lally, that those first victims may have been the

lucky ones. They suffered only death. They did not have to endure heartbreak as well."

"Your heart is heavy, as is mine, but this is no time to shed tears for ourselves. Four people in this family have already died. Miriam and her mother alone survive. We are the only ones still well and we must care for them. With the servants' help, I will manage the house. You must oversee the business."

"August is a poor month for cotton. Certainly this August, when men are too busy building coffins to worry about picking cotton."

"This pestilence will not last forever. When it ceases, cotton will be king once more." She saw the doubt in Nathan's eyes and added, "We must think positively, otherwise we might just as well lie down and wait for the sickness to take us."

In the morning, Leonora checked on Anna and Miriam. Although both had slept through the night, they still seemed drained of energy. She instructed Rebecca to take breakfast up to them. At midday, she looked in again. Miriam, exhausted by her grief, and lingering under the effects of the sedative, continued to sleep. Anna sat by the window, gazing down at the front garden. Leonora pulled up a chair and sat beside her.

"My husband was very fond of that garden," Anna murmured. "He enjoyed caring for it. He said New Orleans had many exotic trees and flowers, the like of which he had never imagined when growing up in Germany. He often talked of shipping plants to Germany because he believed their color and aroma would have a beneficial effect on the German people. 'Such loveliness, Anna,' he would say, 'will make the Germans less ferocious and more appreciative, like the people of New Orleans, of the finer things.' Who will appreciate the garden now that he is gone? And who will manage the business?"

"You do not have to worry about the garden. Samson will take good care of it. Nor do you have to worry about the business. Nathan has gone to the countinghouse today, to prepare for when the first shipments of cotton come down the Mississippi."

Anna nodded as her tired brain accepted the news. "You and your cousin are good and decent people. My husband recognized that on the ship which brought you from England. That was why he invited you to stay here. We were looking forward to attending your weddings as much as we would have looked forward to attending the weddings of our own children."

"You will still attend those weddings."

"I wonder," Anna said, "what we have done for God to punish us like this."

Patting the older woman's hand, Leonora silently asked the identical question.

While Leonora organized the Lowensohn household, Nathan reopened the countinghouse which had been closed for three weeks, ever since the city's newspapers had finally admitted the existence of an epidemic. He saw Gershon everywhere, sitting behind a desk while making entries in a ledger, looking through the window across Canal Street to the *Vieux Carré*, or standing at the door to welcome a planter with whom he did business. No matter how many times he shook his head to dispel the vision, he could not drive it from his mind. Gershon Lowensohn's ghost would live on in this building just as the spirit of Jean-Pierre Vanson lived on in the house on Esplanade.

There was little for Nathan to do but look ahead. No ships would bring cotton to the levee until the epidemic was over. But the moment that happened, the instant Bronze John left the city, madness would ensue. Boats would line up to deposit their white cargo. The presses, idle for the past three months, would begin operating again. Brokers for foreign mills would arrive, and the commercial whirl of New Orleans would continue as before, with barely a thought spared for those who had perished. He would need to contact the planters Gershon had represented, inform them of their factor's death and convince them that he could continue the business relationship to their mutual advantage.

Could he? Had he learned enough in the past two years to carry on the business? As well as selling the planters' cotton he would need to arrange shipment of whatever supplies they needed, lend money if necessary. His head reeled at the complexity of it all. Under Gershon, everything had seemed so straightforward. Now, the well-ordered world of commerce was nothing but chaos.

And in the middle of it all, he was to be married!

The wedding date had not been changed. Nathan's marriage to Marie-Louise, and Leonora's to Antoine, would still take place on October the twenty-ninth. Perhaps that was what had kept them sane in the midst of all this insanity! He and Leonora continued to take instruction from *Abbé* Francois at the Presbytere. Antoine and Marie-Louise met them there, as if sharing such an experience would strengthen their love. Nathan accepted the *Abbé*'s teachings at face value, regarding them merely as a means to please the woman he loved. He cared only that he would make the correct responses during the wedding service. Leonora did not take the instruction so lightly. She believed that religious leaders had a duty to advise, to answer questions. When she asked the *Abbé* what the people of New Orleans had done to deserve such harsh treatment, he had demanded to know who she thought she was to question God's decisions. Leonora had left the cathedral that day in an angry mood, telling Nathan that the rabbi at the Maiden Lane Synagogue in London would never have answered her question in such arrogant fashion.

Although the wedding date had not been altered, Jean-Pierre Vanson's dream of a celebration that all New Orleans would remember had long since faded. Many of those friends he had intended inviting were now in mourning or dead themselves. Others, who traditionally left the city in May or June, to spend the summer in cooler places, were not returning until the epidemic broke, and only God knew when that would be! The wedding would be a very private affair now.

Then Nathan's blood turned cold. He had been concerned

with the wedding day. What of the wedding night? Would even the joy of Marie-Louise's heavenly body opening to receive his love be enough to make him forget the horror he saw all around?

August passed. The toll continued to rise. In the third week of the month, more than thirteen hundred people died. A similar number perished the following week. Corteges blocked every street. All roads led to the city's overflowing graveyards. For those men and women who had so far escaped the fever's deadly touch, there was nothing to do but carry on. And pray that their good luck continued.

Leonora was grateful for the work involved in running the Lowensohn house; it gave her brain something other than death to dwell on. She rose early each morning, even before the servants. She helped Delilah prepare breakfast and took a tray to the rooms of Anna and Miriam. Of the two, Anna was making a much faster recovery. She came down regularly each morning after breakfast. When the weather allowed, she walked around the garden as if seeking the memory of Gershon there, and when the rains returned to force her inside she found comfort in continuing the embroidery Sarah had started. Once, when Leonora fussed around her, she patted her hand and said, "My husband did not bring you here to be our servant." And Leonora had answered, "When you are well, I will let you wait on me."

Miriam, though, had barely left her room in the two weeks following her father's death and she had not been out of the house once, not even to sit on the front porch which had been her favorite place. When Leonora talked to her, she found the golden-haired girl full of self-doubt and remorse.

"I keep asking myself why everyone else died and I survived. I feel confused, Leonora. I feel guilty at still being alive."

"Instead of being confused and guilty, Miriam, you should be grateful and determined."

"Determined?" Miriam stared at Leonora as if she were mad. "How can a tragedy of such magnitude make a person determined?"

"You should be determined to achieve something with your life, something your father, and Henry, and Sarah, and Martha would be proud of. Of an entire generation, you alone are left to carry the standard. You cannot drop it in the dust because you feel too confused and guilty to hoist it on your shoulder."

Miriam made no reply, but Leonora saw tears glisten in her green eyes. She wondered if her words had achieved any effect.

Nathan continued to travel to Canal Street every day. Sitting at the desk which had been Gershon's, he pored over the previous year's records. Cotton would be blooming now on the plantations. Soon, the picking would start. Bales would stand on river landings ready to be loaded and shipped to the levee. It was a cotton factor's responsibility to advise his planters when to sell to get the highest price, but there was little point in even considering selling times and prices now. Not until New Orleans was a healthy city once again.

He knew some people thought New Orleans would never recover from this epidemic. Pessimists called for the Crescent City to be abandoned as a plague den and left to fall back into the river from which it had grown. Nathan considered such men scaremongers. They were no better than the scoundrels who filled the taverns that still remained open. Living with a wild abandon in case death was ready to visit them, they raised their glasses to toast passing corteges and made bets on who among them would be the first to die.

Nathan believed the city would recover. It was too important to do otherwise. Any city with such access to trade routes—any city which shipped the dollar value of merchandise that New Orleans did—could not fail to recover. And when that recovery occurred, Nathan intended to be a part of it.

Chapter Twelve

Not until the beginning of September did the miracle for which New Orleans had prayed all summer finally occur. Fatalities from yellow fever diminished, down to seven hundred and forty-nine the week ending September the third, little more than four hundred the following week, and two hundred and twenty-one the week after that. Simultaneously, the weather improved. The rains ended, refreshing breezes swept across the city from Lake Pontchartrain. Gifts of food and money poured in from all over the country, while many who had survived the worst days of the epidemic puffed out their chests like victorious warriors.

At Waverley, the triumph of survival was tinged with sadness. The Lowensohns had suffered more than most. Death had swept through five times. Yet among the sadness was determination to carry on. Leonora worked on Miriam's feelings of guilt and confusion by stressing to the girl that she had an obligation to shape a life which would revere the memory of those who had died. Simultaneously, Nathan involved Anna in her late husband's business. He took her to Gershon's bank where documents required her signature. They visited Gershon's lawyer who drafted a contract specifying Nathan's duties as manager of the cotton factoring firm. Only when Nathan told the lawyer to include a clause stipulating that he was to be paid a wage while all profits went to the Lowensohn family did Anna speak out.

"As a manager, you deserve a share of the profits, Nathan."

Nathan disagreed. "Your husband may no longer be with us, but no legal document has ever been drawn up assigning even a single share in the business to me. Any profits will remain in the family."

"Nathan, do you believe that you are in debt to this family forever for the little kindness we showed you and your cousin?"

"Nothing could ever repay that *little* kindness."

Anna tried a final time. "Soon you will be a married man with new responsibilities. Even a manager's wage will not be enough for you and your wife to live properly."

"My responsibilities will not be that awesome. We will live in the Vanson family home, as we always planned to. Leonora and Antoine will share the house with us—"

"How naive you are!" Joy and anguish engulfed Anna. If she could be blessed with another son, she would unhesitatingly choose Nathan. "A wife as lovely as Marie-Louise will need more than a roof over her head and food on the table. She will need dresses and jewelry to accentuate her charm. Nathan"— Anna's dark brown eyes shone—"I will wager your manager's pay that Antoine does not plan to treat Leonora in such spartan fashion."

Nathan started to laugh. He could never remember a woman lecturing him like this. He wondered whether his own mother, had she lived, would have talked to him in such a fashion. Then he found himself hoping that she would have talked to him exactly like this. "I think I would be wise not to accept such a wager."

"Good. Have the clause read," she told the lawyer, "that Mister Solomon will receive forty percent of any profits." She turned to Nathan. "There, now you have good reason to work hard."

Nathan did to Anna what he had always dreamed of doing to his own mother. He kissed her.

The good news continued. Yellow-fever deaths proceeded to decline. In the last week of September, Antoine visited the countinghouse brandishing a copy of that morning's *Picayune*. "Look, Nathan, one hundred and twenty-five fatalities last week. Have you walked along the levee? It is wonderful to see ships lining up there again. The smoke and sparks coming from those stacks is the best medicine New Orleans could have."

"I will breathe that smoke tomorrow, when I sail upriver. I have hired clerks to work in the countinghouse, and now I must visit the planters to make sure those clerks earn their money."

"How long will you be away?"

"Perhaps a week."

"Alphonse and his family should be here by the time you return. We will welcome them in true New Orleans style, with an evening to remember. My father's spirit will not object to mourning being cast aside for such a joyous occasion."

Nathan returned home on October the eighth, the same day the *Commercial Bulletin* declared New Orleans to be as healthy as any city in the Union. Less than fifty had died that week. Everyone knew it would be only a few days before the figure dropped to zero. Standing at the rail of the sternwheeler, Nathan could believe such good news. Beneath a bright afternoon sun, the levee was as busy as it had been that day two years ago, when he and Leonora had arrived in the city. As he watched bales of cotton coming off half a dozen boats, he questioned whether an epidemic had really occurred. The scene before him appeared so normal. At any moment he expected to see Gershon walking among the bales, instructing laborers to load his merchandise onto a cart and take it to the press. As he remembered the man who had done so much for him, he felt a lump form in his throat, and only then did he recall the worst moments of the fever's savage reign.

A reception committee waited. Antoine wore a new beige suit with a matching hat. Leonora and Marie-Louise shaded themselves with turquoise parasols. It was a color that suited their complexions admirably and they carried it through to the new dresses and bonnets they wore for the occasion. Nathan kissed Leonora on the cheek, shook Antoine's hand and clapped him on the shoulder, then he turned to Marie-Louise.

"I saw you the moment we rounded the last bend in the river. You stood out like a beacon on a dark night, and never was such a light more welcome." Before Marie-Louise could reply, Nathan drew her close and pressed his lips down onto hers. Her parasol fell to the ground as she clung to him. Fifteen seconds passed. The world could have ended in that time. The levee could have broken, all of New Orleans could have disappeared beneath the waters of the Mississippi, and neither Nathan nor Marie-Louise would have known or cared. When the embrace ended, their faces were flushed and their hearts hammered inside their chests.

"I am not certain, *ma chère,*" Nathan whispered, "that I can wait until this month is ended."

"Nor I. Each tomorrow will seem a thousand years away."

Still holding Marie-Louise's arm, Nathan turned to Antoine. "Where is your brother Alphonse with his family?"

"In Paris." Antoine pulled a sheet of white vellum from his pocket. "Nothing in the world, not even the marriages of his sister and brother, could make him visit this plague-infested hellhole. He will be glad to receive us should we visit France."

"Well damn him!" Nathan said.

"Precisely. Even without him we will have an evening to remember. The only people who matter are right here."

Antoine drove Nathan and Leonora to Waverley. As the vehicle stopped by the marble carriage block, Anna and Miriam came out to meet them. Nathan was cheered to notice how much better they both looked. Anna's bearing was more upright, Miriam's golden tresses had regained some of their luster.

"Was your journey successful?" Anna asked.

"All of Mister Lowensohn's clients were saddened to hear of this family's tragedies. They offer their condolences and assure us of their continued patronage."

"Thank you, Nathan. I do not know how we would have managed without your kindness and consideration."

Nathan smiled. He and Leonora owed the Lowensohns so much that every opportunity to repay a portion of that debt formed an occasion for joy.

Antoine kept his word, and the evening was truly memorable. It began with a carriage ride around the *Vieux Carré*. Nowhere did they see evidence of the deadly epidemic that had transformed summer into hell. The streets were full of people enjoying themselves. The cries of vendors filled the air. Strolling musicians played their tunes and performed their dances in the yellow gaslight. On elaborate ironwork balconies, families sat enjoying the balmy October night.

"New Orleans has a remarkable capacity for recovery," Antoine said as the carriage rolled along St. Peter Street.

"And its citizens, especially here," Nathan observed, "have an equally exceptional talent for pushing unpleasantness into the furthest recesses of their memories."

Further proof of that talent was evident when the carriage reached at Congo Square, where slaves danced every evening before the cannon signaled them to find their homes. Onlookers, many in evening dress, filled the square, clapping hands and tapping feet to an increasingly frantic rhythm beaten on the skins of drums. In the center of the square, four ebony-colored men and a mulatto woman in a skimpy white dress danced with wild passion. Antoine instructed the carriage driver not to stop.

"Those slaves perform a tribal fertility rite their ancestors once danced in Africa," he told his companions. "Our less savage dance will be a giving of thanks for having survived."

They ate dinner at Victor's, a Victor's that pulsed with life and excitement. Waiters wove their way adroitly between tables filled with elegantly attired men and graceful women. There was no sense of mourning here, either, but neither were the trying times of the past few months forgotten. The meal was constantly interrupted by men wishing to offer condolences to Antoine and Marie-Louise on the death of their father. Antoine accepted the condolences easily, but Marie-Louise grew increasingly agitated by the constant reminders of her father's death. After the fourth such interruption, she was close to tears. Nathan sought a way to lift her spirits. His gaze fell upon the calves feet *à la Pascaline* the waiter had just placed in front of her.

"Do you not know that you should never eat the feet of an animal?" he whispered. "God only knows what muck it has stepped in." When Marie-Louise took only one mouthful before pushing away the plate, Nathan looked horrified. "Please do not let me stop you from enjoying your food. I am certain those particular calves feet were thoroughly scrubbed before they were cooked."

Marie-Louise gave him a shining smile. "If you ever talk so disgustingly at our dinner table, it will be your tongue that is thoroughly scrubbed."

From Victor's, they traveled to the Salle d'Orleans ballroom. Only once did Nathan allow Marie-Louise out of his arms. That was when Antoine insisted upon one dance with his own sister. "Very soon you will have her all to yourself, my friend. Surely you would not begrudge me a solitary waltz with her."

Watching them dance away, Nathan decided they made a handsome couple. Anyone not knowing they were brother and sister could be forgiven for believing they were two young people very suited to each other and very much in love.

"Are you going to stand and gape, or are you going to dance with me?"

Nathan turned to Leonora, who stood beside him. "Only you would have the nerve to ask a man to dance." He took her onto the dance floor. She was smaller than Marie-Louise, slimmer, and she felt as light as a feather in his arms. He could never remember dancing with her before, and he questioned why he could have allowed himself to commit such an omission. Enslaved by his infatuation for Marie-Louise, he sometimes forgot just how much Leonora meant to him.

"In three weeks' time we will be married, Nathan. Do you have any qualms?"

"None at all. The prospect of marrying Marie-Louise imbued me with the strength to endure even the worst times." He stared into Leonora's dark eyes. Did she, at this late stage, harbor misgivings? Surely not. "And you, Lally? Are you worried?" She paused, and Nathan knew doubts did exist. He tried to reassure her. "Antoine is a handsome young man who loves you deeply. He will spare nothing to make you happy."

"I love him just as deeply, but . . ." Her face tightened into a grimace and she shook her head in frustration.

"What is it, Lally? What disturbs you?"

"Do you recall the New Year's ball, asking whether I had doubts about taking instruction in Catholicism?"

"Of course." How could he ever forget? Only minutes later, he had challenged Raymonde Perrault to a duel.

"I did have doubts, but I thought my love for Antoine would overcome them. Now, as the time draws near, I worry that I am doing something terribly wrong. I remember cousin David's wedding to Charlotte in London. I think of the ceremony performed that day, and I feel sad and jealous. Can you imagine that, feeling jealous of anything to do with that pompous clod?"

Nathan tightened his grip on Leonora. "Any fear you have now means nothing when compared to the bliss you will share with Antoine. The wedding ceremony with its Catholic prayers will be over in minutes. Your happiness with Antoine will last forever."

Some of Leonora's customary cheer returned. Nathan exploited it. "Do what the Marranos did in Spain when they were forcibly converted to Catholicism. Say Catholic prayers aloud to please the Inquisition while whispering Hebrew prayers to yourself."

Leonora began to laugh. She could always rely on her cousin to dispel her darkest doubts.

They did not leave the Salle d'Orleans until after two in the morning, legs weary from too much dancing, stomachs full of food, heads light with wine. The carriage returned Nathan and Leonora to the Garden District. Antoine stepped down to help Leonora alight. He held her briefly, kissed her good night and promised to visit her late the following morning. If the weather held, they would ride along the Shell Road and enjoy lunch at one of the lakeside restaurants. Inside the carriage, Nathan's farewell to Marie-Louise was lengthier. His arms encircled her body while her hands locked behind his neck to draw his face close. The tip of his tongue pierced her sweet lips. Their mouths widened and Marie-Louise moaned softly as she felt the hardness of his body press against her.

"Mon amour." She clung to him tenaciously. "No man has ever been as happy as I will make you."

The carriage moved as their bodies shifted on the seat. Nathan remembered where they were. Reluctantly, he drew back, envisaging in the darkness Marie-Louise's pale face now flushed with passion, her eyes wide and moist with yearning. "Until tomorrow, my darling," he whispered.

"Until tomorrow." As he opened the carriage door and stepped down, she touched a hand to her lips and blew him a kiss.

He fell asleep dreaming of Marie-Louise's lips, and crying out in protest why time took so long to pass. He slept until ten-thirty, stirring only when Leonora knocked on the door to remind him that Antoine and Marie-Louise would be returning at midday for a drive to the lake. Dressed in a pale blue suit with a white shirt and patterned silk vest, he ventured downstairs. Leonora, Anna, and Miriam had already eaten. Nathan chose to have breakfast on the front porch. He ate lightly, not wishing to spoil his appetite for the lakeside lunch. Miriam joined him, and he described the ride through the *Vieux Carré* the previous evening. "There must be something wonderful about a city, Miriam, where people recover so quickly from such awful tragedy."

"Perhaps it is just in the old part of the city that such rapid healing occurs. Here, my mother and I continue to live with broken hearts." Seeing Nathan's face lengthen, she touched his arm. "I know you are trying to cheer me, but it will need more than a few weeks to heal our pain."

Miriam's gentle reminder that she and her mother remained in mourning caused Nathan a twinge of guilt. Had he the right to enjoy himself, to be in love, when such misery remained? "Always remember, Miriam, if there is anything Leonora or I can do. You only have to ask."

Her hand tightened on his arm. "You do enough already. Your happiness softens the most bitter moments for us—" She broke off and turned toward the front gate as the rumble of wheels and the sound of hooves grew louder. Nathan watched her, wondering if she was pretending that Henry was coming home.

An open phaeton came into view. Only one person rode in it, Antoine, slapping the reins and cracking the whip as if he were in a race. Where was Marie-Louise? Nathan pushed back from the table and ran down the steps as the phaeton swung around by the carriage block. When Antoine shouted his sister's name, Nathan jumped up into the still moving vehicle. The reins slapped across the horse's back, and the phaeton picked up speed.

"What is the matter?" Nathan yelled.

"Marie-Louise is sick. She shivers and shakes like someone with the fever. Our doctor is with her now. He thinks it might be something she ate. I pray to God Almighty that he is right!"

Nathan looked back to the house. Miriam had run inside to alert the others. He screwed his eyes shut. Not Marie-Louise! Not now, not after everyone was declaring the damned disease to be over! Surely not!

Antoine drove at breakneck speed to Esplanade, barely missing accidents at almost every intersection. Followed by Nathan, he ran into the house and up the stairs to Marie-Louise's bedroom. The room was stifling, the windows closed. The Creole doctor, a thin, white-haired man, was bent over Marie-Louise.

When Nathan saw the cruel cup he held, he knocked it out of his hand.

"You will not use such barbaric methods on her!"

"Do you to presume tell me my business, *monsieur?*"

"Bleeding did not work with *Monsieur* Vanson and it will not work with his daughter. If you can prescribe nothing more effective, pick up your damned bag and get out of here!"

The doctor left. Nathan threw open the windows to let in fresh air, then knelt beside the bed. He took Marie-Louise's hand from beneath the covers and held it. Her skin was cold and clammy. Perspiration covered her forehead and upper lip. He peered into her face, anxious to see that paleness of complexion. *"Ma chère,* can you hear me, can you understand me?"

Marie-Louise's head moved. The tip of her tongue traced the outline of her lips. She gave Nathan's hand a weak squeeze. *"Mademoiselle* regrets she will be unable to take lunch at the lake today. She apologizes profusely."

"There is nothing to apologize for. When you are well again we will have a dozen lunches there." He looked up at Antoine, who stood on the other side of the bed, and whispered tensely, "Do you notice any change in her coloring?"

Antoine shook his head. He, too, had sought the ominous buttery hue in his sister's skin.

"Thank heaven for that." Nathan turned back to Marie-Louise. "One among us ate and drank too heartily last night, but soon you will be well again."

"If you stay beside me, I will be well sooner."

Nathan remained by the bed for fifteen minutes, holding Marie-Louise's hand until she drifted off to sleep. As he tucked her hand beneath the covers, Rosa knocked on the door to say Leonora had arrived.

Leonora entered the room, explaining that Samson, the gardener, had brought her from Waverley. She stood over the bed, gazing down at her future sister-in-law. "Does she have—?"

"We do not know," Antoine answered. "We pray it is something she ate, and nothing more."

"Does anyone remember what she ate last night?" Nathan asked. "What did she have that we did not?"

Antoine's eyes narrowed as he recalled dinner at Victor's. Leonora waved a hand excitedly. "The calves feet *à la Pascaline!* Surely you remember chiding her, Nathan."

"Of course! Do you recollect that, Antoine?"

"Now I do." Despite his sister's condition, Antoine smiled. "You were joking, yet you succeeded in deterring Marie-Louise from eating more than a mouthful or two."

"Yes, but a mouthful or two was enough to cause this." He stood up and walked to the door. "Leonora will stay here with you while I fetch Doctor Mathieson, our doctor. You see, he will have Marie-Louise back to her old self by morning."

An hour later, Nathan returned with Edward Mathieson. After hearing the tale of the calves feet *à la Pascaline,* Mathieson concurred that Marie-Louise's illness could indeed be food poisoning. He gave her an alcohol-based medication which he said would both settle her stomach and help her to sleep until the illness had passed.

Nathan spent the remainder of the day and all of the night at the Vanson home, dozing fitfully in a chaise longue beside Marie-Louise's bed. He was at her side when she awakened at seven o'clock on Monday morning. Her skin was dry and cool. Her first words were to complain that she was weak with hunger. Nathan hugged her, oblivious to the sourness that clung to her body. Had he noticed, he would have declared it to be the sweetest aroma he had ever inhaled. "You may eat as much as you want of anything you want," he told her, "just as long as you never touch calves feet again." Then he did something he could not remember doing since he was a young child. Lifting his eyes, he thanked God for delivering his beloved Marie-Louise from harm.

Nathan ate breakfast with Marie-Louise and Antoine. There was no need to encourage her to eat. She was clearly ravenous and it was not until she had finished a plate of bacon-wrapped calves liver, preboiled in butter and cooked in a red wine sauce, that she pronounced herself satisfied.

From the Vanson home, Nathan went to the countinghouse on Canal Street, then to the levee to supervise the unloading and transportation to the presses of cotton for which he was agent. Despite the lack of sleep, he felt full of energy. Marie-Louise was recovering, and that was enough to recharge his body and his mind. He remained at the levee until late afternoon, when he returned to Waverley to bathe and change. That evening, he and Leonora were to take instruction from *Abbé* Francois. He hoped Marie-Louise was well enough to accompany them; her presence always made the old priest's tedious tuition more bearable.

Marie-Louise did feel well enough. She came with Antoine to the Presbytere just as Nathan and Leonora arrived. Nathan had never seen her look so beautiful. Framed by the inky blackness of her hair, the fair skin of her face shone like ivory. Her eyes held a luminous quality that brightened up the small, drab room where the *Abbé* gave his lessons, and for a moment Nathan regretted that after tonight there would be only two more such guidance periods. He could listen to the *Abbé* forever if only Marie-Louise were present.

The tuition ended just after eight o'clock. The two couples left the Presbytere discussing where to eat dinner. "Religious education gives one a hunger for good food and drink," Nathan declared. "It is too bad that none of us can learn the trick of turning water into wine."

"Too bad indeed," Antoine responded. "We could transform the entire Mississippi into a gigantic river of claret. Of course, you'd have to find another way of bringing your cotton to the levee, because ships would be banned from the river for fear of contaminating the wine."

"The poor fish would never swim in a straight line again," Leonora protested.

"Perhaps not, but imagine how splendid they would taste," Antoine said. He looked at Marie-Louise, who held Nathan's arm. "What do you think of that, sister? How would you like to eat fish naturally seasoned with the finest claret?"

Before she could answer, Marie-Louise shrieked with surprise and stumbled. Nathan grabbed her arm to stop her from falling. She stood up straight, suddenly giddy. "Excuse me, I must have tripped over something."

In the gaslight, Leonora sought an obstacle that could have caught Marie-Louise's dainty shoe. She saw nothing. "Do you feel all right now?"

"Of course," Marie-Louise answered gaily. "I feel wonderful. And quite hungry." She linked arms once more with Nathan. "Let us decide quickly where we will eat, before my stomach growls in a most unladylike manner."

Two blocks further, Marie-Louise stumbled again. This time, Nathan could not save her. She fell heavily. Antoine, Leonora, and Nathan surrounded her anxiously. Her eyelids fluttered; her breathing was uneven. She tried to get up only to fall again. "You will have to forgive me," she murmured as she sat quite inelegantly on the *banquette*, "but all of a sudden I do not feel well. Do you think it could be God punishing us for making fun of Jesus turning the water to wine?"

Leonora took charge. "Nathan, you and Antoine take her home. I will fetch Doctor Mathieson." She hailed a passing cab, gave the driver Mathieson's address on Carondelet and urged him to hurry. Carrying Marie-Louise between them, Antoine and Nathan ran the final two hundred yards to the Vanson home on Esplanade.

Forty-five minutes passed before Doctor Mathieson arrived. He wore evening dress. Leonora had caught him as he prepared to go out for dinner. When he examined Marie-Louise, she complained of a nagging headache which had started in the past half hour, a harsh dryness in her mouth and a soreness in her throat. The doctor confronted her brother, Leonora, and Nathan.

"Her temperature is only slightly elevated. She probably has nothing more sinister than a chill. It could be a resurgence of the food poisoning she suffered yesterday. In light of recent events, however, we cannot discount her illness as the onset of the fever. I will prescribe quinine and return to see how she is in the morning." With that promise Mathieson left to enjoy his delayed dinner.

While Leonora returned to Waverley, Nathan sat up once again with Marie-Louise. Antoine remained by Marie-Louise's bedside with his friend. While she slept, the two young men encouraged each other by repeating the *Commercial-Bulletin*'s claim of two days ago that New Orleans was now as healthy as any city in the Union. When Antoine went to bed at midnight, Nathan remained gazing at the sleeping figure of Marie-Louise. At two-thirty, when he could no longer force his eyes open, he made himself as comfortable as possible in the chaise longue and fell asleep. His last thought was that the next morning would duplicate the last, and Marie-Louise would awaken complaining of hunger.

Marie-Louise stirred at seven o'clock, not hungry, but thrashing about in the bed and crying out in pain. Nathan snapped awake, instantly alert and as frightened as he had ever been in his entire life. Even in the dim early-morning light he could see the dreadful yellow tint of Marie-Louise's skin. He did not need a medical degree to know that Dr. Mathieson's most pessimistic scenario had come true.

Mathieson arrived two hours later to confirm Nathan's diagnosis. By then, Leonora was also at the house to offer support to her cousin and her fiancé. The doctor admitted that Marie-Louise's earlier sickness, which they had attributed to food poisoning, had indeed been the onset of yellow fever. "Sometimes the fever never yields its grip, from its first caress until its final choking hold. At other times, it disappears for a day or so, and the victim believes he is suffering from nothing more serious than a chill or upset stomach. And sometimes," Mathieson continued, "the victim has the strength and luck to fight it off and emerge as healthy as before. With the aid of a competent doctor, of course."

Mathieson's manner offered some comfort, but such confidence did not endure. Throughout the day, Marie-Louise's condition failed to improve, and in the evening, when Mathieson returned, she showed definite signs of deterioration. Her eyes were bloodshot, her skin a darker yellow, her temperature higher. When Mathieson administered more quinine, Nathan asked if some other remedy was available.

"Every doctor has his preferred medicine," Mathieson answered. "Mine is quinine. I have known it to be quite effective in some cases."

"I was thinking of something other than medicine. Would bleeding be beneficial?"

"Nathan!" Antoine shouted his friend's name. "You attacked the doctor who has treated this family since I was a child because he wanted to bleed Marie-Louise."

"That was Sunday. This is Tuesday, when it is time to consider every alternative open to us."

"Bleeding will be of no use," Mathieson said.

"Then what will be of use?" Nathan demanded.

Fatigue etched the doctor's lined face. In the middle of an epidemic, death was difficult to accept. It was even harder when that scourge was allegedly over. "Perhaps prayer."

Nathan spent a third consecutive night in the chaise longue beside Marie-Louise's bed, but this time he did not sleep. He spent every minute staring at the body of Marie-Louise, sometimes still, sometimes trembling in the fever's grip. Morning came, and Marie-Louise's condition had worsened further. Her skin was darker, her veins swollen, her temperature higher still. Delirious, she shouted and threw herself around on the bed. From her lips and nose oozed blood. She retched into a bowl held by Nathan who stared morbidly at the black vomit she brought up. Dr. Mathieson visited again to administer more quinine. His prognosis that Marie-Louise might yet recover had a hollow ring. Nathan knew she was going to die, if not that day then the next. And he knew what must be done before that happened.

That evening, while Antoine and Leonora maintained a vigil by Marie-Louise's bed, Nathan left the Vanson home and walked to the Presbytere. He found *Abbé* Francois starting his evening meal of black bread and cheese. When the priest expressed surprise at seeing his visitor on a Wednesday instead of the normal Monday or Thursday, Nathan said, *"Abbé,* I need you for more important matters than teaching me how to be a good Catholic. My cherished Marie-Louise is dying from the fever. Death is determined to cheat me out of marrying her. I want you to deprive death of his hideous triumph by marrying us now, before she dies."

"Such a union would be a mockery. God would never bless it."

"What does it matter whether God blesses a union which is already doomed?" Nathan walked to the table and stood over the priest. "You will be a mockery to the spirit of your cloth if you fail to help fellow human beings in their hour of need."

The priest looked up from his plate into the face of a man who would accept no refusal. "I will come with you, my son."

The *Abbé* accompanied Nathan back to Esplanade. Antoine and Leonora were still by Marie-Louise's bedside. The doctor had returned and was about to administer a sedative that would calm Marie-Louise's delirium. Nathan stopped him, then kneeled beside the bed. "Marie-Louise, can you hear me?"

Bloodshot eyes sought him out. Nathan saw a wildness he had never imagined possible, and he feared that even this attempt would fail. Never mind what the priest believed about such a marriage being a mockery that God would never bless. God had nothing to do with this. The devil had gained the upper hand here, just as he had gained it all over New Orleans this summer. It was the devil doing the mocking, not Nathan.

"Marie-Louise, *Abbé* Francois has come to marry us. Do you understand?" Was it his imagination or did the wildness fade a fraction? Did reason still exist in Marie-Louise's frenzied mind? In such delirium, did there remain any vestige of the love she had known for Nathan? "Do you understand, *ma chère?"*

She struggled to sit up. Leonora pushed a pillow against the headboard to make her more comfortable. "If you wish to make me your wife," Marie-Louise whispered, pausing between every other word, "I think we had best make haste."

The effort of sitting up and speaking exhausted her. She closed her eyes and leaned back. Nathan held her hands as though by such contact he could infuse her with his own strength. "Hurry!" he hissed at the priest.

Abbé Francois glanced nervously at the people around the bed. He had never officiated at such a wedding before. He turned his attention to the wedding couple. To the groom, kneeling by the bed, pale-faced, brown eyes brimming with tears. To the bride, yellow-skinned, red-eyed, her body drained of strength.

"Hurry!" Nathan spat out the word again.

The priest nodded in assent. Dispensing with the opening ritual, he began in the middle of the wedding service. "Wilt thou have this woman to thy wedded wife, to live together——?"

"I will!"

"Wilt thou have this man to thy wedded husband, to live together after God's ordinance in the holy estate——?"

Like Nathan, Marie-Louise interrupted before the question could be fully phrased. "I will."

"Who giveth this woman to be married to this man?"

"I do," Antoine stated firmly.

"Repeat the vows after me."

Still holding Marie-Louise's hands, Nathan followed the priest's words. "I, Nathan, take thee, Marie-Louise, to my wedded wife, to have and to hold——"

This time, *Abbé* Francois, aware of the urgency, cut Nathan off. Turning to Marie-Louise, he instructed her to repeat his words. Her eyes turned to Nathan, hoping she could convey all her love with the words she would say. She did not feel cheated. The only sadness she felt was for Nathan, who would be a widower so soon after being a groom.

"I, Marie-Louise, take thee, Nathan, to my wedded husband . . ." She paused, as if the words required too much effort. She felt Nathan's cool dry hands inside her own, and she prayed to God that he would be fortunate enough to find another woman whose love would be as deep as her own.

"The ring?" *Abbé* Francois asked. "Is there a ring?"

"A moment." Antoine ran from his sister's bedroom to the room where his father had slept. He returned with a thin, plain gold band. "This belonged to our mother," he said, giving it to the priest. "She would have wanted it used in such a manner."

The priest passed the ring to Nathan who slipped it gently onto Marie-Louise's finger. Hearing someone sniff, he glanced up from the bed. Leonora held a hand to her eyes to stem tears. Antoine's arm cradled her shoulders.

"Join your right hand to hers," the priest told Nathan. When this was done, *Abbé* Francois rested his own right hand upon their hands. "Forasmuch as Nathan and Marie-Louise have consented together in holy wedlock, and have declared the same before God and in the presence of this company, I pronounce them man and wife. In the name of the Father, the Son, of the Holy Ghost. What God has joined together, let no man put asunder."

The *Abbé* stepped back, his duty, for the moment, finished. Leaning across the bed, Nathan kissed Marie-Louise upon the cheek. His lips felt like they had touched an open flame.

"Nathan . . ." Marie-Louise whispered his name. *"Mademoiselle* regrets . . . no, no! *Madame* Solomon regrets that she will be unable to keep her promise."

"What promise was that?" He wiped perspiration from her forehead before it fell into her inflamed eyes.

"That no man has ever been as happy as I will make you."

Somehow he found the courage to smile at her. "You have already made me happier than any man has the right to be."

"Thank you." She gazed around her bedroom, determined to acknowledge everyone. "Leonora, my brother loves you very much, and I am grateful for that. Had it not been for his love,

I would never have known Nathan. Antoine, promise me that you will do nothing foolish to break Leonora's heart."

"I promise you."

The bloodshot eyes lingered a moment on Mathieson. "Doctor, I thank you for all you have done on my behalf." Her gaze moved to *Abbé* Francois. The old priest whom Nathan had dragged from his supper at St. Louis Cathedral had made no move yet to return to his interrupted meal. Marie-Louise understood why. He had completed only half of his work.

"Abbé." Marie-Louise's voice was faint as the last of her stamina faded. "I thank you for coming here tonight to perform this service. I will keep you no longer than necessary."

"Take all the time you want, my child."

Marie-Louise turned back to Nathan. "Husband, I feel so tired. Please hold me while I go to sleep."

Sitting on the edge of the bed, Nathan wrapped his arms around Marie-Louise and clutched her to him. Her eyes closed. Her breathing became shallow, and she slumbered peacefully against his chest. Very gently, Nathan lowered her to the bed. Mathieson felt her pulse, finding it faint but steady. He looked at Nathan. "She could pass away at any moment. She could also linger through the night."

Nathan turned to the priest. *"Abbé?"*

The priest stepped forward to finish his task. Mathieson left the room, to wait outside. Antoine and Leonora, arms clasped comfortingly around each other, followed. Nathan waited, unsure whether to remain. He was Marie-Louise's husband, but he did not know whether he had any place in this religious ceremony that was so foreign to him. Oblivious to Nathan's presence, *Abbé* Francois continued with his work. Nathan left the room, to join those waiting outside.

Five minutes passed before the priest emerged from the room. "She is ready to meet God," he said simply.

Nathan led the way back into the bedroom. Marie-Louise lay exactly as he had left her, lips parted slightly, eyes closed in the waxy yellow face. Mathieson lifted her hand, nodding as the faint pulse registered. Antoine and Leonora stood by the bed. Nathan knelt on one knee, hands clasping the left hand of Marie-Louise on which he had so recently placed the ring. "Does anyone have the time?" he asked.

Mathieson checked his pocket watch. "Ten minutes of ten."

Nathan thanked the doctor and returned his full attention to Marie-Louise. Was it his imagination or was her face, so torn with the pain of fever these past days, more serene? Had the *Abbé*'s incantations brought peace to her body and her soul?

No one spoke. No one moved except for Dr. Mathieson, who, every few minutes, broke the stillness of the tableau to check Marie-Louise's pulse. Her breathing came even weaker now, barely disturbing the plane of her chest. Again, Nathan asked the time, surprised when Mathieson told him it was eleven twenty-five.

At ten minutes before midnight, Marie-Louise's pulse was so faint that Mathieson had difficulty finding it. He passed a mirror over her mouth, showing the trace of condensation on the silvered glass to those around the bed as if it were a trophy. He repeated the performance five minutes later, and again at midnight. When he passed the mirror across Marie-Louise's mouth five minutes after midnight, it came away dry. A huge gulping sob escaped from Leonora before she buried her face in Antoine's shoulder. Antoine held her tightly, his own face turned away from the bed so that others would not see the rapid movement of his eyelids as he fought in vain to blink back tears.

Nathan saw none of it. He knew nothing of anyone else's grief, for the instant Mathieson showed the dry mirror he had dropped his head onto Marie-Louise's peaceful body and wept.

Chapter Thirteen

Other than that single moment of anguish on seeing the absence of breath on the mirror, Nathan succeeded in checking his emotions. Much needed to be done before he could afford himself the luxury of open grief.

Antoine was not so adept at suppressing feelings. He wept copiously after his sister's death, finding his only solace in a bottle of Madeira. Once, when Nathan suggested that he go to bed, Antoine turned on his friend, demanding to know why Nathan, unlike himself, was not smitten by grief. "Are you bereft of tears already for my sister? Is that how much you loved her? And you . . ." He turned on Leonora, whose tears had also ceased. "Did you love her so little as well that you can stand dry-eyed?"

"Leonora and I are dry-eyed not because of a lack of love for Marie-Louise but because we have had more experience than you at coping with such devastating tragedies."

After finishing the Madeira, Antoine passed out. Nathan carried him to his room and set him down on the bed. Antoine's eyes flickered open. Recognizing Nathan, he apologized. "Grief causes a man to act strangely, my friend. Please forgive me."

"There is nothing to forgive."

Antoine's eyelids dropped, and he fell asleep again. Nathan left the room and closed the door. He needed sleep as well. It was almost three o'clock. The new day, when Marie-Louise would be laid to rest alongside her father and mother, would be as exacting as the night had been.

While Leonora slept in the room which had been Jean-Pierre's, Nathan slumbered on a sofa in the parlor overlooking the courtyard. He slept until eight-thirty, when noise from the courtyard awakened him. He looked out of the window to see two men carrying a burnished casket. Simultaneously, Rosa entered the parlor with the news that the undertakers, alerted by Dr. Mathieson, had arrived.

"I will take care of them," Nathan said. "Arouse *Monsieur* Antoine and *Mademoiselle* Leonora." He led the undertakers to Marie-Louise's room. Instead of entering the room with them, he waited outside. He wanted to carry through life the picture of Marie-Louise he remembered from their first meeting, and he feared that if he looked upon her now he would bear forever the image of death.

"*Monsieur* Nathan . . . !" Rosa hurried toward him, her dark, lined face alive with panic. "I have awakened your cousin, but I cannot find *Monsieur* Antoine."

"What?" Nathan strode past Rosa to Antoine's room. The bed was rumpled, proof that Antoine had slept in it, but there was no sign of the young man. "He is nowhere in the house?"

"I have not seen him, and I rose at five."

"Have the other servants search every room for him."

The search ended with no sign of Antoine. As Rosa reported the results to Nathan, Leonora emerged from the room in which she had slept. When Nathan told her that Antoine had disappeared, she did not seem overly perturbed.

"He is distraught, as we all are. He may have gone for a long walk to clear his mind. He may be visiting places which hold a special significance. He might even be at church. He will return soon."

By midday, when the undertakers prepared to leave for the cemetery, Antoine had not returned. Nathan ordered the men to wait. An hour passed, then another, and still Antoine did not appear. At last, Nathan had no choice but to allow the funeral to proceed. Leonora did not accompany him. She returned to Waverley to inform Anna and Miriam of Marie-Louise's death. All the way to the cemetery, Nathan expected to see Antoine. He could not understand his friend's absence. No brother and sister had been closer than Antoine and Marie-Louise.

The cemetery was less crowded than it had been. The number of yellow-fever deaths had fallen the previous week to only forty, and that morning the New Orleans board of health had declared that the disease no longer existed as an epidemic in the city. Such statistics were small comfort for those who buried their dead today. Nathan stood silently as *Abbé* Francois chanted the litany that accompanied the placing of Marie-Louise's casket beside those of her mother and father in the aboveground vault. Even after hours of instruction, the prayers meant little to Nathan. Before the vault was closed, he stepped up to place a red rose on Marie-Louise's casket. "Thank you," he whispered.

He returned to the Vanson home to find Anna and Miriam waiting for him. Anna gave him a tight hug. "Nathan, I cannot tell you how sorry I am."

He found comfort in the older woman's touch. She and Miriam had surmounted their own grief in order to help him. How could he fail to be fortified by such friendship?

Miriam took her mother's place in his arms. Tears from her eyes transferred themselves to Nathan's cheeks. He recalled what he had told Marie-Louise, and he repeated the sentiment to Miriam. "Do not cry for me. I have already enjoyed more happiness than most men can expect."

"Nathan, would you prefer to mourn for your wife here or at Waverley?" Anna asked.

"In this house, where the memories are strongest," Nathan answered. "Also, we must remain here for when Antoine returns." He turned to his cousin. Her face was pale and gaunt; puffy shadows filled the space beneath her eyes. Seeking to reassure her, he returned her own words of encouragement. "Antoine will return soon, you will see."

Leonora nodded, but she no longer believed it. Unable to cope with the death of his adored sister, Antoine had run away. Even now, he could be on a boat traveling upriver toward Natchez and St. Louis. Would he ever return to New Orleans? Did the love he had professed for Leonora mean anything? Would she ever see him again? Or would her memories, like Nathan's, be of a few short happy months before tragedy swept everything aside?

Anna and Miriam stayed for the remainder of the day and into the evening. At dinner, the memories were particularly poignant for Nathan. He saw the spirit of Marie-Louise in a dozen different instances, sitting in a chair opposite, laughing at a joke, sharing with wide eyes the latest piece of spicy gossip. As they finished the meal, Rosa entered the dining room to tell Nathan he had a visitor in the courtyard. Mystified, he got up from the table and went outside. Leonora also left the table, to look through the window, but she was unable to recognize the shadowy figure talking to Nathan.

Nathan knew the man, though. It was Georges Mercier, owner of the gambling club on Chartres. "I regret to be the bearer of sad tidings, *Monsieur* Solomon, particularly so after your recent misfortune."

"Antoine?"

"He arrived at my club early this afternoon, behaving like a man possessed by the devil. His clothes were torn and dirty, his hair was unkempt, his eyes wild. One man told me that by midday he had already fought two duels, killing one adversary and wounding another he accused of insulting him."

Nathan closed his eyes in pain. Mercier continued. "I tried to make him leave, to return home, but he insisted on playing cards. He challenged three men, one after the other, accused them of trying to cheat him. Two accommodated him immediately, in the courtyard. One quit when Antoine's sword pierced his arm. The second was run through the heart."

"And the third?"

"The third was not a Creole. He was an American. Instead

of selecting the *colichemarde,* he chose double-barreled shotguns. Obviously, it was not a duel to be fought in my courtyard. They went there and then to The Dueling Oaks. The American, far more proficient with firearms, killed Antoine."

"Where is the body now?"

"Outside, in a carriage. It lies already in a casket because I do not believe it is something you would wish to see. You would do better to remember your friend as he was."

"Thank you."

Leaving Mercier in the courtyard, Nathan returned to the house to tell Leonora as gently as possible that Antoine, unable to bear the loss of his sister, had taken his own life by shooting himself in the head.

Antoine was interred early the next morning. Leonora insisted on accompanying Nathan to the cemetery. He had not wanted her to do so. On learning of Antoine's death, she had broken down and cried for fully thirty minutes, her body shaking like someone in the grip of the fever. Nathan worried that the sight of Antoine's coffin being placed beside those of his parents and his sister would prove too much for Leonora to bear.

During the journey to the cemetery, Leonora did not say a single word. She sat in the carriage, face white and devoid of all expression. At the cemetery, she held Nathan's hand. The service seemed interminable as though *Abbé* Francois was intent on compensating for the time restrictions placed upon him by the sheer volume of funerals he had supervised during the epidemic. Now that interments were the exception and not the rule, he could take his time and linger lovingly over every Latin word. As the service progressed at a snail's pace, Leonora clutched Nathan's hand even more fiercely. She felt herself adrift in a sea of raging emotion. Nathan represented her only lifeline. If she let go, she would be swept under and lost forever.

At last, the *Abbé* finished. He turned to the two mourners, asking if they wished to add anything. Nathan shook his head.

Marie-Louise's burial the previous day had drained him. He had no grief left, no words to say. Leonora released her cousin's hand and stepped forward to stand in front of the open vault. Nathan watched, curious how she intended to bid Antoine farewell.

In a quiet, tremulous voice, Leonora began to recite the psalm Gershon Lowensohn had said at the shipboard service for little Frances Meagher. The Hundred and twenty-first Psalm. *Abbé* Francois's eyes opened wide, first in astonishment, then in disapproval as he understood that the time spent tutoring these English cousins had been completely wasted. The words Leonora used were not those of Gershon Lowensohn aboard *The Wandering Jew.* She recited the psalm as she had remembered it from London. In Hebrew. When she finished, she cast a final glance at the open vault before turning away and walking toward the carriage.

The carriage went not to Esplanade but to Waverley. Antoine's death had caused Nathan to change his earlier decision to mourn for Marie-Louise in the Vanson home. Neither he nor Leonora had the resolve to enter that house again. At least, not now. Later, in a week or so, when feelings had settled, they might be able to face the ghosts that waited there. For the time being, the staff would maintain the house.

For much of the journey to the Garden District, Leonora said nothing. She sat silently, as she had done during the ride out to the cemetery. Only when the carriage rolled along Calliope toward the junction with Prytania Street did Nathan try to draw her out. "You made the *Abbé*'s hair stand on end when you recited that psalm, Lally. I thought he was going to drop dead with a heart attack. We would not have had far to carry him, would we?"

Nathan's bleak humor worked. A weak smile crossed Leonora's pale face. "I had to say something in farewell to dear Antoine, but everything the *Abbé* taught me flew from my mind like leaves before the wind. All I could think of was the Hundred and twenty-first Psalm, and the only language I could say it in was Hebrew. Do you know why, Nathan?" She turned in the seat to face him. When he shook his head, she said, "You cannot escape from what you are, Nathan. We were foolish to even try."

"We are people, Lally. Human beings. We were not trying to escape from that."

"We turned our backs on what we were. We rejected our birthright because we wanted to be something else. Sometimes . . ." Leonora's voice faltered; her eyes turned misty. "Sometimes I wonder if all that has happened is not some kind of punishment."

Nathan fell silent. In her grief, Leonora was using a logic that defied any argument.

During the following days, while the cousins mourned their loss at Waverley, Leonora continued to seek comfort in her past. On Friday evening, she asked Anna Lowensohn for candles. Anna and Miriam watched curiously as Leonora lit the candles while reciting from memory prayers she recalled Harriet Solomon saying in London. Nathan also watched, experiencing his own confusing mix of memories. He wondered what Marie-Louise would have made of this ancient observance. Would she have been as perplexed as *Abbé* Francois? As horrified? He doubted it. Marie-Louise had been above such destructive prejudices. So had her brother.

The very next morning, Nathan came down to find that Leonora had already left the house. She returned after midday, having spent the morning with the Dispersed of Judah congregation which worshipped in the former Episcopalian church on the corner of Canal and Bourbon streets. Nathan did not need to be told where she had been. He could tell from the serenity in her dark brown eyes. Leonora was finding relief from her heartache in the embrace of old traditions.

Ten days passed before they gathered the courage to have Samson drive them to the Vanson home. The door was opened by an ashen-faced man whose body bent to one side like a twisted tree. He walked with the aid of a heavy cane. Assuming he was the lawyer managing the Vanson estate, Nathan addressed him courteously. *"Monsieur,* I am Nathan Solomon and this is my cousin, Leonora. We are part of the Vanson family. For a tragically short time, Marie-Louise Vanson was my wife."

The man's response was explosive. "Hell will freeze over before I consider you a part of my family!"

Nathan stared hard. A likeness did exist, not to Antoine or Marie-Louise, but to Marcel. The fleshy nose, the glowering, dark eyes. Was this sick-looking man Alphonse? Had he decided after all to come from Paris? Why was he so antagonistic?

"Is the Hebrew prince's memory so short that he fails to recognize me?"

Nathan gasped. It was Marcel! He had not seen Antoine's brother for almost a year, since New Year's Day when he had seconded Raymonde Perrault. How could a man change so much in so short a time? Had grief wrought this transformation? Had tragedy wiped the color from Marcel's face, turned his robust body lame? Then Nathan recalled the other duel that had taken place beneath The Oaks that day. Antoine, in settling his long-standing feud with Marcel, had left his brother a cripple.

"Why do you come here? My family has already paid heavily for its obsession with you."

"My cousin and I seek mementoes of the happiness we knew within these walls."

"Nothing within these walls belongs to you. It is all mine."

Nathan paid no attention; this bully no longer held any fear for him. Taking Leonora by the hand, he pushed past Marcel and entered the house. First, Nathan went to Marie-Louise's room. The emerald bracelet he had given to her the previous Christmas rested in a jewelry box. He pocketed it. In Antoine's room, Leonora found the initialed gold ring that had been her gift. The last room they visited was the parlor overlooking the courtyard. Nathan remembered vividly his first visit to this room, when Antoine had invited him for dinner. Nothing had changed. The furniture stood where it had always stood. The same horde of tiny ornaments covered the tables; the same paintings decorated the walls. For a moment, Nathan stood in front of the Jacques Amans portrait of Madame Mathilde Vanson. Had Marie-Louise lived, would she have looked like this in twenty or thirty years? In 1873 or 1883? Feeling cheated, he turned away and crossed the parlor to the other Amans portrait, that of Marie-Louise painted before she left New Orleans for her year in Paris. He would always treasure the copy given to him the previous Christmas by Marie-Louise, but he wanted the original as well. When he gazed at that, he could picture Amans straining every fiber of his artistic genius to capture such incredible beauty on canvas. He turned to Marcel.

"Do you object to me taking this portrait of my wife?"

When Marcel shook his head, Nathan stood on tiptoe to remove the painting from the wall. "Thank you. We are ready to leave."

Marcel followed the cousins to the door. As he stepped outside, Nathan turned around, unable to resist a final dart at the man who had gone to such lengths—even bloodshed—to block his romance with Marie-Louise. *"Au revoir, mon beau frère."*

Marcel bristled. Color flooded dangerously across the ashen face. Nathan hoped Marcel would take offense at being called "brother-in-law." He would be more than happy to offer him satisfaction and finish the work his friend Antoine had started. The flush of color disappeared as quickly as it had arisen. Marcel closed the door firmly behind Nathan and Leonora.

"Did you really expect him to rise to your bait?" Leonora asked as she climbed into the carriage. She held the Amans portrait as Nathan pulled himself into the vehicle.

"No. Antoine was right when he said that no one will ever challenge the man who ended Raymonde Perrault's career." As the carriage began to move, Nathan turned around to look at the house where he had met Marie-Louise and where he had watched her die. Leonora followed suit. Her memories of this house were as poignant as his own.

"Lally . . ." Nathan saw she was looking at the initialed gold ring she had taken from Antoine's room. "I have a question for you, and I want you to think very carefully before you answer."

Her hand closed around the ring. "Ask me your question."

"Would you want to return to England?"

Her answer came immediately. "To do that, after all we have endured in New Orleans, would be a betrayal. Of ourselves and of those dear to us. Even with the heartbreak, what we have here is more important and more satisfying than anything we had in England. Why do you think I would even consider such an idea?"

"I have watched you search the past to find comfort."

"Lighting Sabbath candles? Attending a Sabbath service? Do you call that searching the past? No, Nathan. That is accepting my heritage."

Nathan clasped his cousin's hands. "Lally, do you still believe that what we lost could be some kind of punishment?"

"No, Nathan, I do not. But never again will I ignore what I am. Never again will I pretend to be something I am not." She sat back, staring through the window as the carriage crossed Canal Street. Nathan looked through the other window, toward the Mississippi. During the past year, they had crossed Canal Street many times, but this time they were doing more than leaving the French Quarter and entering the American section. They were drawing the curtain upon a chapter of their lives that had promised so much happiness and had delivered only sorrow.

Part Two

1857–1865

Chapter Fourteen

A soft breeze fanned the two candles on the sideboard, causing the flames to dance and send wild shadows flickering across the walls of the dining room at Waverley. Rebecca quickly closed the window that admitted the draft. Turning to the five people seated at the long table, the housekeeper shook her head and said, "Don't want to bring down bad spirits by having the wind blow out them candles, do we?"

"No, Rebecca, we most certainly do not want that," Anna answered, amusement momentarily brightening her somber brown eyes. She waited for the large Negro woman to leave the room before saying, "Poor Rebecca. Ever since we started lighting candles on Friday night, she worries about them being blown out."

Leonora appeared perplexed. "Where did she ever get the idea that misfortune would occur if the candles were extinguished?"

Before Anna, Miriam, or Nathan could think of an answer, Marcus Barnett, the fifth person at the table, supplied one. "Somewhere in her tribal history must reside the fear that the doused flame of a torch courts bad luck."

"I do not think I have ever heard of such a fear," said Miriam, who sat on Marcus Barnett's right.

"There are probably a million Negro fears we know nothing about," Marcus replied. He chuckled dryly before adding, "Do you not find it odd that no matter what civilizing influences they are exposed to in this country, slaves are incapable of ridding themselves of the ignorant superstitions of Africa? You only have to see them dance in Congo Square to understand that."

"Mister Barnett, Rebecca is not a slave." The words flew like darts from Nathan's lips. Five and a half years in New Orleans had done little to alter his speech, and the reprimand was delivered with the crispness of a barrister making his point in an English law court. "She is a free woman of color who works at Waverley because she chooses to do so, just as Delilah, Naomi, Bathsheba, and Samson do. They are members of this household, not slaves. Kindly remember that."

Marcus Barnett's swarthy face darkened even more. Above a sharp, aquiline nose, black eyes gleamed with a sudden fire. Recovering his composure quickly, he tried to make light of the rebuke by saying, "Occasionally I find it difficult to separate my business dealings from my social engagements."

"Then I suggest you make an extra effort to rectify that shortcoming." Nathan disliked the tall young man who had called on Miriam for the past two months. Despite his greatest efforts to hide his feelings, that disdain sometimes became evident.

"Forgive me." Although Marcus addressed the apology to everyone at the table, he looked at Miriam as if only her absolution mattered. "Believe me, I would do nothing to jeopardize my welcome in this house."

Miriam's response was a warm smile. Nathan nodded stiffly, and the awkward moment evaporated. Naomi entered the room carrying a large tray which she set on the sideboard. As she began to serve portions of baked red snapper, Nathan glanced around the dining room. His eyes focused on the chair at the head of the table. It was empty, as were three other chairs. Three and a half years had passed since yellow fever had devastated Waverley, but its victims were never forgotten for long. At every meal, empty chairs recalled Gershon, Henry, Martha, and Sarah. No one ever thought to sit on one of those chairs. They were reserved, painful monuments to precious lives that had been snuffed out so tragically.

Nathan needed no empty chair to recall his loss. The Jacques Amans portrait of Marie-Louise graced his bedroom wall, watching over him while he slept. It was the last thing he saw each night and the first object on which his eyes focused when he awoke. The copy, given to him on Christmas of 1852, hung in the countinghouse. If that were not enough, he had the emerald bracelet to look at and to hold. His time with Marie-Louise seemed so recent and, simultaneously, so long ago. Only last week he had dragged *Abbé* Francois from his supper to perform the wedding ceremony, yet a millennium had elapsed since that meeting beneath The Oaks with Raymonde Perrault. Despite the warm March evening, an icy finger caressed Nathan's spine as he recalled his twenty-first birthday. Would he ever again love so fiercely? Ever again find a woman he could want with a passion strong enough to kill?

At twenty-five, Nathan knew he was vastly different from the rash young man who had challenged Perrault. Twin patches of gray, appearing less than a month after Marie-Louise's passing, streaked the light brown hair at his temples. Faint lines crept out from the corners of his eyes; deeper passages arced from his nose to the corners of his mouth. The fine scars left by Perrault's *colichemarde* remained as thin white lines. In 1853, he had been impetuous. Now he was a mature man who acted only after careful thought. Grief and hard work had wrought the change. Grief over Marie-Louise, and the hard work with which he had stifled that grief. Supporting the family who had sustained him and Leonora when they arrived in New Orleans filled his hours. When not at the levee or countinghouse, he visited clients' plantations. He was the man of Waverley now, responsible for the well-being of those who lived within its walls. Though not related by blood, he was Gershon's successor, and he was convinced that if Gershon's soul ever elected to fill the empty seat it would be most satisfied with what it saw.

As Naomi finished serving, Rebecca returned to the dining

room. Leonora, still intrigued by the housekeeper's concern about candles, questioned her on it. Rebecca answered simply. "Those are holy candles, Miss Leonora. They light God's way to this house on the Sabbath so we can thank Him for the blessings He's given us. If we let holy candles go out before they're ready to go out, maybe before the good Lord's even had a chance to visit our home, we're opening the door for the devil himself."

"So much for tribal fears," Nathan murmured caustically.

"I said quite possibly," Marcus Barnett protested. "I never claimed it was certain fact."

Leonora was touched by the housekeeper's philosophy. "That is a beautiful belief, Rebecca. I had never considered candles in that light."

Miriam burst out laughing. "Oh, Leonora, that is the worst pun ever uttered in this house!"

"I thought it was very good," Nathan said as his cousin's cheeks turned red. "Did you intend to make a pun, Lally? Or was it just a slip of the tongue?"

"A slip of the tongue." Leonora's blush yielded to a slightly flustered smile. "You know puns never come out the way they're supposed to when you think about them beforehand."

Nathan treasured Leonora's happy expression. Smiles danced across her face more readily these days, proof that she was fully recovered from the shock of Antoine's apparent suicide. In those dreadful months following the deaths of Marie-Louise and Antoine, Nathan had worried so much about his cousin that he often forgot his own sadness. Bouts of depression had led Leonora to withdraw into herself for long periods. A full year passed before this despondency lessened, and even then Leonora was far from the cheerful and optimistic girl Nathan had once known. Only when the passing of the second year coincided with a further improvement did he ultimately understand what was happening. Leonora was grieving for Antoine in Creole fashion, a year of full mourning followed by a year of half mourning.

Like her cousin, Leonora had also used work as a tool against sorrow. Six months after Antoine's death, she had visited the countinghouse on Canal Street to ask Nathan for tasks to fill her time. Giving her lists of insurance, storage, drayage, and wharfage expenses incurred by planters whom the firm represented, he told her to tally the different categories. He expected the chore to take at least an hour. Instead, Leonora returned the figures to him in half that time. Surprised, he had his chief clerk, a man called Tom Harris, double-check her count. Forty minutes later, Harris reported that the figures were correct. When Nathan asked Leonora why she had never divulged such an aptitude for figures before, she answered simply that no one had ever asked her to do so. In Ludgate Hill, Samuel Solomon had been interested only in her ability as a seamstress; he had not needed a clerk. From that day on, Leonora spent two or three days a week in the countinghouse, helping Harris cope with increasing bookkeeping chores.

If she found comfort in work, though, she discovered even greater peace in another area: the traditions of the past. The act of lighting Sabbath candles on the Friday evening following the deaths of Marie-Louise and Antoine was now a regular occurrence. So was attending the synagogue. At first, Leonora had gone alone, but within a month, Anna, and then Miriam, had taken to joining her. All three women professed to find harmony there, as though by communing with a higher power they could understand in some way the tragedies that had befallen them.

Because of the women's involvement with religious tradition, Waverley soon took on a spiritual air. Candles burned on festivals as well as the Sabbath. Jewish periodicals were mailed to the house, Jewish topics discussed. Even the servants knew the difference between Passover and the Day of Atonement. Nathan alone remained aloof from this spiritual rebirth. As a young boy coping with the loss of his parents, he had found few answers in prayer. As an adult emotionally scarred by more tragedy, he discovered no answers at all. Nor did his attitude to religion soften when he remembered that Miriam had met Marcus Barnett through the synagogue. Marcus's father, Isaac Barnett, a founder member of the congregation, had effected the introductions. He viewed the match as an economic alliance. The Lowensohns were successful cotton factors, and Isaac Barnett, who had come to New Orleans from Charleston in 1833, was a prominent trader in another valuable Southern commodity. Slaves.

Again, Nathan regarded the empty chair at the head of the table. What would Gershon Lowensohn have made of this resurgence of Jewish tradition? Would he have considered it a return to the fear and superstition that had trapped Jews behind ghetto walls for so many centuries? Or would he have seen it as the means to recover from tragedies too outrageous for the human mind to accept? Then Nathan wondered what Gershon would have thought of Marcus Barnett, the slave-dealer's son. Would he have welcomed Marcus to Waverley as a fine prospective son-in-law? Nathan did not think so. Gershon Lowensohn had never been duped easily, not by a dishonest planter who hid rocks in cotton bales to make them heavier, or an inappropriate suitor for his daughter's hand.

As dinner finished, conversation around the table turned to the recent presidential inauguration of the Democratic Party's James Buchanan, who had defeated the candidates of the populist American Party and the newly formed antislavery Republicans. The campaign had been bitter with Republicans demanding the repeal of the Kansas-Nebraska Act and opposing the extension of slavery into the new territories. Southern states had responded by vowing to leave the Union.

"I hope Buchanan remembers it was our threats to secede that won him office," Marcus stated. "The notion of some fifteen states pulling out of the Union terrified the rest of the country into voting sensibly."

"You mean voting for the Democrats," Miriam said.

Marcus gave a piercing laugh. "Now I ask you, was there any other sensible choice?"

"Before you laugh too hard," Nathan said, "you would do well to remember that John Frémont and the Republicans polled a surprisingly high number of votes for their first campaign. They might do a lot better in eighteen-sixty."

Marcus scoffed at the warning. "Then we *will* secede, and believe me, we will be more prosperous as a separate country outside the Union than we ever were as part of it. But I seriously doubt if such drastic measures will ever be needed."

"Why not?"

"Because of the Supreme Court's Dred-Scott ruling that a slave is property, and his master's ownership is constitutionally protected across the country. Even if a slave enters a free state, he remains his master's property." Marcus leaned back in the chair, hands clasped across the front of his gold-and-red silk vest. "We have been fighting a hard battle ever since the Stowe woman wrote that libelous garbage, *Uncle Tom's Cabin*. With Dred-Scott, the pendulum finally appears to be swinging back in our favor."

"For libelous garbage, *Uncle Tom's Cabin* achieved a truly remarkable popularity," Leonora pointed out.

Marcus dismissed Leonora's claim by saying, "Abolitionists and black Republicans bought the book by the dozen to give to their friends for Christmas. Sometimes"—he gave his sharp laugh again—"I believe you and your cousin must be abolitionists."

Nathan stiffened as he recalled a scene from the shop on Ludgate Hill, standing over a bolt of cloth while his cousin Alfred accused him of being a Chartist. "Do you always find it necessary to label people who disagree with your point of view?"

"I give labels only when they fit. Tell me, Nathan, if secession occurred, where would you stand? With us? Or with the Yankees?" Marcus waited ten seconds for a reply, aware that the eyes of Anna, Miriam, and Leonora were on Nathan. "You cannot give me your answer, can you? Never mind, we all know what it is. You are an abolitionist because you do not support the platform on which the wealth of the South is based."

At last, Nathan found his voice. "*Your* wealth! *Your* wealth and your *father's* wealth, not the wealth of the South!" He knew he was violating the cardinal rule he had learned from Gershon Lowensohn, that of never criticizing men who owned slaves. But Marcus Barnett and his father Isaac were different. They did more than own slaves, they traded them for profit like farmers selling livestock. "Slavery is an aberration, Marcus, it has no place in this country or in any other country—"

"But it is here! And we will fight to make certain it remains, because it is part of our way of life. Slavery is the cornerstone of our economy."

"Tying up millions of dollars in human property is the cornerstone of stupidity. That money could be used for land improvement and other investments to help the South keep up with the rest of the country instead of falling far behind it." Nathan paused to draw breath. "Slavery will die, Marcus. I pray that common sense and the goodwill of decent men, not force of arms, will be the cause, but slavery *will* die. When that occurs, planters will find that they are no worse off. Their earth will be as bountiful as ever. They will continue to grow cotton and sugar and rice, but instead of investing huge sums of money to buy, feed, and house slaves, they will pay wages to workers. The only group of people hurt will be those who deal in this human traffic." Nathan's mouth curled up at the corners. "Is that why you so despise the thought of abolition, Marcus, because it will close your father's lucrative business? Is that why you are such a fire-eater, with your constant threats of secession?"

When Marcus swallowed hard, Nathan knew he had scored a point. He fully believed his own conviction that little would change if slavery ended. The South's major products would remain in demand. Cotton would still be king. But those, like the Barnetts, who made a living out of slavery would have to find new work. They had the most to lose, and Nathan did not feel the slightest sympathy for them.

Miriam rose to Marcus's defense. "How dare you treat my guest so rudely in my home?" she demanded of Nathan. "I insist you apologize to Marcus immediately!"

"I did not realize that honesty could be so easily confused with rudeness, Miriam. Please excuse my candor." A smile softened Nathan's words. He understood Miriam's feelings. After suffering the loss of her father, brother, and two sisters, she had found some happiness with Marcus. Even Nathan had to admit that he was a personable enough young man, attractive, and attentive to Miriam. Perhaps she even loved him, or thought she did, and she feared that Nathan's hostility might drive him away.

Silence followed Nathan's words. Anna, who had listened to the argument uncomfortably, capitalized on the momentary break to suggest they leave the dining table and adjourn to the parlor. Nathan and Leonora followed. Marcus declined, saying he and Miriam wished to enjoy the balmy March evening with a ride. Miriam concurred, leaving little doubt that they both preferred a carriage ride to remaining in Nathan's company. In the rear parlor, Nathan apologized to Anna.

"I regret spoiling dinner by arguing with Marcus, but his views leave me with little choice."

"He is young. Like many young people his views are extreme."

"He is just three months younger than me. It is not his age that fashions him so, but his background."

"I never understood," Leonora said, "how a man such as his father, a deeply religious man, could be a slave dealer. How many times each year is reference made in prayer to the Children of Israel's bondage in the land of Egypt? Surely, that memory should be hateful enough to make any one of us abhor slavery, yet Isaac Barnett prospers by it."

Anna smiled at Leonora's confusion. She had spent more time in America than the young Englishwoman, and better understood the divergent rationalizations of the slavery dispute. "Some rabbis preach that the Bible favors the custom of slavery. They claim Negroes are the descendants of Ham, and therefore the curse of Noah is applicable to them. Those are the rabbis heeded by religious men such as Isaac Barnett. Then there are rabbis who preach against slavery by saying that the Biblical image of a slave is not what is seen in the South, but a person in whom the dignity of human nature is respected. Those are the rabbis religious abolitionists heed. Our peculiar institution has succeeded in dividing the clergy as it divides everyone else."

Leonora nodded in understanding, but Nathan shook his head. Anna's explanation only cemented his feelings about religion. God's word could be made to mean anything a zealot wanted it to mean! "People like Marcus with their extreme views frighten me. Can he and his fellow fire-eaters not see that secession would destroy our trade with the Upper Mississippi Valley, the trade on which New Orleans depends so heavily?"

"They do not care," Anna said. "Their honor, their right to live as they wish, is more important to them."

"The future frightens me," Nathan confessed. "I see fanatics lining up like warring armies, Southern fire-eaters and Northern abolitionists who will succeed in tearing this country apart."

Leonora studied her cousin intently. "If that day should ever come, which side would you take?" She had posed the same question as Marcus, one which Nathan always avoided asking himself. It made him uncomfortable to even think about it. He sat silently for several seconds, just as he had done earlier.

"Nathan . . . ?" This time Anna asked the question. "Which side would you favor?"

Nathan sighed. "In less than six years, I have experienced more life in New Orleans than in twenty years in London. As much as I abhor the extreme views of the fire-eaters, their home is the same as mine. I would have to ally myself with them."

* * *

Miriam ignored Nathan for the entire weekend, turning her head away whenever they met. Her conduct reminded him of the time she had learned of his romantic interest in Marie-Louise. Instead of being irritated by such behavior, Nathan was amused. He found the golden-haired girl's anger and obstinacy appealing, a challenge to make her acknowledge him. If they passed in the house, he complimented her on the clothes she wore. When they sat at the table, Nathan found reasons to speak to her, whether it was to ask her to pass something, or to seek her opinion on an item of food. Each time, Miriam met his probe with silence, making it pointedly clear that she wanted nothing whatever to do with him.

On Sunday, Marcus Barnett came to Waverley to take Miriam for a ride. As Miriam settled into the front seat beside Marcus, Nathan stepped down from the front porch and walked around to the other side of their phaeton. His manner toward Marcus was as congenial as it had been hostile two days before. "You have chosen a fine day for your drive. Would you mind if I availed myself of the back seat?"

Miriam turned away to stare at the porch, where Leonora watched from the comfort of a wicker sofa. Marcus, though, was taken in by Nathan's apparent change of attitude. "I see no reason why you should not," he replied.

Nathan smiled. "Before committing yourself, should you not ask Miriam whether she minds my company?"

At the use of her name, Miriam swung around in the seat. Instead of chiding Nathan, she assailed Marcus. "How can you talk to him after he treated you so rudely on Friday night? Do you not see what he is doing? He is mocking you!" She snatched the reins from Marcus and slapped them across the horse's back. The phaeton jerked forward before settling down to a steady pace.

"Have a wonderful time!" Nathan called out as the phaeton reached the gate, Miriam glared over her shoulder. Nathan chuckled. He was succeeding. That grimace full of fury was the closest Miriam had come to acknowledging him since Friday.

"Why do you tease Miriam so?" Leonora asked as Nathan climbed the stairs to the porch.

"Because it makes her even angrier than she is already, and I think Miriam is at her most attractive when she is very angry."

Leonora gazed speculatively at her cousin as he sat next to her on the wicker sofa. Was what she had once envisioned finally happening? Had Nathan, at last, taken notice of Miriam in the way Leonora had always known he would? No longer was Miriam a spoiled and precocious child. Nearing twenty, she was a woman who turned heads wherever she went. "You will have many more opportunities to witness that pleasing anger if you continue to treat Marcus as you did the other night."

"Marcus!" Nathan repeated the name disparagingly. "That slave-dealer's son is beneath her. Miriam can do much better than him."

"You have no business involving yourself in Miriam's affairs. Whom she sees has nothing to do with you."

"I disagree. Because of a cruel twist of fate, all that happens here has everything to do with me." When Leonora giggled, Nathan looked pained and asked what she found so funny.

"England is thousands of miles away, Nathan, yet I swear I just heard the dignified voice of our Uncle Samuel." Leonora's mirth proved too volatile to hold. She fell back on the sofa, clutching her sides as laughter turned her face bright red.

For the rest of the day, Leonora teased Nathan by calling him "Uncle Samuel." He took it good-naturedly because her humor contained no malice. Leonora understood that the welfare of Waverley's residents was foremost in his mind, but she would always be ready to remind her cousin not to take himself too seriously. The knowledge that such a safety valve existed pleased him.

Next morning, they traveled together to Canal Street. Samson, who now filled the role of coachman as well as gardener, drove the carriage. At the countinghouse, Leonora worked on updating the account of a planter named James Wilson, who was expected at midday. Nathan spent three hours at the wharf, supervising the unloading and transportation to the presses of cotton bales belonging to his clients. The hectic period was over. Business was slow now, down to a trickle which would peter out in some eight weeks' time when the season's final shipments reached New Orleans.

He returned to the countinghouse just before noon to find James Wilson waiting. A tall, fair-haired man with sharp blue eyes set in a square and bony face, Wilson owned Fallowfields, a three thousand-acre plantation on the Red River on which he grew cotton and tobacco. For eight years, he had been a client of Gershon Lowensohn. Following Gershon's death, he was the first planter to agree to continue working with Nathan.

After greeting the planter, Nathan said he would have the accounts brought in immediately. Wilson held up a calloused hand. "Hold up there. I need time to get my breath back first. Millicent has just about run my feet clean off me!"

"When did you arrive?"

"Friday afternoon. Every minute since then, I've been sitting through plays and operas that Millicent cannot possibly leave New Orleans without seeing. And when I tell her I would like some time to myself"—he gave Nathan a broad wink—"to try my luck at the tables, I learn she has a shopping expedition all planned out for me."

Nathan smiled sympathetically. James Wilson's wife Millicent was no different from any other planter's wife. The plantation's own social life—the visits to neighbors, the banquets and the balls—fell a long way short of what the Crescent City offered. To many plantation families, the voyage to New Orleans aboard a riverboat was tantamount to being released from prison. "Are you accompanied on this trip by your daughters?"

"Of course." Wilson had two daughters, seventeen-year-old Angelina, and Sally, a year younger. "Once Millicent has done with her own shopping, it will be the turn of the girls. I'll be lucky if I get to go home with a new hat!"

"I think we can help you pay for all these extravagances." Nathan called for Leonora. When she brought in Wilson's account, Nathan sat down at the desk and started to go over the figures. Wilson paid close attention. During the season, Nathan had sold four thousand bales of Wilson's cotton for forty thousand dollars. From that he deducted the factor's commission of one thousand dollars, as well as expenses incurred in processing the cotton. Wilson's net was almost thirty-seven thousand dollars, a sum with which he expressed satisfaction.

"I will remain at the Saint Charles with Millicent and my daughters until Friday morning," the planter told Nathan once their business was over. "I would be grateful if you could perform one more service for me before I leave."

"Certainly."

"Our cook is growing old. The kitchen is too much for her to handle on her own. I realize this is short notice, but could you find me a replacement who could accompany us back to Fallowfields on Friday? I will pay a thousand dollars or more."

"I will do my best to have a new cook waiting for you on the morning you sail." Working as a cotton factor necessitated Nathan's occasional presence at slave auctions to purchase field hands and house servants for those planters he represented. It was a task he loathed. He always returned from the auctions dejected by even such brief contact with the traffic in human flesh. He confided to Leonora that he only bothered to bid successfully when he knew the planter for whom he acted treated his slaves well. If he harbored doubts, he deliberately allowed his offers to be outbid. James Wilson was one of those for whom he bid effectively. He cared for the hundred slaves he owned. Despite laws to the contrary, all of his house servants could read and write. So could many of his field hands, who lived in whitewashed log cabins where they had organized their own family structures. Wilson paid bonuses to those who worked hard, gave everyone a week off at Christmas, supplied whiskey for regular dances, and always made certain adequate food and medical treatment were available. Nothing would ever alter Nathan's belief that slavery was wrong, but the Fallowfields slaves were certainly better off than most Yankee millworkers or those *free* men and women who worked for English shopkeepers.

"Thank you, Nathan. Perhaps you and your cousin will be our guests for dinner on Thursday night," Wilson said as he prepared to leave.

"We would be delighted." Nathan shook Wilson's hand at the door and closed it behind him.

Nathan set about fulfilling Wilson's wish immediately. He sent Tom Harris, his chief clerk, to seek a cook among the hundreds of slaves held in the dealers' depots surrounding the St. Charles Hotel. Two hours later, Harris returned to say he had found half a dozen women described as cooks. Nathan asked about references. For James Wilson, he wanted a cook with sparkling credentials.

"Only one woman has notable references," Harris answered. "Her name is Mary, and she cooked for a rice planter in Georgia. The planter fell on bad times and had to sell his slaves, so she was brought down here."

Nathan understood. Slaves fetched a far higher price in the fertile Gulf states than they did farther north. New Orleans dealers regularly traveled to the mid-Atlantic states to buy slaves they could sell for a huge profit in the deep South. "When will this Mary be sold?"

"Midday on Thursday, at Banks Arcade." Harris handed Nathan a poster. Printed at the top in large block letters was the message: VALUABLE GANG OF HEALTHY NEGROES. Beneath was a description of the Negroes—men and women, field hands and house servants—followed by the time, date, and place of the sale.

At the very bottom of the poster, below the words SALE POSITIVE AND WITHOUT RESERVE. TERMS CASH. was the name of the auctioneer. ISAAC BARNETT.

Banks Arcade was a block-long, three-story brick building on Magazine Street. The glass-covered arcade, from which the building claimed its name, ran down the center of the building between Gravier and Natchez streets. The auction block was set up in the middle of the arcade, where the midday sun highlighted it like a heavenly ray shining down on a sacred altar. Standing off to one side, under the supervision of Marcus Barnett, were the slaves who waited to be sold. The men sported high hats and tailcoats supplied for the occasion by Isaac Barnett. The women wore cheerfully colored dresses made of calico. Two boys no older than ten wore shirts and long pants tucked into high socks.

Nathan arrived at five minutes to twelve to find some fifty men and a handful of women waiting for the sale to begin. Isaac Barnett had a reputation for bringing quality merchandise to the auction block. Despite that high standing, Nathan had never bought slaves from Marcus Barnett's father. Until the previous Friday night, when Leonora had admitted her feelings of confusion to Anna, he had never fully understood why. Now he did, and all because of the Children of Israel. No descendant of those Israelites who had endured slavery in Egypt had any business trading in human flesh. Today Nathan had no choice. He needed to keep James Wilson happy. If Wilson were to take a new cook back to Fallowfields, only one slave dealer could fill the need.

Promptly at twelve o'clock, Isaac Barnett mounted the block to stand in the sun's rays. He was a short, stocky man with thick white hair, bristling sideburns, a red face and blue eyes that twinkled with a welcome for his customers. "Ladies and gentlemen, I promise you will not be disappointed with the twelve Negroes I have to offer you today. First, we have John, a strong, young field hand who gathers as much cotton as any two other men. Marcus, send John up here so we can all see how fine a specimen he is."

Marcus Barnett prodded one man with a coiled blacksnake whip and pointed toward the block. Obediently the Negro ascended the steps. Somber-faced, he stood well over six feet tall, with a powerful chest and shoulders that threatened to split his borrowed coat. Isaac Barnett was dwarfed but not intimidated. "Do I have an opening bid of one thousand dollars?" When no such bid was immediately forthcoming, he harangued the crowd. "You all have had the opportunity to inspect John. You know as well as I do that he is a good, hard-working nigger who will repay your investment a hundred times over."

The man in front of Nathan raised a hand. "Seven hundred and fifty." Instantly, another hand shot up. Eight hundred was heard. Two more offers quickly took the price up to the one thousand dollars for which Isaac had first asked. He stood smugly on the platform, waiting for bidding to go even higher. Even John, the slave being auctioned, appeared to take an interest in the proceedings. As the bidding reached twelve hundred and fifty dollars, the solemn black face smiled with quiet pride at the price he commanded.

Nathan had deliberately timed his arrival to coincide with the beginning of the auction. The inspections that occurred before the sale sickened him. When he sought slaves for his planters, he never made such inspections. He considered it demeaning. He had a simpler and more efficient way of ensuring that he bought only the best. He made certain the dealer knew that he represented several planters, all of whom from time to time purchased slaves. Should he ever feel cheated, he would never patronize that dealer again.

John was sold for fifteen hundred dollars to the owner of a sugar plantation on Bayou Lafourche. Isaac closed the deal with a lusty "Give the lucky man his merchandise, Marcus!" The planter stepped up to the block to pay Marcus and receive John's ownership papers. Isaac never touched money at the sales. As the founder of the business, he considered himself above such coarse matters.

The next three sales passed quickly—two field hands who brought more than a thousand dollars each, and a housekeeper who went for seven hundred and fifty. An older Negro woman who stood lethargically on the platform attracted little interest. When one man shouted out to ask if she was sick, the woman nodded her head. Marcus prodded her with his whip. "Give her a taste or two of the cowhide and she'll brighten up real quick," he assured the crowd. The woman went for three hundred dollars. Then followed a lengthy bidding contest for two beautiful mulatto girls who were eventually sold for two thousand dollars each.

Isaac Barnett rubbed his hands as the girls were led away by their new owners. "Those were a delight for the eyes, but now we come to a delight for the stomach. Marcus, send Mary up here."

Marcus returned to the diminishing group of slaves. He touched his whip to the arm of a stout woman and motioned her toward the block. The two young boys in blouses and long pants clutched at the skirt of the woman's calico dress. Marcus struck at them with the whip. One yelped in pain. The woman named Mary swung around. Marcus blocked her way, pointing to where his father stood on the block. Slowly, and with a certain melancholy dignity, Mary climbed the steps.

Before Isaac could seek an opening bid, a woman at the front of the crowd thrust up a hand. "Five hundred dollars!" Other bids followed. Nathan remained silent, ready to enter the auction only when he sensed interest falter. At nine hundred and fifty dollars, the bidding slowed. As Nathan prepared to offer a thousand, the Negro cook named Mary stunned the crowd into silence by stepping uncalled to the front of the block and speaking in a loud, clear voice.

"Are you fine ladies mothers? Are you gentlemen fathers?" She stared out over the crowd, aware that every eye was upon her. "I ask you, would you want your children to be taken from you? Would you want them to grow up in a strange world without a mother, as my sons will have to do? Buy me, if you wish, and I promise that I will be the best cook your kitchen has ever known. But I beg of you to buy my children with me."

Marcus's face darkened. He looked ready to lash out at the woman. As Isaac pulled her back from the edge of the auction block, Nathan's hand shot up. "Two thousand!" he shouted, more than doubling the previous bid. "Two thousand dollars for Mary and her two sons!"

Heads swung toward the fresh voice at the rear of the crowd. Marcus's thin lips curled into a sneer as he recognized the new bidder. "Well, well, if it's not the Crescent City's very own black Republican. Are you going to give these three niggers their freedom the instant you leave Banks Arcade?"

A buzz of disapproval grew around Nathan. He ignored it. "I made a bid! Is it recognized?"

"Two thousand dollars!" Isaac Barnett called out. "For Mary the cook and her sons. Do I hear an advance on two thousand?"

Nathan looked around the crowd. He doubted if anyone would top his bid. Even by New Orleans's inflated slave prices, by far the highest in the country, the two boys were not worth the additional thousand dollars he had just offered.

"Two thousand once! Two thousand twice . . . !"

Marcus interrupted his father to finish off the ritual. "Two thousand sold! Mary and her two sons sold for two thousand dollars to Mister Nathan Solomon, the well-known abolitionist."

Nathan pushed his way through to the auction block. As he checked the papers, he said to Marcus, "I will thank you not to make this ordeal more reprehensible than it is already."

Marcus was enjoying himself too much to stop. "Forgive me, but it is not every day we have an abolitionist as a customer. Quite a shame really."

"What is a shame?"

"Just when I was starting to think that your sanctimonious speeches about the evils of slavery might be right, you turn up here to buy some prime black flesh for yourself."

"I made this purchase on behalf of a client."

Marcus shrugged. His dark eyes shone with delight at Nathan's embarrassment. "Whichever way you want to look at it, you and your kind are nothing but damned hypocrites."

Nathan did not answer, because he had the nagging suspicion that Marcus might be right.

Once the money was paid and the papers exchanged, Nathan took charge of Mary and her sons. As he led them from Banks Arcade for the short walk to the countinghouse on Canal Street, he asked the boys their names.

"Peter," answered one.

"Paul," said the other.

"Peter and Paul," Nathan repeated. The memory of Gershon Lowensohn giving biblical names to the Waverley servants brought a smile to his face. The Georgia rice planter who had owned Mary and her sons had done exactly the same, only he had chosen names from the New Testament.

Nathan's smile gave Mary courage to speak. "I prayed a man as good as you would hear my plea and buy us for his own home."

"You will not be working in my home. You will work for a planter named James Wilson, on the Red River."

"Is he as good a man as you?"

"If he were not such a man," Nathan answered, "I would not do business with him."

Mary and her sons remained at the countinghouse for the remainder of the afternoon. At five o'clock, Nathan took them to Waverley, where they would spend the night before being turned over to James Wilson the next morning. When Leonora asked her cousin what he would do should Wilson not want the two boys, Nathan had an answer ready. "We will keep all three, give them their freedom, and have them work as paid servants. I will not be a party to breaking up a family."

Nathan and Leonora met Wilson and his family for dinner that night at the St. Charles Hotel. While the planter's two daughters, Angelina and Sally, excitedly described to Leonora their week in New Orleans, Nathan told James and Millicent Wilson that he had succeeded in finding them a new cook.

Millicent clapped her hands in delight. "That is wonderful news. Tell us about her."

"Her name is Mary, and I will bring her to the levee in the

morning. I fear, however, that I may have spent too freely of your money."

Wilson's eyes narrowed. "How much did you spend?"

"Two thousand dollars. That sum includes Mary's two young sons, Peter and Paul."

"I do not recall saying that I needed two houseboys as well."

"I know, but this woman beseeched us from the block not to separate her from her sons. It was the most eloquent speech I have ever heard, more articulate than that of any politician seeking office, or any preacher asking salvation for his flock. No decent man could fail to be moved."

Millicent Wilson, a thin woman with fair hair and a pinched narrow face, rested a hand on her husband's wrist. "A happy cook makes a loving kitchen, and we can always find room for two more pairs of helping hands."

"Tell me, what would you have done had I refused to take this cook and her sons from you?" Wilson asked. When Nathan gave the same answer he had given earlier to Leonora, Wilson's stony face softened. "That is the reason I continued my association with this firm after Mister Lowensohn's death. I saw in you a decency which would never let you cheat me."

Next morning, before the Wilsons boarded the sternwheeler for the return voyage to Fallowfields, Nathan turned over Mary and her two sons, Paul and Peter, to their new owners. As she climbed the ramp onto the boat, the cook turned around. "I'm nothing but a poor black woman," she told Nathan. "I don't have money. I don't have anything. All I have is my belief in God and my prayers. And as sure as the Lord hears those prayers, he'll repay you a thousand times for the good deed you did yesterday for me and mine."

Nathan watched the boat until it passed around the bend in the river and was lost to sight. The cook's blessing echoed in his mind. He could never remember being blessed by anyone. And even had he been blessed—by a priest, by a rabbi, by any learned so-called man of God—he doubted if their benedictions would have carried the same weight as the blessing of a simple Negro servant.

The instant he returned to the countinghouse, he blurted out the odd occurrence to his cousin. "She blessed me, Lally. Mary the cook, who I bought for the Wilson family, blessed me."

"Why do you sound so surprised? You stopped the separation of a mother from her two sons. You performed a good turn for her, and how often does someone do such a thing for a slave?"

Nathan's wonder turned suddenly to anger, and his voice sharpened as he recalled the auction. "You should have seen Marcus, strutting around with his whip, pushing people this way and that as if he were some kind of god. Isaac Barnett is reprehensible enough, the way he sells people like cattle, but Marcus exceeds his father for cruelty. He enjoys degrading slaves before he sells them. I know he would willingly have used that whip if he thought the marks it left would not lower the price. Really, Lally, it is too bad that Miriam has never seen Marcus at work. She sees him only when he is at his most charming. If she ever saw him with his father at a slave auction, she would soon think twice about her infatuation. Damn, it does annoy me the way that rascal fools her."

Leonora remembered her thoughts of the previous Sunday, after she had watched Nathan tease Miriam. She was right. Nathan most certainly had noticed the beautiful young woman Miriam had become, even if he did not realize it himself. "Why not do something to show Marcus's true side to Miriam?"

Nathan laughed bitterly. "Right now, Miriam would sooner shake hands with Satan than listen to anything I have to say about Marcus."

Marcus visited Waverley that night to share the traditional Friday-evening meal. As the first course was served, he confessed to Miriam how surprised he had been the previous day. "Next to John Brown, Nathan was just about the last person I expected to see at one of our auctions. Imagine my amazement when this wonderfully high bid came in, from Nathan of all people!" Smiling broadly, he looked across the table to the subject of his banter. "I trust the planter for whom you acted was satisfied with the cook and her two young sons."

"Mister Wilson was very satisfied," Nathan answered coldly.

"Excellent. Can my father and I expect to see you again? Like every business, we rely on satisfied customers returning."

This time, Nathan did not reply. He was unsure whether Marcus was genuinely courting further trade or simply using the opportunity to remind Nathan that he considered him a hypocrite. The lack of response did not faze Marcus. He carried on talking to Nathan, keeping the subject tied closely to the auction. "My father and I leave for Savannah on Monday. We expect to return with excellent merchandise. Should any more of your planters be in the market for our merchandise, you could do them a fine service by recommending them to us."

"Thank you. I will be sure to remember it."

Miriam's green eyes locked onto Nathan. Her voice was as sweet as molasses. *"You* bought slaves? How could you possibly do such a thing after all your fine speeches against slavery?"

While Nathan tried to decide whether Miriam's question was spontaneous or rehearsed, Marcus's laughter rang out. "Nathan understands the fine line between high principles and business, Miriam. He understands it, and he walks it very well."

Unlike Nathan, Leonora had little doubt that Marcus was behind the question. The buying of slaves was nothing new to Miriam. She knew Nathan performed such tasks, as her own father had done. Looking at Anna Lowensohn, Leonora said, "Walking that fine line has done little to harm the fortunes of this household, do you not agree?"

Anna looked along the length of the table, at the four young people who sat there, and at the four empty chairs. Being trapped in an argument she did not understand made her ill at ease. It was like a continuation of the squabbles she remembered from long ago, when Miriam, infatuated with Nathan, learned he loved someone else. Was the shoe now on the other foot? Was Miriam, with one young man firmly in tow, now the object of Nathan's interest? At times like this, Anna missed her husband most. She considered herself practical, but Gershon had always been more adept at untangling such riddles. "The Sabbath is supposed to be a day of rest," she said at last. "Let us refrain from discussing the tiresome matters which engage us all week long."

Conversation diminished as the five people at the table concentrated on the meal. Every so often, Leonora glanced at Miriam and pondered Nathan's description of Marcus at the auction. Marcus did allow Miriam to see only his gentlemanly traits, while he concealed from her the harsh business side of his character. And Miriam, in her innocence—and in her joy at finding a young man who courted her as ardently as Marcus apparently did—ignored reality. She avoided the ugliness of the world Marcus populated because she was terrified of losing him. She shielded her eyes with a blindfold that allowed her to see only the aspects of Marcus she wanted to see.

It was time to remove the blindfold and let Miriam see the entire man. Leonora had enough faith in Miriam to know what the result would be. And when that time came, she hoped her cousin removed his blindfold, too.

Marcus and his father were away for four weeks. Miriam, her social life disrupted, stayed close to Waverley, filling her time with reading and embroidery. During those four weeks, Leonora worked hard to reestablish the warm friendship she had once shared with the golden-haired young woman, the rapport that had been eroded by the entrance into their circle of the abrasive personality and fire-eating philosophy of Marcus Barnett. When she saw Miriam embroidering, she recalled the perfection of Sarah's work. Miriam fell into the conversation immediately, admitting how jealous she had been of her younger sister's needle skills. Soon, the two young women were discussing Waverley as it had been before 1853, laughing as humorous memories surfaced, falling silent as they remembered the epidemic, and then recovering when Leonora pointed out that those who had died would surely want to be remembered with laughter, not with tears.

One evening, Leonora saw Miriam immersed in a book. On learning the book was *Ivanhoe,* she reminisced about the day she had arrived at Waverley, and Nathan had made the connection between the house and Sir Walter Scott. Miriam, too, remembered that day clearly. "Do you recollect how Henry acted?" she asked. Setting down her book, she stood up, squared her shoulders and lowered her voice. "I am Henry, my father's only son. Not only have I finished school, but I work with my father. I am, if I say so myself, absolutely indispensable to him." Laughing, she fell back onto the sofa, where Leonora hugged her tightly.

"Henry was a pompous devil, wasn't he?" Leonora said.

"He was indeed." Miriam wiped tears from her eyes. Her face turned somber. "I still miss him. I miss them all so terribly."

"So do I. But when I feel myself growing too sad, I thank God for the presence of those the fever spared." She gave Miriam a smile that brimmed with affection. "I thank Him that you are still here to be my friend. I thank Him that your mother is still here, and I thank Him for sparing Nathan. Nathan and I have been through so much together. Had he died, I do not think I would have had the strength to go on living by myself."

Miriam did not return the smile, and Leonora could see that mention of Nathan disturbed her. "You were quite taken with my cousin when we first arrived, were you not?"

"That was a long time ago," Miriam answered tartly. "Before he grew too big for his breeches."

"Oh? I had not noticed such a growth."

Miriam was stunned. "How could you fail to notice? Since my father's death, your cousin has assumed the role of the man of this house. He has stepped into my father's shoes as though he were not his boarder but his son. He passes judgment on everything that happens here. Nothing can be bought without his approval. Nothing can be sold. Why, he even has the nerve to regard himself as an authority on my friends! I invite as a dinner guest an eminently respectable young man, and Nathan insults him."

"Perhaps Nathan feels disappointed."

"Disappointed?" Miriam's hostility abruptly changed to interest. "What do you mean?"

"He might believe you can do much better for yourself. I certainly think you can." Leaving Miriam to reflect on that, Leonora got up and walked away.

Miriam pondered the advice for the remainder of the evening. Before retiring, she knocked on Leonora's door to ask if she could speak to her. "Did you mean that," she said, perching on the edge of Leonora's bed, "about Nathan feeling I can do better for myself?"

"I meant every word. There are many handsome young men in New Orleans, Miriam. Do not throw yourself at the first one who smiles at you."

"Where is your handsome young man?" Miriam regretted the quick question instantly. In the light from her candle, she saw sorrow pass swiftly across Leonora's face. "Forgive me. It was a silly thing to say. Your heart still grieves for Antoine." She rose from the bed and walked to the door. Before closing it, she looked back into the bedroom. "If you come across any of those handsome young men, be sure to let me know."

"I certainly will," Leonora called after her. She lay back, completely satisfied. Two things had happened. Miriam had doubts about Marcus. And, for the first time, rancor had not tinged her voice at the mention of Nathan's name.

Chapter Fifteen

Late on a Thursday night, in the middle of a drenching spring downpour, Isaac and Marcus Barnett returned to New Orleans. By noon the next day, posters appeared both in the business district of New Orleans and in the *Vieux Carré*. Block capitals declared in English and French: TOP QUALITY! OUR LARGEST OFFERING EVER! Smaller letters described the credentials of the fifty-two slaves the Barnetts had brought back from Georgia. Skilled carpenters and builders; tireless house servants; cooks who would not disgrace the kitchens of the finest hotels; strong, industrious field hands. All would be auctioned without reserve at two o'clock the following Wednesday. Not at Banks Arcade, where Isaac had conducted his last sale, but in the more grandiose setting of the rotunda of the St. Louis Hotel.

Miriam saw Marcus on the day after his return, when he came to Waverley for dinner. As everyone sat down, Marcus made a show of giving Miriam a swan-shaped gold-and-enamel brooch he had bought in Savannah. Face flushed with pleasure, Miriam passed the brooch around the table for the others to see. Leonora held it the longest, examining it minutely as if seeking flaws. When she handed it back, she said, "I remember our first evening in this house, when Nathan gave you gold."

"I remember, too!" Miriam answered brightly. "He gave me a gold English sovereign because it was my fourteenth birthday. I still have it, locked away upstairs with all my jewelry."

"I am quite flattered," Nathan said.

"You are?" Since talking to Leonora, Miriam had tempered her hostility toward Nathan. She responded to him when he spoke to her, and although such conversations were short they had allowed her to rediscover many of the points she had considered attractive in him. Like now, staring into Nathan's brown eyes, Miriam saw the same warmth that had initially captivated her, the hint of laughter as he had produced the gold coin and passed it across the table.

"Yes. I am flattered that you kept it as a souvenir of our first meeting instead of spending it."

Marcus felt himself being eased out of the conversation. Absent for a month, he had expected Miriam to hang on his every word. Instead, she was allowing her interest to be diverted. By Nathan, of all people! Eager to regain her attention, Marcus began describing the towns he and his father had passed through on their trip to Savannah. Each town, he swore, was a hotbed of secessionist sympathy. "Those fools in Washington would do well to make the journey my father and I made. They would realize that the promise to leave the Union is not an empty threat."

Soon after dinner finished, Marcus professed to feeling tired. After arriving home late the previous night he had risen early to begin work on the upcoming sale. As he bade good night to Miriam, he told her he would not be able to see her again until after the auction.

Frost touched Miriam's green eyes. The specks of amber became chips of ice. "Why not?"

Desperately, Marcus tried to retrieve the situation. After a four-week break in their relationship, Miriam was not about to accept another intrusion happily. "The work that goes into organizing a sale as large as this will consume all my time. Rest assured, though, after next Wednesday I will take you wherever you want to go, and I will have the money to buy whatever your heart desires. That brooch I brought you from Savannah will seem like a paltry bauble."

Leonora, who overheard the conversation, said, "Perhaps Miriam would like to attend the auction, Marcus. Would you be interested in doing so, Miriam?"

Before Miriam could answer, Marcus shook his head. "Miriam has no reason to attend. Unlike your hypocritical cousin, she is not in the market for our merchandise."

Leonora hid a smile at Marcus's abrupt refusal. Wednesday was the auction. She decided that Wednesday would also be an opportune time to enjoy luncheon with Miriam and her mother at the St. Louis Hotel.

The day of the auction dawned bright and clear. With no bookkeeping work to do at the countinghouse, Leonora declared to Anna and Miriam that it was far too nice a day to spend at Waverley. "Why do we not," she said on the spur of the moment, "have our midday meal at the Saint Louis Hotel, and then go for a carriage ride?"

Anna and her daughter consented immediately, never guessing that had it been raining Leonora would have declared it to be too miserable a day to stay indoors.

Samson let them off at the hotel's main entrance on St. Louis Street at twelve-thirty, with instructions to collect them two hours later. Passing through the hotel's enormous vestibule, the three women entered the restaurant, where they were shown to a table by the window. As they sat down, Leonora pivoted in the chair to look around.

"Four years have passed since I was last in this hotel," she said, "yet nothing seems to have changed."

"I have seen many changes over the years," Anna said. "When we moved to New Orleans from New York, the City Exchange was being constructed where we sit right now. Quite magnificent, but short-lived as it burned down some three or four years after it was completed. It was rebuilt to the original plans, but the name was changed to what it is today, the Saint Louis Hotel. We Americans"—she lowered her voice to barely a whisper—"like to think that the Saint Charles Hotel is its equal in every way, but we fool ourselves."

"Why did you choose the Saint Louis instead of the Saint Charles?" Miriam asked Leonora. "You rarely visit the old quarter of town because of the memories it contains."

Leonora smiled. "I thought it time I put those memories to rest. And this building holds a host of bittersweet memories for me." All during the journey from Prytania Street, she had worried that Miriam would connect the luncheon invitation to Isaac Barnett's slave auction. The carriage had passed posters advertising the sale. There had even been two posters outside the main entrance of the St. Louis Hotel, but neither Miriam nor her mother had paid any attention to them.

"Was it not here, during the New Year's Eve ball, that the fencing master challenged Nathan?" Anna asked.

"You have it the wrong way around. It was Nathan who made the challenge. Upstairs, in the ballroom. Antoine and I were outside at the time, taking the air on Royal Street. When we returned, the air was filled with a fevered excitement because some blockhead had just challenged Raymonde Perrault. Imagine our terror when we learned that blockhead was my cousin!"

"He must have loved Marie-Louise very much," Miriam said.

Leonora wondered if a touch of wistfulness colored Miriam's comment. "He did. He would let no man insult her, even when the insult had been made with the deliberate intention of drawing him into a fight in which he would surely be killed."

As the meal progressed, Leonora called up other recollections of that New Year's Eve ball. Remembering how she and Nathan had been feted from the moment they entered the ballroom, she said, "Had we been the president and his lady, we could not have received more attention." She described the questions about her wedding dress—would it be made in Paris or in New Orleans? She mentioned being asked about her and Nathan's loyalties, were they to America or to England? She spoke of the interest in where the two couples would live once they were married, in the *Vieux Carré* or above Canal Street? And finally, as the meal ended just before two o'clock, she recalled the conversation she had shared with Nathan while leaning against the platform in the hotel rotunda where at this very moment Isaac and Marcus Barnett were preparing to begin their largest slave auction ever.

"Nathan talked to me about converting to Catholicism, because he knew the subject troubled me deeply. Earlier, we had been asked if we would convert, and Antoine answered that Judah Benjamin did not convert when he married a Catholic Creole woman. Nathan asked me what I would do if Antoine changed his mind, if he became less accommodating. He asked me what mattered more, Antoine or my heritage?"

Miriam, caught up in the drama of that moment so long ago, leaned forward. Leonora noticed that she wore on her green dress the swan-shaped gold-and-enamel brooch Marcus had given her. "How did you answer?"

"I told him Antoine was more important than any heritage. I made a mistake by believing that. You cannot change what you are, and you only fool yourself by trying. Of all that happened here at that New Year's Eve ball, that moment in the rotunda was the most important. More momentous, even, than Nathan's encounter with Raymonde Perrault." She sat back and sighed, as though the dredging up of such painful memories had sapped her energy, but when she spoke again her voice was firm. "While I am in this hotel, I wish to stand once more in the rotunda. I would like the chance to relive that conversation with Nathan."

"I doubt if it will be as quiet as you remember it from that night," Anna said. "If the rotunda is not being used for a political meeting, then some auctioneer has taken it over to sell land, houses, stocks, or some other kind of property. It surely is the most popular spot in all of New Orleans."

"Oh, Mother, do not be so unromantic," Miriam chided. Leonora's recollections had struck a responsive chord within the golden-haired young woman. Miriam knew that if a thousand people filled the rotunda, Leonora would have ears and eyes only for what had happened on that night more than four years ago.

After settling the bill, they left the restaurant. Leonora led the way to the rotunda. Beneath the huge dome stood a large crowd, its attention focused on the raised platform in the center of the rotunda. The platform was empty, but there was no mistaking the excitement and anticipation of the people who waited for the sale to begin.

"I wonder what they could be selling to draw so many people," Anna murmured as she stood on her toes in a vain effort to see between the hats and heads of the men and women gathered there.

"I really have no idea," Leonora answered, simultaneously marveling at how naive Anna and Miriam were. They had lived in New Orleans for so many years, yet they had never attended a slave auction. Neither had she, but thanks to Nathan she knew just how obscene the spectacle was.

"Shall we find out what is being sold?" Miriam suggested. "Who knows, it might even be something worth bidding for."

Excusing herself in both English and French, Leonora eased her way through the crowd. Behind came Anna, holding Miriam's hand so they would not become separated. After half a dozen steps, their progress was thwarted by a group of four tall and portly men who, despite Leonora's pleas, refused to budge.

"Does this chaos recall for you what happened on that night so long ago?" Anna asked.

"All I have to do is look up there"—Leonora lifted her head to stare at the hollow earthenware pots that formed the rotunda's roof—"and I can remember absolutely everything."

Just then, one of the four men moved. Miriam pushed through. Half a dozen rows of people still separated her from the auction block, but between their heads a new view opened. To one side stood a large group of Negro men in top hats and tailcoats and women in bright dresses. Her voice filled with an odd mixture of confusion and revulsion. "It must be a slave auction." And then her mouth dropped open in shocked surprise as she recognized Isaac Barnett climbing the steps to the block, and Marcus herding the slaves toward the block with his blacksnake whip.

"Welcome, my friends, to Isaac Barnett's largest-ever slave auction! *Bienvenu à—*"

Miriam's shock became a surging anger that blotted out Isaac's greeting. She swung around to Leonora, her voice a breathless, virulent whisper. "You knew! That was why you had us come here today, because you knew!"

Leonora answered coolly. "Do not be angry with me for trying to open your eyes fully."

"My eyes are open enough, thank you very much!"

Next to Miriam, an elderly woman hissed for her to be quiet. Isaac was describing his first piece of merchandise, a maid named Hannah. The dispute was forgotten as the three women from Waverley looked once more toward the auction block. Prodded by Marcus's whip, the maid called Hannah slowly climbed the steps to stand beside Isaac. She was a cumbersome woman with gray in her hair and a tired stoop to her body. Bidding began at three hundred dollars. Each time the price edged up, Leonora glanced at Miriam. The eyes the golden-haired young woman claimed to be sufficiently open had narrowed to slits. The normally generous mouth was stretched into a thin, straight line.

Hannah was sold for five hundred dollars to a man who stood a few yards from Leonora, Miriam, and Anna. As the buyer stepped forward, Isaac pointed to him and cried, "Marcus, give the lucky man his merchandise!" The three women shrank down before realizing they could not be recognized from the block. The hats they wore kept their faces shaded; the people clustered around them assured anonymity.

Isaac was in top form as he continued with the auction. Strutting around the platform like an actor debuting at the Théâtre d'Orléans, he cajoled bidders into offering more. Every sale closed with his exhortation to Marcus to give the lucky customer his goods. To Leonora's right, Anna watched with detached interest. But Miriam, on Leonora's left, became increasingly agitated as Isaac worked his way through the first four sales. The flash of antagonism toward Leonora was forgotten in her preoccupation with what was taking place. She flinched with every new bid, and at the end of each sale, when Isaac called out Marcus's name, her hands balled up into rigid fists. Leonora wondered how many more sales she would endure before something snapped.

"Let us leave," Leonora whispered as Isaac reached the fifth item on his list. There was no need for Miriam to see more.

Anna moved, ready to go. Miriam, transfixed by the events on the auction block, shook her head. When Leonora repeated the words, Miriam turned angrily. "You brought me here to see this, now let me see it!"

The fifth slave for sale was a slim mulatto in her middle teens named Roberta. Bright eyes danced saucily in a light brown, heart-shaped face. Thick black hair fell softly to her shoulders. When her name was called, Roberta sauntered slowly toward the block, hips swaying in time with some unheard beat. She knew the gaze of every man in the rotunda was fixed upon her. At fifteen, she understood what men wanted. She would give it to them. Give them something to look at, and ensure a bidding frenzy that would secure her future as some white man's protected paramour. Isaac waited patiently, aware that every movement of her hips, every flutter of her eyelashes, added another hundred dollars to her eventual price. Marcus, though, lacked his father's knowledge and experience. As Roberta passed him, he grabbed her right arm.

"When my father calls your name, girl, you'd better run if you know what's good for you."

The mulatto stared contemptuously into the thin face and dark, brooding eyes of the slave-dealer's son. "I do not run for any man. When that thing between their legs gets hot and angry, they run for me."

A thundercloud settled over Marcus's face. No person of color, free or slave, had ever spoken to him like that. He did not hear his father call him to let the girl proceed, nor did he notice the sudden silence that had fallen upon the crowd. He gripped Roberta's arm harder, watching in satisfaction as she winced. "You'll do what I tell you to do, girl."

Roberta's left hand flew out. Marcus jumped back, shouting in pain and rage as the mulatto's fingernails left red furrows down the right side of his face. He struck out with the blacksnake whip. The lash curled around the girl's ankles. Marcus pulled back to send her crashing to the ground, flicked the whip free and brought it down sharply across her back. The crack of the whip was lost in the instant shriek of pain. Marcus drew his arm back again. Before he could strike a second time, a figure in a green dress burst from the stunned crowd. Miriam's eyes were no longer slits. They were saucer-round in shock and fury. The thin, straight line of her mouth was open wide, screaming as she launched herself at Marcus.

The attack took Marcus completely by surprise. He did not recognize Miriam until the instant she crashed into him. The whip flew from his hand as they tumbled to the floor. Marcus landed underneath, the breath slammed out of his body by the force of the attack. He tried to shout her name. The first syllable trailed off into a scream as her fingernails followed the raw and bloody trails left by the mulatto girl, and then the scream ended in a shrieking plea for help.

Isaac, showing surprising alacrity for a man in his fifties, jumped down from the block. He had recognized Miriam the instant she had burst through the crowd, but like everyone else he had been too stunned to intercept her. "Have you gone mad?" he shouted as he struggled to lift her from his son. "Leave him alone at once!"

Miriam's fury was too powerful for Isaac alone to overcome. Two other men joined him. Between them they pulled Miriam off Marcus. She relaxed in their grip, staring scornfully at the man she had once considered marrying. He got up cautiously.

Blood ran down both sides of his face. He looked into Miriam's eyes, as if seeking some explanation for the sudden and ferocious attack, then he swung around and stalked away. When he stumbled over the huddled figure of Roberta, the crowd finally found its voice and laughter filled the rotunda.

"Do not forget your whip!" Miriam called after him. "No one will recognize you without that badge of authority! And do not forget this either . . . !" She unpinned the swan-shaped brooch from her dress.

Marcus turned around just as Miriam drew back her arm and flung the brooch with all her strength. It flashed across the five yards separating them to strike him in the chin, slicing a gash in the swarthy skin. Face dripping blood, Marcus stormed out of the rotunda and left the St. Louis Hotel.

Roberta rose slowly to her feet, nursing a sore shoulder where Marcus's single stroke had landed. Isaac gestured for her to rejoin the waiting group of slaves. Miriam shook herself free and turned to look for the two women with whom she had stood before Marcus's assault on the young mulatto had pushed her rage beyond manageable bounds. She saw them at the front of the crowd. Very calmly she said, "I think we had best be going. Samson will worry if he returns and we are not there to meet him." Linking arms with her mother and her friend, she walked away, turning her head just once to address Isaac.

"Please inform your son that his presence is no longer welcome at Waverley."

Nathan returned to Waverley that evening unaware that Leonora had duped Miriam and her mother into attending Isaac Barnett's slave auction at the St. Louis Hotel. He found his cousin waiting on the porch with the news that Miriam wished to speak to him in the rear parlor. When he asked her why, she said one word: "Marcus." Nathan entered the house, puzzled over the meaning of Leonora's cryptic message, and the enigmatic smile with which she had accompanied it. Had

Miriam an announcement to make regarding her relationship with the slave-dealer's son? Did she want his blessing? And did she really expect him to give it?

In the rear parlor, Miriam sat on the sofa where Nathan had first seen her on the day he had arrived in New Orleans. He blinked his eyes and formed an image of Miriam sitting properly with her two younger sisters, while Henry stood by the fireplace examining the marble-and-bronze clock that still sat there. "Leonora said you wished to see me about Marcus."

Miriam stood up and walked slowly toward Nathan. He watched her draw closer, his gaze rising from her narrow waist to the amber-flecked green eyes that dominated her face, then to her hair. Miriam's hair had never looked as glorious as it did at this moment. Catching the low evening sunlight that streamed into the room, it resembled a crown of shimmering golden fire.

She stopped a yard away. "I want to apologize."

"Apologize?" The confession jolted Nathan. An apology had been furthest from his mind.

"You were right, and I was wrong. Leonora tricked my mother and me into attending Isaac Barnett's slave auction today at the Saint Louis Hotel. I saw for myself what Marcus was really like." Miriam described the scene for Nathan, from the opening of the auction to Marcus's attack on the mulatto girl named Roberta. "Marcus Barnett will never be welcome in this house again. So help me, if that scoundrel ever dares to come through the gate, I will take a shotgun to him."

Nathan found such imagery too hard to accept. Laughing, he said, "I doubt if such drastic measures will ever be needed."

Miriam saw nothing funny. Her face remained devoid of humor. "You were right about Marcus all the time, and I was a fool to make an enemy of you by defending him."

"No matter how hard you tried, Miriam, you could never make an enemy of me. You have apologized enough, and we can forget all about . . . about . . . now what was that scoundrel's name?" A smile finally replaced Miriam's serious expression.

Nathan held out his hands for Miriam to take. "There, that is better. Profuse apologies do not suit you. Besides, are we not all entitled to make fools of ourselves occasionally?"

"Did you ever do such a thing?"

"On the day I came here I made a fool of myself by looking into a girl's green eyes and giving her a gold sovereign."

Miriam squeezed Nathan's hands. "The girl is now a woman."

"I had noticed. And I am still willing"—he leaned forward to kiss her on the forehead, then the tip of her nose, and finally her lips—"to risk making myself look a fool."

She threw his own words back at him. "Are we all not entitled to make fools of ourselves occasionally?"

From that moment, Nathan and Miriam were rarely apart. In the morning, when Nathan ate breakfast, before leaving for work, Miriam was sure to be at the table. She visited the countinghouse daily, and in the evenings, when Nathan walked in the garden, Miriam always accompanied him. He remembered his amusement when a precocious fourteen-year-old girl had found excuses to be where he was. Now he welcomed the similar attention of a beautiful young woman in her twentieth year.

It took only two weeks for Nathan to realize how deeply in love he was with Miriam. That understanding came on the second Sunday of May, a dazzling spring day full of bright sunshine and invigorating breezes that gave no hint of the humid summer that would soon engulf New Orleans. They drove a chaise along the Shell Road to Lake Pontchartrain, where resorts and restaurants busily prepared for the coming season's influx of visitors from the city. After eating lunch, they stood looking north across the lake toward Livingston and St. Tammany parishes.

"Miriam, I was not teasing when I said two months ago how

flattered I was that you had kept that gold sovereign all this time. I really did take it as a compliment."

She regarded him quizzically, uncertain why he would bring up the subject at this particular time. He had removed the pale blue hat that matched his coat, and the breeze from the lake ruffled his light brown hair. Was it her imagination, or were those twin gray streaks at the temples more pronounced? Would his hair be white by the time he turned thirty? She found the idea attractive, a young man's face topped by a silver crown. "What makes you think about that gold coin now?"

"I gave it to you because it matched the color of your hair. Now I have another piece of jewelry to give you, one that matches the color of your eyes." He withdrew from his pocket the wide emerald bracelet he had bought four and half years before.

"Nathan . . ." Miriam's voice trailed away as Nathan placed the bracelet upon her right wrist. "It is the most exquisite piece of jewelry I have ever seen. Thank you."

"I have to tell you, it once belonged to someone else—"

She cut him off by pressing a finger to his lips. "I know. You bought it for Marie-Louise. Nathan, if giving me this bracelet means that you love me as much as you loved her, then I can ask for no more." She saw sadness creep into the corners of his eyes at the mention of the Creole girl. He was looking at the lake, but Miriam knew he saw Marie-Louise's face. How could he do otherwise, when he had her portrait in both his room and in the countinghouse? "Please believe me when I say I do not worry about feelings you still have for Marie-Louise. She was your first love, and no man or woman ever forgets that first love. I know I will never forget mine. I adore him to this day."

Curiosity replaced the sadness. Nathan turned from the lake to look at Miriam. "Tell me about your first love."

"Handsome. Strong, but gentle at the same time. And very, very honorable. He would accept no insult, and he would work from dawn to dusk to repay a debt."

"He sounds like a wonderful man. How could you possibly reject him?"

"I did not." She leaned forward to kiss Nathan on the cheek. "Do you not understand—it is you!"

Nathan's stomach tightened into a trembling knot as he reached out to embrace Miriam. He had hoped . . . !

"You are my first love, Nathan, and you will be my last love. This I promise you."

"And I love you as intensely as I loved my first love."

They kissed and clung to each other. When they broke apart, breathless and flushed, Nathan silently vowed to remove the painting of Marie-Louise from his bedroom wall. The Amans portrait, and the copy which hung in the countinghouse, had served their purpose.

Chapter Sixteen

Little more than a month later, in the middle of June, Nathan married Miriam in a traditional ceremony at Waverley. The weather cooperated. The sky was clear, the air dry, and a gentle northerly breeze rippled the trees. As she kissed her new husband for the first time, Miriam whispered that God had sent a favorable omen by blessing their wedding with a continuation of their day at the lake.

Nearly a hundred people attended the luncheon that followed the ceremony. Nathan's clients mixed with members of the synagogue Miriam attended with her mother and Leonora. There was no sign, however, of Isaac or Marcus Barnett. Nor did anyone turn up to fill four chairs that remained conspicuously empty throughout the luncheon. Those close to the family knew the significance of those chairs. Other guests simply assumed that four people had failed to show up. A pity. It was their loss because the day was one to be treasured.

Throughout the day, Anna Lowensohn was torn by the twin emotions of joy and sorrow. When she looked at the bride and groom—Miriam in white, with the emerald bracelet worn over a sleeve, and Nathan in black trousers and frock coat, bright white shirt and black bow tie—her heart swelled. Ever since the yellow-fever epidemic, she had regarded Nathan as a son. Even before that . . . almost from the day he had arrived in New Orleans. And now she had him as a son-in-law, and no mother could ask for a finer, more caring and generous husband for her daughter. But each time Anna's eyes fell upon the four empty chairs, a lump formed in her throat, and her heart weighed heavily inside her chest. Gershon should have been at Waverley today to give his daughter away. Henry should have been here as the best man; and Sarah and Martha as bridesmaids.

Anna was not alone in her feelings of turmoil. Leonora, too, knew such inner conflict. All through the ceremony she had blinked back tears of joy. When the ceremony ended, she was the first to kiss Nathan and Miriam, and wish them well for the future. She wanted only bliss for the cousin who, since childhood, had been her dearest friend. If Nathan was happy, then she, too, was happy. Yet as she watched Nathan and his new bride mingle with the guests, an odd sensation pricked her. It took her several minutes to realize that it was jealousy. She envied Miriam because, deep within her soul, she understood that Nathan meant much more to her than a best friend. She was in love with him, and had been so ever since they were children flung together beneath their uncle's roof. She recalled the times he had read to her in Samuel Solomon's shop, when the sound of his voice had lulled her into believing they were somewhere else, somewhere far more pleasant. Even the early-morning journeys to Ludgate Hill had been less onerous because of Nathan's company. How often had she pretended that they were going not to their uncle's shop but to their own establishment? And not as cousins, but as husband and wife?

As she looked at the newlyweds talking to James and Millicent Wilson, who had traveled from Fallowfields for the wedding, Leonora wondered if Miriam understood just how fortunate she was.

Nathan and Miriam spent their wedding night in a stateroom aboard the *Eclipse*, an elegant riverboat which carried them north from New Orleans. The rocking of the vessel, the steady beat of the wheel and the sound of water slapping against the hull were conducive to their lovemaking. They discovered each other cautiously at first, and then with a kind of wonder that soon yielded to a joyous frenzy. As Nathan felt his strength pour out in a wild, exhilarating rush, he heard from far away a cry of jubilation and the words, "I knew! I knew!" When he asked Miriam what she knew, she laughed and kissed him.

"From the moment we met, I knew that one day we would be here together."

Nathan returned the kiss. "I am grateful that you did not reveal the thought the instant it occurred to you. Your father would surely have thrown me out of the house."

Exhausted by their lovemaking, Nathan soon fell asleep. Miriam remained awake, smiling dreamily as she cradled his head to her breasts. Somehow, the entire day seemed illusory. The wedding was unreal. So were the days preceding it. At any moment she feared she would awaken and find herself alone in her bed at Waverley. But when she looked down and saw Nathan, and remembered the warmth and fullness of him inside her, she knew this was no dream. Still smiling, she fell into a deep and restful sleep.

After disembarking at Memphis, Nathan and Miriam took a series of trains through Tennessee, Alabama, Georgia, Virginia and Maryland. In Baltimore, they boarded a train to New York. For both newlyweds, it was their first trip to New York. Based in a third-floor suite at the white-marble St. Nicholas Hotel on Broadway and Broome Street, they toured the city, barely able to believe that two such diverse population centers as New York and New Orleans could be part of the same country. They shopped at A.T. Stewart on Broadway, ate at Delmonico's on South William Street, and gazed with wonder at exhibits on display at Barnum's Museum. One afternoon, they rode out to the Croton Reservoir on the west side of Fifth Avenue, between Fortieth and Forty-second streets. Standing on top of the reservoir's high walls, they gazed east and west to the East River and the Hudson, and north toward the villages of Yorkville, Harlem, and Manhattanville.

Among the city's many exceptional buildings, one struck a profound note with Nathan. Opposite Latting's Observatory and Ice Cream Parlor on Forty-second Street was a massive structure erected four years earlier for the 1853 World's Fair.

"New York has copied London's Crystal Palace," Nathan told Miriam as they gazed at massive panes of glass reflecting the bright sunlight. He related how he and Leonora had first met Americans inside the Crystal Palace, and how those meetings had been the impetus for them to flee.

"Then our being here as man and wife is because of the building on which this one is based," Miriam said. She touched a hand to her lips and blew a kiss toward the building. "One day we will build a home of our own, with many windows, and we will call it the Crystal Palace. And only we will know the significance of the name."

They left the St. Nicholas Hotel after three days and took a cab to the docks where they boarded a Cunard steamer. Nine days later, as the sun broke through an early-morning mist, the steamer entered the River Mersey.

Liverpool had not changed. Massive stone buildings lined the river. Forests of masts rose above the walls enclosing docks. As the steamer neared Prince's Dock, Nathan saw a square-rigged packet heading toward the Irish Channel. Steerage passengers lined the rail, cheering and waving as they passed the Cunard steamer. Nathan's heart went out to them as he waved back. "I pray their voyage is more comfortable than the one endured by Leonora and myself," he said to Miriam.

"Pray, instead, that their fortunes follow your own. That they leave England in steerage and return in cabin class. And pray they have the luck, as you did, to meet on the voyage a man as wonderful as my father."

The steamer docked. After disembarking, Nathan and Miriam were driven with their baggage to Lime Street Station. They had to wait an hour before completing in reverse the journey Nathan had made six years before with Leonora. That night, their first on dry land in more than a week, they slept at

Brown's Hotel in Dover Street. They rose early the next morning. Over breakfast, Nathan asked Miriam how much she thought he had altered in the past six years. She stared at him across the table, taking in every feature. The obvious difference was the widening streaks of gray at his temples. They added years to his twenty-five. So did the deep lines that curved from his nose to the corners of his mouth. The faint scars from that day beneath The Oaks lent him an air of danger that had not been apparent six years before. He was thinner, too, the angles of his face more defined, the chin and nose sharper. The leanness made him seem taller.

Nathan grew impatient with her inspection. "Come on, Miriam. If you had not seen me for six years, would you recognize me?"

"No. I do not think I would."

"Good. In that case, neither will my uncle and my cousins. Today"—Nathan folded his linen napkin and pushed himself back from the table—"we go shopping."

The previous night, when they had arrived at the hotel, Nathan had been too tired from the long journey to realize how distinctive he now appeared in the country of his birth. In the morning, the difference struck him immediately. Miriam's clothes—her bright yellow full skirt and jacket, with matching bonnet and parasol—could have been worn by any fashionable Englishwoman, but his own clothes set him apart. The predominant color among Englishmen seemed to be black. Black coats, black trousers, black hats. Nathan's pale blue coat and trousers, his multicolored vest, and royal blue hat drew attention to himself the instant he left the hotel. He felt like a rainbow among a sky full of thunderclouds.

After walking a hundred yards, Nathan hailed a hansom cab. He gave the driver instructions for Ludgate Hill and sat back to see what had changed about the city from which he had fled. The answer came quickly. Nothing had altered. The streets were as crowded as ever, filled with every conceivable kind of horse-drawn vehicle. Soot covered the red bricks of buildings;

horse manure filled the streets. Miriam giggled as she pointed out to Nathan a sight she had never seen—a young boy earning money by sweeping a way through the horse droppings so an old man could cross the street. Nathan smiled automatically but he was far from sharing his young wife's amusement. With each sight, the memories were coming faster, and he wondered whether this return trip would be such a triumph after all.

The cab stopped outside S. Solomon and Sons. As Nathan paid the driver, he noticed a policeman approaching. He swore it was the same officer he and Leonora had seen those mornings they had opened the shop. The constable's eyes passed over the couple without recognition. So did David Solomon's eyes when Nathan and Miriam entered the shop. Nathan had no trouble recognizing his cousin, though. The six years had added to David's likeness to his father. David was stockier. His hair had thinned, and the sideburns that framed his round face showed gray.

"Good morning. May I help you?"

Miriam removed her bonnet, but Nathan did not take off his hat. Its presence on his head helped foil identification. "Thank you. My wife and I seek gifts to take back to friends in New Orleans."

Miriam glanced at Nathan, amazed initially by his sudden adoption of an accent that any native-born Orleanian would have considered natural. David's face widened into a beaming smile of pleasure. His tone became positively obsequious. "We do so enjoy serving American customers. Their fine tastes and appreciation of quality make our work a pleasure. Of course, our humble shop must pale beside the American emporiums we hear so much about, but perhaps we can find an item or two that will give you pleasant memories of our country."

Nathan squeezed Miriam's hand as they followed David further into the shop where he showed them a selection of ivory-topped walking canes. While Miriam paid close attention, Nathan looked around. His uncle was upstairs, sitting in the office which overlooked the trading floor. Alfred was busy with another customer on the other side of the shop. Both men had seen him but, like David, they had noticed nothing unusual.

"I think we would prefer to see some cotton goods," Nathan told his unsuspecting cousin. "In New Orleans I am in the business of selling Southern cotton to English brokers. I am sure our planter friends would like to see what use is made of their cotton."

David beckoned to a clerk and told him to bring samples of cotton goods. While they waited, Samuel descended from his upstairs office. He introduced himself to Nathan and Miriam. "Forgive me for eavesdropping on your conversation with my son, but I understand you are in the cotton trade. Allow me to welcome you both to London. We are always pleased to see Americans here."

"Surely not all Americans," Nathan answered, amazed at how easily he fooled both his cousin and his uncle. The accent was the final touch. Coupled with the facial changes and the hat that kept his eyes in shadow, he was a complete stranger to David and Samuel. "I will warrant that those people from the North can try your patience. Do you remember," he said, turning to Miriam, "just a few years ago when that Yankee woman tried to foist that ridiculous garment on all other women?"

"Bloomers?" David inquired innocuously.

"That's it. An incredibly ridiculous piece of clothing."

"I would never allow my wife to be seen in them," David answered pompously.

"Nor I mine," Nathan agreed with another look at Miriam. She had no idea what was going on, only that they were standing in the shop of the uncle who, with bad grace, had raised both Nathan and Leonora. Nathan wondered if David and his Charlotte had any children yet. Was Samuel a grandfather? Alfred an uncle? Perhaps he should ask, so that he could offer congratulations.

The clerk returned with swatches. Nathan glanced through them, rubbing the occasional sample between thumb and forefinger. "Sometimes it is difficult to believe that there is any connection between the wet, stinking bales that line the levee and the fine, finished fabric we see here. British mills, I am sure, can transform even the most miserable staple into a cloth fit for a president. Or a king." Handing back the swatches, he said, "We will return on another day to choose gifts for our friends. Thank you for your time."

"Not at all," Samuel said as he saw them to the door.

Outside, Miriam asked what the pantomime inside the shop had been about. Nathan explained the ridicule of everything American that had taken place during the Great Exhibition six years before. "I think their derision, more than anything, prompted me to travel to America. If they made so much fun of America, then it had to be a marvelous place."

"Perhaps I should go back to thank them, otherwise I would surely have never met you."

"You will have another opportunity."

Nathan waved down a passing cab and told the driver to take him and Miriam to Russell Square. When the cab stopped in the square's northwest corner, Nathan sat wordlessly for almost a minute, studying the small-windowed stucco building with its terra-cotta ornaments. Compared with the grandeur of Waverley, the Solomon home looked very dull and ordinary indeed. At last, Nathan climbed down, paid the driver, and faced the house.

"When Leonora and I left this house six years ago, my aunt told us to take the first step quickly because it was the hardest. The second and third steps would come easier. Her advice was good then, and it is just as good now." Taking a deep breath, he grasped Miriam by the arm and marched up the steps. Suddenly he was at the top, confronted by the front door. He reached for the bell and pulled down sharply. From deep within the house came muffled chimes. The door opened. A uniformed maid surveyed Miriam and Nathan without recognition.

"Mrs. Solomon, please," Nathan said pleasantly. "Mrs. Harriet Solomon."

"Whom should I say is asking for her?"

Behind the maid, in the darkness of the hallway, Nathan glimpsed movement. The maid stepped back and Nathan saw a woman with a round, gentle face and soft brown eyes. For a long moment, Harriet Solomon stood in the doorway, staring at the unexpected visitors. Finally, she uttered Nathan's name.

Nathan rushed toward his aunt, arms outstretched. He had known she would recognize him; had she not, he would have been truly disappointed. Samuel and his two sons had not placed him because they had thrust him from their minds the instant he had left the house. Well, perhaps not Samuel, who was still short one hundred and twenty-nine gold sovereigns, but even then he would not have spent time thinking about his nephew as Harriet would surely have done, imagining how life was treating him, how age was changing him.

Aunt and nephew hugged each other tightly until at last Nathan remembered he was not alone. "Aunt Harriet, I would like you to meet Miriam, my wife."

Harriet gazed solemnly at the golden-haired figure dressed in sunny yellow, like a mother first seeing the girl her son has brought home. "You have a very beautiful wife, Nathan. And you, young lady"—Harriet embraced Miriam—"are married to a very handsome and remarkable young man."

"Thank you. I know that already."

Harriet stepped back two paces to get a better view of the couple. Then she pulled them into the drawing room and sat them down on a sofa by the window. "Leonora, how is Leonora? Where is she?"

"At home, in New Orleans."

"That is where you live, in New Orleans? Tell me about New Orleans. Tell me about Leonora, about yourselves, about everything that has happened in . . . how long has it been?"

"Six years, Aunt Harriet."

"Six years?" Harriet was genuinely shocked. "Where are you

staying? How long have you been in London? Have you eaten?" Before Miriam or Nathan could answer any of the questions, Harriet called for the maid to bring in refreshments. She swung back to her nephew. "Uncle Samuel will be surprised to see you."

"He has seen me and spoken to me already, and he did not recognize me. David, also." Nathan told his aunt about the visit to the shop. "Does David have children?"

"Your uncle and I still wait to be grandparents. David has yet to become a father. Alfred, of course, remains unmarried."

"Of course," Nathan concurred. He could no more see Alfred as a husband and father than he could see himself still living in England. He felt tremendous pity for his aunt. Harriet would dearly love to hold her grandchildren, to spoil them as, perhaps, she had never been allowed to spoil her own children.

Harriet shook her head, still amazed by Nathan's sudden appearance. "I am delighted to see you after so much time, but why have you come? Is there a special reason for this visit?"

"I have come to keep the promise I made, to repay Uncle Samuel the money I took."

"He has long ago forgotten about that. He said he considered it your wedding gift, yours and Leonora's." Harriet smiled at Nathan's look of skepticism. "Now tell me everything that has happened since you surprised us all, *especially me*, by leaving here in the middle of the night with your cousin."

Over food and drink, Nathan recounted everything he could remember. The voyage from Liverpool, his and Leonora's acceptance by the Lowensohn family, their relationships with Antoine and Marie-Louise Vanson, and the tragic endings. Harriet and Miriam dabbed their eyes with lace handkerchiefs as Nathan related the deathbed wedding service performed by *Abbé* Francois.

"Thank God you were spared from that terrible plague," Harriet whispered. "We read about it here, of course, but we had no idea that you and Leonora were in New Orleans. Had I known, I would have worried myself to death. And you . . ."

She turned to Miriam and held the young woman's hands. "How terrible for you to lose your father, your brother, and your sisters. I am so sorry."

Nathan continued the tale, bringing his aunt through the last four years to his wedding to Miriam. When he looked at the clock on the marble fireplace, he was shocked to see that two hours had passed. Harriet thrust more food upon them, then insisted that they come to Russell Square that evening for dinner. "The family will be here. I will say nothing, so you may surprise them."

Nathan accepted. Not for a minute did he believe that Samuel had written off the money quite so easily. Tonight he would repay his debt.

At seven o'clock, they were back at Russell Square. In place of the yellow dress, Miriam now wore dark green, while Nathan had exchanged his pale blue for black. He did not object to wearing black for dinner; he just opposed wearing it, like the English seemed to do, all day long. In his hand, he carried a small leather bag secured by a drawstring.

Harriet answered the door. With a whispered message that no one was expecting them, she led them through to the drawing room. "We have two special guests for dinner," she announced proudly.

Samuel stood with his back to the window. Charlotte and David sat next to each other on a sofa, while Alfred slouched in a high-backed chair. They all turned toward the door as Harriet made her announcement. The faces of Samuel and David, always so alike that the two men could be mistaken for brothers instead of father and son, reflected identical puzzlement as they recognized Nathan and Miriam from that morning's visit to the shop. Samuel looked from the young couple to Harriet, seeking an explanation why two Americans who had bought nothing should be described as special guests.

Nathan supplied the explanation. "Good evening, Uncle Samuel. Good evening, cousins."

Alfred sat up in his chair, a broad smile suddenly covering his face. "Well, I never! The prodigal cousin has returned!"

"Nathan?" David asked. "Is our cousin Nathan the man who claims to work in the cotton trade in New Orleans?"

"Your cousin Nathan," Harriet answered. "Paying us a visit with his charming wife, Miriam."

Nathan, enjoying the instant of surprise, flicked his eyes from one person to the next. Alfred had lost weight. The once curly brown hair was thin and streaked with gray. Lines creased his face, and the sharp blue eyes which Nathan remembered being so full of biting humor had lost much of their gleam. Nathan thought his cousin looked dissolute. At the age of thirty, his profligate life had caught up with him. Charlotte had grown plumper and more homely than Nathan remembered her. Nathan doubted if she and David ever would have children; money would be their comfort. His gaze fastened on Samuel at the window.

"Uncle Samuel, I have come to repay the money which I borrowed from you."

Samuel's face turned red. "Borrowed?" He barely managed to utter the word.

"One hundred and twenty-nine pounds." Nathan offered the leather bag to his uncle. "In there you will find one hundred and seventy-two pounds, seventeen shillings and fivepence, which equals the principal plus interest of five percent per annum, compounded."

Taking the bag, Samuel gently spilled the contents onto a leather-topped table. As he sorted gold from silver and copper, Harriet's voice stopped him. "Samuel, remember what you said."

Samuel looked up from the money, his expression that of a child caught misbehaving. Slowly, his guilt changed to a wan smile. "My dear, I was merely seeing if our nephew's arithmetic is as sharp as the sarcasm he displayed in his letter to me. 'I do not use the word theft,' " Samuel quoted with such perfection that Nathan knew his uncle still had the letter and referred to it occasionally, as if to keep his anger fresh, " 'because I have no intention of depriving you permanently of your money.' "

"Never mind the arithmetic. Remember what you said."

Samuel shoveled the coins back into the bag. "Half of this belongs to you, to you and your wife. Your wedding gift. The other half is your cousin Leonora's wedding gift."

"Thank you, Uncle Samuel," Nathan said. Miriam added her thanks, with the assurance that Leonora would receive the money with Samuel's best wishes when she married. Warmed by both Miriam's gratitude, her refined charm and a smile that brightened the gloomy room, Samuel even forgot for a few moments that the gift had been his wife's idea and not his own. Nathan introduced the rest of the family, finding enjoyment in their reactions. Alfred clasped Miriam's hand while gazing deeply into her green eyes and swearing he had always known his cousin Nathan would marry such a lovely young lady. David, like his father and brother before him, also fell prey to Miriam's allure. He asked so many questions about New Orleans that Nathan finally realized his cousin just wanted to hear Miriam speak; he was captivated by her accent, the soft pronunciation of her words. Charlotte, too, realized it, and as David struggled to think of one more question, his wife stepped in front of him to congratulate Miriam and welcome her to the family. Nathan turned away to hide a smile. He would not want to be in his cousin's shoes later that night, when he had to confront Charlotte alone.

During dinner, Nathan and Miriam took turns answering the questions. Charlotte and Harriet showed interest in the homes of New Orleans, the style of decoration, the furnishings. When Miriam described Waverley, Charlotte asked who would live in such a house.

"We live there. It is the house my father built, the home of a merchant."

"American merchants would appear to live in far greater luxury than their English counterparts," Charlotte said with a meaningful glance at her husband, and once again Nathan decided he would not want to be in his cousin's place later that night.

Alfred interrupted the women's questions with his own queries about entertainment. Nathan described the racetrack at Metairie, the dance halls, and the gambling clubs he had once frequented in the *Vieux Carré*. He saw envy in Alfred's eyes as he described the game he had watched at Mercier's, when Antoine had caught the riverboat gambler cheating.

"You seconded a man in a duel?" Harriet whispered fearfully.

Before Nathan could reply, Alfred pointed a finger at Nathan's face. "I do not remember those narrow, white scars on your face. Do they result from such an affair of honor?"

"They do indeed," Nathan answered in an even tone, and no one at the table mentioned dueling again, although Miriam swore she saw in the eyes of the men a new respect for her husband.

The questions from David and Samuel centered around business. They wanted to know about stores Nathan had seen, the merchandise they stocked, their operating procedures. Samuel, who had followed with interest the confrontation between the free states and the slave states, was particularly interested in the commercial climate prevailing in the South. When Nathan reiterated his belief that the conflict would be resolved peacefully, Samuel sighed in relief. Like all merchants he worried about his source of cotton.

Charlotte inquired about Leonora, and Miriam spoke warmly of the friendship she shared with the young woman. When Nathan added that the factoring business could never manage without Leonora's bookkeeping ability, Samuel's eyebrows lifted.

"Your cousin possesses the skills necessary to keep accounts? Why did she never make that skill known to me?"

"Because you never asked her, Uncle Samuel. You were only interested in Leonora's worth as a seamstress. You were not interested in her skill as a clerk."

Samuel accepted the veiled rebuke by lowering his head. When he lifted it again, his blue eyes shone with derision. "And what of your interests, Nathan? Does your heart still bleed for every battered soul on God's earth? Do you continue to weep for every hungry child? How difficult it must be for you to cling to such noble ideals in a place where everyone owns slaves."

"Not everyone, Uncle. I do not."

"Perhaps not, but you willingly work with cotton planters, the very people who do."

"While you willingly buy their produce," Miriam interjected.

"I do, my dear. I most certainly do. Unlike your husband, though," he added with a wide smirk that was echoed by both his sons, "I have never claimed to be a champion of the oppressed."

"Do you still pay your outworkers the princely sum of threepence a shirt?" Nathan asked.

"I pay them whatever I can get away with paying them, the same as every other shopkeeper. You can rest assured, however, that your friend Mary McBride has received no work from me since you left. Nor has she received work from other shopkeepers."

"She has not been seen," David added. "When we passed the word that she was not to be given work, we learned that she had abandoned that hovel she lived in, taken her brood of ragged children and fled."

Nathan savored his next words. He knew they would signify the end of the evening, the conclusion of this brief and only partly welcome family reunion. Nonetheless, he savored them. "She fled because I told her to flee. When Leonora and I left here that night, we visited Saffron Hill before we boarded our train at Euston. We gave Mary McBride forty-three of the gold sovereigns and told her to flee with her children immediately."

Samuel stood slowly, his face darkening with each inch he rose from the chair. "You gave my money to that woman?"

"No, Uncle Samuel. Leonora and I gave her *our* money. Money you had always intended for us to have as wedding gifts.

I am sure she used it wisely." Standing up, he held out a hand to Miriam. "It might be difficult to find a cab if we leave later. Good night, Uncle Samuel. Alfred, David, Charlotte. I enjoyed seeing you all again."

Other than a nod and a cynical smile from Alfred, Nathan's farewell drew no response. Harriet saw them to the door. When Nathan began to apologize for his behavior, Harriet interrupted him. "You have no need to make amends. Your uncle was begging for precisely the response you gave him. He and David might be better people if they came up against more of your kind of man, and less of the kind they can browbeat and bully into submission." She wrapped her arms around Nathan and Miriam and hugged them tightly. "Thank you both so much for coming to see me. And be sure to tell Leonora that I think of her constantly."

"We will," Miriam assured the older woman.

Harriet released them from her embrace and watched them walk down the steps to the street. At the bottom, they turned to wave. She waved back and blew them a kiss, then quietly closed the door. Holding Miriam by the arm, Nathan began to walk. As they left Russell Square, Nathan looked back at the house in the northwest corner. Gaslight glowed dimly through the windows of the dining and drawing rooms. Nathan imagined what was going on inside. "I wish I could be a fly on the wall," he told Miriam as they continued on their way to the cabstand.

"Would you hear anything worthwhile?"

"I would hear the wagging of tongues. Not my Aunt Harriet, of course. She is above such malicious gossip, but the others will be at it, talking about you and me as if we were the most scandalous couple on the face of the earth. My uncle. My cousin David and his wife Charlotte, whose sense of propriety has taken a terrible beating tonight. And Alfred, before he leaves to visit his latest disreputable haunt."

"Did you see the look Charlotte gave David when I described Waverley? And the envy in Alfred's eyes at your tales? They tried to counter by questioning how you could maintain kindness and sympathy while living among slavery, but you turned the tables on them when you said you had given a third of the money to that seamstress. Did you?"

Nathan nodded. "Had I not, she would surely have starved thanks to my uncle organizing such a disgraceful boycott against her." He turned to look back again, but the northwest corner of Russell Square was no longer in view. "When I was young, Miriam, I thought Alfred and David were far more fortunate than me. Their parents lived while mine and Leonora's had died. They were wealthy, while I lived on the scraps they threw. Now I know better. They have nothing. Alfred follows an empty, dissolute life. David is married to a woman who is an image of himself. Their marriage might produce wealth, but it will produce neither children nor happiness. I am fortunate, Miriam, because I have you. In a few weeks with you, I have experienced more happiness than David and Alfred will know in a hundred lifetimes."

Nathan and Miriam stayed in London for another two weeks, after which they traveled north to Manchester to visit mills which bought cotton from Nathan's clients. From there, they made the short journey to Liverpool and the Cunard steamer that would return them to New York. When the ship pulled out into the center of the River Mersey, Nathan stood at the rail to watch the imposing buildings of Liverpool slip by. Once he closed his eyes and heard Leonora's excited shout and saw red-shirted sailors dancing through the rigging, but when he opened them again he saw smoke belching from the ship's stack.

He reflected on the visit. He and Miriam had enjoyed London. It had been her first visit. His own, too, because his earlier nineteen-year sojourn had occurred in a different lifetime. They had attended plays and operas, and shopped in every store, it seemed, but S. Solomon and Sons. Although they had not seen Samuel or his sons again, they had met twice with Harriet.

They had parted the last time, on the day before leaving London, by promising Harriet that if she did not have a grandchild she would, one day, have a great-niece or -nephew to hold. An American great-niece or -nephew. Harriet's eyes had turned misty as she made a promise of her own. When that day came, she would make the voyage to America to hold the child.

Nathan and Miriam returned to New Orleans in early September, after an absence of more than ten weeks. The worst of the summer was over. Already breezes from the lake could be felt, banishing the city's cloying humidity and hinting at the autumn that soon would follow. With a feeling of excitement, Nathan watched the first cotton bales on the levee. Those bales were heralds of a new season, the couriers of New Orleans's annual rebirth. As he watched the white piles grow, he knew no man could be happier than he was at that moment.

He was wrong. He found that out a month later, when his happiness turned to ecstasy at Miriam's news that she was expecting his child.

In March 1858, Miriam gave birth to a boy with a red, wrinkled face and a circle of fluffy golden hair that surrounded his head like a heavenly halo. She wanted the child's name to memorialize her brother Henry but, simultaneously, she preferred something less formal. Henry sounded too royal, too pretentious. Nathan offered Harry, the familiar name of England's King Henry the Fifth. Miriam repeated the name twice before looking down at the baby in her arms. "Would you want to spend the rest of your life as a Harry?" she whispered. When no response was forthcoming, she turned back to Nathan. "Harry likes Harry."

The arrival of the child caused an upheaval at Waverley. Anna's exhilaration at becoming a grandmother was equalled by Leonora's thrill at being an honorary aunt. Each morning, Nathan watched the two women inspect his son, seeking changes from the previous day. They competed with each other to see who could first spot Harry smiling, crawling, and finally, as he turned a year, walking. Nor were the servants immune from the excitement. Delilah prepared special dishes which she claimed would help Miriam regain her strength. Samson carved wooden ornaments to hang over Harry's crib, while Rebecca urged Naomi and Bathsheba to keep the house spotless. "You've got to be extra watchful for dirt when there's a baby in the house," the housekeeper told the two maids. "A tiny speck of dust that don't mean a thing to you or me will make the little one sick."

With joy came a single moment of agonizing sadness. On the very day of Harry's birth, Nathan wrote to his aunt in London, reminding her of the promise she had made. Four months later came a letter from his cousin David. Written in a stiff, upright hand, the letter did not include a single word of congratulations for Nathan on the birth of his son. Instead, it told him that his aunt had died from pneumonia at the beginning of March. When Nathan shared the news with Leonora, they both cried.

Two years after Harry's birth, in March 1860, Miriam and Nathan were parents again, to a baby girl whose green eyes were the mirror of her mother's. There was no discussion about a name because Miriam had decided long ago what a girl should be called. "Our daughter," she told Nathan, "shall be called Louise."

Nathan was stunned. He had expected Miriam to choose Martha or Sarah, thereby remembering her sisters who had perished in the yellow-fever epidemic of 1853. He had never considered that she would want the child named after Marie-Louise.

Miriam understood her husband's shock. "Nathan, I know what Marie-Louise meant to you, and what her memory continues to mean. That day at the lake, when you gave me the emerald bracelet, I said I did not worry about any feelings you still harbored. It is right that Marie-Louise will always live on in your heart, and it is just as right that she will live on in name as well."

A lump blocked Nathan's throat. Moisture filled his eyes. He questioned whether he, were the roles reversed, could have shown such understanding. The girl he had deemed so spoiled and precocious had become a wonderful, compassionate woman.

Each time Nathan saw his children—Harry alive with the energy of a two-year-old, and Louise sleeping peacefully in her bassinet—that same realization recurred. With it came comparisons. Creole blood had blazed through Marie-Louise's veins, while Miriam displayed cool, dependable strength. Nathan saw more evidence of that each day as she cared for their children. Under her attention, major crises became minor, and minor crises no reason for tears at all. Once, Nathan's comparisons set Marie-Louise in Miriam's place. How would the Creole girl have reacted to losing four family members? Would she, like Miriam, have grown into a stronger person? Or would she have acted as irrationally as her brother Antoine had done? Terrified of living without those she loved, would she have courted death until it accommodated her?

Nathan never drew that particular parallel again, because he knew what the answer would be.

Chapter Seventeen

The summer of 1860 was the hottest most Orleanians could recall. Once the spring rains ended, blistering heat set in. Humidity levels soared while energy fell. Today's tasks were put off until tomorrow, and tomorrow's tasks deferred until next week. The wealthy sought refuge at the lake, or in cooler, more northerly climes. The poor carried on as best they could. In crowded areas, sporadic cases of disease occurred. They were treated quickly, the victims isolated until they recovered or died. In 1860, there would be no repeat of the epidemic that had ravaged New Orleans seven years earlier. Besides, many new drainage ditches had been dug since then. Sodden filth no longer covered the ground in such profusion.

Those who earned a living from cotton had no complaints. A record two and a quarter-million bales had passed through New Orleans the previous year, and prospects for the coming season appeared even better. The exceptional summer had guaranteed an outstanding crop. Coupled with the unquenchable demands for raw cotton from European mills, the current harvest would surely make 1860–61 the most successful season ever.

Even the storm that battered the city at the start of October failed to dampen spirits. Buildings were flooded. Many of the streets became tributaries of the Mississippi, and people paddled to destinations instead of walking or riding. In the second week of October, when the St. Charles Theater opened, patrons were so enchanted by Campbell's Minstrels that they overlooked the theater's gloomy, water-damaged interior. The same held true at Vannuchi's Museum where crowds admired wax figures of President Buchanan meeting the Japanese ambassadors, Louis Napoleon conferring with Garibaldi, and old John Brown and his gang of murderers. More crowds flocked to the Spalding and Rogers Museum where a hippopotamus, the first such monster ever brought to America, was on display. The one event that best signified the start of the city's social season was the opening on November 8 of *The Barber of Seville* at the Théâtre d'Opera, where as many people showed interest in the theater's newly frescoed proscenium and dome as came to listen to Rossini's masterpiece.

Nathan's appreciation of opera had flourished in the eight years since Gershon Lowensohn had taken him to see *William Tell*. Except for the period of his deepest mourning for Marie-Louise, he had seen every production to pass through New Orleans. With Miriam, Leonora, and Anna, he attended the opening night of *The Barber of Seville*, but for once his mind was not fully on the performance. Only Leonora noticed his apparent distraction. When she asked him what was wrong he answered with an enigmatic: "We live in a fantasy world, Lally. While a massive storm gathers above our heads, we watch opera and hum its melodies."

Throughout the second act, Nathan contemplated that storm, an upheaval made even more turbulent by the national election two days before. While the city had supported Unionist candidates, John C. Breckinridge, the choice of the breakaway Democratic wing, had picked up enough of the outlying vote to carry the rest of the state. That result was academic, because the national election had been won by a man whose name had not even appeared on the ballot in Louisiana. Abraham Lincoln.

Next morning, Nathan received a visit from James Wilson who was in New Orleans with his wife and daughters. After settling accounts, the two men discussed the effects of the Republican Party's election triumph. Nathan remarked on the moderate stance taken by many of the city's newspapers. "The *Bee* claims to support the continuation of the Union as long as it is possible to preserve it, while the *Commercial Bulletin* declares that it would never consent to a dissolution of the Union. Is that what the editors really believe, or do they seek, at this late stage, to soothe emotions that have run riot for so long? Personally, I fear it is far too late for such restraint to be shown now."

Wilson nodded in agreement. "Now that the die is cast, everyone wants to be seen as the voice of reason and sanity." He told Nathan that he had listened to Stephen Douglas, the unsuccessful Democratic presidential candidate, speak outside the St. Charles Hotel only the previous day. "When Douglas pointed out that, despite Lincoln's victory, the Democrats still controlled both houses of Congress, he struck me as a man throwing water over a small fire which he feared would become a furious blaze. Like you, I believe such shows of responsibility are too little, too late. Our fire-eaters will never allow their torches to be doused now."

"If secession comes . . . if war comes . . . what will you do?"

Wilson's red face hardened. His blue eyes froze. "As much as I value our trade with the Upper Mississippi Valley, I will never forget that I am a Southerner first and a businessman second. When the bugle calls, I will turn over the running of Fallowfields to my wife. I will be among the first you see in uniform. And I trust that you will be among the first I see."

Nathan recalled his words to Anna and Leonora on the night four years ago when they had pressed him to take sides. He had no choice but to fight for the South. He just hoped that he and Wilson were wrong, and that it was not too late for the voices of moderation to be heeded.

His hope was in vain. Restraint quickly yielded to defiance and open challenge. By mid-November, the secessionist blue cockade—a pelican button with two streamers—was a common sight. Newspapers which had preached moderation after

Lincoln's election grew hostile to the North. Even the *Picayune* switched sides to join the fire-eaters it had once vociferously opposed. Unionist hopes suffered a major blow on Thanksgiving Day when the Reverend Benjamin Morgan Palmer condemned the abolitionists in a two-hour sermon and declared the South was fighting for God and religion. Palmer's sermon was reprinted and distributed across the entire South. As the flames of separatism flared from this new fuel, Nathan read in the once-moderate *Bee* what everyone in the city knew already: that New Orleans was now a hotbed of secessionism.

Explosions rocked the city on December 20. Nathan and Leonora ran from the countinghouse to find the air full of smoke. Cannon were being fired at the foot of Canal Street to celebrate South Carolina's secession from the Union. As the smoke cleared, and echoes of cannon fire faded, the Pelican flag appeared. In January, the roar of cannon filled Canal Street again. The state convention, meeting in Baton Rouge, had passed the Ordinance of Secession, and the connection with the Federal Union was dissolved. Louisiana, the sixth state to secede, was now an autonomous nation. At Waverley, Nathan opened a bottle of champagne. After pouring glasses for himself, Miriam, Leonora and Anna, he made a solemn toast. "To Louisiana. A free, sovereign, and independent power. And may God help us all."

Both Leonora and Miriam smiled. Even nonbelievers called upon the Almighty when peril threatened.

Before secession, the state had taken Forts Jackson and St. Philip below New Orleans, the United States arsenal at Baton Rouge, and a revenue cutter. Following secession, the new nation of Louisiana seized all remaining Federal property within its borders. Militia units occupied Forts Pike and Macomb and secured the United States Mint and Customs House in New Orleans, along with more than six hundred thousand dollars in cash. While this occurred, the *True Delta* offered its readers another blinding glimpse of the obvious by pointing out that everything in the city appeared to be progressing rapidly toward a war establishment.

A new flag was needed for the new nation. Louisiana adopted a standard containing thirteen stripes—six white, four blue, and three red—and a five-pointed yellow star on a red field. The flag represented the state's history, the thirteen stripes of the original Union, the Tricolor of France, and the red and yellow of Spain. Now it owed allegiance to none of them.

For almost two months, Louisiana remained an independent nation. Then, on March 21, by ratifying the constitution of the Confederate States of America—created at the Montgomery meeting of the Southern states—it joined the Confederacy. Each morning that Nathan went in to the countinghouse, he saw preparations for war. Weapons appeared in almost every hand. Hastily formed military units, commanded by officers taken from the city's upper class, drilled in the streets. Auctions and bazaars raised money to outfit the soldiers. Above the crisis and urgency, he sensed a festive atmosphere, as if the Orleanians believed they were going not to war, but to a carnival. Did they not know that men bled in war? That men lost arms and legs, and often died?

A week after Louisiana joined the Confederacy, Nathan was surprised to see James Wilson enter the countinghouse. The Red River planter's cotton yield had been shipped early, in November, when Wilson had visited New Orleans with his family. This time, Wilson had not come with his family. Nor was he wearing his normal attire. Keeping the vow he had made to Nathan at their last meeting, Wilson was dressed in a gray uniform.

"Colonel James Wilson at your service, sir. I have been given the honor of a commission in the army of the Confederate States of America, with the charge of leading a regiment. Join me, Nathan. Be among the first to carry the flag in this noble and God-blessed quest for freedom."

Nathan shook his head. "I still hope that cooler heads prevail and war will be averted."

"Look around you and tell me that you really believe what you say. Those men drilling in the street, those women raising money by giving their valuables to be auctioned . . . do you really believe there is any other way to establish our freedom than by armed conflict?" He grasped Nathan's hand and shook it. "When the guns sound in anger, I will be back to ask you again. Do not disappoint me a second time."

Standing in the doorway of the countinghouse, Nathan watched Wilson stride down Canal Street toward the river. In the four months since Nathan had last seen him, Wilson had changed from planter to soldier. What did his wife, Millicent, and his two daughters, Angelina and Sally, think about it? Both girls had married in the past year. Had their new husbands marched off to war as quickly as their father had done? His thoughts turned to Miriam, and he wondered how she would react if he went home to Waverley that night and declared that he had joined the fight. The scene terrified him, and he did something he had not done for a very long time. He prayed. Despite the war preparation he saw all around, he closed his eyes and offered up a silent prayer that war never came. Because he knew what his answer would be when Wilson returned to ask again.

Nathan's prayer went unheard. Less than two weeks after Wilson's visit, on April 12, 1861, Confederate artillery at Charleston, South Carolina, opened fire on Union-held Fort Sumter. When the fort surrendered after three days, the crash of cannon echoed along Canal Street once again. Abraham Lincoln's call for seventy-five thousand troops to force the South back into the Union failed to frighten the people of New Orleans. Neither did the blockade of the city at the end of May by Federal ships stationed at the mouth of the Mississippi. Brave men and fast cutters would run the Yankee blockade. And if that failed, other ways would be found to export the South's cotton and sugar. The second American Revolution had begun, and nothing would dampen the enthusiasm of those called upon to fight it.

Enthusiasm turned to jubilation as Confederate forces routed the Union army at Bull Run. The belief spread quickly that the war would be over soon. The Federal government would have no alternative but to recognize the independence of those states in the Confederacy. In the meantime, geography and strategically placed forts would protect New Orleans. Tom Harris, Nathan's chief clerk, had been born in the city. His grandfather had fought in its defense against the British, and he considered himself an expert on the city's military security. Certain that Nathan and Leonora were concerned over the possibility of a Federal attack, he sought to reassure them. "No army can march overland against New Orleans. It must be carried within striking distance, as the British were. General Pakenham chose the route through the Mississippi Sound, marched across the narrow swampland between Lake Borgne and the river, and was defeated soundly when he attacked Old Hickory's defenses below the city. Should the Federals try the same route, Fort Bienvenu will give them a fine welcome. If they choose to move through the passes into the lake for an attack from the north, Fort Pike on the Rigolets and Fort Macomb on Chef Menteur will halt them. And if they come up the river, their deep-draft warships must navigate the shallow bar at the mouth, and the two forts, Jackson and Saint Philip, twenty-five miles upstream."

Nathan congratulated Harris on his expertise, and assured the chief clerk that he had, indeed, set his own and Leonora's mind at rest. The very next day, promising to return the instant the war was over, Harris joined the Confederate army. Nathan turned over the chief clerk's duties to Leonora, although, with the season finished, there was little work to do. He hoped there would be more when the next season began, but with Union ships continuing their blockade, he was beginning to doubt it. Abraham Lincoln, the despised President of the United States, was far stronger than most Southerners gave him credit for. He was a man who would refuse to go down in history as the president under whom the nation had disintegrated.

Bull Run had filled the South with hope, but Nathan could not drive from his mind the old English adage that a single swallow did not make a summer.

During those first months of the War for Southern Independence, Louisiana worked at a frenzied rate. All kinds of military equipment was assembled in government warehouses. Factories were built to manufacture those goods which the Federal blockade had cut off. Food crops were planted. Boats scoured the rivers and bayous for scrap iron to be shipped to foundries in New Orleans for war supplies.

Early one Sunday in September, three horsemen dismounted in front of Waverley. One was a colonel in the Confederate army, another a captain. The third wore a black coat and trousers, and a wide-brimmed black hat. The colonel rapped authoritatively on the door. Rebecca answered, and took the visitors through to the rear parlor, asking them to be seated while she fetched Nathan.

Rebecca knew exactly where to find Nathan, in the bedroom his children shared. Sunday morning was his favorite time, the one moment of the week he could be alone with his daughter and son. During the rest of the week, he felt lucky to steal a minute or two with them. Even in summer, when no cotton gathered on the levee, he was busy with obligations to his customers. So each Sunday, he did his best to compensate for any neglect. He always started the precious day the same way, looking closely at each child as if seeking changes from the previous week. Had Harry's hair darkened or was it still as golden as his mother's? Had Louise's eyes remained so green? The boy, three and a half years old and quite accustomed to his father's weekly routine, stared back as if looking for similar changes in Nathan. The girl, two years younger and bursting with the novelty of self-propulsion, rarely kept still long enough to be inspected. Nathan made a game of chasing her, until he trapped her in a corner of the room where he could hold her while he scrutinized her face. She always smiled when he did that, rewarding his effort with a wide and wet chubby-cheeked beam that made him hug her tightly. No one interrupted his Sunday-morning frolics with his children. Not Miriam, not Leonora, not Anna. They all knew how important the time was to him. So when Rebecca knocked on the door, Nathan knew she had good reason.

"Three men are here to see you, Master Nathan. A colonel, a captain, and a man in black."

"Where is my wife?"

"She picks flowers in the rear garden with Mistress Leonora."

"And her mother?"

"In the kitchen with Delilah."

Nathan nodded in satisfaction. He knew nothing of the captain or the man in black, but he was certain he knew the colonel's identity. James Wilson was making the return call he had promised to make once the guns sounded in anger. Nathan did not want the women of Waverley to hear his conversation with Wilson. If he did enlist—and deep down in his heart he knew the allegiance he owed this city left him with no alternative—the decision might sit badly with the women. Nathan preferred to face that problem after Wilson and his companions had departed.

Wilson swung around the instant he heard Nathan's footsteps cross the hall. "Our righteous struggle for independence goes well, Nathan. Join now and share the glory with us."

Nathan looked at Wilson, then at the two men accompanying him. The man in black was a total stranger, but the soldier with the captain's insignia was very familiar. He was the last person Nathan expected to see at Waverley.

"Allow me," Wilson said, "to introduce my aide, Captain Barnett. The other gentleman is Major Moore, of the Confederate Signal Service."

Nathan saw the smirk that appeared on Marcus Barnett's face at the introduction. Wilson's aide! Instead of giving the slave-dealer's son the satisfaction of recognition, Nathan turned to Major Arthur Moore, a short, sturdy man with a tidy dark brown beard. "Delighted to make your acquaintance, Major."

Moore's handshake was crisp and dry. "And I, sir, am just as delighted to meet you."

"I believe that you and Captain Barnett already know each other," Wilson said.

"Be sure that it is only because he comes as your aide that I tolerate his presence."

Marcus's smile grew condescending. "Surely if a grudge is held, Nathan, it should be mine. After all, it was not *I* who married the young lady *you* intended to make your own. How is Miriam? Is she still the same little spitfire?"

"I would thank you not to ask after my wife, nor any other member of this family." Nathan saw with satisfaction the scar across Marcus's chin where Miriam's brooch had struck him. "I would also thank you to leave because I do not wish my wife to be upset by seeing you in this house."

Wilson stepped between the two men. "Captain Barnett, I think it best you wait outside." When the front door closed, Wilson turned his attention to Nathan. "Forgive me. I was unaware of any friction between the pair of you."

"It occurred several years ago. However, if he is your aide, I could not possibly serve with you."

"I appointed Captain Barnett as my aide because he raised money to outfit my regiment. His presence will be no problem, though, because Major Moore was hoping you would serve with him."

Moore stepped forward. "The Signal Service not only passes information, it gathers it. I am recruiting foreign nationals sympathetic to our cause. You are, I trust, sympathetic."

Before Nathan could answer, Wilson said, "You will find no more sympathetic a man in all of New Orleans."

Moore's square face broke into a cheerless smile. "I need to hear it from him, sir."

"My sympathies lie with the South," Nathan answered.

"I am recruiting foreign nationals to act as agents in major Northern cities such as Washington, Baltimore, Philadelphia, and New York. Especially New York, where antiwar Democrat Copperheads are powerful. At one time, the Copperheads even proposed that New York secede from the United States, constitute itself as a free city, and receive the whole and united support of the Southern states. Our agents in New York, as well as reporting information on troop movements and allied activity, will provoke unrest against the Union among elements already opposed to the war."

"I have spent but three or four days in New York, and that was several years ago. I know little about the city."

"Therefore New York knows little about you!" Moore exclaimed triumphantly. "That is why you are such an exemplary choice. When Colonel Wilson first mentioned you as a possible agent, I saw the potential immediately. You will enter New York as an English businessman seeking to profit from the war. We will provide you with the necessary papers to support that background. Once you are settled, you will be contacted by the liaison through whom you will pass information and receive instructions."

As Nathan contemplated the offer, Wilson spoke. "Nathan, I would dishonor a long and warm relationship if I did not make known to you the dangers of such an assignment. Captured spies are subject to being tried and hanged."

"I understand that, but if Major Moore's confidence is any indication, surely such a dreadful possibility will never arise."

"I find it gratifying that you have such faith in me, but the risk of exposure is always present."

Despite Moore's admission, Nathan's mind was already made up. He would have served willingly in the line, although not beside a man like Marcus Barnett. Being asked to spy added a dash of excitement to what he already considered a moral obligation.

Miriam found neither excitement nor moral obligation in her husband's decision to spy for Major Arthur Moore. When Nathan revealed his plans to her shortly after the departure of Moore and James Wilson she was astounded. She let fly with a fury verging on hysteria. "Are you that desperate for me to become a widow? For your son and daughter to have nothing of their father but memories of a few minutes' play each Sunday morning?"

Nathan reached out to grasp Miriam's shoulders. She had been outside, picking flowers, and he questioned whether anger or the early-morning sun was responsible for the flush of color that suddenly bloomed in her normally pale face. "How will you become a widow, Miriam? Why will our children be fatherless?"

"Because spies are hanged," she answered with such immediacy that Nathan wondered whether she had been eavesdropping.

"Spies are hanged only if caught. I will not be caught."

"All right. Suppose God grants you such good fortune, you will still be away for years. Your children will forget you."

"Not years, Miriam!" Nathan's tone became as forceful as his wife's. "This war will be over in a matter of months! Bull Run demonstrated that the Yankees cannot fight. My work will help bring the war to an end even sooner."

The raised voices drew an audience. Anna entered the rear parlor with Leonora a few steps behind. "The sound of your argument reaches all the way to the kitchen. Is it so important that you wish the servants to hear every word?"

Miriam sought help from her mother. "My husband has decided that his duties to his adopted country are more important than his responsibilities to his wife and children."

Anna turned to her son-in-law. "You are joining the army?"

"No, Mother. Much more dangerous. My husband is a spy."

"May I speak?" Nathan asked. Anna turned toward him. "Four years ago, in this very room, I said that if war came I would fight for the South. The time has come to keep that promise."

"You made no such vow in my hearing," Miriam argued.

Nathan thought back to the night he had argued with Marcus Barnett over slavery. "You were not here. You had gone riding. If you remember, you were furious with me because you felt I had been rude to your beau over dinner."

"Oh, him," Miriam said disdainfully. Nathan wondered how she would react if she knew Marcus had been here only minutes earlier. He decided that she would have thrown him out even before Nathan had asked him to leave. She had never forgiven his cruelty at the St. Louis Hotel.

"What about the business?" Anna asked.

"No cotton will leave New Orleans until we win this war and end the blockade," said Nathan. "Besides, Leonora is perfectly capable of managing for the few months I will be away."

Miriam swung around to look at Leonora, seeing in the young Englishwoman her last possible alliance. "Do you want your cousin to risk his life for a war he claims is already won?"

"I do not want my cousin to risk his life for anything," Leonora answered calmly, "but I would be the last to stand in his way when he follows an honorable course."

Nathan felt an instantaneous burst of warmth for his cousin. Lally knew him better than anyone. Their years together and their shared experiences provided her with a unique understanding of his feelings. Better even than Miriam, who was his wife.

Miriam accepted defeat. The anger left her eyes. Sadness took its place. Nathan's throat tightened, and his stomach performed an uncomfortable somersault. He would do anything to drive away that sadness. Anything but the one deed that would surely succeed. "I will come back a hero," he promised. "A hero you and Harry and Louise can be proud of."

"We are proud of you already."

"Then I will make you even prouder." He kissed Miriam gently on the lips, held her for a long minute, then went upstairs. He had to prepare for his two new careers—English businessman and Confederate spy.

Chapter Eighteen

Accompanied by Major Arthur Moore, Nathan left New Orleans a week later. While traveling overland to Savannah, he concentrated on perfecting his new identity. When he eventually reached New York through the circuitous route Moore had planned, Nathan Solomon would be just a memory, an old coat to be slipped on again only when he returned to New Orleans. He would be Nathan Cox, a Manchester cotton broker pragmatic enough to believe the Union would put down the rebellion by the cotton states. His reason for visiting the United States would be the establishment of new supply sources once hostilities ceased.

Immediately before the two men parted company in Savannah, Moore told Nathan the name of his contact in New York. "He is a man who will call himself John Harold Bentley."

"How will he know where to find me?"

"He will know. He will watch for you on the ships that dock in New York. He will follow you to your hotel and contact you when he feels the time is appropriate."

They shook hands and separated. Moore went north to Richmond. Nathan boarded *Neptune's Maid,* a fast cutter that was set to sail at nightfall. Union ships waited outside the harbor to intercept blockade runners, but the cutter's captain was experienced at evading them. He had taken *Neptune's Maid* past Union blockaders half a dozen times before.

An hour after dusk, *Neptune's Maid* slipped out of the harbor. Low clouds obscured a sliver of a moon. Not a light showed on board the ship, not a sound was heard. Standing at the quarterdeck rail, Nathan peered into the gloom. Once he saw the lights of a ship. Another time, shouted commands leaped at him from the darkness. Every moment he expected to hear the roar of cannon, to see muzzle flashes and feel shot slamming into wood all around him. He heard nothing. Nothing but the creaking of timbers, the whistle of the wind, and the whispered orders that carried no further than the men for whom they were intended. When dawn crept up over the eastern horizon, Savannah was far behind. That morning, as *Neptune's Maid* rode all alone, Nathan started his disguise. He did not shave.

Neptune's Maid carried Nathan to Nassau, St. Thomas, and finally Havana, where he transferred to a British steamer bound for England. Five weeks after leaving New Orleans, he stood once more on the Liverpool waterfront. His beard, now complete, was streaked with gray. When he looked in a mirror, a hairy face he did not recognize stared back. He grew more confident about his ability to deceive. If he could not recognize himself, who would be able to identify him?

He stayed in Liverpool three days until, as Nathan Cox, he boarded a New York-bound Cunard steamer. He kept his own company during the voyage, remaining in his cabin as much as he could, mentally preparing himself for the task that lay ahead. Those times he could not avoid mingling with the other passengers, he volunteered as little as possible about himself, even to the point of rudeness. He remembered advice given to him by Major Moore, that an agent's worst enemy was his own loose tongue.

As the steamer drew within sight of the American coast, Nathan hunched over the rail. It seemed only yesterday he had occupied a similar position as he and Miriam returned from their wedding voyage. They had been starting a new life then, full of hope for the future. Now Miriam was in New Orleans with their children, and Nathan was preparing to risk his life.

Landing was a formality. Nathan presented his forged papers and was passed through. While waiting for his baggage to be placed aboard a cab, he scanned the men gathered at South Street, trying to decide which was John Harold Bentley. The cab took him to the St. Nicholas Hotel, on Broadway and Broome Street. Every minute or so, Nathan looked back but he failed to spot an obvious tracker. Had Major Moore's man slipped up and missed the ship? If so, Nathan would be stranded in New York without a contact. What would he do then? He calmed himself by remembering that he was a novice in the profession of spying, while the man who had sent him was a veteran. Bentley was out there and would make his presence known at the proper time.

At the St. Nicholas, Nathan stayed in the same third-floor suite he had shared with Miriam. He thought he recognized several members of the staff from four years ago, but no one remembered him. Not that he expected them to. Thousands of guests had passed through the hotel since he had stayed with Miriam. None, probably, had taken such pains to disguise himself on his return visit. He kept close to the hotel, venturing out only for a brisk walk to keep his senses alert. On the second night, after returning from such a walk, he received a sealed envelope from the desk clerk. He gained the security of his suite before opening the envelope. It contained a short letter from a man calling himself John Harold Bentley, asking Nathan to meet for dinner at Gosling's on Nassau Street at eight o'clock the following night.

Nathan entered Gosling's at ten minutes before eight. After giving Bentley's name, he was guided to an empty table. For five minutes, he sat alone, feeling uncomfortably exposed, then a tall, gray-haired man approached. "How do you do, Mister Cox?" The man pulled out the chair opposite Nathan and sat down. "I am John Harold Bentley."

"Your friend Arthur Moore said you would be able to help me acquire cotton, Mister Bentley. In fact, he said he would bet every hair of his bright red beard on it."

A smile crossed Bentley's thin face. "My friend Arthur Moore has a dark brown beard."

Nathan returned an equally wintry smile. "So he does."

They ate dinner slowly, talking about everything but the war taking place just a few hundred miles to their south. To an eavesdropper, their conversation was that of two men who might or might not be associated by business. On finishing the leisurely meal at ten o'clock, Bentley suggested they adjourn to Nathan's hotel suite where they could discuss their business in greater privacy. He collected a black opera cape from the cloakroom, which he flung around his shoulders with a dramatic flourish, then followed Nathan out of the restaurant. Reaching the hotel, Nathan led Bentley to the third floor.

"When I followed you from the dock, I noticed that you went straight to the Saint Nicholas," Bentley said as he accompanied Nathan along the gaslit third-floor corridor. "Was that the cab driver's recommendation or your own idea?"

"I stayed here with my wife when we were first married."

"Did you?" A warning sounded in Bentley's voice. "Coming back constitutes a risk."

"Do not worry," Nathan said as he unlocked the door. "Four years have passed. Besides, I did not wear a beard then. No one remembers me."

"I trust your confidence is not misplaced. Many men before you have kicked and squirmed at the end of a rope for such errors of discretion."

Pulling out the key, Nathan swung back the door. The light from the corridor failed to penetrate the sitting room. He stepped inside, fumbling for a match with which to light the lamp that sat on a table close to the door. The match flared into life. Blinded by the sudden light, he heard Bentley's gasp of surprise. Figures darted into motion as the match dropped from Nathan's fingers and fell to the ground, plunging the room once more into darkness.

"Raise your hands! You are both under arrest!"

Bentley shoved Nathan deep into the sitting room, flung back his cape and pulled a cumbersome Colt revolver from his trouser waistband. Twice the gun roared, filling the room with noise and light and smoke. Three revolvers answered. A shout of pain came from the direction of the door. Flame blossomed from the muzzle of a fourth revolver. Fire burned Nathan's eyes and a white-hot sword slashed across his forehead. He staggered back, clutching at his face. The blackness of the room closed in on him. He felt himself falling and floating, plunging down a deep well and then drifting on a cloud. His last conscious thought was one of failure. Despite the beard, despite the passage of four years, someone had seen him and remembered him after all.

He regained consciousness with his head strapped onto a blacksmith's anvil. The slightest movement brought the smithy's hammer crashing down. He opened his eyes slowly, one at a time. Lamplight filled them. He was no longer in the St. Nicholas. This room had none of the hotel's luxurious fittings. His bed was a straw mattress on a cold stone floor. The only furniture he could see was a wooden table and three chairs. Iron bars adorned the single window. More iron bars formed a door. Ignoring the pain, he raised a hand to his face to find a wide, heavy bandage drawn tightly around his head.

A man in a blue uniform looked in, saw Nathan move his head and shouted out that the prisoner was awake. Moments later, the barred door opened. The guard entered with a fat, red-faced man carrying a black bag. When Nathan recognized the guard's blue uniform as that of the Union army, the incident at the St. Nicholas came flashing back. His assignment had ended in abysmal failure, and he had fallen into the hands of the enemy.

The red-faced man knelt down beside Nathan and asked how he felt. When Nathan answered "Terrible," the man laughed. "I'm not surprised. You've been unconscious for nearly two days. I had a hell of a job patching up the new parting a bullet gave you and picking out a parcel of powder from your forehead."

"You did better than your partner," the guard volunteered. "He's feeding the worms right now."

Very gently, the doctor removed the bandage and inspected the wound. "That's coming along nicely. I daresay you'll be fit to travel in a couple of days."

"Where?"

"Washington," the guard answered.

"What reason do I have to be in Washington? I have business in New York, not Washington."

"Some people there want to talk to you. They want to find out why Mister Nathan Cox of Manchester is really Mister Nathan Solomon of New Orleans."

Two days later, handcuffed and escorted by four soldiers, Nathan traveled by train to Washington. He felt much better. The pain inside his skull had subsided to a dull throb. The powder burns across his forehead were healing, and the red-faced doctor, after a final examination, had declared the scalp wound to be mending well.

A dozen soldiers met the train at Washington. They escorted Nathan to the Old Capitol Prison where he was locked in a cell whose only light came from a small barred window set high in the wall. Sitting on one of the cell's two chairs, he contemplated his predicament. He had been brought here so Union spy catchers could question him. They would be unlucky. He had been exposed to only one other Confederate agent, the thin, white-haired man who had identified himself as John Harold Bentley. Bentley was dead anyway, killed before he could pass on information. All Nathan knew was the objective of his mission, to contact Democratic Copperheads and stir up antiwar sentiment. His arrogance at staying in a hotel where he could be recognized had cost the life of Bentley. He would be damned if he'd give the Yankees anything else. Not the reason for his presence in New York. Not the name of the man who had sent him. Nothing, not even the drippings off the end of his nose!

Three hours passed while he hardened his resolution. At last, the cell door opened. Two men entered. One had the body of a giant and the face of a monster. His left eye shone brightly, a twinkling sapphire in a rosy, weather-beaten face. His right eye was covered by a patch. The right side of his face, from the bottom of his jaw to his hairline, was a mass of scar tissue, a red and purple blaze twisted together like the relief map of a mountain range. He wore an army uniform, with a sergeant's yellow stripes sewn on the sleeve. Next to the soldier, the other man looked frail. His face was thin, his dark beard neatly trimmed, his shoulders stooped. His strength was in his sharp blue eyes. They flicked over the prisoner, storing details in the brain that lay behind them.

While the scarred sergeant stood, the other man took the seat opposite Nathan. "I am Major Allen. I am to the Union what Major Arthur Moore is to the Confederacy." Nathan's eyes widened involuntarily. Allen smiled. "There is very little we do not know about you, Mister Solomon. You were sent here, ostensibly an English businessman, to wreak havoc behind our lines. The fact that we caught you is proof that our spy system is better than your own. The only matter that remains to be settled is whether you choose cooperation or a hangman's noose."

Nathan sat up straight. "I demand to see the British ambassador. I am a British citizen who is being illegally held. When the British government finds out—"

"Demand all you want. Your words will go no farther than this cell. How can the British government help you when it cannot hear you? We are the only ones who will hear you, and what we want to hear are the names of your contacts. In New York, and back in that traitor's nest you call the Confederate States of America."

"My name is Nathan Cox. I am a director of—"

"Please." Allen held up a hand. "Do not insult me. I will return tomorrow to talk to you again, but before I go let me give you a word of warning. If you do not cooperate, we will try you as a spy and we will hang you. And if you attempt to escape, the sergeant here will take great pleasure in dissuading you from such foolish action. Show him your eye, Sergeant." Allen watched revulsion cover Nathan's face as the sergeant lifted the patch to reveal a shriveled eye socket. "The sergeant received that souvenir at Bull Run, Mister Solomon, a burning torch ground into his face. Ever since then, he has diligently sought ways to exact his vengeance."

Nathan tried hard to control his fear. The sergeant's single eye had just swept over him, and the awful gaze was like the devil's breath.

Allen returned with the sergeant the next day and every day after that for a week. Each time, Nathan met his questions with silence. He knew nothing but the objective of his mission. If he admitted that and nothing more, Allen would never believe it was all he knew. Allen would think Nathan was offering a sprat to satisfy him, and it would only make the Union major more certain that his prisoner was holding back. Nathan failed to see how he could be any worse off by maintaining total silence.

On either side of Nathan's cell were three other prisoners, each in a separate cell. Two spent their waking hours calling out to each other. Their names were Robert Clark and Johnny Barrow, spies who had already been tried and sentenced to death. Despite their own impending fates, they shouted encouragement to Nathan each time they saw Major Allen and the large scarred sergeant pass their cells. The third prisoner, who occupied the cell next to Nathan, made no noise at all. Nathan learned that the man was a Confederate soldier from South Carolina called Billy Harrison who had been captured a week earlier in a Union raid into Virginia. Badly wounded in the raid, Harrison was being tended daily by an army doctor in the hope he would recover and give information on Confederate forces.

When Major Allen made his eighth visit to Nathan's cell, he had no questions to ask. He ordered the sergeant to bring Nathan from the cell. The adjoining cells were quiet, as if the occupants were asleep. Nathan found out the real reason for the silence soon enough. Guided by the sergeant, he walked to a window overlooking a yard. A weak November sun shone brightly on a double set of gallows. As Nathan watched, an army corporal placed cloth bags over the heads of two men and adjusted nooses around their necks. Two other men stood on the platform, an officer and a chaplain who rocked back and forth in prayer. The corporal stood by a long lever. At a signal from the officer, he pulled it back. The trapdoors fell. The ropes snapped tight as the two men dropped through.

Allen turned to Nathan. "You should find the cells more peaceful now. Your fellow spies, Clark and Barrow, have met their maker." He motioned for the sergeant to lead Nathan back to his cell. "You will be making the same journey unless you come to your senses in very short order."

"I have nothing to say that I have not said already."

"Very well. Be it on your own head."

That evening, Nathan was told he would be tried the next morning by a military court on the charge of spying.

The trial began at nine o'clock. When the colonel in charge of the tribunal read the charge, Nathan interrupted him. "My name is Nathan Cox. I am a British businessman illegally held by the United States government. When my government learns of this, British troops will mass on the Canadian border, and the Confederates will have gained a truly terrifying ally."

The colonel was unfazed. "Rest assured, if we were not fully certain that you are Nathan Solomon—cotton factor of New Orleans, recruited as an agent by Major Arthur Moore of the Confederate Signal Service—we would not have wasted our time in arresting you and bringing you here."

Nathan fell back on silence. His guilt was as obvious as the sun in the sky.

The trial lasted less than an hour. At the end, the colonel pronounced sentence. "Death by hanging." The sentence would be carried out in seven days, giving him time to reflect, time to change his mind about cooperating with his captors.

Only after Nathan had been back in the cell for an hour did the court's decision finally sink in. In a week, he would be dead. Seven days. One hundred and sixty-eight hours. How could he make the time take longer to pass? By counting days as the sun rose each morning and shed its light through the small barred window? Or counting hours on his gold pocket watch? He remembered stories of condemned men paying the executioner at London's Tower Hill to be sure his blade was sharp and his aim true. Would he need the watch to bribe the hangman to make his own death agony as short as possible? He thought of Miriam. What was it she had asked when he agreed to spy? "Are you so desperate for me to become a widow? For your son and daughter to have nothing of their father but memories of a few minutes' play each Sunday morning?" Miriam had known, and he had been a fool.

Finally, his mind drifted south to the Confederate troops in Virginia. Surely in a week they would have attacked Washington. Everyone knew the Yankees couldn't fight. The Confederates would rescue him. He would never keep that date with the gallows.

Major Allen and the scarred sergeant visited his cell that evening. "You are thinking right now how you can break that date with the hangman," Allen said. "You are thinking about those rebel troops to the south, and you are wondering how long it will take them to attack Washington and set you free?"

"How did you know?"

"Clark and Barrow thought the same. They boasted that I'd never see them hang. Gray uniforms, they said, would march into the White House before they set foot on any scaffold." Allen placed his foot on the second chair and stared down at Nathan. "This is the last time you will see me, Nathan Solomon. The last chance you will have of saving your neck. I have other spies to catch and hang."

Nathan looked past Allen, concentrating on the wall where images appeared of those he loved, of those who would grieve for him. Above all he saw his children's faces, Harry's golden hair, Louise's green eyes. A hard lump filled his throat. He swallowed awkwardly and brushed at his eyes, surrendering himself in that moment to the inevitability of his own death.

"Burn in hell," he told Allen.

The spy catcher laughed. "You will be burning there long before the devil catches me." Without another word, he left the cell. The sergeant's one good eye lingered on Nathan before he followed Allen out of the cell and locked the door.

Nathan counted days. No new prisoners were moved in. The only sounds he heard were made by the doctor who continued his daily calls on Billy Harrison, the wounded Confederate soldier in the next cell. The only visitor Nathan had was the scarred sergeant who brought in meals. When Nathan asked questions, the sergeant replied gruffly, his words often difficult to understand because of the scar tissue that deformed one corner of his mouth. The longest answer he gave was to Nathan's question about the condition of Billy Harrison. "Doctor's wasting his time. Boy ain't gonna live no matter what he does." He lifted Nathan's gold watch from his vest and tucked it into his own pocket. "And that fine piece of jewelry is wasted on you. I'll be telling the time with it long after you're no longer concerned with the hours and minutes of this world."

At nine o'clock on the evening before he was due to hang, Nathan asked the sergeant for pen and paper. It was time to perform the task he had deferred until the last moment, the composing of letters to Miriam and Leonora. He wrote first to Miriam, telling her that he loved her with all his heart and begging her forgiveness for the way he had deserted her and the children. As he started to write to Leonora, he became aware of a commotion in the next cell. The doctor had already visited once, earlier in the day. Something important must have happened to make him return. Nathan set down the pen and listened. After two minutes, the doctor left. Nathan's cell door opened and the sergeant entered.

"Told you the doctor was wasting his time. That rebel boy next door just died."

"You will have one less man to hang."

"Prisoners of war don't swing from the end of the rope. That's reserved for spies like you." The sergeant stood by the door, head cocked to one side, listening. Satisfied that no one else was nearby, he said, "I'll daresay that Major Allen and those officers who tried you were not as gullible as those Irish peasants ten years ago who thought you'd stolen your fine clothes from the Earl of Clarendon."

Nathan dropped the pen in shock. "Flaherty!" The man's full name came surging back. "William Patrick Flaherty, is that you?"

"Himself. No wonder you didn't know me, not when one of your fellow rebels burned off half my face."

Nathan had not recognized Flaherty, nor had the Irishman's distorted speech yielded any clue to his geographical background. "You sailed to New Orleans as I did. You should be wearing the gray, not the blue."

"New Orleans?" Flaherty spit on the floor. "I could not stand the place. It was hell on earth, hot and damp and filled with bothersome insects. I bought passage on a boat going north. I ended up in a town called Cincinnati. Work was hard to find. When I came to the end of my money, I joined the army. I liked being a soldier. I was a damned good one, and if it weren't for this mask of horror and this burned-out eye, I would still be out there fighting. Instead, I'm stuck here guarding spies like you who wait to hang."

The instinctive pleasure at seeing Flaherty faded. Once he had been a friend, but none of that rapport remained. "I will not keep you long. My second letter will be finished in a few minutes."

The Irishman laughed. "Tear up your letters of farewell. Do you think I'd let you die at the end of a rope? You did a lot of Irishmen a good turn on that boat, and I'd be a sorry fellow if I failed to return the favor when I had the chance. I'm sergeant of the guard here. My word is law, and I've just decreed that you and Billy Harrison next door are going to change places."

He opened the door and passed into the corridor. Nathan heard the door of the adjacent cell thrown back, followed by a man grunting as though bearing a heavy load. When Flaherty reappeared, he carried the lifeless body of a dark-haired man dressed in undergarments. A two-week growth of beard covered his pasty face. Dirty, bloodstained bandages encased both legs. As Flaherty set the man gently on the floor, he told Nathan to move into the next cell. "You'll find Harrison's uniform on the bunk. Put it on."

Billy Harrison's former cell smelled like a butcher's shop late on a hot Louisiana day, when the meat had spoiled. Nathan threw up on the floor as the putrid stench forced its way down his throat and into his stomach. Flaherty returned a few minutes later. "You can live with the stink for a few hours. By tonight, when Nathan Solomon next door has been declared dead from poison and Billy Harrison in this cell has enjoyed a remarkable recovery, you'll be on your way to a prison camp where you'll spend the rest of the war. And this Irishman will be even with the only Englishman he's ever owed a favor to."

"But how—?"

"I told you, my word is law here. Absolute bloody law. The officers leave the running of this place to me because they're too damned well groomed and finicky to offend their very proper senses by coming down here. Now get your fancy civilian clothes off and slip into the late Mister Harrison's uniform."

"Even if you convince everyone that Harrison is me," Nathan said as he undressed, "who will vouch that he committed suicide by poisoning himself?"

"The same doctor who'll soon write a report that Harrison has recovered from his wounds and is doing nicely. And as Harrison did not trade incarceration for information, I'll have him shipped off to a prison camp where he belongs." Seeing confusion remain on Nathan's face, Flaherty laughed. "Did you really believe that I'd stoop so low as to take your gold watch for myself? That was the doctor's payment for being part of this. Harrison was going to die. His legs had gone rotten on him, and his blood had carried that rottenness clear through his body. That's what you smell in here. The only worry I had was whether he would die before you were due to dangle." Flaherty took Nathan's clothes and walked to the door. "So I gave him a gentle nudge to make sure."

Nathan turned around and threw up again, not with disgust this time but with relief. So strong was the feeling, he did not even spare a thought for the real Billy Harrison who had received the gentle nudge from Flaherty. He inspected the dead man's gray uniform. It smelled of stale sweat and blood and decay. Nathan forced himself into the trousers, knowing that his life depended on it. Then the jacket. Everything was loose, but it did not matter. No prisoner of war weighed what he should.

From the cell now occupied by the dead man, Nathan heard the doctor's voice. It was followed by banging, metal on metal and wood on wood. Flaherty returned to Nathan carrying a sheet of paper. "You're one of the few men ever to see his own death certificate. You committed suicide rather than face the noose, fed yourself poison you'd concealed on your person, and now your body's on the way to potter's field." Nathan looked at the document. Although the doctor's signature was illegible, his own name stood out clearly. "If there's a chill running down your back right now, think how much icier it would be if Billy Harrison hadn't offered his life to save yours."

Nathan saw Flaherty one more time, shortly before dawn when the sergeant led him in irons from the cell for transferral to a prisoner-of-war camp. "Remember, you are Billy Harrison from now until it's safe to say otherwise. Nathan Solomon is dead, buried, and forgotten."

"Can you get word to my family that I am alive?"

Flaherty shook his head. "Not even if I knew of a way to get letters across the lines. Your family will have to worry like the families of everyone else."

As they approached the military escort waiting for Nathan, Flaherty offered one more piece of advice. "So far, you've made two terrible mistakes in your life. Being born an Englishman and then siding with the rebels. Do your damnedest not to make a third." He shoved his charge toward the escort. Hampered by leg irons, Nathan fell to the ground. "This piece of rebel scum's all yours, boys. Shoot the bastard if he so much as even thinks about escaping!"

A soldier pulled Nathan to his feet and shoved him into a wagon. As the escort started moving, Nathan looked back. Flaherty had disappeared, already back inside the prison where his word was law. Nathan's eyes turned eastward, where the first rays of the sun were breaking through the mantle of the night. Had it not been for the scarred Irishman, he would have been ascending the gallows at this very moment. Instead, he was on his way to a prisoner-of-war camp. Nathan gazed at the sun's first rays and prayed for his family to be strong, and for a blessing to fall on the head of William Patrick Flaherty.

Nathan spent four years as Billy Harrison, Confederate soldier and Union prisoner of war. The first eighteen months passed while he was incarcerated at Fort McHenry, near Baltimore. He was there in May 1862, when news came of the fall of New Orleans to Union forces under General Benjamin Butler. The guards joyfully declared that the mother of all American rivers would soon be flowing under the Union flag once more. A dozen prisoners from Louisiana pestered guards for more information, but Nathan remained disinterested. He was supposed to be Billy Harrison, and Harrison came from South Carolina, not Louisiana. New Orleans would mean nothing more to him than a Confederate city that had fallen into Union hands. But beneath the mask of indifference, Nathan's mind seethed with worry over Miriam, her mother, Leonora, and the children. What would their life be like under occupation? How would they manage? How would they survive until he returned?

Those questions were still unanswered when Nathan was moved, in the summer of 1863, to Fort Lafayette in New York, a grim, old coastal fortress. The quarters were small and perpetually damp; even during the height of summer, he found it impossible to be truly warm. The drinking water, drawn from dirty cisterns, was foul. Each glassful contained up to a dozen tadpoles which had to be removed before the water could be swallowed. The only moments of comfort were provided by sympathetic New Yorkers who regularly sent in food, clothing, blankets, and cases of wine.

In the spring of 1864, Nathan was transferred deeper into Yankee territory, to Fort Warren in Boston. Although he stayed there only two months, he finally heard genuine news from home. Several of the Confederate soldiers confined at Fort Warren had been captured during the defense of Vicksburg in the winter of 1862–63. They told Nathan that their commander had fallen while leading a charge against Union positions. The commander's name had been Wilson. Colonel James Wilson. Nathan wondered about Wilson's aide, Captain Marcus Barnett. Had the slave-dealer's son also died? He could not ask for fear his interest would arouse suspicion.

The final move was across the top of the country from Fort Warren to Camp Douglas, Illinois, where Nathan sat out the remainder of the war. Rumors continually filled the camp of Confederate victories, new weapons, and foreign alliances which would force the North to cease its war against the states which had chosen independence. There was even talk of the opening of a second front near to Camp Douglas itself by Southern sympathizers flooding across the border from Canada. But it was obvious even to the most die-hard Southerner that the North was winning. The Union was an industrial society; the South was agrarian. For every cannon and rifle the South could make, the North could manufacture twenty. And king cotton, no matter how many fortunes it had created, made rotten ammunition when stuffed down the barrel of a gun.

When the war ended on April 9, 1865, with the Appomattox meeting of Lee and Grant, prison guards relayed the news. Some men cheered at the knowledge that soon they would go home, whatever home was after four years of fighting had ravaged the South. Others grew moody in defeat. Nathan neither cheered nor sulked. He felt only gratitude to have survived. A week later, that gratitude turned to sickness as word of Lincoln's assassination swept the camp. The country had suffered enough already. This murder by a frustrated actor who sought to play on a larger stage seemed particularly senseless. The struggle was over. It was a time to heal.

Six weeks after the war ended, Nathan took the amnesty oath of President Andrew Johnson and was released. With no money, with nothing but Billy Harrison's oversized, stinking, threadbare uniform on his back, Nathan joined the hundreds of thousands going home. Freed of the camp's restrictions, he took notice for the first time of his own condition. His beard straggled down to his chest. His hair, shaggy and unkempt, had turned completely white. His body itched from fleabites, and the shoes he had worn for the past four years raised blisters on his feet.

He came to a small town where he knocked on doors of houses and offered to work for food. A gray-haired widow gave him a meal for chopping wood. When he finished the work, she asked how far he was going. He told her New Orleans, a thousand miles away. She looked at the clothes he wore, at his shoes, at the gauntness of his body, and she took pity on him.

"Did you fight at Shiloh or Antietam?" she asked.

He shook his head. "No, ma'am, I did not."

The woman searched Nathan's eyes before deciding he told the truth. "I had two sons. They joined the army the day the president called for volunteers. One died at Shiloh, the other at Antietam. Their clothes still wait for their return. I will bring them out, and you may see what fits you."

When the widow reappeared, Nathan protested that he could not take the clothes without working for them. He stayed at the house, repairing everything that had needed fixing since the woman's sons had gone off to war. He patched a corner of the roof where rain seeped in; he mended fences and dug drainage ditches; he fixed broken windows with a skill that surprised himself, for he had never performed such manual work before. Each day the woman cooked him three full meals, and when he left the house at the end of June, he had regained some of the weight four years of prison life had stolen from him. He still had the beard, but now it was well trimmed as was his hair, and he wore Sunday-best coat and trousers that fitted passably well. In his knapsack he carried another suit and a spare pair of shoes. He had no money but he did not care. Clean and well fed once more, he felt he could walk all the way back to New Orleans.

He only had to walk as far as St. Louis. There, curiosity took him to the city's busy dock. One million miles might just as well still separate him from New Orleans, but if he could see the boats that navigated the river between St. Louis and the Crescent City he would feel much closer. More than a dozen vessels were moored at the dock. The first one he saw forced his eyes open with amazement. The *Eclipse*, the boat on which he and Miriam had spent their wedding night, had survived the war. When he climbed the gangplank, a ship's officer asked what he wanted.

"Is your captain the same man who commanded the *Eclipse* eight years ago?"

"He is."

"Then I wish to see him. Where may I find him?"

"You may find the captain right here," said a voice from Nathan's right. "State your business and be brief about it."

Nathan turned to find a burly red-faced man with a snow-white beard. "Captain, I am Nathan Solomon of New Orleans. Eight years ago my wife and I spent our wedding night aboard this ship. If you do not remember me from that voyage, then surely you—"

"The cotton factor! I carried many of your bales, Mister Solomon. What are you doing in Saint Louis?"

Nathan beamed at the recognition, the first in four years. "I am returning from the war. I could accomplish that return in greater haste with your assistance. I have no money, but—"

Again the captain interrupted. "We sail full, but if you do not mind sleeping on the deck . . ."

Nathan accepted gratefully. He could think of no better way to return to New Orleans than by sailing down the Mississippi.

Chapter Nineteen

Nathan returned to New Orleans midway through September. The river was alive with cotton-laden boats, and it took him a few moments to realize that the season was just beginning. A war had been fought, a country split and reunited, and still cotton came downriver on schedule. He would be home just in time to help Leonora in the countinghouse. How many of the business's old customers had, like James Wilson, died? How many still owned their plantations? Could those owners work the land without their slaves?

The *Eclipse* approached the final bend of the river. Nathan pressed against the rail impatiently, willing more speed from the vessel. At last, it cleared the bend and New Orleans came into view. The sight ripped Nathan's breath away. The central tower and the twin belfries of St. Louis Cathedral rose like welcoming arms. The white houses of the Garden District reflected the sun in a bright smile of welcome. Even the cramped tenements by the river looked warm and inviting. He dashed down the gangplank as soon as it was lowered. The instant his feet touched firm ground, and much to the amusement of his fellow passengers, he dropped to his knees and kissed the earth. He was home.

He stood up and looked around, unable to believe how little the city had altered. A bitter, bloody, four-year war had been fought, and everything seemed just the same. Bales of cotton lined the levee. White men discussed business while gangs of Negroes loaded bales on carts for transfer to the press. Nothing had changed at all.

No . . . ! Wait . . . ! Nathan's eyes fixed on a blue uniform, moving up, inch by inch, from the trousers to the jacket and finally to the coal-black face beneath the peaked cap. Everything was *not* the same. New Orleans had been occupied. Some of the Union soldiers who still remained were Negroes, and those Negroes loading cotton bales now worked for wages, just like white laborers did.

The Negro soldier looked at Nathan. "Been away long?"

"Four years, courtesy of Union prisons."

An odd expression, an amalgam of smile and sneer, passed across the soldier's face. "Welcome home."

Carrying the knapsack in one hand, Nathan walked up Canal Street, searching for identifiable changes. He found one when he drew abreast of the countinghouse doorway. A shining brass nameplate proclaimed it to be the office of a lawyer. Confused, Nathan pushed his way inside. A reedy, pale-faced clerk asked what he wanted.

"What happened to the business that was here?"

"The countinghouse of Lowensohn? It's gone. Years ago."

"Where?"

The clerk shrugged. "I have no idea."

Nathan left the office, fearful of what else he would find. He looked across Canal Street to the *Vieux Carré*. What had changed there? Had the old part of town, which had withstood the shock of many different administrations, survived this one as well? He turned in the other direction and walked toward the Garden District. His pace was slower now. Anxiety had blunted the edge of his anticipation. The joy of returning home had been superseded by trepidation.

Even before he reached Prytania Street, some sixth sense prepared Nathan for a shock, told him that if the countinghouse had passed to new occupants, then Waverley, too, would have changed hands. If it had, so be it. He would meet the new owners, he would talk with them and learn of his family from them. But even six hundred senses could not have readied him for the stunning jolt that waited.

Mouth open, Nathan stood by the gate and stared in disbelief. Waverley did not have new owners. It had no owners at all. The ornate wrought-iron fence surrounded a jungle of untamed plants. All that remained of the house was the front wall, where pillars rose to support a roof that no longer existed. The sight ripped at his heart and he turned away, unable to look any longer. He walked along Prytania Street to the next house. It was as he remembered it. So was the next, and the next, and every house in the street. Every house but his own. In one garden he saw a woman pruning roses. He stopped to ask her about Waverley. She told him that the house had burned down two years before.

"What of the people who lived there?"

"The women and the children? They left before it burned."

"How long before?"

"Soon after Butler and his men occupied the city."

"Where did they go?"

The woman shrugged. Many people had moved during the occupation; who knew where they were now? Nathan thanked her and retraced his route to the city center, wondering with every step how to trace his family. Would they be listed at city offices, on electoral rolls or tax lists? Perhaps there was a record of their move from Waverley, before fire had destroyed the house?

By the time he reached Canal Street, he knew exactly how to find them. Every morning, the French Market came alive with people selecting the freshest food for their tables. Even the war could not have altered that New Orleans tradition. If his family still lived in the city, he would find them there.

Three mornings passed while Nathan stood watch in the French Market. In the afternoons and evenings he worked at the wharf among the laborers he had once employed. No one recognized him, and he was thankful for the anonymity. At night, he slept in a room shared by four men. Before dawn, he was up and on his way to the French Market once again. On the fourth morning, his fortune changed. Standing by a stall piled high with glistening fresh fish, he saw a boy and girl dart through the crowd. At first he gave them no more than a glance before moving his attention to the faces of the shoppers who poured into the market. Suddenly his eyes flicked back to the boy, to the long golden hair that whipped around his face as he chased the girl. His son Harry had such hair, golden like his mother's. Before he could see the children's faces properly, and compare them against four-year-old memories, they ran behind the fish stall. Nathan ran around the other side to meet them. The girl came first, green eyes shining in a face alight with laughter. The boy came steps behind, never seeing Nathan, intent only on the girl he chased.

Nathan grabbed the boy and lifted him off the ground. "Are you Harry?"

Frightened by the unfamiliar bearded face, the boy shrieked in terror. A hand dropped onto Nathan's shoulder. Thin fingers gripped like talons, and a woman's voice demanded angrily that he release her son. Still holding the boy, he turned around. Gray streaked the shimmering golden hair. Lines of worry and fatigue marked her face, spinning out from eyes that no longer gleamed with such vitality, and curving from a mouth that was thinner and more downcast than Nathan remembered. Her clothes were old and shabby. The long purple skirt showed signs of recent repair. Nathan's head felt light, and his stomach trembled.

"Miriam, do you not know me?"

The woman did not hear his question. Again she demanded loudly that he release her son. Nathan saw other people closing in on him. The owner of the fish stand stood closest, an arm raised threateningly, the hand gripping a stout stick. Two yards away, the little girl with the green eyes—his little girl!—stood thumb in mouth as she watched the sudden drama.

"Miriam!" Nathan shouted her name. "Do you not recognize your own husband?"

The fish-stand owner lowered his hand and turned to Miriam. "Is this man your husband?"

"My husband died in a Yankee prison."

Nathan set the boy down. "Your husband stands here before you, the man who came home expecting to find his family waiting to welcome him at Waverley."

The name of the house struck a chord with Miriam. Stepping closer, she peered at Nathan's face. Hesitantly, she touched his beard, then she lifted his hat and saw the white hair. A shriek burst from her lips and she threw herself into his arms, burying her face against his chest. "We thought you were dead! We were told you were dead, that you had committed suicide by taking poison on the night before you were to be hanged as a spy."

"Who told you that?"

"Marcus Barnett."

"Marcus?" Before Nathan could ask where the slave-dealer's son belonged in this, he remembered the two children. They were looking up at him, more secure after seeing their mother's sudden acceptance of the bearded stranger. The crowd which had gathered menacingly at Miriam's first angry outburst, dispersed. "Harry, Louise, do you also not know me?"

The five-year-old girl regarded her father uncertainly. At the end of some dark tunnel flirted an indistinct memory. No such doubt assailed her seven-year-old brother. Past his initial fright, he brimmed with confidence. "You had no beard and your hair was not so white," the boy said. "I liked you with no beard. You came upstairs at our old home and played with us."

"Would you like me to come upstairs and play with you now?"

"You're silly," Louise said.

"I am? Why?"

"Because you can't go upstairs where we live right now."

"That's right," Harry said earnestly. "We all live in the same place now."

"We all lived in the same place before."

"What he means, Nathan," Miriam said softly, "is that we all live in one room now."

"You, the children, your mother and Leonora all in one room?"

Harry chimed in before Miriam could answer. "Of course Grandma Anna is not in the room with us. She's dead."

While Nathan tried to accept the latest shock, Miriam took his hand and led him away from the children. "Much has happened since you left, none good."

"Leonora?"

"Well, thank God. Her job pays the rent on the room in which we live and puts food on our table. I do not know how we would exist without her."

Putting his arms around Miriam, Nathan told her not to despair. He was home and soon the family would enjoy its former affluence, but even as he offered comfort, he questioned how to achieve such a return to prosperity. Perhaps New Orleans had not changed much on the surface, but below the veneer nothing was the same. He led Miriam to a refreshment stand where he ordered coffee for himself and Miriam and fruit drinks for the children. Over the coffee, Miriam related the ill fortune which had enveloped the family since Nathan's departure four years earlier.

"From the moment you left, we heard no word of you, Nathan. We tried to make ourselves think that this was as it should be. We comforted ourselves by believing that as a spy you had to make yourself invisible and could not afford the luxury of contacting us in any way. This conviction succored us through the first few months, but it no longer proved a shield when Butler and his Union troops occupied the city in May."

"I was at Fort McHenry when I heard of the city's fall. My worst days were already over, but I feared that yours were just beginning."

"They were. Beast Butler earned his nickname well. He hanged a gambler called Mumford for tearing down the Union flag, and he issued an order that allowed his troops to treat the women of New Orleans as if we were prostitutes. But the worst was the Confiscation Law, which he applied rigorously to anyone refusing to swear allegiance to the Union. We swore allegiance, Nathan, your cousin, my mother, and myself, because we had children to consider. And those swine still stole Waverley from us."

"But if you cooperated, how could they take the house?"

"Because one man stepped forward and pointed out to Butler that Waverley was the home of a convicted Confederate spy. It was then we learned you had been caught within days of arriving in New York. That you had been tried and convicted for spying, and that you had taken poison to cheat the hangman."

Nathan's mind staggered as he combined that information with Miriam's earlier words. Words came slowly as a chilling truth grew evident. "You mentioned Marcus Barnett's name before."

"It was he who told Butler."

Still the picture was not fully clear. "But Marcus was James Wilson's aide? Surely he fought alongside him at Vicksburg? How could he have been here?"

"Marcus was not at Vicksburg. He bought favor with Union commanders by feeding them information. When New Orleans fell to Federal troops, he appeared as a very powerful man in the new administration. I almost felt sorry for his father. He was so shamed by his son's perfidy that he took his own life a week after the city's fall."

The slave-dealer's suicide meant nothing to Nathan. He could think only of his own betrayal. On the road to Savannah with Major Moore . . . the running of the blockade . . . the voyage to Liverpool, and the following voyage to New York . . . ! Every moment of that long and hazardous journey had been spent moving toward an eventual trap, a snare that had been set before he had taken the first step from New Orleans. Marcus Barnett, the loudest, most objectionable fire-eater of all, a Union spy! At least, Nathan now knew that he had not been responsible for the death of John Harold Bentley. His own carelessness had played no part in it at all. Treachery had!

"Marcus was only half right. His betrayal led to my arrest and conviction, but a man who was already dead took my place in the condemned cell while I took the dead man's identity. The next time you pray, ask God to bless the soul of a man named Billy Harrison."

"Marcus told me that he could save Waverley if I treated him with the respect that was his due. Instead," Miriam said with satisfaction, "I spit in his eye. We were given a day to leave Waverley. We could take only what we could each carry in one case. No jewelry, not the emerald bracelet you gave me, not even my wedding ring. Can you imagine our pain as we spent our final night in the house where we had lived for so long? As we looked for the last time at all the furniture and the paintings? As we explored the memories? It was too much for my poor mother. That night, in the very bed where my father had died, she joined him."

Tears bloomed in Nathan's eyes. He had loved Anna Lowensohn like a mother. "What happened to the servants?"

"They wanted to join us. They were prevented from doing so by the colonel who moved into Waverley. He told them they were no longer slaves. They were free and he wanted them to work for him. When they protested that they had never been slaves at Waverley, the colonel refused to believe them. He ordered them to remain there and serve him and his guests as they had served us. This colonel, he did not care for the house as we had done. Samson, whom I used to see occasionally, told me that the colonel would not let him tend to the garden. He wanted him only as a coachman, to carry the colonel's guests to and from Waverley, and the garden could go to hell. Almost every night the colonel held a party in the house. Then one night, a year after we had been evicted, a tremendous fire left Waverley looking the way it does now. Some say the fire was started deliberately by the colonel because he had received orders to move elsewhere. Four of the servants—Samson, Rebecca, Delilah, and Naomi—died in the blaze. Only Bathsheba, the other maid, survived. I have no idea where she is now or what she is doing."

"And Marcus? What does he do?"

"His treachery has been well rewarded. He helps to oversee the port and takes a little for himself from every cargo that moves in or out of New Orleans."

"Where does he live?"

"On Melpomene. He resides in a very pleasant residence he Butlerized from its legal owners."

Nathan's eyes narrowed. "I will visit that pleasant residence soon enough. A day of reckoning is long overdue between Marcus Barnett and myself."

Holding Nathan's arm, Miriam walked with him away from the market. Harry and Louise followed, their attention fully taken with the man who had introduced himself as their father. Both children were thrilled to have their father home again. How often had they listened with envy to stories told by other children about their fathers' exploits in the war? The best they could do was create fictitious adventures for their own father. All too often they were caught out in a lie and their faces burned with shame. Now they would have stories, real stories! Their father had been a prisoner of war, a spy, a man who came within an inch of being hanged. The other children's tales would never surpass that!

Miriam showed Nathan the family's home on the ground floor of a house on Camp Street. Into a single room was crowded a wood stove, a table and four chairs, and a battered chest of drawers. Miriam and Leonora slept in this room, on mattresses filled with Spanish moss which they set upon the floor. The children slept on cots in a tiny alcove separated by a curtain from the main room. Nathan thought of Mary McBride in Saffron Hill; half a world away, and such poverty still existed. A lump blocked his throat as he remembered the splendor of Waverley. How had his family fallen to this? The lump disintegrated, and new thoughts occupied him. Optimistic thoughts. How unfortunate were they really when all they had lost was property, when the only death they had suffered was that of a fifty-two-year-old woman who had succumbed, like her husband nine years before, to a broken heart? Thousands of families had lost sons and brothers and fathers. Sometimes, in the greatest tragedy of all, they had lost them fighting against each other.

"Compared with the places I've called home these past four years, this is a palace," Nathan declared. "Truly a palace, in which I will be king and you, Miriam, will be my queen. And you and you"—he lifted his giggling children into the air—"will be my prince and princess."

Despite the bleakness of their situation, Miriam laughed. "What will Leonora's title be?"

"She will be a duchess. If you tell me where she works, I will give her the splendid news myself."

"She is at Thompson's, on Tchoupitoulas Street."

Nathan remembered Thompson's, a millinery store where Miriam, Anna, and Leonora had always bought their sun bonnets. "What does she do there?"

"She is a salesperson serving the women with whom she once shopped. When she applied for the job, the proprietor told her it was beneath a lady's dignity to work. Your cousin replied that although she was certainly a lady, she could no longer afford the dignity that accompanied the title. The proprietor gave her the job."

Late that morning, Nathan pushed open the door to Thompson's. Leonora stood at a wood-and-glass counter, selling a hat to an elderly woman. Like Miriam, she had altered in the past four years. The short hair was as curly as Nathan recalled it, but strands of gray now streaked the black. The once-firm shoulders drooped as if the last four years had beaten her down, and when she wrote details of the transaction in a ledger, she donned dainty gold-rimmed spectacles to aid her eyesight.

"May I help you, sir?"

Nathan turned around to see another clerk. "No, thank you. I wish to see Miss Solomon."

The clerk left. Nathan returned his attention to his cousin. How old was she? If he was thirty-three, Leonora had to be thirty-one. How could time have passed so quickly?

Finished with her customer, Leonora closed the ledger and removed her glasses. As she watched Nathan approach, a smile filled out the lines in her face. "Welcome home. I never believed those awful lies Marcus Barnett told us."

Nathan could not control his amazement. White-haired, bearded, with all the changes four years privation had wrought, and Leonora had known him! "You did not? Miriam did."

Leonora held out her hands. Nathan took them, feeling their cool dryness inside his own. "I have known you longer, and I was sure that my clever cousin would never allow himself to be hanged. Caught, perhaps. Hanged, never."

"Do you remember William Patrick Flaherty from *The Wandering Jew?*" When Leonora nodded, Nathan said, "He is the guardian angel who saved my life. Without his charity, which he had little business offering to a Confederate agent, I would surely have ended my days on a rope."

"After you left, I prayed three times a day for God to watch over you. Even when that scalawag Marcus told us you were dead, I kept on praying because I knew God would not disappoint me. The Irishman was the tool He chose to answer my prayers." She looked at the clock on the wall. "It is time for my midday break. Walk with me and tell me everything that has happened."

The sun filled Tchoupitoulas Street with brightness and warmth. Remembering the dark and dreary days he had spent in northern prisons, Nathan suggested that instead of seeking shade they walk in the sunlight. As the heat penetrated his flesh and bones, he described the past four years for Leonora. "I have no doubt that Marcus was responsible for my arrest. Major Allen, the Union spy catcher, must have been waiting for me as I disembarked from the steamer in New York. He had me followed to see what contacts I made, then set an ambush at the Saint Nicholas. I damned myself for carelessness in staying at a hotel where I might be recognized but it wasn't that at all. It was Marcus. He will answer for his treachery, Lally. Believe me, he will answer for it."

"Nathan, leave his punishment to God."

"I can see how God has already punished him. Miriam tells me he grows rich by supervising the port and lives in a beautiful house he stole from its rightful owners."

Leonora did not doubt Nathan's intention to challenge Marcus to a duel. Such valiantly foolish encounters had not ended with the war. "The Irishman Flaherty took pains to save your life while making it appear you were dead. If you demand satisfaction from Marcus, he will not meet you on a field of honor. He will have you arrested. You were a spy who was to have hanged. Do not give him the chance to carry out the sentence."

Nathan said no more about settling his account with Marcus, but Leonora could see he had not forgotten. His anger lay just below the surface, a desire for revenge that could erupt at any moment. She hoped time would dull that anger and make Nathan aware of the foolishness of taking such a dangerous course.

After half an hour, Nathan saw Leonora back to the store. He returned from there to Camp Street to find Miriam alone in the room. Harry was at the school he had started the previous year while Louise played at a friend's home. As Miriam prepared food, Nathan told her that not only had Leonora recognized him, she had not been surprised to see him.

"Your cousin is a stronger woman than I am," Miriam admitted as she set bread, cheese, and fruit on the table. "Perhaps it is because her life was harder than my own. When Marcus told us you were dead, she looked him straight in the eye and called him a liar. She never lost hope that one day you would come home." She watched Nathan eat the simple meal, happy at the sight of his enjoyment. "We have a little money saved. I will use it to buy more food, and this afternoon I will create a meal that will remind us of Waverley. I will use every trick I ever learned from Delilah, and tonight you will eat like a king."

"What if this kingly feast tires me? Where will I sleep?"

A spark shone in Miriam's eyes. "With your queen."

"With others present in the royal chamber, it will be difficult to add to the royal line."

Miriam looked from Nathan to the moss-filled mattress on which she slept. "The prince studies and the princess plays."

"While the duchess sells hats to old women." Nathan rose from his chair, took Miriam's hand and led her to the mattress. "I did not tell you the name of the boat on which I traveled from Saint Louis. It was the *Eclipse.*"

"Our *Eclipse?*"

Nathan nodded. "The *Eclipse* on which we made Harry. If we close our eyes and pretend to hear the slapping of water on the hull, we can make believe we are back in our stateroom."

"I have no need for staterooms, Nathan. I would make love to you anywhere."

They made love on the moss-filled mattress. Miriam's eyes remained wide open, filled with the images of the room in which two women and two children lived. Nathan's eyes were closed. Once again he heard the sound of water, smelled the mahogany and leather of the stateroom, and saw the opulent upholstery of the bed on which he had first made love to Miriam.

Only when their lovemaking reached its climax did they share a feeling, that of relief as the pain and misery of the last four years were swept away in a joyful release.

Long before the evening meal was ready, the heady scent of spices filled the room. Pots bubbled merrily on the stove. The windows were wide open to let the heat escape. Every so often, Miriam offered a morsel from one of the pots to Nathan and the children. When Leonora returned from work late in the afternoon, she stood in the doorway and inhaled the fragrant aroma. She remembered meals like this from long ago. "Delilah must be looking down from heaven and smiling," she said. When Miriam turned around to offer a taste of trout poached in wine sauce, Leonora saw the sparkle in her eyes and knew that Nathan had truly returned.

Miriam kept her promise. Despite the modest surroundings, the evening meal was reminiscent of Waverley. At any moment, Nathan expected to see Bathsheba or Naomi appear with some new delicacy from Delilah's kitchen. Soon after the meal ended, Harry and Louise climbed into their cots in the curtained alcove. The day's excitement had exhausted them. Nathan waited for Miriam and Leonora to kiss the children good night before he entered the alcove. He sat down in the narrow space between the cots. Holding the hand of each child, he began to tell them tales about the war, not horrific stories of battlefields awash with blood and gore, but anecdotes of camaraderie, of heroic efforts by men to save the lives of friends. Despite their fatigue, the children willed themselves to stay awake and listen to their father, little knowing that his tales were invented. He had seen no fighting at all. His accounts stemmed as much from his own imagination as they did from tales he had heard in prison. Only when he reached the final story, as his children's eyelids began to droop, did he recount the truth. He told of a spy saved from the hangman's rope by a man he had befriended a dozen years before.

As he finished the tale, he looked from one sleepy child to the other. "Do you understand the lesson of that story?"

Harry nodded vigorously, his sleepiness momentarily forgotten, in the thrill of knowing the answer to his father's question. "You should always be good to people because one day they might have the chance to be good to you."

"Right. Never turn away from a chance to do a man good. Live your life that way and you will be happy."

"Are you happy?"

"The happiest man in the world." Smiling hugely, Nathan

kissed his son and daughter and left the alcove, drawing the curtain behind him. Miriam and Leonora watched him emerge.

"You look like a man who has found a chest full of gold," Miriam said.

"I have found riches far beyond gold. I have rediscovered the love of my children." He sat down at the table and poured himself a cup of thick black coffee. "The problem now is to decide where to enjoy those riches, for we cannot remain here."

Miriam's eyes widened in horror as Nathan's meaning became clear. "Leave New Orleans? Never! It is my home!"

Leonora's reaction was less emotional. "It is our home, too, Miriam. Mine and Nathan's, filled with bittersweet memories as any home should be. But we must look to the future, and, like Nathan, I question whether that future lies in New Orleans."

Miriam shook her head. "How can you speak so? New Orleans made us wealthy once before, and it will do so again."

"Slavery created that wealth," Leonora argued. "Although we did not personally subscribe to slavery, we profited from it."

"New Orleans's most glorious days are in the past," Nathan said factually. "They ended when the Union blockade began. The city will never regain its old prestige and wealth. As railroads and canals link the country, its value as a port diminishes."

"Most importantly," Leonora added, "New Orleans is not safe for Nathan. In another city, his name will mean nothing, but here it is the name of a Confederate spy who is supposed to be dead. Even taking another name would not help because there is always the possibility of recognition. I recognized him, so there is no guarantee that no one else will."

Miriam fell silent. Leonora had just given her the one reason she could not refute. Her love for the city came second to her love for her husband. When she spoke again, it was to ask where they would move. "Do we go to New York? To Philadelphia, or some other Northern city unscathed by the war?"

"No!" Nathan answered sharply. "I have seen enough of Northern paradises to last a lifetime."

"Where else is there?"

"Atlanta," Leonora said.

"Atlanta?" Miriam repeated. "It was destroyed by Sherman, burned to the ground as he began his murderous march to the sea."

"Like the phoenix, Atlanta springs already from the ashes. People I meet in the shop swear that Atlanta's geographical importance as a railroad junction is already transforming Sherman's funeral pyre into a bustling city."

Miriam turned to Nathan. "What do you know of Atlanta?"

"Only what I heard from the prisoners of war who came from there. Without exception, they bragged about their city's freshness as enthusiastically as any proud Orleanian ever boasted of his city's history and traditions."

Uncertain now, Miriam turned to gaze at the curtain which shielded her two children. "Will they enjoy growing up in Atlanta as much as I enjoyed growing up here?"

"I never heard an Atlanta soldier mention yellow fever," Nathan said. "This family, especially, should take that into consideration."

Miriam remained unsure, unable to envision living in a city that did not have a port. Finally, she forced herself to smile. "If we are to make a fresh start, it will be easiest to do so in our present state, when we have nothing to encumber us."

A thousand memories blossomed in front of Nathan. Images of the *Vieux Carré*, of Waverley, the levee piled high with cotton, and voyages along the Mississippi passed before his eyes. He saw again the Vanson family, Marie-Louise as she had been after returning from Europe. He sat again at the dinner table in the Lowensohn home, enjoying the sight of Henry teasing his sisters.

Nathan blinked once to drive the memories far away, and raised his coffee cup in a salute. "To a new life in Atlanta. *Au revoir*, New Orleans."

remembered his vow to Leonora, and he knew that if he had a pistol to hand, he would shoot the slave-dealer's son through the eyes and damn the consequences. Instead, he turned away and

Chapter Twenty

Three months passed before the family set out for Atlanta. Nathan continued his laborer's job at the wharf while Leonora carried on as a clerk at the Thompson's store on Tchoupitoulas. Miriam spent her days caring for the children and keeping house as if nothing had changed. If anyone noticed the addition of a man to the small family unit, they asked no questions. Miriam, in turn, made no mention of the fact that her husband had returned. Leonora was right. In Atlanta, the name of Nathan Solomon would mean nothing, but in New Orleans it was the name of a spy who had cheated the executioner by taking poison. It was wise to heed the old adage of letting sleeping dogs lie.

Once, as he worked, Nathan saw Marcus Barnett. Plumper than Nathan remembered, and finely dressed in black coat and trousers, he looked every inch the officious director of a busy port. He was not alone. Two men accompanied him on a tour of the wharf. Marcus paid no attention to Nathan. White men doing the work of slaves were two a penny these days, and there was nothing remotely familiar about the sunburned, white-haired, bearded figure. Nathan paid attention to Marcus, though, and to the two men with him. They spoke with Northern accents, carpetbaggers come south to bleed the land a second time. Marcus, eager to line his own pockets even more, was their willing stooge. As he watched the three men, Nathan remembered his vow to Leonora and he knew that if he had a pistol to hand, he would shoot the slave-dealer's son there and then, and damn the consequences. Instead, he turned away and concentrated on the new and wonderful life he would make for his family in Atlanta.

But he did not forget the vow. As the time drew near for the family's departure from New Orleans, he spent some of the money he had saved on the purchase of a Colt Army revolver. He took the gun back to Camp Street, hiding it with ammunition in a chest that contained clothes and some Mardi Gras masks with which the children played. Closing the chest, he recalled the man who had demonstrated the weapon at the Great Exhibition fourteen years before. God grant him the easy expertise that man had shown!

The acquisition of the revolver did not remain a secret for long. Next morning, after Nathan had gone to work, Miriam found the gun. She lifted it from the chest, frightened by the sight and feel of it. When she showed it to her husband's cousin, Leonora handled the heavy weapon with an easy familiarity.

"You know of such things?" Miriam asked as Leonora checked that each of the gun's chambers held a cloth cartridge incorporating the powder charge and a separate bullet.

"The proprietor of the shop keeps one in case we are robbed." Seeing Miriam's concerned expression, she added, "Do not fear, the gun cannot be discharged until the caps are inserted."

"Why would Nathan have such a weapon?"

"He must have bought it for our protection on the journey to Atlanta. The route will be filled with soldiers returning home. In such troubled times it is best to be prepared."

Although she appeared to accept Leonora's explanation, Miriam knew better. Nathan had not bought the gun for protection. He had bought it for revenge, for the long-overdue day of reckoning with Marcus Barnett. When did he intend to make his move? In a week they would be on their way. Would he wait until the last moment and make retribution his final act in New

Orleans? Or would he do it as quickly as possible? Either way, Miriam knew Nathan could not win. The instant Marcus recognized him, he would summon assistance. And even if, by some miracle, he did kill Marcus, he would still forfeit his life.

"If our journey will be so dangerous, perhaps I should know how this weapon works," Miriam said.

Leonora demonstrated how to load the brass percussion caps and cock the hammer. With the caps removed and the weapon made harmless, Miriam practiced cocking the hammer to advance a chamber and prepare the gun for firing. Her hand was small and the motion awkward, but after half a dozen attempts she felt comfortable. Leonora replaced the weapon in the chest.

That night, Miriam willed herself to stay awake. Just before midnight, she lifted her head and listened carefully. On the mattress beside her, Nathan slept peacefully. Across the room she heard Leonora's untroubled breathing. From the curtained alcove came the lighter sound of the children's breathing. She tiptoed to the chest, removed the revolver and percussion caps and dropped them into a cloth bag. As an afterthought, she took one of the Mardi Gras masks, a silver-coated image of a lion's face. Step by careful step, she walked toward the door, treading with extra caution as she passed close to Leonora's mattress.

Suddenly, an iron band encircled her ankle. "Where are you going?" Leonora hissed as she gripped Miriam's ankle with all her strength.

"It is too warm in here. I need to walk in the fresh air."

"With a gun?"

Miriam crouched down, glancing nervously toward Nathan. Had he awakened yet? "Nathan did not buy it for our journey. He bought it for Marcus. He will surely die if he tries to avenge himself on Marcus."

"And you think you can save him by killing Marcus yourself? I knew what you intended doing the moment you asked me how to operate the gun. Give it to me, and we will yet find a way to dissuade Nathan from carrying out this mad act of retribution."

Taking the revolver from the cloth bag, Miriam held it out by the barrel. Leonora sat up, hand outstretched. Instead of passing over the gun, Miriam suddenly swung it at Leonora's head. She bit back her own scream of pain as she heard it slam into bone. The gun weighed three pounds. Without so much as a whimper, Leonora dropped down onto the mattress. Miriam knelt over the still body, relieved to hear steady breathing. The blow had only been enough to stun. "Forgive me, Leonora, but you do not know your cousin if you think you can dissuade him from his honorable course." She left the room, pausing outside just long enough to insert the percussion caps and cock the hammer.

Light filled the windows of Marcus's house. At the gate, Miriam had to jump back as a carriage clattered past. Another followed. A party was just ending. Miriam reached into her bag for the silver lion's mask and held it up to her face. She passed the gate and walked beneath spreading live oaks toward the house. A third carriage stood in front of steps leading up to the porch. Three men were boarding. At the top of the steps stood Marcus. He saw Miriam emerge from the shadow of the trees.

"What have we here?" he cried out. "A masked lady! Surely it cannot be Mardi Gras already."

One of the men in the carriage leaned out the window. "You crafty devil, Marcus, saving the best until last. I've a damned good mind to come back into the house and share her with you!"

Marcus lifted his hand in a salute. The coachman cracked his whip, and the carriage moved off. Marcus came down the steps for a closer look at this unexpected guest. "And who might you be, my fair lioness?" He reached for the mask. Miriam stepped back, out of reach. She noticed that his walk was unsteady.

"Do you not remember inviting me?" she asked.

"If I had invited someone as enchanting as you, I would have made certain my staff was up to wait upon you. As it is, I gave them leave to go to bed an hour ago."

"Let them sleep. I am here to wait upon you." She walked

past him, up the steps to the porch and into the house where she found herself in a large hall, similar to that of Waverley, with a wide stairway sweeping up to the second floor. Laughing, Marcus pursued her. He had never been one to spurn opportunity. Miriam turned from the hall into a high-ceilinged parlor furnished with exquisite rosewood furniture. She wondered about the house's real owners. Did they now live in virtual poverty, like the owners of Waverley? Her resolve strengthened. Marcus, completely unaware of the danger to himself, followed her into the parlor and closed the heavy door.

"Now, my pretty lioness, there is nowhere for you to run. Let us see the face of one who wishes to wait upon me."

Miriam turned coy. "Your servants might grow envious if they hear another waiting upon you."

"Their quarters are in the back. They will hear nothing. Come, let me see if your face is as beguiling as your manner."

Miriam dropped the mask onto the floor and stepped toward Marcus. He stared at her, knowing he should be familiar with the faded golden hair and the alluring green eyes. The whiskey he had drank that night slowed his thinking so that five seconds passed before recognition came. "You! What do you want here?"

Letting the cloth bag hang heavily from her arm, Miriam peeled off a glove, drew back her hand and slapped Marcus across the cheek. His initial look of puzzlement gave way to a smile, then a raucous laugh. "You seek a duel? You, a slip of a woman who would be blown away by the slightest breeze, challenge me?"

"I demand satisfaction for your betrayal of my husband."

"Satisfaction?" Marcus's laugh grew more piercing. He stepped back until he reached the wall and leaned against it while his body shook with mirth. "Leave here now while blood still flows through your body. It is not my custom to accept challenges from women, especially those as stupid as yourself."

Miriam's voice grew dangerously low. "Do not mock me. As you see"—she withdrew the cocked Colt from her bag and held it with both hands—"I am quite prepared to back up my challenge."

The sight of the gun sobered Marcus. "You fool. If you so ardently wish to join your husband, I would be less than a gentleman to deny you. Put aside your weapon until I am ready to face you."

Lowering the revolver, Miriam watched Marcus cross the parlor to a cabinet. He pulled opened a drawer and extracted a gun that was the twin of the one Miriam held. "As we have no seconds, we will have to agree on the rules ourselves," he said. "I would suggest that we stand back to back, walk five paces, then turn and fire. And keep firing, if necessary, until our revolvers are empty. Or we could defer this meeting until daylight. Then you could seek your satisfaction outside, where the beauty of this house would not be damaged."

"I am sure this house's rightful owners would be most pleased to know that its thief is so worried about its welfare."

"Damn you." He stepped right up to Miriam and stared down at her. His eyes were red. A wave of whiskey-laden breath poured from his mouth. "Let us be done with this farce!"

Miriam turned around, heart pounding in fearful anticipation. She knew how Nathan had felt that morning beneath The Oaks, when he had fought for Marie-Louise's honor. Gripping the pistol with both hands, she began to walk with a slow, measured tread.

"One!" Marcus's voice called out the first step.

The caps! Had she inserted them properly, the way Leonora had showed her?

"Two!"

Her hands shook. The gun wavered. A voice from within screamed at her to keep calm.

"Three!"

Her right leg trembled. The knee turned weak. She stumbled. A roaring explosion filled the room. An unseen hand plucked at her hair, and in front of her eyes a gold-framed wall mirror shattered into a thousand shards. Regaining her balance, she swung around, blood boiling in rage at this treachery. Six yards away, Marcus stood with his mouth hanging open in surprise at having missed. As Miriam raised her gun to eye level, he scrambled feverishly to cock the hammer of his own weapon.

Miriam did two things at once. She closed her eyes and pulled the trigger. The report was thunder in her ears. Her hands flew upward and she staggered back from the force of the recoil. When she opened her eyes again, Marcus lay sprawled against a couch. His revolver rested a dozen feet away from his outstretched right hand. His left hand cupped a huge bleeding wound in his stomach. He looked up as Miriam approached.

"Help me," he whispered. "Help me."

"Marcus, can you hear me?"

He nodded and repeated his plea for help.

"My husband never poisoned himself. He returned to New Orleans three months ago."

Shock replaced the agony that covered Marcus's face. Then despair, because he understood that Miriam could never allow him to live with that information. She thumbed back the hammer, aimed at Marcus's head and closed her eyes again. The recoil staggered her once more. When she recovered her balance, she glanced once at Marcus and breathed deeply to steady her stomach. Without looking at the body again, she removed two cartridges and two percussion caps from Marcus's gun to replace those from her own revolver, then she left the house.

She returned to the room as quietly as she had left it. Leonora was awake, sitting up on her mattress and holding a cold, damp cloth to her head. Miriam knelt beside her. "I am truly sorry if I hurt you. Had there been any other way—"

"You have given me a violent headache which will surely last for a day or two. Do I suffer for a good reason?"

"Marcus has a worse headache, one that will surely afflict him for all eternity."

Leonora reached up to hug Miriam, understanding how

shaken and frightened the young woman must be. She wondered if Nathan would ever know just how lucky he was. Few men had wives so courageous as to risk themselves in such a manner.

Miriam replaced the revolver in the chest and laid down beside Nathan. In his sleep, his arms came out to meet her. She snuggled into them and closed her eyes, shivering as she finally understood the reality of her actions. Her movements disturbed Nathan. He awoke and softly asked if she felt all right.

"Just a dream," she whispered. She ran her fingers through his white hair and held him tightly, finding reassurance in his closeness. Nathan would approve of what she had done. She would never tell him, of course, but as a businessman he would approve.

She had just made sure that when the family departed from New Orleans, they would leave behind no outstanding debts.

Part Three

1870–1882

Chapter Twenty-one

The steady pattern of the marshal's footsteps echoed along Garnett Street. His voice rang out to tell those people still awake that it was one o'clock in the morning and all was well in Atlanta. From an open window, Nathan watched the law officer proceed to the intersection with Whitehall Street before disappearing from view. All might be well at street level where the marshal patrolled, but it was a different tale on the second story where the Solomon family lived.

A woman's cry pulled Nathan from the window. He swung around to stare fearfully at the door of the bedroom he shared with Miriam. The cry came again, louder this time and filled with suffering. Nathan trembled. Sweat beaded his forehead and drew his shirt to his body. He did not recall such sounds of pain attending the birth of Harry twelve years before, or Louise two years later. But Miriam had been young then, her body stronger, better prepared for the rigors of childbirth. The struggle of the last nine years had aged her beyond the thirty-three she was. She should not be enduring such strain again.

Nathan's heart leaped as the bedroom opened. Leonora stepped out, closing the door before he could see inside. Words flew from Nathan's lips. "Is she all right? Has anything—?"

"Not yet. Nothing has happened yet." Leonora clasped her cousin's face with her hands. They were freshly dried and smelled of strong soap. Behind the gold-rimmed glasses she wore more frequently now, her brown eyes looked tired. Gray streaked the curly hair that clung damply to her scalp. "Find yourself something to do, Nathan, otherwise you will go mad standing out here and listening to Miriam's cries."

"I want to cry with her as if the pain were mine."

"Go out for a walk. A long walk." She pushed him toward the stairs leading down to the street. "When you return, God willing, Miriam's cries will be replaced by the lusty wails of your youngest child."

Nathan walked slowly along Garnett Street, following the route taken by the marshal. He listened to see if he could still hear the man's cries, but the only noise that carried on the humid September night was that of a locomotive leaving Union Depot five blocks away. Upon reaching the intersection with Whitehall Street, he looked back. No one waved to him from the lighted window. Nothing had happened yet. Childbirth was like a kettle on the fire. The more you watched, the longer it took to boil; the less you watched, the quicker everything happened.

Consoling himself with that thought, he turned north on Whitehall and walked toward the city center, stopping to look in shop windows illuminated by gas lamps. Quite suddenly, he stared up at the nearest lamp, his eyes concentrating on the flickering yellow flame. In the center of the city, people took gas lamps for granted now. As night fell, they shone their brightness on the street, but it had not been that way when Nathan had arrived in Atlanta with Miriam, Leonora, and the two children at the beginning of 1866. Oil lamps had been the sole source of lighting in stores, offices, and homes, and the streets had remained dark. Nathan remembered the jubilation nine months later that had greeted the lighting of gas lamps along Peachtree Street and the houses lining it. It was the first gaslight seen in two years, since the fall of the city. The Atlanta Gas Light Company's return to business was evidence of the city's determination to recover from the savage destruction Sherman's army had wrought.

Such encouragement was timely. In 1866, Nathan and his family had needed all the cheer they could get. Their first view of Atlanta had filled them with a despair that was slow in dissipating. Having spent all their money to make the journey from New Orleans, they found at their destination a dirty wreck of a city, a wasteland of rubble from which cheaply constructed buildings sprang up like weeds in the spring. Wooden shanties, far removed from the fine commercial buildings of Canal and Carondelet streets, lined the city's business thoroughfares. Wagons and carts jostled for space on roads that oozed with mud. The sight had been too much for Miriam. Tears had filled her eyes and choked her voice as she stated what was on the mind of everyone in the family.

"This is Atlanta? We left New Orleans for *this?"*

Curling a comforting arm around Miriam's shoulders, Nathan had stared glumly at the chaotic scene. What had made them come here? The gossip Leonora had heard in the millinery shop? The tales he'd listened to while in prison from soldiers who called Georgia home? Their Georgia did not exist anymore. Sherman had seen to that. Before Nathan could think of words to console Miriam, Leonora had dipped deeply into their feeling of hopelessness to find a single heartening thought. "Do you not see what all those carts and wagons carry? They are filled with lumber and brick. These miserable buildings that stand here now are only temporary, put up to provide shelter until stronger, permanent structures can be erected." Lifting her head, she breathed in deeply. "I feel something about this city, Miriam. The air is full of energy. It is as though a miracle is taking place around us."

Nathan had grabbed at the straw offered by his cousin. "Do you hear that, Miriam? Would you want to return to New Orleans and miss being part of such a miracle?"

The question had brought a wan smile to Miriam's face. "I thought miracles came only with burning bushes. It would appear that this one comes with bricks and lumber."

The energy felt by Leonora swept across the city in the

following years. The number of stores in the city reached two hundred and fifty, leading to the revival of the Atlanta Board of Trade. A new newspaper, the *Constitution,* was launched. Atlanta, with its rail accessibility, took over from Milledgeville as state capital, and the unfinished opera house at Forsyth and Marietta became the capitol. City limits were extended to a mile and a half in every direction from the general passenger depot as Atlanta's population doubled from its 1860 figure of almost eleven thousand.

But while the Solomon family saw the miracle occur all around, they were never fully included in it. If the streets of the new Atlanta were paved with gold, as those of London were once supposed to have been, the luster did not rub off on them. For the first year, they lived in two rented rooms, little better than the accommodation they had left behind on Camp Street. Leonora found work quickly, as a seamstress in a company making men's pants in a tin building on Forsyth Street that was so rickety it swayed and sang in the wind. She remained there for a year and a half before being offered employment in a new millinery shop on Whitehall Street, between Hunter and Alabama streets. From there she brought home tales of women spending money on elaborate headgear that would have paid the rent for a week on the two rooms the family shared.

Nathan's first job used skills he had discovered while staying at the widow's home near Camp Douglas. He worked as a bricklayer, taking pride in the completion of each wall that went into the construction of the commercial buildings springing from the rubble of Sherman's Atlanta. Each night he came home with callouses on his hands and the conviction in his mind that one day he and his family would live in a fine house. Not a wooden one, such as those that filled Atlanta, but a brick one. His construction career ended abruptly after a year when he fell off a ladder, breaking two ribs and an arm. He did not work for eight weeks and the family, which had just taken larger lodgings on Thompson Street, was forced to live on Leonora's earnings. Nathan returned to work as soon as the bones healed, but as he climbed a ladder he realized his fall had caused more than physical damage. When he looked at the ground fifteen feet below, terror and dizziness overcame him. The hod of bricks fell from his shoulder and he half climbed, half fell to the ground. For a week he tried to overcome the fear, but each time he set foot on a ladder it returned. The supervisor took him aside. He was sympathetic, but Atlanta was erecting buildings taller than one story. If Nathan wanted to work on those buildings, he would have to conquer his phobia. When he could climb a ladder again, he would be welcomed back.

The fear stayed. Nathan could lean out of a second-story window and feel no panic at all, but the moment he set foot on a ladder it returned. He never ventured onto a building site again. Instead, he found work as a traveling salesman for a dry goods store on Decatur Street, owned by a German named Ephraim Gottfried. Driving a rig laden with Gottfried's merchandise, Nathan took the store to rural areas. He enjoyed the life, meeting farmers and villagers and providing them with a valuable service while earning more than a bricklayer could ever hope to earn. Enough, after a year, to move the family into their most comfortable residence yet, the second story of a large wooden house on Garnett Street, where they lived now.

He worked long hours, often being away from home for two or three nights at a time, and he saved money diligently at the Atlanta National Bank because a new dream filled his mind. Not to live in a fine brick house but to be like his employer, Ephraim Gottfried, proprietor of his own dry goods store.

Miriam thrilled to the idea. Brought up in luxury, the struggle of the last few years had been especially hard on her. She would never let Nathan know how much she missed the wealth and comfort she had known in prewar New Orleans. He might think she blamed him for their present modest surroundings when nothing was further from the truth. Fate had been doubly cruel in its dealings with their family. An average man would have rolled over and died, but Nathan was not an average man. He had fought back, and this latest ambition to have his own store was proof of his determination to regain everything the family had lost.

Leonora reacted to the idea quite differently. With gentle humor, she reminded Nathan of his feelings half a lifetime before. "Uncle Samuel would surely feel gratified to hear how your opinion of shopkeepers has changed. From regarding them on the same level as slave drivers, you now want to be one."

This time, Leonora's bubble-bursting skill was wasted. "Believe me, Lally, when I open my store, I will do right all the things Uncle Samuel did wrong."

Recalling that conversation as he walked along Whitehall Street toward the center of Atlanta, Nathan spared a rare thought for his English family. He had not been in contact with them since his aunt's death. Harriet had been the only sympathetic link with the Solomons of Russell Square, and with her passing Nathan's interest had ended. He did not even know whether Samuel, his own father's brother, was still alive, whether David now managed the store, or whether Alfred still pursued his licentious inclinations. Nor did he want his uncle's family to know how badly he had fallen. They had been impressed to the point of envy in 1857 when he and Miriam had visited London. To learn that Waverley had been lost and its owners thrown out into the street to survive as best they could might replace that envy with cruel satisfaction.

The sound of the marshal's voice calling out the hour of two o'clock jerked Nathan back into the present. He looked around, surprised to find himself at the railroad tracks north of Alabama Street. Should he rush home? Would anything have happened yet? He strode a few paces south before remembering Leonora's supplication to take a long walk. A locomotive rumbled along the track, Nathan turned to watch. He would do better to arrive home after the baby's birth. If he were there before, he would only get in the way.

The locomotive passed. Nathan crossed the tracks, his mind once more exploring the past. Saving toward his own store was one thing. Saving enough to open it was a different matter. Two years of scrimping and saving had left him woefully short of the thousand dollars he considered necessary to rent the premises for such a store and stock it. A thousand dollars! It might as well be a million. A thousand dollars was a magical sum, far beyond the reach of most people. Only recently had Nathan heard of the small number of Atlantans who actually earned that much in a year. Three hundred and fifty-two people out of a population approaching twenty-two thousand. Even with Leonora's savings, he was only halfway toward the magic number.

Dear Lally . . . Nathan's heart softened as he considered his cousin. They owned little more now than when they had left England nineteen years ago, yet Leonora never complained. She faced each crisis with firmness and optimism and worked until it was no longer a crisis but an experience from which she drew strength. She deserved more from life, Nathan thought. Much more. He would have sold everything he owned to give her the happiness she richly merited. She worked so hard that all too often she ignored her own satisfaction. There had been no man in her life for seventeen years, not since Antoine. Sometimes Nathan looked at his cousin through a bittersweet lens and decided that all these years later she remained in love with the dashing young Creole who had first stolen her heart. At other times he used a more pragmatic perspective. His cousin might have mourned Antoine to the exclusion of all other men for five years, perhaps even until the outbreak of the War Between The States, but after that fate had dictated her personal life. Who could seek love in a New Orleans terrorized by an occupying force? Survival, not romance, had been foremost in Leonora's mind, just as it was now.

Miriam, who attended services with Leonora in the rented premises used as a synagogue by the city's newly chartered congregation, told Nathan of single men who approached his cousin there. Men whose families had lived in Georgia for thirty or forty years, and recent German immigrants who had moved south after the war. "All eligible men," Miriam had said, "and some of them quite wealthy. Yet your cousin spurns them all. Why, she even told one persistent man that he was profaning the Sabbath by using God's house as a social club."

Nathan chuckled at the memory. He could just see Leonora taking a stubborn would-be suitor down a peg or two. He could just as easily understand their interest. At thirty-six, she still represented an excellent catch for any marriage-minded man, but she was interested in none of them. It was as though she had made the decision that Nathan, Miriam, and their children were all the family she would ever want or need. Frequently she told her cousin and his wife that she regarded their children as her own, but Nathan knew that could never really be. No matter how much she loved her young cousins, they could never replace children that had grown from her own body. Nathan wondered how deeply Leonora had been hurt by never having children. No one would ever know because she kept such feelings to herself. His cousin had never been one to impose her own sadness on others.

At last, Nathan began retracing his steps. He walked slowly at first, then quicker when he heard the marshal's voice in the distance calling out three o'clock. Surely his child had been born by now. Along Whitehall Street his stride became a gentle jog, and then a run. By the time he reached Garnett Street, his legs were weak, his lungs ached and his clothes were soaked with sweat. He slowed to a walk, gasping for breath and wiping sweat from his face. Ahead of him, a single second-story window showed light. From the square of brightness, a shadowy figure leaned out, looking up and down the street.

"Nathan!" Leonora's excited shriek was louder than anything the marshal could muster. "Harry and Louise have a brother!"

Finding a last reserve of energy, Nathan broke into a run. He reached the house and raced up the stairs to the second floor, bursting through the door into Leonora's arms. "When?" he managed to gasp.

"An hour ago. I have been looking out of the window for an hour. Where did you go?"

"You told me to take a long walk! Remember?"

"And you listened to me? What kind of man heeds such terrible advice when his wife is ready to present him with a child?" She opened the door and stuck her head inside. "The proud father is here."

Miriam lay in the bed, holding a white-wrapped bundle in her arms. Two other women were also in the room, stout, gray-haired Bertha Gutheim who, with her husband, owned the house in which the Solomon family lived, and Emily Ruffin, a fair, thin-faced woman in her late twenties who lived on the floor above the Solomons. Both women had come the instant Leonora had called for help. There was little they did not know about bringing a child into the world. Bertha Gutheim had four children, all married now, and a dozen grandchildren. Emily had three children, two boys and a girl aged between three and eight. Tonight, those three children had company while they slept—Harry and Louise, who had been taken upstairs by Emily the instant she learned that Miriam had gone into labor.

"He can come in and see what he's done," Bertha said. Her loud voice contained an odd mix of accents, a little of the Atlanta which had been her home for twenty years, and a lot of her native Germany. "Tell him it's all cleaned up. You know how finicky these big strong men get over something as simple and natural as childbirth."

"I'll be getting back upstairs," said Emily, whose speech had no foreign inflection whatsoever. Emily's father had worked on the railroad that was Atlanta's original *raison d'être*, and she had been born less than a mile from where she now lived, when the bustling city had been a sleepy railroad terminus called Marthasville. "I'll send your children down in the morning."

While Leonora thanked both women for their help, Nathan entered the room. His heart went out to Miriam as he saw her lying in the bed. The once-golden hair had faded to a streaky ginger. Her face was pinched and lined, and gleaming with perspiration. As Nathan looked at her, he understood Bertha Gutheim's loud, good-natured humor. The man's role as family head and breadwinner paled when placed beside the pain and suffering a woman endured.

Some of the tiredness left Miriam's eyes when she saw Nathan. She held the wrapped bundle out toward him. "Come say hello to your son."

Taking the baby in his arms, Nathan crooned softly. The baby's face was red and shriveled. Dark brown hair fell over the forehead. Jet black eyes shone like two tiny buttons. An extra wave of happiness swept over Nathan. He loved his other children as deeply as any father did, and he knew he would never be able to replace the four years that had been torn from his relationship with them, but deep down he had always wanted one child who resembled his family. Brown-haired and dark-eyed like himself and Leonora. Now he had one.

The need to save enough money to open his own dry goods store seemed even more urgent now.

The baby was named Jacob, to honor Nathan's father. Ten and a half years had passed since Louise's birth, and to have a baby in the house again was a novelty. Not only for the adults, but for the children as well. They stood staring at their baby brother for long periods. Harry wanted to know if his face has been as red while Louise, showing early maternal instincts, pestered Miriam to allow her to hold Jacob. Miriam did so, but she stayed beside Louise the entire time. She need not have worried. Louise held the baby as tenderly as any mother could have done.

The Solomon's second-floor home became engulfed by a constant stream of visitors. Ephraim Gottfried, Nathan's employer, came every day with gifts from his store. Sometimes he brought toys; at other times, he carried an item for the kitchen, a saucepan or some plates. Nathan suspected that his employer simply picked up whatever was handy as he left the store to visit

Garnett Street. A short, plump man with white hair and a round face with cheeks like rosy red apples, Gottfried encouraged Nathan to take time off to celebrate the arrival of his third child. He would be on the road again soon enough, and working with a vengeance. Gottfried knew Nathan wanted to open his own dry goods store. What store drummer didn't? No matter how much a man enjoyed a life on the road, one day he would want to settle down. Especially a man with three children.

Bertha Gutheim and her husband were also frequent visitors. Adolph Gutheim, a tall, thin man with fingers like long, dry twigs, was a watchmaker by profession. He conducted his trade at a shop around the corner on Whitehall Street. He and Ephraim Gottfried had been friends as boys in their native Frankfurt, and their lives had been entwined ever since. In 1848, they had left Germany with their wives and children to eventually settle together in Atlanta, and together they had fled from their homes in 1864 to live in encampments in the woods as the Union army laid waste to the city. There, togetherness had ended. During the exile, Gottfried's wife, Wilhelmina, had died. Gottfried still blamed Sherman personally for her death. He failed to see where his house and shop had military value. Burning them was a crime. So was forcing him and Wilhelmina, a couple well into their fifties, to exist like foraging soldiers. Gottfried returned to Atlanta full of hate for the North, a passion that grew even sharper as the city struggled to its feet under the heavy shackles of Reconstruction. He retaliated the only way he could, by giving preferential treatment to any man who had fought for the South. He had chosen Nathan over a dozen other applicants for the job because he had spent four years in prison for the Southern cause. Furthermore, it was he who had recommended the Gutheims as landlords to Nathan. "My friend Adolph's name is German for good home, and he will provide that for you and your family."

The other frequent visitors were the Ruffins from the floor above. Emily dropped in a couple of times a day. Her husband

Frank came by after his evening meal, usually with a sample from his job at the City Brewery, where he drove a delivery wagon. Frank Ruffin was the strongest man Nathan had ever known. Years of loading and unloading kegs of beer had given him massive arms and shoulders. With fiery ginger hair and a freckled face that turned uncomfortably red in the long summer, he was an impressive sight. Fortunately, that strength was coupled with a warm nature and an eagerness to use his might to help others. Sometimes, Nathan wondered how Frank and Emily felt being a Gentile family on a block that was rapidly becoming a Jewish enclave. Every month, it seemed, a new family from Germany or Austria-Hungary moved into the square comprising Garnett, Whitehall, Brotherton, and Forsyth streets.

Living in a predominantly Jewish neighborhood was a new experience for Nathan. He had never known such separation before, not in Russell Square or in New Orleans. Adolph Gutheim and Ephraim Gottfried were familiar with it, though. They told Nathan of the Frankfurt Jews who had once lived behind ghetto walls. Despite being freed by Napoleon, the Frankfurt community continued to live a tightly knit existence, as much for shelter against outside prejudice and influence as from choice.

Nathan wondered if the same thing was happening in Atlanta.

Nathan returned to the road a week after Jacob's birth, hungry for business. The more he sold, the more he earned, and the closer became his dream. He left Atlanta on a horse-drawn wagon loaded with the latest merchandise Ephraim Gottfried had bought from the wholesale warehouse in Charleston— spices and blankets, kitchen utensils and hair brushes, needles for a woman's nimble fingers and hammers for a man's strong hand. He visited villages and farms north of the city, where his regular calls were eagerly awaited by white farmers in their homes and newly emancipated Negroes in flimsy shacks. To them all, Nathan represented more than a traveling salesman for a dry goods store in Atlanta. He was a farmer's contact with the state capital, able to discuss the latest punitive policies pursued by the Republican brigands who daily bled Georgia. For the farmer's wife he was a style guide, offering advice on the latest fashions being worn not only in Atlanta but in Baltimore and New York. He never sold such clothes to the farmer's wife, though; he just sold her the fabric and the pattern, and she made the dress herself.

On this trip, Nathan spoke only briefly of politics and fashion because he had another topic of conversation. His son, Jacob. Customers shared his excitement as he described the baby for them. Some pressed gifts on him for the child. One farmer's wife brought out a woolen shawl she had made for herself. "Give this to your wife so that she will not be cold this winter."

A Negro woman whose husband worked at a sawmill gave Nathan a tiny doll. The body was carved from wood. Dyed cotton formed the hair. Tiny red stones that danced with fire created the eyes. "Hang it where your baby sleeps, Mister rolling store-man," the woman said, using the name by which all the Negroes knew Nathan. "Its magic powers will keep bad spirits away."

Marcus Barnett's face suddenly appeared, and Nathan heard again the comment about slaves never being able to rid themselves of the superstitions of Africa. "Thank you very much," he told the woman, and accepted the gift graciously.

Nathan was away for three days and two nights, eating and sleeping at the farms he serviced. His wagon was almost empty and his order book full as he drove southeast along Marietta Road. It had been a good trip. He would be able to deposit another few dollars in that special savings account at the Atlanta National Bank, another few dollars toward his own store. What would he call the store? Names danced through his mind as he cradled the reins in his hands and watched the horse plod easily toward Atlanta. N. Solomon? N. Solomon and Sons? No, too pretentious, too reminiscent of his uncle's shop on Ludgate Hill. A store name needed to be more than just a glorification of its owner. It should be an attraction that drew people, like London's Crystal Palace had done. He would ask his children, that was it. Whenever he had a choice of children's novelties to load onto the wagon, he always asked Harry and Louise for advice. Harry, a lively, inquisitive child, usually decided instantly, while Louise thought deeply about the choice. Despite their different ways of reaching a decision, they usually agreed. When their choices differed, though, Nathan usually learned later that Harry's instinctive reaction had been correct. His son was a natural merchant.

A farm off to the left attracted Nathan's attention. It had been deserted for as long as Nathan had traveled this road. Now a man in trousers and high boots stood repairing a fence that had been broken for years, and on the roof of the farmhouse a hundred yards distant two more men patched a leak. Nathan pulled on the reins. No matter how badly he wanted to get home, he would not let pass an opportunity to make a new customer. The horse stopped. Nathan set the brake and climbed down. The man mending the fence looked up from his work as Nathan approached. He removed a wide-brimmed straw hat from his head and wiped sweat from a scalp covered by thinning fair hair.

"Looking for someone, mister?"

Nathan took off his own hat and fanned his face with it. His silvery-white hair stuck to his head, and his neatly trimmed beard felt heavy with sweat. "First time I've seen men working this property in a long time."

"I'm the new owner, bought the place for me and my boys to work. We're going to make a real good farm out of it. Raise some hogs. Grow some corn and greens, maybe even some cotton."

"King cotton's made a lot of fortunes in the past, and it'll make just as many in the future."

"You sound like you know a little bit about it yourself."

"Once I did, but these days I'm in a different line of work."

The man held out his hand to Nathan. "My name's Thomas Hopkinson. Those boys working on the roof are George and Jamie."

Nathan took Hopkinson's hand. "I'm Nathan Solomon. I work for the dry goods store of Ephraim Gottfried."

"Gottfried, huh?"

"That's right." Nathan saw the farmer's two sons climb down from the roof and walk toward their father. "There's not a better store in all of Atlanta. If we can't get something for you, then it's not available. I'm on the way back to Atlanta right now, but I've got a few items left in the wagon. And what I haven't got, I can always order for you."

Hopkinson's dry, leathery face broke into a wintry smile. Ice touched his pale blue eyes. "I guess I'll find everything I need at the country store."

Nathan gave the farmer good advice. "You don't want to deal with country stores, Mister Hopkinson. Railroads and wholesalers run them. You'll have to mortgage your crop to pay their exorbitant prices. Before you know where you are they'll own this land and you'll be nothing more than a field hand working for them. Buy from me and keep your land."

The two boys took places behind their father like troops backing up a general. One held a hammer. The other carried a steel bar he had been using to pry up rotten wood. "You don't seem to understand, Mister Solomon, but I guess that's because you're a foreigner and you don't speak our language too well. I know the country store charges too much, but at least I'm being robbed by one of my own kind, a man who belongs in this country." Hopkinson turned to his sons. "This is Mister Nathan Solomon, boys, who works for the Atlanta dry goods store of Ephraim Gottfried."

"Daddy." The boy carrying the hammer spoke. "Solomon and Ephraim are names from the Bible."

"That's right. You'll see a lot of this kind around now, foreign Israelites come down from the North to bleed the land and make us white men slaves of the niggers."

Blood throbbed through Nathan's veins. "This Israelite spent four years in a Union prison."

"For what? Smuggling from one side to the other to make yourself a tidy profit?"

"For being a patriot."

"Patriot? You and your kind don't know the meaning of the word. If you did, that Israelite Judah Benjamin wouldn't have fled the country. He'd have stayed to face the consequences like President Davis and the rest of the Confederate cabinet did. Now get off my land. Your kind ain't welcome here."

Jamming his hat on his head, Nathan climbed aboard the wagon and slapped the horse into motion. His face burned with anger. His head felt light. No one had spoken to him in such a manner since Marcel Vanson had insulted him eighteen years ago. Certainly, he had heard the slurs that the heat of war had created. Judah Benjamin—at one time or another Attorney General, Secretary of War, and Secretary of State for the Confederacy—had been attacked by both Union figures and by opponents in the South. Nathan had dismissed such ethnic snubs as bottom-of-the-barrel politics, but now he challenged that belief. Had he chosen to ignore a feeling that had always existed in the country? Or had the turmoil of war brought it to the surface?

Nathan's anger had not died by the time he reached Atlanta late that afternoon. After taking the horse and wagon to the livery stable used by Gottfried, he entered the store to hand over the money he had collected and requisition merchandise to fill the new orders. As Nathan started counting, the store owner's hand closed over his own, forcing him to stop. "Forget the money," Gottfried said. "Is everything all right?"

"Of course it is. I sold almost everything."

"I do not mean with business. I mean with you."

"I am tired, that is all."

Gottfried held Nathan's hand. "Go home. Play with your children, that is the best rest a man can have. Tomorrow you will come in here rejuvenated. We can count money and fill orders then."

Nathan carried his rage home. How dare Thomas Hopkinson treat him with such disrespect? Did he not know that Nathan had almost paid with his life for his support of the South? Miriam, like Gottfried, noticed instantly that something was wrong. Rigid lines etched Nathan's sunburned face. His eyes were hard. He sat in a chair by the window with the *Constitution* clutched in his hands. He did not go into the bedroom to see his youngest child, and when Harry and Louise, on their return from school, tried to involve him in a game, he told them he was busy reading the newspaper. Miriam had never seen him reject his children before, but when she asked him what was wrong he offered the same answer he had given Gottfried. He was tired, that was all.

He kept his anger bottled up until after the evening meal. Only when the children were in bed did he let it spill out. Through clenched teeth he told Miriam and Leonora of his meeting with Thomas Hopkinson and his sons. "I have no idea what this man did during the war. Perhaps he was a hero, perhaps he was a deserter. Who knows? I know only that he has no right to malign either me or Ephraim Gottfried. We lost more than he ever did."

Miriam tried to calm her husband. "Nathan, how many people did you see on this journey? How many treated you with respect and how many insulted you?"

"Just one man insulted me. That was enough to offset all the goodwill I received, all the gifts and all the good wishes on Jacob's birth. I felt as if I were unwelcome in this country, that my achievements and sacrifices were meaningless."

"Listen to Miriam," Leonora said. "You met one ignorant, bigoted farmer. If he wants to get robbed by what he calls one of his own kind at the country store, do not deny him the privilege. Let him lose his farm to the wholesalers and the railroad concerns that own the store. At least he won't be able to say he was robbed by a Jew."

"Yes, he will," Nathan replied with gloomy conviction. "That kind of man will always be able to say he was robbed by a Jew."

Leonora regarded her cousin curiously. Was Nathan finally acknowledging his own heritage? Accepting it not from desire but because it had been forced upon him? His next words, delivered in a bitter, biting tone, proved the accuracy of her conjecture.

"In thirty-eight years, I have never really considered myself to be a Jew. I am sure there are thousands just like me, tens of thousands even, Jews who have forgotten they are Jews. But I ask you, does such absentmindedness really matter?" He looked from Miriam to Leonora before answering his own question. "Of course it does not matter, because for every one of us who forgets he is a Jew, there will always be a man like Thomas Hopkinson only too ready to remind him."

Nathan went to sleep that night still dwelling on his clash with the farmer. When Jacob's cries drew Miriam from the bed at two in the morning, Nathan also awakened. Eyes closed, he listened to the sound of Miriam feeding their son. When she returned to the bed, he began to talk softly. Miriam shrugged off her tiredness and willed herself to stay awake and listen. Nathan's voice sounded different. The harsh edge of anger had yielded to a softer tone.

"My Uncle Samuel and your father were very dissimilar men, Miriam. Your father was as admirable as my uncle was loathsome, yet they had a common characteristic. Neither of them was ever bothered by the malice of men like Thomas Hopkinson."

"My father never met a man like Thomas Hopkinson."

"He must have done. So must my Uncle Samuel. The very fact that they never spoke of such men proves they were not disturbed by them, as I was today."

"I cannot understand why something that did not bother your uncle should bother you. You are twice the man he ever was."

Nathan smiled in the darkness and reached out to hug his wife. "My uncle had a shield I do not possess at this moment. He had wealth, as your father did. Wealth is a thick wall which the most hideous lies and insults cannot penetrate."

Miriam shivered. She had never heard Nathan speak this way. He had always wanted the best for his family, but he had never spoken of amassing wealth as a defense against a hostile world. His altruistic attitude had been altered by his encounter on Marietta Road. Deep inside him, something had changed.

"Money *is* the answer, Miriam, but instead of hiding behind it, you use it as a weapon. You use it to better the lot of all men, even men like Thomas Hopkinson. Only then can you erase such senseless hatred from their ignorant minds. Our store will be the foundation of that wealth. It will be a store where people want to work because they are treated fairly. It will be a store that grows as this city continues to grow. Our store will be as much a part of this city as any hospital, library, or church."

Miriam relaxed in Nathan's arms. Her husband's benevolent attitude had not changed at all. The encounter on Marietta Road had only served to strengthen it.

Chapter Twenty-two

Saving enough to open the store became an obsession. The family economized wherever possible. Miriam looked at a worn dress and wondered if she could get another year's wear from it. Leonora found a second job, doing bookkeeping for a lumber yard, and Nathan thought twice before bringing home a toy for the children.

That was the hardest economy of all. He hated himself each time he denied his daughter and his two sons in such a manner. Depriving them seemed such false thrift. What damage could the purchase of a doll or a bat and ball possibly do? Would it cause the opening date of the store to be put back a day or a week? Yet a week might well make the difference between success and failure. In a city blooming as quickly as Atlanta, opportunities rewarded only those alert enough to snatch them. Later, when the store was established and successful, the children would understand and appreciate the sudden hardship. The only area where the family did not scrimp was education. Somehow they still found the money to send Harry and Louise to private schools.

Nathan worked longer and harder than he had ever done before, continually seeking new customers for the dry goods store of Ephraim Gottfried. The more he sold for Gottfried, the more he earned; the more he earned, the closer drew the dream. He expanded his route to take in additional communities, competing for their business not only with salesmen from other businesses but with the country stores springing up at every crossroad. Each time he made his northwest swing and journeyed along Marietta Road, he slowed down as he passed the farm owned by Thomas Hopkinson and his sons. In the winter, he saw smoke curling from the farmhouse chimney. When spring came, crops pushed their way through the earth, and hogs roamed around in pens. The new owners were making a success of their venture. Those times Nathan saw Hopkinson working in the fields, he doffed his hat and called out, "Thank you, Mister Hopkinson!" The farmer stared back uncomprehendingly, unaware that he was being thanked for focusing Nathan's mind and giving him a purpose in life.

Simultaneously, Nathan began participating in his local community by joining the Hebrew Benevolent Society, which had been revived after the war. His involvement, though, did not extend as far as religious observances. Despite entreaties from his wife and cousin, he did not join the congregation in prayer. A bigot's insult had forced him to face his own identity and heritage, but he considered himself a secular Jew—Jewish by tradition, not by religion. Besides, Saturday was the best day to catch up on work at Gottfried's store, to follow up the orders he had taken the past week, and prepare for the coming week. Later, when he had his own store, and when the family lived in a fine brick house with as many servants as they had enjoyed in New Orleans, he would have time to go to the synagogue and thank God for such blessings.

Toward the end of 1871, the saving and self-denial paid off. Leonora told Nathan of a building for sale on Whitehall Street, next to a hardware store and close to the millinery shop where she worked. On the ground floor had been a bookstore. Above it was a two-story dwelling that was far roomier than the flat on Garnett Street where the family lived now. On the top floor, where the building narrowed, were two bedrooms. On the main floor was a kitchen, living area, and two more bedrooms. Nathan met with the building owner. An agreement was reached to buy the building, and Nathan made a down payment with part of the money he had saved at the Atlanta National Bank. More money went to remodel the store to make it more in keeping with fabrics and fashions than books. As the store took shape, an old problem arose. The name. Nathan put the dilemma to his family. Miriam suggested the obvious, that he give the store his own name. Harry and Louise were more original. The eleven-year-old girl proposed that the shop be named "White Hall" after the street on which it stood, while her older brother opted for the more exotic "Solomon's Bazaar."

Nathan shook his head. "I want a name that will stand out and attract people." He looked at his cousin. "Do you remember twenty years ago how people flocked to the Crystal Palace, Lally? That is how I want them to flock to us. With the right name, they will."

"Then why not call it Nathan Solomon's Crystal Palace?" Leonora suggested. "Surely no more appropriate name exists. After all, it is because of that exhibition that we are here."

Miriam clapped her hands. "That is a wonderful name! Why, when we outgrow this store, we will build a new store, an enormous store with thousands of windows to reflect the light like a real crystal palace!"

Nathan had four hundred dollars left. With that, and with the credit wholesale houses would give him, he had hoped to stock the Crystal Palace's empty shelves and counters. Instead, he took eighty dollars from his stockpile to purchase an ornate crystal gaselier, which hung from the ceiling at the front of the store. Perhaps his dream was not a palace yet, but the title that graced the storefront—a small and plain Nathan Solomon's above a large, ornate Crystal Palace—was half correct.

The Crystal Palace was due to open on a Monday. The weekend preceding the opening was the longest Nathan had ever known. He had plenty of time to contemplate his actions and worry whether he had done everything possible to ensure success. The family's savings were all gone. He had left

Ephraim Gottfried's dry goods store two weeks before, and Leonora had just given up both her millinery and bookkeeping jobs to work for her cousin. With no money coming in, the entire future of the Solomon family rested on the success of the Crystal Palace.

As Miriam and Leonora prepared to leave home on Saturday morning to attend the Sabbath service, Nathan spoke to them. "Ephraim Gottfried always told me that the first customer of the day is the most important. If the first customer buys, then it will be a good day. But if the first customer does not buy . . ."

"Do you not remember that Uncle Samuel had a similar superstition?" Leonora asked. "He always tried to serve the day's first customer himself, to make sure he made a purchase."

Nathan's white hair shook as he nodded eagerly. "That is right. Can you imagine, then, how important the Crystal Palace's first customer will be? Today, when you speak to God, ask Him to make sure our first customer on Monday buys something."

The two women promised they would.

Monday morning arrived at last. Before six o'clock, Nathan was downstairs in the store to make a final check of the merchandise-laden counters. On the shelves, empty boxes filled in the space that would have been taken by merchandise bought with the money he had used for the crystal gaselier. He knew the shop was small, yet it suddenly appeared as big as Union Station, a vast space he must continually empty and fill if he were to succeed. And right now, part of his stock comprised empty boxes!

As dawn's light spread across the city, he stepped out onto Whitehall Street. The crisp, cold January morning made him shiver. He looked up. The sky was clear. Neither rain nor snow would mar his store's grand opening. A good omen, the second such sign Nathan had seen. The first had been the massive celebrations that weekend to commemorate the inauguration of Governor James M. Smith. Smith, the former Speaker of the

Georgia House, was a Democrat. The man he replaced, Governor Rufus Bullock, was a Republican who had resigned under threat of impeachment. Although Federal troops remained in Atlanta, the end of the despised Republican rule signaled, to all intents and purposes, that in Georgia the Reconstruction era was over.

Again, Nathan raised his eyes to the clear sky. Fine weather, and Democrats running the state once more. Two good omens! Now if only Miriam's and Leonora's prayers were answered, and the store's first customer made a purchase . . . !

Promptly at seven-thirty, Nathan unlocked the front door of the Crystal Palace. With him were Leonora and Miriam, both businesslike in dark dresses, and Harry and Louise who hoped to see the store's first customer before they left for school. Fourteen-month-old Jacob remained upstairs, playing by himself in a pen Nathan had constructed. For fifteen minutes, all five people watched men and women walk past the store without giving it so much as a second glance. Finally, a young, fair-haired girl, no more than eight or nine, stopped outside. She looked curiously at the sign, then at the windows, and then through the wood-and-glass door into the shop itself. The gleam of the crystal gaselier attracted her and she pushed the door open.

Nathan stepped forward. "Good morning. Welcome to the Crystal Palace. What can we do for you?"

The girl looked around nervously, confused by the reception committee that greeted her. "My mother sent me out to buy some white cotton thread."

Leonora fetched some and pressed it into the girl's hand. "That will be five cents, young lady."

The girl stiffened. "My name is not young lady," she said as she handed across the nickel her mother had given her.

"What should we call you then?"

"Clarissa. I am Clarissa Jenkins from Hunter Street."

Miriam held back a smile at the girl's primness. "Thank you,

Clarissa Jenkins from Hunter Street. We hope to see you again."

"You will," the girl replied gaily. "I'll come back to see your pretty light."

Clutching the white cotton thread, Clarissa slipped out of the door and skipped along Whitehall Street. Watched by Nathan, Miriam, and the children, Leonora stared in awe at the nickel in her hand. "I think God heard our prayers," she whispered. "He heard them and sent a little girl called Clarissa Jenkins to give us His answer."

Nathan took the coin from his cousin and held it beneath the gaselier. At the beginning of the month he had turned forty. During those forty years he had earned money by cleaning and running errands for his uncle, by working as a cotton factor, by laying bricks, and by working as a drummer. Today, for the first time in his life, he had earned money in a manner which he had once despised. He had earned money as a merchant.

"Congratulations." Miriam stepped forward to kiss her husband. When she stepped back, Leonora kissed him on the cheek. His son and daughter stood watching, unable to fully appreciate the significance of that first five cents. Miriam waved her hands at them and told them they had better start out for school. As they left the shop, she called after them. "Don't forget to tell your friends and your teachers that your father's shop is open for business!"

Within five minutes, the Crystal Palace made two more sales. Bertha and Adolph Gutheim entered the store seconds ahead of Ephraim Gottfried. The Gutheims bought a blanket. Gottfried spent more than ten dollars on some lengths of cloth.

"Why would you buy cloth from me?" Nathan asked.

Gottfried smiled. "I have a customer coming at noon for just such cloth as this. I could never order it in time from a wholesaler, so I take it from you instead."

Nathan understood. The Gutheims and Gottfried had made their purchases out of superstition. They knew the importance of the day's first customer, and each had tried to be that customer, to buy something to ensure the store's success. Nathan loved them for it, and would never dream of telling them that they had been beaten by a young girl named Clarissa Jenkins. He held up the money for Leonora and Miriam to see. "We have been open less than half an hour, and already we have fifteen dollars."

Leonora looked at Miriam. "Perhaps now would be a good time to tell my cousin that he will need to make more than that."

Miriam took Nathan's free hand and pressed it to her stomach. "Can you feel your fourth child move, Nathan?"

Nathan glanced up at the gaselier above his head. Every omen was good today.

As hard as he tried, Nathan could not drive from his memory Miriam's cries of suffering at the termination of her last pregnancy, and his own consequent feelings of guilt for making her endure such strain. This time, he treated her like a fragile piece of china. When she worked in the store, he hovered nearby to see she did nothing that might conceivably jeopardize her condition, and when she remained upstairs, cooking or caring for little Jacob, he left customers in the middle of transactions to run up and see she was all right. Frequently, Miriam protested that she was not an invalid. Each time Nathan gave her the same answer. "The less you exert yourself now, the more strength you will have later. And the more strength you have later, the easier time you'll have of it." After a while, Miriam stopped protesting. She also stopped calling her husband by his name. Instead, she referred to him as Doctor Solomon.

Although she complained about the constant attention, Miriam appreciated it deeply. How many other women had such sensitive and understanding husbands? Very few, she would warrant. Each time she saw a pregnant woman struggling with shopping, she felt lucky. Nathan would not let her carry even the lightest item. When she shopped, he sent Harry or Louise to accompany her. If they were busy, Leonora went along. The further Miriam went into her term, the more pronounced became Nathan's care and concern. He would not even let her go for a short walk on her own!

At the start of her ninth month, while returning home with Leonora from a short stroll, Miriam said, "If I had to go out and there was no one to accompany me, I think Nathan would close the store and go with me rather than let me venture out alone. The way he fusses over me, the way he cares, makes me realize I am the luckiest person in the world."

"You are," Leonora replied immediately, then she laughed and reached out to squeeze Miriam's hand. As Miriam joined in the laughter, she stored Leonora's instant response away in her mind. Nathan, with all he had done during his life, knew so much about so many things, yet there was so much more he did not know.

"Leonora, you have known Nathan longer than I have. Tell me, have you ever seen him happier than he is now?"

"My cousin works fourteen hours a day in the store. When he is not there he constantly thinks of it. I guarantee that even while he sleeps, he dreams how to improve it. No"—Leonora shook her head—"I have never seen him happier than he is now."

"Neither have I." Blinking in the bright June sunlight, Miriam recalled the day twenty-one years ago when the two English cousins had entered her life. She had turned fourteen that very day. That first evening at the Waverley dinner table, Leonora had not even existed for Miriam. She had seen only Nathan. Everything about him had been different and utterly fascinating. His English accent, his looks, his thin, earnest face and dark, compassionate eyes. She had watched his every movement and hung on his every word. He had given her the gold sovereign that evening as a birthday present, and she had clutched it all night long while she slept, pretending it was a lucky talisman and wishing on it not for a piece of gold but for Nathan himself, envisioning the wonderful life they would have together. That birthday dream had taken many years to come true, and since wish had become fact little, other than those first three years of marriage, had gone as she had dreamed. The worst was when she had believed him dead. That, followed by her own mother's death, had made her want to crawl away like an injured animal and die. Had it not been for her responsibility to Harry and Louise, she would never have survived the war. God, in His wisdom and mercy, had given her those children to prolong her own life, so that she would be there to greet her husband when he returned from the dead. And He had given her Jacob and the child she carried now—a new, young family when her two older children were almost fully grown—as proof that there was a life and future for them in this town that rose so quickly from the ashes of war.

Reaching the store, Leonora held open the door. Miriam stepped through to stand beneath the glittering crystal gaselier. Nathan looked up from the cloth he was showing to a gray-haired woman. Miriam's face was flushed and damp and he instantly questioned the wisdom of her taking the air in the heat of June. "I think you should lie down and rest," he said.

For once, Miriam agreed without protest. The short walk in the sun had tired her. She would rest for half an hour and feel the better for it. She walked through the store to the stairs leading to the dwelling above. Leonora followed. Nathan returned his attention to the customer. Moments later, he heard the sound of something falling, followed by a cry of pain and the clear tone of Leonora's voice calling his name. He dropped the cloth and ran to the rear of the store. Halfway up the stairs, Leonora crouched over the fallen figure of Miriam. Nathan lifted Miriam in his arms and carried her up to the bedroom where he set her gently on the bed.

"Miriam . . . ?" Nathan whispered the name. "Miriam . . . ?"

Slowly the green eyes opened. The flush had disappeared, and Miriam's face was now deathly white. She spoke in a hushed voice. "What happened?"

A sigh of relief burst from Nathan's mouth. Terrifying images had danced in front of his eyes as he had seen Miriam lying on the stairs. "You fell," Leonora answered.

"How silly of me." Her eyes fastened on Nathan. She reached out to clasp his hand. "Perhaps I should listen to Doctor Solomon more often than I do and take better care of myself."

Nathan tried to slow his own pounding heart by making light of the moment. Holding Miriam's wrist with his right hand, he lifted his watch from his vest pocket with his left. "Doctor Solomon recommends rest and unswerving obedience to his advice."

"I promise. Go back downstairs before you lose a customer."

"I will stay with Miriam," Leonora said.

Nathan returned to the gray-haired woman who had waited patiently. When he explained that his wife had fallen on the stairs, the woman sympathized. The moment the customer left, Nathan walked quickly to the back of the store. As he reached the stairs, he heard Leonora's footsteps coming down.

"Doctor!" she gasped on seeing him.

Nathan smiled. Obviously the crisis was past. "I will be right up."

"No, you fool!" The insult flew out before Leonora realized what she said. "Your wife needs a real doctor! She's having the baby now!"

Miriam gave birth three hours later to a boy so pitifully weak and underweight that he barely breathed. The doctor summoned by Nathan gave the newborn, still bloody baby the most cursory examination before offering his professional opinion that the family should christen the child as quickly as possible so that it would not be buried without a name or hope of salvation. Grabbing the doctor by the shoulders, Nathan rushed him down the stairs, through the store and flung him out onto Whitehall Street with the shouted admonition that his baby son needed to be neither christened nor consigned to the grave just yet. Harry and Louise, returning from school at that very moment, stood openmouthed at the unique sight of their father losing his temper. Noticing them, Nathan snapped his fingers.

"Go to Garnett Street. Find Mrs. Gutheim! Tell her your mother's had a baby and we need her help! Run!" He clapped his hands and his son and daughter raced toward their old home. Nathan ran back upstairs to his wife and baby son. Damned doctors! The man must have learned his trade during the war. If he couldn't cut off a limb or cauterize a wound he was lost.

Bertha Gutheim arrived fifteen minutes later, red-faced and out of breath from rushing. She took charge immediately, banishing Nathan and the two older children down to the store, and instructing Leonora to care for Jacob, who, confused by all the noise and excitement, was sitting on the floor and screaming with all his might. Then she closed the bedroom door, hiding herself, Miriam, and the newborn child from view.

An hour later, she came down to the store with the news that Miriam and the baby were sleeping. "Nathan, I would be a liar if I told you that your baby is well formed and blessed with health. Poor thing, he was born too early and did not have all the time he needed to prepare for the hardships of life. To survive even until tomorrow . . . ?" Bertha shrugged her heavy shoulders. "He will have his mother's love, this I know, but more than his mother's love, he will need a miracle." She kissed Nathan on the cheek. "My husband and I will pray for such a miracle."

That night, long after the house was silent, Nathan let himself out onto Whitehall Street and began to walk south, away from the city center. The heat of the day had been replaced by a cool breeze from the north. A bright three-quarter moon lit the streets. Tears stung Nathan's eyes. He could cry now, alone on a deserted street where no one would see him. All day long, he had been strong, sharing that strength with his wife and cousin and children. Now, as he walked, he could let the tears flow.

It crossed Nathan's mind that he had walked on the night Jacob had been born. There was little similarity between that night and this. Jacob was a fit child, just like his older brother and sister. This youngest one was sickly, born too early. What was it Bertha Gutheim had said? Born without all the time needed to prepare for life's hardships? Like Nathan, the German watchmaker's wife knew that no mother could care for a child more lovingly than Miriam, but would loving care alone be enough? To live, the child would also need a miracle. How did miracles happen? Bertha said she was going to pray for one. Perhaps he should, too, but where? Should he go to the hall used by the Hebrew Benevolent Congregation, where Leonora and Miriam worshipped? At this time of night it would be closed. Locks would deny him the opportunity to pray.

Crossing East Peters Street, he found himself before Trinity Methodist Church. In forty years he had never taken a great deal of notice of any house of worship. Neither St. Paul's Cathedral, near his uncle's shop in London, nor St. Louis Cathedral in New Orleans—where he was to have married Marie-Louise—had raised little more than a passing curiosity and appreciation of architecture. Standing in the shadow of Trinity Methodist Church, however, Nathan sensed for the first time in his life the peace and fulfillment found by so many others. He stood for fully five minutes, staring at the building and letting his mind float free. The fear and worry that had plagued him since his son's birth seemed lighter, as though an unseen hand had brushed it away.

Slowly, he retraced his steps. Instead of returning to the house, he let himself into the shop. For a few seconds, he stood perfectly still, uncertain of the wisdom of his chosen course. Prayer was something new to him. Seeking help from anyone, let alone from a deity he was not even sure existed, filled him with confusion. He had not sought help when he had fought and triumphed over Raymonde Perrault. Nor had he looked for it during the war, when a hangman's rope had beckoned. But then only his own safety had been at risk. This was the well-being of his child, which he held in far higher esteem than his own welfare. Kneeling on the shop floor, he closed his eyes and let his forehead rest on the counter's cool wood.

He did not pray. He spoke in a calm, even tone as though he were not on his knees in supplication but sitting in a parlor chair, and the God whose help he sought was not a divine being but a close friend.

"I've blamed You and cursed You for much ill fortune. For my parents dying. For Marie-Louise dying. Yet when good luck came my way, I never even gave You a thought. Perhaps You were there when Gershon Lowensohn made his presence known on board the ship. Perhaps You were also there when overconfidence caused Raymonde Perrault to grow careless, and when William Patrick Flaherty decided to repay a favor." Nathan drew his head away from the counter, opened his eyes and looked around in the darkness, suddenly embarrassed that someone might be in the shop to hear him. "If I never thanked You for such blessings, forgive me. I thank You now, and I ask for one more. Upstairs is a child so weak he might not live through the night. He has done nothing to deserve such a fate. Help me, and help that child. Give me the miracle that is his only hope."

Nathan stood up, dusted dirt from his knees and went upstairs. He felt tremendously relieved, as though he had passed the responsibility for his son on to a higher level.

The baby boy did not die that night. Nor the following night, or the night after that. And for each night he did not die, and for each day he gained a little strength, Nathan prayed. He knelt on the floor of the shop and thanked God in that same conversational tone for sparing the life of his youngest child.

On the fifth night of such furtive prayer, Nathan sensed he was not alone. As he finished thanking God for bringing his son through another day, he opened his eyes and looked around to see a woman's outline.

"Please carry on," Leonora whispered.

"I have just finished."

"A pity. I enjoyed listening to you."

Nathan's voice grew sharp. "Do you laugh at me, Lally?"

"No. I smile at the beauty of your prayers."

"You heard no prayers, Lally. You eavesdropped on a private conversation."

"Conversation?" Leonora's dress rustled as she knelt beside Nathan. "I heard but one voice."

Nathan's momentary flash of anger evaporated. "I heard two, but then the answers to my questions are meant only for my ears."

"I do not need to hear those answers. I can tell what they are by the way your son progresses." In the darkness, Leonora reached out to hold her cousin's hand. "You cannot do everything on your own, Nathan. There is no shame in asking for help."

"Thank you, Lally." He squeezed her hand fondly, glad now that she had discovered his secret. He had no doubt that she had been praying also, as had Miriam, the other children, and everyone who cared for the Solomon family. He alone among them all was the last to realize the power faith could wield.

Chapter Twenty-three

For the first weeks of his life, the youngest Solomon child lived with no name. That he lived at all was enough for Miriam and Nathan, who watched with wonder the tiny improvements each day made. Flesh filled out the shriveled face and scrawny limbs. Tiny lungs drew in deeper breaths. Pitifully weak whimpers grew into lusty cries. Only after a month, when doubt over his survival no longer existed, was the baby named. Nathan chose a name that reflected the miracle wrought by a mother's love and a father's prayers. He selected William, to honor William Patrick Flaherty whose reappearance at the Old Capitol Prison had truly been a miracle, and, through its more familiar version, to honor a rebel soldier from South Carolina called Billy Harrison. He followed William with Gershon, in memory of his father-in-law.

Watching his youngest son sleep peacefully, Nathan said, "You will grow up big and strong like the William for whom you are named. And if you temper that strength with the compassion and generosity that was your grandfather Gershon's, you will become a truly great man."

Nathan's prayers, which he had begun with the premature birth of his son, did not cease as William slowly recovered from nature's treachery. Late each night, just before going to bed, Nathan knelt on the store floor to communicate with the God he had found late in life. Prayer made life's hardships easier to manage. Faced alone, each problem seemed a mountain; somehow those mountains were less daunting after discussing them from his knees. Every Friday, Miriam and Leonora asked him to accompany them to that night's service at the Hebrew Benevolent Congregation. He always said no, preferring his own simple, conversational style of prayer to the formalized worship he would find in a synagogue. Alone, he knew his words were heard. In the middle of a crowd, his voice might be drowned out.

The more Nathan knelt and talked, the more he learned about himself. And the more he learned, the more numerous were the blessings he discovered. The greatest blessing of all was his family. No matter how successful a man became, if he had no family with which to share those triumphs, his life was a desert, a wasteland bereft of all joy and warmth. With four children, Nathan knew he was truly blessed.

The store, his very own Crystal Palace, was another blessing. He worked harder now than he had ever done, but he did not mind. A man appreciated the blessings for which he worked. Those that were thrust upon him were all too often taken for granted. Six days a week, Nathan opened the store at seven in the morning, often staying open until nine at night. Most of the time, Leonora worked beside him, while Miriam came down to help during the busiest periods. In the afternoon, when school was over, Harry and Louise performed odd jobs. But the bulk of the work fell on Nathan. Even when he closed the doors at night, he was far from finished. He could spend another hour in the stockroom, checking inventory and inspecting new shipments of goods, tasks he could not attend to during the day. As proprietor, he had to be on the floor the entire time the store was open. Customers expected to see him there. It gave them confidence to know that, no matter who was serving them, they could always turn to the owner. To Mr. Nathan. Thank God for Leonora. Without her bookkeeping and administrative skills, Nathan knew he would never be able to manage. Yet another blessing, to have such a loyal, wonderful cousin as

Lally. If only a tenth of the good things Nathan wished for his cousin came true, she would marry a prince and live in a palace.

Because he worked so hard during the week, Sunday became increasingly important to Nathan. It was the one day he could spend with his family and it quickly developed into a routine. Every Sunday began with a communal breakfast. The entire family, except for the two youngest children, Jacob and William, crowded around the small dining table to share a leisurely meal. Miriam cooked, using the spices of New Orleans she found stocked by Atlanta's produce dealers. Conversation always accompanied the meal, as members of the family caught up on the previous week's news. Nathan recounted business stories. Miriam talked of Jacob and William, who remained her main responsibilities during the week, while Harry and Louise discussed schoolwork with Leonora. Nathan never failed to be amused at how his two older children went to Leonora for such help and not to him. They knew which family member to ask when it came to schoolwork.

After breakfast, the family went out. Miriam pushed William in a baby buggy that had room for Jacob if his tiny legs grew tired. The idea was to leave, if only for a few hours, Whitehall Street and the Crystal Palace behind them. Frequently, their first stop was the skating rink where the railroad crossed Forsyth Street. That was Harry's and Louise's favorite spot. The moment they put on roller skates, a fierce competition raged between brother and sister. Harry was bigger and stronger, six inches taller and at least twenty pounds heavier, but Louise's determination kept her right on his tail as they flew around the rink, arms swinging and wheels buzzing. Every outing to the rink included at least one tumble which threw Miriam's heart into her mouth, but the worst either skater ever received was a grazed knee or elbow, which they considered a small price to pay for such exhilaration.

From the rink, the family visited Oglethorpe Park to row on the lake, or crossed the trestle bridge over Clear Creek to picnic at Ponce de Leon Springs. Miriam was so taken with the taste of the spa water at the Springs that she ordered it for home. At both places Nathan was sure to run into customers of the Crystal Palace. When he exchanged greetings with them and talked for a minute or two, he was more than a storekeeper—he was part of a burgeoning community. And each time he pulled at the oars of a boat on the lake at Oglethorpe Park, or enjoyed a lazy picnic at Ponce de Leon Springs, he counted his blessings again. Among all the men he knew, he was truly fortunate.

Nathan's blessings continued to mount. By the end of his first year in business, the Crystal Palace was firmly established. His credit was good with the wholesale houses. Returning customers brought friends with them. Such success was no fluke. Atlanta had too many dry goods stores to allow such accidents. From the day he opened, Nathan had gone out of his way to please his customers. On one wall was a sign that read: NO CUSTOMER LEAVES THE CRYSTAL PALACE DISSATISFIED. No matter what item a customer returned, from the cheapest reel of thread to an expensive length of linen, the Crystal Palace took it back without question. More importantly, he abolished the haggling that accompanied each transaction. Every storekeeper Nathan had known, from Samuel Solomon to Ephraim Gottfried, marked their wares with a coded price below which they refused to sell. They began a transaction by asking a higher price, then allowed themselves to be beaten down. Often, the eventual price was above the coded figure, giving the merchant a larger profit while leaving the customer uncertain whether he had snared a bargain or paid too much. Nathan waited six months, until the Crystal Palace had gained some customer loyalty, before announcing with window signs and newspaper advertisements a one-price policy: BY ESTABLISHING A SINGLE PRICE, AN INNOCENT BABY CAN BUY AT THE CRYSTAL PALACE AS ECONOMICALLY AS THE WORLD'S MOST EXPERIENCED, ASTUTE SHOPPER.

Many customers appreciated the change because it removed uncertainty, but there were also those who missed the bargaining. One was a schoolteacher named Rose Strickland, a middle-aged spinster who bought dress fabrics and patterns from the Crystal Palace, and never failed to spend at least ten minutes haggling over prices.

"You are truly a Philistine, Mister Nathan," she declared on a visit to the store shortly after the one-price policy had gone into effect. "Negotiating is an art and you have destroyed it."

"Negotiating is for politicians, Miss Strickland, not shoppers. One of the reasons for our new policy is that there is nothing I hate more than to see customers leave here wondering if they got the best price possible. I want them to know they got the best price without having to work for it."

The schoolteacher was not so easily mollified. "I think having a single, inviolable price removes much of the pleasure from shopping, Mister Nathan. What is the point of visiting a store without the fun of jewing down the price?"

Nathan's face showed a tolerant amusement. "Miss Strickland, another reason for the Crystal Palace's policy change—which you, as a schoolteacher, should appreciate more than anyone—is to remind people that the word *Jew* is not a verb but a proper noun."

Miss Strickland had a thin face which rarely, in the course of a day's work in school, smiled. But now it did, slightly at first, then breaking into a wide, bright beam. "Thank you, Mister Nathan, for finding such a novel way of correcting my appalling misuse of the English language."

"You are quite welcome, Miss Strickland."

Nathan recounted the story to his family over the next Sunday breakfast. Everyone laughed when Harry asked, "At what other dry goods store can you get a paper of pins, a spool of thread, a card of buttons, and a grammar lesson at one and the same time?"

In the weeks leading up to Christmas, Nathan was especially grateful that he had instigated his one-price policy earlier in the year. The store was never empty, and in the five minutes he would have wasted haggling with a customer he now completed two other sales. He was so busy he even temporarily relinquished his traditional Sundays. Instead of spending them with the family, he worked in the stockroom, attending to the chores he normally would have done each weekday evening. But the Crystal Palace stayed open so late each night that he barely had the strength, after closing the store, to crawl upstairs and fall into bed, let alone take inventory and check new deliveries.

Only when Christmas Day arrived did Nathan rest. He sat at a window overlooking Whitehall Street, hearing the joyous sound of bells and watching people make their way to church in celebration of Christ's birthday. Christmas had fallen on a Wednesday, and Nathan was quite enjoying the novelty of taking off a weekday. As he listened to the bells, an idea occurred. He went down to the store and chose a doll wearing a crinoline and sun bonnet with a paper parasol clutched in a tiny hand; it was the only one remaining from a shipment of a dozen such dolls he had ordered especially for Christmas. He took it to Hunter Street where Clarissa Jenkins lived in a two-story wooden house with her parents and two older brothers. Clarissa's father, Alfred Jenkins, opened the door. A tall, heavy man with a gleaming bald head, Jenkins told Nathan that Clarissa was at church with her mother. Nathan handed him the doll. "When she returns, please give her this with the message that she will always remain the Crystal Palace's first and favorite customer. Each year, God willing, we will give her a bigger and better present."

Returning home, Nathan felt pleased with himself. He may have learned much from Samuel Solomon and Ephraim Gottfried, but this idea was all his own. Clarissa was a frequent visitor to the store. Sometimes she came with her mother, a chubby woman with graying hair and a round, smiling face. But most of the time she came alone, just, as she had promised, to admire the crystal gaselier. The girl loved to listen to Nathan describe London and New Orleans. She also loved to talk, about her home, her family, her school, about anything that came into her mind. Pride entered her young, high voice when she spoke of her father who drove one of the new horse-drawn streetcars that ran along Peters Street between Whitehall Street and the Yankee Barracks. Only rarely did Clarissa buy anything, and then it was an item that cost five or ten cents. It did not matter to Nathan. Clarissa would always be his first customer. And no matter how many customers a store served over its lifetime, only one could be the first.

Harry left school the following summer, three months after his fifteenth birthday, and joined his father in the Crystal Palace. His arrival coincided with the beginning of a worldwide depression that made itself felt even in the normally ebullient Atlanta. Four of the ten banks with offices in the Gate City failed. Companies went bankrupt. Among them was the Decatur Street dry goods store of Ephraim Gottfried. On the day he was to be evicted from the premises he had occupied since returning from the woods after Atlanta's burning, Gottfried tore a sheet into strips, fashioned a rope and hanged himself. Nine years earlier, Sherman had driven him from his store and home. No one would drive him out again.

Nathan attended the funeral. Many of the mourners he saw there were merchants like himself and Gottfried. Sprinkled among their words of regret at Gottfried's death were expressions of concern that their establishments might soon close their doors. Wholesalers, choked for credit by manufacturers, were squeezing their retail customers. Nathan left the cemetery feeling fortunate that he had no sales clerks to pay. When it came to tight times, nothing surpassed a close family willing to pitch in and help each other.

As 1873 passed, the depression tightened its grip on Atlanta. More firms closed. Real estate values, which had soared since the city's rebuilding, suddenly stagnated. Among the hardest hit were the farmers who came to Atlanta to sell their produce and buy the goods and merchandise necessary to operate their farms. The depression caused a decline in the value of their crops while their debt to suppliers remained as large as ever. Because the Crystal Palace's operating expenses were less than those of merchants with paid staffs, Nathan could afford to be flexible. He offered regular customers credit against future crops and bartered goods for produce. Scissors for a ball of butter, a length of calico for half a dozen chickens which he sold elsewhere. Somehow, he always found the money to pay his own bills—in the Atlanta of 1873 that was no mean feat—and when Christmas came he took Clarissa Jenkins another doll, bigger and better than the one he had given to her the previous year. Nothing would make him break his word to the Crystal Palace's first customer. This time, Clarissa was at home, expecting Nathan's visit, and he returned from Hunter Street with a present of his own, a freshly baked apple pie.

Business showed no sign of improving in 1874, and the men who prophesied that the slump could last for another five years were no longer ridiculed as malcontents and pessimists. To survive in such a climate Nathan knew he needed more than the help even a close-knit family could supply. While other merchants favored economic retrenchment by decreasing inventory, Nathan went on the offensive. He added men's and women's clothing and children's toys to his standard dry goods, then completely reorganized his advertising policy. Instead of taking advertisements that did little more than call attention to the Crystal Palace's existence, he copied Samuel Solomon by crafting announcements that snatched at the public's attention because of their very triteness. The first appeared in the *Constitution* in the spring of 1874, under the title THE SEVEN WONDERS OF ATLANTA. Listed below were these phenomena: Atlanta's free mail delivery; its mineral spring; its uniformed police; its fire department; the new iron bridge at Broad Street; the beauty of its ladies; and, most importantly, how cheaply gentlemen's underwear is sold beneath the glittering gaselier at Nathan Solomon's Crystal Palace on Whitehall Street . . . !

The last line changed every couple of weeks to reflect a new bargain. To complement the advertisements, Nathan took another leaf from his uncle's book. He had the store's small delivery wagon refurbished. Each side carried the announcement currently running in the *Constitution,* while on top rested a facsimile of the crystal gaselier. Soon, the wagon, driven either by Harry or Louise, who joined the store in the summer of 1874, became as familiar a sight in Atlanta as the hat-shaped carriage had been in London. As Nathan grew older, he found his opinion of Samuel Solomon altering. Nothing could ever make him admire his uncle as a man, but he was learning to respect him more as a merchant.

Despite Atlanta's commercial gloom, Nathan kept his promise to Clarissa Jenkins again in 1874. By being aggressive while other storekeepers had hesitated, Nathan had enjoyed his best year yet, achieving success in a time when business failures were more common than summer flies. Simultaneously, he had learned a valuable lesson: mediocre businessmen rode out bad economic times; shrewd businessmen profited from them. On Christmas Day, he delivered to Clarissa's home on Hunter Street an intricate dollhouse, and returned with another freshly baked pie.

Nathan's choice of gift amused Miriam. "A doll in eighteen seventy-two, another doll last year, and now a dollhouse," she said as they lay together in bed that night. "Do you not think that our first customer might be too old to play with dolls?"

"You played with dolls and a dollhouse when I first knew you, and you were fourteen."

"It was a different world back then, Nathan, a world unsullied by pestilence and war."

"What would you give Clarissa?"

"She is eleven or twelve, almost a young lady. You should give her something a young lady would appreciate. Perhaps a silver-backed hairbrush or a piece of jewelry."

"A silver-backed hairbrush or a piece of jewelry! Do you know what kind of year I would need to afford those presents?"

"Another one like you had this year." She turned over and snuggled close to Nathan as a gust of wintry wind rattled the windows and filled the room with sudden cold. "Stop trying to pretend you had a terrible year. I know better."

"Did you believe it would be such a splendid year?"

"Always. I never doubted for a moment your wisdom of expanding while others contracted. I am a businessman's daughter, remember?"

"And a businessman's wife." Nathan drew her closer to him, needing the warmth of her body to drive away the cold that seeped into the bedroom and found its way through the blankets and his nightshirt.

"Are you happy to have Harry and Louise in the store?"

"As happy as any father can be. And I will be even happier when Jacob, also, joins us. I have such plans for him. I watch him play. He takes things apart and puts them back together better, I swear, than they were before. Jacob will design and build a new store, a new Crystal Palace that will be a landmark."

Miriam laughed at Nathan's enthusiasm. "Jacob is four, and already you plan his life." She started to ask if he had such grandiose ideas for William, but sadness seized her as she thought of her youngest son. William had never shrugged off the shock of being ejected from his mother's womb a month before his lease was up. Thirty months later, he lacked the explosive energy of other children his age. He had been slow to walk and slow to talk. He needed to rest often, and his communication went little beyond pointing to an object and uttering a single word. Miriam knew he would never grow to be powerful like the William after whom he was named. She could only hope that he turned out like the grandfather whose memory he also honored, then his strength would not be in his body but in his brain.

"Do you really think I try to plot my children's lives?" Nathan asked. Without waiting for an answer, he added, "I wish I could fashion the lives of other people. That way I could bring happiness to those who really deserve it."

Resting on her elbow, Miriam tried to see Nathan's face in

the darkness. A change had come over his voice, a softness, an anguish almost, as though he now felt the sadness that had swept over Miriam at the mention of William. "Whose life would you change, Nathan? Who deserves happiness?"

"Surely you know. My cousin."

"Why do you think she is not happy?"

"How can she be? Just look at her, Miriam. Leonora would have made a wonderful wife to some fortunate man, a wonderful mother to some lucky children. Instead, she is forty years old, her life is more than half over, and she has no one."

Miriam wondered what had caused Nathan's sudden lapse into sentimentality. Was it scrutinizing his own good fortune and realizing that the cousin who had accompanied him every step of the way from England had not shared in it? "She considers us her family. She treats our children as her own."

"Then she is cheating herself, but Lally has always been cheated. Like me, a railway accident cheated her of parents. The fever cheated her of happiness when it plucked Antoine from her arms. Traumatic times cheated her of the chance to find another man to love, and now she cheats herself by ignoring the interest of eligible men. At seventeen, when we left England, my cousin possessed the courage of a lioness. But now, at forty, I think courage has deserted her."

"Nathan, how can you be so blind? Courage has not deserted Leonora. She has not shown interest in a man because for more than twenty years she has met no man who compares well to you."

"To me? What reasoning is that?"

"Your cousin is in love with you. Antoine was the only man to ever make her forget you, and he died."

Nathan could not bring himself to believe what Miriam said. "Give me proof of your wild allegations."

"Leonora went out of her way to show me what a swine Marcus Barnett was. She did not do it for my benefit. She did it for you. She knew you desired me, and therefore she wanted to see the two of us together. Nathan, no woman can love more deeply than to ensure the happiness of the man she loves, even if it means sacrificing her own chance at bliss."

Nathan groaned softly in pain. Did Miriam speak the truth? All these years he had made excuses for his cousin's lack of interest in men, using the same rationalizations he had just given to Miriam. Had he really been so blind, or had he known the truth and not wanted to accept it? Closing his eyes, he rode again with Leonora in the horse-drawn omnibus from Bloomsbury to Ludgate Hill to prepare Samuel Solomon's shop for the business day. Once their work was done, he recalled, he read aloud to Leonora. She always asked him to read for her, claiming that the stories became alive when told—Leonora's exact words rushed into his mind—by her handsome older cousin.

The scene changed. Nathan saw Leonora demanding that he take her with him to America. He remembered trying to persuade her to stay, but could he, in truth, have succeeded in his flight without her aid? She had helped him every step of the way.

Nathan felt the moist warmth of Miriam's lips caress his forehead. "I am not upset that another woman loves you," she whispered. More kisses followed, one on each eyelid, on his nose, his chin, and finally his lips. "In fact, I feel complimented. Leonora is a lady of impeccable taste, and knowing she feels so strongly about you endorses my own good judgment."

Miriam's revelation made Nathan take more notice of his cousin. It shamed him to realize how he had always taken Leonora so much for granted, but was that not often the fate of such selfless people? Goodness and decency were accepted without question while rudeness and bad taste drew notice and, all too often, admiration. Leonora was the most selfless person Nathan had ever known, always putting the happiness of others before her own. Had she not done that with Miriam and Nathan, pushing them together because she understood Nathan's feelings toward the golden-haired girl? Pushing them together even when, as Miriam had pointed out, she was in love with Nathan herself?

Even armed with Miriam's information, Nathan saw nothing different in Leonora. She behaved toward him in the store and in the house with the same warmth she had always shown. She loved him, certainly, but it was the depth of that love which remained in question. Did she love him as Miriam did? Or did she love him the way Nathan loved her, as a cousin, with a familial fondness which Miriam—and through her, himself—had mistaken for something far stronger?

In 1875, the slump showed signs of easing, and Nathan began to give serious thought to expanding the store. By enlarging inventory, he had drawn more customers to the Crystal Palace. If he added even more lines, he would attract more customers still. He envisioned a store—a magnificent store with a range and depth of inventory like no other!—where a customer could buy everything he needed.

In the fall of 1875, Nathan got his chance. The hardware store next to the Crystal Palace became a late casualty of the depression. When the bank foreclosed, Nathan stepped in with an offer. Carpenters and painters began work on the newly acquired property. When they finished at the beginning of December, the Crystal Palace sign extended over two establishments—the original shop which confined its business once again to dry goods, and the new store which sold everything from clothing to crockery and cutlery. Leonora and Louise worked together in the dry goods section. Harry and Miriam sold in the new store. And Nathan ran from one to the other to greet customers.

On Christmas Day, Nathan attended to a task that had become an enjoyable annual ritual, the delivery of a gift to Clarissa Jenkins. Mildred Jenkins, Clarissa's mother, opened the door for Nathan. She took his hat and coat and showed him through to the living room. In front of a roaring fire, puffing contentedly on a pipe, sat Alfred Jenkins. He stood up as Nathan entered, and extended his hand.

"A merry Christmas to you, Mister Solomon."

"To you as well, Mister Jenkins. I'm glad to find you looking so well. I had not seen you lately, and I was wondering whether you were all right."

"I'm surprised Clarissa did not tell you I had been moved. She's a regular old gossip who tells tales all over town. I am no longer on the run to the Yankee Barracks. The company shifted me to the new line out to Ponce de Leon Springs."

Nathan nodded. "A delightful destination. No doubt we will see you when spring comes."

"Just as long as the company hasn't seen fit to move me again," Jenkins said with the dry smile of a man who knows such things are possible. He turned to his wife. "Clarissa is probably telling her entire life story to our new boarder. Call her down before she frightens him away." As Mildred left the room, Jenkins returned his attention to Nathan. "What with our sons being married and on their own now, we decided to put our empty room to good use. Took in a boarder a few weeks back. Pleasant young fellow who works for the Atlanta *Daily Herald*. Farm boy originally, quiet and respectable on the surface, but he can be real outspoken when he sets his mind to it. I'll wager he's got some fires burning down in his belly."

"He'll have to if he's ever going to make himself heard at a ruckus-raising newspaper like the *Daily Herald*."

Mildred returned with Clarissa. Wearing a long green dress, and with her fair hair swept back into a bun, Clarissa looked very grown up indeed. "Merry Christmas to you, Clarissa," Nathan said as he held out a small package. "Thank you again for being the Crystal Palace's first customer."

Clarissa unwrapped the package. A delighted shriek burst from her lips as she saw a silver brooch in the shape of the crystal gaselier which had first attracted her. Pinning it to her dress, she swung around to show her parents. "Had I known how well stores treated their first customers, I would have been first through the door of every store in Atlanta. Thank you, Mister Nathan, and a very merry Christmas to you as well!"

"I swear you'll spoil our daughter for any young man," Mildred told Nathan in mock rebuke. "She will expect such gifts from everyone."

"Clarissa brought me much luck. She deserves such gifts." Nathan looked past Mildred as a young man entered the room. Wearing black trousers and jacket, he was as tall as Alfred Jenkins but considerably slimmer. His light brown hair was cut short. A thin mustache covered his top lip, and above a long, thin nose, his blue eyes held a cold and distant look. Nathan stared, knowing he had seen the Jenkins boarder before, but unable to identify him.

"Clarissa, why don't you show your lovely gift to Mister Hopkinson?" Mildred suggested.

The girl whirled around, eager to show off her new treasure. "Look what Mister Nathan gave me, all because I was the first customer ever to go into his store four years ago. I only bought a few cents' worth of thread, and he's been buying me Christmas presents ever since! How can he make a living doing that?"

The young man named Hopkinson studied the brooch for several seconds before raising his eyes to look at Nathan. "Do not worry your pretty head about merchants, Clarissa. They always manage to make a living somehow."

Alfred Jenkins burst out laughing. "Told you he could be real outspoken, didn't I? Mister Hopkinson, this is Mister Solomon, who owns the Crystal Palace on Whitehall Street. Mister Solomon—"

"We already know each other," Nathan cut in as recognition finally came. So did the young man's first name. George, that was it. George, the older son of Thomas Hopkinson, the bigot he had met on Marietta Road. How could he ever forget? He smiled at the uncertainty he saw on Hopkinson's angular face as the farmer's son also searched his memory. "Five years ago, I drove a wagon for Ephraim Gottfried. I stopped by soon after your father had taken over the farm, and he sent me packing because he disliked the sound of my name."

At last, Hopkinson placed Nathan. "You don't have to worry about him sending anyone packing anymore. He lies under the farm now. Him and my little brother Jamie."

"I'm sorry. What happened to them?"

Nathan's expression of regret drew a skeptical glance from Hopkinson. "My father lost the farm two years ago when this depression started. Prices he got for his crops went way down and he couldn't pay what he owed to the merchants. So they took over the farm, and my father and my brother had to go to work for them if they wanted to eat. Work harder than any nigger slaves ever worked, seven days a week until they were so weary they dropped. One night last winter, there was a fire. The farmhouse burned down, with my father and Jamie in it. Some people think the smoke got to them before they could get out, but I know better. I reckon they were so damned tired they didn't have the strength to wake up and save themselves."

"How did you get out?"

"I wasn't there. I left before the merchants stole it. I was never cut out to be a farmer, but I still wanted to help them. I thought I could best do that by giving them a voice in the city and the state."

"On a newspaper?" Nathan's voice assumed a hard edge. "It wasn't every merchant who took your father's farm, Mister Hopkinson. It was the country store he insisted on dealing with because he would rather be robbed by what he so proudly called one of his own kind than buy from a foreigner or an Israelite. It was the railroads and the wholesalers who owned that store who enslaved him and your brother Jamie. If he had bought from the likes of me, he would have gotten honest prices and good credit, and he might still be alive today." When Nathan paused to draw breath, he noticed Alfred and Mildred Jenkins watching the exchange with growing concern, and Clarissa fiddling nervously with her new silver brooch. "I thought the stock-in-trade of newspaper people was fact, Mister Hopkinson. Let me share one with you. There are good and bad merchants, as there are good and bad reporters. Your father was ill-advised enough to allow his prejudices to guide him in the wrong direction."

Hopkinson's face reddened with anger. He opened his mouth to respond, then swung around and stalked from the room. Moments later, Nathan heard the crash of feet on the stairs, followed by the slamming of a door. He turned to the other three people in the room. "I apologize for spoiling your Christmas."

"Told you he could be outspoken, didn't I?" Alfred Jenkins said to Nathan. "But then I reckon you're not backward in that department either, are you? Clarissa, why don't you show Mister Solomon what you made for him?"

The girl opened the drawer of a cabinet set against the wall and withdrew a rolled piece of cloth. "No apple pie?" Nathan asked in surprise.

"This took much more time, Mister Nathan. It took a whole year, but I'm afraid it only shows the old store because I started it when that was all you had."

Nathan unrolled the cloth and held it with both hands at arm's length. Clarissa's gift was a work of embroidery depicting the store Nathan had opened four years earlier. He could believe it had taken the girl a year to complete because he knew the effort that went into a work like this. Miriam's sister, Sarah, had been a skilled embroiderer. Nathan remembered her sitting for hours on end at Waverley, painstakingly inserting the minute stitches that comprised such a work of art. If anything, this was even finer. The detail was so acute—right down to his own name, small above the larger "Crystal Palace"—that he felt he could have been staring at a photograph.

"Thank you, Clarissa. I will have a frame made for it. And please do not worry about it showing only the old store. That is the most important part of the store because it is where you were our first customer."

He walked home with the embroidery tucked carefully beneath his arm. The unexpected gift gave him such a feeling of warmth that he even forgot the clash with George Hopkinson. And when he did remember later that day, he refused to let the memory upset him. The son would not do as the father had done.

Four days later, Nathan hung the framed embroidery in the new store, with Clarissa's name below it. When she came in later that day, she gasped with pleasure at the sight of her name written in a sign-painter's flowing script, then told Nathan that George Hopkinson no longer boarded at her parents' home.

"My daddy threw him out. Wouldn't do it on Christmas Day or the following day, because it was a Sunday and Daddy said it wouldn't be the Christian thing to do. But first thing on Monday, before he left for the streetcar depot, he went up to Mister Hopkinson's room and told him he wasn't welcome to remain in our house anymore. I heard it all. When Mister Hopkinson asked why, my daddy told him that he would not stand for our friends to be treated so rudely."

In some ways, Nathan felt sorry for George Hopkinson. The young man had lost both his father and his brother, and Nathan could identify with such tragic losses. But his empathy went no further, for in the Hopkinson family the apples fell very close to the tree. Thomas Hopkinson had been a bigot whose prejudices went little farther than the stretch of Marietta Road which fronted his farm. The son was far more dangerous than the father, because as a newspaper reporter his bias would have a wider audience.

It was a relief to know that for every George Hopkinson, there was at least one Alfred Jenkins.

Chapter Twenty-four

Nathan routinely read the *Constitution*, the newspaper in which he advertised the Crystal Palace. After the meeting with George Hopkinson, he added the *Daily Herald* to his list. He saw Hopkinson's name regularly, sometimes linked with stories about Atlanta's business climate but more frequently appearing on articles concerning the difficulties faced by Georgia's farmers. One particularly biting piece described the funerals of farmers, who were buried, Hopkinson pointed out, in Northern-made clothes and Northern-made coffins. Even the shovel used to dig the grave and the headstone used to mark it came from the North, while Georgia provided nothing but the body and the hole in the ground. In Hopkinson's stories, farmers were hard-working, heroic folk locked in a struggle against overwhelming adversity. Nathan wondered how long it would be before the reporter's resentment towards banks and merchants found its way more openly into his stories. Or had he already tried to color the stories with his own prejudices, only to have the editor delete such references for fear of alienating the merchants and banks which advertised in the newspaper?

After a few months, Hopkinson's stories ceased altogether as the *Daily Herald* folded. In vain, Nathan sought Hopkinson's name in other publications until a friend at the *Constitution* told him that the farmer's son had left Atlanta. Satisfied that any threat Hopkinson presented had disappeared with his departure, Nathan pushed the young man from his mind.

The closing of the *Daily Herald* was a rare failure in an Atlanta rebounding from the depression. Population continued to boom. New banks opened for business. The two major hotels, the Kimball House and the Markham, were filled with drummers representing manufacturers in northern cities, and in a move guaranteed to boost the spirits of all Atlantans, the last Federal soldiers were withdrawn after the national election of 1876. With the soldiers' departure went the last traces of occupation. For the first time in more than a decade, the city was completely free.

Atlanta greeted 1877 with joy and well-founded optimism. The installation of the first telephone line, connecting Union Station with the passenger agent's office of the Western and Atlantic Railroad, aroused curiosity and wonder. Every form of recreation drew crowds. The lake at Oglethorpe Park swarmed with rowing boats. Throngs filled Ponce de Leon Springs to take the waters, and picnic in the summer sun. Baseball teams battled before excited fans, while those folk with a gentler, more sophisticated nature chose the opera and theater for their entertainment. At the end of September, as if to complete the summer of resurgence, President Rutherford B. Hayes visited Atlanta and spoke from the Markham Hotel's balcony of the need to achieve warmer feelings between the South and North.

For the Solomon family, 1877 signified the end of Nathan's communal Sundays. Everyone still assembled over Sunday breakfast, but the two oldest children no longer shared in the remainder of the day's activities. Harry, at nineteen, and Louise, at seventeen, had found social interests outside the family. They belonged to a group called the Meyerbeer Society, young men and women who gathered on Sunday afternoons in each other's homes for musical and literary afternoons.

In mid-October, two months after Harry and Louise had joined the Meyerbeer Society, it met for the first time in the Solomon home. The joint hosts made known that they wanted only club members to be present at the meeting. "You *will* be out this afternoon, won't you?" Louise pointedly asked her parents as they gathered over breakfast that morning.

"Of course we will," Miriam answered. "Have we not already told you so at least a dozen times?" She remembered how it had been when she was young and wanted privacy in a large family. Henry had always managed to pop up in the middle of whatever she was doing, and Sarah and Martha were never far behind. Miriam would not want to do to her own children what she had disliked herself. Despite her good intentions, though, her curiosity was aroused when she noticed the preparations being made for the meeting. Louise baked cakes to be served with tea, while Harry went around the parlor straightening antimacassars on the backs of chairs, and dusting the piano.

Just before noon, Nathan walked along Whitehall Street to the livery stable where he kept the store's delivery wagon and a horse and buggy. It was a warm, dry fall day, and he wanted to make the most of it. He returned with the buggy to collect Miriam, Leonora, and the two youngest children, then they set out for Ponce de Leon Springs. They took with them a picnic lunch, and left behind a promise that they would not be home before five, when the meeting of the Meyerbeer Society would have finished. But as they ate their lunch, Miriam looked anxiously at the sky where streaky cirrus clouds began assuming far more ominous shapes.

Afterward, while the two women sat on a blanket beneath the spreading branches of an oak, Nathan played ball with his youngest sons. When he heard thunder rumble in the distance, he looked up in annoyance. He hated it to rain on Sunday and spoil the little time he had with his youngest children. Playing with Jacob and William was a journey into the past, back to when Harry and Louise had been this young. Only he had never played with Harry and Louise then. Those years had been stolen from him. A whole generation of fathers, in the South and the North, had lost those years.

Holding the ball, he looked from one boy to the other. There was no doubt these two were brothers. They shared the dark hair and brown eyes of Nathan's family, unlike the older children, who followed the Lowensohns. "Who wants to catch the ball?" When both boys thrust their hands into the air, Nathan tossed the ball between them. Before William had covered more than a couple of steps, Jacob had run half a dozen paces and flung himself through the air to swoop on the bouncing ball and claim it for his own. Grass stains covered his clothing, and sweat shone on his face. William was as clean as he had been when they left the house. He never seemed to get dirty. Sometimes, Nathan wondered if William really enjoyed these outings. Given the choice between playing ball or looking through a book at words he could not yet read, Nathan was certain his youngest son would opt for the book.

Thunder rumbled again. Miriam looked up at the rapidly darkening sky. She called Nathan's name and suggested they leave the park to find, instead, some recreation under cover, a concert by one of the city's musical societies, or a rehearsal for a play. Another clap of thunder filled the sky, much closer this time. William screamed in terror and clasped his hands to his ears. That was enough for Nathan. The youngest boy was especially sensitive. While thunder and lightning delighted Jacob, it terrified William. Holding a child with each hand, Nathan started running toward the buggy. Miriam and Leonora, arms full of picnic debris, followed.

The storm broke when they were still half a mile from Five Points. Rain lashed down and lightning danced across a gray sky. Forgetting all about finding alternative entertainment, Nathan aimed the buggy for Whitehall Street and home. He stopped outside the store and helped Miriam, Leonora, and the children down. They entered the building while Nathan returned the horse and buggy to the stable. Only as he ran home through the teeming rain did he remember the promise he and Miriam had made to Harry and Louise.

He took the stairs two at a time. A sight both funny and odd greeted him in the parlor. His cousin and Miriam, each holding the hand of a child, stood perfectly still, sodden clothes dripping water onto the wooden floor. Just as motionless, but dry and seated, were the members of the Meyerbeer Society. One girl with long dark hair and a bright yellow dress sat at the piano. Next to her, frozen in the act of leaning forward to turn the page of a score, sat Harry. Five more young men and women formed a semicircle around the piano, while Louise stood paralyzed in the act of offering around a tray of chocolates. Each group stared at the other, as if uncertain about the validity of its presence in the house.

Louise was the first to move. She straightened up, the tray of chocolates still held out in front of her as though she were offering them to the intruders. "You promised . . . !"

Miriam, remembering as Nathan had done on his way from the stable, threw her hand up to her mouth. "I'm sorry! We forgot!"

"But you promised!"

"What will your friends think," Leonora asked, "if you force your parents, your two brothers, and me to remain out in weather as foul as this? Not very much, I'll warrant."

Harry rose from the stool. His carefully brushed golden hair shone with pomade. He spoke with a strict formality his parents had never heard before. "I regret that your afternoon at Ponce de Leon Springs was ruined. Please change into some dry clothes and join us. Ella was about to play Chopin's Polonaise."

"Thank you. We would love to listen." Leonora was being more than polite. Ella Hirsch was a skillful pianist, who had excelled in music at school. Although she now worked in her parents' grocery on Decatur Street, she continued to practice diligently, dreaming that one day she would play professionally.

The three adults changed their clothing and returned to the parlor, leaving William and Jacob to play in their room on the top floor. The recital began. After the first few notes, Nathan no longer felt annoyed about the interruption to his afternoon's enjoyment with his two youngest sons. He wished his own children could play half as well as Ella Hirsch. Louise read music aptly enough to press the right keys in the right order, but her playing was mechanical, devoid of style or harmony. That surprised Nathan, because she showed talent in other artistic fields. Harry, on the other hand, showed no interest at all in music. Playing piano, he claimed, was for girls; if his friends saw him at the keyboard, they would die laughing. At least, that had been his attitude until today. Turning pages for Ella, Harry looked like the most conscientious music lover in the world.

The muscles of Nathan's face began to form a smile. He held it back in case anyone thought he found the music amusing. No wonder Harry had gone around dusting! No wonder his normally unruly hair was so carefully combed! And that stilted speech! Cupid had been busy. The god of love had shot an arrow straight through Harry's heart and made him fall in love with Ella Hirsch. Why else would he sit there turning pages whenever Ella inclined her head toward him?

Nathan glanced at the other six young people. Every one of them listened raptly to Ella's Chopin recital. They were paired off into three couples. Louise sat next to a young man with dark, curly hair named Lionel Selig. Nathan knew Lionel's parents, who operated a drugstore at Five Points. He knew the parents of every one of his children's guests, They were all members of the Hebrew Benevolent Congregation.

It struck Nathan that of all the young people present, only Harry and Louise had an American-born parent. He had been born in England, and the parents of Harry's and Louise's friends were all from Germany, like most of the older members of Atlanta's Jewish community. You could never guess the parents' birthplaces from the sons and daughters, though. Born during the country's most turbulent period, they spoke without their parents' accents and dressed like any other person of their age. They didn't think of themselves as Germans, as most of their parents still did. They regarded themselves as Americans.

Nathan looked at Harry once again as the young man turned another page, then moved his gaze to Louise. Each had inherited one of Miriam's physical characteristics. Harry had her golden hair, while Louise had her green eyes. Beyond that, they had nothing in common. Harry had grown into a burly young man who lifted a heavy oak counter in the store as easily as he picked up a dozen shirts. Louise, despite the sense of adventure and fierce competitiveness which had characterized her younger years, was dainty and elegant, as any young lady should be. She sat now with her eyes half closed, her head moving from side to side in time with Ella's playing. Despite earlier efforts to suppress it, a smile blossomed over Nathan's face. Harry and Louise did have something in common after all! Cupid's arrow had not stopped at Harry. It had scored a direct hit on his sister as well, because while Louise sat listening to Ella's playing, she held the hand of young Lionel Selig.

Ella finished her recital with a flourish that filled the room with triumphant sound. She stood up and turned to face her audience. Nathan joined in the applause, clapping his hands enthusiastically, thinking not of what he had just heard, but what he had just seen. A musical young lady whose father owned a grocery, and a young man with a drugstore. If Harry and Louise married these young people, the Solomon family would never want for medicine, food, or music again!

Suddenly Nathan felt far in advance of the forty-five he was. Thank God, he murmured, for Jacob and William who were still young enough to let him believe that he, too, was young.

The Meyerbeer Society continued to gather every Sunday afternoon. New faces appeared and old ones vanished to return again after a short absence. Sometimes, as many as eighteen people squeezed into a member's home while at other times a meeting drew no more than six. The only members to attend every meeting were Harry, Louise, Ella Hirsch, and Lionel Selig. For them, the society was more than a musical and literary group. It represented the center of their social lives. The drugstore belonging to Joseph and Sophie Selig, and the grocery operated by Ella's parents, Max and Leah Hirsch, maintained hours similar to those of the Crystal Palace. Because so little time remained between the opening and closing of such stores for young people to meet and socialize, every opportunity had to be exploited.

Nathan was not the only one to notice the affection existing between Harry and Ella, and Louise and Lionel. When he visited Selig's Drugstore, Lionel's parents commented on the growing friendship. "Do you notice how our children see so much of each other?" Joseph Selig asked. He was a thin, bald-headed man whose back was bent from stooping. His wife, Sophie—equally thin with wavy gray hair and twinkling blue eyes—added her own voice to that of her husband. "Maybe your daughter and our son are meant for each other?" Nathan just smiled, and told Sophie Selig that whatever was meant to be would be.

At the Hirsch grocery store, speculation was also rife. Leah Hirsch, a small, quiet woman with fading auburn hair, enjoyed the relationship between her daughter and the Solomon family's oldest son. Each time she saw Nathan, she expressed pleasure that Ella and Harry saw each other. "Two very nice young people, your son and our daughter. They go well together." Max Hirsch was the opposite of his wife. A heavy man with a red face, thick black hair, and a bushy mustache, he could hoist a sack of potatoes onto each shoulder and carry them the length of Decatur Street without breathing hard. His manner was equally forthright, and he believed no one in the world was good enough for an only daughter who was talented as well as beautiful. "Have you explained to your boy how lucky he is to have a wonderful girl like my Ella even look at him?" he once asked Nathan in all sincerity, and Nathan replied just as earnestly, "It is your daughter who is lucky, Mister Hirsch. Harry has only to smile, and every young lady south of Richmond will come running."

When Nathan described that encounter, Miriam and Leonora applauded his reply. "You must be the first person ever to put that braggart in his place," Miriam said. "He is a good-hearted man who will help anyone in need, but he is so full of himself."

"Would you mind such a man as your son's father-in-law?" Leonora asked.

Miriam considered the question. "Not at all. We would not have to live with him, would we?"

"I would mind neither the Hirsches nor the Seligs," Nathan told his cousin. "They are all good people, and you can wish for no more. But are we not rushing our children into adulthood before they have had a chance to fully enjoy their youth? Louise is only seventeen, and Harry is but two years older."

"I was married when I was nineteen," Miriam said.

"I would have been married at nineteen, too," Leonora added.

"Then let Louise reach nineteen before you start marrying her off, and let Harry reach the twenty-one I was when the *Abbé* married me." Despite the mild rebuke to his wife and cousin, Nathan could see the two young couples eventually marrying. They shared none of the wild passion he remembered from his own courtship of Marie-Louise. Nor did they show the intensity that had characterized his relationship with Miriam. His children and their sweethearts were taking their time to fall in love, getting to know each other instead of diving headlong without any consideration of the consequences. Post-war Atlanta was quite unlike antebellum New Orleans. It fostered a very different kind of life, a very different kind of love.

While Nathan watched his two oldest children fall in love, he enjoyed witnessing his youngest two grow more independent. As the fall of 1877 turned to winter, the Sunday outings spent lazily enjoying the sunshine gave way to entertainments of a more vigorous nature. Jacob took to skating like Harry and Louise before him, tearing fearlessly around the rink, and seemingly oblivious to any possibility of harm. He embarked upon any adventure in the same manner. There was not a dog that scared him, a tree he would not try to climb. William was the opposite. At the rink, he found it hard to keep his balance on the wheels. When he fell, tears sprang from his eyes. Jacob would not let him quit. He was William's older brother, and any restraint on the younger boy's part would reflect badly on him. Each time William wanted to stop, Jacob exhorted him to continue. If that failed, he taunted him with cries of cowardice.

More than once, Miriam tried to intervene between the brothers. She feared for William's safety when she saw him driven on by Jacob. She wanted to tell the older boy to be gentle with his younger brother, to explain that William was not as strong as he was, that perhaps he would never be as strong. He needed protecting, not bullying. But each time she attempted to step in, Nathan stopped her.

"Let them be," he told her one December afternoon as Jacob goaded William into climbing onto the bottom branch of a magnolia tree. "An older brother is the best example any boy can have."

"Did David provide such a good example to Alfred?"

Nathan ignored Miriam's reference to his cousins in England. One was a pompous bore, the other a libertine; neither provided an example for anyone. "The trouble is, Miriam, that you come from a family of three girls and only one boy, so you would not understand."

"I only understand that I do not wish to see William hurt because he is pushed beyond his limits."

"William will know when he goes far enough. You would be amazed at how aware even a young boy is of his limitations." Nathan smiled as he saw William finally manage to get a leg over the magnolia's limb. A little push from Jacob and the youngest Solomon son straddled the branch triumphantly. "Look how William laughs, Miriam, and then tell me that you really believe he is in any danger. At seven, Jacob might have more wisdom than we do when it concerns his younger brother."

* * *

At Christmas, Nathan and Miriam invited the Selig and Hirsch families for dinner. In the morning, while Miriam, helped by Leonora, cooked the dishes she had learned from Delilah in the kitchen of Waverley, Nathan made his traditional journey to Hunter Street with a gift for Clarissa Jenkins. This year he gave her a colorful silk shawl. Draping it around the shoulders of her pale blue dress, she swung around to show her parents.

"I swear you are the prettiest young lady in Atlanta," Mildred Jenkins told her daughter. "Young men will soon be lining up three deep outside to ask for your hand in marriage."

"On that day," Nathan said, "the Crystal Palace will set aside a singularly beautiful gift for its favorite customer."

Clarissa was not enamored by her mother's vision. At fourteen, she had aspirations that went far beyond an early marriage and a handful of children tied to her apron strings. She could marry and raise a family later, after she had tasted something of life. "I have left school, Mister Nathan, and I wish to work in a store. Will you employ me in the Crystal Palace?"

Nathan would have loved to say yes, but with Miriam, Leonora, his two oldest children, and two sales clerks he had hired since the depression lifted, he had all the help he needed. As successful as the store was, its profitability could be upset by hiring one person too many. "I'm sorry, Clarissa, but we do not need any additional help right now."

"Very well. I will just have to find work at another store."

"It will be their gain and my loss."

"It will, Mister Nathan. It surely will."

After promising to supply a reference should Clarissa need one, Nathan left the Jenkins house. Walking home, he chuckled at the girl's assurance. She believed she would go far, and he agreed with her. He related the story to Miriam and Leonora, and told it again that afternoon when the family's guests arrived. Max Hirsch declared that Nathan had done the right thing by not accepting Clarissa's request. "No store owner in his right mind would employ a worker with that much cheek!"

"Normally I would concur with you," Nathan replied, "but

this time I think you are wrong. Clarissa will do very well for herself, and I might just live to regret that her accomplishments were not achieved while working for the Crystal Palace."

At six that evening, thirteen people squeezed around the dinner table. Nathan sat at the head, with Harry on one side and Louise on the other. At the opposite end, flanked by the two youngest boys who were allowed to stay up late, sat Miriam. Along one side sat Leonora and the Hirsch family. Facing them were Lionel Selig and his parents. Each dish drew praise from both sets of visitors, causing Miriam to blush.

"I have eaten nothing like this in my entire life," Sophie Selig enthused as she tasted chicken breast braised with apple brandy and cream. "Where did you learn to create such dishes?"

"From a woman called Delilah in New Orleans. Besides being our cook, she was a wonderful teacher."

Joseph Selig chuckled. "I will wager that no one else in Atlanta eats as well as we do today."

"That is because no one else has Miriam to conjure up such magnificent meals," Nathan said, smiling the length of the table at his wife. He liked the sensation of enjoying a leisurely meal with so many people. Tonight was special. He knew that some might think thirteen at a table tempted ill luck, but Nathan held no such superstitions. So many people added luster to the meal. The only way to improve it would be with servants to fetch and carry so that Miriam, Leonora, and Louise would not have to keep leaving the table. He wondered if that had been on Miriam's mind when she mentioned Delilah? One day soon they would have the money to move to a larger home, on Washington Street, which was becoming the place of choice to live in Atlanta. A home on Washington Street would not be complete without servants.

Max Hirsch's heavy accent filled the room. "Does it not strike anyone as odd how we, as Jews, are celebrating the birth of Christ?"

"Do not talk nonsense," Joseph Selig said. "We celebrate nothing. We are having dinner, that is all."

"A special dinner, while all around us Gentiles have similar special dinners. We may not have become Christians, but we have adopted their culture and become assimilated into their society." The grocery store owner turned to Nathan. "What do you think? Are we celebrating Christmas, or are we not?"

"I think we are," Nathan answered after weighing the question for several seconds. "Not because we believe in it but because we are happy for our Christian friends and neighbors who do treasure it as a holy day."

"What a difference to Germany," Sophie said. "There we used to fear for our lives on such holy days. Especially Easter," she added with a barely perceptible shudder.

Her husband and the Hirsches nodded in agreement. Their American-born children knew of pogroms only from their parents' tales. True, there had been moments during the War Between The States when such prejudices had arisen. Aside from the attacks on Judah Benjamin, there had been famous incidents involving two Union generals, Butler and Grant. Benjamin Butler, the despised occupier of New Orleans, had launched outbursts against Jews for smuggling medicine across Lake Pontchartrain to Confederate forces, and Ulysses S. Grant had issued his notorious Order Number 11 banishing Jews as a class from the Department of Tennessee in order to halt trading between the Union and the Confederacy. Grant's order had done nothing to stop such commerce because Gentile merchants, freed of Jewish competition, had traded even more vigorously and profitably. Nor had Grant's order remained law for long. Lincoln had rescinded it the instant he learned of it.

"Fortunately, America is not Germany," Nathan told Lionel's mother. "Look how Atlanta's Christian community celebrated two years ago when the Hebrew Benevolent Congregation laid the cornerstone of the new synagogue. The mayor attended. So did the city council and the police. A brass band escorted a procession of Masons, Odd Fellows and B'nai B'rith members, and a Protestant minister gave the opening prayer. It was a fine example of one group of people appreciating the traditions and beliefs of another."

Leonora laughed at her cousin's enthusiasm. "I do not recall seeing you there. Either for the opening, or at any time since."

"I continue preferring to pray alone. Too many voices clamor for attention in the synagogue. Mine might be lost among them."

"I am sure your every word is heard." Leonora returned to her meal, remembering when she had seen Nathan on his knees in the store as he prayed for the newborn William. Quite possibly, he held a greater belief in a supreme being than anyone at the table, yet he never attended services while everyone else did. It was more than anxiety over his voice being lost among so many. He simply disliked formal worship. And who was to say his way was wrong? Still, Leonora puzzled over what it would take to draw her cousin into the handsome brick-and-stone synagogue of the Hebrew Benevolent Congregation, whose distinctive Moorish architecture dominated the corner of Forsyth and Garnett.

The meal finished just before eight. While Leonora, Louise, and Ella cleared the table, Miriam put Jacob and William to bed upstairs. Afterward, Ella sat at the piano. Her first two pieces were Schubert *lieder,* accompanying her father who sang in a sweet, melodious baritone. She played the songs from memory, which obviated any need for Harry to turn pages. He sat a yard away, staring at her as though terrified she would miss a note without his help. When she finished the second song, and Max Hirsch accepted applause for his singing, she turned around to her audience. "Is there anything you would like me to play?"

"Your father has a indisputably fine voice," Nathan said, "but play something we all know."

Ella swung back to the piano. Her fingers danced across the keyboard to form "The Girl I Left Behind Me." Harry started the singing, followed by his father and Lionel, and then by the other two men. The women remained silent, content to let the men enjoy what was so obviously a man's song. Halfway through, Ella stopped playing. Without turning around, she said: "Would you prefer something you can all sing?" Her fingers caressed the keys again, and the ten men and women clustered around the piano burst into song simultaneously. Miriam sang loudest of all. She had lived longest in the South, and "Dixie" meant more to her than anyone. Nathan, too, sang lustily. Had he not spent four years in prison, and come within a whisker of being hanged?

From "Dixie," Ella played her way through half a dozen wartime jewels, including "The Southern Marseillaise," "Cottage by the Sea," and "Banks of the Blue Mozelle." At the end, her face was flushed with pleasure and exertion. Harry fetched her a glass of punch. She sat on the piano stool, sipping it gratefully. When she finished, Harry suggested that he, Lionel, Ella, and Louise go out for a walk. Miriam protested that they were all quite mad to leave a warm house for a cold, raw night, but Leonora touched her arm.

"They are young and in love," she whispered. "In the coldest wind, they will be warm. They have done their duty by spending time with us old people, now let them be alone."

Harry helped Ella with her cape. Lionel did the same for Louise. Nathan looked through the window as the four young people emerged onto Whitehall Street and began walking north toward Five Points. He remembered another Christmas, seeing Leonora and Marie-Louise walking with Jean-Pierre Vanson. How many years had passed? Twenty-five already? The three of them walking along Esplanade because Jean-Pierre wanted to try out his new gold-topped walking stick, and what better way to do it than with a pretty girl on each arm?

The evening ended at ten o'clock, just after the two young couples returned. Tomorrow was a business day. The Crystal Palace would open at its regular time. So would Joseph Selig's drugstore and Max Hirsch's grocery. Leonora climbed to the top floor, looking in on the two youngest boys before retiring for the night. Nathan and Miriam went to their own room. They undressed quickly and slipped into their nightgowns. Miriam removed the long-handled warming pan which she had placed in the bed twenty minutes earlier. The bed was as toasty as the room was cold. Lying beneath the fluffy quilt, they held each other tightly. Miriam asked Nathan if he had enjoyed his Christmas. He nodded. Everything about it had been perfect.

"Your cooking, as always, was wonderful. So was the company and the entertainment. Even Max Hirsch's voice was flawless."

"I never knew he could sing so well," Miriam said. "I have heard him at the Concordia Club, of course, but tonight his voice had a marvelous tone. And Ella playing those lovely old songs. It felt so good to sing them again, to sing them with other people. You know, don't you"—her voice dropped to little more than a whisper—"that thirteen sat at the table tonight?"

"It was the first thing I noticed. I worried that someone might be superstitious. Thank God no one was."

Miriam laughed. "This is Atlanta in eighteen seventy-seven, not a witch-burning New England town of two centuries ago. The number thirteen has no magical properties. It does not bring bad luck." She kissed Nathan and rolled onto her side. Within a minute she was asleep.

lally. If only a tenth of the good things Nathan wished for his
cousin came true, she would marry a prince and live in a palace.
Because he worked so hard during the week, Sunday became

Chapter Twenty-five

The Crystal Palace was busy the next day as Nathan sold
cheaply merchandise he had explicitly ordered for Christmas.
Midway through the morning, Clarissa Jenkins entered the
store, wearing her new silk scarf over a dark green dress. When
Nathan asked if she wished to buy anything, she shook her
head.

"I am on my way to Regenstein's to ask for a job."

"You would approach a competitor of mine?" Nathan asked
in mock outrage. Regenstein's, opened just along Whitehall
Street six years before, was hardly that. The store specialized in
millinery, and Nathan was friendly with the two brothers, Julius
and Gabriel, who owned it.

"You would not give me a job when I asked you yesterday."
Clarissa's blue eyes sparkled. "But it is not too late to change
your mind, you know."

Nathan smiled at the girl's determination. "I would dearly
love to hire you, Clarissa, but who would I dismiss to make a
place for you? And how would that man tell his family he could
no longer feed or clothe them because he had lost his job? Just
tell either Mister Julius or Mister Gabriel that I sent you along,
and you will have no trouble."

Twenty minutes after Clarissa's departure, Leah Hirsch visited to thank Nathan for his hospitality the previous day. Behind her came Rose Strickland, the schoolteacher. Rather than

have Harry or one of the other sales clerks serve her, she waited patiently for Nathan to finish with Leah. The grocer's wife was in no hurry. After twice telling Nathan how much she and Max had enjoyed themselves the previous day, she looked around nervously and dropped her voice to a whisper.

"We were talking last night, Max and me, after we got home, and we both agreed that we like your Harry very, very much."

"His mother and I like him, too."

"No, no . . . you know what I mean. Max and I would be more than happy to have him for our Ella."

Nathan smiled. "Does Max still want him to go down on his knees twice a day and thank God that Ella even looks at him?"

Leah made a disparaging motion with her hand. "You should know Max by now."

"I do. I do. Give him my regards when you get back to Decatur Street."

Leah left. Nathan turned to Rose Strickland who sought new cutlery to replace the set she had inherited from her parents fifteen years ago. As Nathan showed her two different patterns she asked if he had enjoyed his Christmas.

"Very much, thank you, Miss Strickland. And yourself?"

"Oh, I had a wonderful time. I went to my brother's home as I do every year." She pondered the cutlery, uncertain which pattern she preferred. "Did you really enjoy Christmas, Mister Nathan? After all, it is not a holiday Israelites traditionally celebrate, is it?"

"I enjoy honoring the festivals of my friends and neighbors."

"What a delightful sentiment. I'll have this pattern, Mister Nathan. Thank you so much."

Nathan placed the cutlery in a box and took Miss Strickland's money. As he made change, he saw Miriam approach with the two younger boys. Jacob recognized Miss Strickland, who taught him arithmetic. Very politely, he said how nice it was to see her and asked how she felt. She returned the greeting before turning to William. "When will we be seeing you in school along with your big brother?"

William looked away shyly, and Miriam answered for the boy. "Sooner than you probably wish, Miss Strickland. Having two Solomon youngsters on your hands at the same time might prove to be more than even you can manage." She turned to Nathan. "I have to go to Selig's drugstore. Shall I leave Jacob and William with you, or would you prefer that I took them with me?"

Nathan looked toward the front door as two more customers entered. "Take them with you. It will be too busy for them to be in here."

"I will walk with you," said Miss Strickland. "I have business myself at Selig's."

Clarissa returned five minutes later to tell Nathan she had been given a job at Regenstein's, starting the following day. Delighted at her success, Nathan asked if the two brothers, recognizing her abilities, had already made her store manager. The girl laughed. "Perhaps next month. In the meantime, I have to sweep the floors, dust the counters, and keep the stockroom tidy. But I suppose everyone has to start at the bottom."

"They do indeed, Clarissa. I began by driving a hat-shaped wagon around London in all kinds of terrible weather. When I wasn't doing that, I was either cleaning or collecting and delivering work from seamstresses who lived in London's dirtiest, most plague-infested slums."

"I told them that I came with your recommendation, Mister Nathan. I said that you thought very highly of me and would willingly give me a position at the Crystal Palace if it did not mean dismissing a man with a large family to feed." She looked uncertainly at Nathan. "Do you think I exaggerated?"

"Not at all, Clarissa. I think very highly of you indeed."

The girl blushed at such praise. "I'm going home now, to tell my mother about getting a job. She'll be so pleased." Waving goodbye to Nathan, she left the store. Five minutes later she was back, her face stretched taut with anxiety.

"Mister Nathan! Mister Nathan!"

Nathan looked away from the customer he was serving, annoyed by the interruption and simultaneously alarmed.

"Mister Nathan! There's been an accident! A terrible accident at the railroad tracks—"

Nathan heard no more. Shouting Harry's name, he rushed past Clarissa, flung open the door and started to run north toward the point where the Western and Atlantic tracks crossed Whitehall Street. Harry, after calling for his sister and aunt to follow, raced after Nathan who was already fifty yards ahead. This day, Harry's youth was no match for his father's fear and anxiety. Nathan ran as though a hurricane blew at his back. Visions of his youngest sons danced before his eyes, cruel visions of broken, bloody bodies. His lungs drew in great gulps of air and his feet barely touched the ground. He flew across Alabama Street, darting between carts and buggies. Ahead, a stationary train blocked traffic. Spewing stream impatiently, the locomotive was stopped just west of Whitehall Street. Its six cars stretched back toward Union Station, blocking both Whitehall and Pryor streets. Nathan stopped five yards short of the train, head swinging left and right as he looked around in confusion. If there had been an accident, there should be signs of it. Where was the crowd? Where was the excitement that always accompanied such events?

Harry caught up. Gasping for breath, he leaned on his father's shoulder for support. Nathan listened carefully. Above the hiss of escaping steam came a different sound. Shaking off his son's arm, he strode to his right until he reached a break between the cars. Looking through, he saw the crowd he had expected. Followed by Harry, he scrambled between the cars to come out on the other side of the train. At least two hundred people gathered there, milling around like ants whose nest has been disturbed. Three policemen tried to establish order, repeatedly calling for the bystanders to disperse. As Nathan started to push his way through, a woman's voice called his name. In the shadow of the train stood Rose Strickland, who had left the store a short while ago with Miriam and the two younger boys to walk to Selig's drugstore. Nathan's heart slowed to normal when he noticed that the schoolteacher held William in one hand and Jacob in the other. Thank God! Despite his horrifying visions, nothing had happened to them. And then his heart skipped a couple of beats. Why was Miriam not looking after the boys? He elbowed his way through the crowd, not caring who he hurt in his mad scramble to reach the center. Why was the schoolteacher holding his sons? Why were they both crying? Where in God's name was Miriam?

The last line parted, and Nathan saw Miriam. She lay on the ground, curled up on her right side like a sleeping child. Her neck was turned to the left so that she faced upward. Her green eyes were fixed open, staring but unseeing at the sky above. Calling her name just once, Nathan dropped onto his knees and lifted her body in his arms. Her head dropped back at a sickening angle. Harry, tears brimming in his eyes, stood helplessly behind his father.

"Make way for the doctor! Make way!" A policeman pushed through the crowd, followed by an elderly man clutching a black bag. While Nathan held Miriam, the doctor lifted her wrist. As he sought her pulse, he noticed for the first time the peculiar angle of her neck, and saw Nathan slowly, sorrowfully, shaking his head. The doctor lowered Miriam's hand. His fingers touched her face to close her eyes.

"There is nothing either of us can do," the doctor whispered. He removed Miriam's body from Nathan's grasp and set it gently on the ground. Harry helped his father to stand. Holding on to each other, they stared down at the body as the enormity of the tragedy began to manifest itself.

Nathan's self-control vanished. His voice, aching with sorrow, eclipsed even the panting of the locomotive as he swung around to face the crowd. "What happened here? Why is my wife lying here like this? Will someone tell me what happened?"

Harry tried to pull his father away from Miriam's body. Nathan fought against his son's guidance. He wanted to remain by his wife's lifeless body, and he wanted answers from the people who had gathered. The doctor and a policeman came to Harry's assistance. Between them, they led Nathan through the crowd into the shadow of the halted train. Rose Strickland stood in the same spot she had occupied a few minutes before, with William in one hand, and Jacob in the other. The cutlery she had bought that morning at the Crystal Palace lay forgotten at her feet. At the sight of their father, the boys wrenched themselves free of the schoolteacher's grasp and ran to him. He knelt down to hold them without really knowing whom he held.

Despite the commotion around her, Rose Strickland's angular face remained perfectly composed. She was quite accustomed to dealing with crises, no matter how great their magnitude. Gazing down at Nathan holding his children, she spoke in a calm, factual monotone. "Mister Nathan, a truly terrible thing has surely happened, but you must not think of blaming either of your sons."

Nathan stared uncomprehendingly at the woman, his grief too raw for him to understand the implication of her words. Harry asked her what she meant.

"The accident, of course."

Harry glanced at his brothers sheltering in their father's arms. Were Jacob and William—God forgive him for even thinking such a thing!—in some way responsible for their mother's death?

The schoolteacher's tone never changed as she related what had occurred at the point where the railroad crossed Whitehall Street. "A train was just pulling out of Union Station. We had time to cross, but Jacob and William wanted to watch the train pass. Your mother agreed, but told the boys they had to stand very still. She was carrying some produce she had just bought. My hands, too, were occupied with the cutlery I had purchased. As the train approached, Jacob challenged his younger brother to run across the track. Before either your mother or I could do anything, the two boys raced off. Jacob reached the other side easily but William faltered. In the middle of the track, with the

461

train only ten or fifteen yards away, he froze in fear. He stood there like a small animal hypnotized by a snake."

Nathan looked up, eyes wide open as the schoolteacher's words registered. He did not say a word, but his grip around his sons tightened like a vise.

"Your mother rushed out onto the track. She lifted William in her arms and threw him to safety, but she was not quick enough to save herself. The locomotive's pilot hit her and pushed her aside. The train was not going very fast, it had just left the depot after all. Nine times out of ten, she would have received nothing more than some cuts and bruises, or perhaps a broken limb. Unfortunately"—at last, Miss Strickland's voice showed a trace of emotion—"this was the tenth time. It was not the boys' fault, I swear it. It was just one of those terrible mishaps that no one could do anything about."

Harry heard a scream. He turned away from the schoolteacher and saw his sister staring in horror at Miriam's body. Leonora stood beside her, arms reaching out to comfort the girl. Harry looked again at his father and younger brothers. All three clung to each other, shaking as they cried. Harry took a deep breath to quell his own tears. His father was too stricken with grief to help those around him. He had to be the man of the family now.

The same people who had visited the Solomon home on Christmas returned the following evening, their demeanor as solemn and grief-stricken as it had been lighthearted and festive the day before. Leah Hirsch and Sophie Selig busied themselves preparing food. Joseph Selig looked more stooped than ever, as if burdened with guilt because Miriam had been on her way to his drugstore when the tragedy occurred, and Max Hirsch told everyone that he had petitioned the town several times to make the railroad tracks safer. "Until bridges cross those tracks at Pryor, Whitehall, and Forsyth streets—especially Forsyth—accidents like this will continue to occur," he repeated angrily.

Only Alfred Jenkins, who had come with his wife and Clarissa, seemed to pay attention to the grocer. As a streetcar driver, he knew too well the dangers of railroads intersecting streets. Even then, he did little more than nod agreement to Hirsch's words and tell him he was perfectly right and something should be done.

Leonora and Harry sat on either side of Nathan, shielding him from the people who came to call. They both worried for Nathan's welfare. He leaned forward in the chair, shoulders bent, head down, eyes fixed on the floor. He had spoken no more than a dozen words since the accident, responding to the most heartfelt expressions of sympathy with little more than a numb stare. Given food, he had taken one bite before pushing it away, muttering that it tasted like sawdust. Leonora believed her cousin should take a sedative. Louise had taken such a drug, given to her by the same doctor who had pronounced her mother dead. Now she lay sleeping on her bed, her mind temporarily freed of the suffering that would plague it the moment she awakened. Nathan needed to do the same. He needed to rest, to gather his strength for the ordeal tomorrow would bring, when Miriam would be buried at Oakland Cemetery. But when Leonora proposed the idea of a sedative to Nathan, he regarded her as if she were mad.

"How can I can sleep when I have lost a wife for a second time?" he asked before lowering his eyes to the floor once more. The angry outburst was the most he had said all day.

As the visitors prepared to leave, Harry looked over the top of his father's head to Leonora. "Do you think you should see that the boys are all right?"

Carrying a lamp, Leonora climbed to the top floor. William and Jacob had gone to bed two hours earlier, still full of the horror of seeing their mother hit by the train. Harry had sat with them for thirty minutes, talking softly, trying to drive the devils from their minds. Leonora marveled at the fortitude shown by her cousin's oldest son. How many nineteen-year-olds reacted so strongly to such adversity? From the moment of the accident, Harry had assumed all responsibility. He had shepherded the family back to Whitehall Street, dealt with the police and the undertaker, and had contacted the Hebrew Benevolent Congregation to arrange for the funeral. Now he sat downstairs, shielding a father too grief-stricken to care for himself. When, Leonora mused as she opened the door to the boys' room, would Harry have time to indulge his own sorrow? When would he find time to shed the tears that were such a necessary part of healing?

Both boys were still awake. Leonora set the lamp on a table, pulled up her long black skirt and sat on the edge of the bed the boys shared. Jacob asked who was downstairs. When Leonora mentioned names, he wanted to know the reason for so many visitors. "People come to a party, like we had yesterday. It's not a party today," he said with youthful petulance. "Mama's dead. What are they doing here?"

"Good friends share your sorrow as well as your happiness," Leonora answered, uncertain whether Jacob would be able to understand. She looked at William, who held a thumb comfortingly in the corner of his mouth. His eyes were red and puffy, and his cheeks were streaked with the marks of fresh tears. Both boys had darted across the tracks in a continuation of their games of daring, but William had been the one to pause, frozen, as the train bore down on him. How much did he remember of that? And how much did he blame himself for Miriam's death?

As if to echo Leonora's thoughts, William removed his thumb and spoke. "If I had not stopped, Mama would still be alive."

Leonora's throat constricted. She reached out for William. "No, darling. Do not think that. One thing had nothing to do with the other."

William shook his head vehemently. "Jacob said Mama died because we ran in front of the train, and because I stopped."

Shocked, Leonora let go of William. No wonder his eyes were so red and puffy. Jacob must have tortured him with such accusations until the very instant she entered the room. This was taking the game of teasing his younger brother to grotesque extremes. She turned to Jacob. "That is a most spiteful thing to say. You should be ashamed of yourself."

Jacob stared defiantly at his father's cousin. "But we did run in front of the train, didn't we? And William did stop, didn't he?"

"I never want to hear you say that again! Apologize to your brother at once!"

Jacob's eyes dropped from Leonora's face. Almost inaudibly, he murmured, "I'm sorry, William. I didn't mean it."

Leonora stood up, collected the lamp and left the room. Her mind was in a turmoil. Despite the whispered apology, she knew that Jacob still believed William was primarily to blame for their mother's death. They had both crossed the tracks in front of the train, but only William had frozen. She needed to speak to Nathan about this. No matter how badly he felt for himself, he had to do something about this right now, otherwise seeds of destruction would be sown in the family he cherished.

When Leonora returned downstairs, the visitors had gone. Harry stood by the window, looking north along Whitehall Street toward the tracks. Nathan continued to bend forward in the chair, staring at some imaginary spot on the floor. Leonora sat next to him and asked him what he thought about. To her surprise, he grew talkative, replying not in the monosyllabic sentences he had used to answer earlier questions, but at length.

"I think about the number thirteen, Lally. Thirteen sat at our table yesterday. Last night, before going to sleep, I mentioned it to Miriam and said I was glad that our guests were not superstitious. Miriam scorned the idea and said that this was modern Atlanta, not some seventeenth-century, witch-burning New England town. She said that the number thirteen had no magical properties, no ability to bring bad luck. Now I wonder."

On the verge of chiding her cousin for harboring such beliefs, Leonora recalled an experience of her own from the previous day. She had wondered what it would take to bring Nathan into the new synagogue at Garnett and Forsyth streets. Now she knew. He would surely have to go there to offer up a prayer of mourning for Miriam. Had she, by making that simple speculation, tempted fate, as Nathan believed he had done with his concern over the number thirteen? Age-old superstitions might not be so stupid after all; perhaps that was why they endured through the ages.

"Nathan, you need to talk to Jacob and William. They believe that what happened was their fault."

A spark gleamed in Nathan's eyes. "God forgive me, Lally, but that was my first reaction, too. When Miss Strickland explained what had happened, I thought the same thing. I remember Miriam complaining about the way Jacob goaded William. She feared that William would hurt himself trying to meet his brother's challenges. But it was not William who was hurt, was it? He has escaped unharmed while Miriam is dead."

"You are wrong, Nathan. William has been hurt. Badly so. Jacob, too. If you do not go up there and explain to them that Miriam's accident was not their fault, they will go through life blaming themselves and each other. Is that what you want, for your youngest sons to ruin their lives in such a way? I am certain it is not what Miriam would want."

Nathan stood up and walked toward the stairs. His cousin was right. What had happened was not the boys' fault. It was no one's fault, because no one had intentionally caused the misfortune to occur. It was an accident, a tragic, ill-fated accident, just like the one that had killed his and Leonora's parents thirty-seven years before. The family needed to help each other now, not apportion blame. He climbed the stairs slowly, forming in his mind the assurances he would give his sons. He would stay in their room all night, if necessary, to be certain they understood. Miriam's life had already been destroyed. He would not stand by while his two youngest children destroyed their lives as well.

* * *

Nathan spent two hours with Jacob and William. He sat between them, cradling each with one arm. Compensating for his earlier silence, he talked ceaselessly. He told the boys he knew exactly what had happened on the railroad tracks, but he did not blame either of them. Harry and Louise had been just as daring when they were young, racing around the skating rink, constantly challenging each other. That was how children grew up, Nathan explained. Through challenge, through pushing themselves and each other beyond their self-perceived limitations.

While Jacob accepted Nathan's explanation, and the absolution it contained, William remained unconvinced. Twice the boy mentioned falteringly that he had stopped in the middle of the tracks, stopped as the train approached because he had been terrified. Each time, Nathan assured him that fear was nothing of which to be ashamed. Boys grew into men not through passage of years, but by confronting and defeating that which made them afraid. When Jacob asked his father if he had ever failed to overcome any fears, Nathan shook his head and smiled. He had conquered every fear that had ever plagued him, he told his sons, because he saw no point in admitting that, eleven years after falling from a ladder, he could not bring himself to climb one.

Nor could he confess that after last night's dinner, he would never again sit at a table where twelve other people sat.

Jacob's behavior grew muted in the period immediately following Miriam's death. Rather than running everywhere, as was his custom—up and down the stairs, through the store, and along the street—he walked solemnly. He no longer filled every spare moment with the boisterous play he had always enjoyed. Instead, he absorbed himself with jigsaw puzzles, drew with a pencil on sheets of paper, or played with toys he took from his father's store. His favorite was a fire engine of painted tin, pulled by two galloping horses. He sat on the floor for hours at a time, pushing the toy in one direction and then another to extinguish fires that burned only in his own imagination. Once, he would have scorned such staid pastimes, but with his mother's death so fresh in his mind, sedate endeavors appealed to him.

The change in attitude lasted for only three weeks. In the middle of January, a brief snowstorm left Atlanta's streets invitingly white. Unable to resist so much temptation, Jacob rushed outside and scooped up a snowball which he flung gleefully at the driver of a printing company's delivery wagon before fleeing back inside the store. Enraged, the driver followed him into the Crystal Palace, demanding that he be thrashed. Nathan placated the man and sent him on his way. Instead of complying with the driver's wishes, he hugged the boy, grateful that any guilt Jacob might have harbored about his mother's death was disappearing.

William's recovery was slower, and took a different, more meandering route. Jacob's accusation on the day of the tragedy lodged in the youngest boy's memory. Despite Leonora's intervention, and Jacob's subsequent apology, William could not rid himself of the feeling of culpability. Had he not frozen with terror, there would have been no reason for his mother to leap into the path of the train. Therefore, because he had stopped— and only because of that—his mother had died. Nothing could be more simple. Or more devastating.

A quiet child by nature, William withdrew further into himself. Jacob's challenges, which had once drawn spirited reaction, now elicited only a sulky demand to be left alone. Soon, Jacob did just that. Approaches from his sister and oldest brother fared similarly. William made it as clear as any five-year-old could that he wanted to be on his own. As he learned to read, he spent more and more time buried in books, losing himself in the make-believe worlds that existed in the printed word. He discovered an even greater pleasure in unraveling problems that challenged his mental ability. While Jacob found excitement in skating, in climbing trees and playing with a bat and ball, William realized a similar thrill in working with figures. Leonora was the first to notice this talent when William asked her to give him three numbers of less than ten. The third number had barely passed her lips before William supplied her with their total. For a boy not yet six, it was a notable achievement. Leonora remembered that her own fluency with figures had been discovered by accident, and she was determined that William's similar flair would be groomed early. When she explained how to divide and multiply, he grasped the concepts with the speed of a hungry dog snatching a bone. Soon, he was manipulating columns of figures, adding and subtracting, multiplying and dividing. Not on paper, as his father and eldest brother did in the store, but in his head. It was as if his mother's death had freed his spirit and allowed him to be the boy he wanted to be. No longer was he obliged to join in the bustling, bruising games young boys were expected to play. Now he could do as he pleased. He would never be as strong as other boys, but he felt amply compensated by the power he had discovered in his own brain.

Nathan healed slowest of all. He saw Miriam everywhere he looked, attending to a customer in the Crystal Palace, cooking in the home above it, or walking along Whitehall Street each time he left the store. Her spirit was always with him, but each time he reached out, it disappeared like a puff of smoke to leave him empty and alone. Enviously, he watched the comfort given to Harry by Ella Hirsch, and to Louise by Lionel Selig. The grocer's daughter and the drugstore owner's son visited the Solomon home every night for a month after Miriam's death. They never failed to spend time talking to Nathan, but he knew he was not the reason for their visits. They were paying their respects to him before consoling the two young people they had come to see. Nathan had no doubt that the Meyerbeer Society had produced a pair of love matches, and he decided that his daughter and oldest son were lucky. So young, and already they had found their perfect partners. Some people went through their entire life without having such good fortune. He hoped they were spared the heartbreak he had endured, not once, but twice.

Business days were the easiest for Nathan to get through. The Crystal Palace kept him busy from early morning to late at night, but after he closed the doors he had to deal with memories that never let him be. As he lay awake each night, scenes of his life with Miriam unfolded on the ceiling above him. He tried to select the episodes he wanted to watch, like a man choosing books he wished to read at a library. He had two favorites. One was from 1851, when he had given a young and sparkling Miriam the gold sovereign. The other came fourteen years later, finding Miriam in the French Market on his return from four years' captivity. Her golden hair had faded and worry lines had bitten deeply into her fair skin, but Nathan had never seen her look more beautiful. As he grew tired, though, and his eyes began to close, he lost control of what he viewed. Then on the ceiling above his head loomed the one scene he would give everything to forget, that of Miriam lying like a broken twig beside the train that had killed her.

Sunday was Nathan's most difficult time. Not long ago, the entire family had spent the day together, beginning with one of Miriam's breakfasts and continuing with an outing. Then it had been Nathan's favorite day. Now he absolutely dreaded it. Leonora tried once to keep the Sunday tradition alive by preparing the kind of breakfast Miriam had always made. Nathan sat down to eat. In the middle of the meal, he pushed himself back from the table and ran down to the street. Harry followed, but Nathan shook him off. He fetched the horse and buggy from the stable and drove out to Oakland Cemetery, where he spent two hours kneeling by the newly turned grave and talking softly to Miriam.

He went there every Sunday after that, often returning with red eyes and a tear-streaked face. Leonora watched her cousin with increasing anxiety. God only knew that he was entitled to his grief, but he was allowing it to blind him to the needs of others. He did not notice his own children anymore. Harry and Louise had Ella and Lionel to help lift them from their most depressing moments. Jacob and William had no one. With their mother gone, they looked to their father for love and guidance only to find that he ignored them more often than he noticed them. Leonora did what she could to fill the void left by a dead mother and a father so deep in self-pity that he could not even see his own children's distress. She took over Miriam's responsibilities. She cooked and performed the numerous tasks necessary to make a house a home. When Jacob or William cried, she consoled them; when they misbehaved, she chastised them. On Sundays, when Nathan made his journey to the cemetery, Leonora took the youngest boys out. While Jacob skated or climbed or chased a ball, Leonora played arithmetic games with William.

A year after Miriam's death, a headstone was placed at the grave. Once the short ceremony was over, Nathan told the rest of the family to return home in the carriage that had brought them to the cemetery. He would follow in the horse and buggy. As they moved away, he leaned over the grave, hands flat on the stone made colder by winter's chill. He did not notice Leonora detach herself from the group of people walking toward the carriage, not did he see her step close enough to hear his whispered words.

"A year has passed since you were taken from me, Miriam, and time has not even begun to heal the hurt. How long"—his voice broke and he took one of his hands from the stone to wipe tears from his eyes—"will this pain last?"

"It will last for as long as you indulge yourself with sorrow," Leonora said.

Nathan straightened up, face white with shock as if the words he had heard had come from the ground below his feet. When he turned and saw Leonora standing beside him, color rushed back into his cheeks. "You eavesdrop on me again, Lally? You listen to words that are meant only for Miriam?"

Nathan's anger did not faze Leonora. She answered in a voice that was as calm and even as Nathan's was dangerously low. "Yes, I eavesdrop on you again, and I prefer what I heard you say the last time. You spoke to God then, and your words made sense. Miriam is dead, Nathan. She cannot hear you. You should be grateful that I listen, otherwise your question would fall onto the deaf earth and be wasted. At least, I can give you an answer. The pain will never cease as long as you deliberately inflame the wound. You have to continue with your life, Nathan. You have lost Miriam. You have grieved for her. Now you must—"

"Forget her?"

"No. You will never forget her. Neither will I. But you must put the living before the dead. For the past year, you have done the opposite. You have grieved for Miriam and for yourself to the exclusion of everyone else. Think, Nathan, do you know anything about your children? Much has happened to them in the past year, but have you seen any of it?"

Nathan's anger yielded to uncertainty. He looked from Leonora down to the freshly installed stone, as if Miriam could help him.

"Do you know that Harry and Louise wish to marry?"

"I knew they were serious about Ella and Lionel, but . . ."

"They are more than serious. They are discussing marriage. A month ago they came to me for advice—"

"Why did they come to you?"

"When they tried to speak to you, they were discouraged by your coldness. They could not get through the wall you have erected around yourself."

Nathan tried in vain to recall Louise and Harry approaching him. For the past year his life had circled around the store and his visits to the cemetery. He recollected little else.

"They wanted to know how long they should wait before marrying. They asked me how much time should pass between Miriam's death and their weddings."

"What did you tell them?"

"I said at least a year, perhaps as much as two. The extra year was for you, in the hope that you would recover enough to enjoy watching your oldest children take a husband and a wife."

The self-pity which had begun to lift settled again on Nathan like a cloak. "I pray they have more luck than I did."

Leonora's brown eyes lost their customary warmth. She could never remember reproaching her cousin before. Nor could she ever recall cursing, but she did both now. "Stop feeling so damned sorry for yourself, Nathan Solomon, and start thanking God for the damned good fortune you've had!"

"Good fortune?" Nathan looked at his cousin as though she were mad. "I have lost two wives, what good fortune is that?"

"A million men would happily give ten years of their lives to know the joy of loving so strongly. Not twice, as you did, but just once! And those same million men would give another twenty years to be married to a woman who loved her husband so much that she even killed for him!"

The instant she realized what she had said, Leonora flung a hand to her mouth. She was too late. Nathan's eyes narrowed in curiosity. "What do you mean? Whom did Miriam kill for me?"

Leonora noticed the change that had suddenly swept over Nathan. He was so intrigued by her words that he had forgotten all about the feelings of anguish which had been rekindled by the headstone consecration. Her slip of the tongue, her betrayal of a secret she had held for twelve years, might be for the best. "Do you not remember the killing that shocked New Orleans just before we left? The duel on Melpomene—"

"Marcus Barnett?"

"Yes, Marcus Barnett. Miriam and I both knew why you had bought a revolver. Not to protect us on our journey to Atlanta, but to avenge yourself on the man who had betrayed you. And we knew that even if you killed Marcus, you would never escape."

Nathan's mouth hung open. "Miriam challenged him to a duel, and defeated him?"

Leonora nodded. She related the events of that night, how she had caught Miriam leaving the room on Camp Street, how Miriam had knocked her senseless, and how she had recovered and waited, praying for Miriam's safety, until at last she returned. "She wore a mask to visit his home. She waited until he sent his friends away before she removed the mask. And after she killed him she had the presence of mind to take two cartridges from his weapon so that you would never know your gun had been fired."

Stunned, Nathan looked down at the earth beneath which Miriam slept and slowly shook his head. "Do you know, Lally, when I learned of Marcus Barnett's death I had this wild notion. I was working on the wharf, and I rushed home at the first opportunity to check my revolver, to see whether the chambers were still full. They were, and I laughed at myself, laughed that I could have been so stupid to even consider that you or Miriam had gone to Melpomene. I remember thinking Marcus must have been shot by someone else with a grudge against him. A man like him must have many enemies." Slowly, a smile formed upon his face, bemused at first, then filling with pleasure. Leonora watched. A long time had passed since she had seen her cousin smile.

"You are right, Lally. I am truly blessed. I fought a bloody duel to preserve the honor of my first love, and my second love fought an equally dangerous duel to keep me safe. If I am ever fortunate enough to discover such powerful love again"—he caressed the headstone a final time with his hand before leaving the grave to walk toward the waiting horse and buggy—"in what ways will it be demonstrated?"

Leonora followed, holding out her hand for Nathan to help her into the buggy. Neither of them spoke during the journey back to Whitehall Street, but Leonora could not help likening the journey to another she had made with Nathan in a horse-drawn vehicle. That journey had taken place twenty-five years before, as they left the *Vieux Carré* for the final time to return to the Garden District. Crossing Canal Street, she had seen a curtain falling on a chapter in their life, a chapter which had promised joy and delivered only heartbreak. She knew better now. Joy and heartbreak were inseparable. They went hand in hand. The greater the joy, the deeper the heartbreak that would eventually accompany it.

She saw a similar curtain falling now. Another of life's chapters was coming to an end, and Leonora was glad to see it finish.

Chapter Twenty-six

Harry Solomon married Ella Hirsch at the end of June, eighteen months after Miriam's death, and three months after his own twenty-first birthday.

The ceremony took place in the synagogue of the Hebrew Benevolent Congregation, at Forsyth and Garnett streets. Beneath the wedding canopy, Harry and Ella listened to the rabbi intone the wedding vows. On one side of the bridal couple stood the bride's parents, Max Hirsch smiling broadly, and Leah dabbing a lace handkerchief to her eyes. On the other side Nathan stood with Leonora, who substituted for the groom's mother.

Noticing the smile on Max's face, Nathan wondered what he found so pleasing. Did the grocer smile with pride because his only daughter, with her gentle brown eyes and long brown hair, made such a beautiful bride? Or did he smile because he finally understood that Ella had been as fortunate in her choice as Nathan's son had been in his? Nathan turned his eyes toward Harry. The groom's blazing golden hair was covered by a high black hat, and a powerful body filled out his black coat. Nathan had never seen his oldest son so handsome. He felt a lump in his throat and blinked quickly to drive back tears. If there was a hereafter, two sets of grandparents—his own mother and father, and Anna and Gershon Lowensohn—would be looking down with pride and happiness. And beside them, just as proud and just as happy, would be Miriam.

As Harry placed the wedding ring on the forefinger of Ella's right hand, Nathan heard someone sniff back tears. Leonora, too, was overwhelmed by the occasion. She might be filling in for Miriam, but she was as involved as any real mother could be. She had attended every event in Harry's life, from his birth through to his wedding. She had even been present for occasions that the boy's own father had failed to attend. In the formal sense, she was Harry's first cousin once removed, but in reality she was his surrogate mother. If his real mother could not attend, there was no one better suited than Leonora to stand beneath the *chuppah* at his wedding.

The seven benedictions were said. A glass was placed on the ground before the groom. Nathan heard again the sound of sniffing. He reached out, and as Harry brought his foot crashing down on the glass, Nathan squeezed his cousin's hand fondly.

After the ceremony, the marriage was celebrated with dinner at the Concordia Hall. Before everyone sat down, Lionel Selig formed the wedding party into a group for a photographic memento of the occasion. Lionel was obsessed with photography. He spent far more time experimenting with wet collodion plates and pyrogallol baths than he did working in his father's drugstore. Bidding the wedding group to remain perfectly still, he removed the cover from the camera lens.

Nathan found himself beside Max Hirsch. Looking straight ahead, he spoke without moving his lips. "You smiled all through the ceremony. At what did you smile?"

"I smiled because I was thinking of all those young ladies from here to Richmond who will cry themselves to sleep tonight." Just then, Lionel signaled that the process was complete. Max laid a heavy arm on Nathan's shoulder and turned him to face a group of young men and women, all friends of the bride and groom. "Do you think any of those young people will have such a splendid beginning to their married lives as your son and my daughter?"

Nathan shook his head. Harry and Ella had a wonderful start to their marriage. Over the years, Max had invested profits from the grocery store into real estate, which he rented out. As a wedding gift, he had given one of his houses, on South Pryor Street, to Ella and Harry. Nathan, for his part, had completely furnished the house and had, at Leonora's suggestion, conferred the title of manager of the Crystal Palace upon his twenty-one-year-old son.

Following their wedding, Harry and Ella went to New York for a week. At night, they attended shows at theaters along the Rialto, between Madison Square and Forty-second Street, and during the day they either toured the city or shopped "The Ladies' Mile," the stretch of Broadway running from Twenty-third down to Eighth Street. When they returned to Atlanta, Ella's trunks were filled with clothes, and Harry's mind brimmed with ideas which he yearned to share with his father.

"New York is unbelievable," he told Nathan the instant he returned to work. "Instead of allowing trains to interfere with traffic, they have them running in the air. And what bridges! Magnificent works of architecture, all of them! They will soon be finished with an incredible structure that will span the East River to connect New York to Brooklyn. You should see New York, you really should."

"I have seen it. Twice." Harry's enthusiasm made Nathan think of himself almost thirty years before, brimming with excitement over his visit to the Great Exhibition. "I visited New York with your mother after our marriage. We were on our way to England. The second time, I was an unwilling guest of the Union government during the War Between The States. I hope the drinking water has improved since I was last there, because ours had tadpoles swimming in it."

"New York was a village then. Now it is a vibrant city. You should see the stores. No, not stores, palaces of commerce. Walk through A.T. Stewart, James McCreery, Arnold, Constable and Company, or Lord and Taylor's, and your brain will come alive with merchandising ideas that will place you a decade ahead of everyone else in Atlanta. I brought back examples of their advertising for you to see, eye-catching announcements from which we can learn."

"Show me," Nathan said.

Harry unrolled a copy of the New York *Daily Graphic*, opening it to a large advertisement. The artwork showed a beach on which four adults and two children wore bathing suits ending at the neck, ankles, and wrists. The promotional copy boasted that the best and cheapest bathing suits in New York could be found at Lord and Taylor's, on Broadway and Twentieth Street, where such items were a specialty.

"Do you not agree that it is eye-catching?"

Nathan nodded. "Possibly the most eye-catching advertisement I have ever seen."

Harry beamed at the praise inferred in his father's words. "Why do we not have such an advertisement in the *Constitution?*"

Nathan began to chuckle. Hands on his hips, he rocked back and forth as the chuckle became a laugh so loud that Leonora and Louise came running to learn the source of the joke. He held out the advertisement for them to see. "Harry wants us to have such an advertisement for bathing suits in the *Constitution.*"

Immediately, Leonora saw the source of her cousin's amusement. She regarded Harry with fond indulgence. "Have you decided yet how to transform Atlanta into a city surrounded by sea and beaches where such fashionable bathing suits could be sold in the quantity necessary to justify such an expensive advertisement?"

Harry felt his face begin to burn. As he stammered an excuse for ignoring regional distinctions, Nathan clapped him on the shoulder. "You might be wrong this time, but you can rest assured that you will be right more often than you're wrong."

In the following weeks, Nathan smiled often at the memory of the bathing-suit incident. It was a sign of a son eager to show that his father's faith in making him manager was not misplaced. Both Nathan and Harry knew that the title was merely symbolic. Nathan still supervised every aspect of the Crystal Palace. Not an item was bought without his approval, nor a price set, but the title of manager gave Harry the confidence to express ideas. Before, he had been a sales clerk. Now he was the acknowledged second-in-command, ready to step in should the leader falter. Which was exactly what Nathan wanted. One day, God willing, the Crystal Palace would belong to his three sons, and Harry, as the oldest, would shoulder the greatest responsibility. Nathan had not forgotten Louise, but he did not see his only daughter being involved with the store beyond her marriage to Lionel. Lionel had no interest in retail, not even in the drugstore his father operated. He wanted to make photography a career, and Louise would help him.

Nathan missed seeing his oldest son in the house. Harry had always been in such a rush to go somewhere or do something that the house seemed quiet without his presence. Having Ella for a daughter-in-law compensated for the loss, though. She visited the store often, always wearing the latest fashions. Sometimes, Nathan teased her by saying that he did not recognize such a dress or such a jacket as being part of the Crystal Palace's inventory. Each time, Ella unashamedly told him which store it came from. Once Nathan remarked upon a colorful silk scarf by saying that he did not remember ordering anything so exquisite for the Crystal Palace.

"It comes from Regenstein's," Ella told her father-in-law. "Clarissa Jenkins sold it to me yesterday. They must have just let her begin selling, and she is doing very well at it. She persuaded me to buy this when I had only gone in to browse."

Clasping his hands behind his back, Nathan did his best to act the stern family patriarch. "Now that you are married to Harry, do you not think it appropriate that you buy your clothes at the Crystal Palace?"

Ella looked across the store to where Harry supervised the stocking of shelves. "My husband works extremely hard for his money, and I think I am entitled to spend it wherever I see fit."

Only with difficulty did Nathan keep a straight face. The

moment Ella had gone, he told the story to Leonora. Later that day, and with equal pleasure, he related it to Max Hirsch. And the next time he knelt on the floor of the store, he thanked God that his oldest son had married a woman with her own mind, and not some thin-lipped shrew with ice-cold water in her veins.

Six months after Harry's wedding, in the week between Christmas and the New Year, Louise married Lionel Selig. Once again Leonora stood beneath the wedding canopy with Nathan, and once again Nathan envisioned two sets of grandparents and a mother observing the ceremony with pride and happiness.

Like Harry and Ella before them, Louise and Lionel went to New York. Instead of bringing back trunks brimming with clothes, they returned to Atlanta with cases of photographic equipment, including the new gelatin dry plates that were supplanting the inconvenient wet collodion plates. Four weeks after their wedding, on the last Saturday of January 1880, Lionel and Louise opened a photographic studio on the top floor of a building on Whitehall Street, diagonally opposite the Crystal Palace. Within five minutes of turning the sign to read OPEN, they had their first customers. Nathan and Leonora brought in Jacob and William for a family portrait. The two older children had flown the nest. It was time to concentrate on the younger boys.

Under Louise's guidance, Nathan and Leonora sat on chairs. Above them, a large skylight allowed sunshine to fill the studio. The boys stood, Jacob next to his father, and William beside Leonora. Louise fussed around them, pushing and prodding each member of the group until she found the position she liked. "Is this how you divide responsibility?" Leonora asked as Louise took her arm and placed it around William's shoulder. "Lionel makes the pictures only after you arrange the scenery?"

"I have artistic talent," Louise answered, "while Lionel has technical aptitude. What he does to make a picture appear on the dry gelatin plate is all magic to me, but he cannot arrange a scene as elegantly as I can." She made a last adjustment, resting Nathan's hand on Jacob's shoulder. "There, now you are perfect. Remember to keep very still. Do not even breathe."

She stepped back, leaving the four of them to face the camera. Removing the lens cover, Lionel counted off fifteen seconds before closing the lens again. "There, now you may all breathe again."

"I was breathing the whole time," Jacob retorted.

"Then you will be the one who looks funny," Lionel told his young brother-in-law.

Lionel was correct. When he brought the finished picture to the Crystal Palace, Nathan, Leonora, and William appeared just as Louise had arranged them, every feature clear and distinct. Nathan's white hair and neat beard had a reddish tinge, a color also picked up by the streaks of silver which prevailed in Leonora's hair. Lionel explained that the silver chloride in the paper caused the reddish tone. Only Jacob's image failed to come out sharply. The shape of his mouth was indistinct and there was a blurriness to his eyes. When Lionel apologized for the fault, Nathan clapped his son-in-law on the shoulder.

"If you had managed to keep Jacob perfectly still, I would have been concerned for his health. He cannot remain in one place for five seconds, let alone fifteen."

Nathan liked the picture so much that he gave it pride of place on the sideboard. He enjoyed the idea of having a photographer in the family. It was a good trade, one that would carry Lionel and Louise comfortably into the future. Too bad there had been no photographers in the family before. What wouldn't he give for such lifelike pictures of other people who had meant so much to him?

Each time Nathan looked at the picture, he chuckled. Jacob's motion, while the other three people maintained rigid poses, gave the picture a natural mood. The middle Solomon son stayed still for no one. Not at school, where Miss Strickland constantly rebuked him for fidgeting. Not at home, where he was forever on the move like a caged animal yearning for freedom; nor outdoors, where he still viewed every tree and fence as a challenge. The two younger boys were exact opposites. Lionel's photograph had caught the differences perfectly. Jacob, with his moving eyes and moving lips, and his thin, wiry body, was the very essence of perpetual activity, while his brother's face wore the kind of somber expression one associated not with a seven-year-old boy but with an elderly judge.

In the spring of 1880, the family resumed the Sunday outings which had been suspended after Miriam's death. While Nathan played with Jacob, Leonora and William amused themselves with mental games. William still liked to solve mathematical problems, but as his reading improved and his vocabulary increased, he grew fond of puzzles formed around words. He enjoyed spelling quizzes and being tested on word meanings. Most of all, he liked a game Leonora had shown him, where he had to find words inside another word. While Jacob chased a ball, William stayed absorbed for half an hour at a time, chewing on the end of a pencil and studying a word Leonora had given him to discover what other words it contained. On the journey home, the two boys competed with each other. William spelled words he had learned that afternoon and recited their meanings, while Jacob described how far he had thrown a ball or how fast he had run.

"What is more important?" Jacob demanded of his father one Sunday after both boys had exhausted tales of their differing prowess. "Being able to run and catch, or knowing the meanings of words?"

"They are equally important."

"How can that be? Surely one has to be more important than the other."

"Muscles need brains to tell them what to do," Leonora explained, "while brains need muscles to carry out their ideas."

Jacob jabbed himself in the chest and then pointed to his

father. "So you and I are the muscles of the family, while they are the brains?"

"That's right," Nathan answered. "We are the muscles and they are the brains." Suddenly he felt glad that he had resumed the routine of taking the children out on Sundays. Glad, too, that his four children had been born in two distinctly separate periods—before and after the War Between The States—and in two separate towns. He had known parents to grow empty and ineffectual when their children left home to begin families of their own. He was luckier than those parents, because such a fate could not befall him. Although his two older children were married and completely independent of him, his younger two still needed the help and advice of a father.

Not a Sunday outing passed without Nathan thinking of Miriam. Her absence no longer caused the great, gaping wound that had once torn him apart. He continued to miss her, but with a poignancy made bearable by the knowledge that her spirit watched him continually, and approved of the way he brought up their children. Sometimes, he felt as if Miriam were standing close behind. If he turned quickly he would be able to see her before she disappeared. No matter how quickly and how unexpectedly he turned, he always failed to catch her, and then he smiled at his own foolishness for believing he could. Often, he wondered how deeply Jacob and William missed their mother. During a slack moment at the store, he confided to Leonora that he wished to learn about his sons' feelings but he was scared of reawakening old horrors.

"God forbid," he told his cousin, "that Jacob and William should ever remember that once they had held themselves responsible for their mother's death."

"Children have a wisdom of their own, Nathan. If they want to talk about it, they will find a time and a way."

"When it comes to children, you also have a wisdom. A truly remarkable wisdom because—"

"Because I have no children of my own?" Leonora inquired.

Nathan felt his face burn. "Forgive me, but that is exactly what I thought."

"I have four children, Nathan, the same four you have. Perhaps they are not mine physically, but be assured that they are most certainly mine emotionally and spiritually."

Nathan cursed his stupidity. He had always known that Leonora looked on his and Miriam's children as her own—they were the only family she had—and his foolish, insensitive remark must have sounded as if he disputed her right to such a notion.

The time and the way of which Leonora spoke occurred during a summer outing to Oglethorpe Park. Nathan hired a boat and rowed gently across the lake. Leonora and the two boys shared the narrow bench seat facing him. In the center of the lake, Nathan stopped rowing and left the boat drift. "I swear the oars were lighter when we all came here a few years ago, before Harry and Louise became involved with their Meyerbeer Society."

"The oars were no lighter," Leonora answered. "Your muscles were younger and stronger back then."

"I remember those times," Jacob declared. "William and I were too small to go in the boat, so we waited on the shore. You and Mama," he told Leonora, "took turns looking after us. One week you would stay with us while Mama went in the boat, and the next week you went in the boat while Mama stayed with us."

"Who did you prefer looking after you?" Nathan asked.

Jacob's answer was instantaneous. "Mama."

"Why?"

"Because she was our mother, of course," Jacob replied with the irrefutable logic of a child. Suddenly, his face was robbed of its customary vitality. Wistfulness appeared, narrowing his eyes and forcing his mouth into a downward curl. His voice lost its high, childish tone. It became grown-up, and doleful. "Children at school tease me because I have no mother."

Nathan felt his son's pain. It ripped through him like a red-hot knife. "How do these children tease you?"

"They say that Mama went away because I was bad. I fight them to make them stop saying such things, but they still tease me." Tears glistened in the boy's brown eyes. "It isn't true what they say, is it?"

"Of course it is not true," Leonora told the boy. She marveled at the cruelty of children, and simultaneously she contemplated whether Jacob remembered his equally cruel treatment of his younger brother. Children could inflict greater pain on each other than adults could ever do.

Nathan's thoughts paralleled those of his cousin. If the children at school upset Jacob with such vicious gibes, he dreaded to think what they did to William. The younger boy was far more sensitive. And, because of his frailty, less capable than his older brother of standing up for himself. "Do these children say such cruel things to you as well, William?"

"They used to, but they have stopped now."

"Why?" Nathan's puzzlement showed in his face. How did William succeed where Jacob, with his fists, failed?

"When they said my mother had gone away because I was bad, I told them that it didn't matter because I had another mother to take her place." He turned to Leonora and hugged her. She hugged him back, pressing his head to her bosom. Then she embraced Jacob as well. When she looked at Nathan, a gleam of triumph lit her eyes.

She was right. They were her children every bit as much as they were his.

The boat ride at Oglethorpe Park opened Nathan's eyes. For forty years, from the instant a tragic train wreck had forced them to share an uncle's grudging charity, he had taken Leonora for granted. She was his cousin, nothing more. Dependable, always there like a familiar piece of furniture or a picture on the wall. Now, for the first time, he noticed her as a woman.

Guided by this new perspective, he watched everything she did. He grew fascinated at the way she reacted with Jacob and William. How had he ever failed to notice the tight bond that existed between Leonora and the two younger boys? Every morning she rose early to make them breakfast, and she never allowed them to leave for school without first checking that they wore the clean clothes she had put out for them. They always kissed her as they left, and when they returned each afternoon they kissed her again. Leonora and Miriam had been as close as sisters, sharing laughter and sharing tears. Now that Miriam was gone, Leonora had stepped in to fill the void, to assume the other woman's responsibilities as though it were the most natural thing in the world for her to do.

The older children treated Leonora with just as much love and respect. At least once a week, Harry brought her an enormous bunch of flowers to brighten up the office she shared with Nathan. When Louise and Lionel decided to redecorate the photographic studio, they sought Leonora's advice before asking Nathan. And when, at the end of 1880, Ella discovered that she was pregnant, Harry flung his arms around Leonora and shouted, "You're going to have a new cousin! A second cousin . . . no, no, a first cousin once or twice removed! Oh, the heck with it! That's too much of a mouthful for any man to say or figure out! You're going to be a grandmother!"

Watching Leonora's face flush with pleasure and excitement, Nathan finally realized he was the last person in the world to understand exactly how large a role his cousin played, and just how barren and meaningless his life would be without her.

The baby was born in June 1881, a long and skinny brown-eyed boy with a red face and a lusty, ear-piercing cry that would have qualified him, ten years earlier, for the job of marshal. Ella named him Benjamin, to honor the memory of a paternal grandfather she had never known.

A month after Benjamin's birth, Harry and Ella brought the baby to Lionel Selig's studio for a family portrait. Ella's parents were there, as were Nathan and Leonora. For once, Max's bluster was absent. He told Nathan that his heart wept with joy because the child had been named for his father. Nathan nodded. He understood perfectly. His own four children memorialized those dear to him.

Louise arranged many groups for Lionel to photograph. First, she had Ella hold the sleeping baby, then Ella and Harry together with their child. Next, it was the turn of Leah Hirsch to hold her first grandson, then Leah and Max. Finally, Louise turned to Leonora and Nathan.

"Before my nephew awakens and spoils the scene by moving, let us make a picture of him with his other grandparents."

Leonora sat with the baby in her arms. Nathan stood beside her, back rigidly straight, eyes fixed on the camera. As Lionel prepared to expose the plate, Nathan moved, resting one hand gently on his cousin's shoulder. A broad smile stole across his face. The joke had been forty years in the making, but at last he understood the punch line.

The photograph of himself with Leonora and his grandson became Nathan's favorite. Lionel made two prints for his father-in-law. One sat on the sideboard with other family pictures. The other Nathan kept in his office at the Crystal Palace. When business was quiet, he sat and studied the picture. His own smile, appearing just as Lionel uncovered the lens, fascinated him. Louise's artistic placing of the subjects had nothing to do with that smile. In all the pictures made that day, only this one showed such a jovial expression. Ella and Harry appeared serious. So did Max and Leah Hirsch. After all, being a new mother and father, or a grandparent for that matter, was a very serious affair. But Nathan had smiled because he had recalled

Miriam revealing how Leonora loved him, and he had finally understood the joke.

After a week of watching Nathan study the picture, Leonora asked her cousin what he found so fascinating. "I hope the novelty of being a grandfather fades soon, Nathan, otherwise the Crystal Palace will surely suffer."

"Why do you say that?"

"Before, you spent every available minute in the store. When it was busy, you served customers, and when it was slack, you stood in the doorway to greet people as they passed along Whitehall Street. Now you seem to occupy yourself by staring at that picture. I am sure that if Max Hirsch spent so much time looking at his picture, hungry people would soon start shopping for their groceries at other places."

Nathan ignored the rebuke. "Do you think, Lally, that one day Benjamin will show this picture proudly to his friends?"

"I see no reason why he should not. You, with that flower stuck in the buttonhole of your frock coat, cut a very elegant figure—"

"As do you."

Leonora shook her head. "No. Lionel's skill with a camera is brutal when used on me. It brings out every line in my face, every gray hair on my head."

"Lally, I have known you forty years and I never realized until now that vanity was a fault of yours."

"It is not. It just seems unfair that white hair looks so debonair on you and so aging on me."

"Nonsense. It looks as well on you as it does on me. To tell you the truth, I believe we make a very handsome couple. Do you not agree?"

Leonora held the picture at arm's length, appraising it critically. "I have seen worse, I must admit."

Nathan took a deep breath to quell the sudden quaking in his stomach. "Shall we scandalize our children, Lally?" It seemed so natural to use the possessive pronoun that included Leonora.

She set the picture down on Nathan's desk and turned to

stare at him, intrigued by the trembling note that had crept into his voice. What was he so nervous about? "How would we do that?"

"By marrying." Nathan watched his cousin lift her hand to her mouth, too late to stifle the gasp that leapt unbidden from her lips. "Do you not understand why I smiled so when the picture was being made?" he asked, taking Leonora's face in his hands. "I smiled, darling Lally, because I had just realized how deep was my love for you, and how empty my life would have been without you."

Leonora looked up into the white bearded face. How long had she waited to hear her cousin say those words? How many years of dreams had been filled with such visions? "We are first cousins, Nathan," was all she could think of to say. "Our blood is too close. We will produce idiots."

"In royal circles, first cousins marry all the time. It is the accepted practice."

"Yes, and royal circles consistently produce a preponderance of idiots."

"Do not worry." He kissed her tenderly on each cheek, then on the forehead. "We are far too old to concern ourselves with producing idiots."

Leonora's body went limp as she felt Nathan's arms slide around her waist. Her dreams would not be fully realized after all. Nathan would be fifty on his next birthday. She had just turned forty-seven. The wild and youthful passion which had filled her dreams would never rule this union. It would be much stronger, a partnership based on trust and harmony and a deep, abiding love that had lasted forty years and would, God willing, endure for another forty.

Five months later, on the first Sunday of 1882—and the day after his fiftieth birthday—Nathan stood once more with Leonora beneath the wedding canopy of the Hebrew Benevolent Congregation. This time, the marriage service they witnessed was their own.

Throughout the ceremony, Nathan's face was covered with a smile, a broad and beaming expression of happiness that grew brighter with every passing minute. This union had so many odd twists that no man could fail to be amused by it. How many fathers asked for their children's approval to marry? Not that he had ever doubted it would be given. Harry, Louise, Jacob, and William already looked on Leonora as a second mother; marriage served only to make the relationship formal. Nor had the children been surprised. After learning of the news and offering his congratulations, Harry had simply asked what had taken Nathan and Leonora so long to decide.

As Nathan slipped the wedding ring onto Leonora's right index finger, images of two earlier marriages passed before him. He saw again the brief ceremony at Marie-Louise's deathbed in the *Vieux Carré,* and the wedding four years later at Waverley. Both marriages had ended in tragedy, the second after twenty years, the first in less than twelve hours. Yet he would change nothing, for both had given him heartwarming memories he would carry to the grave.

Leonora's heart leaped as she felt the ring slide down the forefinger of her right hand and heard Nathan say that she was now consecrated unto him according to the law of Moses and of Israel. She blinked back a tear and swallowed hard. Dear God, she didn't want to cry here, not when the vision she had carried throughout her life was finally being realized. Crying would spoil everything. She let her mind float free, seeking some recollection that would stop the tears. Christmas of 1879 came to her, when Ella's and Lionel's parents had visited the Solomon home. Over dinner, they had discussed Atlanta's tolerance, how the city's Christians had celebrated with their Jewish brethren the setting of the synagogue's cornerstone, and Leonora had wondered what it would take to draw her cousin into that house of worship. The following day, when Miriam died in front of a train, she had found out, and she had agonized over the possibility that her thoughts had tempted such brutal fate. But since that hateful day, Nathan had entered the synagogue three more times. Each a happier occasion than the last. And this time . . . Leonora's tears became a deluge. She no longer cared, for these were tears of joy. This time for the most wonderful occasion of all.

A glass was placed on the floor in front of Nathan. As he raised his foot to crush it, he saw two more people beneath the wedding canopy. Two women, one with golden hair and green eyes, the other with lustrous black hair and the dark flashing eyes of a Gypsy.

He brought his foot down to crush the glass into a hundred pieces, and the two visions disappeared.

Part Four

1902—1913

Chapter Twenty-seven

A Locomobile traveled north along Whitehall Street at a steady eight miles an hour. High in the buggy seat, the driver manipulated the steering lever to guide the machine past slower horse-drawn traffic. Approaching the new railroad viaduct linking Whitehall and Peachtree streets, the vehicle passed a three-story building with tall glass windows that threw back the July sun's brilliance like enormous mirrors. In front of the building's entrance stood an elderly man with thick white hair and a neatly trimmed white beard. His feet were planted twelve inches apart, and his hands were clasped behind his rigidly erect back. The Locomobile driver tempted fate by removing his hand, if only for one precarious instant, to wave to the white-haired man who stood like a soldier at parade rest.

"Good morning, Mister Nathan! The best of luck to you today!"

Nathan waved back. "Good morning to you, sir! Your good wishes are most appreciated."

Turning his head, Nathan watched the Locomobile disappear across the viaduct into the northern part of Atlanta. A year after its debut on the Gate City's streets, the steam-powered, chain-driven Locomobile remained a novelty. Three of them drove around the city now, and wherever they went they turned heads. Nathan was no different from anyone else. He was curious about the new machines. They signified the move away from the exploitation of animal power to the use of energy that flowed from the genius of man. Electrification of the streetcar lines linking Atlanta with outlying towns had freed the red-tailed Mexican mules that had originally pulled the cars. Machines such as the Locomobile would do the same for horses. Nathan chuckled quietly as an amusing thought occurred. First the Negroes had been liberated, and then the mules. Soon it would be the turn of the horses.

An elderly woman in a black dress stopped beside Nathan. "Would that be Graham Courtney, Mister Nathan?"

"I believe it was, Miss Strickland."

The schoolteacher shook her head in exasperation. "A member of the State House of Representatives should know better than to risk his life on one of those infernal machines. He'll leave young Clarissa wearing widow's weeds the way he carries on."

Nathan suppressed a smile at Miss Strickland's description of Clarissa. He supposed that to a schoolteacher—even to a retired schoolteacher as Miss Strickland now was—any pupil she had taught remained young eternally. The truth was that the Crystal Palace's first customer that Monday morning thirty years ago was now the mother of a sixteen-year-old son named Alexander, and married to a lawyer whose political career could take him right into the governor's mansion. Clarissa had done well, and Nathan liked to think that much of her good fortune stemmed from his refusal to hire her. Instead of working at the Crystal Palace, she had gone to Regenstein's. There, as a twenty-year-old salesgirl, she had caught the eye of one of the store's regular customers who saw in Clarissa's fair-haired, blue-eyed beauty and pleasing manner a young woman she would like to introduce to her son. The son was Graham Courtney. Six months after the introduction the young couple were married. During the wedding, Clarissa had described Nathan as the man she and her new husband had to thank. They had met and married only because Nathan had not given her a job.

Clarissa might no longer be young, but one thing had not

changed. Every Christmas, Nathan still gave her a present. The previous year he had sent a china tea service to her home on Peachtree Street, and he expected to eclipse that next Christmas. Providing the new store—the new Crystal Palace that had thrown open its doors that very morning—proved to be the success he anticipated.

"I do not understand why you had to go and get all busy with this new store, Mister Nathan," Miss Strickland complained. "I could barely keep up with all the changes you kept making to the other one. I'm seventy now, you know," she admitted with coy candor.

"So am I, Miss Strickland. So am I."

"You are?" She eyed Nathan skeptically. Her own hair had gone iron gray when she was nearing sixty, making her suddenly aware of her increasing age. She had rarely noticed Nathan growing older because his hair had been white for as long as she could remember. "Then you should know all about the difficulties of climbing so many stairs."

"That is why our new store has elevators, Miss Strickland."

"I detest entering such contraptions, Mister Nathan. What if they get stuck between floors? If the cable snaps? If a fire breaks out? It was hard enough shopping in your old store when you expanded it to two floors. This"—she eyed the new store's three stories warily—"will be nigh on impossible."

"We got as much out of the original store as we could, Miss Strickland. We expanded it by building a second floor. My family even moved so the living quarters could be converted to store space—"

"Yes, yes, I remember. You bought a house in Inman Park, on Edgewood Avenue, once Joel Hurt made it accessible by running his electric trolley line out there."

"That is right, and still we did not have sufficient room. It was time to move the Crystal Palace, that was all. To a bigger, better building. When the viaduct opened, this whole area of Whitehall Street opened up with it, so here we are."

The schoolteacher remained unconvinced. She distrusted

change, and Atlanta was full of it in 1902. "Will you continue to give me your personal attention in this bigger, better building, Mister Nathan?"

"Please forgive me, Miss Strickland, but just this once I hope you will accept Harry's personal attention. Today, I plan to stay out here to welcome my old and cherished friends such as yourself to my new store."

Miss Strickland shook her head, disillusioned even more with the new Crystal Palace, but she went in just the same, eager to see how much better it was than the store she had patronized for thirty years. Nathan clasped his hands behind his back once more, contentedly rocking back and forth as he waited to greet customers drawn to the new store by a massive advertising campaign. The day was full of special one-time offers, silk sold for the price of linen, imported lace for the price of cotton. Manufacturers' representatives were demonstrating machines designed to make life easier, while prizes were being given to customers fortunate enough to be standing in the right place at the right time. Nathan had no doubt that by the time the doors closed that evening, two thousand people would have passed through them. He would be disappointed if he did not know the name of every single one.

In the midst of all the excitement, a wave of sadness suddenly engulfed him. What a pity that Miriam was not here to see all this. A building with tall, gleaming windows, just like the real Crystal Palace. Just like Miriam had once envisaged it.

Memories of Miriam made him glance northward. Had the city government been thinking of Miriam when they built the viaduct? Of Miriam and the many like her who had died at that crossing in the unequal clash of flesh and steel? Would she be alive today if action had been taken twenty-four years earlier? He tried to push the wretched questions from his mind, knowing that if he dwelled on such matters he would also torment himself with asking why a medical breakthrough made six months ago by an army surgeon named Walter Reed could not have occurred fifty years earlier: the discovery that mosquitoes, those damned pests of New Orleans, caused yellow fever.

The sound of his name being called rescued Nathan from his musing. Max and Leah Hirsch approached, arm in arm like two young sweethearts. Max shook hands with Nathan, then stepped back to allow his wife to kiss Nathan on the cheek. "Do you stand out here to make sure no one has the nerve to walk along Whitehall Street without entering your store?" Max asked.

Nathan smiled at the question. Although the passage of years had altered Max's appearance—the thick hair had vanished, leaving nothing but a shining red scalp, and the lustrous black mustache had turned gray—it had done little to dull his personality. In his late sixties, Max was as full of bluster as he had been in his forties, when his only daughter had fallen in love with Nathan's oldest son. "I stand out here to enjoy a wonderful day, while my sons do all the work. And one day in the not so distant future, my sons will stand out here, while my grandsons labor."

"Our grandsons," Max said. "At least, some of them."

"I stand corrected. Our grandsons." He had so many grandchildren that he was losing count. Sometimes he thought that Harry and Ella must have made a wager with Louise and Lionel to see who could produce the largest family in the shortest amount of time. Each couple had three children. Following the birth of Benjamin in June 1881, Harry and Ella had added two more, Rose in March 1883 and Edward in December 1884. Keeping pace, Louise and Lionel had quickly produced three of their own: Harriet, after Samuel Solomon's wife, in October 1882; Albert, eleven months later; and Aaron, thirteen months after that in October 1884. Benjamin, the oldest grandchild, already worked in the store. Despite a far better education than his own father had enjoyed, he had started in the same place as Harry—sweeping floors and stocking shelves. Nepotism did not exist in the Solomon family.

"Lucky is the man who has many sons," Leah said. The words, spoken with a gentle smile, contained a trace of regret.

Nathan understood. The Hirsches had no sons to take over their grocery business, and Ella, their only daughter, had no interest. Why should she, when her husband managed the Crystal Palace? Despite his age, Max Hirsch refused to sell the grocery business. He worked as hard now as he had done thirty years ago, certainly harder than the men he employed. Early each morning he visited the produce market to buy the day's stock. He spent the remainder of the day in the store, leaving it reluctantly to the hired help for half an hour or so when Leah called him upstairs for a meal. Leah worried about him constantly. Her worst fear was that one day she would call Max's name and he would not come. He would not answer because he had dropped dead in the store, dying where he had lived. That had happened to Joseph Selig, the father-in-law of Louise. While serving a customer in his drugstore three years earlier, Joseph Selig had collapsed on the floor with a hand to his heart and a surprised expression on his face. Sophie, his widow, had lived for only five months before joining him.

The Hirsches entered the new Crystal Palace to see for themselves what all the fuss was about. Nathan remained outside, pondering Leah's words. Her remorse made him appreciate his own good fortune all the more. Max and Leah had no sons while he had three, all of whom worked with him in the business. Harry, the oldest at forty-four, and living with Ella and their three children in a house on Capitol Avenue, bore most of the responsibility. He supervised the daily operation of the store, from hiring staff to approving the decisions made by buyers. William, the youngest, was now thirty. Still single, he lived with Nathan and Leonora in their home on Edgewood Avenue. His expertise centered around figures. He was the Crystal Palace's comptroller. From his office on the top floor, he made up the payroll, tallied receipts, settled accounts of suppliers, paid tax and utility bills, and supervised the thousand other items that comprised the firm's financial affairs.

If Nathan had any concerns at all about his sons, they centered on Jacob. Now thirty-one years old, the middle son had resisted settling down with the determination worthy of a mule. He had grown up in the Crystal Palace and wanted to see something else. If not of the world, at least of Atlanta. And instead of selling, he wanted to build, to create with his hands what he envisioned with his mind. Nathan, indulgently, had given the boy his own way, and from the age of fifteen Jacob had held a series of jobs that included repairing streetcars at the car barn on Exchange Place, erecting exhibits for the Piedmont Exposition of 1887, and building sets for DeGives Opera House. Although he enjoyed the work, his greatest passion had centered around sports, especially baseball. From early spring to late fall he had played on amateur baseball teams, swinging a bat and chasing a ball with the same gusto he had shown as a boy, and he considered it the high point of his life when the local professional team had signed him on. Unfortunately, his career had come to an abrupt end during the first season, before he could even win a regular place on the team. A collision at second base left him with a badly broken right leg. When the bone healed, his right leg was an inch shorter than his left, and he walked with the aid of a cane.

Only then did Jacob enter the family business. Not on the operations side, like Harry; nor on the financial side, like his younger brother. Instead, he involved himself with store maintenance, getting down on all fours and squeezing himself into uncomfortable positions to make repairs. An obvious penchant for such toil overcame the lack of any formal training. He learned as he went, and soon he was as familiar with building work as any tradesman. When Nathan announced plans for the new store he wanted to open at the northern end of Whitehall Street, Jacob was more excited than anyone. While Harry schemed with buyers to fill the vast new space with money-making merchandise, and William scrutinized each expense to find where money could be saved, Jacob oversaw construction. He supervised the installation of drum-type electric elevators, while all the time telling his father how a moving stairway shown two years earlier in Paris would soon make such cages redundant. He inspected the work of carpenters and bricklayers, compared each finished section with the architect's plans, and castigated painters at the faintest hint of a brush mark. And finally, when all the work was done, he performed one chore himself. He removed the crystal gaselier from the ceiling of the old store and used it as the basis for an ornate electrical lamp in which half a dozen incandescent bulbs burned brightly to illuminate the lobby of the new Crystal Palace.

Frequently, Nathan puzzled over how Jacob came by such artisan's skills. Harry's commercial talents were simple to understand—merchants appeared in the families of both his mother and father. William's dexterity with figures was just as easy to comprehend. It could be traced directly to Leonora's influence. Nowhere in the family, however, was there a hint of the mechanical aptitude Jacob enjoyed. His skill, his ability to understand concepts that his father could not even begin to fathom, came like a bolt out of the blue.

Nathan also wondered how long Jacob would remain with the store, or in Atlanta for that matter. Harry and William would happily spend their lives with the store, inheriting from their father the obligation to give Atlanta's shoppers a fair deal. Jacob was different. He did not want to be limited by boundaries—he wanted to smash right through them. Even his marriage a year earlier would not tie him to the city of his birth. If anything, it would have the opposite effect, for Helen, the young woman Jacob had taken as his wife, came not from Atlanta but from New York.

"Daydreaming already of the store that will be even grander than this one, Mister Nathan?"

Startled, Nathan swung around to see a petite young woman in a narrow-waisted yellow dress with puffed sleeves, and a wide hat with the uncurled ostrich plumes that were all the fashion. He had not heard her approach, and he could see from the mischievous glint in her dark brown eyes that she was enjoying his surprise.

"So help me, Helen, but I was just thinking of you."

"Good thoughts, I hope."

"How could you ever appear in any other light?" Nathan stooped to kiss his daughter-in-law on the cheek. The ostrich plumes got in his way, tickling the end of his nose. He stepped back, stifling a sneeze. Helen laughed. When Nathan recovered, she removed the hat and invited him to try again. This time he was more successful. "Perhaps you should check that hat at the door," he told Helen when she replaced it on her wavy brown hair. "Some people might consider it a lethal weapon."

"Only men who are trying to steal a kiss would consider it so. There . . ." She patted the hat into place. "How do I look?"

"Attractive enough for any man to risk a feather in his eye."

"Thank you. Jacob promised to take me to lunch. Will I find him clean and respectable?"

"The last time I saw him he was as clean as you or me. Mind you, that was when the store opened, just as I stepped out onto the street. In those three hours . . . who knows? The elevator could have broken down. He could have found a plumbing problem that needs his attention—"

"In that case I had better find him quickly, before he covers himself in grease and grime."

Chuckling, Nathan watched Helen enter the store. Every time he saw the young woman he understood what had attracted his son to her. Although ten years younger than Jacob, she had a vitality that matched his own. Neither of them seemed to sit still and relax for more than a minute. At their home on South Pryor Street, Jacob could always be found tinkering with some piece of machinery. Nathan swore he took apart perfectly serviceable items just to see if he could improve their efficiency and design. Simultaneously, Helen was always engaged in half a dozen different projects, running the gamut from involvement in local theater to volunteer work with charitable organizations throughout the city.

They had met two years earlier, when Jacob had visited New York to attend an engineering exhibition. On the day before his return to Atlanta, he had sought gifts for his family. Next to the St. Cloud Hotel on Broadway, where he stayed, was a small shop specializing in theatrical memorabilia. The shop was owned by Helen's parents, and Helen herself had waited on Jacob. He had left there an hour later, unable to remember a single one of the half-dozen gifts he had bought. He knew only that he would return to New York to see Helen again.

During the lengthy train journey back to Atlanta, Helen had rarely left his thoughts, and when he reached home he talked of her incessantly. To his distress, however, his preoccupation with the young woman caused amusement. Harry wanted to know if this Helen had a pressure gauge fitted into her ear, otherwise how could Jacob communicate with her? Before the laughter died, William asked his older brother whether Helen was steam- or electric-powered. Nathan, seeing Jacob's face go beet red, called a halt to the teasing. Unless he was very much mistaken, love had hit his middle son with all the force of a steam hammer.

A month later, Jacob had returned to New York, and every month after that, staying a week at a time in the St. Cloud while he paid court to Helen. After six such visits, he brought her back to Atlanta to meet his family. They married three months later beneath the same wedding canopy that had covered Jacob's two brothers, his sister, and his father more than twenty years before. To all appearances, Helen had settled well in Atlanta, but Nathan knew she missed the bustle of the bigger city. Atlanta might be an exciting place but it paled beside New York. Helen missed her family as well, her parents, two younger brothers, and a younger sister. Nathan wondered how long it would be before she persuaded Jacob to move up to New York, convinced him that greater opportunities existed for his engineering skills in the North than in the South?

From Jacob, Nathan took to musing about his only daughter and her husband. Pride swelled his chest each time he saw one of Lionel's family portraits on the sideboard or mantelpiece of an Atlanta home. Only a few days ago, he and Leonora had visited Clarissa and Graham Courtney, at their home on Peachtree Street. The moment they were led into the drawing room, Leonora had tugged at his arm and pointed to a new portrait of Clarissa, her husband, and their teenaged son, Alexander. Amused by the sudden show of excitement, Graham asked if they could recognize Lionel's pictures with no more than a single glance, and Leonora had laughingly replied that the combination of Lionel's photography skills with Louise's subject compositions was unmistakable. Despite the effort of managing a home and raising three children, Louise rarely missed being present for one of Lionel's sittings, because everyone in Atlanta knew that a Lionel Selig picture was incomplete without a Louise Selig arrangement.

Nathan wondered how long it would be before Lionel Selig pictures were no longer available in Atlanta. He was sure that Lionel and Louise, like Jacob and Helen, would eventually forsake the city. Not to open another studio like they had on Whitehall Street, but to pursue a new kind of film technology that had become an obsession with Lionel. Seven years ago, at the International Cotton States Exposition held at Piedmont Park, Lionel had watched in amazement as living pictures flickered on a screen. The pictures drifted in and out of focus, and the spotty film broke frequently, yet the brief exposure to such technology was enough to capture Lionel's interest. Still photography had furnished him with a good livelihood, but moving pictures had captured his imagination. What would it take, Nathan wondered, to make him quit the one and immerse himself in the other?

Given the right circumstances, two of his children would leave Atlanta to lead their lives elsewhere. Jacob pushed, perhaps, by a wife who wanted to return to the city of her birth; and Louise led by a husband chasing a new technology. Two would leave, and two—Harry and William—would remain. Two out of four was not so terrible. Besides, the country was shrinking every year. Places that had once seemed as far away as the moon were now nothing more than a long railroad journey. And the telephone that linked Nathan's home to the Crystal Palace would soon join the entire country. Nathan decided to ask Jacob how it would all be done. His middle son would surely know.

At twelve-thirty, a victoria carriage stopped outside the Crystal Palace. High on a raised seat sat a smartly turned out Negro groom. The single passenger was a woman wearing a turquoise dress and matching hat with the ubiquitous ostrich plumes. Before the groom could jump down to help the passenger, Nathan stepped forward. Opening the victoria's door, he held out his hand. "Welcome to the new Crystal Palace, my lady."

"Thank you, sir," Leonora said. Smiling, she took Nathan's hand and stepped down.

Nathan treasured the smile. Whenever he looked at Leonora he did not see a woman whose hair, beneath the plumed hat, had turned gray. Nor did he see a woman whose face bore the lines and etchings of sixty-eight years of life's experiences, whose faded eyes required the help of gold-rimmed spectacles. He saw instead a young woman with smooth skin, sparkling black eyes, and curling black hair, the same young woman who had brightened up so many omnibus rides on miserable London mornings. Furthermore, he knew that Leonora viewed him not as a white-haired old man of seventy but as a young quixotic figure trying to right the myriad wrongs he saw occurring all around him.

The twenty years of marriage to Leonora had been the most serene of Nathan's life, like a long and welcome rest after a period of sustained activity. He supposed that in a way his first fifty years had been just that, a hectic mixture of pleasure and pain, joy and sadness, exhilarating triumphs and devastating setbacks. The last twenty, when age had blunted the well-honed edge of youthful passion, had been far more placid. He had created nothing in those twenty years, but he had taken immense satisfaction in watching what he had planted in earlier years grow to fruition. The new store was not his individual accomplishment. His three sons had played major roles in its development, cultivating it from the seed their father had nurtured. They had done the bulk of the work, but like good sons they wanted their father out front to greet the customers and enjoy the plaudits. They knew how much he merited such pleasure.

Holding Leonora by the arm, Nathan led her to the entrance of the new Crystal Palace. A tall Negro in a frock coat and high hat pulled back the door to allow them entry to the lobby. Leonora's eyes fell on the crystal gaselier Jacob had converted to electricity. Large incandescent bulbs burned brightly, driving shadows from corners where sunlight failed to reach.

"Is there anything particular that madam would like to view?"

Leonora studied the varnished billboard directing customers to the various departments. Her head swam. Men's and women's clothing. Bedroom furnishings. Dry goods. Housewares. Hardware. Draperies. The list seemed endless. She had been part of the planning for this store, preparing meals for Harry, Jacob, and William when they gathered at Edgewood Avenue to discuss proposals and problems with their father. She had witnessed the various stages of construction, visualizing how it would be when the last sheet of glass was set into its pane, the last shelf fitted to a wall. But now that she saw it all for the first time without the dust and dirt, without the builders and painters, without the bare walls and unfinished fixtures, she had difficulty taking it all in. "Nathan, have you really filled all three floors with merchandise," she whispered, "or have you just padded the shelves with empty boxes as you did thirty years ago?"

"There is no longer a need to pad. Our credit is good enough with suppliers that we could fill every shelf and every counter ten times over if we wished."

Leonora squeezed Nathan's hand. "Our Uncle Samuel would be most proud if he could see you now."

Nathan laughed. In old age he was magnanimous enough not to deny Samuel Solomon such a simple pleasure.

Harry greeted them as they moved from the lobby into the store. The golden crown he had inherited from his mother was liberally splashed with silver, and his round face and stocky body bore testimony to Ella's cooking skills. Each time Nathan saw his oldest son at work he considered him the model of a successful storekeeper. He acted the role, too, remembering the names of every customer, their children's names, even their children's birthdays. A dozen years ago, when the store was still in its original site farther south on Whitehall Street, Harry had conceived the idea of cataloging the birthdays of customers' children, and sending each a little gift on the special day. The simple scheme had created enough goodwill to ensure the Crystal Palace of another generation of customers.

"Has it been a good day?" Leonora asked.

"You should ask that question of my father. He has been standing outside all morning, counting customers."

"Greeting customers, not counting them," Nathan said.

Harry gave his father a skeptical glance. "I would wager that you know within ten people how many customers have passed through our doors today."

"And I would wager that I know within five," Nathan replied.

"Show me around, please," Leonora told Harry. "If I like your manner, young man, I might even deign to buy something."

"What is there to buy," Harry asked, positioning himself between his father and Leonora, and taking their arms, "for the woman who has everything already?"

Leonora laughed brightly. Harry spoke the truth. She did, indeed, already have everything she had ever desired—a husband she loved, and children she adored. Children? After twenty years of marriage to Nathan, Leonora was still unsure of her exact relationship to Harry, Louise, Jacob, and William. Were they still first cousins once removed, or did the title of stepson and stepdaughter override that designation? It was all so confusing that she had long ago decided to refer to them simply as her children. She was sure that Miriam would not mind. On the contrary, Miriam would be delighted that another woman loved her children, the flesh of her flesh, as dearly as she had loved them.

Holding his father and Leonora by the arm, Harry guided them through the store, proudly describing each department. Wherever Leonora looked she saw the unfamiliar faces of new sales clerks. And so many; were other stores in Atlanta short-staffed today? Every one of the clerks was busy attending to a customer, while more shoppers waited to be served. It was all a sight, she knew, guaranteed to warm Nathan's heart.

The final stop on the tour was the third floor. Beyond the millinery department lay the store's administrative section. Harry led his guests past the buyers' offices to the room from which William oversaw every financial transaction of the Crystal Palace. From the ceiling, a skylight poured sunshine onto a heavy oak desk which was completely obscured by ledgers full of painstakingly neat entries, by accounts and invoices, by correspondence from banks and suppliers. Behind the desk sat William. At thirty, he was as slight and fragile as he had been at ten. Thick glasses covered his eyes, and a transparent green eyeshade shielded him from the brightness that streamed through the skylight. The mountain of paperwork dwarfed him, but it did not daunt him. As his three visitors entered, he held up his left hand, palm outward, while he operated an adding machine. The fingers of his right hand flew across the keys, pausing only to crank a lever at the side. When he finished, he called out a name. A woman dressed in black eased her way into the room past Harry, Nathan, and Leonora. She took the strip of paper William ripped from the adding machine and returned to her own office. William stood up to welcome his guests properly.

"Your fingers fly across that machine like Paderewski's fingers fly across a piano," Leonora said.

"The music I create is far sweeter. Especially today, when I am playing for the first time in such a grand auditorium."

"We are a success?" Nathan asked.

"We are an indubitable success."

"Good. We will leave you to continue tabulating it."

They left William's office and entered the millinery department on their way back to the ground floor. Suddenly, Nathan felt Harry's grip tighten on his arm. Ahead of them, one of the newly appointed sales clerks argued heatedly with a middle-aged woman holding a hat similar to the one Leonora wore. Nathan knew the woman well. She had patronized the Crystal Palace for more than ten years. He remembered talking outside to her not thirty minutes ago. Before he could learn the cause of the argument, Harry stepped forward.

"Good morning, Mrs. Johnson. Is there something I can do to help you?"

"Mister Harry, I bought this hat just a few minutes ago. Before I could even leave the store I noticed that one of the ostrich plumes was marked. There, do you see?" She shoved the hat beneath Harry's face. He could barely see a blemish, but he said nothing. "I wanted to change it, but your sales clerk had the nerve to tell me that many plumes have such marks."

Harry looked at the clerk. "Why were you arguing with Mrs. Johnson?"

"I was not arguing, Mister Harry. I was trying to resolve the lady's complaint."

"No, sir! You were most certainly not! Kindly give the lady whatever she wants. That is the only way we resolve complaints at the Crystal Palace." He turned to Mrs. Johnson, bowed slightly, and rejoined Nathan and Leonora. "It is amazing how many of our clerks regard a complaint about merchandise as a personal insult, an attack upon their very integrity. They act as if the cost of the goods they take back comes out of their own pocket. Tell me, why is that?"

"Because, being good sales clerks, they identify themselves completely with the store for which they work," Nathan answered. "That is all well and good for other stores, but when they come here they have to learn to temper that loyalty with strict adherence to the Crystal Palace's golden rule."

"That the customer is always right," Harry said.

"Correct. If you and your brothers never learn anything else from me, just remember that one thing." He gave Harry's arm an affectionate squeeze and continued with the tour.

Chapter Twenty-eight

Inman Park, developed by Atlanta businessman Joel Hurt, was the city's first suburb, and Edgewood Avenue, where Nathan and Leonora had moved to from Whitehall Street, was the thoroughfare along which Hurt operated the electric trolley line that made such suburbs feasible. On summer evenings, Nathan liked to sit on the deep porch that wrapped itself around the lower level of the house and watch the trolleys on their journeys between downtown and the car barn on Edgewood and Elizabeth streets. Each time one rumbled past on its path of steel, he reminded himself that the war had been over for only thirty-seven years, and he pictured in his imagination how Atlanta had looked when he had arrived with Leonora, Miriam, Harry, and Louise. From a devastated dust bowl of a ruin to this . . . ! A bustling, modern city with a population topping one hundred thousand, and an efficient street railway that made it possible for a man to live far from work. If miracles did happen, he was fond of telling people, then God had certainly been busy in Atlanta.

The house on Edgewood Avenue was as large as Waverley had once been. Tall brick chimneys climbed from three sides, while sharply angled, half-timbered gables added a dramatic silhouette to a roof of scalloped wooden shingles. Intricate lattice work edged the porch. Each door and window was surrounded by ornate scrollwork that was carried through to the interior of the house on mantels, cornices, and the mahogany balustrade leading from the spacious entrance hall to the second floor.

Nathan had one complaint about the house. The dining room was too large for regular use. He, Leonora, and William never used it for just themselves. They preferred eating in the cozier atmosphere of the breakfast room, where their own voices and the servants' footsteps did not create echoes, and where they did not feel like three chessmen marooned in the middle of a gigantic board. The one night of the week that Nathan enjoyed the dining room was Friday, when the entire family visited. Only then, with upward of a dozen people sitting around the burnished mahogany table, with the tinkle of silverware on china, and the murmur of half a dozen simultaneous conversations, did the emptiness disappear from the vast room. Only then did it feel like a dining room was supposed to feel.

On the Friday following the opening of the new store, the family gathered as usual at Edgewood Avenue. Pride imbued Nathan as he looked down the long table from his position at its head. What more could a man want than to have such a large and loving family? Along one side sat Harry, Ella, and their three children, Benjamin, Rose, and Edward, with William next to them. Along the other side sat Louise and Lionel, with their daughter, Harriet, and their two sons, Albert and Aaron. Beyond them sat Jacob and Helen. At the far end of the table, facing Nathan through the corridor of his children and grandchildren, sat Leonora.

Two young mulatto sisters named Bessie and Suzannah served the meal. They were the daughters of the Solomon family's groom, Alonzo, and the housekeeper, Fanny. The fifth member of the domestic staff—Lucy, the cook—was the housekeeper's cousin. The two mulatto sisters shared a spontaneous happiness. Smiles seemed to lie just below the surface, ready to burst out like sunbeams at every opportunity. Nathan noticed that they always shone brightest for the men at the table, and most radiantly of all for his oldest grandchild, Benjamin. Nothing Benjamin asked was too much trouble for the sisters. Nathan knew that if his grandson asked Suzannah and Bessie for the moon, they would carry a long pole and net to the roof of the house and do their best to snare it for him.

Nathan could not blame the sisters for their infatuation. His oldest grandson's good looks were almost Mediterranean. Soulful dark brown eyes anchored a hawklike face that turned golden-brown in the sun's rays. Thick black hair, parted in the center and swept back over his ears, rested on the collar of his shirt. At twenty-one, Benjamin fully understood the power of his appearance. Half the eligible young women at The Temple, as the synagogue was called since its move that year to new premises at Pryor and Richardson streets, were in love with him, and in the past year two liaisons had taken place within the walls of the Crystal Palace. Unwise liaisons. The first time, when Benjamin had taken up with an eighteen-year-old stockgirl, Harry had come to his father for advice. Nathan had told his son to get rid of the girl, but to give her a month's money because she was not solely to blame. Then he had counseled Harry to deduct the sum from Benjamin's wages. Loss of money might teach his grandson what common sense could not. Six months later, Harry caught Benjamin in a similar situation. He discharged the girl with two months' pay. When telling Benjamin that the money would be deducted from his wages, he promised that a month's earnings would be added to the severance pay of each and every female employee with whom he caught his son in the future. Nathan smiled inwardly as he recalled Harry telling him the story. Benjamin had finally gotten the message.

As dinner finished, Nathan spoke softly to Bessie, the older of the two sisters. She left the room, returning a minute later with a box of polished wood. Taking the box, Nathan rapped with a knife against a glass.

"This week, as you all know, has been successful beyond even my wildest expectations. In fact, I am already so accustomed to our new address that I have difficulty recalling our old store."

"If your memory is so weak," Louise said to her father, "I am sure that the Selig Studio has some pictures to remind you."

"On a point of principle, I refuse to pay the Selig Studio's exorbitant prices for pictures I allowed taken of my store."

"We will give you a special family rate," Lionel promised his father-in-law.

"Fifty percent more than anyone else pays," Harry quipped.

Nathan waited for the laughter to subside before he opened the box Bessie had brought him. Inside were gold brooches and smaller gold stickpins, all bearing the same design. "Many years ago, I gave a silver brooch with this motif to a girl who may one day be the first lady of our state. To commemorate our new store, I thought it fitting that you all should have one. To avoid confusion, the first name of each of you is engraved upon the back." He gave the box to Harry, who took the stickpin with his own name before passing the box to Ella. As Nathan's gaze followed the box around the table, his face mirrored each recipient's smile of pleasure.

Louise took the last brooch and pinned it to her dress before passing the empty box back to her father. Nathan noted that his daughter's green eyes shone as brightly at forty-two as they had when she was twenty. Although her early life had not been without its suffering and tragedy, twenty-two good years of marriage had surely compensated for any hardships. Nathan was certain that his daughter and son-in-law loved each other every bit as deeply as they had done during the meetings of the Meyerbeer Society. Three children had cemented that love. Harriet, the oldest, was nearing twenty and helped her parents in the studio. Her dark curly hair, brown eyes, and vivacious personality reminded Nathan uncannily of a young Leonora. He saw nothing odd in such a resemblance. After all, had Lally's features not reminded him of his own father? His father's looks had jumped diagonally to his sister's daughter. A generation later, looks had jumped diagonally again, with Leonora's image manifesting itself in the granddaughter of her cousin. Such family characteristics did not extend to Louise's two sons, though. Eighteen-year-old Albert was short and stocky, dark-haired, with a pugnacious set to his jaw. Aaron, a year younger, was a thin, pale-faced youth with wispy brown hair.

The opposite held true for the three children of Harry and Ella, where family features had skipped the oldest but settled in the other two. While Benjamin, with his Mediterranean charm, bore no resemblance to anyone Nathan could remember, his younger sister and brother did. Nineteen-year-old Rose and seventeen-year-old Edward shared the golden hair their father had inherited from Miriam. What a legacy that was, Nathan marveled. A golden shimmering crown, more brilliant than any of the brooches or stickpins he had given away that evening.

As Nathan turned to Jacob and Helen, he tried to picture how their children would look. Married a year, they gave no sign yet of starting a family. Nathan hoped they set about it soon. At seventy, a man could not expect to see many more years. If Jacob and Helen wanted him to spoil their children as he had spoiled his other grandchildren, they would have to hurry.

Finally, Nathan's gaze fell upon William. Watching his youngest son fiddle with the stickpin, he wondered whether he would ever have a family of his own. William showed no interest at all in marrying and settling down. His enjoyment centered around displaying his mental prowess. When not working at his office in the Crystal Palace, he found other ways to exercise his skills. He played half a dozen different games of cards equally well, memorizing every hand and then recalling entire sequences an hour or a day later. He played chess with the same ruthless efficiency, logging every contest in a small book although Nathan suspected that he could record the games equally well in his head. William blended mental agility with a prodigious memory. At any game, he was a fearsome opponent. It was too bad that he did not apply himself so diligently to life, to marrying and raising a family.

Nathan pushed back his chair and stood up. The remainder of the family followed suit. Led by Leonora, the women moved into the parlor. The men followed Nathan onto the porch where Bessie had set out glasses, a bottle each of brandy and Madeira and a jug of lemonade. Such a division after the Friday-night meal was customary. Men had their own affairs to discuss. So did women. Nathan had no idea what the women talked about. He had once asked Leonora, and she had answered, "Women's business." He had not asked again because he felt that Leonora and the other women of the family were entitled to their privacy. Leonora was not so reticent. She always asked about the men's discussion.

On this night, the men discussed politics. In the early summer of 1902, while the main Washington topic was the decision to pay forty million dollars for the rights to build a canal through Panama, the citizens of Atlanta were still recovering from the shock of the Pittsburgh Riot when a former policeman named Samuel Kerlin had been attacked by a group of armed Negroes led by a man Kerlin had once sent to the chain gang. Kerlin's cries had drawn assistance from police officers and soldiers, and the episode had ended in a fearsome gun battle which left six men dead, another half dozen wounded, and an entire city block burned to the ground.

Two months after the incident, its shadows continued to darken Atlanta. While reasonable men of both races pleaded for calm, extremists did their best to keep the pot boiling. Lionel related how he had been approached in the studio only that day by two white men who swore that they had information concerning an uprising by armed Negroes.

"If such a thing were in the wind, the police would surely know of it," Nathan told his son-in-law.

"Perhaps so, but these men told me that many people are so unnerved by the possibility of an uprising they have discharged their servants for fear of being poisoned by the family cook, or done to death in their beds by the gardener or the coachman. I did not let Louise know this, of course."

Nathan had also heard such stories, but he put little faith in them. "Such men are alarmists. Pay no heed to them."

"Are you that sure of your own servants?" Lionel asked.

Nathan called Bessie's name. When the maid appeared, he asked her to fetch her father. Five minutes later, Alonzo joined the men on the porch. Nathan wasted no time. "Alonzo, what do you know of Negroes arming themselves to kill white people, and of servants planning to murder their employers in their beds?"

Alonzo shook his narrow head and rolled his eyes. "I haven't heard nothing about such things, Mister Nathan."

"Are you and your family happy here?"

"Yes, sir, Mister Nathan. We're all so happy here that we reckon we're part of your family. If you don't mind, of course."

"Of course not. Thank you, that was all we wanted to know." He waited for Alonzo to leave before turning to the others. "There, we have as much likelihood of being butchered in our beds by Negro servants as mankind has of walking on the moon. I trust that none of you has acted rashly upon this spiteful rumor."

"Rumors of a Negro uprising bother me less than the animosity I feel from some of Atlanta's white citizens," Albert told his grandfather. "At the Georgia Institute of Technology, young men reject students whose families are recent arrivals in America. They say they should go back to where they came from."

Nathan understood exactly what was happening. Thirty-five years ago, everyone had pulled together to drag the city from Sherman's ashes. Now that Atlanta thrived, its citizens had enough time on their hands to indulge in class distinction. The Piedmont Driving Club and the Capital City Club were fine examples of such distinction. Neither had a Jewish member, although a Jew had been a founder of the Gentlemen's Driving Club, as the Piedmont Club was first called. "Tell them that the families of your mother and your father date back to long before the War Between The States. Then ask these students what their grandparents were doing then. Digging peat in some Irish bog, I'll warrant. Or herding sheep in Scotland."

Edward, Harry's younger son, who studied with his cousin Albert, said, "Length of time is not the criterion. Heritage is. These people feel that an Anglo-Saxon whose family came here last year has more right to be in America than any Catholic family. Than you or any of us, no matter when our ancestors came."

"There is an even greater and more dangerous hostility toward us," Benjamin said. "From the lintheads, the cannon fodder of the cotton mills who, having nothing themselves, seek to blame their misery on those more fortunate."

Nathan nodded slowly. His family, especially his grandsons, saw crises all around. They looked to him for explanations, for the oil with which to soothe troubled waters. "To understand any situation, you must first study the period in which it occurs. Tremendous change is taking place in Atlanta right now. During the last decade, we experienced a depression that was far worse than the one we went through twenty years before."

"It affected agricultural activity particularly badly," William pointed out. "Thousands of farmers lost everything."

"And they came here, to Atlanta, to the growing city that shines like a star in the night sky. They came here, lured by the new industrialism which they expected to support them as farming had once done."

As Nathan paused to sip from his glass of brandy, Harry took up the conversation, saying the words he knew his father would have said. As the oldest son, he had the duty to keep the family together, to soothe its fears and solve its problems. "The beliefs of these new city dwellers have been formed from childhood in an Anglo-Saxon environment by religious ministers who preached that agrarian life was good and holy, while city life was evil and godless. Still, the city's evil was preferable to starvation, so they came here in their thousands to seek work in factories. But when they saw those same factories swallow their wives and daughters—saw the women of the family going out to work—they felt that their traditional position as family breadwinner had been eroded."

Nathan set down his glass. "These men who have already lost all material things now see their pride stripped away as well. They seek people to blame for their misfortune. Negroes are an obvious choice because of their visibility, but Negroes do not own the mills and factories that employ these men. Nor do they own the stores. In some cases, we do, and believe me when I say that we most surely stand out to people raised to be xenophobic. Though white, we are neither Anglo-Saxon nor Christian. Many of our community, even myself, are foreign-born, and still speak with noticeable accents. To a people fiercely aware of their own Anglo-Saxon heritage, we represent the perfect scapegoats, ready to carry the blame for all the upheaval that industrialism and the move from rural areas to the city has caused."

"How do you fight such ill feeling?" asked Aaron, the younger of Lionel's and Louise's sons.

"With compassion," Nathan answered immediately. "These people have lost everything, so you try to help them start again. Instead of dismissing them as lintheads, you regard them as proud people struggling to put their lives together. You give them respect, and hope they repay you in kind. If they are ignored, if they feel their lives are truly hopeless, they might well become faithful followers of some demagogue who wants to ride such discontent to high political office. Then the tide might turn against all successful men, especially us, and all we have worked so hard to achieve will be in jeopardy."

Benjamin's mouth dropped. The darkly handsome features went slack. "You mean that we could lose the Crystal Palace?"

"We could lose far more than that. It has happened in other countries. Ask your mother's parents."

A long silence followed. Nathan's eyes moved from one man to another, from son to son-in-law to grandson, and he wondered what thoughts passed through their minds. Fear, that such animosity could exist toward them? Worry, that it might drive them from their homes? Or determination to fight it? He, for one, would never move, no matter how uncomfortable

Atlanta became. He had moved enough already, and Atlanta's Oakland Cemetery—in a spot beside Miriam—was where he would rest for all eternity. But he would never blame the others for wanting to go elsewhere, to a city where the climate was less unstable.

Harry was the first to speak. "I do not care what happens. I will never leave this place. I may not have been born here, but this city is my home."

"Mine, too," said William. "Doubly so, because I was born in Atlanta."

"Like you, William, I was born here," Lionel said, "and I have built up a successful business here. But if trouble arose I would not put Louise and my family at risk by staying here. My photography is a portable skill, and what I do here I could always do elsewhere. Besides"—he gave a dry chuckle, as if to temper the urgency of the discussion—"being so comfortable with the Selig Studio hampers me from pursuing my interest in motion pictures. The shock of being forced to move might be just what I need to jar me out of my complacency."

Harry grew irritated that his brother-in-law did not share his own loyalties. "Your motion pictures are nothing but a fad. No one takes them seriously—"

"No? Is that why the Star on Decatur, and the Eldorado on Marietta are always full?"

Harry refused to be swayed. "They have novelty value, nothing more. The length of the pictures is too limited to be of real significance. They are good only as chasers, a signal to vaudeville audiences that the show is over and it is time to leave the theater. When theater owners think of a better way to finish the show, motion pictures will lose that purpose as well."

"The length is growing," Lionel asserted. "Three hundred to six hundred feet is common now, and soon it will be double that."

Before Harry could respond, Nathan pointed a finger at Jacob. He wanted to keep to the original topic. "What about you?"

"I love the new store dearly, but my first loyalty is to Helen. If she felt frightened by events here and wished to return to New York, I would accompany her."

"What would you do in New York?" Harry demanded.

"Like Lionel, my skills are highly portable."

"If you think New York is waiting with open arms for a man who can repair a broken elevator, then you are in for a rude awakening. You would do better to stay here with your family, where there is a market for your ability."

Deadlock, thought Nathan. Two of his children would stay, and two would go. Harry and William would remain with the Crystal Palace, inheriting from him the obligation to serve the people of Atlanta, while Jacob and Louise would leave. Nathan felt depressed. Knowing that he had prophesied such a division only a few days earlier did little to lift his spirits.

Later that evening, after the family had left, Nathan sat with Leonora on the porch. He spoke of the joy his gifts had brought, and he asked Leonora if she remembered when he had first given such a brooch—a silver brooch, not gold—to Clarissa.

"Of course I do," she answered. "It was the fourth Christmas gift you gave her—"

"The fourth? Surely it was the third. First I gave her a doll, and then a dollhouse—"

"You gave her two dolls and then a dollhouse."

Nathan chewed his bottom lip as he forced himself to recall every detail of those early years. "So I did," he said at last. "Do you remember what I gave her the year after the brooch?"

"No. Do you?"

"I wish I did, but I do not. Is my memory becoming feeble?"

"No." Leonora reached across the table to hold his hand. "You have far more than most men to remember, that is all."

"Thank you, Lally."

Still holding his hand, Leonora asked her customary question. "What did the men talk about tonight? It must have been a weighty subject because your expression is so serious."

"We talked about the canal being built in Panama," Nathan

answered quickly. "Forty million dollars it will cost. It is hard to imagine so much money. I know it is a worthwhile investment, but I worry if the day should ever come when the people of Panama grow hostile toward the United States and refuse us passage through the canal we built and paid for."

"Forty million dollars for a canal would not mask your face with such sadness, or cause your voice to echo with unhappiness."

Nathan forced himself to laugh. "You see what is not there."

"No, Nathan, I have known you too well for too long to be deceived. Why are you so despondent?"

He reached deep inside his imagination for another story, another lie so Leonora would not know the worries that gripped her family, and he remembered watching William toy with the gold stickpin. "I took a good look at William tonight, Lally. He went through hell as a child and is still not strong. God compensated for that weakness by giving him a sharper intelligence than most other men. Nonetheless, William remains only half a man. A wife is what he needs to make him complete. That is why I am despondent, because I worry I will die before William marries. I am frightened of leaving him alone."

When he saw the understanding in Leonora's eye, he knew the lie had been accepted.

The men of the Solomon family continued the custom of gathering on the porch after eating Friday dinner, but no one brought up the subject of leaving Atlanta again. The topic had created harsh feelings. Harry, who had declared his intention to remain in the city and face problems could not understand how anyone else could do otherwise. William had said he would stay, which was exactly what Harry had expected, but the declarations of his younger brother and his brother-in-law had shocked the oldest brother. He could think of only one word to describe men who would desert a family at the sign of trouble. He regarded them as traitors, and his attitude toward them grew chilly until Nathan expressed his own belief that Lionel and Jacob were bound to leave Atlanta sooner or later. The threat of trouble really had little bearing on their decision.

Each morning, Nathan continued to be driven in from Edgewood Avenue to spend three or four hours welcoming friends to his new store. When weather permitted, he stood on the sidewalk, where he could talk to everyone who passed. If rain or heat made outside activity impossible, he positioned himself just inside the store, greeting shoppers and pointing them to the different departments. All was well with the world as long as Crystal Palace patrons could see Nathan on duty.

While Nathan remained busy greeting customers, Leonora filled her time with charitable pursuits. She involved herself with both the Hebrew Orphanage on Washington Street, and the Hebrew Ladies Benevolent Society which, among its philanthropic works, sought to assist immigrants from Eastern Europe. These new immigrants shared little with the coreligionists who had preceded them from Germany. Stubbornly orthodox in belief, they were shocked by the Reform brand of Judaism prevalent at The Temple. English words had replaced Hebrew in the liturgy; the ritual robes and prayer shawls had been abandoned; men prayed bareheaded; and Holy Day observances had been cut from two days to one. Why, there was even talk of a Sunday service to accommodate those members unable to attend the traditional Friday-night and Saturday-morning observances. Discomfited by this unusual form of worship, the newcomers soon formed their own, more traditional congregation, but they still needed help from the established community. And the established community, aware that its own members could all too easily be confused in the eyes and minds of Gentile Atlantans with these odd-looking strangers, was only too willing to help transform the newcomers into self-supporting Americans.

A year after the opening of the new Crystal Palace, the tide of immigration to America was quickened by a violent pogrom in the Russian city of Kishinev. More bloodbaths followed. The

Reform and Orthodox congregations acted together to resettle some of the new refugees in Atlanta. Nathan had always given money willingly, but as the pogroms continued, Leonora urged him to become more involved.

"This time more than money is needed. You are an articulate, persuasive man. Let your voice be heard."

Nathan did. A week later, at a benefit to raise money for resettlement, he told a group of wealthy Gentile and Jewish Atlantans that the clothes of the new immigrants might be bizarre, their language indecipherable, and their manners unfamiliar to Americans. "But remember this—in the veins of the humblest Hebrew who disembarks at New York flows the blood of priests and prophets. His bearing might be unpolished and his demeanor unrefined, but his basic ideals are akin to your own."

As Nathan stepped down from the dais to rejoin Leonora, a young man approached. After identifying himself as a reporter named John Parkins, he complimented Nathan on the passionate eloquence of his speech, then added immediately, "Even you, though, will have to admit that these Eastern European Israelites are a peculiar-looking lot."

"Young man, you commend me on my speech but it is obvious that you have not digested a single word of it. Do not be fooled by appearances. These people are thrifty and hardworking, sober and industrious. They will toil while you play. In half a dozen years, when they live in fine houses and you still exist in a rented room, you will ask how such a thing came about. If your mind is so inclined, you might even subscribe to the slander that these people must have taken shortcuts, broken the law, or cheated their way to success. Otherwise how else could they have achieved so much while you achieved so little?"

"Perhaps then," another voice said, "you will remember this conversation and you will understand precisely why."

Nathan, Leonora, and the reporter turned to see Graham Courtney and Clarissa standing beside them. Clarissa looked tiny next to her husband. The Georgia State Representative stood well over six feet tall, a spare man with gray-spattered fair hair and pale blue eyes in a square, bony face. He reminded Nathan of James Wilson, the owner of Fallowfields.

"You agree that these newcomers will benefit Atlanta, Mister Courtney?" the reporter asked.

"I would stake my political career upon it."

"Really? Then perhaps you would be kind enough to explain what benefit are those foreigners who operate the dives where Atlanta's Negro loafers hang out, drinking all day while plotting the mischief they will commit that night."

"Can you swear that every Baptist is an epitome of virtue?" Courtney retorted. "Every Methodist? Every Episcopalian? I warrant not. You will find among these immigrants the same cross section of good and bad you will find in any group."

As Nathan listened to the exchange, it occurred to him that he had never seen the reporter before. "What newspaper did you say you represent, Mister Parkins?"

"The newspaper I write for is called *Awaken*."

The Solomons and the Courtneys stared blankly at each other. "I'm afraid we are totally unfamiliar with your newspaper," Leonora finally said.

"*Awaken* is a new weekly publication, less than a month old. You will hear of it, though." He reached into his jacket pocket and withdrew a folded newspaper. "Please accept a complimentary copy. You might appreciate it enough to subscribe."

Nathan took the folded newspaper, slipped it into his own jacket pocket and promptly forgot all about it. As Parkins walked away, Leonora turned to Courtney. "We are extremely grateful for support such as yours."

Courtney seemed embarrassed by such praise. Clarissa took his hand and squeezed it. "I meant every word I said to that young man. My admiration for the Hebrew people has been recorded many times. I have said that while we see beggars of every other nationality and religion on our streets, we never see your people begging. If they do, they beg only of their own. And if charity is given, it is given as charity should be given. Secretly, and hidden from the rest of the world. I believe that the Jew makes a desirable citizen. Few of his kind inhabit the penitentiary or ally themselves with the vicious or criminal class. That is because obedience to the rule of law is part of his religion. I have stated this in the House. I will challenge anyone to disprove it in the Senate if I am elected, and God willing, I will continue to state these truths one day from the executive mansion at Peachtree and Cain. Your people have a friend in Graham Courtney."

"Thank you." As Nathan uttered the automatic words of gratitude, he could not help reflecting that Graham Courtney represented perfectly the anomaly that had overtaken Atlanta. He belonged to both the Piedmont Driving Club and the Capital City Club, organizations which excluded from their membership the very people for whom Courtney declared his admiration from the floor of the Georgia House of Representatives.

In the thirty-eight years since the war, a social wall had been erected. Jews and Gentiles worked together to improve Atlanta, but their cultures had become socially separated.

Only as he prepared for bed that night did Nathan remember the copy of *Awaken* given to him by John Parkins. He unfolded the newspaper and spread it out. It was a single sheet, nothing more. Four pages, certainly no competition to the city's three established newspapers, the *Constitution*, the *Journal*, and Hearst's *Atlanta Georgian*.

Skimming through the stories, Nathan quickly spotted a common theme—populism, a political doctrine that was slowly losing the favor it had enjoyed the previous decade when William Jennings Bryan had lost his bid for the White House. Stories critical of government for being the pawn of Wall Street, big money, and the railroads ran alongside articles praising farmers who still worked the earth while new industrial smoke blotted out the sun above them. With the populist platitudes came racial attacks. Nathan read two editorials. One called for farm subsidies and an eight-hour working day; the other demanded stern action against drunken Negroes who were molesting white women in the street.

Nathan was not at all surprised when he noticed that the publisher's name was George Hopkinson.

Chapter Twenty-nine

As much as Nathan detested the philosophy of *Awaken* and the man behind it, he could understand its appeal to whites who considered themselves underprivileged. Not only millworkers and factory hands—many of whom needed to have the stories read to them because they were illiterate—but men as responsible as clerks and insurance agents, police officers and carpenters. Populism, despite its national disintegration, continued to draw plenty of followers among Georgia's needy. So did bigotry, and the need to have someone else to blame.

The weekly newspaper quickly moved up from its single-sheet, four-page format. By the spring of 1904, a year after its launch, *Awaken* had filled out to a healthy twenty-four pages, with sufficient advertising to pay its costs. The influence George Hopkinson wielded through his newspaper became evident that summer, when Graham Courtney ran for the Georgia State Senate on a platform of bringing more industry to the state. His opponent took an old-fashioned populist stand. While established newspapers reported the contest objectively, each issue of Hopkinson's publication carried an attack on Courtney. Articles linked him with every populist bugaboo—the financiers of New York, the railroads, factory and mill owners, and immigrants who would take American jobs. For good measure, Hopkinson threw in a few bugbears of his own. Although Courtney was not a Catholic, *Awaken* tried to have its readers believe that the candidate was part of a Vatican conspiracy to subvert American civilization and abolish the liberties of its citizens. And believe they did, to the point of clamoring for more information on Courtney's Vatican connections, which Hopkinson was only too happy to supply from his own active imagination.

On a gray and rainy day a week before the election, Clarissa shopped at the Crystal Palace. Nathan was at his station just inside the door. Clarissa kissed him on the cheek as she always did when visiting the store. When Nathan asked how she was bearing up under the strain of the election campaign, Clarissa said, "I am grateful that Mister Hopkinson's scandalous paper has only one more publication date before election day. How much more nonsense can he possibly put in one copy?"

"I am amazed that your husband has not chosen to sue."

"We discussed it, Mister Nathan, but what value would be served? To sue a man like Hopkinson only serves to legitimize him. Furthermore, his writings have brought forth so many men with feelings similar to his own that we could not be certain of receiving an impartial hearing."

Nathan understood perfectly. Hopkinson's tirades had tapped a fertile vein of hatred. Right behind the dislike of Negroes he had discovered an aversion to Catholicism which he was milking for all he was worth.

"He has never forgiven my family for what my father did to him, telling him that he was no longer welcome to stay in our home on Hunter Street," Clarissa said. "Now he sees his chance to pay my family back, and he is taking it with a vengeance."

"All that happened almost thirty years ago. Where has he been hiding all this time? He disappeared from Atlanta when the *Daily Herald* failed, not long after your father threw him out. No one had seen or heard of him until he turned up here with that damned piece of gutter journalism he now publishes."

"Graham had men check on him. He worked on different newspapers throughout the South, in Alabama, Florida, the Carolinas, Tennessee. He always wrote for papers that followed the populist line, standing up for farmers and criticizing businessmen, favoring agrarian priorities over industry."

"Quite understandable, I suppose, after what happened to his father and brother."

"He even worked on the campaigns of populist candidates during the movement's heyday in the nineties. As populism faded, he found his message falling into disfavor."

"Where did he find the money to launch a newspaper? Even a weekly? Reporters are hardly in the same financial league as railroad magnates."

Clarissa smiled. "He found it by being a hypocrite. George Hopkinson, hater of the rich, wed some fifteen years ago the only daughter of a cotton mill owner in Alabama. The woman was as ugly as sin, to hear Graham's investigators tell it. The owner of the mill died soon after, some illness that ate away his insides until he looked like a parchment-covered stick. The sickness must have been hereditary, because the daughter died from it, too, about three or four years ago. George Hopkinson put aside his populist leanings long enough to get his hands on his late wife's money. It was enough to build a beautiful home halfway between here and Marietta—bigger even than the governor's executive mansion—and start that dreadful newspaper that caters to the sick prejudices of so many people."

Clarissa's mention of the executive mansion reminded Nathan that Graham Courtney had his eye on the state governorship. Did George Hopkinson also see himself living at Peachtree and Cain? "The platform of a newspaper is often the stepping-stone to political office, Clarissa. Were your husband's researchers able to learn if such is the case with Hopkinson?"

"Most definitely he has political aspirations, but not for the governorship. Hopkinson is in his early fifties, too old to waste time campaigning for state office. He has his eyes on the United States Senate."

Nathan chuckled deeply. "Then I think we have little to worry about, for Mister Hopkinson will need a much higher stepping-stone than a yellow rag like *Awaken* to gain entry into that exclusive club."

Clarissa's claim that George Hopkinson had ambitions to become a United States Senator piqued Nathan's interest. More than a year had passed since *Awaken* had first come to Nathan's attention, yet in all that time he had never seen the man who published it. Hopkinson worked from the home he had built, and when he ventured out from it, he did not visit the city, which he detested; he mixed with country folk, the farmers and the small-town people who, he hoped, would one day get him elected.

On the Sunday after Clarissa's visit, Nathan had Alonzo drive him out along Marietta Road in the victoria. It was the first time Nathan had ridden far in that direction for many years. He stared avidly at all the new buildings which had taken Atlanta far beyond its original boundaries, and every so often he told Alonzo how much had changed since the days he had driven Ephraim Gottfried's wagon along this road to service rural customers.

Nathan was not surprised when he saw the location of the house George Hopkinson had built. It was located on the very spot where the Hopkinson family home had stood thirty years ago. Where once had been a modest farmhouse now rose a white-columned residence that would not have looked out of place among the Grecian designs of the Garden District. At a table on the front porch sat a man, head bent as he wrote with a pen on a sheet of paper. When Nathan had Alonzo stop the victoria at the bottom of the long drive, the man looked up. Tall and thin, with flowing gray hair, he stepped down from the porch and walked toward the road. When he was twenty yards away, Nathan realized it was George Hopkinson.

Hopkinson did not spare Alonzo a glance. The Negro groom did not even exist for him. "Do you seek someone, sir, or are you just admiring my home?"

"Neither," Nathan answered. "I was merely wondering if you still bought everything from the country store, like your father did, because he didn't mind being robbed by one of his own kind."

"Should I know you?" Hopkinson's sharp blue eyes narrowed as he tried to place his visitor.

"We last spoke some thirty years ago, when you warned young Clarissa Jenkins about the folly of being overwhelmed by a merchant's generosity."

Hopkinson nodded in recognition. "Ah yes, that was before her father evicted me because he did not like the truths I told about his friends. I have more truths to tell about you now, and a far louder voice with which to tell them."

"If they are anything like the truths you tell about Graham Courtney, I will not lose sleep worrying."

"You should, because my supporters are increasing all the time. They are loyal folk who are grateful to me for the heritage I give them."

"Heritage? Since when is page after page of fevered, vicious slander a heritage?"

Hopkinson smiled coldly. "I see that like all of your class, you have no understanding of the ordinary people who are the backbone of this country."

"Tell me about them."

"Certainly. These people have little material wealth. My writings open their eyes to a heritage they have never fully considered. I make them aware of their birthright of white superiority. I show them that it is a tradition they can pass on, a legacy they can bestow upon their heirs. Your class bequeaths riches, money, property, stock in the companies that profit from this new, destructive industrialism. Because of me, the readers of *Awaken* are now able to leave a legacy to their children—the knowledge that they are superior to Negroes."

"That is not a treasure. It is a hate that will poison the air of Atlanta for generations to come." Nathan turned back to the victoria. Alonzo opened the door and held out a hand to help his passenger board.

Hopkinson was not finished. "What poisons Atlanta is people like you who import the dregs of Eastern Europe as cheap labor to deprive white Christian Americans of the work they need to feed their families."

Alonzo cracked the whip and the victoria started the return journey to Atlanta. From behind, fading with each turn of the wheels, came Hopkinson's continuing tirade. "I will ruin you as I am ruining Courtney. Once I have stopped his bid for the State Senate, I will focus my readers' attention on the likes of you."

George Hopkinson's attacks failed to stop Graham Courtney from winning election to the Georgia State Senate, but Clarissa's husband's margin of victory was far narrower than his supporters had anticipated. Hopkinson's rabble-rousing weekly publication wielded more influence than many moderate Georgians cared to acknowledge.

Courtney kept the promise he had made to Nathan at the benefit to raise money for resettling Eastern European refugees. In the State Senate, he spoke of the advantages of inviting such industrious and law-abiding people to become citizens of Georgia. As much as Nathan appreciated reading the reports of such speeches, he still found it incongruous that he would never hear Courtney declare the same sentiments on the floor of the Capital City Club or the Piedmont Driving Club that he expressed so enthusiastically from the floor of the Senate.

At the beginning of 1906, a year after Courtney took his seat in the Senate, Nathan became a grandfather for the seventh time when Jacob and Helen presented him with a grandson named Burton. Holding the baby for the first time, the thought crossed Nathan's mind that his newest grandson might feel confused as he discovered that all his cousins were old enough to be his aunts and uncles. Unless William married and fathered children, of course, but Nathan was more doubtful than ever of that occurring.

The birth of Jacob's and Helen's child signaled the start of a period of celebration within the Solomon family. At the end of February, Rose, the only daughter of Harry and Ella, married a young man named Daniel Morris who had worked at the Crystal Palace for five years since coming to Atlanta from Birmingham, Alabama. Within three months—and much to Harry's relief—Rose's older brother Benjamin stood beneath The Temple's wedding canopy to marry Caroline Helman, daughter of an Atlanta doctor. Three months after that, in the middle of August, Harriet, the only daughter of Louise and Lionel, married Saul Jaeger, whose German-born parents owned a small hardware store on Decatur Street.

During each ceremony, while Leonora wiped tears from her eyes with a lace handkerchief, Nathan glanced toward his youngest son as if to ask why William was not standing beneath the canopy. Sometimes, William caught Nathan looking at him. He smiled awkwardly because he understood exactly what was passing through his father's mind, and he fiddled with the gold stickpin he had been given after the opening of the new store. The stickpin had become William's worry bead. He wore the bauble every day, caressing it whenever crises arose. He fondled it during tense moments in chess and card games, at hectic periods in the Crystal Palace, and during those times, like now, when Nathan's eyes accused him of not living up to his father's expectations.

As Nathan returned his attention to the wedding ceremony, he told himself he should be content that William thought enough of the gift to wear it all the time, and perhaps he should stop torturing himself by wishing for what would never be.

The happiness of the Solomon family was a single ray of sunlight piercing the dark clouds of fear and anger that gathered over Atlanta that summer of 1906. Rarely did a week pass without a newspaper reporting an assault on a white woman by a Negro man. Provocative descriptions of such incidents raised public anger to boiling point. The editorials in *Awaken* were particularly fiery. Describing Negroes as a subspecies fit only for manual labor, George Hopkinson wrote that "without the restraints and disciplines of serfdom, they are no better than wild animals. A man-eating tiger should be regarded with more trust."

At the beginning of August, Hopkinson switched to a new tack, one which he knew would horrify his xenophobic readers more than anything that had gone before. "Those of us familiar with the perils of the Negro problem must stand together to ensure that freedom and political power do not give him encouragement in his foul quest for mixing the races." Every week after that, *Awaken* harped on the theme of race mixing; and every week, circulation rose. Hopkinson had found a volatile recipe, and he was resolved to keep mixing the ingredients until he caused an explosion.

The explosion occurred on a Saturday late in September, a day on which Atlanta newspapers had carried lurid stories of four attempted assaults on white women by Negro men. Just before six o'clock, Nathan stood in the lobby of the Crystal Palace, waiting for Alonzo who would soon collect him and take him home to Edgewood Avenue. Suddenly, the doors swung back. Lionel pushed his way past the frock-coated Negro doorman. His face was pale, and he breathed as heavily as a man who has just run a race.

Lionel grabbed his father-in-law by the arm. "Close the store! Send everyone home before it's too late."

"Too late for what?" Shaking himself free of Lionel's grip, Nathan opened the door and looked up and down Whitehall Street. He saw nothing out of the ordinary.

"I was just at Pryor and Decatur, ordering supplies for the studio. A crowd has gathered there, two or three hundred men, many of them drunk. They attack any Negro who comes in sight. They drag Negroes from streetcars and beat them. I saw one Negro messenger pulled off his bicycle and attacked. If the police had not rescued him, he would have been killed. The crowd grows bigger all the time with people flocking to it like pins drawn to a magnet."

Nathan's face turned as pale as Lionel's. "Alonzo! I must stop him before he leaves the house." He sought out Harry. With Lionel following, they took the elevator to the third floor. In Harry's office, Nathan placed a telephone call to his home. Leonora answered. When Nathan asked for Alonzo, Leonora said that the groom had already left. She asked if anything was wrong, and Nathan answered that he could have saved Alonzo a journey because Lionel had offered to drive him home.

While his father talked on the telephone, Harry explained the situation to his department heads. "Tell our customers what is happening. Ask them to leave as quickly as possible in case the trouble spreads south of the railroad tracks." Finished with the department heads, Harry sought out William. "Collect all the money and lock it in the safe. You can do a proper accounting when the trouble is over."

Accompanied by Jacob and Lionel, Nathan went downstairs and stood outside the store. A faint breeze carried the sounds of angry shouting from the junction of Pryor and Decatur. To Nathan's ear, the noise sounded greater than that made by just three hundred people. It was more like the roar of a capacity crowd at a Crackers' baseball game.

"Look!" Jacob pointed excitedly toward the viaduct. "There is Alonzo!"

His father and brother-in-law turned to look. Alonzo stood up in the low carriage, slapping the reins across the backs of the two horses that pulled it. A hundred yards behind the carriage raced a yelling crowd of two dozen men. Clubs and ax handles danced in their hands.

Nathan turned to the Negro doorman. "Go inside. Find the other Negro employees and tell them to leave immediately. Not by this entrance, but through the basement."

The doorman needed no second bidding. Weaving his way

past customers leaving the store, he ran inside to seek out the men who swept and cleaned. Nathan, Jacob, and Lionel looked north again. Alonzo was only fifty yards away, still urging more speed from the horses. At the last moment, Alonzo pulled back on the reins and shouted a command. The horses stopped. Fear widened Alonzo's face as he looked down at his employer.

"Climb aboard, Mister Nathan. We don't have time to waste!"

"I will climb aboard when I am good and ready. In the meantime, you will sit there and wait for me."

"Mister Nathan . . .!"

"Kindly do as I say. No mob will make me run."

While Alonzo glanced nervously over his shoulder, Nathan stood behind the victoria, arms folded resolutely across his chest. Jacob and Lionel joined him.

The first men slowed as they reached the victoria. As uncertainty replaced the blood lust in their eyes, Nathan grasped the moment. "If you men have nothing better to do than run amok and terrify my horses, I am sure that the judicial system could find you plenty of work on the prison farm."

One man stepped forward, a shaggy blond giant with red-rimmed eyes and greasy coveralls. The smell of liquor filled the air as he spoke. "We don't want your horses. We want that nigger driving them!"

"Why? What has he done to you?"

The blond man's mouth dropped open in amazement. Another rioter thrust his way to the front, a skinny red-bearded man who clutched a heavy hammer. "What business is it of yours?"

"It is every business of mine. That Negro belongs to me. If you diminish his value by as much as one cent, I will sue you all for everything you own. Do you want to see your wives and children going barefoot next winter because of your stupidity?"

The crowd backed off, leaving only the red-bearded man. His blue eyes bored into Nathan, trying to see if a weakness existed in the lined face that looked at this moment as if it were cast from granite. After thirty seconds, he shook his head and swung around. "Let him keep this nigger if it's so damned important to him. We can find plenty of others, can't we, boys?"

With a roar of assent, the mob started running toward the viaduct and the northern side of town. Nathan waited until they had passed from view before turning around. "Forgive me, Alonzo, for turning the clock back fifty years."

The groom's face was gray and sweaty. As he jumped down to open the door of the carriage, his body trembled. "You can turn the clock back as far as you want, Mister Nathan. You just talked those white men out of lynching me."

After boarding the victoria, Nathan addressed Jacob and Lionel. "Return to your families as quickly as you can. I will warrant this madness is not over yet."

Alonzo made a lengthy detour to avoid crossing the tracks near the city center. When the carriage eventually reached the house, Nathan saw Leonora waiting agitatedly on the porch. She came down the steps as quickly as she could and held onto him for the longest time before saying, "You lied to me, didn't you, when you telephoned about stopping Alonzo before he left the house. You did not mention the trouble at Decatur and Pryor streets."

Nathan kissed her gently on the forehead. "I did not want to alarm you. Besides, you can see that Alonzo is safe and sound. Whatever trouble there is stayed out of our way."

William reached home an hour later, having ridden the electric trolley after he, Harry, and Jacob had closed the store. He told his father that the mob had grown. It numbered at least a thousand men now.

The telephone rang. Nathan answered. The caller was Jacob. His home on South Pryor Street was closest to the trouble spot. He could keep the remainder of the family informed. "Men run up and down the street, knocking on the doors of houses to demand that the residents turn over their Negro servants."

"Have they knocked on your house?"

"Fifteen minutes ago. I confronted them with a shotgun, and they ran."

"Are the police in evidence?"

"Their presence is spotty. I think they have more to do at the center of the riot."

In the earpiece, Nathan heard hammering. "More visitors!" Jacob shouted. Nathan stayed on the line, listening. A sudden explosion made him drop the earpiece. By the time he picked it up, Jacob was back.

"What was that?"

"Helen saw them off with a blast of buckshot over their heads. Every house in the street is like an armed camp. Guns poke from every door and window. They will not come back again."

The moment the call finished, Nathan summoned the operator to connect him with Harry's home on Capitol Avenue. Ella answered, assuring her father-in-law that their neighborhood was peaceful. Nathan remained by the telephone, placing regular calls to his children to check they were in no danger. When at last he heeded Leonora and went to bed, it was past midnight. He fell asleep, satisfied that the turmoil had been contained.

Only when he arose on Sunday morning did he learn how wrong he was. The morning newspapers were full of the mob violence that had turned downtown Atlanta into a slaughterhouse. At Marietta and Forsyth, two Negro barbers had been hauled from their shop and murdered. A Negro porter had been killed near Union Depot, while another Negro caught alone on the Forsyth Street bridge had been beaten to death. The bloodiest attack of all had come at Marietta and Peachtree where a crowd of rioters had boarded a streetcar in search of Negro passengers. When the mob left, seven Negroes lay on the floor, three of them bludgeoned to death.

As Nathan digested the news reports, Jacob telephoned to say he had just returned from touring the center of town. Debris covered the streets. Vehicles had been overturned, shop windows smashed. Six hundred soldiers from nearby Fort McPherson stood guard to maintain order. Despite the military presence, the unrest continued for two more days. When peace finally returned to Atlanta, twelve people—ten black and two white—were dead and seventy injured.

On the following Friday, there was no doubt in anyone's mind what the topic would be when the men and women of the Solomon family divided after dinner. As the men took seats on the porch, Jacob remained standing. He wasted no time on a preamble.

"In a civilized city, no woman should ever have to resort to firing a shotgun to protect her home and person from a drunken mob. The events of the past week were terrifying, and neither Helen nor I ever want to witness such fearful sights again. Whether or not New York waits with open arms"—he looked from his father to Harry—"for a man who can repair elevators, that is where I am taking Helen and Burton. I will not have my family exposed to the terror that has torn Atlanta apart and made us an unenviable front-page story in the world's newspapers."

Nathan nodded. "I cannot find it in my heart to blame anyone for wanting to move their family far away from such madness. Lionel? Have you and Louise talked this matter over?"

"I am already negotiating the sale of the Selig Studio."

"What about your children?"

"Albert and Aaron have said they will accompany us to New York. Harriet will do whatever her husband wishes to do."

Saul Jaeger, Harriet's husband, sat next to Lionel. He was a short, chubby man with thinning black hair and a rosy face. "My parents are elderly. They need help with their hardware store. I am an only child, so I will stay, but if something like this should ever happen again . . ."

"Harry?" Nathan had no doubt what his oldest son's answer would be. Harry would stay with the Crystal Palace until the store's walls came tumbling down.

"My family will remain. Benjamin works in the store, so does my son-in-law, Daniel. Their lives are here, as is my own."

"William?"

The youngest son smiled sheepishly. "Where would I go?"

The breakup of the family happened so quickly that Nathan and Leonora barely had time to feel sad. Two houses and a photography business were sold, and within three weeks of the race riot the families of Jacob and Louise were ready to leave for New York. Only when Nathan bade farewell to his daughter and middle son at the newly opened Terminal Station did he fully understand what was happening. As the train jerked into motion, Leonora saw him blink back tears.

"You will all come visit us in our new homes!" Louise called out as she leaned from the window of the slowly moving train.

"I am too old to make such a journey," Nathan protested.

Jacob thrust his head and shoulders through the window beside his sister. "Then we will return every New Year's Day for your birthday! All of us!"

"God has witnessed that promise," Leonora said. "You cannot go back on it now."

"We will not."

Harry reached up to clasp the hands of his brother and sister. He walked beside the train for a few steps. "Like our father I cannot find it in my heart to blame you for wanting to do what you think is best for your families. Good luck!" He released their hands as the train's speed increased.

Nathan reached for Leonora's arm as the train rolled out of the depot. "Will we ever see them again?" he asked softly.

"You heard what they said. They will return on every New Year's Day to help you celebrate your birthday."

Nathan laughed as the absurdity of such a promise made itself clear. "I am seventy-four years old, Lally. How many trips do they expect to make?"

Within three weeks, letters arrived at Edgewood Avenue.

Nathan read them and passed them on to Leonora. "Our children have settled well into their new lives."

Leonora shook her head. "Read them for me, Nathan."

Nathan fell back onto a response he had used when they were young. "A young lady should be able to read for herself, Lally."

Leonora removed her gold-rimmed glasses. "My eyes are tired, Nathan. Please tell me what they say."

Nathan took Jacob's letter first. As he scanned the words, he realized that he had not seen Leonora read anything for several weeks, since long before the race riot. Were her eyes failing her? He found it difficult to believe because his own sight was still so remarkably acute. "Jacob, Helen, and Burton are staying with Helen's parents until they find a home of their own. Helen's parents are shopkeepers like ourselves. They sell theatrical merchandise. And Jacob has found employment as an assistant radio operator with a wireless-telegraph company."

"Assistant radio operator? What does he operate?"

Nathan scoured the letter, trying to find an explanation. "It is a gadget to transmit noises—or signals, as Jacob calls them—through the empty air."

"Without a wire?" Leonora could grasp the concept of a telephone, where conversations were transmitted through a cable, but Jacob's new job mystified here.

"That is what he claims here."

"Tell me what Louise and Lionel do. I might be able to better understand them."

Nathan switched letters. "They live in Brooklyn. Lionel works for a company called Technograph. The company makes motion pictures, he writes, at a studio out in the wilds of Flatbush, wherever that is, and it is more exciting than he had ever imagined. He tells us to mention to Harry that not only will motion pictures continue to be used as chasers for vaudeville, they will even outlast vaudeville."

"Perhaps," murmured Leonora, "God will allow us to live long enough to see one of Lionel's motion pictures."

Jacob and Louise kept the promise they had made as the train carrying their families pulled out from the terminal. On New Year's Day they returned to Atlanta to celebrate their father's seventy-fifth birthday. They came back again on New Year's Day 1908, when Jacob told his father that he had been promoted to radio operator. The new position entailed sacrifices, Jacob admitted, but he and Helen both agreed that they were worthwhile. When Nathan asked his son what kind of sacrifices, Jacob explained that he spent a lot of time away from home, in isolated outposts and on ships as an operator for the shipping companies which used his firm's radio system.

Nathan did not like what he heard. "Since when did you allow this radio mumbo jumbo to take precedence over your family?"

"My family still comes first. They are the reason I do this work. I am getting in at the beginning of an industry that will be bigger even than the railroads. One day, my family will live in luxury because of sacrifices made now."

Nathan let the subject drop. If the wife agreed, what right did the father have to argue? Maybe there was something to all this sending of messages across hundreds of miles of empty air. Like Leonora, he understood none of it, but obviously Jacob did, and that was all that mattered.

Later that year, Nathan's interest turned once more to politics as Graham Courtney, after four years in the State Senate, ran for Governor of Georgia. Once again, his supporters represented industrialists and business leaders, men who wanted to see Georgia in the forefront of the technological advances that were sweeping the country. Courtney's populist opponent was backed by the people who feared such progress, and their most strident voice belonged to George Hopkinson.

Hopkinson's editorial onslaught against Courtney was even

more slanderous than it had been four years earlier, during the State Senate campaign. To the readers of *Awaken*, Courtney was the candidate of race-mixers, the candidate of the Vatican, and the candidate of New York Jewish interests who were intent on stealing the jobs of white Christian Americans by importing hundreds of thousands of Eastern European coreligionists who would work for next to nothing.

Even when Courtney's populist opponent repeated Hopkinson's charges, Clarissa's husband refused to lower himself to such standards. He ran his campaign on a simple promise—to take Georgia forward into the twentieth century instead of letting it slip back into the dark ages. When the votes were counted, Nathan knew he would be sending Clarissa's next Christmas present to the executive mansion at Peachtree and Cain.

On New Year's Day, only Louise traveled from New York to Atlanta to celebrate her father's seventy-seventh birthday. Jacob was unable to come. He did not want to leave Helen who was expecting their second child. Louise told her father that both Jacob and Helen were hoping that he and Leonora would travel up to New York in the spring when the baby was born.

Nathan looked to Leonora. "Would you like to make such a lengthy journey?"

"How was the weather when you left, Louise?"

"Snow covered the ground and an icy wind filled the streets."

Leonora shivered. "It does not sound very appealing."

"It will be far nicer in the spring," Louise promised.

Nathan knew he could endure such a long rail journey, but he worried about Leonora. Perhaps it was his imagination, but she seemed frailer. The bouncy curl had gone from her gray hair, leaving it thin and stringy, and her eyesight was deteriorating steadily. She wore glasses with stronger lenses, but they did little. When Nathan saw her perusing the newspaper, he knew she was only scanning the headlines and gazing at the pictures. The small type of the stories defeated her. When she found a headline that kindled her interest, she asked Nathan to read the applicable article for her. If he were out, she waited for him to return. Occasionally he wondered if she recalled how he used to read for her at their uncle's shop on Ludgate Hill. Life had come full cycle.

"Are trains comfortable?" Leonora asked.

"Inside our own compartment you would never know that you were not staying at the finest hotel. Unless, of course, you tried to go out for a walk in the fresh air."

Leonora nodded her head. "I think I would like to go. God willing, I shall."

"God willing, you shall indeed."

Nathan's eighth grandchild was born at the beginning of May, a baby girl named Rhea by her parents. Nathan and Leonora made train reservations the instant they learned of the birth. A week after the child was born, they were in New York, taking turns to cradle Rhea in their arms, smiling down at the round red face with its solemn brown eyes and button nose, and admiring the golden ringlets.

While in New York, Nathan and Leonora were feted by Lionel and Jacob. Two days after their arrival, Lionel took them out to Flatbush, where they spent the day watching a western being filmed in Technograph's glass-roofed studio. In the first scene, a fight between two cowboys was so authentic that Leonora jumped in fright when they fired their guns. Lionel seemed to have a dozen different responsibilities. He played a minor role in the film. When not acting, he strode around the set with a megaphone yelling instructions. Every so often, he stood by the stationary camera, critically surveyed the actors on the set, and shouted: "Ready! Shoot!"

During a break, Lionel explained that after two years with Technograph, he had worked his way up from cameraman to a director. "We make seven or eight films a week here, one- or two-reelers using our own company of actors. If we find we're a body short, I can always fill in."

"And are you happy?"

"Never happier. I don't make as much money as I did at the Selig Studio, but I will. One day I will own my own film company, and then the Selig Studio will seem like peanuts."

"And your sons? Albert and Aaron? What do they do?"

Lionel laughed. "You mean you did not even know your own grandsons?" He snapped his fingers and two young men in cowboy outfits joined him. Nathan gasped. He had just watched these two face each other in a gunfight no more than ten yards away, and he had not recognized either of them.

"A long time ago, I planned for my children to take over the Selig Studio," Lionel said. "Now they will take over a motion picture studio that I will open sometime in the next few years. Not only Aaron and Albert, but Harriet and Saul if they want to leave Atlanta."

The next day, Jacob gave Nathan and Leonora a demonstration of his skills. He took them to a radio station located on the top floor of a tall building on lower Broadway where he donned earphones and began transmitting. Nathan looked at Leonora and smiled. "Now we know why Jacob and Lionel came to New York. Lionel, so he could pretend to be a cowboy and shout 'Ready! Shoot!' through a megaphone, and Jacob because he wanted to cover his ears like it is the middle of winter and play a one-finger symphony on a telegraph key."

He fell silent as Jacob swiveled in the chair and held up a hand. "Please! I cannot hear the signals!"

"What signals?"

Jacob beckoned his father to come close. Removing the earphones, he held them to Nathan's ear. "Those signals."

Nathan listened, then stepped aside for Leonora to hear. "I hear crickets singing in the middle of the night," she said.

Jacob took back the earphones. As he listened, he jotted down a series of dots and dashes before transmitting his own message in the same unintelligible code. When he finished, he read through the message he had received. "Those crickets you hear are on board the *Atlantic Star*, which is in the middle of its

547

maiden voyage from Southampton to New York. It will dock in New York in three days' time."

"You can contact a ship in the middle of the Atlantic Ocean?" Nathan asked in astonishment.

"This is nineteen-hundred and nine. Eight years have passed already since the first radio signal was successfully transmitted from England to Newfoundland. Many ships have radio now. They are no longer alone in the middle of the sea."

Three days later, Nathan and Leonora accompanied Jacob and Helen to the dock to watch the *Atlantic Star* berth at the end of her maiden voyage. A carnival atmosphere prevailed. While sirens of smaller craft blasted a welcome to the liner, fire hoses sent ribbons of water soaring into the air. Three-year-old Burton, held securely by his father, jumped up and down in excitement. His baby sister, less than two weeks old, slept peacefully in a baby carriage through all the pandemonium.

Jacob pointed up at the liner's towering superstructure. "Do you see the antenna? That is what plucks signals from the air."

Nathan saw, but Leonora strained her failing eyes to no avail. Even through her stronger glasses, the upper area of the *Atlantic Star*'s superstructure was indistinct. She could make out objects at close range, although not well enough to read, but distances defeated her; the farther an object, the more blurred it became. She sought to turn the discussion away from the antenna she could not see. "Look how large the ship is, Nathan. It is just as well it has this wireless radio. If something happened, God forbid, help could be summoned and hundreds of lives could be saved."

Jacob laughed. "On a ship this size, the figure would be closer to thousands."

Leonora held Nathan's hand and squeezed it gently. "Do you remember the boat we sailed on? It was no bigger than . . . than one of this ship's lifeboats."

Nathan squeezed back. "It was a lot bigger than that, Lally, but you are allowed a slight exaggeration after fifty-eight years." Gazing up at the liner, he wished he were thirty or forty years younger. He would love to cross the ocean once more, and take Leonora with him. They were both too old for such travel now, even on a floating palace such as this. The return journey to Atlanta was all they could manage.

He looked again at the antenna and reconciled it with the signals he had heard through Jacob's earphones. There was so much waiting for his children and his grandchildren to see and hear and experience, and he envied them deeply.

Chapter Thirty

Soon after returning to Atlanta from New York, Leonora's sight, which had been deteriorating gradually, took a sharp turn for the worse. Outlines of objects grew more indistinct. Colors became difficult to identify. Greens merged with yellows and blues, and slowly turned to gray and then to black. At last, on a sunny August day, as she shared with Nathan a wicker settee on the front porch, Leonora admitted aloud what she had only whispered to herself.

"Nathan, I fear that I am losing my sight completely."

The words came as no surprise to Nathan. He had known for a long time that Leonora's eyesight was deserting her. To hear her make the simple confession, though—to know that she had resigned herself to going blind—tore at his heart. He tried to find words of consolation, but all he could manage was a choked, incoherent snatch of a sentence. Leonora reached for his hand.

"Do not feel sad for me. I have been fortunate enough to see far more wonderful sights than most people. Seventy-five years have passed in front of these eyes. They are tired, that is all, and they need to rest."

Nathan heard the rumble of a streetcar approaching along Edgewood Avenue. He turned his head to look. From forty yards away, he could discern the number of the Georgia Electric Company car. His own sight was as sharp as it had ever been. If only it were possible to give one of his good eyes to Leonora. . . .

"When my sight is gone, Nathan, will you be my eyes?"

"Of course. I will study a dictionary for an hour every day so that I may be able to describe objects in words so colorful that you will feel you are seeing them for yourself."

"Thank you. I could ask for no more."

A tear trickled from the corner of Nathan's left eye as he peered a few months into the future. How well would he be able to describe the looks of his first great-grandchild, the baby Benjamin and Caroline were expecting in October? And a month or so after that, the first child of Rose and her husband Daniel Morris? "Lally . . ." Nathan's voice was hushed, as though he could not believe his own words. "In just a few months, our Harry will be a grandfather twice over. And Ella— the grocer's daughter he married what seems like only months ago—will be a grandmother. Until now, I never realized just how old I had grown, and just how quickly seventy-seven years have passed."

He closed his eyes for an instant and captured the image of Harry's wedding as Lionel had once captured it on a wet collodion plate. So many of the older generation were gone now. Miriam. The Seligs. Max Hirsch, who had died the week after Nathan and Leonora returned from New York, struck down by a heart attack while arguing with a wholesaler at the produce market. And Leah Hirsch, who had gone to bed the very next night, never to awaken. So many had gone, and so many had appeared to take their places. Life went on.

"Do you remember, Nathan, how Ella replied to your suggestion that she buy her clothes only at the Crystal Palace?"

"I do. She told me that her husband worked hard for his money and she would spend it wherever she liked!" Nathan began to smile at the memory, but the expression faded as the image of Leonora's blindness filled his thoughts. Mere words, no matter how colorful and descriptive, could never compensate for sight. Still, Nathan vowed to do his best to fill Leonora's mind with the visions her tired eyes could never see.

Nathan's routine changed. Instead of going in to the Crystal Palace each morning to greet customers and keep an eye on store operations, he stayed at home until midday. He spent an hour reading stories from the newspaper to Leonora. Being able to censor the news, he chose only stories that would not dishearten her. He told her of the discovery of the North Pole, and the altercation between Dr. Frederick Cook and Commander Robert Peary over who had reached it first. He described the flight by an aviator named Louis Blériot across the English Channel. He read to her of George M. Cohan's new musical *The Man Who Owns Broadway,* and said he would learn when the music would be available; perhaps Ella would like to play some of the tunes for the family. The news he did not share with her included the bloody battles in the steel industry between striking workers and law enforcement officials, the underground explosion that killed four hundred miners at Cherry, Illinois, and British fears that Germany was preparing for war.

After reading the newspaper each morning, Nathan had Alonzo prepare the victoria carriage. As the internal-combustion engine made inroads in Atlanta, horse-drawn vehicles were losing popularity. Both Harry and William drove cars, Harry a Pierce-Arrow, and William a Maxwell roadster, and the Atlanta Taxicab Company had started operation that year with eight vehicles. Despite the move to mechanical propulsion, Nathan still preferred the sedate comfort of the victoria, and Leonora, to whom sound was doubly important now, favored the clip-clop of hooves to the rattle and thunder of an engine. They rode around for an hour or two with Nathan describing at length even the most insignificant sights. Only after they returned to the house did Nathan have Alonzo drive him to the store. In the evening, after dinner, Nathan returned to being Leonora's eye by reading aloud a chapter or two from a book.

At the end of October, Nathan's oldest grandson Benjamin and his wife, Caroline, became parents. Not to one child, but to two. Nathan's excitement as he described the twin boy and girl communicated itself to Leonora. When he talked of blue eyes, she could see blue eyes! When his words depicted tiny hands with delicate fingers and flawlessly shaped nails, she could see them perfectly! Five weeks later, at the beginning of December, she listened just as avidly to Nathan's description of the baby girl born to Rose and Daniel. As Leonora felt Nathan place her hand on the baby's head, so she could feel the warmth and smoothness of the skin, she swore she could visualize every member of this youngest generation with her mind as clearly as she could ever picture them with her eyes.

"Two of our married grandchildren have children of their own," she told Nathan the following morning as Alonzo took them on their daily drive. The air was chill, and they sat with a blanket across their legs beneath the opened top of the victoria. "Why do Harriet and her husband Saul wait? They have been married three years already, you know."

"Perhaps children are not in their plans just yet," Nathan answered, amused by Leonora's impatience. "They both work at Saul's family's hardware store on Decatur Street. They might feel that business is not good enough for them to begin a family just yet."

"Saul should have joined the Crystal Palace. Harry would have found a position for him. He would have earned enough there to start a family."

"Too many family members in a business can lead to the ruination of both the family and the business."

"Perhaps you are right." Leonora breathed in deeply of the cool air. "I sense rain," she said, and Nathan knew she was probably correct. With the fading of her sight had come increased awareness in other areas. Her hearing, for a woman in her seventies, was acute, and she seemed to be able to sense changes in the weather long before anyone else could.

On New Year's Day, when Nathan turned seventy-eight, the entire family gathered at Edgewood Avenue. When Louise remarked that the journey from New York seemed to pass quicker each year, Jacob pointed out that the travel time between New York and Atlanta would be sliced in half when men made the trip by air. All the adults swore immediately that they would never be caught dead in a flying machine. All except Jacob, that is, who said that not only would he ride in one, he would learn to operate it!

While family members exchanged news, Nathan sat beside Leonora describing the changes he noticed in the children and grandchildren he had not seen since his visit to New York the previous spring. At forty, Jacob showed gray in his dark brown hair. When Nathan suggested that his middle son might take after him, Leonora laughed and said the gray came from worry over all the ships with which he was constantly in radio contact.

"Helen looks almost girlish next to Jacob, with her wavy brown hair and petite figure."

"She is entitled to look almost girlish, Nathan. She is ten years younger than Jacob."

"Rhea has grown tremendously since we were in New York. Then she was a few days old, and now she is a chubby, happy baby with ringlets of fat circling her arms and legs."

Leonora laughed at the vision that appeared in her head. "What of Burton? How has he changed?"

"He has grown two or three inches. You know, I think he looks like the image of Jacob as a child."

"You mean he has become an intense little boy who cannot keep still for a second?"

Nathan took his eyes off Jacob's son and looked at Leonora. Was she fooling him? Pretending to be blind when she was not? No. He dismissed the idea as ludicrous. No one would pretend to be so handicapped. He was doing his job well, that was all.

"How about Louise and Lionel, and their two sons?" Leonora whispered. "Have they altered since we saw them in New York?"

"Louise's brown hair has more gray in it now, but her green eyes shine just as brightly. I think she looks"—Nathan paused as a lump momentarily blocked his throat—"as her mother

would have looked at such an age. She is a beautiful woman."
He flicked his gaze to Lionel, who stood talking with William.
"Lionel has put on weight. The watch and chain he wears
across his front is more prominent now. Albert, too, seems
heavier, but Aaron is just as thin as ever."

"How old are they now?"

"Albert is twenty-seven, and his brother is a year younger."

Leonora drew in her breath. "They will be marrying any day
now and starting their own families. Soon, this house will not
be big enough to hold all the guests to your birthday parties."

Nathan laughed. "How much longer do you think these
parties will be necessary, Lally?"

"Long enough for Jacob to be able to operate his own flying
machine and bring everyone down from New York with him."

The reunion contained one major news item. After talking to
Louise and Lionel, Harriet and Saul Jaeger approached Nathan
and Leonora. "When Benjamin and Caroline, then Rose and
Daniel had children, did you wonder why Saul and I waited?"
Harriet asked.

"Not at all," Nathan answered as he gently squeezed
Leonora's hand. It was too bad, he thought, that she could not
see the smile that danced around his lips and eyes.

"Saul and I dearly want a child, but so far we have been
unlucky. So we are adopting a child."

Quite suddenly, Harriet began to cry. Saul wrapped his arms
around her, holding her until the tears had passed. "My wife
cries," Saul told Nathan and Leonora, "because she feared that
her parents and grandparents would not love an adopted child
as dearly as they would love a child that carried their own
blood. Please assure her, as her mother and father have already
done, that such a fear is baseless."

Nathan drew Harriet closer. Taking Leonora's arms, he
placed them on his granddaughter's shoulders. Leonora spoke
softly to the young woman she could not see. "Any child you
and Saul call your own, we will regard as our own, too."

The annual reunion ended on the second day of the year,

when the families of Jacob and Louise boarded the train for the return journey to New York. Alonzo drove Nathan and Leonora to Terminal Station to see them leave. Leonora listened to the snorting of the locomotive and the rumble of the wheels, and in her imagination saw the train pulling out of the depot with Jacob's and Louise's families leaning from the windows and waving. She felt she hadn't missed a thing. Nathan had truly become her eyes.

Leonora grew to rely more and more on Nathan, but instead of feeling like a blind person forced to depend upon the sighted, she regarded herself as lucky. How many other women had such a caring, loving husband to read for them, to color the birds whose songs she heard, and to describe in careful detail the thousand scenes she could no longer see for herself?

When a rare ice storm struck Atlanta in February, Leonora thrilled to Nathan's description of tree branches wreathed in shimmering jewels. In April, on Confederate Memorial Day, she held tightly onto Nathan's arm as they walked slowly along a Peachtree Street festooned with gray and blue bunting. When Nathan identified the colors of Southern regiments which lined the street, Leonora recalled earlier Confederate Memorial Days, when her own eyes had been her guide.

"The reviewing stand faces Five Points Square, does it not?" she asked.

"It does, surrounded by the flags of Georgia regiments."

"Are the Georgia flags still those that were flown during the War Between The States?"

"They are, Lally, still torn and rent by shells fired at Gettysburg and Shiloh."

Leonora breathed in deeply. On such days, it was so easy to remember Atlanta as it had been forty-five years before, and to recall New Orleans beneath the heel of Beast Butler.

Although Nathan had never worn a uniform, he considered himself as much a veteran as any man who had fought for the lost cause. In past years, he had marched, but this year he refused to leave Leonora. Instead, he stood and watched, describing for Leonora the passage of the veterans—whose number decreased every year as time took a toll Union guns could not—in front of the reviewing stand from which Governor Graham Courtney saluted them.

In the first week of May, Harry masterminded a special promotion centered around the World's Fair which was taking place in the Belgian capital of Brussels. For every day of the week the promotion lasted, the Crystal Palace staged different foreign exhibits. Leonora attended every one, listening to Nathan describe English china, French silks, Italian lace, and Irish crystal. She did not need his assistance to taste the multitude of dishes created in cooking demonstrations, or to listen to music played by performers from half a dozen different countries.

The international week ended on Saturday with a special presentation of food, fashion, and music. Knowing how big a crowd the final day would draw, Leonora decided not to go. Even with Nathan's arm to guide her, she felt uncertain among crowds. Nathan spent most of the day in the store. As he walked around, one detail struck him. Not once did he see an idle sales clerk. This day was the busiest in the history of the Crystal Palace, busier even than the day he had stood outside to welcome his friends to the grand opening. Every hour he broke away from his inspection to go up to the third floor and use the telephone in Harry's office to describe the excitement to Leonora.

After each call to Leonora, Nathan popped his head into William's office to learn how his youngest son was faring under the pressure. The financial center of the store always looked the same. Sunshine streamed in through the skylight while William, eyes covered by a green shade, made the adding machine dance. His assistant, a pretty red-haired girl named Valerie Riley, was equally busy. Whenever Nathan looked in, Valerie was conscientiously copying figures into ledgers, licking the end of her pen as she checked and double-checked each entry. Only once, midway through the afternoon, did Nathan notice a change. William's shirt collar was open. His necktie lay discarded on the desk. The youngest Solomon brother had forsaken formality for comfort.

"Hectic day?" Nathan asked.

William removed the eyeshade and used it as a fan, waving it back and forth in front of his face. "The most hectic I have ever known. At the rate customers are pouring in to the store, it will be past midnight before I get everything balanced. I will have to cancel my bridge game tonight."

"I will work late, Mister William," Valerie offered. Her yellow dress caught the sun pouring through the skylight and bounced it back onto the opposite wall, where it spread like buttercup dust. "I will stay until it is time to catch the last trolley to Decatur. My parents won't mind as long as they know where I am."

William acknowledged the girl's offer with a smile. Valerie did not expect to work overtime for nothing, but it was good to know that she was willing to put in extra hours.

"You need not work past midnight," Nathan told his son. "Tomorrow is Sunday. The store is closed. You can play bridge tonight and come in tomorrow to bring the books up to date."

Valerie withdrew the earlier offer. "I am afraid I cannot work then. On Sunday, I attend church."

"I would not dream of asking you to do otherwise," William told the girl. "We will do what we can tonight, then I will finish alone tomorrow."

Nathan left, thinking of the girl. She was only fifteen, and combined intelligence with a pleasant nature and a willingness to work. Her parents operated a small dairy farm in the town of Decatur, six miles to the east. Instead of working with cows, Valerie had chosen commerce. Nathan believed the Crystal Palace had done well to hire her straight from school, before she could be snapped up by another store that recognized her qualities.

Just before six, Alonzo drove Nathan home in the victoria

carriage. Sitting down for dinner with Leonora, Nathan told Fanny, the housekeeper, to remove one of the three places she had set because William would not be home until much later. After eating, Nathan gave Leonora a synopsis of everything that had happened at the store that day, then read aloud two chapters from Ellen Glasgow's *Battle-Ground*. Although both Leonora and Nathan had read the book before, Glasgow's studies of Virginia at the time of the War Between The States made a second reading just as enjoyable as the first. The only disturbing note to Nathan was the sympathy the author showed to an agrarian people whose way of life was disappearing. As he read, he could not help thinking of Georgia's uprooted tenant farmers, whose misery was so cynically exploited by George Hopkinson.

At ten-thirty, when Nathan and Leonora retired, William had not returned home. Both fell asleep almost immediately, but the sound of an automobile roused Nathan shortly after midnight. He heard the closing of the front door, and William's footsteps as he climbed to the wing of the house he used for his own.

The next morning, William did not come down until after breakfast had been served. Followed by Suzannah, who carried a tray with a cup of coffee and two slices of toast, William walked out onto the porch, where Nathan sat reading to Leonora from that morning's newspaper. As Suzannah set the tray on a wicker table, William bade his father and Leonora a good morning.

"Did you work until midnight?" Nathan asked. He saw that his son was already fully dressed, wearing a dark gray business suit and tie, as though he intended to return to the store the instant he finished breakfast.

"Very nearly. Valerie left shortly after nine, and I put in another two and a half hours. The cleaners must have been glad to see me go, I'll tell you. Twice they came into my office expecting it to be empty, and twice I had to ask them to leave.

I suspect the night watchman was glad to see the back of me as well. Once I was gone, he could sleep with impunity."

"You do Sam Joyner an injustice," Leonora said. "He is the first Negro we ever hired for such a responsible position, and we hired him precisely because he was responsible."

William shrugged in acceptance of the rebuke. Even without sight, there wasn't much that Leonora missed. He sat down and began to eat, chewing quickly on the toast and washing it down with coffee. Nathan watched, puzzled. There was something different this morning about William, something missing. Only as William finished the hasty meal, and stood up to leave, did Nathan realize what troubled him.

"Where is your gold stickpin? You always wear it."

William clutched at his necktie, the same tie he had worn the previous day. Without a word, he turned around and left the porch. He returned ten minutes later, lips drawn into a tight, agitated line. "I cannot find it anywhere. I looked on my chest of drawers, in the pockets of the suit I wore yesterday. I even checked the shirt I threw into the laundry, to see whether I had inadvertently pinned it to the fabric."

"You removed your tie yesterday, while you were working," Nathan said. "I saw it on the desk."

"I put it on again as I prepared to leave for home." William gazed up at the sky as though trying to recollect every moment of the previous night. "I was so tired last night that I do not remember whether I pinned the tie to my shirt or not."

Seeing how upset William had become at the possibility of losing the gold stickpin, Nathan said, "It will turn up soon enough. And if it doesn't, I will get you another one just like it. You deserve something for working so hard this week."

Nathan's attempted absolution failed to cheer William. The stickpin had been a gift, a memento of a specific occasion. No substitute could ever truly replace it. "I had better be going, otherwise I will be working until midnight again. With any luck, I will find the stickpin sitting on my desk."

From inside the house, Nathan heard the telephone ring.

Moments later, Suzannah emerged onto the porch. For once, her infectious smile was absent. "Mister Nathan, your son, Mister Harry, wishes to speak to you. He says it's urgent. Real urgent. About the store."

Nathan's first fear was that there had been a fire at the Crystal Palace. He called for William to wait, then walked quickly to the front hall, where the telephone was located. When he returned two minutes later to the porch, his face was white. Something far worse than a fire had occurred.

"What did Harry want?" Leonora asked.

"The store was broken into during the night. The police notified Harry. William will drive me to Whitehall Street, where Harry will meet us. I will return as quickly as possible."

William waited for his father to climb into the Maxwell, then asked him what had been stolen. For a few seconds, as the Maxwell rolled along Edgewood Avenue, Nathan offered no response. When he did eventually speak, his voice was low.

"Nothing was stolen. I told your stepmother there had been a break-in because I did not want her to worry any more than was absolutely necessary. She will know what happened soon enough, once the newspapers get hold of it."

"Get hold of what?" William decided his father was making no sense at all. "I do not understand what you are getting at."

"Sam Joyner was making his rounds this morning. He went down to the basement, to the boiler room. Behind one of the furnaces, he found a body. A woman's body. She had been murdered. He alerted the police, who notified Harry."

They reached the Crystal Palace in record time. Parked outside was a black Hudson with two uniformed patrol officers lounging against the hood. As William brought the Maxwell to a halt behind the Hudson, Harry's black Pierce-Arrow appeared from the other direction. One of the patrolmen led the three men into the store and down to the boiler room. Four furnaces supplied heat to the store. By the furthest furnace, peering at an object neither Nathan nor his two sons could yet see, stood Sam Joyner and two other men. One was tall and dark-haired, the other overweight and bald. All three men turned at the sound of approaching footsteps. The watchman appeared terrified. His dark skin had a grayish hue, and his hands shook visibly.

The bald man introduced himself as Detective Joseph Hill, and his colleague as Detective Tom Green. "Sorry to drag you all the way down here on a Sunday morning, but we've got a murder on our hands. We're hoping you might be able to give us some help in solving it."

"Supplying us with the victim's identity would be a good start," said the other man.

Nathan sucked in his breath as he stepped forward to look. No wonder Sam Joyner shook with fear. The murdered woman was white. Harry joined his father. He closed his eyes and gritted his teeth at the sight before him. A piece of rope was knotted tightly around the victim's throat. Her eyes were fixed wide open. Her tongue poked obscenely between lips that had been ground bloody by her own teeth in the futile struggle for life.

William was the last to look. His eyes did not take in the rope, the victim's discolored, bloody face, or her tightly clenched hands. All he could see was the dress hiked up over her hips. The bright yellow dress that yesterday had caught sunbeams streaming through the skylight and bounced them back onto the opposite wall like buttercup dust. He turned around and threw up a cup of coffee and two slices of toast.

"Valerie," Harry whispered. "Her name is Valerie Riley."

"She work here?" Detective Hill asked.

"Yes. She was employed in my brother's office."

Both detectives turned to the white-faced, perspiring William. "Can you tell us where and when you last saw her?"

William felt faint, sure he would be sick again. He removed his thick glasses and wiped his face. His knees trembled, and he held on to his brother's arm for support. "I last saw her just after nine on Saturday night. Upstairs, as she left my office."

"The store was no longer open for business?"

"No."

"Why was she leaving so late?"

"She was working overtime. We had been very busy and needed the extra time to finish up the books. I was coming in today to complete the work."

"Who else was in the store?"

William searched his memory and could find only one name. He looked at Sam Joyner. The Negro night watchman flung himself onto the floor, clutching at William's legs. "No, Mister William! It wasn't me that did this! Don't let them take me, please!"

The two detectives reached down to jerk Joyner upright. As Nathan listened to the Negro's continuing screams of denial, he, like the police, had little doubt that the murderer was already in custody.

While Harry remained in the basement, watching the police go about their business, William went up to his third-floor office to see if he had left the gold stickpin on his desk. It was not there. As he drove his father home, William decided not to finish the books today. He had no stomach for work after seeing his pretty red-haired assistant lying in the boiler room. He would get back to the books tomorrow, or the day after. No one would blame him for being late under such circumstances.

Leonora was still sitting on the porch when they reached the house. The instant she heard footsteps, she demanded to know about the robbery. Nathan waited until he was seated beside her before explaining the true nature of the crime.

"The police have taken Sam Joyner into custody."

"Have they charged him with the murder?"

"I do not know, but it can be only a matter of time until they do so."

Leonora shook her head in sorrow. Would the first Negro given a responsible position by the Crystal Palace turn out to be a murderer? "If he did kill the girl, why would he alert the police to the crime? Surely he would be the first person they would suspect."

"Who knows what occurs in the mind of a man who could commit such evil? Perhaps he thought the police would not believe a man could be so stupid as to call attention to his own crime, and therefore they would not suspect him." He closed his eyes and pictured the dismal scene again. No punishment was too severe for a man who could perform such a barbaric act.

Leonora turned to where William sat. "The attack must have taken place moments after poor Valerie left your office. Did you hear nothing at all?"

"I was too engrossed in my work to hear anything." He shook his head slowly. Last night was a complete blur. He had worked so hard and come home so tired that he remembered little. He did not recall driving back to Inman Park. For God's sake, he could not even remember where he had put his gold stickpin, and that was his most treasured possession. He never felt fully dressed unless he wore it. He looked down to see the fingers of his right hand stroking his tie, seeking the piece of jewelry they always found there. Standing up, he said that he was going to his room, to search again for the missing stickpin. Nathan made no comment. He knew his son was seeking something to take his mind off the gruesome sight in the boiler room.

At one-thirty, Harry telephoned to tell his father that the girl's body had been removed so that a medical examination could be performed. "The two detectives, Hill and Green, remain here, seeking evidence. They told me they are certain that they have the right man, and they expect a full confession before the day is out."

"That is when the police department's real problems will begin," Nathan said. "When they have to protect Sam Joyner from a lynch mob."

* * *

Joseph Hill and Tom Green drove out to Inman Park at eight-thirty that night. The housekeeper took the detectives through to the parlor, where Nathan and William played chess, while Leonora sat by a phonograph, listening to Caruso sing "Vesti La Giubba."

Detective Hill took charge. "Sorry to interrupt your Sunday evening—"

Nathan cut him short. "You seem to spend a great deal of your time apologizing to people. I understand from my oldest son that you are certain you hold the right man and expect him to confess. Is that why you are here, to inform us you have the confession, and that the case is closed?"

Hill shook his bald head. "Not yet. We discovered a few facts we thought you might like to hear. For instance, did you know—" He broke off and looked at Leonora. "Are you sure you want the lady to listen to all this?"

Leonora answered for herself. "Whatever concerns the Crystal Palace concerns me. Please carry on."

Hill waited while William turned off the phonograph. "The girl may have been murdered where she was found, but the initial attack did not take place there. Wood splinters embedded in the skin of her face indicate that she had been dragged to the boiler room from somewhere else."

"Dragged from where?" Nathan asked.

"From the first floor of your store. Men's clothing."

"That's close to the exit."

"Right. Which led us to assume that whoever was seeing her out couldn't make up his mind until the last moment whether or not to assault her. Another couple of seconds, and she would have been safe. We found skin and hair on the corner of a counter there, as though she cracked her head against it. Probably while she was struggling with her assailant."

"How do you know the hair and skin belonged to Valerie?" William asked.

Detective Green spoke for the first time. "Who else was assaulted in your store last night? Bruises and lacerations on her

565

scalp are consistent with injuries she would have received had she hit her head on the counter. We also found traces of blood on the floor. They led from the counter, down the stairs to the basement."

"So she did not die from strangulation," Nathan mused.

"She died from strangulation, all right," Green said. "The blow to her head knocked her unconscious, then she was dragged down to the boiler room. We think the assailant intended to rape her down there. Instead, he panicked and strangled her."

Leonora, who had listened to the story with mounting revulsion, asked, "Why are you telling us all this?"

"Because we think we've been laboring under a misconception all this time. We assumed it was Sam Joyner, the night watchman, who was showing Valerie Riley off the premises, and it was Sam Joyner who assaulted her. Now we aren't so sure."

Nathan felt the first, slight touch of fear reach out from his stomach to caress his spine. "Why not?"

Hill pulled an object from his jacket pocket and tossed it onto the chessboard. "Does that belong to anyone?"

William's mouth dropped with shock. "My stickpin!"

He reached out for the gold pin, but he was not quick enough. Hill's beefy hand snatched it back. "We thought it belonged to you. Your name's engraved on the back."

"Then let me have it."

"Sorry." Hill smiled coldly as he dropped the stickpin into the pocket from which he had taken it. "It's evidence. Belongs to us now."

Leonora strained toward the sound of voices. "What kind of evidence is it?"

"The dead girl's hands were clenched shut. You remember that, don't you?" Hill asked the two men.

"I remember," Nathan said, while William stared at the pocket which held his stickpin.

"When we pried her hands open, we found that inside the

right one." The detective's gaze settled on William. "You look sick. You going to throw up like you did this morning?"

William took a deep breath to settle himself. His clothing clung to his body; his glasses slipped down his sweat-covered nose. "It was you who escorted Valerie down from the third floor, wasn't it?" Hill said. "It was you who assaulted her. What happened—did she tear this bauble off your clothing during the struggle?"

"I lost that stickpin yesterday."

"So you say."

William pulled his tie free. "This is the tie I wore yesterday. Do you see a tear in the silk that would have resulted in the stickpin being ripped from it?"

"We've only got your word it's the tie you wore yesterday."

"You have mine as well," Nathan said. "I remember seeing my son wear that tie yesterday."

"Sure," Green murmured. "I'll bet your wife remembers seeing him wear it as well."

Nathan's worry found an escape in anger. Pushing himself out of the chair, he strode toward the dark-haired detective. "You might think that being a police officer gives you the right to be insolent. Not in this house it doesn't. Now get out!"

Hill stepped between his colleague and Nathan. "We were just about to leave. But we're taking your son with us. We think he can help us by answering a few more questions."

Chapter Thirty-one

Detective Joseph Hill's words signaled the beginning of Nathan's blackest nightmare. Nothing he had lived through in his seventy-eight years could have prepared him for the anxiety and bitter grief that lay in ambush for him.

Within a minute of the two detectives taking William from the house, Nathan was on the telephone to Harry. He told his oldest son what had happened. Harry was as disbelieving as his father. Not only was he sure that his youngest brother had not committed the murder, he doubted if even the thought of such a heinous crime had ever entered William's mind. Harry promised his father that he would immediately arrange for a lawyer to meet William at police headquarters. "I will contact Lawrence Travis and ask if he'll deal with it himself, or otherwise send his best man."

Harry's assurance of direct action made Nathan feel slightly better. Lawrence Travis was one of Atlanta's best-known trial lawyers. He was a senior member of the law firm which handled the Crystal Palace's legal affairs. If anyone could put a halt to this madness, it was Travis.

William returned to the house shortly after midnight, not with the police but with the lawyer Harry had summoned. Leonora was asleep, but Nathan had forced himself to stay awake. He hugged his son, then shook the hand of the lawyer.

"Thank you for going so quickly to my son's assistance."

Travis was a big man with a florid face, a regal beak of a nose, and a bald head fringed by gray. "I loathe injustice," he said. "Especially when it happens to my friends. Not for a moment do I believe your son could be guilty of such an outrage."

William related the evening's events for his father. "I was in a room with the chief of detectives and the two men who came here. They were all asking questions. I didn't know where to look first. Then I heard a great commotion, a voice calling my name and shouting for me not to say a word to anyone. It was Mister Travis. He burst into the room and demanded to know why the police were harassing me when they should have been looking for the real killer. I was never so glad to see anyone."

Travis took up the story. "The chief of detectives, a man named Bobby Taylor, told me the police had reason to believe William was a genuine suspect. I said surely the girl must have fought for her life. Surely she would have left scratches on her killer. I had your son remove his shirt, then asked the detectives to show me the marks of such a struggle. There were none. They asked William to make a statement, which he did, and they let him go soon after that. I do not think we have seen the end of this, though. The newspapers were there, for one thing. They took photographs of William as he was brought in, and again as he left. Then there is that damned stickpin. Everything revolves around it. If we could account for it being in the girl's hand, the police would have no case at all."

The following morning, all three Atlanta daily newspapers carried pictures of William being brought to police headquarters. One headline screamed, IS THIS THE MONSTER? For the first time, Nathan felt glad that Leonora was blind, and that he could censor the news he read to her.

Instead of going to the store to finish work he had not touched since Saturday, William, certain that every finger would be pointed at him, refused to venture out of the house. He did not leave it until eight that evening, when the same two detectives escorted him to police headquarters for more questions. When he arrived, he found Lawrence Travis already waiting. In the lawyer's watchful presence, William answered the same questions he had answered the previous night. Half a dozen times he was asked about the stickpin, and each time he denied any knowledge of how it could have come to be in Valerie's hand. By nine-thirty, he was home again.

Valerie was buried the next morning, three days after her murder. Hundreds of mourners filled the small cemetery at Decatur; family and friends mingled with curiosity seekers who wanted contact with what was rapidly becoming Atlanta's most notorious crime. Twenty-four hours later, many of the same crowd squeezed their way into the room where the inquest was held. At the very front sat Valerie's father, Jim Riley. Yesterday he had buried his daughter; today he wanted to see the wheels of justice begin to turn. The witnesses waited outside. The first to be called were the two detectives, Hill and Green, who testified how they had gone to the Crystal Palace on Sunday morning in response to a call from Sam Joyner. When a bright yellow dress was shown to them, they identified it as the dress worn by the murdered girl. Jim Riley's tear-filled blue eyes followed his daughter's dress as it was set aside on an empty chair. Although his ears took in every word of testimony, his gaze remained fixed on the dress.

The county physician informed the six-man coroner's jury that Valerie had met her death through strangulation at around nine o'clock on Saturday night as she left the store. She had not been raped; she was, in fact, a virgin. In a detached voice, he asserted that she had also suffered a head injury, but that, he conceded, could have been unintentional. He had no way of knowing whether she had fallen and banged her head on the counter while struggling, or whether the murderer had deliberately injured her.

Testimony continued in a cold, factual manner until Sam Joyner, the night watchman, took the stand. His evidence, delivered in quaking tones, destroyed any belief the Solomon family had that justice would prevail. He wove a tale of being called down to the boiler room at nine o'clock by William, whom he found standing over the girl's body, wringing his hands in horror. "He said to me that a terrible accident had happened," Joyner told the jury. "He said he needed help to get rid of the body. He meant to burn it. He gave me money to do the job, then left. He couldn't stand to look at the body anymore." Not once did Joyner say that William had admitted killing the girl. He just kept repeating the phrase, "A terrible accident." The insinuation contained in those words was as clear as crystal. Joyner continued by saying that William had spoken to him one more time before leaving the store around midnight. "He checked on me to see if I'd done it. I told him I would, and he left. But I couldn't. I stayed in the boiler room all night, sweating over what I had promised to do. I knew it was wrong, and when morning came I called the police."

When Joyner finished testifying, his eyes swept briefly across the crowded room. They passed over Nathan without the slightest hint of recognition or remorse.

William testified last. As he identified himself, Jim Riley's gaze finally left his daughter's yellow dress. No longer were his blue eyes moist. As they focused on William, they narrowed and turned as hard and gray as flint. A father's grief had been surpassed by hatred for the man he believed had killed his daughter. William's evidence bore little resemblance to that of the night watchman. He repeated what he had told police in earlier statements, emphasizing that he had no idea how his gold stickpin came to be in Valerie's hand.

After deliberating for no longer than ten minutes, the coroner's jury recommended that William be held pending further investigation by the Fulton County Grand Jury.

The next day, Atlanta's newspapers feasted on the recommendation of the inquest. One story told of women at the Crystal Palace deliberately avoiding William because he made sexual overtures to them; another quoted a former employee who claimed to have seen nude pictures on William's desk. But even these tantalizing tales, nothing more than traditional circulation-boosting tactics, faded into insignificance on Friday, six days after the murder, when George Hopkinson's *Awaken* was published.

Hopkinson spread pictures of the principals in the case across his newspaper's front page. At the top, surrounded by a thick black border, was a picture of Valerie, her eyes glancing upward like Marguerite ascending to heaven in the final act of Gounod's *Faust,* Below the martyred Valerie, staring out hostilely, were Sam Joyner and William. With this issue, Hopkinson exceeded even his own crude standards. The front-page headline comprised two words: UNHOLY TRINITY. The equally sensational story described a young, pure Southern virgin's murder at the hands of her wealthy Jewish employer, who was aided at every step of the way by his Negro hireling.

Hopkinson had never sold as many papers as he did that Friday. Every mourner who had attended Valerie's funeral bought one. So did every man made uncertain by changes he saw sweeping across Georgia. On street corners, men read that Friday's edition of *Awaken.* In bars and restaurants, they pored over it while seated at counters or tables. The newspaper protruded from jacket pockets and shopping bags. So great was the demand, Hopkinson had to rush another edition onto the streets.

With a dreadful trepidation, Nathan witnessed the growing interest in the case. How long would it take before Hopkinson's shameful manipulation of his readers replaced genuine concern with mob hysteria? And for that hysteria to goad the authorities into taking frantic, ill-conceived action? Nathan remembered his ride along Marietta Road to Hopkinson's newly built mansion. The publisher had vowed then to ruin Nathan as he was ruining Graham Courtney. Nathan had scoffed at the threat, and his derision had seemed well-founded when Hopkinson's attacks on Courtney failed to stop Clarissa's husband reaching either the State Senate or the executive mansion. Now, Nathan was forced to ponder whether Hopkinson's threat against himself carried greater danger.

A grand jury indicted William on a charge of murder, and he was held in the county jail. A trial date was set for early July. Nathan and Harry visited him every day, and they met with Lawrence Travis almost as frequently. The news the lawyer gave them was anything but encouraging. Newspaper reports, as Nathan feared, had created a wave of hysteria. In mid-June, Travis told Nathan that it would be next to impossible to find twelve impartial jurors; he hoped that by the trial date, some of the passion would have been spent. Of more import was the decision taken by the county solicitor general, Richard Holmes, to personally prosecute the case. Holmes, who viewed his office as a stepping-stone to political power, never personally handled cases he thought he might lose. Nathan's biggest worry, though, centered on Sam Joyner. The Crystal Palace's night watchman had disappeared completely; even his family claimed to know nothing of his whereabouts. It was Travis, eventually, who found out that the night watchman was being held in the same place as William, the county jail.

"On what charge?" Nathan demanded.

"They call it protective custody. The police are worried about his health. They claim that until William is found guilty, Sam Joyner would be lynched the instant he stuck his face outside the county jail."

"Since when do the police give a hoot about a Negro being lynched? They're keeping him hidden to stop us learning why he changed his original story to such a damning pack of lies."

Travis could do nothing but agree. Piece by piece, the prosecution was putting together its case against William, all of it based on coincidences, outright lies, and one condemnatory piece of evidence—the gold stickpin.

Mail flowed daily between Atlanta and New York as the remainder of the Solomon family kept up with the news and gave support. When Jacob and Louise promised to come for the trial, Nathan did his best to discourage them from making the journey. As much as he wanted William to have family close to him in such a stressful period, Nathan felt a growing undercurrent of resentment against the group of people to which the accused man belonged. At the store, business had dropped off considerably. At first he had considered it a natural reaction by people to stay away from the site of a murder, but a conversation with Clarissa opened his eyes to the real reason. She showed him a printed card. With mounting anger he read aloud the message it contained.

"Carry me with you all the time. Look at me whenever you reach for money, and remember to spend it only in a store owned by a Christian American. Do not spend your hard-earned money in the stores of foreign Israelites who defile our pure young women and would mongrelize our race by having us mate with Negroes. Look at me each time you shop, and remember."

When Nathan asked Clarissa where she had obtained the card, she told him that a man had given it to her at Five Points. "He is one of dozens who hand out such cards, Mister Nathan. They are printed by George Hopkinson."

A week before the trial was due to start, Nathan finally saw the man he had been seeking since the grand jury had indicted William. Walking with Lawrence Travis along a corridor in the county jail after visiting his son, Nathan came face-to-face with Sam Joyner. Despite being thirty years older than the night watchmen, Nathan grabbed Joyner by the shoulders and shook him like a dog with a bone.

"You, not my son, should be the one who stands accused of murder!" Nathan shouted. "You should be the one who hangs!"

Joyner's eyes widened in terror. "For God's sake, Mister Nathan, I would hang if I didn't do what they told me to do, if I didn't say what they told me to say! So would half my family—"

The sentence was cut off as two patrolmen shoved Nathan aside, grabbed Joyner by the arms and hustled him along the corridor and up a flight of stairs. Nathan felt a hand fall on his shoulder. He turned around to see the squat, bald figure of Detective Joseph Hill.

"What are you doing here, Mister Solomon?"

"Visiting my son."

"Then get on with it, and stop intimidating witnesses, otherwise your visiting privileges will be withdrawn."

Astounded by Hill's words, Nathan could only watch as the detective followed Joyner and the two patrolmen along the corridor and up the stairs. Afterward, in Travis's Hudson, Nathan turned to the lawyer. "The police are behind Joyner's lies, aren't they? They cannot see further than that gold stickpin in Valerie Riley's hand, so they are forcing people to perjure themselves to make sure William is found guilty."

"You are half right. The police are behind Joyner's change of story, but they are not doing it to support their own theory of the gold stickpin. They are doing it to pacify the mob that George Hopkinson has riled up. We live in desperate times. Industrial growth frightens thousands of farmers. That fear feeds a terrible, surging anger—"

"I know all that," Nathan answered gruffly.

Ignoring the interruption, Travis carried on in his best courtroom manner. "And that terrible, surging anger expands like a heated gas until it is ready to explode. Unless the explosion is channeled in a certain direction—"

Again, Nathan broke in. "Channeled? Toward William? You mean my son is to be a scapegoat to placate these people?"

"Precisely. The police and the solicitor general's office believe your son is guilty, make no mistake about that. They believe it because they want to believe it, because it is so convenient for them to believe it. A young white girl has been murdered, Mister Solomon. Usually, the lynching of a Negro is sufficient to soothe the outraged feelings such a crime engenders, but not this time. This time the mob is too angry, too out of control to settle for just a nigger.

"It wants a Jew to hang."

* * *

Jacob and Louise ignored their father's wishes and came to Atlanta at the beginning of the second week of July. From the moment they stepped off the train, they felt something different about the Gate City. The mob fury following the murder of Valerie Riley had been mentioned in New York papers, but none of the stories had readied Jacob and Louise for the wall of hate they felt the instant their feet touched the ground. Atlantans spoke of nothing else. The porter who carried their bags from the train described the upcoming trial as the biggest event to occur in Atlanta since The Cotton States and International Exposition of 1895. The cab ride to Inman Park was even more upsetting for William's brother and sister. The driver, an overweight, fair-haired man with oceans of sweat staining his shirt, considered himself a one-man guide and welcoming committee to Atlanta. "Yes, sir! Folks are flocking in from all over for this trial. There's going to be a real celebration when the jury finds that little pervert guilty of killing that poor girl. Him and his family can get all the money they like from their rich kinfolk up in New York to pay for all kinds of fancy lawyers, but it won't make a patch of difference."

"Who says they have rich kinfolk up in New York?" Jacob asked, glad that his accent was still of the South.

"Why, Mister Hopkinson says so, in *Awaken*. See for yourself," he offered, passing a copy to his passengers.

"And what if this jury finds him not guilty?" Louise asked between clenched teeth. Like the rest of her family, she had no doubt of William's innocence.

"What jury in its right mind would do that? He killed her as plain as the nose on your face, then tried to pay that nigger night watchman to help him cover it up. Both deserve to hang."

When Jacob pointed out his father's house on Edgewood Avenue, the cab driver did a double take. "That house! The pervert's family lives there. Wait a minute, I picked you up—"

"From the New York train, that's right. Do we look rich?"

"Rich enough to take a cab instead of the trolley."

"Perhaps," Jacob answered. "But most certainly not rich enough to leave you a tip." Taking his sister by the arm, he walked up to his father's house. Let the cab driver call him names; the fat man in the sweat-stained shirt could say nothing worse than he had said already.

Two days later, the trial began. At precisely ten o'clock, William entered the stifling courtroom. He stopped for a second to adjust his glasses, then walked to the defense table, taking the single empty seat next to his father. The other three seats at the table were taken by Lawrence Travis and two of his associates. Behind the table, but inside the rail separating the participants from the spectators, sat William's two brothers and his sister. Leonora remained at home, sitting in her natural darkness and praying for her stepson's acquittal.

"How do you feel?" Nathan whispered.

William glanced over his shoulder to the benches packed with followers of George Hopkinson. "Like a Christian about to be thrown to the lions."

Travis turned to his client. "A better analogy would be, like a lion about to be thrown to so-called Christians."

The judge entered. His first official act was to order the bailiffs to open the windows. Immediately, the courtroom echoed with the noise of the crowd outside. Richard Holmes made the opening statement for the prosecution. A tall, sandy-haired man, he had appeared with increasing frequency in *Awaken,* described as the bearer of justice's sword. Holmes did not object to such exposure; since the murder, George Hopkinson's newspaper had become, if not the city's most widely read publication, certainly its most talked about. As Holmes detailed the points he would prove, cheers filtered in to the courtroom. When Travis declared in ringing tones his intent to show that the prosecution's case rested on coincidence, exaggeration, and outright lies, the cheers changed to catcalls. The judge, settling on a compromise of noise and comfort, ordered the windows to be half closed.

Detective Joseph Hill began the proceedings by detailing how he and his partner, Tom Green, had been called to the Crystal Palace on Sunday morning by Sam Joyner. Under Holmes's careful questioning, Hill wove a tale of how they had first suspected the night watchman. All that changed when the gold stickpin with William's name engraved upon it was found clenched in the girl's hand, as though she had ripped it from her assailant during a struggle. Green repeated his partner's story word for word, adding for good measure how he had considered William to be excessively nervous, both at the scene of the crime, where he had been sick, and at home when the police had asked him about the gold stickpin. Nothing Lawrence Travis asked in cross-examination could shake either of the two detectives. They had their stories down so well, Nathan reflected, that Holmes must have rehearsed them at least a dozen times. So did the chief of detectives, Bobby Taylor, who described how agitated William had seemed during questioning.

"Far more agitated than any innocent man has a right to be," the thickset chief of detectives said. Travis leaped to his feet to protest such conjecture. The judge upheld his objection, but Nathan knew the damage was done.

The state's next witness, and its most damning one, was Sam Joyner. He was on the stand for almost two days, repeating his testimony over and over again. As he told his story, a low rumble of anger shook the courtroom. Like the detectives before him, he refused to be shaken by Lawrence Travis. When William's lawyer brought up the confrontation in the county jail between Joyner and Nathan, the night watchman stoutly denied ever saying that the police had forced him to lie. "Why would I say such terrible things about the police when they're the only people looking out for me?" Joyner cried out. "They're keeping me in jail for my own protection, because they know what can happen to a colored man when there's even the slightest possibility that he did something awful to a white girl."

Travis could respond with nothing sharper than, "I am cer

in that every colored man in this county is relieved to know e police are so attendant to his well-being."

More police officers gave evidence. Medical experts added eir voices. Religious figures who confirmed the victim's good-ss and virtue were followed by a seemingly never-ending ing of witnesses who could attest to William's dissipation and pravity. All were former employees of the Crystal Palace, omen and girls who swore that William had made lewd ad-nces toward them, and men who claimed they had seen such lvances take place. Travis went after each witness, pinning em down as to the reason for their leaving the store's employ. 'ithout exception, each one had been fired. A former elevator echanic who swore he had heard William make indecent ggestions to a fourteen-year-old girl was exposed by Travis as living been dismissed for drinking on the job. A twenty-five-ar-old seamstress who testified that William had tried to fon-e her several times admitted under Travis's harsh oss-examination that she had been dismissed for theft. Worst all, a sales clerk fired a month after the murder for continual teness, claimed that Valerie Riley had on several occasions mplained to him about sexual advances made by William.

"She said that working with William Solomon was like hav-g an octopus in the office with her," the fired sales clerk said, inning at the roar of laughter his comment aroused.

Travis exploded. "Does it not strike you as strange that a girl ho had made such complaints would happily offer to work ertime with William Solomon that Saturday?"

The sales clerk just shrugged.

When Travis pointed out to the court that evidence from such itnesses was not only tainted but probably perjurious, rousing itcalls from outside the courtroom almost drowned his voice.

As Travis ridiculed such evidence, Nathan studied the faces the jurors. On not one did he see disgust or outrage at being d to. He saw only a grim determination to believe every criminating word, no matter how tarnished it might be. With silent sigh, he turned away and gazed at his youngest son.

These people were intent on hanging William. Travis had bee[n] right when he had said the mob wouldn't be satisfied with [a] Negro this time. It did want a Jew to hang.

When Holmes eventually rested the prosecution's case, th[e] trial had finished its second week. Travis knew that if he ha[d] two months with which to work and twice the number [of] tainted witnesses the prosecution had brought forward, h[e] would still not win acquittal for his client. Nonetheless, he trie[d.] He began his defense by calling William's father. Nathan wa[s] a respected man in Atlanta, a leading commercial figure wh[o] had come from New Orleans to the Gate City when it wa[s] struggling to rise from the ashes of Sherman's visit. His tes[ti]mony might repair some of the damage done by the lies of th[e] prosecution's witnesses.

Led by Travis, Nathan recalled the international week put o[n] by the Crystal Palace to celebrate the World's Fair. He describe[d] the frenzied pace of the promotion's final day, his visits [to] William's office, and Valerie's offer to work late. He remem[-] bered hearing William return home, but he did not see him un[til] after breakfast the next morning. He recalled William sayi[ng] that Valerie had left shortly after nine, and that he had final[ly] stopped working just short of midnight. "He mentioned th[at] Sam Joyner must have been glad to see him leave, because th[e] night watchman could then go to sleep with impunity. My wi[fe] chided William for this remark, saying that he was doing Joyn[er] an injustice." It was obvious from the distaste in Nathan's voi[ce] as he mentioned Joyner's name that he did not agree wit[h] Leonora. He still believed Joyner to be the guilty party.

Travis switched to the gold stickpin. Nathan described ho[w] William had been so busy that, for once, he had removed h[is] tie and the pin. Nathan had seen it lying on the desk. Trav[is] asked if Joyner could have picked it up. Nathan answere[d] truthfully that he doubted it; the night watchman had littl[e] reason to enter William's office, especially if William was pre[-] sent. When Travis asked if Nathan thought Valerie might hav[e] taken it, a chorus of jeers erupted from the spectators, picked u[p] immediately by the crowd outside and amplified tenfold. Nathan waited for the noise to subside before answering that it was possible for Valerie to have taken the pin.

"William Solomon is a man of quiet, refined taste, a man who excels with his brain rather than with physical strength," Travis said. "When you saw him on Sunday morning, did you notice anything that might have led you to believe he could have committed a bestial murder just twelve hours before?"

"No, sir," Nathan answered with conviction. "I most certainly did not."

Holmes, in his cross-examination, treated Nathan with respect; there was nothing to be gained by attacking an elderly man who had been a part of the city's rebuilding.

When Nathan stepped down, Travis called a witness who he hoped would be able to sway the jury if not by her evidence, at least by her courage in appearing. He called Leonora. After being helped to the stand, she repeated the oath, her head moving from side to side as if she could see every person present in the courtroom. As Travis began talking, her sightless eyes fastened upon him. He concentrated on her blindness, asking if she had heard anything untoward in William's speech that Sunday morning, the day after the murder? Had she sensed anything strange about his manner? To both questions, Leonora answered no. When Travis finished, Holmes declined to cross-examine. To interrogate an elderly blind woman would serve no purpose for his case.

After Leonora, Travis called Harry to the stand. The oldest Solomon brother reiterated what his father had said. When Holmes, in cross-examination, asked for an explanation of why William had been so violently sick on seeing the body, Harry looked at him as though he were mad. "William is not accustomed to seeing people who have been brutally murdered. Perhaps a policeman is acclimated to such violence, but a normal, decent man such as my youngest brother is not." Roars of derisive laughter arose from the packed benches inside the courtroom, and from the street.

When Harry returned to his seat, he patted his youngest brother reassuringly on the shoulder. William glanced up and smiled. Harry wished he could give such encouragement to himself. Like his father, he knew there could be only one outcome to this mob-dominated, distorted trial.

Following Harry, Travis summoned more than two-dozen witnesses, friends, and associates of William, who could attest to his good character. They ranged from school friends who had known him for more than twenty years, to current employees of the Crystal Palace. As Holmes listened to the reams of praise Travis elicited from these witnesses, he glanced occasionally toward the members of the jury. Not once did he see their expressions change. Their minds were made up already, and no amount of testimony that William Solomon was incapable of such a crime would change them.

The last person to speak for the defense was William himself. Disallowed by law from testifying in a capital crime on his own behalf, he elected to make a statement to the jury, on which he could not be cross-examined. He spoke for three hours in a calm, measured voice, detailing everything that had happened to him since the day of Valerie Riley's murder. He denied ever treating a female employee with anything but the proper respect. If his concern over his missing stickpin seemed exaggerated, it was because the pin was a highly treasured gift from his father. He explained that Valerie's murder had been a tremendous shock to him, especially so because it might have occurred simply because she had offered to work late.

"Had I insisted on being a gentleman by walking her down to the door and seeing her out onto the street, she would be alive today, and the insidious accusations made against me would never have arisen. Instead, I listened to her when she said she could see herself out of the store. Because of that one lapse—that single departure from the code of a gentleman—she lies dead and I stand accused of a crime which those of you who know me well realize I could never have committed." He looked from the jury to Jim Riley as he said those words. Then was no compassion in the stare returned by Valerie's father. The blue eyes were as steely and unforgiving as they had been all through the trial. William took a deep breath and carried on.

"The testimony given by Sam Joyner amounts to nothing more than a pack of vicious lies. Never did I call him down to the boiler room. Never did I admit to him that there had been any kind of an accident. Never did I offer to pay him money to dispose of a body. I have no idea whether these lies are Sam Joyner's own doing, to divert attention away from himself because he was the first obvious suspect, or an attempt by the police, for whatever reason, to wreck the life of an upright man."

William's final words constituted a plea. "Put aside the hysterical stories you have read in *Awaken*. Put aside Sam Joyner's lies. Put aside the spiteful inventions of men and women who were dismissed from employment at the Crystal Palace. Heed only the truth, and send me where I belong—home to my father's house." As he stepped down, only the sound of sobbing broke the silence that filled the courtroom. Looking past the defense table to where his family sat, William saw Louise dabbing a handkerchief to her eyes. Before sitting down, he bent to kiss his sister on the cheek.

The judge called for a recess. As Travis collected his papers, he turned to William. "You did very well. Let us hope that tradition rules the outcome of this case, and that the jury believes the word of a white man over the word of a Negro, especially when it is the white man telling the truth, and the Negro who is lying."

Despite the hope he expressed to William, Lawrence Travis already knew the outcome of the trial. Tradition had no place in it, and at the beginning of the fourth week, after closing arguments for the prosecution and defense, he was far from surprised when the jury, following just ninety minutes of deliberation, returned a guilty verdict.

Nathan watched Richard Holmes approach the jury box and

poll each member of the panel. Each juror to whom he asked, "Is this your verdict?" unfailingly replied, "It is."

Travis leaned toward William and Nathan. "We'll start work immediately for a new trial. This mockery of justice will never be allowed to stand."

The same raucous crowd assembled inside the courtroom and out in the street the next morning, eager to witness the judge pass sentence. The anger that had energized the mob for the twenty-two days of the trial had yielded to merriment. The beast had been trapped and caught; now it could be put down.

Staring down at William from the bench, the judge asked if he had anything to say before sentence was passed. William replied only that he was totally innocent of any crime. The judge proceeded with his sworn duty. Reading from a sheet of paper he declared that on Tuesday, September 13, William Solomon was to be executed by the Sheriff of Fulton County, between the hours of 10 A.M. and 2 P.M. "That he be hanged by the neck until he is dead, and may God have mercy on his soul."

William slumped back against the chair. September 13 was little more than six weeks away. Nathan leaned toward his son and whispered, "When a Union judge condemned me to death for spying, he gave me a week to think about it. If I, without the benefit of the best legal brains in Atlanta, could cheat the hangman in a week, you, with six weeks, and Lawrence Travis to help you, will have no problem breaking your date."

Travis immediately notified the judge that he intended to file a motion for a new trial. After consulting a calendar, the judge said he would hear arguments on September 7, six days before the scheduled execution. When Travis returned to the defense table with the welcome news that the time of the execution was already extended, Nathan nudged his son's arm.

"What did I tell you? No rope had my name on it in the War Between the States, and no rope has your name on it forty-nine years later in Atlanta."

What Nathan did not say was that William Patrick Flaherty, the very man whose name William bore, was not in Atlanta perform the miracle again. This time, the condemned man's fate rested solely on legal brains and the capricious whims of jurists.

Waiting for appeals to be heard was even harder on Nathan's nerves than the trial had been. While Jacob and Louise returned to New York to continue with their own lives, and Harry soothed his anxiety by working at the store, Nathan spent most of his time at home with Leonora. The customs he had adopted to help Leonora cope with her blindness fell by the way. Only on infrequent occasions did he read to her from the newspaper, and rarer still were their carriage rides with Alonzo. Nathan's mind was preoccupied with counting days, with planning visits to William's cell at the county jail, and with meeting lawyers. Leonora understood. When William's conviction was recognized for the injustice that it was, Nathan would have time for her again. But as the weeks passed she withdrew into herself, and became a prisoner of her own failing body.

The first execution date passed while arguments for a new trial were being heard. Travis claimed that William had been denied due process because the jury had been influenced by the mob. When the motion was denied, Travis took the case to the Georgia Supreme Court, again claiming mob interference with justice, and pointing out that more than one hundred errors had been made in the original trial. The Georgia Supreme Court examined the appeal before deciding that insufficient reason existed for a new trial. For the second time, William appeared before a judge to be sentenced. His new execution date was Tuesday, March 14, 1911. He had cheated the hangman out of six months, but he was no nearer being free.

While Nathan sat at home, glumly counting off the days to the new execution date, George Hopkinson's *Awaken* protested furiously at the delay. Hopkinson dipped his pen in vitriol. 'While the spirit of a butchered Christian girl cries out from heaven for vengeance, a cruel game of appeasement takes place on earth." Every issue carried a condemnation of Lawrence Travis. When Travis took the case to the United States District Court, Hopkinson slammed the lawyer as a disgrace to Atlanta, and a foul blot upon the good name of the State of Georgia. He kept the anger of his readers at boiling point by writing that the exoneration of William Solomon was the first step in turning Georgia into an autonomous Jewish state within the United States. "Their new Israel will be here!" Hopkinson screamed. "Their new Jerusalem will be Atlanta! And their first president will be the pervert murderer William Solomon!"

The more Hopkinson ranted, the more the rednecks listened. With his flowing gray hair and furious tirades, he came across as an Old Testament prophet consigning evildoers to the fiery pit. Hopkinson reveled in such fame. After a year of feasting on the murder of Valerie Riley, the circulation of his newspaper had increased tremendously. He was a wealthy man, and when he made his bid for the United States Senate, every right-thinking citizen in Georgia would vote for him.

The second execution date slipped past as the case was appealed all the way up to the United States Supreme Court. There, at the end of 1911, the trail ended when, by a majority decision, the justices decided to allow the state of Georgia to conduct its own business. William's only hope of avoiding the third execution date, on February 14, 1912, was a commutation of sentence from Governor Courtney.

Nathan went with Travis to the county jail after the United States Supreme Court had rejected the appeal. They found William surprisingly calm, far calmer than Nathan remembered being when he had faced death in the Old Capitol Prison in Washington. When Nathan remarked upon his fortitude, William answered, "God has helped me come to terms with my fate. He knows, as I do, that I am innocent, but a price must be paid for the tragedy of that poor girl's death. If the price is to be my life, so be it."

"Do not be so quick to make your peace with the Almighty," Travis said. "I will be most surprised if Governor Courtney does not commute the sentence to life imprisonment. Both the Georgia Supreme Court and the United States Supreme Court rejected us, not by unanimous decisions, but by majority decisions. Doubt existed in both courts, and such doubt must enter into the governor's judgment when he considers our appeal."

"I will pray that you are right," Nathan murmured.

Travis gave a dry smile. "It can do no harm."

Governor Graham Courtney announced that he would hold hearings beginning on January 22, 1912, to consider commuting William Solomon's sentence to life imprisonment. Immediately, he was besieged by letters. While men of conscience begged for leniency, George Hopkinson distributed form letters for his supporters to send to Courtney, to demand that the death sentence be carried out without further delay. Elements of the same mob that had persuaded a jury to find William guilty now surrounded the executive mansion.

The decision confronting Courtney was the toughest he had faced in three years as governor. The Solomon family were his friends; every Christmas, when a package arrived for Clarissa from the Crystal Palace, Courtney felt the same lump in his throat. But the majority of Georgia's citizens—swayed by Hopkinson's diabolical manipulation—wanted William Solomon to hang. Even those who did not share Hopkinson's fanaticism desired to see the affair ended once and for all. They were embarrassed by all the attention the case had received; what should have been a Georgian matter had been turned into a national *cause célèbre* by Northern newspapers.

On the evening of January 30, after eight days of reflection, Courtney told Clarissa that he was close to reaching his decision. Asking not to be disturbed, he locked himself away in his study. Clarissa went to the telephone and placed a call to the house on Edgewood Avenue.

Nathan's stomach lurched when he heard Clarissa's voice. "Has the governor made a decision yet?"

"Not yet, but he is close. He is in his study now, on his knees to ask God for guidance in reaching the proper decision."

"Thank you for letting me know, Clarissa." Nathan replaced the earpiece on the hook and went into the parlor to join Leonora. She sat on a loveseat by a window overlooking the garden, gazing out into the dark with sightless eyes. Nathan sat beside her. "What do you do, Lally?"

"I listen to the rain."

"Oh?" he said, surprised. He, with perfect sight, had not even noticed it was raining. The light from the room enabled him to see raindrops dancing off the petals of rose bushes close to the windows. "That was Clarissa. Her husband is near to making his decision."

Leonora reached out to take Nathan's hand and squeeze it. "He is an honorable man. He will make the right decision."

"Of course he will." He gazed at Leonora, thinking how cruel the past two years had been to her. The once faint wrinkles on her face had become deep lines, etched by the grief and worry that had overtaken the family. The path of veins marked the translucent skin. Her back was stooped, and her walk unsteady. What would she think of him if her eyes could only let her see him? His white hair was no longer a lion's mane. The pink of his scalp shone through. His beard, grown initially as a spy's disguise, was thin and wispy. Strong hands which had once constructed buildings, could now barely hold a pen. Arthritis had twisted his fingers into claws. He looked like a man of eighty should look, not that he counted birthdays anymore. The family had not gotten together for the past two. How could they, when one member languished under a sentence of death?

He stood up. Leonora asked where he was going. Smiling tenderly, he said, "I go to join Graham Courtney on his knees." Leaving Leonora in the parlor, Nathan walked slowly to the porch. He stood for a minute watching the rain fall, then he retreated to a secluded corner of the porch where he lowered himself gently onto his knees and began talking in a low voice.

"Thirty-nine years ago, I asked You to save the life of my

youngest son. Now I am asking again. You know he could never have committed the crime of which he was found guilty. There is no violence in him. I am not asking You to punish the guilty. Just protect the innocent. Guide Graham Courtney as he struggles with his conscience to make the right decision."

Slowly, he rose to his feet, dusted the knees of his trousers, and returned to the house to sit beside Leonora once more. They sat together for more than an hour until Fanny, the housekeeper, entered the parlor.

"The governor's wife wishes to speak to you, Mister Nathan."

"Thank you." Heart pounding in his chest, Nathan walked to the front hall. "Clarissa?"

"Mister Nathan, Graham has decided to commute William's sentence. He will make it official in the morning."

"God bless him." Nathan replaced the telephone on the table, dropped down onto the chair beside it and began to cry.

Courtney announced his decision at nine o'clock the next morning. Outside his home, the mob, which had stayed through the night, showed signs of turning violent. Chanting "Courtney, Courtney, King of the Jews!" hundreds of angry men marched toward the executive mansion. They stopped only when armed troops leveled rifles at them.

The instant the decision was made public, Nathan placed a call to Harry at the Crystal Palace. So much excitement bubbled in Nathan's voice that Harry did not have the heart to tell him that he already knew. The news was all over town. Harry promised to leave the store immediately and collect his father from Inman Park so they could visit William together. While Nathan waited, he called Courtney, to thank him. When Harry arrived, the two men drove to the county jail. Armed guards were in evidence there as well. Nathan and Harry were allowed in to see William.

"This is the last time we will be visiting you here," Harry told his brother. "I am glad. I was growing tired of seeing this building. To visit you in the future, at the prison at Milledgeville, will be a pleasant outing in the country."

"I, too, will be happy to see the country," William said. "To be honest, I had given up all hope of ever getting out of here, except . . . You know what I mean." He looked at his father. "Mister Travis is confident that without time pressing down so urgently, he will be able to unearth new evidence that will lead to my eventual freedom. How much are his fees, and the fees of his associates costing?"

Nathan deflected his son's concern by saying, "Do not worry about cost. Just be grateful that we could afford to hire the best lawyer in Atlanta."

As the visit ended, William first hugged his brother, then his father. "Before I leave here this evening, I will write to Governor Courtney to thank him. I owe my life to the fact that among all these hate-filled men who call themselves Christians, Governor Courtney is truly a Christian."

"Amen to that," Harry murmured.

That evening, a festive air prevailed in Nathan's home. A long night had finally passed; the gray light of dawn filled the eastern sky, and soon the brightness of the sun would drive away the dark. Harry and Ella joined Nathan and Leonora for dinner. After the meal, Ella sat down at the piano in the parlor and played for half an hour. While Harry turned pages, Nathan sat with Leonora on the loveseat. They held hands, and as Nathan listened to the music and looked at Leonora, he swore he saw some of the lines fading from her face.

Harry and Ella left at ten forty-five. Leonora retired soon after, but Nathan remained awake and alert. He was too excited to sleep. He stood out on the porch, breathing in the crisp night air. The sky was cloudless and filled with glowing stars. He looked up and whispered, "Thank you."

Eventually, he went to bed at three o'clock. Even then, he could not sleep. Where was William now? Was he already at the prison that would be his home until justice was served and a pardon given?

Sleep did not come for another four hours, until seven o'-clock, as the household servants went about their daily routines. Less than an hour later, the sound of chaos dragged Nathan from that sleep. He tried to focus his sleep-filled eyes on the commotion taking place before him. Leonora stood at the bottom of the bed, eyes screwed shut, hands jammed over her ears as though she were blotting out a loathsome noise while she shrieked at the top of her voice. Next to her stood Fanny, the housekeeper, teeth gleaming brightly in a wide-open mouth.

"Wake up, Mister Nathan! You got to wake up!"

Nathan struggled to sit up in bed. "What is it? What the hell is going on?"

"It's your boy, Mister Nathan! It's Mister William!"

"What about him?" Why should Fanny be worrying about William? Surely she knew his sentence had been commuted!

"A group of men attacked the automobile taking him to Milledgeville. They killed one of the deputies who was riding with your son, then they took Mister William to Decatur and they . . ." Fanny's eyes and mouth grew even wider.

"Lordy, Mister Nathan, they've gone and lynched your boy! And then they left his body on that poor girl's grave!"

Leonora stopped shrieking. She turned around to face Nathan. Her arms reached out for him. Mind swimming with Fanny's news, Nathan threw back the covers and stood up. Leonora walked toward him. He held out his arms. Their fingers touched. Leonora shrieked one more time, a piercing, agonized scream that embraced every torture of hell. The scream died away, and, before Nathan's horrified gaze, she collapsed onto the floor.

Fanny reached the fallen woman first. She felt for a pulse, then pressed her face to Leonora's mouth. When she looked up at Nathan, tears streaked her black skin.

"Lordy, Mister Nathan," was all she said.

Chapter Thirty-two

Nathan grieved for two people: the son who had been ripped away from him by the frenzied violence of a mob, and the woman who had fled with him from England more than sixty years before, the loving cousin who had become his loving wife.

Like soldiers rallying around a fallen leader, his family gathered around him. Not just his daughter and his surviving sons, who mourned on their own account, but his grandchildren and great-grandchildren. The house on Edgewood Avenue was filled as it had never been filled before, as four generations came together, to lament and to lend one another strength.

The presence of his family comforted Nathan. He spent his time in either the parlor or on the porch, content to watch the activity all around him. Sometimes, he became bewildered by the tumult so many people caused, but he accepted that a man of eighty was entitled to a little confusion now and then. He discovered that he had trouble remembering names. Not the names of older family members. Those were imprinted upon his memory like all events from so long ago. No, it was the names of the young people that escaped him, the seven little ones who romped through the big house like it was an oversized playground built just for them. He called his oldest son.

"Harry, refresh my memory. What are the little ones' names?"

Harry did not question his father's request. He understood

hat among the elderly, fresher memories vanished long before old remembrances faded. All except one. His father would never forget the vision of Leonora reaching for him while uttering that final tortured scream. That memory, and the events surrounding it, would never dim. "The boy and girl staring at the picture Lionel made of my wedding to Ella are Burton and Rhea, Jacob's children. The two girls and the boy who play hide-and-seek around the furniture, their names are Roberta, Deborah, and—"

"And Jonathan, that's right," Nathan said as the cloud screening his memory momentarily lifted. "Roberta and Jonathan are Benjamin's and Caroline's children, aren't they?"

"That's right. Benjamin's and Caroline's three-year-old twins. And Deborah is their cousin, the child of Rose and Daniel. She is two months younger."

"Your grandchildren, eh? My son's grandchildren. What of Edward? When will he marry and give you more grandchildren?"

"When he feels the time is right." Harry twisted his head and pointed with his chin to two older boys who faced each other over the chessboard on which Nathan had battled William. "Do you not remember the names of those two young men?"

"Tell me one."

"Walter."

"And his younger brother, Arthur." Nathan nodded his head and smiled contentedly. His memory had not really gone; it just required an occasional prod. How could he ever forget the two boys Harriet and Saul had adopted at the beginning of 1910 from the Hebrew Orphanage on Washington Street? Walter and Arthur had lost their parents and a sister in a fire. Even now, after more than two years in their new home, they remained shy and withdrawn. Nathan understood. He and Leonora must have been the same when they were taken into the home of their aunt and uncle.

"Does it not strike you as odd," Harry asked, "that Harriet, who was named after your aunt, and her husband are bringing up two children who are not their own, as your Aunt Harriet did?"

"Perhaps that was why Louise and Lionel named her Harriet, so she would grow into as loving a person as my aunt."

As Harry walked away, Nathan sat back in his chair. If a man was to be favored with grandchildren and great-grandchildren, the least he could do to show his gratitude for such a blessing was remember their names! As he looked around the busy house, he recalled an aphorism he had once heard, that the value of a man or woman could be judged by the friends and family left behind. Leonora had left plenty. Her spirit and her love, if not her actual blood, flowed through every person here.

Among the many callers to Nathan's home were the Courtneys, the governor and Clarissa. Courtney had received William's letter the day after the lynching. "It was the most poignant piece of correspondence I have ever read," he told Nathan on his first visit to the house. "I had taken what I believed was the right course, and I had failed. Yet as I felt myself awash in misery, I received your son's letter. He did not know it, of course, but he was thanking me for doing my best, if not for succeeding."

"You succeeded," Nathan assured the governor. "Sadly, this was one time when the power of evil overcame the power of good."

The next time Courtney and Clarissa visited, the governor told Nathan that he had ordered the cutting down of the oak tree on which William had been lynched. "I gave the order because I fear it will become a shrine, a gathering place for the sick people who committed this outrage. Already, dozens of bouquets are left each day on the grave of poor Valerie Riley. She is becoming a saint to these people."

"They care more for her in death than they ever did in life," Clarissa said.

After two weeks, when the period of sharpest grief was over, Jacob and Louise returned with their families to New York. Harry drove Nathan to the station to see them off. As the train began to move, Jacob cried, "We will all return at the end of the year to help you celebrate your eighty-first birthday."

Nathan did not believe he would live to see another birthday, not without Leonora, but he refused to allow his children to see that. "God willing!" he called out. "God willing."

At the beginning of April, two months after William's death, Nathan had an unexpected visit from the man who had led the team that defended his son. Lawrence Travis carried news which he wanted Nathan to hear.

"Does the name James Brooks mean anything to you?"

Nathan shook his head. "Should it?"

"Your son, Harry, would know the name. He knows everyone who works for the Crystal Palace, no matter how lowly a position they occupy. James Brooks is a cleaner—at least, he was."

"He was dismissed?"

Travis chuckled dryly. "Rather permanently, I'm afraid. He died last night as the result of knife wounds received during a fight in a saloon on Decatur Street."

"I do not think—" Nathan was about to say that the store would have no trouble replacing a cleaner, but something about Travis's demeanor made him bite his tongue.

"He did not die immediately. He lived for half an hour with the blood pouring out of him onto the floor of the saloon. But he knew he was dying, and he was terrified of meeting his maker without first having the opportunity to cleanse his soul. He begged for a minister. One came from the Wheat Street Baptist Church. The poor devil didn't know what he had let himself in for. Brooks confessed to a string of crimes. He was still confessing when the devil took him. The minister contacted me, because he thought I would be interested in one particular crime to which Brooks confessed."

Nathan grimaced. He knew what was coming.

"On the night Valerie Riley was murdered, William said he worked so late that the night watchman, Sam Joyner, must have been glad to see him go. He also said that the cleaners had tried to get into his office to do their work, and he had told them to leave."

"He mentioned the cleaners?" Travis's face bore a look of incredulity. "He mentioned them to you, but never thought to mention them to me?"

"He must have assumed they had finished their work and left the building. He worked so hard and for so long that he had trouble remembering anything that night."

Travis nodded curtly. "The other cleaners might have gone, but Brooks had not. When he entered William's office to clean it, he saw the gold stickpin lying on the desk. While William's back was turned, he stole it. Afterward, he remained in the closed store to see what else he could steal. All he had to worry about was Sam Joyner, and he was just one man. When Valerie came down alone, she saw him. She started to run, but he grabbed her. She fell against the counter and hit her head hard. Thinking she was dead, he dragged her down to the boiler room. When he found out she was not dead, but just unconscious, he strangled her with a piece of cord. Before letting himself out of the store, he had the presence of mind to clench Valerie's hand around your son's gold stickpin."

"Then Joyner had nothing to do with the murder?"

"The police were obsessed with that stickpin. And the solicitor general was obsessed with making a reputation for himself not by prosecuting a hapless Negro night watchman, but by successfully prosecuting the son of a wealthy merchant. Together, they bullied and browbeat Joyner into giving that damning testimony. And when the newspapers jumped on it, especially when George Hopkinson decided he could use it to sell hundreds of thousands of copies of *Awaken*, the skids beneath William were well and truly greased."

Nathan shivered. His son had died, his entire family had been torn apart with anxiety and grief, and for what? To satisfy the desires of ambitious men? "Where is Sam Joyner now?"

"He left Atlanta soon after the trial. I suspect he was paid off and told to disappear with the warning that it would be more

an his life was worth to show his face here again. I tried
:eping track of him in case we won our appeal for a new trial,
it I have no idea where he is. He might even be dead."

"I hope he is," Nathan murmured. "I would hate to think of
.at lying scoundrel enjoying life while my son lies murdered in
grave." He looked sharply at Travis. "What do you intend
oing with this information?"

"I am going to purchase full-page advertisements in all of
tlanta's newspapers. Including *Awaken*. Each advertisement
ill contain my sworn statement attesting to the deathbed con-
ssion of James Brooks. After all you paid for my services, the
ery least I can do is continue working to clear your son's
ame."

"Thank you, Mister Travis."

The *Constitution*, the *Georgian*, and the *Journal* carried Travis's
dvertisement. Only one newspaper refused to do so. When
ravis sought to buy space in *Awaken*, George Hopkinson re-
cted him. Instead, he mentioned Travis editorially, describing
ae lawyer as he had done before as a tool of those who would
irn Georgia into the new Jerusalem. "Let other newspapers be
oled by the fantasy of a simple-minded Negro seeking salva-
on in the hour of his death by confessing to the defilement and
aurder of that poor little girl from Decatur," thundered Hop-
inson. "Our readers are not so gullible. No matter how many
es are told down through the years, we will always know who
illed Valerie Riley."

Nathan read Hopkinson's column, but he refused to allow it
) upset him. The bigots and hatemongers who subscribed to
waken would always believe the trial had produced the correct
erdict; a thousand full-page advertisements to the contrary
ould never change their minds.

Nathan saw Hopkinson just once. It was during the summer,
hile being driven by Alonzo in the low victoria carriage that
vas now a rarity among the city's motorized traffic. As they
assed the Empire Building at the junction of Marietta and
road streets, Nathan noticed a small crowd listening to a

speaker. He instructed Alonzo to draw nearer. Only when th
carriage was twenty yards away did Nathan identify the strider
voice that pierced the air. For two minutes, he listened t
Hopkinson rant about Wall Street bankers and railroad trus
before he realized what the publisher was doing. He was seel
ing votes, launching his campaign for election to the Unite
States Senate. As Nathan listened, a sudden excitement too
hold, and an idea gripped his mind. A mad idea that had n
place in modern Atlanta, where an innocent man could b
lynched; a mad idea that belonged only in the past wher
Nathan often felt more comfortable.

"Help me down," Nathan told Alonzo. His joints were sti
these days, and he could neither board nor step down from th
carriage without assistance.

Alonzo held Nathan's arm as he descended to the groun
"Thank you, Alonzo. Kindly wait for me." Nathan tugged a
the jacket of his beige mohair suit to be certain it was straigh
adjusted his wide-brimmed straw hat, then walked slowly tc
ward the back of the crowd. Men and women parted to mak
way for the old man who asked for passage with a soft, "Excus
me, please. Excuse me." Soon, Nathan found himself at th
front, facing Hopkinson, who stood on a low platform. On on
side of the publisher flew the flag of Georgia; on the other, th
Stars and Bars of the Confederacy.

Hopkinson was in the middle of a tirade against New Yor
financiers controlling Georgian industry when Nathan inter
rupted him. "Sir, does the presence of the Confederate fla
signify that you fought for the South in her moment of greates
need?"

Hopkinson stared down at the old man whose bearded fac
was kept in shadow by the brim of his straw hat. "Had I bee
old enough, I would have gladly served my country, sir. I woul
have gladly served and gladly fallen." Hopkinson inclined hi
head at the murmur of applause that greeted the remark.

"As a man who did serve his country and spent four years i
Union jails, I do not believe you would have done either.'

athan removed the hat so Hopkinson could see his face. "You ould have done then what you do now, sat behind a desk and vented lies to make other men kill and die for you." Before opkinson could react to the accusation, Nathan reached up to ap him across the face. A stunned silence came over the owd. They watched eagerly to see how Hopkinson would act.

The publisher rubbed his cheek for a few seconds, his eyes ancing over the crowd in front of him. "A duel?" he said at st. "You challenge me to a duel? What century do you live in, d man?"

"A century where scoundrels like you found their just deserts aiting beneath The Oaks."

Hands gripped Nathan's arm. He turned to see the dark, oncerned face of Alonzo. "Come along now, Mister Nathan. ll take you home."

"Wait, Alonzo. I have business to finish here."

"No, sir, you don't," Alonzo whispered. "Six years ago, you ved my life when the mob was after me. Now I can return the vor."

"Go on!" Hopkinson shouted at the groom. "Take your aster home before he upsets me enough to take him up on his aallenge."

Nathan allowed himself to be led through the crowd. As lonzo helped him into the carriage, Nathan said, "I would ave killed him. Pistol, *colichemarde* . . . it doesn't matter. I would ave killed him."

"Sure you would, Mister Nathan," Alonzo said. "Sure you ould." He climbed into the driver's seat and slapped the reins cross the horse's back. Nathan turned around to watch Hop- nson harangue the crowd in his search for votes. Alonzo ould not have interfered. If Hopkinson had refused to accept ae challenge, he would have been branded a coward in the yes of the very people whose votes he courted. And if he did ccept, he would have signed his own death warrant. Like

Raymonde Perrault, Nathan would have fought only to the death.

By the time the carriage reached Inman Park, the excitement had left Nathan. His hands shook and his legs trembled as Alonzo helped him down. "Thank you, Alonzo. You saved an old man from making himself look an old fool."

"You didn't look like a fool to me. You looked like a proud man who wanted revenge. You know"—the groom did something he had never done before to his employer, he winked—"I reckon you might have killed him at that."

As summer turned to fall, Nathan began to believe that he would live to celebrate one more birthday. The heat of summer had been beneficial to him, easing the pains that plagued his joints and bones. Additionally, he swore that his memory was improving. Not once had he been forced to ask Harry to supply a name. He began to take a greater interest in the world around him. He tried to spend an hour or two each day in the store, and he forced himself to return to the habit of reading the newspaper each morning. It was difficult at first, without Leonora beside him to listen to the stories he so carefully selected. He forced himself to continue, and as he worked himself back into the habit, he grew amazed at the things he learned were happening not only in America but around the world. An assassin's bullet meant for Progressive Party presidential candidate Theodore Roosevelt had been diverted by a glass case. War was imminent in the Balkans. Thousands crowded into New York's Times Square to see baseball scores flashed on the New York *Times*'s electronic bulletin board. All this was happening, and he knew nothing about it. What if someone spoke to him about such news? He would just stare dumbly at them, and they would regard him as a fool. An old fool. That particular description troubled Nathan the most.

In late October, a familiar name appeared in a front-page headline in the *Constitution*. Nathan stared at the paper for few seconds while trying to recall the significance of the *Atlantic Star*. Suddenly it struck him. The *Atlantic Star* had been the ship he and Leonora had seen complete its maiden voyage from Southampton to New York three years ago. Jacob and Helen had taken them to the dock to see it arrive, and Jacob had pointed out the radio antenna which allowed the liner to keep in contact with other ships, and with radio stations on shore.

As he read the entire headline, his heart skipped. The *Atlantic Star*, with more than two thousand passengers aboard, had struck an iceberg at full speed and was sinking! Its SOS had been picked up fourteen hundred miles away in New York by a radio operator who had contacted other ships in the area to organize a rescue.

Suddenly Nathan trembled with excitement. "Look, Lally! Look!" he cried, before realizing he was completely alone. He spoke again, but this time softly. "Can you guess the name of the radio operator, Lally? Jacob Solomon, that's who."

He called Alonzo to take him to the store. Harry should know about this immediately. Imagine, the young man who had once serviced the Crystal Palace's elevators now supervised a mammoth maritime rescue operation. Together, he and Harry sent a congratulatory telegram to Jacob. He did not receive it until three bone-weary days later, when he finally left his post after collecting the names of the seven hundred survivors rescued by radio-carrying vessels. Nathan had never felt so proud.

Not all the news was so uplifting, though. In November, Nathan threw aside the *Constitution* in disgust when he read that George Hopkinson's political wishes had been fulfilled. The publisher of *Awaken* would be one of two men to represent the State of Georgia in the United States Senate. Georgia was entering a dark night, thought Nathan, but it would see the sun once more as long as men like Harry and Graham Courtney continued to call the state their home.

As December dawned, Nathan began anticipating his eighty-first birthday. He was pragmatic enough to know that it might be the last time he saw the entire family together, and he felt grateful for the opportunity. To have seen them all for a final time earlier in the year, following the deaths of William and Leonora, would have been a painfully sad way to say farewell.

At Christmas, Nathan saw to his time-honored custom of selecting a gift for Clarissa. Remembering that the Courtney's only son, Alexander, had become father to a baby girl six months earlier, Nathan selected from the store's toy department the largest doll he could find, then instructed Alonzo to deliver it to the governor's home. With it he sent a note reminding Clarissa that it had been a doll from the Crystal Palace he had first given her more than forty years before. Now she could give a doll from the very same store to her new granddaughter.

On New Year's Eve, Jacob and Louise arrived with their families. It was the first time Nathan had seen Jacob since the sinking of the *Atlantic Star* had transformed him into a hero. Nathan pestered his son with questions about the baffling business he was in. Jacob answered eagerly. "The tragedy of the *Atlantic Star* brought radio to the forefront. At the same time, it brought me to the forefront. The company has placed me in charge of all radio operations, at more than twice the money I was earning before. The only trouble is, it's not enough."

"Not enough?" Nathan repeated in astonishment. "What do you want—to be president of the company?"

Fire glowed in Jacob's eyes. His intensity overwhelmed Nathan. "New opportunities are opening up, opportunities my company does not envisage. I see radio being more than a means to transmit signals from ship to shore. It will become an entertainment medium. In ten or fifteen years, every American home will have a radio receiver. Music, plays, debates, even sports events will be broadcast into people's homes. It will be a whole new world, and I will be in the forefront once again."

Nathan winked at his daughter and son-in-law. "Do you see how a little fame has turned our Jacob's head?"

"No more than it has turned my husband's," Louise answered. "Lionel, tell my father what you have brought for his birthday."

Lionel's chest expanded with pride. "I have arranged to hire a projector and screen so you may see a copy of a motion picture I have just directed for Technograph. It is by far and away the most important motion picture I have ever worked on."

"What is the name of this most important motion picture?"

"Oliver Twist."

"I know it well," Nathan said. "I read the book by Charles Dickens many, many years ago, when I was younger than either of your sons. It was an excellent story, the favorite of both Leonora and myself." He smiled inwardly as he remembered reading chapters of it to Leonora. They had both found so much of themselves in that story, orphans cast into an unfamiliar world. "I will have to see if you have improved upon it."

"I have," Lionel answered with conviction. "I have."

Over dinner, Louise told her father why *Oliver Twist* was so important to Lionel. "It is his final picture for Technograph. In a few weeks, Albert, Aaron, Lionel, and I are leaving New York to travel to California."

"What is there? Earthquakes?"

"Earthquakes trouble San Francisco. We are going to Los Angeles, where Lionel will open his own studio. Independent companies have established themselves there to find freedom from the Motion Picture Patents Company. Lionel believes that one day Los Angeles will be the motion picture capital of the country."

"Like your brother Jacob believes that one day every family in America will find their entertainment coming out of a radio receiver."

"Lionel is fifty-four years old. If he does not make the move immediately, he will have missed his opportunity."

"Go to California. Go there and be successful. Just watch out for the earthquakes."

"That's San Francisco," Louise repeated. "Not Los Angeles."

Nathan went to bed soon after dinner. He did not wish to

stay up to celebrate the New Year; he would have celebrations enough tomorrow. He fell asleep immediately, and slept so deeply that he did not even hear the festivity that greeted the birth of 1913. The only disturbance to his sleep came from a dream, one that centered around the title of Lionel's new picture. Nathan's subconscious painted a familiar scene from long ago, the interior of his uncle's shop on Ludgate Hill. He saw himself and Leonora sitting by the stove as they stole their few precious minutes before the rest of the staff arrived. He was reading aloud from *Oliver Twist*. Their favorite part of the book had been Oliver asking for a second helping. The line "Please, sir, I want some more," had been a special term between Nathan and Leonora, a catch phrase to remind them just how much they shared with Dickens's resourceful orphan. He hoped Lionel had not left it out.

Nathan arose early on New Year's Day. The adults continued to sleep off the celebrations of the previous night, while Jacob's two children ate in the breakfast room. Nathan joined them, happy at the opportunity to be alone with his two youngest grandchildren whom he saw all too rarely.

After eating, he looked at Burton and Rhea and said, "Who has ridden in an automobile?" Both thrust their hands into the air. "All right, who has ridden in a horse-drawn carriage?"

No hands showed this time, and Nathan spared a moment of pity for generations of children yet to come who would never know the joy of riding in a horse-drawn vehicle. "How many of you would like to ride in a carriage?" Again the hands went up. Nathan called for Alonzo to prepare the carriage, then he asked Fanny to make sure the children were warmly clothed.

Outside, breath from the two horses hung like clouds in the chilly air. Nathan sat next to Rhea, holding her tightly, while Burton perched beside Alonzo on the elevated driver's seat. Alonzo flicked the reins across the horses' backs and the carriage jerked into motion. As they passed the first pedestrians,

Nathan called out, "Happy New Year!" Soon, both children were shouting the greeting with him.

They returned to the house after almost two hours to find the adults eating breakfast. When Helen asked where they had been, Burton answered that they had seen the governor's mansion, the speedway, and the home of the man who had written the Uncle Remus stories. Helen clasped her hands together in wonder. "My, you have been busy. I wouldn't be the least surprised if you were too tired to watch the picture with us this afternoon."

Immediately, she was beset by protesting children. Nathan watched the clamor with a smile on his face and a warm feeling in his heart.

Around midday, the rest of the family arrived. Harry and Ella were first, followed soon after by their unmarried son Edward, and their two married children, Benjamin and Rose, with their families. The last to arrive were Harriet and Saul, with their two adopted sons, Walter and Arthur. Everyone, from the oldest adult to the smallest child, had a gift for Nathan on his eighty-first birthday. He derived the greatest pleasure in accepting presents from the children, assuring each that his or her gift was the most wonderful he had ever received. When the children had finished making their presentations, Nathan wore a new pair of slippers over two new pairs of socks. Two new monogrammed handkerchiefs lay on his lap. A new bow tie fitted snugly around his neck, while three-year-old Rhea tidied his thinning white hair with a new silver-backed brush. Every so often, Helen urged her daughter to be careful. "If you brush so hard, your poor grandfather will have no hair left at all."

Nathan waved at his youngest daughter-in-law. "Leave the girl alone. She tears out less hair than my barber does." He winced as Rhea tugged at his hair to make a liar of him, and then he laughed. Having his hair pulled by a little girl did not hurt. On the contrary, it was a reminder of just how lucky he was to have such a wonderful family. A man like George Hopkinson might have power, but he had never known this kind of love. Nathan knew which was more important.

The picture show began at three o'clock in the afternoon. Lionel had set up the borrowed projector and screen in the parlor. The children sat in a semicircle on the floor, close to the screen. The adults fanned out behind them. Nathan sat in the center, comfortable in a Queen Anne chair.

"Lionel, do you have to shout 'Ready! Shoot!' before the picture begins?" Nathan asked.

"An audience doesn't need instructions. They're smarter than actors." Lionel threaded the film into the projector and asked Harry to draw the heavy drapes.

Nathan heard the whir of machinery and saw a beam of light dance across the parlor onto the screen. He watched in fascination as images appeared, and he wondered where all this new technology would eventually lead? Perhaps Jacob had only recognized half the future when he spoke of entertainment coming into homes through a radio receiver. Would there be a machine to bring pictures such as this into the home?

"Are you enjoying the show?" whispered Louise, who sat behind her father.

"Perhaps it is not as satisfying as the book, but it is pleasant nonetheless. Look!" He pointed at the screen. "There is Mister Bumble. I would know him anywhere."

He continued watching the film, comparing it with the book he had read so many years before. If only Dickens were alive today to see his works translated to this new medium. Perhaps the world of motion pictures would have given him ideas for new plots, new stories. Nathan felt his eyelids start to drop. The early-morning carriage ride had tired him more than he had realized. He forced himself back into wakefulness. After all the trouble Lionel had gone to, he would feel insulted if his father-in-law fell asleep during the showing. He fought the tiredness by searching his memory for scenes comparable to those he witnessed on the screen. Mary McBride's home in Saffron Hill would have provided a good background for Lionel to use. Nathan wondered if the slum still existed, along with all those other pitiful areas of London where the destitute waited for hunger or disease to strike them down. A shudder passed down his back as he remembered Fleet Ditch. Good God, more than sixty years later he could still smell the stench of the open sewer carrying waste to the Thames.

Suddenly, Louise's whisper was full of concern. "You shivered. Do you want a blanket?"

"No, no. I shivered because your husband is a genius. He has created a work so powerful that it evokes memories for me." He turned back to the screen, drawing again on his own recollections as he watched the story unfold, and fighting the tiredness that continued attacking him. His obstinacy failed to match the fatigue. His eyes closed and his head dropped. Once more, he rode in a horse-drawn omnibus from Bloomsbury to Ludgate Hill. Once more, Leonora sat beside him. A gray and greasy fog filled the air, concealing the soot-stained red-brick buildings. He felt Leonora clutch his arm, and heard her ask if the fog had made them very late.

"It is only ten minutes past six, Lally," he heard himself reply. "We have plenty of time."

His eyes opened wide. The fog had gone. Instead of being in a horse-drawn omnibus, he was in a room with many people. Adults. Children. All watching pictures flicker on a screen. Strange pictures of people who could not speak. Their mouths opened and closed, but no sound came.

A hand touched his arm. He tried to turn around but his body refused to obey instructions issued by his brain. His throat tightened, and he struggled for breath.

"Papa?" Louise left her chair and knelt beside him, looking anxiously at his face in the flickering light thrown back from the screen. "Papa, are you all right?"

Her urgent whisper cut across the whirring of the projector. Other heads turned. Harry jumped up to pull back the drapes, and Lionel stopped the projector, but not before Nathan had seen one wonderfully familiar picture. A ragged little boy holding out an empty bowl.

"Look, Lally!" he cried excitedly. "Please, sir. I want some more."